T0190320

Communications in Computer and Information Science 1889

Rationale

The CCIS series is devoted to the publication of proceedings of computer science conferences. Its aim is to efficiently disseminate original research results in informatics in printed and electronic form. While the focus is on publication of peer-reviewed full papers presenting mature work, inclusion of reviewed short papers reporting on work in progress is welcome, too. Besides globally relevant meetings with internationally representative program committees guaranteeing a strict peer-reviewing and paper selection process, conferences run by societies or of high regional or national relevance are also considered for publication.

Topics

The topical scope of CCIS spans the entire spectrum of informatics ranging from foundational topics in the theory of computing to information and communications science and technology and a broad variety of interdisciplinary application fields.

Information for Volume Editors and Authors

Publication in CCIS is free of charge. No royalties are paid, however, we offer registered conference participants temporary free access to the online version of the conference proceedings on SpringerLink (http://link.springer.com) by means of an http referrer from the conference website and/or a number of complimentary printed copies, as specified in the official acceptance email of the event.

CCIS proceedings can be published in time for distribution at conferences or as post-proceedings, and delivered in the form of printed books and/or electronically as USBs and/or e-content licenses for accessing proceedings at SpringerLink. Furthermore, CCIS proceedings are included in the CCIS electronic book series hosted in the SpringerLink digital library at http://link.springer.com/bookseries/7899. Conferences publishing in CCIS are allowed to use Online Conference Service (OCS) for managing the whole proceedings lifecycle (from submission and reviewing to preparing for publication) free of charge.

Publication process

The language of publication is exclusively English. Authors publishing in CCIS have to sign the Springer CCIS copyright transfer form, however, they are free to use their material published in CCIS for substantially changed, more elaborate subsequent publications elsewhere. For the preparation of the camera-ready papers/files, authors have to strictly adhere to the Springer CCIS Authors' Instructions and are strongly encouraged to use the CCIS LaTeX style files or templates.

Abstracting/Indexing

CCIS is abstracted/indexed in DBLP, Google Scholar, EI-Compendex, Mathematical Reviews, SCImago, Scopus. CCIS volumes are also submitted for the inclusion in ISI Proceedings.

How to start

To start the evaluation of your proposal for inclusion in the CCIS series, please send an e-mail to ccis@springer.com.

Antonia Moropoulou · Andreas Georgopoulos ·
Marinos Ioannides · Anastasios Doulamis ·
Kyriakos Lampropoulos · Alfredo Ronchi
Editors

Transdisciplinary Multispectral Modeling and Cooperation for the Preservation of Cultural Heritage

Third International Conference, TMM_CH 2023
Athens, Greece, March 20–23, 2023
Revised Selected Papers

Editors
Antonia Moropoulou
National Technical University of Athens
Athens, Greece

Marinos Ioannides
Cyprus University of Technology
Limassol, Cyprus

Kyriakos Lampropoulos
National Technical University of Athens
Athens, Greece

Andreas Georgopoulos
National Technical University of Athens
Athens, Greece

Anastasios Doulamis
National Technical University of Athens
Athens, Greece

Alfredo Ronchi
Polytechnic University of Milan
Milan, Italy

ISSN 1865-0929 ISSN 1865-0937 (electronic)
Communications in Computer and Information Science
ISBN 978-3-031-42299-7 ISBN 978-3-031-42300-0 (eBook)
https://doi.org/10.1007/978-3-031-42300-0

This Springer imprint is published by the registered company Springer Nature Switzerland AG
The registered company address is: Gewerbestrasse 11, 6330 Cham, Switzerland

Paper in this product is recyclable.

Preface

The adoption of innovative scientific methodologies and the implementation of challenging projects that mark future trends in the protection of cultural heritage have initiated a universal and wide-ranging dialogue among scholars, professionals, stakeholders, industry representatives and policy makers, within a holistic approach that fuses competences from the scientific fields of architecture, civil engineering, surveying engineering, materials science and engineering, information technology and archaeology, as well as heritage professionals on restoration and conservation, stakeholders, industry representatives and policy makers. The combined utilization of digital documentation technologies with innovative analytical and non-destructive techniques, numerical, computational and 3D techniques, archaeometric and archaeogene methods, supports the creation of a transdisciplinary multispectral modeling towards the sustainable preservation of cultural heritage. Innovation is enhancing and revealing a critical dimension of the preservation of cultural heritage along with social participation and communication.

The National Technical University of Athens interdisciplinary team "Protection of monuments" (A. Moropoulou, M. Korres, A. Georgopoulos, C. Spyrakos, C. Mouzakis), with scientific responsibility for the Holy Aedicule's rehabilitation of the Holy Sepulchre in Jerusalem, and the Technical Chamber of Greece, in collaboration with international and Greek organizations and universities, organized the 3rd TMM_CH International Conference on "Transdisciplinary Multispectral Modelling and Cooperation for the Preservation of Cultural Heritage: Recapturing the World in Conflict Through Culture, Promoting Mutual Understanding and Peace", on March 20–23, 2023 at the Eugenides Foundation in Athens, Greece, discussing modern trends in the original agora of our technological and democratic roots, with emphasis on digital documentation technologies.

The conference was organized by the National Technical University of Athens in cooperation with the Technical Chamber of Greece, under the patronage of Her Excellency the President of the Hellenic Republic, Katerina Sakellaropoulou, with benedictions bestowed by His All Holiness, Ecumenical Patriarch, Bartholomew I of Constantinople, His Beatitude Archbishop Hieronymus II of Athens and All Greece, and His Beatitude, Patriarch Theofilos III of Jerusalem.

Distinguished scientists and representatives of the National Geographic Society, the Cultural Heritage Finance Alliance, the International Council of Monuments and Sites, ICOMOS, the Organization of World Heritage Cities OWHC, the European Society for Engineering Education, SEFI, the European Construction Technology Platform, ECTP, the International Federation of Surveyors, FIG, the International Committee CIPA Heritage Documentation, the World Monuments Fund, AHEPA Hellas, and other major international and European organizations, associations, networks, universities and research centers in the field of cultural heritage preservation, participated in the international steering and scientific committees of the 3rd International TMM_CH conference.

At the 1st and the 2nd TMM_CH conferences, which were held with great success in October 2018 and December 2021 respectively at the Eugenides Foundation in Athens, with the presence of 350/650 delegates from 22/33 countries from all continents, and over 5000 online attendees, the emblematic rehabilitation of the Holy Aedicule of the Holy Sepulchre in Jerusalem was presented as an exemplary application, in the field of monument protection, of interdisciplinary and multispectral collaboration, as an outcome of innovation, not only on research but also in the implementation process, with emphasis on technological advancements, not only intersecting all the scientific fields of engineers and natural scientists but also initiating an ongoing dialogue with humanities, in domains such as archaeology, theology, sociology, diplomacy and tourism.

Revised selected papers from the above two conferences, pertaining to digital innovation, which enhances and reveals a critical dimension of the preservation of cultural heritage, were published in three volumes of the Springer proceedings series Communications in Computer and Information Science. Specifically, they were published in the volume Transdisciplinary Multispectral Modeling and Cooperation for the Preservation of Cultural Heritage. First International Conference, TM_CH 2018, editors A. Moropoulou, M. Korres, A. Georgopoulos, C. Spyrakos, Ch. Mouzakis, Communications in Computer and Information Science, Vol. 961–962, Springer Nature (2019), and in the volume Trandisciplinary Multispectral Modelling and Cooperation for the Preservation of Cultural Heritage. Second International Conference, TMM_CH 2021, editors A. Moropoulou, A. Georgopoulos, A. Doulamis, M. Ioannides, A. Ronchi, Communications in Computer and Information Science, Vol. 1574, Springer Nature (2022).

Innovative knowledge transfer through practice and education is continuing in the rehabilitation projects in the Holy Sepulchre Church, in association with the National Technical University of Athens, La Sapienza University in Rome, and the Bezalel Academy of Science and Arts in Jerusalem, in cooperation with the Israeli Antiquities Authority, through the Erasmus+ Strategic Alliance EDICULA "Educational Digital Innovative Cultural Heritage related Learning Alliance".

Following on from the achievements of the 1st and 2nd TMM_CH conferences, the latest developments in research and innovation that identify novel trends to build an interdisciplinary approach to conservation and holistic digital documentation of cultural heritage was attempted at the 3rd TMM_CH. The utilization and reuse of monuments, historic cities and sites forms the framework of a sustainable preservation of cultural heritage, in accordance with the principles of a circular economy; in terms of the respect and protection of values, materials, structures, architecture and landscape; with an informed society, able to participate effectively in the policies that will enable the design and implementation of the new strategies required. The importance of computer science, IoT and digital technologies was prominently highlighted, and various case studies were presented.

The issues discussed in the 13 sessions and 13 panel discussions at the TMM_CH 2023 were as follows:

1. Historic cities and centers: new reuse and preservation strategies applying a circular economy
2. Digital heritage: a holistic approach
3. Machine learning techniques for cultural heritage preservation

4A. Emblematic works as a source of innovation and transdisciplinarity
4B. Novel educational approach for the preservation of cultural heritage
5. Art, Archaeology – Archaeometry – Archaeogene
6. Preserving compatibility, the materiality and integrity of structures and architectural authenticity
7. Earthquake protection and structural rehabilitation
8. Resilience of cultural heritage mitigating climate change, natural hazards and pandemic risks and ensuring biosafety
9. New European Bauhaus creative and interdisciplinary initiative
10. Green and blue deal for local and regional sustainable development
11. Institutional framework bridging heritage stakeholders, art, science, and industry
12. Advanced non-destructive and structural techniques for diagnosis, redesign and health monitoring
13. Recapturing the world in conflict through culture, promoting mutual understanding and peace

Sharing knowledge, experiences, and recommendations about sustainable cultural heritage approaches and practices at a moment of great conflicts and climate change, and energy, environment and socio-economic risks, the sustainable preservation of cultural heritage is addressing challenges through mutual understanding and international cooperation.

The TMM_CH 2023 conference was held at the Eugenides Foundation. On-site attendance and oral presentation was required and was organized according to government restrictions against Covid-19. The opening session and all panel discussions, as addressed to the general public, were livestreamed with free access via the conference's YouTube channel and website (https://www.tmm-ch.com/).

The 3rd TMM_CH conference was highly anticipated, attracting researchers from all over the world. It was held with great success, with the physical presence of over 500 delegates and online attendance of 1700 delegates in real time and approximately 50,000 online attendants for the panels. Thirteen sessions and 13 panel discussions with the participation of 142 panelists were organized during the conference, with a visibility of 2–3 million internationally through livestreaming by BCI Media Toronto.

Striving to ensure that the conference presentations and proceedings are of the highest quality possible, the scientific committee only accepted papers that presented the results of various studies focused on the extraction of new scientific knowledge in the area of transdisciplinary multispectral modeling and cooperation for the preservation of cultural heritage. 416 contributions were submitted and 163 papers were accepted for oral presentation and publication by 487 authors from 31 countries, after peer review from three reviewers on average per paper and consequent revisions, with a rate of acceptance equivalent to 40%. Accepted papers were published in this Springer proceedings volume and in special issues of scientific journals in the field of cultural heritage preservation.

The interdisciplinarity in the preservation of cultural heritage implies a holistic documentation with fusion of the various disciplines' data in 3D models. Computer-aided design and computer science advanced methodologies support an interdisciplinary synthesis regarding the assessment of the preservation state and the evaluation of the rehabilitation achieved, in relation to the integrity of materials and structures, throughout the restoration of the authentic architecture. In parallel, new technologies are used to enhance research and education and communicate the reuse and revealing of cultural and natural assets, providing through tourism external economies to sustain local and regional development in a circular way.

Hence, 34 papers presented at the 3rd TMM_CH conference and integrating all the above aspects are published in this book, Transdisciplinary Multispectral Modeling and Cooperation for the Preservation of Cultural Heritage, within the Springer series Communications in Computer and Information Science. The editors would like to express their sincerest appreciation to all of the reviewers and authors who contributed to maintaining the high standards necessary for the implementation of the successful 3rd TMM_CH conference, as well as for the preparation of this book.

We would like to acknowledge all who made the conference possible and successful: the organizers, as mentioned above; the sponsors, Public Power Cooperation, AEGEAS Non-Profit Civil Company, GEK TERNA Group, P. Zafeiri Sons Technical Company, Dalkafoukis House Ltd., Athens Anaplasis S.A., Attica Bank, TITAN Cement Group, EYDAP Athens Water Supply and Sewerage Company, and Eurobank; the Eugenides Foundation for the kind offer of the venues of the conference; the media sponsors, ERT Hellenic Broadcasting Corporation and BCI Media Toronto; the media support offered by DNA Sequence Ltd., PerpetielSI Srl, and the Boussias Media Group; the partners of the Erasmus+ Strategic Alliance EDICULA "Educational Digital Innovative Cultural Heritage related Learning Alliance", coordinated by NTUA, for the co-organization of Panel 4; the organizers of the researchers night at the National Technical University of Athens 2022 and the partners of the research program AEI "Sustainable Development of Less Developed Areas by Creating New Tourism Resources and Products Through Analysis, Documentation, Modelling, Management and Preservation of the Cultural Preserve Using ICT Applications", coordinated by NTUA, PA 2014-2020, for the co-organization of Panel 10; the partners of the research program RESPECT "An Exemplary Information System and Methodology for the Integrated Management, Analysis and Dissemination of Digital Cultural Heritage Data Coming from the Rehabilitation of the Holy Aedicule", coordinated by NTUA, PA 2014-2020, for the co-organization of Panels 2 and 3; and the research program BIOFOS coordinated by NTUA, PA 2014-2020, "TRIQUETRA: Toolbox for Assessing and Mitigating Climate Change Risks and Natural Hazards Threatening Cultural Heritage", for the co-organization of Panel 8.

The conference would not have been possible without the commitment of the NTUA interdisciplinary team for the "Protection of Monuments"; the full cooperation of the TMM_CH editors of this volume; the scientific support of the international steering committee and the scientific committee; the support of the executive organizing committee and the technical system providers; and the valuable assistance of the CCIS team at Springer, to whom we are utmost grateful. We are very proud of the result of this collaboration and we believe that this fruitful partnership will continue.

The next TMM_CH conference has already been announced for 2025.

June 2023 Antonia Moropoulou

Organization

President – General Chair

Moropoulou, Antonia	National Technical University of Athens, Greece

Steering Committee Chairs

Stasinos, Giorgos	Technical Chamber of Greece, Greece
Constanti, Constantinos	ETEK Cyprus Scientific and Technical Chamber, Cyprus
Burnham, Bonnie	Cultural Heritage Finance Alliance, USA
Eskosido, Eli	Israel Antiquities Authority, Israel
Stylianidis, Efstratios	Aristotle University of Thessaloniki, Greece and International Committee CIPA Heritage Documentation, France
Ioannides, Marinos	Cyprus University of Technology, Cyprus
Georgopoulos, Andreas	National Technical University of Athens, Greece and International Council of Monuments and Sites (ICOMOS), France
Gravari-Barbas, Maria	Paris 1 Panthéon-Sorbonne University, France
Hiebert, Fredrik	National Geographic Society, USA
Järvinen, Hannu-Matti	Tampere University, Finland and European Society for Engineering Education SEFI, Belgium
Korka, Elena	Ministry of Culture and Sports, Greece and Hellenic Blue Shield, Greece
Leissner, Johanna	Fraunhofer Gesellschaft, Germany
Minaidis, Lee	Organization of World Heritage Cities, Canada
Oosterbeek, Luiz	Polytechnic Institute of Tomar, Portugal and International Council of Philosophy and Human Sciences CIPSH, Belgium
Rodriguez-Maribona, Isabel	European Construction Technology Platform (ECTP), Belgium
Žarnić, Roko	University of Ljubljana, Slovenia
Di Giulio, Roberto	University of Ferrara, Italy and 4CH Competence Centre for the Conservation of Cultural Heritage, Italy
Matikas, Theodoros	University of Ioannina, Greece

Steering Committee

Achniotis, Stelios	Cyprus Scientific and Technical Chamber (ETEK), Cyprus
Aesopos, Yannis	University of Patras, Greece
Alexopoulos, Konstantinos	Hellenic Army General Staff/Defense and Civil Emergency Planning Directorate, Greece and The Grand Priory of Greece in the "Sovereign Military Order of the Temple of Jerusalem"
Amditis, Angelos	National Technical University of Athens, Greece and European Association for Virtual and Extended Reality EuroXR, Belgium
Anagnostopoulos, Christos	University of the Aegean, Greece
Anagnostopoulos, Dimosthenis	Harokopio University, Greece and Ministry of Digital Governance of the Hellenic Republic, Greece
Anastasiadis, Spiros	University of Crete, Greece and Foundation for Research and Technology Hellas FORTH, Greece
Andrade, Carmen	International Centre for Numerical Methods in Engineering, Spain
Androulidaki, Amalia	Ministry of Culture and Sports, Greece
Antonatos, Alexandros	Hellenic Society for Non-Destructive Testing, Greece
Arabiyat, Abed Al Razzaq	Jordan Tourism Board, Jordan
Arakadaki, Maria	Aristotle University of Thessaloniki, Greece
Aravossis, Konstantinos	National Technical University of Athens, Greece and Ministry of Environment and Energy, Greece
Athanasiou, Stefanos	University of Bern, Switzerland
Avgerinou-Kolonias, Sofia	National Technical University of Athens, Greece and Hellenic Section of ICOMOS, Greece
Avgeropoulos, Apostolos	University of Ioannina, Greece
Avni, Gideon	Israel Antiquities Authority, Israel
Avouris, Nikolaos	University of Patras, Greece
Avramides, Yiannis	World Monuments Fund, USA
Babayan, Hector	National Academy of Sciences, Armenia
Badalian, Irena	Church of the Holy Sepulchre, Israel
Bafataki, Vicky	"Giuseppe Sciacca" Foundation, Italy
Bakogiannis, Efthimios	National Technical University of Athens, Greece and Ministry of Environment and Energy, Greece
Benelli, Carla	Church of the Holy Sepulchre, Israel

Botsaris, Pantelis	Democritus University of Thrace, Greece
Caradimas, Costas	National Technical University of Athens, Greece
Caristan, Yves	European Council of Academies of Applied Sciences, Technologies and Engineering (Euro-Case), France
Chatzarakis, E. George	School of Pedagogical and Technological Education, Greece
Chetouani, Aladine	University of Orleans, France
Cholakian, Paul	Great Priory of Greece in the Sovereign Military Order of the Temple of Jerusalem, Greece
Chondrokoukis, Grigorios	University of Piraeus, Greece
Constantopoulos, Panos	Athens University of Economic and Business, Greece and ESFRI Strategic Working Group in Social and Cultural Innovation, Belgium
Corradi, Marco	University of Northumbria, UK
Correia, Mariana	Portucalense University, Portugal
D'Ayala, Dina	University College London, UK
Daktylidis, Michail	Panhellenic Association of Engineers Contractors of Public Works, Greece
De Vries, Pieter	Delft University of Technology, Netherlands and European Society for Engineering Education, Belgium
Dimakopoulos, Vassilios	University of Ioannina, Greece
Distefano, Salvatore	Kazan Federal University, Russia and University of Messina, Italy
Drdácký, Miloš	Czech Academy of Sciences, Czech Republic and Institute of Theoretical Applied Mechanics, Czech Republic
El Feki, Mostafa	Bibliotheca Alexandrina, Egypt
Erdik, Mustafa	Bogazici University, Turkey
Floros, Andreas	Ionian University, Greece
Forde, Michael	University of Edinburgh, UK
Forest, Emmanuel	Bouygues Group, France
Galetakis, Mihalis	Technical University of Crete, Greece
Gómez-Ferrer, Bayo Álvaro	Valencian Institute for Conservation and Restoration of Cultural Heritage, Spain
Grekas, Aristarchos	National and Kapodistrian University of Athens, Greece and Hellenic Institute of Cultural Diplomacy, Greece
Grigoroudis, Evangelos	Technical University of Crete, Greece
Groysman, Alec	Association of Engineers, Architects and Graduates in Technological Sciences, Israel
Hamdan, Osama	Church of the Holy Sepulchre, Israel

Ioannou, Ioannis	University of Cyprus, Cyprus
Kakali, Glykeria	National Technical University of Athens, Greece
Kaliampakos, Dimitrios	National Technical University of Athens, Greece
Kallithrakas-Kontos, Nikolaos	Technical University of Crete, Greece
Kampanis, Nikolaos	Foundation for Research and Technology Hellas, Greece
Karadimas, Dimitris	Vision Business Consultants, Greece
Karagiannis, Christos	Democritus University of Thrace, Greece
Karapiperis, Christos	American Hellenic Progressive Association (AHEPA), Greece
Karystinos, George	Technical University of Crete, Greece
Kavassalis, Petros	University of Aegean, Greece
Keane, Kathryn	National Geographic Society, USA
Kokkossis, Harry	University of Thessaly, Greece
Kollias, Stefanos	National Technical University of Athens, Greece and National Infrastructures for Research and Technology, Greece
Kolokotsa, Dionysia	Technical University of Crete, Greece
Kordatos, John	Worldwide Industrial and Marine Association, Greece
Koundouri, Phoebe	Athens University of Economics and Business, Greece and European Association of Environmental and Natural Resource Economists, Italy
Koutoulakis, Manolis	Ministry of Shipping and Island Policy, Greece
Koziris, Nectarios	National Technical University of Athens, Greece
Kremlis, George	Espoo Convention, Belgium
Kriari, Ismini	Panteion University of Social and Political Sciences, Greece
La Grassa, Alessandro	Centre for Social and Economic Research in Southern Italy (CRESM), Italy
Lagaros, Nikolaos	National Technical University of Athens, Greece
Lee-Thorp, Julia	Oxford University, UK
Lianos, Nikolaos	Democritus University of Thrace, Greece and Hellenic Section of ICOMOS, Greece
Loukopoulou, Politimi	International Council of Museums (ICOM), Hellenic National Committee, Greece
Maistrou, Eleni	National Technical University of Athens, Greece and Society for the Environmental and Cultural Heritage, Greece
Masi, Alessia	Sapienza University of Rome, Italy and Max Planck Institute for the Science of Human History, Germany

Mavroeidi, Maria	International Committee for the Conservation of Industrial Heritage (TICCIH), Greece
Mavrogenes, John	Australian National University, Australia
Menychtas, Andreas	University of Piraeus, Greece and BioAssist SA, Greece
Mitropoulos, Theodosios	Church of the Holy Sepulchre, Israel
Mouhli, Zoubeïr	Association de Sauvegarde de la Médina de Tunis, Tunisia
Nakasis, Athanasios	Hellenic Section of ICOMOS, Greece
Neubauer, Wolfgang	Ludwig Boltzmann Institute for Archaeological Prospection and Virtual Archaeology, Austria
Nobilakis, Ilias	Network PERRAIVIA, Greece and University of West Attica, Greece
Nounesis, George	National Centre for Scientific Research "Demokritos", Greece
Ntroutsa, Eirini	Erasmus+ Hellenic Agency (IKY), Greece
Oungrinis, Konstantinos-Alketas	Technical University of Crete, Greece
Padeletti, Giuseppina	National Research Council, Italy
Palaitsaki, Nana	Independent Journalist
Panayiaris, George	University of West Attica, Greece
Papageorgiou, Angelos	University of Ioannina, Greece
Papakosta, Kalliopi	Hellenic Research Institute of Alexandrian Civilization, Egypt
Papi, Emanuele	University of Siena, Italy
Pappas, Spyros	ARGO - Hellenic Network in Brussels, Belgium
Paraskevopoulos, Marios	University of Leicester, UK
Petridis, Platon	National and Kapodistrian University of Athens, Greece
Philokyprou, Maria	University of Cyprus, Cyprus
Pissaridis, Chrysanthos	ICOMOS, Cyprus
Potsiou, Chryssy	National Technical University of Athens, Greece
Pressas, Charalambos	University of West Attica, Greece
Prodromou, Elizabeth	Boston College, USA
Re'em, Amit	Israel Antiquities Authority, Israel
Rydock, James	Research Management Institute, Norway
Salakidis, Antonios	PerpetielSI SRL, Romania and DNASequence SRL, Romania
Sali-Papasali, Anastasia	Ionian University, Greece
Santos, Pedro	Fraunhofer Institute for Computer Graphics Research IGD, Germany
Skianis, Charalambos	University of the Aegean, Greece
Skriapas, Konstantinos	Network "PERRAIVIA", Greece
Soile, Sofia	National Technical University of Athens, Greece

Sotiropoulou, Anastasia	School of Pedagogical and Technological Education, Greece
Spathis, Panagiotis	Aristotle University of Thessaloniki, Greece
Stamoulis, Georgios	University of Thessaly, Greece
Stavrakos, Christos	University of Ioannina, Greece
Stylianou, Platonas	Cyprus Scientific and Technical Chamber ETEK, Cyprus
Tapinaki, Sevi	National Technical University of Athens, Greece
Touliatos, Panagiotis	Frederick University, Cyprus
Tournikiotis, Panayotis	National Technical University of Athens, Greece
Triantafyllou, Athanasios	University of Western Macedonia, Greece
Tsatsanifos, Christos	International Society for Soil Mechanics and Geotechnical Engineering, UK
Tsiampaos, Kostas	National Technical University of Athens, Greece
Tsimas, Pavlos	Independent Journalist
Tucci, Grazia	University of Florence, Italy
Tzitzikas, Yannis	University of Crete, Greece and Foundation for Research and Technology Hellas / ICCSCCI, Greece
Tzitzikosta, Aikaterini	Hellenic National Commission for UNESCO, Greece
Varelidis, Petros	Ministry of Environment and Energy, Greece
Varvarigou, Theodora	National Technical University of Athens, Greece and Athens Water Supply and Sewerage Company, Greece
Vergados, Dimitrios	University of Piraeus, Greece
Vesic, Nenad (Amvrosije)	International Scientific Committee for Places of Religion and Ritual (PRERICO), ICOMOS, France
Vlachoulis, Themistoklis	Ministry of Culture and Sports, Greece
Ward-Perkins, Bryan	University of Oxford, UK
Weinblum, Liat	Israel Antiquities Authority, Israel
Yakinthos, Kyriakos	Aristotle University of Thessaloniki, Greece
Zacharias, Nikos	University of the Peloponnese, Greece
Zarafonitis, George	National Technical University of Athens, Greece
Zervakis, Michael	Technical University of Crete, Greece
Zouain, Georges	GAIA-Heritage, Lebanon

Scientific Committee Chairs

Korres, Manolis	National Technical University of Athens, Greece and Academy of Athens, Greece
Georgopoulos, Andreas	National Technical University of Athens, Greece and International Council of Monuments and Sites (ICOMOS), France
Mouzakis, Charis	National Technical University of Athens, Greece
Spyrakos, Constantine	National Technical University of Athens, Greece
Favero, Gabriele	Sapienza University of Rome, Italy
Turner, Mike	Bezalel Academy of Arts and Design, Israel
Baruch, Yuval	Israel Antiquities Authority, Israel
Ioannidis, Charalambos	National Technical University of Athens, Greece
Aggelis, Dimitris	Free University of Brussels, Belgium
Betti, Michele	University of Florence, Italy
Della Torre, Stefano	Polytechnic University of Milan, Italy
Doukas, Haris	National Technical University of Athens, Greece
Kyriazis, Dimosthenis	University of Piraeus, Greece
Liritzis, Ioannis	University of the Aegean, Greece
Osman, Ahmad	Saarland University of Applied Sciences, Germany and Fraunhofer Institute for Nondestructive Testing, IZFP, Germany
Ronchi, Alfredo	Politecnico di Milano, Italy
Zendri, Elisabetta	University Ca' Foscari of Venice, Italy
Doulamis, Anastasios	National Technical University of Athens, Greece
Delegou, Ekaterini	National Technical University of Athens, Greece
Konstanti, Agoritsa	National Technical University of Athens, Greece
Lampropoulos, Kyriakos	National Technical University of Athens, Greece

Scientific Committee

Abuamoud, Ismaiel Naser	Hashemite University, Jordan
Achenza, Maddalena	University of Calgary, Canada
Adamakis, Kostas	University of Thessaly, Greece
Agapiou, Athos	Cyprus University of Technology, Cyprus
Aggelakopoulou, Eleni	Acropolis Restoration Service, Greece
Alexopoulou, Aleka	Aristotle University of Thessaloniki, Greece
Apostolopoulou, Maria	Acropolis Restoration Service, Greece
Argyropoulou, Vasilike	University of West Attica, Greece
Asteris, Panagiotis	School of Pedagogical and Technological Education, Greece

Avdelidis, Nikolaos	Cranfield University, UK
Bakolas, Stelios	National Technical University of Athens, Greece
Balas, Kostas	Technical University of Crete, Greece
Belavilas, Nikos	National Technical University of Athens, Greece
Bettega, Stefano Maria	Superior Institute of Artistic Industries, Italy
Boniface, Michael	University of Southampton, UK
Bounia, Alexandra	University of the Aegean, Greece
Boutalis, Ioannis	Democritus University of Thrace, Greece
Boyatzis, Stamatis	University of West Attica, Greece
Bozanis, Panayiotis	International Hellenic University, Greece
Cassar, JoAnn	University of Malta, Malta
Cassar, May	University College London, UK
Castigloni, Carlo	Polytechnic University of Milan, Italy
Cavaleri, Liborio	University of Palermo, Italy
Chamzas, Christodoulos	Democritus University of Thrace, Greece
Chiotinis, Nikitas	University of West Attica, Greece
Chlouveraki, Stefania	University of West Attica, Greece
Christaras, Basile	Aristotle University of Thessaloniki, Greece
Daflou, Eleni	National Technical University of Athens, Greece
De Angelis, Roberta	University of Malta, Malta
Demotikali, Dimitra	National Technical University of Athens, Greece
Diker, Hasan Firat	Fatih Sultan Mehmet Vakif University, Turkey
Dimitrakopoulos, Fotios	National and Kapodistrian University of Athens, Greece
Dritsos, Stefanos	University of Patras, Greece
Drosopoulos, Georgios	University of Central Lancashire, UK
Economou, Dimitrios	University of Thessaly, Greece
Efesiou, Irene	National Technical University of Athens, Greece
Exadaktylos, George	National Technical University of Athens, Greece
Facorellis, Yorgos	University of West Attica, Greece
Formisano, Antonio	University of Naples Federico II, Italy
Foudos, Ioannis	University of Ioannina, Greece
Frosina, Annamaria	Centre for Social and Economic Research, Italy
Fuhrmann, Constanze	Fraunhofer Institute for Computer Graphics Research, Germany
Ganiatsas, Vassilis	National Technical University of Athens, Greece
Gavela, Stamatia	School of Pedagogical and Technological Education, Greece
Ghadban, Shadi Sami	Birzeit University, Palestine
Gharbi, Mohamed	Institute of Technological Studies of Bizerte, Tunisia
Giannini, Evgenia	National Technical University of Athens, Greece

Groag, Shmuel	Bezalel Academy of Arts and Design, Israel
Hadjinicolaou, Teti	International Council of Museums ICOM, Hellenic National Committee, Greece
Iadanza, Ernesto	University of Florence, Italy
Izzo, Francesca Caterina	University Ca' Foscari of Venice, Italy
Kapsalis, Georgios	National University of Ioannina, Greece
Karaberi, Alexia	National Technical University of Athens, Greece
Karagiannis, Georgios	ORMYLIA Foundation, Greece
Karellas, Sotirios	National Technical University of Athens, Greece
Karoglou, Maria	National Technical University of Athens, Greece
Katsioti-Beazi, Margarita	National Technical University of Athens, Greece
Kavvadas, Michael	National Technical University of Athens, Greece
Kioussi, Anastasia	Ministry of Culture and Sports, Greece
Komnitsas, Konstantinos	Technical University of Crete, Greece
Konstantinides, Tony	Imperial College London, UK
Konstantinidou, Helen	National Technical University of Athens, Greece
Kontoyannis, Christos	University of Patras, Greece
Kourkoulis, Stavros	National Technical University of Athens, Greece
Koutsoukos, Petros	University of Patras, Greece
Kyvellou, Stella	Panteion University of Social and Political Sciences, Greece
Lambropoulos, Vasileios	University of West Attica, Greece
Liolios, Asterios	Democritus University of Thrace, Greece
Lobovikov-Katz, Anna	NB Haifa School of Design, Israel and Technion Israel Institute of Technology, Israel
Loukas, Athanasios	University of Thessaly, Greece
Lourenço, Paulo	University of Minho, Portugal
Lyridis, Dimitrios	National Technical University of Athens, Greece
Maietti, Federica	University of Ferrara, Italy
Mamaloukos, Stavros	University of Patras, Greece
Maniatakis, Charilaos	Water Supply and Sewerage Company of Hersonissos Municipality, Greece
Maravelaki, Pagona-Noni	Technical University of Crete, Greece
Marinou, Georgia	National Technical University of Athens, Greece
Maroulis, Zacharias	National Technical University of Athens, Greece
Mavrogenes, John	Australian National University, Australia
Medeghini, Laura	Sapienza University of Rome, Italy
Milani, Gabriele	Polytechnic University of Milan, Italy
Miltiadou, Androniki	National Technical University of Athens, Greece
Mohebkhah, Amin	Malayer University, Iran
Nevin Saltik, Emine	Middle East Technical University, Turkey
Oikonomopoulou, Eleni	Architect, Greece

Ortiz Calderon, Maria Pilar	Pablo de Olavide University, Spain
Ouzounis, Christos	Aristotle University of Thessaloniki, Greece
Pagge, Tzeni	University of Ioannina, Greece
Paipetis, Alkiviadis	University of Ioannina, Greece
Panagouli, Olympia	University of Thessaly, Greece
Pantazis, George	National Technical University of Athens, Greece
Papagianni, Ioanna	Aristotle University of Thessaloniki, Greece
Papaioannou, Georgios	Ionian University, Greece
Papatrechas, Christos	Institute of Geological and Mineral Research, Greece
Pérez García, Carmen	Valencian Institute for Conservation and Restoration of Cultural Heritage, Spain
Perraki, Maria	National Technical University of Athens, Greece
Piaia, Emanuele	University of Ferrara, Italy
Polydoras, Stamatios	National Technical University of Athens, Greece
Prepis, Alkiviades	Democritus University of Thrace, Greece
Psycharis, Ioannis	National Technical University of Athens, Greece
Rajčić, Vlatka	University of Zagreb, Croatia
Saisi, Antonella Elide	Polytechnic University of Milan, Italy
Sapounakis, Aristides	University of Thessaly, Greece
Schippers-Trifan, Oana	DEMO Consultants BV, Netherlands
Sela Wiener, Adi	Bezalel Academy of Arts and Design, Israel
Seligman, Jon	Israel Antiquities Authority, Israel
Smith, Robert	Oxford University, UK
Stambolidis, Nikos	University of Crete, Greece
Stavrakos, Christos	University of Ioannina, Greece
Stavroulakis, Georgios	Technical University of Crete, Greece
Stefanidou, Maria	Aristotle University of Thessaloniki, Greece
Stefanis, Alexis	University of West Attica, Greece
Tavukcuoglu, Ayse	Middle East Technical University, Turkey
Theodorou, Doros	National Technical University of Athens, Greece
Theoulakis, Panagiotis	University of West Attica, Greece
Thomas, Job	Cochin University of Science Technology, India
Tokmakidis, Konstantinos	Aristotle University of Thessaloniki, Greece
Triantafillou, Athanasios	University of Patras, Greece
Tsakanika, Eleutheria	National Technical University of Athens, Greece
Tsilaga, Evagelia-Marina	University of West Attica, Greece
Tsilimantou, Elisavet	Ministry of Infrastructure and Transportation, Greece
Tsoukalas, Lefteris	University of Thessaly, Greece
Van Grieken, René	University of Antwerp, Belgium
Van Hees, Rob	Delft University of Technology, Netherlands

Varum, Humberto	University of Porto, Portugal
Vayenas, Dimitris	University of Patras, Greece
Vintzilaiou, Elissavet	National Technical University of Athens, Greece
Vlachopoulos, Andreas	University of Ioannina, Greece
Vogiatzis, Konstantinos	University of Thessaly, Greece
Vyzoviti, Sophia	University of Thessaly, Greece
Xanthaki-Karamanou, Georgia	University of the Peloponnese, Greece
Yannas, Simos	Architectural Association School of Architecture, UK
Zachariou-Rakanta, Eleni	National Technical University of Athens, Greece
Zervos, Spyros	University of West Attica, Greece
Zouboulakis, Loukas	National Technical University of Athens, Greece

Executive Organizing Committee

National Technical University of Athens, Greece

Lampropoulou, Antonia	NTUA - EDICULA Erasmus+ Strategic Partnership
Sinigalia, Maria	NTUA, IT at Central Library
Psarris, Dimitrios	NTUA, School of Applied Mathematics & Physical Sciences
Vythoulka, Anastasia	NTUA PhD Candidate - PA Research Program AEI
Keramidas, Vasilios	NTUA PhD Candidate
Roumeliotis, Stergios	NTUA, School of Chemical Engineering

Technical Chamber of Greece

Anagnostaki, Liana	Head of the TCG Directorate of Public Relations, International and European Affairs
Athini, Lilly	Head of the TCG Directorate of Scientific and Development Activity
Pergantopoulou, Alexia	TCG PRIEA Directorate
Haviara, Villy	TCG PRIEA Directorate
Manitsa, Theodora	TCG Department of Governing Bodies' Support
Tsavari, Isavella	Democritus University of Thrace, TCG WG
Erotokritos, Emmanouil	International Affairs, TCG WG
Bairaktari, Eleni	ICME, TCG WG

Technical System Providers

Cosmolive Productions
P. Vrelos
BOUSSIAS Media Group

Contents

Scientific Innovations in the Diagnosis and Preservation of Cultural Heritage

The Preservation of the Heritage of the Petralona Cave Using Multiple 3D Scanning Techniques and Data Processing Algorithms 3
Panagiotis Tokmakidis, Charisios Achillas, Dimitrios Tzetzis, Elli Karkazi, Emmanouil Tzimtzimis, Andreas Darlas, Athanassios Athanassiou, and Dionysis Bochtis

The Restoration of the Main Theatre of the First Ancient Theatre of Larissa, Greece, Assisted by 3D Technologies 13
Dimitrios L. Karagkounis and Sofia D. Tsanaktsidou

Comparing the Methods of Terrestrial Laser Scanning and Photogrammetry for the Geometric Documentation of Stone Bridges Through the Case Study of Tzelefos Bridge 23
A. Fellas and M. Demosthenous

Associating Geodetic Theory to Digital Pottery Reassembly Practice 43
Michail I. Stamatopoulos and Christos-Nikolaos Anagnostopoulos

Advanced Digitization Methods for the 3D Visualization and Interpretation of Cultural Heritage: The Sphinx of the Naxians at Delphi 55
Athanasia Psalti, Marilena Tsakoumaki, Christina Mamaloukaki, Michael Xinogalos, Nikolaos Bolanakis, Christos Kavallaris, Andreas Polychronakis, Katerina Mania, and Emmanuel Maravelakis

Different Geodetic Approaches for the Creation of a HBIM 65
Tsilimantou Elisavet, Pagouni Chara, Iliodromitis Athanasios, Anastasiou Dimitrios, and Pagounis Vasileios

A New Low-Cost Rolling Ball Type Isolation Device for the Protection of Museum Collections 82
Alessia Di Martino, Francesco Cannizzaro, Giuseppe Cocuzza Avellino, and Nicola Impollonia

Documentation of the Leprosarium of Chios 94
Athanasios Iliodromitis, George Pantazis, and Elena Konstantiniu

Digital Technologies for Heritage Conservation Labs Open to the Public. The Case of the CALLOS Project 104
Sophia Papida, Martha Athanasiadou, Kostas Petrakis, Lida Charami, Dimitris Angelakis, Chryssoula Bekiari, Kristalia Melessanaki, and Paraskevi Pouli

Evaluating the Effectiveness of Unsupervised and Supervised Techniques for Identifying Deteriorations on Cultural Heritage Monuments Using Hyper-spectral Imagery 114
Nikolaos Chrysogonos, Kyriakos Lampropoulos, Ioannis N. Tzortzis, Charalampos Zafeiropoulos, Anastasios Doulamis, and Nikolaos Doulamis

Terrestrial Laser Scanning Coupled with UAVs Technologies: The Case of Old Navarino Castle in Pylos, Greece 125
A. Kompoti, A. Kazolias, M. Kylafi, V. Panagiotidis, and N. Zacharias

A Contribution to Palaeocoastal and Beachrock Studies with the Application of Digital Technologies: The Case Study of Romanos Beach in Pylos 137
Evangelia Bilitsi, Vayia V. Panagiotidis, Anastasios Kazolias, and Nikolaos Zacharias

The Digitization of Klissova Islet and the Church of Agia Triada in Mesologgi 146
A. Papoutsaki, V. V. Panagiotidis, A. Kompoti, A. Kazolias, and N. Zacharias

Digital Heritage a Holistic Approach

Crowdsourcing for 3D Digital Modelling: Ioannina City-Chairedin Pasha Sarai Case Study 157
Athina Chroni, Andreas Georgopoulos, and Pavlos-Stylianos Megalooikonomou

A Digital Cultural Landscape: Interpretations on Multisensory Projections 171
Eleni Maistrou, Konstantinos Moraitis, Yanis Maistros, Katerina Boulougoura, Amalia-Maria Konidi, Karolina Moretti, and Margarita Skamantzari

Smart City and Open-Air Museum: A Digital Application for the Promotion of the Old Town of Chania 188
Hippocrates Manoudakis, Ioulia Pentazou, and Maria Bakatsaki

Digitization of Industrial Heritage in Greece 202
Theodora Chatzi Rodopoulou

Built Cultural Heritage and Digital Transition: The New Role of Data and Artificial Intelligence Applications in Administrative Procedures 213
Anna Maria Pentimalli Biscaretti di Ruffia

Design of a VR Environment Optimized for Cultural Heritage Sites and Objects: The Use Case of Its Kale, Ioannina, Greece 222
Christos Bellos, Dafni Patelou, Konstantinos Stefanou, Georgios Stergios, Angeliki Kita, Persefoni Ntoulia, Vasileios Nitsiakos, and Ioannis Fudos

When Technology Meets Heritage 231
Jenny Pange, Alina Degteva, and Vasiliki Manglara

Preservation, Reuse and Reveal of Cultural Heritage through Sustainable Building and Land Management, Rural and Urban Development to Recapture the World in Crisis through Culture

AAGIS: An Archaeoastronomical Approach Using Geographic Information Systems 243
George Malaperdas, Dimitris Sinachopoulos, and Eleni Valianatou

Approaching Climate Resilience in Greek Cultural Heritage Using Geodata and Geoinformatics Tools 255
Athanasios Dimou and Christos-Nikolaos Anagnostopoulos

Salamis Island in the Challenge of a Digital Storytelling 266
Delazanou Maria

Planning to Live Longer: A Model for the Maintenance-Focused Heritage Building Conservation 276
Arturo Cruz, Vaughan Coffey, and Tommy H. T. Chan

A Review of Heritage Building Information Modelling: Classification of HBIM through the Utilization of Different Dimensions (3D to 7D) 287
Efstratios Koutros and Christos-Nikolaos Anagnostopoulos

Environmental and Socioeconomic Pressures and Cultural Heritage Degradation. Evidence from Elounda, Crete Island 298
George Alexandrakis, Stelios Petrakis, Nikolaos Rempis, Antonios Parasyris, and Nikolaos Kampanis

Analysis Between Cultural Heritage, Human Settlements and Landscapes Using Earth Observation and Archaeological Data 308
George Alexandrakis, Georgios V. Kozyrakis, Nikos Paxakis, Antonios Parasyris, Anastasia Vythoulka, Nikolaos A. Kampanis, and Antonia Moropoulou

ICT and Semantic BIM Technologies for the Advanced Documentation and Condition Assessment of Cultural Heritage Sites 321
Marco Medici, Roberto Di Giulio, and Beatrice Turillazzi

Enhancing Heritage Management for Sustainable Development in Insular Areas Through Digital Documentation: The Case Study of the Historic Center of the Megisti Island (Kastellorizo) 335
Aspasia E. Fafouti, Anastasia Vythoulka, Ekaterini T. Delegou, Agapitos Xanthis, Antonios Giannikouris, Nikolaos Kampanis, Georgios Alexandrakis, and Antonia Moropoulou

Delivering Education on the Sustainable Aspects of Heritage 353
Stavroula Thravalou and Maria Philokyprou

Development of a Support System for Improved Resilience and Sustainable Urban Areas to Cope with Climate Change and Extreme Events Based on GEOSS and Advanced Modelling Tools 364
Charalampos Zafeiropoulos, Ioannis N. Tzortzis, Ioannis Rallis, and Anastasios Doulamis

Cultural Heritage Protection and Artificial Intelligence; The Future of Our Historical Past 375
Eugenia Giannini and Evi Makri

AegeanDigital Tourism Tank: Experiences and Products for Enhancing the Sustainable Preservation of Digital Heritage of Cultural Organizations of North Aegean 401
Dora Chatzi Rodopoulou, Athanasia Kadrefi, Christos Kalloniatis, Angeliki Kitsiou, Maria Koltsaki, Anna Kyriakaki, Katerina Mavroeidi, Evangelia Proiou, Maria Sideri, Stavros Simou, Stavros Stavridis, Katerina Vgena, and Mania Mavri

'Orphaned' Monuments or Common Bicommunal Heritage? Conservation of four Gothic Churches in Famagusta Cyprus, Promoting Cultural Understanding, Exchange and Peace 411
Nasso Chrysochou

Author Index 425

Scientific Innovations in the Diagnosis and Preservation of Cultural Heritage

The Preservation of the Heritage of the Petralona Cave Using Multiple 3D Scanning Techniques and Data Processing Algorithms

Panagiotis Tokmakidis[1,2], Charisios Achillas[1,3](✉), Dimitrios Tzetzis[1,4], Elli Karkazi[5], Emmanouil Tzimtzimis[1,4], Andreas Darlas[5], Athanassios Athanassiou[5], and Dionysis Bochtis[1]

[1] Centre for Research and Technology Hellas (CERTH), Institute for Bio-Economy and Agri-Technology, Volos, Greece
c.achillas@certh.gr
[2] Laboratory of Topography, Aristotle University Thessaloniki, Thessaloniki, Greece
[3] Institute of Sustainable Development and Circular Economy, International Hellenic University, Katerini, Greece
[4] Digital Manufacturing and Materials Characterization Laboratory, International Hellenic University, Thermi, Greece
[5] Ephorate of Palaeoanthropology–Speleology, Ministry of Culture and Sports, Athens, Greece

Abstract. Petralona Cave is one of the most impressive caves in Greece (also, at European level), mostly due to the discovery of the Petralona human skull, which is dated back to the Middle Pleistocene, as well as its rich collection of fossilized animal bones and the great number of lower Palaeolithic lithic artefacts. In this work, we focus on the digitization process for the Petralona Cave. This is part of the overall research work that is being realized in the framework of the Cave3 project which is co-financed by the European Regional Development Fund of the European Union and Greek national funds through the Operational Program Competitiveness, Entrepreneurship and Innovation, under the Special Action "Open Innovation in Culture".

Keywords: Digital heritage · 3D scanning · terrestrial scanning · aerial scanning · photogrammetry · cave

1 Introduction

As the field of speleology became an established scientific discipline, advancements in survey instrumentation led to the evolution of various techniques for mapping caves. A review of the literature shows that there has been a longstanding effort to accurately map caves in 3D geometry, but the recent advent of terrestrial laser scanners with short and medium range capabilities represents a relative new phenomenon [1–4]. The paper provides a detailed report on Petralona Cave which is considered as a cultural heritage asset, well-known both as a natural and –at the same time– as a cultural monument. The Cave is located close to the village of Petralona in Chalkidiki, Greece, and was formed

A. Moropoulou et al. (Eds.): TMM_CH 2023, CCIS 1889, pp. 3–12, 2023.
https://doi.org/10.1007/978-3-031-42300-0_1

approximately one million years ago. It stretches over a zone of about 10,400 m^2 and comprises a progression of chambers, high roofs and narrow passages, decorated with stalactites, stalagmites, curtains, columns and other calcareous formations. It is a site of great importance and unique value due to the discovery of the oldest human remain –a human skull dated to the Middle Pleistocene– found so far in Greece and one of the most well-preserved skulls in Europe [5–7]. A wealth of fossilized animal bones, which belong to many species of both small vertebrates and large mammals, have also been found inside the Cave [8–11]. Additionally, a great number of lower Palaeolithic lithic artefacts, knapped by human groups who inhabited the cave, have been revealed during excavations. The Petralona Cave is considered as one of the earliest archaeological sites in Greece and Europe due both to the human skull and the above-mentioned lithic artefacts found within very thick deposits, dated to the Middle Pleistocene. The Cave's findings are of particular importance for the investigation of the early human occupations of Europe, since it is located at the threshold of the European continent, on one of the possible routes of dispersal of early humans [12].

The Petralona Cave is a well-known tourist attraction, welcoming more than 50,000 visitors every year. Unfortunately, only a limited area of the cave is accessible to wheelchair users and visitors with mobility impairments due to its narrow passageways and stairs. The tour visit covers only a small part of the cave, rendering many impressive cave formations invisible to the public. It only supports small groups of visitors ensuring their safety on the one hand and preventing the negative side effects of over-frequentation in the cave's micro-environment, on the other hand. Furthermore, the tour visit does not last long, especially during the peak season. For this reason, the visitors do not have enough time to observe the physical beauty of the Cave.

In the present work, the results of the Cave3 project [13] are highlighted. The project is co-financed by the European Regional Development Fund of the European Union and Greek national funds, through the Operational Program Competitiveness, Entrepreneurship and Innovation, under the Special Action "Open Innovation in Culture". In brief, the Cave3 project focuses on the exploitation of state-of-the-art digital technologies for developing innovative mechanisms to widely disseminate the cultural assets of the Petralona Cave and the Petralona Museum, and also to provide an interactive experience to the visitors. The project focuses also on satisfying the needs of visitors with disabilities, a group with special requirements that should be always considered in the framework of the "culture-for-all" and "tourism-for-all" concepts [14].

2 Exploitation of Digital Technologies to Promote Cultural Heritage

The emergence of digital technologies allows widespread free and equal access to all types of public, regardless of their economic status or the place where they live [15]. Digital technologies also affect experiential learning since those facilitate more immersive participation and deeper engagement with the heritage asset. The objectives set for the design and development of the Cave3 project take into account the principles established by the ICOMOS charter in 2008 [16]. Among others, the objectives also include; (i) the dissemination of the little-known archaeology of the Palaeolithic era to the public, (ii) the creation of a holistic digital museum and educational experience, (iii) the placement of the archaeological and palaeontological finds in various contexts, (iv) the offer of new possibilities for interaction and manipulation of the heritage asset, (v) the illustration of aspects of the cave that are not visible or/and accessible to visitors through the virtual tour of the cave, (vi) the raising of the awareness and the increase of the public sensitivity about the protection of caves and their ecosystems.

Apart from the digitization of the Petralona skull through 3D scanning and digital 3D facial approximation, we also selected a considerable number of the most representative and well-preserved fossilized animal bones and lithic artefacts to be digitized, so as to be incorporated into the digital museum, as well as the tools and application that are being developed in the framework of the project.

3 Digitization of the Petralona Cave

For the 3D digitization of the Petralona Cave, a terrestrial 3D laser scanner and an unmanned aerial vehicle (UAV) were used in combination with terrestrial photography, to achieve the maximum possible resolution of the photorealistic texture of the produced 3D model. In addition, the processing of all the data was realized in a specialized software that simultaneously resolves the scans and photographs, with the use of photogrammetry (SfM) [17]. Photographs were taken with the use of an aerial camera that was installed in a UAV system. To optimize texture quality and enhance the geometry in areas were the 3D laser scanner was unable to survey, a very high-resolution medium format camera was used for ground shots in combination with artificial strobe lighting.

In order to geo-reference the whole 3D survey in the Greek Geodetic Reference System 1987 (GGRS87), artificial ground control points (GCP) where placed in an even distribution along the 3D scanner's traverse inside and outside of the cave and measured using a 1 arc-second precision geodetic total station. The exact position of the initial control points (T1 & T2), from which the TS traverse started, was calculated using GNSS receivers in a fast-static survey mode (Adjustment Accuracy 6mm Horiz. 18mm Vert.), with the use of three (3) additional control points established in the area by the Hellenic Army Mapping Agency (Fig. 1). The initial control points have been georeferenced to GGRS87, but the rest of the TS traverse used to georeference the GCPs was processed without taking into account the linear scale factor of GGRS87 (0.999662 at the area) to avoid deformation and the same applied to the rest of the data processing, thus the final coordinates of the survey refer to a "pseudo-GGRS87" without linear scale. Moreover, several findings from the excavation research in the Petralona Cave were also digitized in the form of high detailed 3D models for their digital display, using a handheld structured light 3D scanner (Artec EVA).

To 3D scan the Petralona Cave and create a colored point cloud of its geometry, a FARO scanner model Focus 3D S120 was used. In total, one hundred and forty (140) scans were carried out with varying scanner resolution. Indicatively, for narrow passages and very closed spaces, a scan resolution of 47 m points was selected for each scan position. For the points where a rocky wall was located at more than 10 m from the scanner, a scan of 174 m points per scan position was selected. This was realized to ensure uniformity in the spatial resolution of the scan data. Due to the fact that the methodology combines scans with photographic images from a medium format camera, it was necessary for the scanner to record as reliably as possible the color during the scans, so that the scans could be photogrammetrically correlated with the terrestrial photography. To achieve this, a suitably adapted, wirelessly controlled, LED light body, both to trim brightness and on/off operation, was embodied in the scanner (Fig. 2).

Fig. 1. Snapshot of the geodetic total station traverse inside the cave.

Fig. 2. Snapshots from the scanning process.

In order to realistically reproduce the actual texture of the Petralona Cave, but also to improve the geometry in blind spots of the 3D scanner, ground shots were taken with a Hasselblad X1D II medium format digital camera, with a 50 Mpixels sensor, 30 mm lens (equivalent to 24 mm in full frame format) and built-in GNSS receiver (Fig. 3). It should be emphasized that the shots were captured in RAW file format. The camera produces files with 16-bit color information and provides the possibility of a dynamic range greater than 14 stops. For the shots, it was essential to use four (4) studio flashes of 200 W s each, with wireless synchronization with the camera. In addition, to fill shadows in several cases, additional portable flashes mounted on small tripods were used. The color temperature in all cases was kept as close as possible (due to the sharp differences in the distance of the rock from the camera and the flashes in each shot) to 5,500°K. In total, more than six thousand shots were taken with the medium format camera so as to fully cover the Petralona Cave.

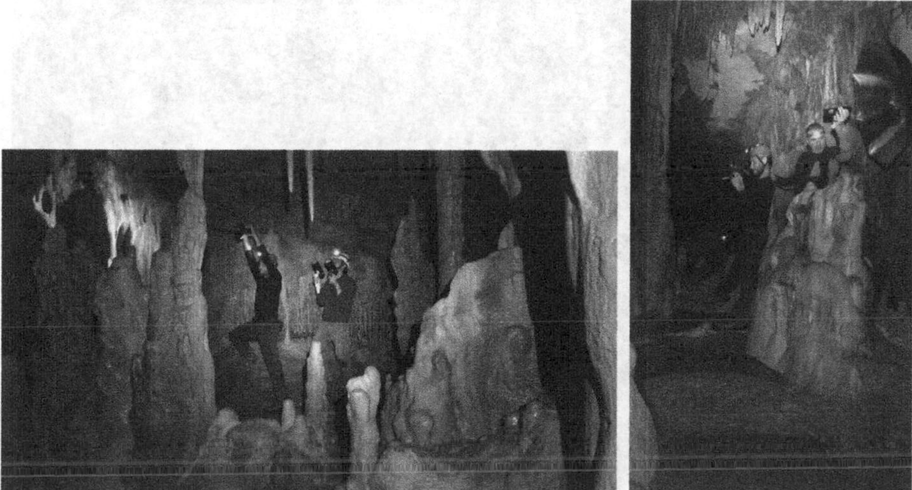

Fig. 3. Use of studio flash with an operator to quickly change position and bounce flash technique in very narrow parts of the Petralona Cave.

To optimally capture the entrance of the Petralona Cave, as well as for 3D rendering purposes of the surface area above it, a professional unmanned aerial vehicle, namely DJI Phantom 4 RTK model, was used. The UAV was equipped with a 20 Mpixels camera which initially flew autonomously at a height of 110 m above ground in order to quickly compile a relief file of the area in DEM (GeoTIFF) format. This file was then uploaded to the UAV's remote controller and two autonomous flights followed that maintained a constant distance of 35 m from the imported digital terrain model (Fig. 4). In this way, the result is homogeneous with the same spatial resolution on the ground throughout the area, despite the strong altitude differences.

The scans were resolved and georeferenced in FARO Scene, the scanner manufacturer's dedicated software. With the use of the aforementioned software, the clouds of each scan location were exported in one file each. The scans from FARO Scene were exported in E57 file format, as this is a generic file format that can be processed with most available software, either commercial or open source. As a next step, the digital images of both the UAV and the medium format camera, were processed in appropriate software (Hasselblad Phocus) and the color-corrected files in.jpg format were obtained. The point clouds of each position of the scanner and the processed photographic images were processed in Reality Capture software (PPI license) and resolved in combination with the measured coordinates of the ground control points. In this way, the overall 3D model of the cave with a photo-realistic texture was produced. This model was cleaned of anomalies in its topology and reduced in resolution using automatic and semi-automatic polygon re-topology techniques in Blender software to an 80-million triangles model. This process was necessary since the original model consists of 1.9 billion triangles with average edge length of 0.0046 m, 796 textures of 8192 × 8192 pixels and would not be easily inter-manipulated, nor compatible with web and mobile applications.

Fig. 4. (a) View of the entrance of the Petralona Cave. View from (b) 110 m above the ground, (c) 35 m above the ground.

The results of the process include both the original high-resolution model, as well as the lower resolution model in.fbx format and the reduced model in.stl format, in order to be 3D printed. The precision of the method for the high-resolution model, allows the possibility of printing and processing at scales up to 1:50. In other words, there is a precision and ground sampling distance in its texture, smaller than 1 cm. In Figs. 5, 6 and 7, the outcomes of the digitization process are outlined.

Fig. 5. Camera shots.

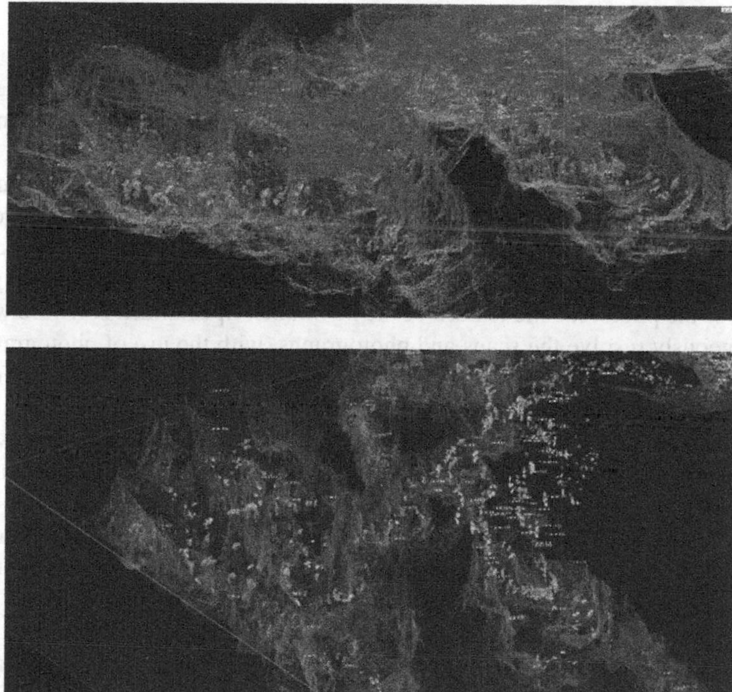

Fig. 6. Views from final 3D model of the Petralona Cave interior (combination of laser scanning and photogrammetry using the Reality Capture software).

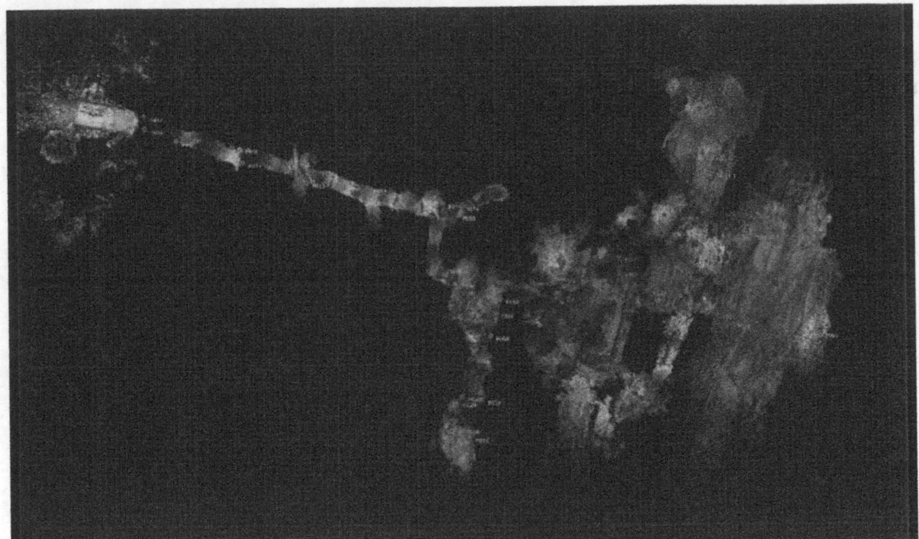

Fig. 7. 3D model of the entire Petralona Cave.

4 Conclusions

The paper presents the digitization process of the Petralona Cave, realized in the framework of the Cave3 project. 3D scanning models of large objects and environments, such as the Petralona Cave, although very complex, are possible as demonstrated in the current work. However, this would be very difficult to survey and details to be captured with the use of conventional surveying techniques, therefore the combination of other, more sophisticated techniques is required. To that end, unmanned aerial vehicle were used in combination with terrestrial photography in order to achieve the maximum possible resolution of the photorealistic texture of the 3D model. Specialized software was used to simultaneously resolve the scans and photographs, with the use of photogrammetry. Photographs were also taken with the use of an aerial camera that was installed in a UAV system to capture the external surroundings. To optimize quality, a second medium format and a camera with a very high resolution was used for ground shots. The wealth of data provided by such techniques, allow for the construction of a 3D representation and photorealistic appearance of the complex Cave's structure.

Using the presented methodology, the Petralona Cave and the surrounding area of its entrance have been surveyed in High Definition Survey, with great precision and photorealistic textures in less than a month on site, including some delays due to weather conditions, and less than three months for processing of the data. A transdisciplinary team co-operated for the needs of this project, something that is a common ground lately for similar large-scale surveys, as this is considered as best practice in terms of efficiency, accuracy and final results.

The Petralona Cave has been documented in great detail and the products of this documentation will be used further for disseminating the Cave, as well as its history and scientific facts to the wide public. The models contain information that can be interactively examined and enhanced for scientific and promotional purposes. A great advantage from such techniques is that caves, which are closed for conservation reasons or damaged from natural disasters, can still be studied and visited once a 3D virtual model has been created. The potential of modelling complex sites, such as caves, open new avenues in heritage applications, for instance virtual restoration or virtualized reality tours. Moreover, novel technologies like Augmented Reality (AR) and 3D printing will support this purpose, with the first visitors of the Museum of Petralona and the Petralona Cave, to experience an immersive and very interesting tour of the Cave and artefacts.

Acknowledgement. The work is co-financed by the European Regional Development Fund of the European Union and Greek national funds through the Operational Program Competitiveness, Entrepreneurship and Innovation, under the Special Action "Open Innovation in Culture" (project acronym: Cave3 | project code: T6ΥBΠ-00247).

References

1. Grussenmeyer, P., Landes, T., Alby, E., Carozza L.: High resolution 3D recording and modelling of the Bronze Age Cave "Les Fraux" in Perigord (France). In: International Archives of Photogrammetry, Remote Sensing and Spatial Information Sciences, Vol. XXXVIII, Part 5, Commission V Symposium. Newcastle upon Tyne, UK (2010)
2. Oludare Idrees, M., Pradhan, B.: A decade of modern cave surveying with terrestrial laser scanning: a review of sensors, method and application development. Int. J. Speleology **45**(1), 71–88 (2016)
3. Núñez, A., Buill, F., Edo, M.: 3D model of the Can Sadurní cave. J. Archaeol. Sci. **40**(12), 4420–4428 (2013)
4. Ullman, M., et al.: Formation processes and spatial patterning in a late prehistoric complex cave in northern Israel informed by SLAM-based LiDAR. J. Archaeol. Sci. Rep. **47**, 103745 (2023)
5. Stringer, C.B.: A multivariate study of the Petralona skull. J. Hum. Evol. **3**, 397–404 (1974)
6. Stringer, C.B.: Phylogenetic position of the Petralona cranium. Άνθρωπος **7**, 81–95 (1980)
7. Κουφός, Γ.: Ο Άνθρωπος των Πετραλώνων. In: Koufos, G., Tsoukala, E. (eds.) Πετράλωνα: *Ένα σπήλαιο μια προϊστορία*, Θεσσαλονίκη, pp. 87–128 (2007). (in Greek)
8. Sickenberg, O.: Revision der Wirbeltierfauna der Höhle Petralona (Griech, Mazedonien). Annales Géologiques des Pays Helléniques **23**, 230–264 (1971)
9. Kurtén, B.: Faunal Sequence in Petralona Cave. Άνθρωπος **10**, 53–59 (1983)
10. Kretzoi, M., Poulianos, N.A.: Remarks on the middle and lower pleistocene vertebrate fauna in the Petralona cave. Άνθρωπος **8**, 57–72 (1981)
11. Tsoukala, E.: Contribution to the study of the Pleistocene fauna of large mammals (Carnivora, Perissodactyla, Artiodactyla) from Petralona Cave, Chalkidiki (N. Greece). PhD thesis, Aristotle University of Thessaloniki. Scientific Annals, Faculty of Physics and Mathematics, University of Thessaloniki 1 (8) (1989). in Greek
12. Darlas, A.: In search of the identity of Petralona cave and its importance for the Greek and European Prehistory. In: Stefani, E., Merousis, N., Dimoula, A. (eds.) 1912–2012. A Century of Research in Prehistoric Macedonia. International Conference Proceedings, Archaeological Museum of Thessaloniki, Thessaloniki, Greece, 22–24 Nov 2012
13. Cave3 project: https://www.cave3.net. Last accessed 20 Jan 2023

14. Tokmakidis, P., Spatalas, S., Tokmakidis, K., Tsioukas, V.: Laser scanning in the service of the visually impaired. In: GEOMAPPLICA Conference, Skiathos island, Greece, 8–11 Sep 2014
15. Salleh, S.Z., Bushroa, A.R.: Bibliometric and content analysis on publications in digitization technology implementation in cultural heritage for recent five years (2016–2021). Dig. Appl. Archaeol. Cultural Heritage **25**, e00225 (2022)
16. International Council on Monuments and Sites: ICOMOS Charter on the Interpretation and Presentation of Cultural Heritage Sites. Reviewed and revised under the Auspices of the ICOMOS International Scientific Committee on Interpretation and Presentation – Ratified by the 16th General Assembly of ICOMOS, Quebec, Canada (2008)
17. Verykokou, S., Soile, S., Bourexis, F., Tokmakidis, P., Tokmakidis, K., Ioannidis, C.: A Comparative analysis of different software packages for 3D Modelling of complex geometries. In: Ioannides, M., Fink, E., Cantoni, L., Champion, E. (eds.) EuroMed 2020. LNCS, vol. 12642, pp. 228–240. Springer, Cham (2021). https://doi.org/10.1007/978-3-030-73043-7_19

The Restoration of the Main Theatre of the First Ancient Theatre of Larissa, Greece, Assisted by 3D Technologies

Dimitrios L. Karagkounis[1](✉) and Sofia D. Tsanaktsidou[2]

[1] Department of Archaeological Projects and Studies, Ephorate of Antiquities of Larissa, Diachronic Museum of Larissa, 41500 MezourloLarissa, Greece
karagdk@gmail.com

[2] Ancient Theatre of Larissa, Ephorate of Antiquities of Larissa, 10-12 Mitropolitou Arseniou, 41223 Larissa, Greece

Abstract. The First Ancient Theatre of Larissa, is one of the largest and most important theatres of Greece, situated in the centre of the modern city of Larissa, in the Region of Thessaly. Its unearthing and restoration have been a long and demanding process spanning almost half a century. In recent years, its restoration has been possible through European co-funded projects, which have also allowed the application of new technologies in designing and executing restoration works. In the current paper, the restoration of the main theatre is discussed, focusing on the challenges that arose during the repositioning of 350 ancient marble seats, 299 of which were repositioned to their original or corresponding positions, as well as the installation of 240 new marble seats, according to the approved restoration study. Also, the new technologies that were implemented in designing and producing the new marble seats are showcased, featuring photogrammetry methods, 3d laser scanning and point cloud imaging as well as CNC machining.

Keywords: Ancient Theatre · Restoration · Anastylosis · Cultural Heritage · 3D Modelling · 3D Laser Scanning

1 Introduction

The First Ancient Theatre of Larissa, Greece, is one of the most celebrated ancient monuments of Thessaly, and one of the largest and most important theatres of Greece. It is located in the centre of the modern city of Larissa, where, until recently, it was buried under blocks of flats and city roads. It is a Hellenistic theatre, constructed in the early 3rd century BC [1, 2]. Its unearthing was made possible with the emergence of co-funded EU projects, since the 2nd Community support framework, which allowed for compulsory purchases and demolitions of modern constructions to take place, in order to save a monument that had been – quite literally, in some cases – encased in concrete foundations and corroded by the effects of tens of cesspits.

The theatre has been unearthed almost in its entirety. The diazoma, a 2 m wide corridor, divides the cavea ("koilon"), into the main theatre and the "epitheatron", the

A. Moropoulou et al. (Eds.): TMM_CH 2023, CCIS 1889, pp. 13–22, 2023.
https://doi.org/10.1007/978-3-031-42300-0_2

cavea's lower and upper section respectively. The main theatre consists of 11 cunei, with 10 staircases ("klimakes") in between. Each cuneus ("kerkida") consists of 25 rows of seats ("edolia"). During the Roman period, the first three rows of seats were removed and repurposed in order to form the podium. The epitheatron is preserved to a small degree in the northwestern part. The orchestra has a diameter of approximately 25m and is surrounded by a closed marble duct, the "evripos" which conveys stormwater. Both retaining walls "anallimata" are maintained in excellent condition, although not fully unearthed. Finally, to the south, the theatre's scene building ("Skene") is situated, a luxurious and well preserved elongated rectangular structure, with a colonnade forming the "Proskenion", one of the few examples of similar Hellenistic buildings that survive to this day.

In this paper, the restoration of the main theatre is discussed, involving the repositioning of 299 ancient marble seats "edolia" to their original or corresponding ("homologous") positions and the installation of 240 new marble seats, according to the approved restoration study "Restoration of the Ancient Theater of Larissa" [3] (Fig. 1). Special mention will be given to the 3D technologies implemented in the process of documenting the current situation, designing, modeling and finally manufacturing the new architectural members.

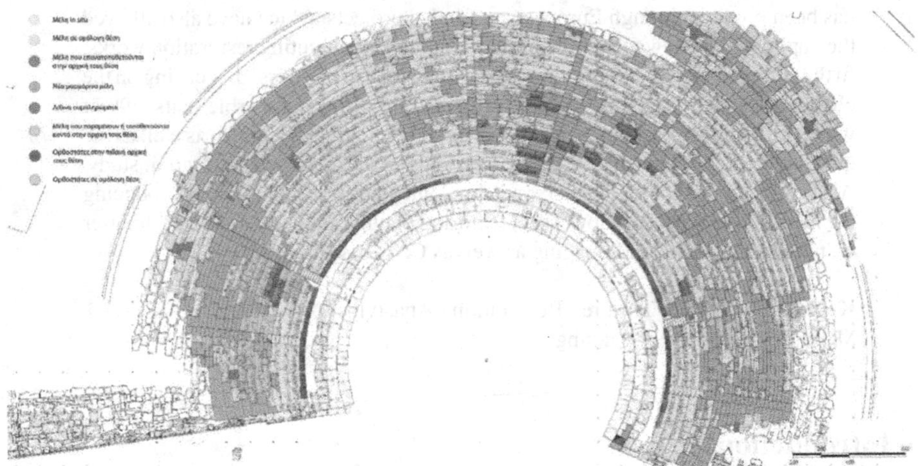

Fig. 1. Plan view of the suggested positions of ancient (purple, blue and green) and new (dark grey) "edolia" as per the approved study. Cyan are considered to be in their correct position [3]

2 3D Modelling Process

In recent years, 3D modelling and digital documentation technologies have been gaining popularity in the documentation and preservation of cultural heritage, in cases of both immobile and mobile monuments and artifacts, especially 3D laser scanning and 3D modelling [4–6]. A brief presentation of the implementation of said technologies in the scope of the Restoration of the First Ancient Theatre of Larissa was carried out by the authors in [7].

In the following sections, the process of digitizing the main theatre and modelling 240 new marble seats is discussed, as carried out according to the approved study [3], by a specialized contractor selected after an open international public tender within the framework of sub-project 3: "Laser scanning – 3D CAD/CAM software", under D. Karagkounis's supervision. All field work had to precede any repositioning of ancient marble seats, due to the project's progress and limited free surrounding space. Ancient seats non-related to the study's provisions were removed, documented, tagged, and temporarily placed in the scene building's rooms.

2.1 Description Of Field Work And Design Process

Field work included topographic surveying, aerial photography with UAVs (Unmanned Aerial Vehicles), terrestrial photogrammetric photography, measurements of the exact dimensions of neighboring existing seats, and 3D laser scanning of the monument.

A total of 6 UAV flights were performed with cross flight plans. Aerial photographs with more than 80% overlapping were acquired in both vertical and diagonal orientations, to cover either side and produce a complete and blind-spot-free photogrammetric 3D model.

The processing of the data from the field measurements included the solution and application of the topographic measurements (Fig. 2), the definition of photostables, the production of orthophoto maps/3D point clouds and meshes with photogrammetric methods and the solution, binding, coloring, and point cloud georeferencing. In total, 32 orthophoto maps were created with pixel size of 0.00022 m. The final orthophoto map has a pixel size of 5.93 mm and a precision of 10.7 mm (Fig. 3).

Fig. 2. Measurements of existing topographic points of the 2017 study

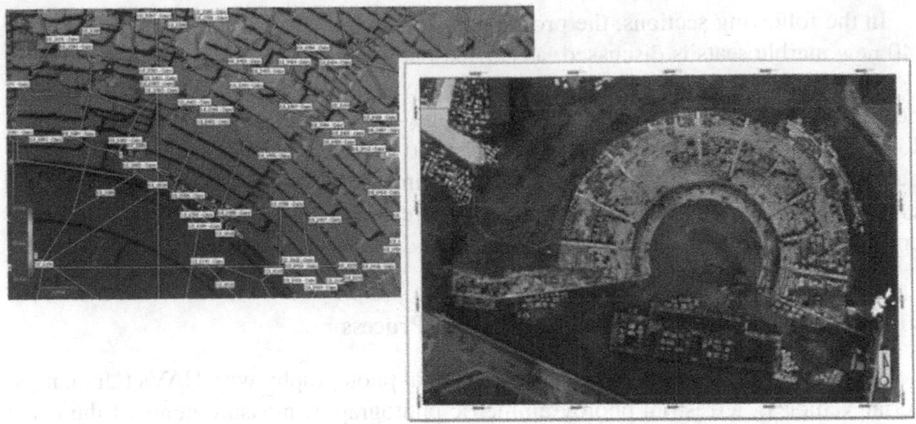

Fig. 3. Digital Elevation Model (DEM) and final Orthophoto map

The processing and design of the 240 new marble architectural members was done in a 3-dimensional CAD environment and exported as the desired solids with open-source 3D design software. The final deliverables include a CAD file and a 3D*.Stl file for each new seat.

The final dimensions of each new seat were derived from measurements of the final three-dimensional clouds with an accuracy of less than 1 mm, considering the assumptions and limitations analyzed in the following Subsect. 2.2. The initial digitization of each new seat's 2D plan view was done on the high-resolution orthophotomap.

The width of the groove was taken from on-site measurements and the terrestrial photogrammetry model. Foot arch radii were extracted from dense point clouds of neighboring seats, where available.

Fig. 4. Terrestrial photogrammetry 3D model

The height of each seat was derived from the height of neighboring existing ancient seats, or from the height difference of the 3D point cloud between the staircase step height and the groove depth, with the base height of the row.

All dimensional measurements were verified with field survey measurements.

In the case of cunei such as KB, KΔ, KΣT and KZ there were rows where all seats were absent and new members were required (Fig. 6). In these cases, the staircase steps on either side were calculated as the beginning and end. Their dimensions were calculated from the average spans of seats of neighboring rows.

All data were georeferenced to the Hellenic Geodetic Reference System 1987 (EGSA'87) with coordinates from the topographic survey.

The final deliverables of the 240 seats in CAD/3D format file were transferred to zero coordinates (0,0) for the needs of importing the 3D model to the CNC machines of the marble members.

2.2 Assumptions And Limitations

For the design of the new marble seats (Fig. 5), specific assumptions based on the study of field measurements and the approved study of the "Restoration of the Ancient Theater of Larissa" [3] were examined and used. The following assumptions were made to derive correct dimensions for the design of the new marble architectural members:

Curves (arches) with a specific radius were used for each series extracted from the terrestrial 3D scan (Fig. 4) and which also agree with the previous study. At various points, differences from the overall curve of the series were observed. The standard seats were designed according to the overall curves of the series.

Dimensional measurements from adjacent ancient seats, where available were used.

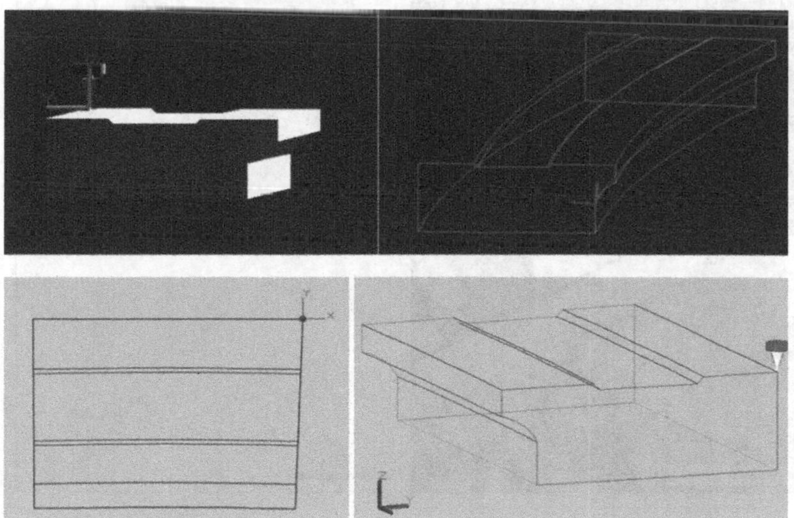

Fig. 5. Typical model and 3D drawings of a new seat

Adjacent seats in a row were designed with the same characteristics so as their joints do not coincide with those of adjacent rows.

It was assumed that the height of the seat's groove is the same as the adjacent scale.

The height and depth of the alignment of the vertical part of the 'foot' of the seat to the point of the beginning of the curvature is the same as the height of the adjacent staircase step.

The curvature at the foot of the seat was measured in the 3D model of the laser scanner or terrestrial photogrammetry in the neighboring ancient seats, if they existed.

In the opposite case, where there were no neighboring ancient seats, the average of the nearest seats was used (Fig. 6). This assumption was also used for other dimensions.

A far as the groove's dimension is concerned, it was decided that its depth should be the same across all new seats and uniform with a value of 0.023 m and in accordance with the approved restoration study proposal [3]. The many different values of the existing ancient seats, adjacent and non-adjacent, contributed to this decision, as well as their complete disparity.

In some cases, it was extremely difficult to conclude on the final seat dimensions, despite the above assumptions and what was provided by the approved study. The main problem was the absence of the correct neighboring seats, as dictated by the restoration study, that would allow for the precise calculation of the seat's lengths, or instances where the neighboring seat, at the time of modeling, would be moved to another position or a fragmented seat will be restored in the future.

It should be noted that all 240 new seats are entirely new, whole members, since circumstances are not mature, at this restoration phase, to proceed with the restoration of fragmented ancient seats.

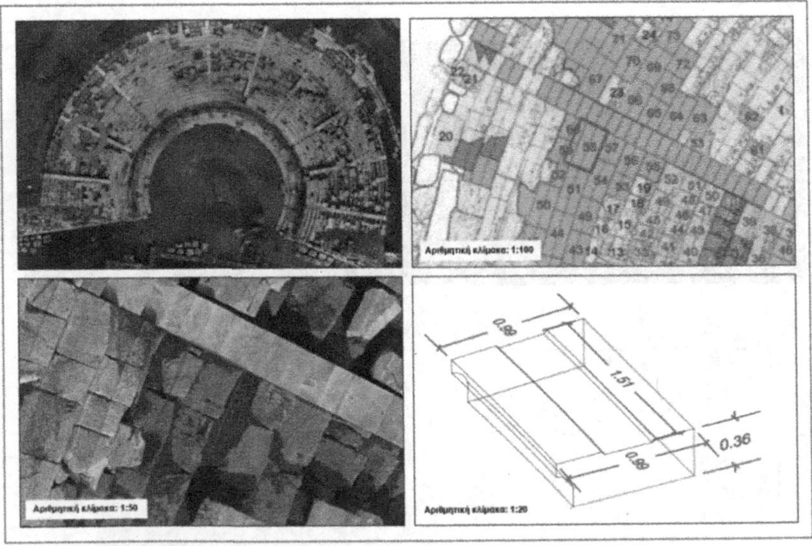

Fig. 6. Proposed outer dimensions of a new "edolio" at cuneus KB

3 Restoring The Main Theatre

3.1 Repositioning Of Ancient Seats

The repositioning of ancient marble seats involved a total of 299 "edolia" (Fig. 8). Of these, 30 were repositioned to their exact position, 64 were placed close to their original position, while 205 were placed in corresponding ("homologous") positions.

For the repositioning of ancient seats, an application study was carried out, as well as detailed documentation of all phases of the restoration process. The application study consisted of identifying each seat in its initial position, and "matching" it to its final position according to the restoration study, cataloging them in tabs.

Fig. 7. Repositioning an ancient marble "edolio" according to the study

In the process of repositioning the 299 "edolia", it was necessary to remove and relocate more than 50 ancient seats that were not included in the approved study but had been temporarily placed in the final positions of some of those 299 seats. As previously mentioned, they were removed, documented, tagged, and temporarily placed in the scene building's rooms. They were later placed in the top rows of the cunei, so that they could be studied and identified in the future.

Each architectural member was documented (Fig. 9) before and after their placement in their final positions (Fig. 7), accompanied by notes regarding study issues or challenges encountered. These happened in several cases of "homologous" architectural members, where technical difficulties arose during placement, such as the impossibility of complete identification of continuous seats in terms of their overall morphology (e.g., differences in the carving of supposedly neighboring seats, inconsistencies with shared dimensions, lack of continuity when it came to the inscriptions they bear).

Fig. 8. Aerial view of the theatre after repositioning of ancient seats is complete.

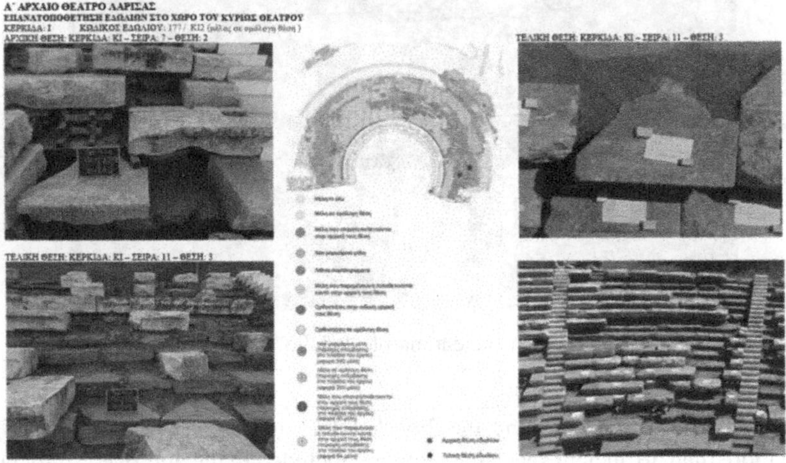

Fig. 9. Documentation of the repositioning of ancient seat "K67" to a corresponding "homologous" place, according to the restoration study [3]

3.2 Installation of New Marble Seats

The process of producing the new architectural members included wet-cutting of the large marble blocks into smaller blocks of 0.40 m height, then the creation of a solid in which each "edolio" is inscribed and finally the programming and processing of the final blocks on a 5 axis CNC machine according to the models created as described in Sect. 2 (Fig. 10). Production was carried out by a contractor selected after an open international public tender in the scope of sub-project 5.

Fig. 10. Manufacturing process of the new marble seats on CNC machine

After their manufacturing, new marble seats, were gradually transferred from the factory to the monument restoration site and were temporarily placed around the orchestra's perimeter, by use of crane trucks. Afterwards, the seats were grouped according to the cuneus they belong to, as dictated by the approved study. The installation process is similar to the one followed with the repositioning of ancient "edolia". Final on-site measurements are taken, and a test placement is done. Any necessary smoothing of surfaces is carried out, the soil substrate is arranged, and the architectural member is lifted and positioned according to the restoration study (Fig. 11).

Fig. 11. Placement of new marble seats "edolia" using a crane truck

4 Conclusions

The Restoration of the First Ancient Theatre of Larissa is an ongoing project that has utilized modern technologies in documentation for the last 20 years. An important breakthrough is the use of 3d technologies in the modelling and manufacturing of 240 new marble seats, thus modernizing, streamlining, and expediting restoration works, while staying within the framework of international restoration guidelines and statements. The combination of complementary methods in 3d scanning, imaging and modelling is proving a useful tool to accurately achieve a high quality of work. Nonetheless, each monument's specific features should be taken into consideration when planning and executing such tasks.

The repositioning of more than 350 ancient seats, was a difficult and time-consuming process that required meticulous planning and exhaustive documentation. The problems encountered highlight the need for more precise studies and the need for more leeway in the cases of restoration works of this scale.

Acknowledgements. The activity presented was conducted under the Project "Restoration of the first Ancient Theater of Larissa – Phase E" that is co-financed by the European Union (European Regional Development Fund – ERDF) and Greek national funds through the Regional Operational Program Thessaly 2014–2020 of the National Strategic Reference Framework (NSRF) 2014–2020.

References

1. Tziafalias, A.: Το αρχαίο θέατρο της Λάρισας, Πρακτικά του Α΄ Ιστορικού-Αρχαιολογικού Συμποσίου. Larissa **1985**, 162–185 (1985)
2. Tziafalias, A.: Το έργο της ΙΕ΄ ΕΠΚΑ Λάρισας, Το έργο των Εφορείων Αρχαιοτήτων και Νεωτέρων Μνημείων του ΥΠΠΟ στη Θεσσαλία και την ευρύτερη περιοχή της (1990–1998), 1η Επιστημονική Συνάντηση, Volos, pp. 91–96 (2000)
3. Karagkounis D, Chatzidakis N, Angeli E.A., Plakotaris I., Karnavezos Ch., Tziafalias A.: Αποκατάσταση του Αρχαίου Θεάτρου της Λάρισας (Restoration of the First Ancient Theatre of Larissa), unpublished study (2017)
4. Bilis, T., Kouimtzoglou, T., Magnisali, M., Tokmakidis, P.: The use of 3d scanning and photogrammetry techniques in the case study of the roman theatre of Nikopolis. Surveying, virtual reconstruction and restoration study. ISPRS – Int. Archiv. Photogrammetry, Remote Sens. Spatial Inform. Sci. **XLII-2/W3**, 97–103 (2017)
5. Efstathiou, K., Bouzakis, K., Efstathiou, C., Basiakoulis, A.: Investigation, reconstruction, and manufacturing of accurate copies of archaeological findings, based on innovated technologies as: 3D scanners, photogrammetrie, X-ray tomography, neutron tomography, CAD systems. In: Symposium: New Technologies in Service to Our Knowledge of Antiquity. Academy of Institutions and Cultures, Thessaloniki (2013)
6. Parfenov, V., Igoshin, S., Masaylo, D., Orlov, A., Kuliashou, D.: Use of 3D laser scanning and additive technologies for reconstruction of damaged and destroyed cultural heritage objects. Quantum Beam Sci. **6**, 11 (2022)
7. Karagkounis, D.L., Tsanaktsidou, S.D.: Digital documentation and 3d modelling in the restoration of the first ancient theatre of Larissa, Greece. In: Vayas, I., Mazzolani, F.M. (eds.) PROHITECH 2021. LNCE, vol. 209, pp. 586–593. Springer, Cham (2022). https://doi.org/10.1007/978-3-030-90788-4_46

Comparing the Methods of Terrestrial Laser Scanning and Photogrammetry for the Geometric Documentation of Stone Bridges Through the Case Study of Tzelefos Bridge

A. Fellas(✉) and M. Demosthenous

Frederick University, 1036 Nicosia, Cyprus
art.fa@frederick.ac.cy
http://www.frederick.ac.cy

Abstract. The technological means used for geometric documentation of monuments are advancing rapidly and the equipment required are becoming more accessible to architects, engineers, archeologists, surveyors, and restorers. Due to the rapid technological evolution there needs to be a continuous evaluation of the various hardware and software available for producing accurate three-dimensional models of monuments.

When a restoration team is presented with the dilemma of which method to use for documenting the geometrical characteristics of a monument, choosing between traditional photogrammetric surveys and terrestrial laser scanning technologies is not apparent. The research presented evaluates the different methods of documentation through the direct comparison of their outcomes.

The case study used for comparing the different methods of geometric documentation is the stone bridge of Tzelefos located in the mountain area of Troodos. The bridge has been declared a monument by the Cyprus Department of Antiquities. In the scope of this study the bridge was documented with three different methods. The first method of documentation was terrestrial laser scanning and the other two methods were photogrammetric with the use of an unmanned aerial vehicle (UAV) and a full frame digital single-lens reflex camera (DSLR).

The different methods are compared based on the time required for the data acquisition, the time needed for processing the data, the cost of equipment, the resolution of the produced geometry, the quality of the texture maps and the effectiveness of each method in dealing with an environment that is densely populated with vegetation.

Keywords: Photogrammetry · UAV · Laser · Scanning · Monuments · Bridge · Stone

A. Moropoulou et al. (Eds.): TMM_CH 2023, CCIS 1889, pp. 23–42, 2023.
https://doi.org/10.1007/978-3-031-42300-0_3

1 Introduction

The Department of Antiquities in Cyprus has classified many stone bridges as important examples of historical bridge construction and declared them as protected historical structures and monuments [1]. A comprehensive survey of the stone bridges of Cyprus is necessary in order to fully appreciate the structural, artistic, and cultural value of these monuments. The survey should include a detailed physical examination of the bridges, their location, the materials used in their construction, their morphological characteristics, and the cultural and historical context of their construction. In addition, a detailed study of the local environment and topography should be conducted in order to better understand the impact of the bridges on the landscape. Furthermore, a photographic and geometric documentation should be undertaken to provide a record of the current condition of the bridges. The results of the survey should be used to inform a documentation, conservation, and promotion strategy for the bridges.

The technological means for surveying bridges, either these are conventional structures or historical monuments, have been evolving with a high rate in the last 50 years [2]. This is mainly caused by the development of digital photogrammetry and terrestrial laser scanning [3]. The technologies supporting these surveying methods regarding the hardware and software needed to process the information produced by the photogrammetric and laser scanning equipment have been dramatically improved over the last 10 years. Both the photogrammetric method as well as the method of terrestrial laser scanning can produce results of high accuracy when it comes to delivering three-dimensional point clouds and models [4]. The choice of which method to use when a survey team is assigned the task of geometric documentation of a stone bridge is not always apparent. Both methods are highly accurate as far as their produced point clouds which are derived from the first stage of processing and can also transfer color information to a three-dimensional mesh model in the second processing stage. Although the two methods have many similarities regarding their final outputs some distinct differences exist that may be of crucial importance to the geometric analysis of stone bridges.

2 Research Aims

The current research aims to compare and analyze the geometric documentation methods of Terrestrial Laser Scanning (TLS) and Photogrammetric Surveys with Unmanned Aerial Vehicle (UAV) and a Digital Single-Lens Reflex camera (DSLR) in terms of parameters such as geometrical accuracy, resolution of projected images, level of vegetation permeation, processing time, cost of equipment, and technical skills needed to successfully complete the surveys.

2.1 Geometrical Accuracy

The comparison of the geometric accuracy of all the methods were executed through the produced point clouds using an open-source point cloud comparison software (CloudCompare). The post processed three-dimensional mesh models with the different methods were be evaluated and compared.

2.2 Resolution and Fidelity of Projected Textures

The different methods were evaluated in relation their produced textures resolution and their textures fidelity and quality.

2.3 Level of Permeation of Dense Vegetation

Due to the common densely populated environment surrounding stone bridges with trees and vegetation the surveying methods were evaluated for their ability to penetrate the vegetation and produce accurate geometric information of the bridges as well as the surrounding terrain.

2.4 Processing Time, Cost of Equipment and Technical Skills Required

The time needed for data collection and post processing of the collected data with the different surveying methods were compared. Also, the very significant factor of cost of surveying equipment was evaluated. The requirements for specialized personal computer specifications were considered in the cost evaluation. The last comparison parameter was the level of knowledge and technical skills needed for the effective use of the different surveying methods.

Fig. 1. Tzelefos bridge aerial photo

3 The Case Study of Tzelefos Bridge

One of the main reasons for selecting the Tzelefos bridge (Fig. 1) as the case study for this research was its inclusion in the list of Class A monuments by the Cyprus Department of Antiquities. The bridge is constructed of stones from the surrounding mountain area and chiseled lime stones at the edges of the arches, and incorporates solid clay bricks in the construction of the underside of the bridge arch. This mixture of building materials was common in the construction of stone bridges in the timeframe between the 14th and 16th centuries [5]. The overall scale of the bridge, spanning 33 m with a width of 3 m, is similar to many stone bridges in Cyprus. The bridge is located deep within the mountain area of Paphos District, at an altitude of 440 m above sea level, and is surrounded by trees, bushes, and low vegetation. Its location in the mountain area can cause weak or nonexistent GPS signals, so this factor needs to be considered when assessing appropriate surveying instruments. In addition, the surveyor or surveying team may need to hike a substantial distance to reach the monument, so the weight and safe stabilization of the equipment is important.

4 Methodology Description

The collection of data was carried out with three different surveying methods: terrestrial laser scanning, photogrammetry with the use of a UAV and photogrammetry with the use of a full frame DSLR (Fig. 2). The processing of the collected data with the three methods followed the same three steps until their final outputs: the generation of a dense point cloud, the generation of a three-dimensional mesh and the generation of a texture that will be mapped on the final digital model. To validate the dataset produced with the TLS, a laser level and laser distance meter was used. The comparison of the different datasets was executed using the open-source software CloudCompare to evaluate the geometrical deviations of the photogrammetric point clouds in relation to the TLS point cloud. The geometric characteristics of the three models, their projected textures, resolution, and fidelity was also be compared. In addition, the percentage of missing geometric information after removing the points relating to trees and vegetation was determined to evaluate the level of vegetation permeation for each method.

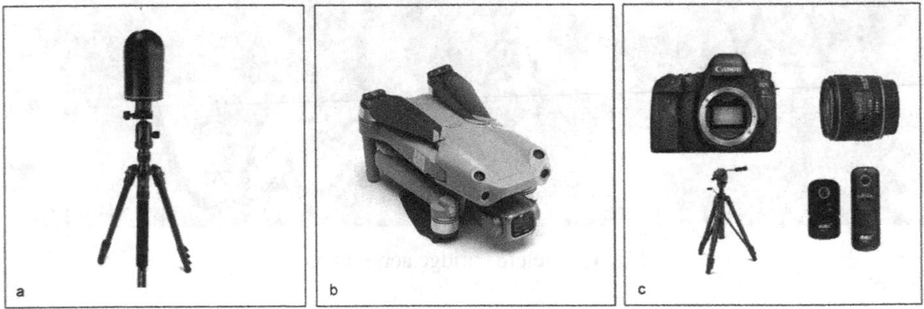

Fig. 2. Main Surveying Equipment, a) Terrestrial Laser Scanner (BLK 360 G1) b) UAV (DJI Air 2s) c) DLSR Camera, Fixed 24mm Lens and Accessories

5 TLS Data Collection and Processing

5.1 Survey Equipment Selection

Before beginning the TLS survey, the most suitable scanner had to be selected for this type of monument. The overall size of the monument and the steep slope of the terrain surrounding the bridge were the main factors that influenced the decision for the type of scanner that was used. The scanner selected was the BLK 360 G1 due to its small size, which would make the stabilization with the use of a tripod much safer than bulkier and heavier scanners. Additionally, as this was a case study for surveying the stone bridges of Cyprus, the fact that some bridges are located deep in the forest and hikes of thousands of meters are sometimes needed to reach, heavy equipment would make it difficult to carry to these remote locations. The scanner selected had a scanning range of 60 cm to 60 m with the optimal scanning range of 10 m with an accuracy of 6 mm at that distance [6]. These specifications made the current model sufficiently suitable for this survey since the monument has a total length of 33 m and the estimated scanning positions were initially estimated to be more than 15, meaning the distance between scans as well as the distance of each scan position in relation to the monument was within the optimal range of the instrument.

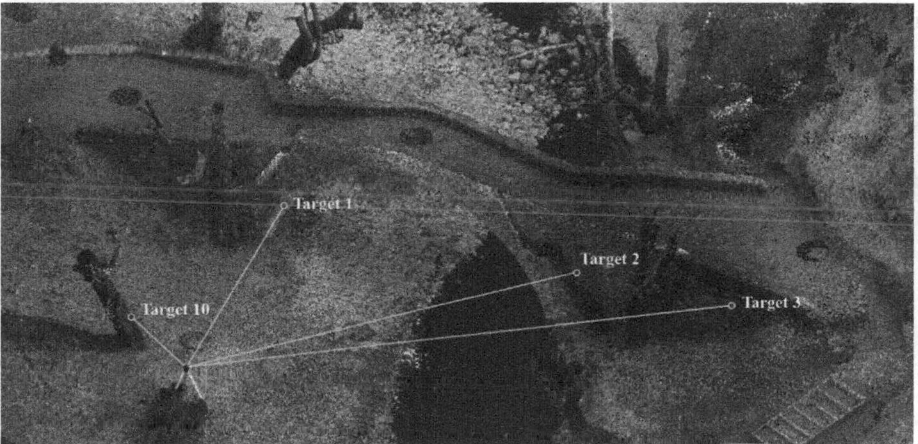

Fig. 3. Targets set in the same horizontal plane using a laser level (Bosch GLR 400H).

Before initializing the scanning, a set of twelve printed targets were placed on the surfaces and in the immediate surrounding area of the bridge. The targets were coded with the RAD system of coding [7] so that they would be automatically registered in the photogrammetric processing software at the next survey sets. The first 4 targets were placed using an automatic laser level instrument. The level used was the model Bosch GLR 400H combined with the Bosch LR 1 receiver [8]. The placement of the first targets with this method aimed to confirm and validate the automatic leveling accuracy of the TLS that made use of its own internal inertial measuring unit to set the horizontal plane.

5.2 Data Collection and Processing

The monument was surveyed with a total of 22 scanner positions, mainly defined by the areas that the tripod could be safely stabilized (Fig. 3). From the scanned positions, a set of 360-degree images was collected that would later be used for colorizing the point clouds produced from these positions. For equipment safety purposes, there were no scanned positions in the area of the river bed. The distances between the scanner and the monument ranged from 1 m to 10 m.

The data collected by the scanner were post-processed in the Leica Register 360 software. Within the software environment, the different scanned positions were registered with a total estimated alignment error of 8 mm, which was an acceptable value for this size of monument. Before the export of the final point cloud produced by the TLS, the automatic self-leveling of the data was evaluated. The 4 targets (numbered 1,3,4 -10) that were placed using the laser level were compared to the coordinates of the same points as produced by the TLS (Fig. 4). The maximum deviation in the vertical (Z axis) was 11mm and that was between the targets 1 and 2. This deviation was noted but no adjustment to the leveling of the final point cloud produced by the TLS was made since the value was within the expected total error considering the GLR 400H error and Bosch LR 1 receiver error estimated by the manufacturer. The GLR 400H laser level has an estimated error by the manufacturer of ±1.6 mm at 20 m, and the receiver has an estimated error of ±3 mm at 20 m. Considering the user errors for both instruments, the final deviation in the vertical axis of 11 mm was considered acceptable.

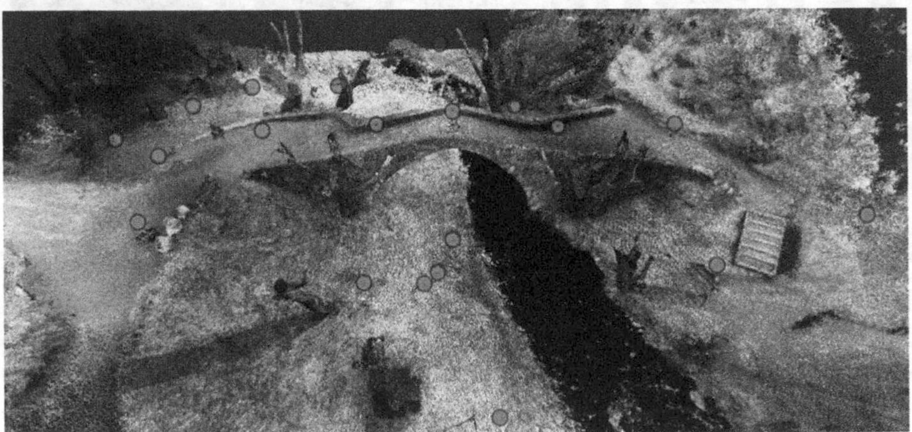

Fig. 4. Terrestrial Scanner Positions

The final verification of the point cloud data from the TLS was conducted using a laser distance meter (Bosch DLE 70). Distances between the four targets with the same Z alignment were measured and compared with the TLS data, with a maximum deviation of 5mm. This deviation was within the range of user error, so no further adjustment of the TLS point cloud was necessary.

After the manual cleaning of the point cloud from points that were further away from the area of interest or were referring to tall tree trunks, branches and crowns, the data was exported in E57 format so that it could later be imported into photogrammetry and cloud compare software. The points referring to the 10 targets attached to the monument and the surrounding area were identified in the TLS software and their coordinates were exported in TXT format and imported into an Excel sheet.

The final step of this process was the insertion of the E57 point cloud in Agisoft Metashape 1.71. The purpose of this step was to further clean the point cloud form unrelated points referring to vegetation and the water surface (Fig. 5) and to produce a colorized mesh from the final set of points. The final points count after cleanup and the reduction of the study area to final plan dimensions of 46 m × 23 m was 64,656,307 points. Setting the mesh generation setting in Agisoft Metashape to high the final mesh that was produced had a count of 12,931,260 triangles. The texture applied to the mesh was automatically derived from the average color values of the point cloud as exported from the TLS software (Fig. 6).

Fig. 5. Selection and removal of points referring to the water surface

5.3 TLS Survey Evaluation

The process of collecting the scanner data in the field took 2 h for the 22 scanned positions. This time can be expected to increase in rougher terrain due to the need for stabilizing the tripod for safety. Despite the difficulties of the topology, the time required for data collection is relatively short compared to other surveying methods such as photogrammetry and total station [9]. The post-processing of the data collected on-site took a total of 12 h, which includes registration of scanned positions, generation of accuracy reports, final point cloud cleaning and textured mesh generation.

The specifications recommended by the Leica software developer for this type of processing are a 3.0 GHz quad core processor with 32 GB of memory and an Nvidia GeForce GTX 680 or better graphics card. The total cost of survey equipment and computer for applying this method comes to about €35,000 with prices for the year 2022 [10]. This cost in relatively high compared to other survey methods. The conventional

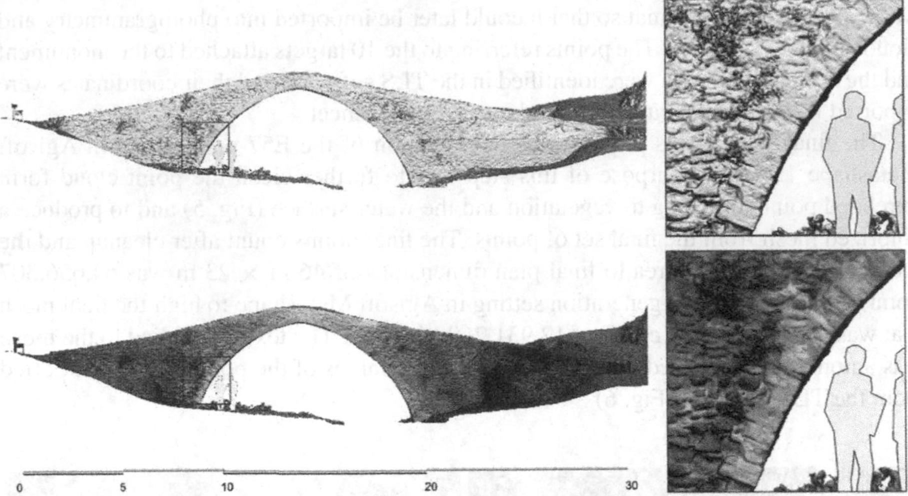

Fig. 6. Terrestrial laser scanner final mesh and textured model (South View)

survey method that uses a total station to set several control points to be completed by adding measurements with distance meters and tape measurements is by far less costly and the personal computer needed to digitize the information is significantly less demanding it terms of specifications. The cost comparison with the photogrammetric methods, which is also less costly, is analyzed in the next stages of this research.

The required knowledge to apply this surveying method is restricted to basic understanding of the hardware and software components as well as basic knowledge of digital modeling and topography. This knowledge to successfully complete a TLS survey of such a monument compared to other survey methods can be characterized as elementary.

6 UAV Photogrammetry Data Collection and Processing

6.1 UAV Selection

For applying the photogrammetric method with the use of an unmanned aerial vehicle the proper UAV was to be selected prior to the survey. The limited air space that a safe flight could be executed due to the dense forest surrounding the bridge was the most significant factor for the UAV selection. Also due to the trees surrounding the bridge, flight paths low to the ground were expected in order to gather the necessary photos to successfully recreate the digital model of the monument. In the case of a large and heavy drone the thrust generated by the propellers would be equivalently high. This force would have as result the steering of dust particles from the ground and ultimately affecting the accuracy of the three-dimensional model.

So, in the early stages of the research, it became apparent that a compromise had to be made as the larger UAV's that can carry large cameras would not be safe to fly in this environment and probably not yield the most accurate results. UAV options with relatively large camera sensors and small weights were evaluated and the UAV with model code DJI AIR 2s was selected.

6.2 Data Collection

Two 20-min flights were conducted by the aircraft to collect all photos, which were downloaded in JPEG and DNG (Raw) formats. Unfortunately, due to the dense vegetation in the area, only 12 of those photos had enough altitude to cover almost the entire area of the bridge, and all of them were taken from the south side. Ideally, the photos should have been divided into two sets of 50%: vertical shots downwards and lateral shots. However, due to the presence of trees close to the monument, it was not possible to take enough pictures with a vertical angle towards the ground. Prior to its first flight, the aircraft underwent a data check procedure during which its geodetic receiver detected 14 satellites and the aircraft automatically entered GPS flight mode, providing enhanced levels of flight safety. Unfortunately, during photography, the UAV lost connection to the satellite data and switched to manual control mode, leaving the motion control inactive and the UAV stationary for some seconds. It was revealed that in areas with no clear view of the sky, the operator must be adequately trained to handle such phenomena.

Fig. 7. UAV camera positions in relation to the bridge and surrounding area

For the completion of the survey 2 flights were executed collecting a total of 454 photographs (Fig. 7). The photographs were collected in DNG and JPEG formats although only the later would be used for the photogrammetric processing. Although the common practice in these types of surveys is to collect the first photographic set with many photographs perpendicular to the ground due to the surrounding trees this was not possible. From the set of photographs only 12 were able to cover the entirety of the monument and this was less than ideal. Also, most of the photographs collected were at a steep angle in relation to the ground due to the low flight paths.

The photogrammetric processing was done in the software Agisoft Metashape 1.71. Despite the less-than-ideal sequence of data collection the first processing step which was creating of the sparce point cloud showed no significant errors or gaps of data in relation to the bridge's geometrical characteristics. This was achieved mainly with the use of high percentage of overlap between each photograph (more than 70%), Another factor that aided towards a successful first step was the relatively high resolution of the UAV camera (5472 × 3648) with a sensor size of 1 inch.

6.3 Photos Processing in Photogrammetry Software

Photo Alignment and Sparce Point Cloud Generation

The initial alignment of the 454 photos in Agisoft Metashape 1.7.1 photogrammetry software was successful, with no errors occurring during the alignment process. The high resolution of the photos (5472 × 3648) and their high density resulted in a sparse point cloud of 2,140,458 points (Fig. 8).

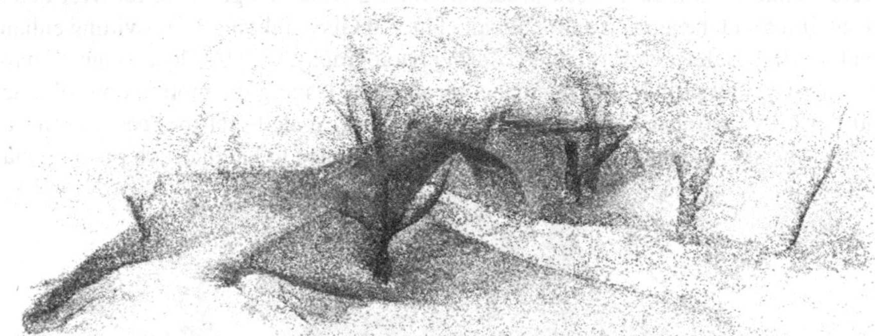

Fig. 8. UAV photogrammetry, sparse point cloud (2,140,458 anchor points)

The outline of the structural elements was visibly clear, with no significant information gaps. Although the initial positions of the photos, based on the data embedded in the photos, had significant deviations from the modified positions after alignment processing, the initial data still helped in the processing since the software had some initial information and did not need to calculate all positions from scratch using only the images as input. The maximum deviation was 36 m and the minimum was 30 cm, which was attributed to the basic referencing system of the UAV, which did not include an additional high accuracy positioning system (RTK).

Dense Point Cloud Generation and Filtering of Unrelated Points

After generating the sparse point cloud, additional points were automatically added to form a dense cloud. Points referring to tree canopies and vegetation were then manually identified and removed. Similarly, points referring to the water of the river were easily identified and removed due to their color contrast and the angle relative to the water surface. Finally, the point cloud consisted of 62,625,303 points spanning an area of 45 m × 20 m.

Definition of Scale and Orientation of the Produced Model

To further refine the scale and orientation of the point cloud, the coordinates of each of the targets 1, 2, and 8 as exported from the laser scanning software were matched to the corresponding coordinates of the photogrammetric model (Fig. 9). This enabled a much more accurate adjustment of the scale and orientation of the model by ensuring the coordinates of each target matched those obtained from the laser scanner. Furthermore,

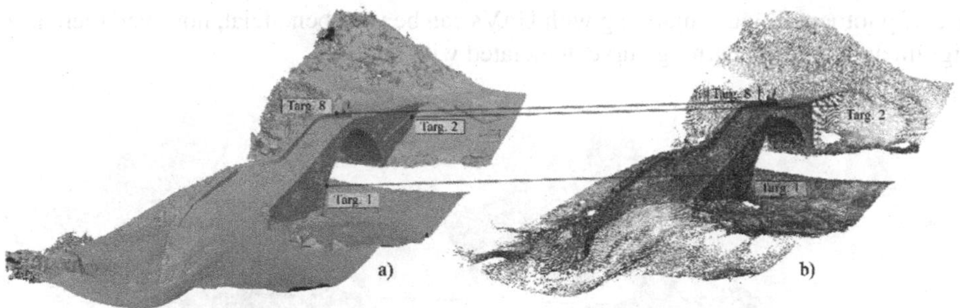

Fig. 9. Rescale and alignment of photogrammetric model base on TLS coordinates, a) Terrestrial Laser Scanner model b) UAV photogrammetry point cloud

this allowed for a more accurate correlation between the laser scan point cloud and the photogrammetric model, providing a much more accurate representation of the 3D geometry of the project area.

Mesh Model Generation and Texture Projection
The production of the three-dimensional surface mesh followed the creation and orientation of the dense cloud. The mesh was automatically calculated by the software with great precision and accuracy, and it comprised 14,141,252 triangles. This number of triangles allows for the viewing and editing of the model on modern computers, and also provides the possibility to adjust both the amount and the resolution of the texture maps displayed. In this case, eight texture maps were created with a resolution of 8192 × 8192 pixels (Fig. 10), offering a significantly higher resolution than the scanning method using a three-dimensional scanner. This feature is highly beneficial when studying the details of the object, since it allows for the examination of fine features that could otherwise be easily overlooked.

Evaluation of the Photogrammetric Method Using a UAV
In addition to the technical training and certification required for the operation of UAVs, the use of photogrammetric mapping with UAVs requires a significant financial investment and specialized knowledge. The cost of the UAV, photogrammetric software, and a powerful computer for data processing can be considerable, with estimates ranging from €12,500 to €20,000. The computer must have certain features such as a 3.0 GHz 24 Core processor with 256 GB memory and GeForce RTX 2080 or better graphics card to ensure accuracy. To further verify the accuracy of photogrammetric methods with UAVs, additional survey equipment such as a total station or GNSS receiver may be necessary. Also, the use of photogrammetric mapping with UAVs requires knowledge of the principles of aerial machines and photographic art. In order to successfully operate and use UAVs for photogrammetric mapping, a person must have a comprehensive understanding of the technology, which can be acquired through proper training and certification. In addition to the technical and financial requirements, a person must also possess the right skills and have a thorough understanding of the photogrammetric process. This includes knowledge of the principles of photogrammetry, aerial navigation, and remote sensing, as well as the ability to interpret and analyze aerial imagery. The

use of photogrammetric mapping with UAVs can be very beneficial, however, there is a significant cost and learning curve associated with it.

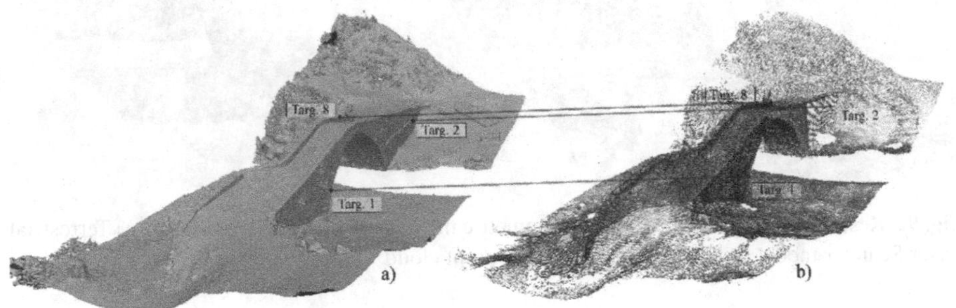

Fig. 10. UAV photogrammetry final mesh and textured model (South View)

7 Photogrammetric Survey Using a DSLR

7.1 Equipment Specifications and Data Collection Methodology

For the photogrammetric mapping of the bridge, a Canon 6D Mark I camera was selected. This full-frame camera has a sensor size of 35.8 × 23.9 mm and a resolution of 20.6 MP, producing photos with a maximum resolution of 4864 × 3648 MP in 4:3 ratio. The images were captured in both JPEG and CR2 (Raw) formats. For optimal stabilization during the photo capture process, a remote shutter activation was used in combination with a tripod of medium size (171 cm height) and low weight (2 kg). A fixed-type lens with a focal length of 24 mm was also used for the photogrammetric mapping.

The 454 photographs were collected using a parallel orientation to the bridge and following its route of passage. Each move was repeated three times to capture the required angles and display the relief of the bridge as much as possible (Fig. 11). The camera settings were determined using an F/18 diaphragm and stabilizing the focusing ring with masking tape. The temperature setting of colors was maintained based on an initial automatic setting. The shutter speed was left as a variable to adjust to the changing light conditions throughout the survey.

7.2 Photos Processing in Photogrammetry Software

The photos were imported into Agisoft Metashape 1.7.1 photogrammetric processing software to generate a point cloud and mesh. The alignment of the 454 photos was completed without errors due to the increased resolution (4864 × 3648) and the increased level of mutual overlap of the information they contain. The generated sparse cloud consisted of 1,170,651 points.

Subsequently, a dense cloud was produced, although it had some gaps in the outline of the study area (45 m × 20 m). These gaps did not affect the geometric characteristics

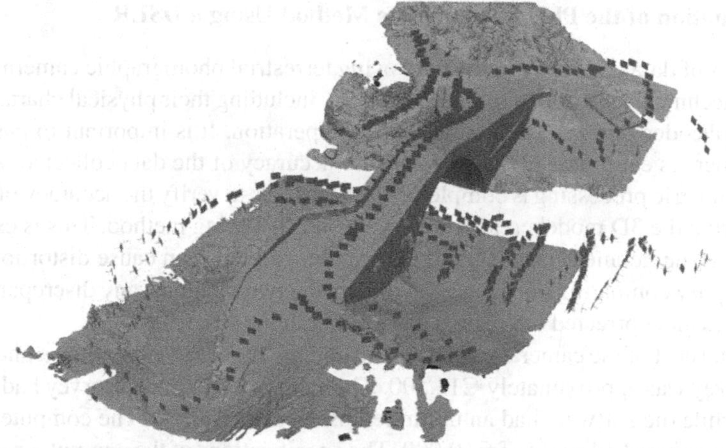

Fig. 11. DSLR camera positions in relation to the bridge and surrounding area

of the bridge. Optically, the points referring to the branches and leaves of the trees were selected and discarded, as well as incorrect points created by the reflections in the water. The final cloud consisted of 73,527,873 points with an area of 45 m × 20 m. The scale and orientation of the model were set by identifying the targets 1,2 and 8 in both models and forcing the photogrammetric model to align them in terms of scale and orientation. The mesh was determined by the automatic calculation of the software with high accuracy, resulting in 18,408,846 triangles. The last step of processing was the creation and display of 8 texture maps with 8192 × 8192 resolution each (Fig. 12). The texture detail also presented similar accuracy to the UAV model.

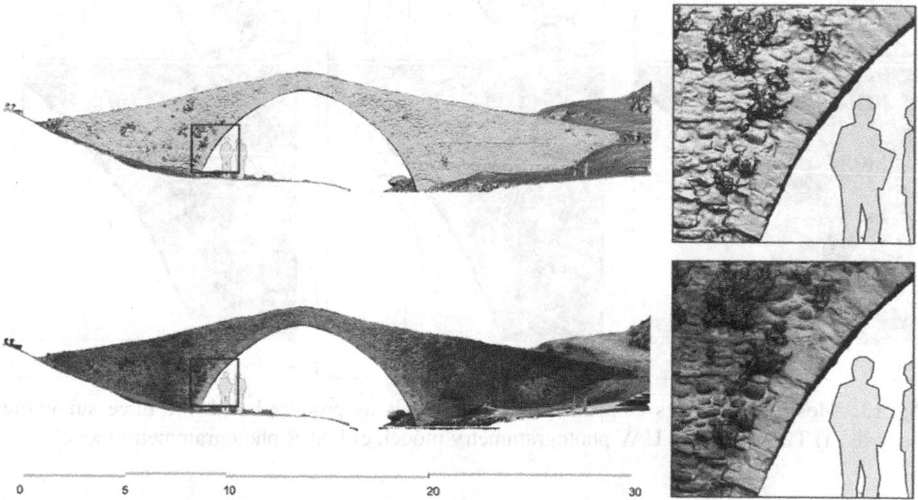

Fig. 12. DSLR photogrammetry final mesh and textured model (South View)

7.3 Evaluation of the Photogrammetric Method Using a DSLR

The process of data collection in the field using terrestrial photographic camera requires extensive technical knowledge of the equipment, including their physical characteristics and the embedded software that controls their operation. It is important to ensure that the equipment is calibrated correctly to ensure accuracy of the data collected. After the photogrammetric processing is complete, it is necessary to verify the accuracy of the data by comparing the 3D model created with a second surveying method. This is especially important as the geometric analysis of the camera and lens can cause distortions in the model [11]. By comparing the data created from the two methods, any discrepancies can be identified and corrected to create a more accurate representation.

The total cost of the camera, software, and computer needed to conduct a photogrammetric survey was approximately €14,500. The camera used for this survey had a cost of €1,000, while the software had an unlimited use cost of €3,500. The computer needed for data processing had a cost of €10,000. The specifications of the computer required to apply photogrammetric methods are similar to those required for aerial photogrammetry.

The knowledge and technical training required to apply photogrammetric methods using a terrestrial camera is less demanding than that of aerial photogrammetry, since it does not involve having to learn how to operate an aircraft.

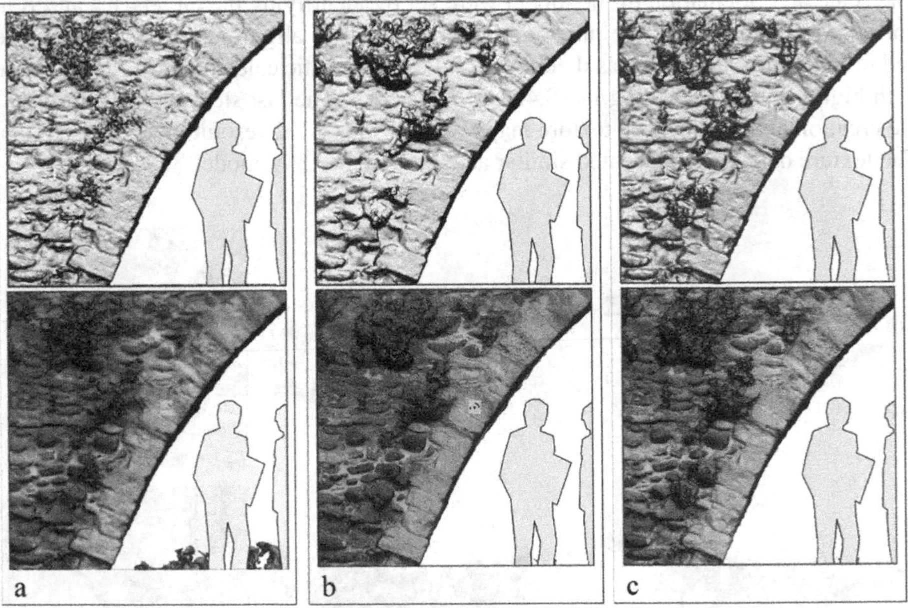

Fig. 13. Mesh and textures comparison of the models as produced with the three surveying methods, a) TLS model, b) UAV photogrammetry model, c) DSLR photogrammetry model

8 Comparing Both Photorammetric Methods to Laser Scanning

8.1 Comparison Overview

It is evident from this study that, although both terrestrial scanning and photogrammetric methods can generate high-resolution point clouds and mesh models of stone bridges, their cost of equipment, total processing time, texture resolution, vegetation permeation level and geometric accuracy still differ, making them worth analyzing and comparing.

8.2 Cost Comparison

When selecting a survey method, various factors must be taken into consideration, such as the type of object being surveyed, the desired geometric accuracy, the desired resolution of the 3D model, and its projected texture. Cost is also a key factor in the decision-making process. The cost of equipment, software, and computers for the three methods analyzed was €35,000 for three-dimensional scanning, €12,500 for UAV photogrammetry, and €11,500 for DSLR photogrammetry.

8.3 Comparison of the Processing Time and Required Knowledge for Each Method

It is evident that three-dimensional scanning requires less processing time and specialization than photogrammetric methods. The researcher applying three-dimensional scanning must possess knowledge of the object being scanned and the parameters governing the software processing of the scanner's data. Additionally, photogrammetric methods are more complex due to the multiple variables in data collection and the need for expertise in topography, photography, and photography equipment. Furthermore, unmanned aerial mapping necessitates aviation policy holders to provide technical training and experience. Ultimately, three-dimensional scanning is much less time consuming and technical less demanding than photogrammetric methods.

8.4 Comparison of the Projected Textures and Mesh Model Resolutions

The mesh resolutions produced through the three mapping methods present some differences. The comparison of the analysis is made in the study area defined by the 45 m × 20 m footprint. The mesh resolution in triangles produced with a terrestrial laser scanner is 22,721,955, with photogrammetry using a UAV is 14,141,252, and with photogrammetry using a DSLR camera is 18,408,846.

The analysis of the mesh resolution is important for the final reliability of the three-dimensional model; however, it is not the only factor that determines its quality. The accuracy of the surface representation, in particular the depth changes that arise from the alternation of structural elements of stones and pebbles, is also a critical factor. Comparing the same areas of the mesh in the south view of the bridge, it appears that the depth rendering of the surface is slightly more distinct as produced with the TLS. However, the meshes produced with the three methods show a similar representation of detail of the structural elements, with the TLS producing slightly more distinct structural elements behind the vegetation. The percentage of triangles that make up the vegetation is also reduced compared to the two photogrammetric methods (Fig. 13).

When it comes to texture in the three-dimensional models, the differences between photogrammetric models and the model generated using a terrestrial scanner are evident. The analysis of the texture produced by the terrestrial scanner is greatly reduced due to two factors: the low resolution and small sensor size of the embedded camera of the scanner and the rendering process of the texture at each point of the cloud. Photogrammetric methods, on the other hand, produce textures of higher resolution and quality due to the higher resolution of photographic cameras and the texture being rendered after the processing of the mesh. Comparing the two photogrammetric methods, it is difficult to discern a substantial difference in the quality of the texture. However, when comparing the textures produced with a UAV and a DSLR camera, the textures produced with the DSLR camera show an advantage, especially when focusing on a scale beyond 1:5 (Fig. 13).

8.5 Comparison of the Level of Vegetation Permeation of Each Method

By removing the points referring to vegetation with the three methods it appears that in the case of using a TLS a much larger part of the surface information remains. This has to do with the great difference in the degree of permeability of the vegetation between the three-dimensional scanning method and photogrammetric methods. With the use of the TLS the largest part of the rays that traverses the dense vegetation returns to the receiver and is recorded as a point in space. In contrast, the photogrammetric method records in a greater percentage the information that is closer to the lens of the photographic device, resulting in surfaces that are behind the dense vegetation remaining as blank information.

The photogrammetric methods among them do not present significant differences as far as the permeability of the vegetation is concerned. There is a small advantage in terms of the percentage of the surface points that remain with the use of UAV and this has to do with the available photographs at a greater distance from the bridge due to the additional height that naturally results from this method of recording.

8.6 Comparison of the Geometric Deviations Between the Photogrammetric Methods and Laser Scanning

Upon completion of the surveys and using the three methods, the final point clouds were imported into the Cloud Compare software in order to compare the deviations in all axes between the point clouds acquired with the terrestrial laser scanner and the two photogrammetric methods.

For the purposes of analyzing the clouds, four deviation maps were generated at plan view and four maps for the south view. The three maps for each view refer to deviations in the X, Y, Z axes and the fourth to the absolute deviations collectively for the three axes. The maps are analyzed in pairs referring to the comparison between the two photogrammetric methods and the TLS method.

At plan view, the first deviations that become visible are those that appear in circular areas below the scanner setups. These deviations are due to the error of the acquired

Fig. 14. Photogrammetric point clouds absolute deviations from terrestrial laser scanning, a) UAV Photogrammetry/TLS comparison, b) DSLR Photogrammetry/TLS comparison

cloud with the terrestrial laser scanning and refer to the gaps that are created from each scanning position. With terrestrial scanning a circular area is left empty automatically by the scanner software. This information is supplemented by the remaining scanning positions which, depending on their distance from the first position and depending on the slope of the scanner to the area of the void created, present the corresponding deviations. The fact that we can identify errors of the terrestrial scanning method smaller than 10 mm through this comparison is indicative of the possibility of photogrammetric methods to produce models of very high geometric accuracy (Fig. 14).

Deviations in the western area of the bridge have been observed when using the photogrammetric method with the use of a UAV. These deviations are of the order of 12 mm to 25 mm. This is attributed to the low height of the UAV in relation to the bridge due to the presence of trees on either side of the western access, leading to an increase of particles in the air which affected the quality of the photographs, thus introducing errors into the final point cloud.

The photogrammetric method with the use of a DSLR present smaller deviations in the Western area but in the Eastern side there are deviations of the order of 13 m with 27 mm. These deviations are due to the inability to stabilize the tripod in the eastern and north-eastern area of the bridge resulting in the shots that concerned this area to be restricted and to have acute angles of capture in relation to the eastern surfaces of the bridge (Fig. 14).

As for the comparison of the data in the Southern View, these do not present significant deviations in the axes (X) and (Z). The deviations that appear are mainly in the axis (Y) and concern displacements of the points on the surface of the order of 12 mm with 45 mm (Fig. 15). These displacements are localized and concern areas that had tree limbs and foliage very close to the surface of the bridge. This forced the capture of the photos at an acute angle in relation to these surfaces. Also, the shading of these areas due

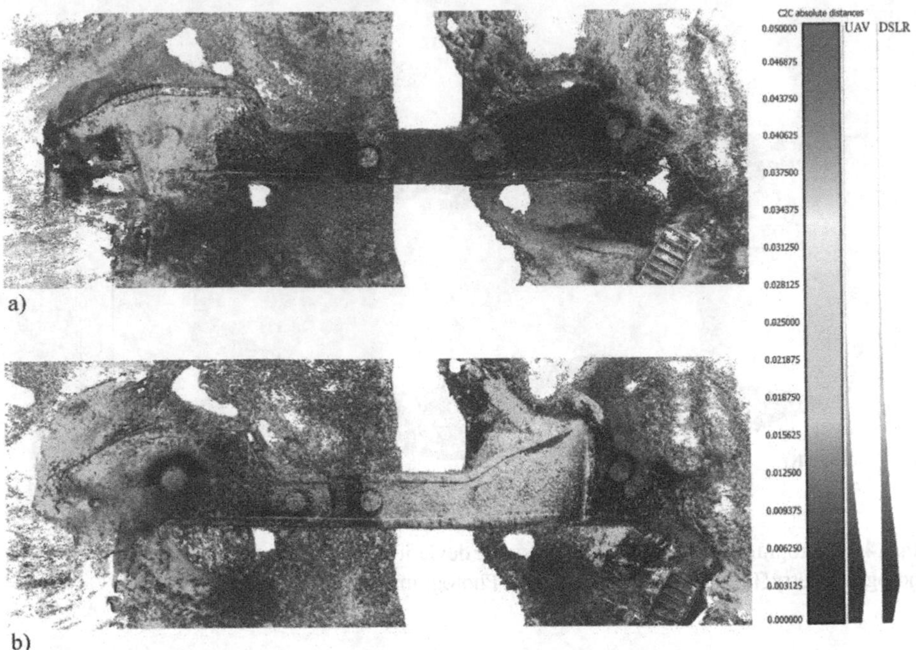

Fig. 15. Photogrammetric point clouds absolute deviations from terrestrial laser scanning, a) UAV Photogrammetry/TLS comparison, b) DSLR Photogrammetry/TLS comparison

to the small distance of the trees from them is a factor that contributed to a percentage of the errors.

Overall, the analysis reveals that terrestrial laser scanning provides the highest level of geometric accuracy with less than 10 mm error, while the photogrammetric methods using UAV and DSLR yield models with a range of accuracy from 12 to 25 mm and 13 to 27 mm, respectively.

9 Conclusion

The parameters that define each method of recording are the desired geometric accuracy, the resolution of the generated model, the cost of equipment, the specialization level of the surveying team, the available time spent at the monument, and the available time for processing the data. In order to facilitate the comparison of the different surveying methods, a distribution table of the parameters defining the recording methods was created (Fig. 16).

This table includes criteria such as accuracy, resolution, cost, and time, which can be used to determine the most suitable surveying method for a particular monument. Additionally, the availability of specialized personnel and the accessibility of the monument are also considered to ensure the accuracy and reliability of the recorded data. Finally, the table provides an overall assessment, considering all parameters, which can be used to identify the most cost-effective and efficient method for recording a monument.

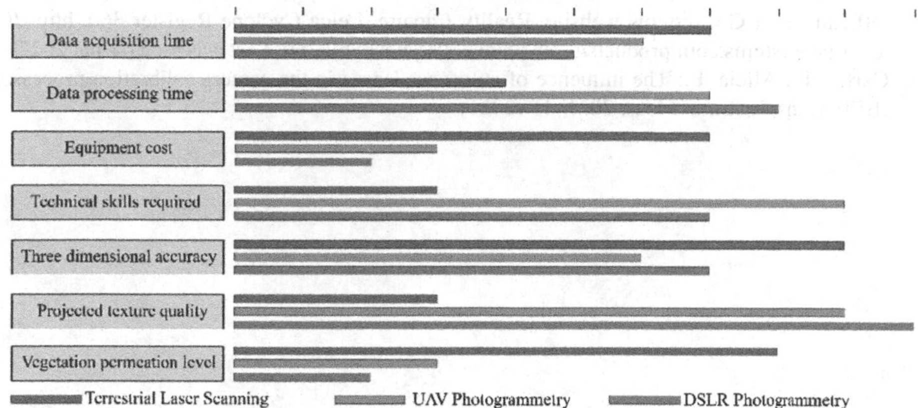

Fig. 16. Distribution table of the parameters of the different surveying methods

From this study, it appears that laser scanning is the most reliable recording method with the highest cost for the equipment. However, photogrammetric methods produce results with much higher resolution and accuracy when it comes to capturing texture and displaying it in a 3D model. Therefore, when finances allow, a combined use of laser scanning and photogrammetric methods may be the best option for obtaining the highest overall result in terms of geometric accuracy and texture resolution and fidelity.

References

1. Official Government Site of the Cyprus Department of Antiquities, List of Monuments, http://www.mcw.gov.cy/mcw/DA/DA.nsf/DMLmonum_gr/DMLmonum_gr?OpenDocument. Last accessed 04 Jan 2022
2. Remondino, F., El – Hakim, S.: Image based modelling a review. Photogram. Rec. **21**(115), 269–291 (2006)
3. Kadobayashi, R., Kochi, N., Otani, H., Furukawa, R.: Comparison and evaluation of laser scanning and photogrammetry and their combined use for digital recording of cultural heritage. Int. Arch Photogrammetry, Remote Sens. Spat. Inf. Sci. **35**(5), 401–406 (2004)
4. Baltsavias, E.: A comparison between photogrammetry and laser scanning. ISPRS J. Photogramm. Remote. Sens. **54**, 83–94 (1999)
5. Papacostas, T.: The Crusader states and Cyprus in a thirteenth-century byzantine prosopography. Identities and Allegiances in the Eastern Mediterranean after 1204, pp. 215–242. Taylor and Francis Ltd (2016)
6. Official Leica Geosystems website, Survey Equipment, Laser Scanners, Scanners, BLK360, https://leica-geosystems.com/products/laser-scanners/scanners/blk360. Last accessed 04 Jan 2022
7. Liu, Y., Xin, S., Guo, X., Suo, T., Qifeng, Y.: A novel concentric circular coded target, and its positioning and identifying method for vision measurement under challenging conditions. Sensors **21**(3), 855 (2021)
8. Official Bosh Professional Power Tools and Accessories website, Lasers https://www.bosch-professional.com/om/en/products/grl-400-h-0601061800. Last accessed 04 Jan 2022
9. Jalloh, Y., Ahmad, A., Amin, Z.M., Sasaki, K.: Conventional total station versus digital photogrammetry in land development applications. J. Environ. Anal. Toxicol. **7**(1), 1–6 (2016)

10. Official Leica Geosystems website, Reality Capture, Leica Cyclone Register 360, https://leica-geosystems.com/products/laser-scanners/scanners/blk360. Last accessed 04 Jan 2022
11. Carlos, R., Alicia, E.: The influence of autofocus lenses in the camera calibration process. IEEE Trans. Instrum. Meas. **70**, 1–15 (2021)

Associating Geodetic Theory to Digital Pottery Reassembly Practice

Michail I. Stamatopoulos(✉) and Christos-Nikolaos Anagnostopoulos

Intelligent Systems Lab (i-lab), Cultural Technology and Communication Department, Social Sciences School, University of the Aegean, Lesvos Island, 81100 Mytilene, Greece
{mstamatopoulos,canag}@aegean.gr

Abstract. Geodesy is a scientific branch of the science of Geography dealing with accuracy and precision in measuring and understanding Earth's geometry, including its orientation in space. It is mainly based on geometric quantities, such as angles, distances, distance differences, directions, curved lines, elevations, elevation differences, and it primarily solves geometric problems, determining the shape and size of our planet and calculating, coordinates on its surface. Similarly to the study of Earth's spatial elements, theories of geodesy can also be transferred to investigate smaller-scale spherical/ellipsoidal objects. To this end, since the shape of ancient ceramic pottery is an ellipsoid formed by the rotation of a potter's wheel, in this paper it is presumed that on a ceramic pottery a similar to Earth's geodetic network may be hypothesized, researched and used. Therefore, in line with all the above, we describe a methodology based on precise geodetic distances that can be extracted from arcs of ellipses deriving from the traces left by the potter's fingers on the internal side of sherds. This can be achieved through high precision digital 3D models that we have previously obtained using photogrammetry and macrophotography (close-range photography). By extracting geometric quantities from each digitally modeled sherd, it is possible to gather local geodetic set of distances, which we will then compare with respective sets of candidate conjoined sherds for successfully arranging them their original position.

Keywords: Geodesy · Ceramic Sherds · Pottery Reassembly · Photogrammetry

1 Introduction

Geodesy is a scientific branch of the science of Geography dealing with accuracy and precision in measuring and understanding Earth's geometry including its orientation in space [1]. Geodesy, deriving from the ancient Greek words "*Geo*..." (Earth: in Greek) and "...*desy*", ("δαίομαι": in Greek, means: divide/distribute), combined with the science of Geometry [2, 3], are sciences, known since antiquity. Basic applications of geodesy are the creation of land, sea and air maps. The measurements implemented in geodesy, are mainly measurements of angles, lengths and elevation differences. Moreover, in order to setup a geodetic network, an appropriate reference system must be defined. In geodesy, *reference system*, is any frame of parameters or coordinates, which is associated with a specific space that is able to unambiguously determine the position of any point within this space.

A. Moropoulou et al. (Eds.): TMM_CH 2023, CCIS 1889, pp. 43–54, 2023.
https://doi.org/10.1007/978-3-031-42300-0_4

In addition to the study of Earth's spatial elements, geodesy can also be used to investigate smaller objects (medium-scale or small-scale objects). Since the shape of archaeological ceramic pottery is an ellipsoid derived from the rotation of potter's wheel [4, 5] and resembles Earth's ellipsoid (geoid), it may be assumed that on every ceramic pottery geodetic network similar to those used for Earth's calculations could be set up, researched and used. The study of the network may be approached through the use of state-of-the-art technologies as photogrammetry, macrophotography (close-range photography) and digital modeling, which are techniques that provide high-precision metrics 3D digital models [6–8].

Fig. 1. On the left, a small-scale ceramic sherd, measuring, 5,9 × 2,6 × 0,6 cm. On the right, in close-up, the stack of arcs.

2 From Concept to Algorithm

2.1 Geodetic Networks on Small-scale Ceramic Sherds

It is well known in archeology that every hand-made pottery which was made on a wheel, has on its inner surface a grid of horizontal traces created by the potter's fingers, during the construction of the pottery (see Fig. 1/left). Moreover and specific to the pottery sherds and to simple geometry, these horizontal traces looks like a stack of horizontal rings (or arcs in the fragments), which are stacked on top of each other (see Fig. 1/right). It is also known that, if using three random points from any arc of a circle, the center of the circle to which the arc corresponds can be safely calculated [9]. After that, if someone applies the same calculation process, on two different arcs of the arc stack of a sherd, with one of the arc at the top of the stack and the other at the bottom of the stack, it is possible to orient the sherd on the 3D space [10–12], in relation to the vertical construction axis of pottery (see Fig. 2/a). This initial orientation of the sherd can then be used to create a small local geodetic network. In particular, for our proposed methodology, we follow the next steps: a) we identify on each of the two arcs of the stack, two points at their ends named, x, y and z, w, b) we create four edges named a1, a2, b1 and b2, from joining the points x, y, z and w with the points k1 and k2 (see Fig. 2/c), which we respectively defined, as centers of the circle of each arc and c) we proceed with the separation of the sherd into two pieces, with the vertical splitting plane of sherd, running through its middle point (see Fig. 2/b), creating four sub-points named y1, y2, w1 and w2.

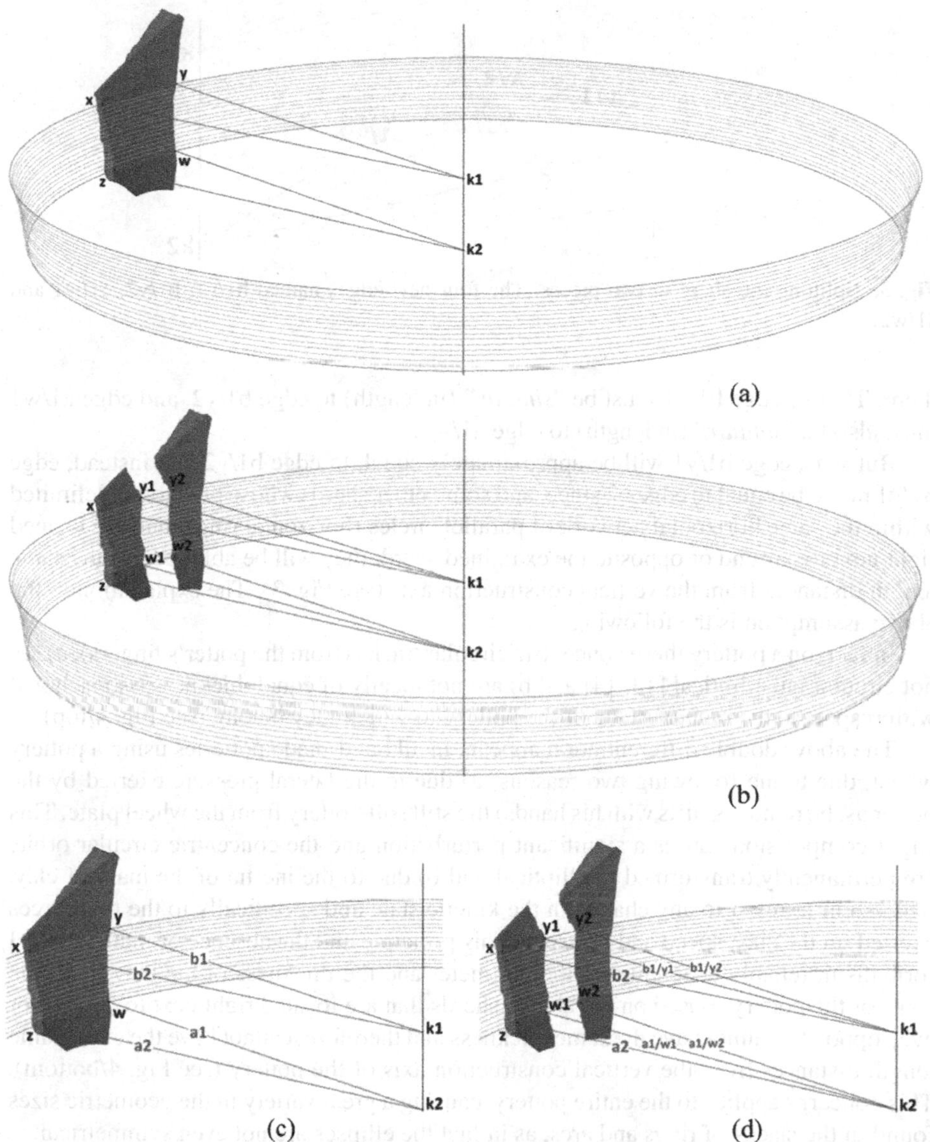

Fig. 2. The orientation process on sherd. The two arcs of the stack, the four initial edges, named a1, a2, b1 and b2.

We could then assume that, the four new sub-edges that are created, b1/y1, b1/y2, a1/w1 and a1/w2 (see Fig. 2/d), will still have some relationship (proximity) between

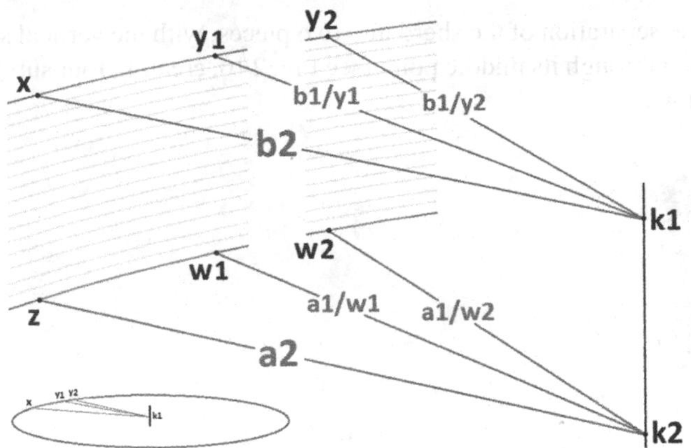

Fig. 3. Splitting the sherd in two pieces. The four new edges named b1/y1, b1/y2, a1/w1 and a1/w2.

them. That is, edge b1/y1 must be "*similar*" (in length) to edge b1/y2, and edge a1/w1 must also be "*similar*" (in length) to edge a1/w2.

But why, edge b1/y1 will be approximately equal, to edge b1/y2 and instead, edge b1/y1 not to be equal to edge b2 since, and some other sherds whose position is delimited within the same horizontal network of parallel circles (horizontal rings) and are located right next to, around or opposite the examined sherd, they will be able to have the same length distances from the vertical construction axis (see Fig. 3). The explanation to the above assumption is the following.

In fact, on a pottery these concentric circular tracks (from the potter's fingers), a) are not circular but elliptical [13, 14] and b) are not locally of equal thickness (isopachous) with respect to the outer surface of the pottery to which they belong (see Fig. 4/top).

The above double differentiation appears in all hand-made potteries using a pottery wheel, due to the following two reasons: a) due to the lateral pressure exerted by the potter as, he removes (lifts with his hands) the still soft pottery from the wheel plate. This slight compression causes a significant perturbation and the concentric circular orbits are permanently transformed to elliptical and b) due to the inertia of the mass of clay, which tent to resist to any change in the kinetic state and specifically to the two forces exerted on the clay, speed and pressure. This principle and the absence of mathematical formalism, reliably differentiates the perimeter and the thickness of the clay in all the rings of the pottery. Based on the above, sherds that are located right next to, around or even opposite, cannot have the same thickness and therefore, cannot have the exact same length distances from the vertical construction axis of the pottery (see Fig. 4/bottom). This concerns applies to the entire pottery, causing a great variety in the geometric sizes found in the stacks of rings and arcs, as in fact the ellipses are not even symmetrical.

Consequently, this unevenness creates an efficient and dense geodetic network of different measurements, which if properly examined and exploited, they can assist in the task of repositioning each sherd to its proper original location.

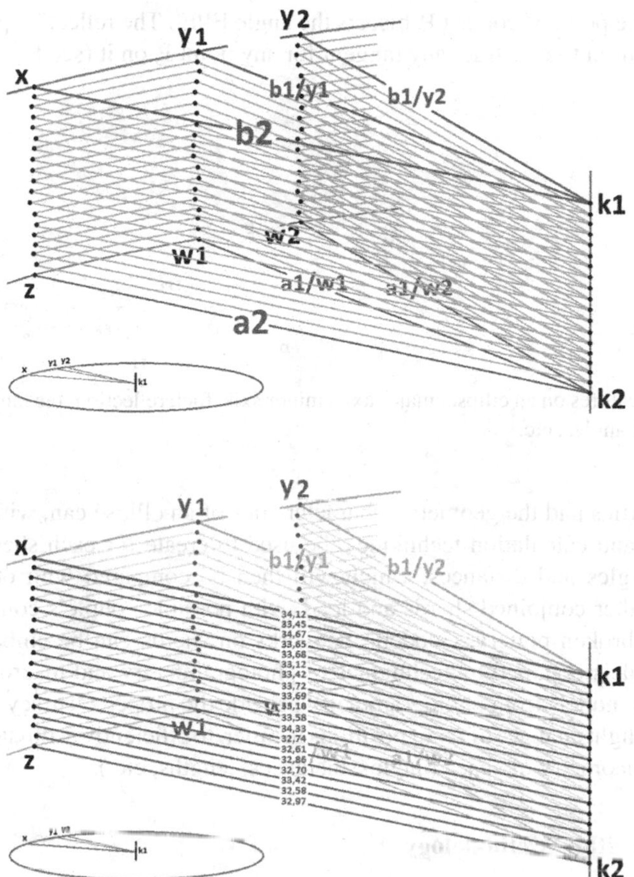

Fig. 4. The small local geodetic network of distances as can be extracted, like a sequence of numbers, from one of the two sides of sherd.

2.2 Geometry of Ellipses

Ellipse is a fundamental geometric element of Euclidean geometry that has a large number of important properties [2, 3, 15]. Ellipse, is the geometric locus of points on a plane, whose, for each point, the sum of their distances from two fixed points E, E′ on plane, remains constant and greater than the distance EE′. The points E and E′ are named, focus points or foci of the ellipse, while the straight segment EE′ itself, is called, focal distance. Moreover, named eccentricity (*e*), the ratio of the distance between the foci E and E′, to the length of the major axis AB, which may be, $0 < e = EE'/AB < 1$. When *e*, tends to zero, the ellipse becomes a circle, while, when *e*, tends to 1, the ellipse becomes a straight line. For any point P on the ellipse, there is a tangent T1T2, which is unique. One of the typical properties of the ellipse is its reflective property. According to this, if a line is tangent to any point P of the ellipse, then, it will form equal angles with the straight segments PE and PE′ (and vice versa) as the normal to the tangent of an ellipse, at the point of contact P, bisects the angle EPE′. The reflective property of an ellipse can be used to construct any tangent for any point P, on it (see Fig. 5).

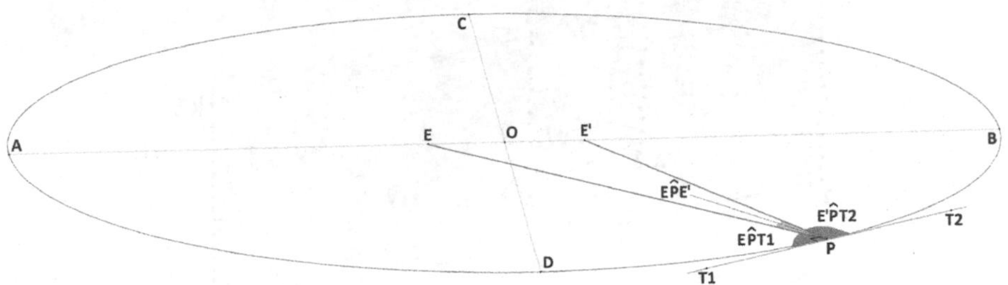

Fig. 5. Major features on an ellipse, major axis, minor axis, foci, reflection, the tangent line T1T2 to point P, equal angles, etc.

The properties and the geometric characteristics of an ellipse can, with appropriate measurement and calculation techniques, be used to create for each sherd a geodetic network of angles and distances, which will then be compared with other geodetic networks of other conjoined sherds and lead, with possible couple's combinations, to reassembly a broken pottery. Geodetic networks on sherds can be embedded on the digital 3D models obtained by techniques of photogrammetry and macrophotography. The 3D digital models from photogrammetry provide the proper accuracy [16] and they can evidence slight changes of point positions in order, to efficiently estimate, differences related to the geometry of space (angles, distances, lengths, etc.).

2.3 The Algorithm Methodology

In order to implement the proposed methodology of embedding the geodesy techniques with the practices of digital reconstruction of fragmented potteries, we can use the 3D digital models of sherds (see Fig. 6) that are created with photogrammetry and the Agisoft PhotoScan photogrammetry software (Agisoft LLC). The editing of the 3D digital models is performed using the Rhino-Rhinoceros digital design software (Robert McNeel & Associates).

The algorithmic process can be described by the following steps and particularly to a digital 3D model of a sherd, that will play the role of the "*guide*", to the whole process:

- the stack of arcs is extracted from the horizontal rings as shown in Fig. 7/a, (for example, the arcs can be extracted, every 1mm),
- the longest arc (in radians) is selected from the stack of arcs (see Fig. 7/b),
- from the selected arc, two focus points will be identified which will define an ellipse, to which the arc is a part. It should be noted that the calculated ellipse is not the actual original ellipse of the arc, but rather a reference ellipse, as the essential aim of the process is to establish a common reference system for all subsequent measurements. Having two hypothetical focus points E and E′ and knowing that infinite ellipses pass through any pair of focus points, then the sought identical ellipse will certainly also pass through them,

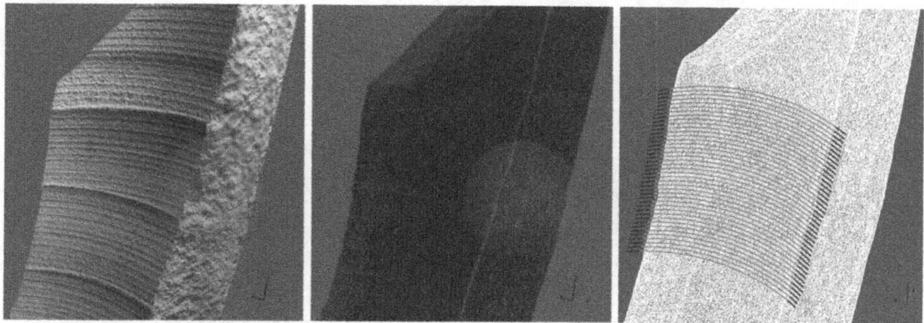

Fig. 6. The digital 3D models, from Agisoft PhotoScan software and Rhinoceros software.

- defined from the tangents, of both ends of the arc, a third tangent at the middle of the arc is calculated (see Fig. 7/c),
- for each of the three arc tangents, a normal vector is defined (at the points P1, P2 and P3) as shown in Fig. 7/d. The normals will be used later in conjunction with the reflective property,
- since the location of the focus points of the requested ellipse is unknown, a random hypothetical focus point E is initially defined (see Fig. 7/e). As the actual ellipse will tend to looks like a circle, this random point may simply be a short distance point from the center of the hypothetical circle (relative to the sought ellipse),
- from the hypothetical point E, a "*light beam*" is originated which is directed towards to the points P1, P2 and P3 (see Fig. 7/e). The angles of incidence to points P1, P2 and P3 create (due to reflective property) corresponding and equal angles of reflection,
- as a result, the three reflections are redirected and focused at the exact same point. This point E′ is the second focus point of the sought ellipse (see Fig. 7/e). According the geometrical properties of the ellipse, then we can assume that, $EP1E' = EP2E' = EP3E'$,
- with the focus points E and E′, two vertical axis of pottery, along with the points P1, P2, P3 of the "*guide*" arc, from the stack of arcs, create a reference system. This reference system can be used to apply the same methodology of measurements and calculations of angles and distances to the remaining arcs of the stack.

As this process ends for the "*guide*" sherd, a small local geodetic network of distances (see Fig. 8/a and 8/b) is created.

From this network, a final result, of two sequences of consecutive length measurements may be extracted. These sequences are the lengths of the external sides (indicatively, for the first arc, the sides $P3E' = 21{,}10$ and $P1E = 21{,}07$) of the stack of triangles (indicatively, for the first arc, the triangles P3E′E και P1E′E), as they are created, by the stack of arcs, the corresponding tangents of their edges and the relation to the common foci EE′. The two sequences of numbers are the distances of the left and right sides of sherd from the (approximate) vertical construction axis of pottery (see Fig. 8/c and 8/d).

The exact same process will then be applied to create a local geodetic network of distances on a second, candidate for matching sherd, with final aim, a following process of successive comparisons, rejections, and matches.

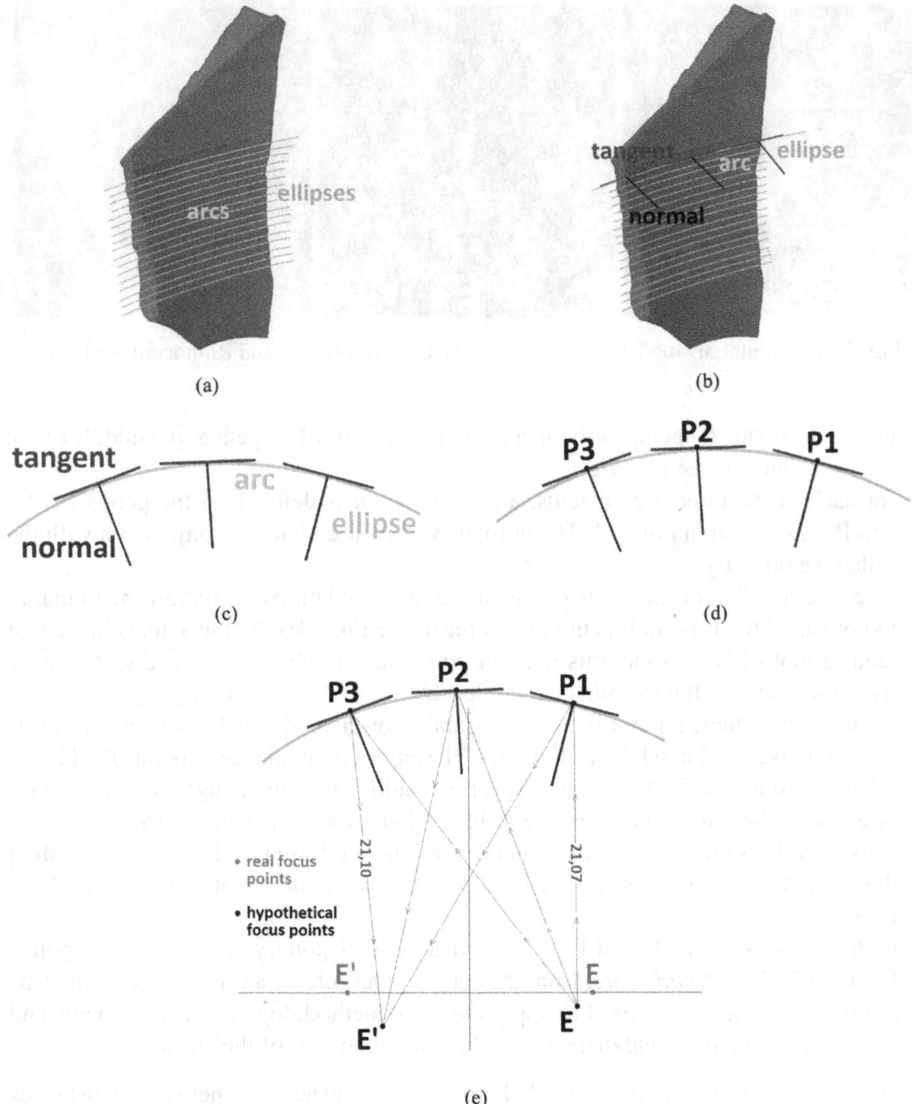

Fig. 7. Drawing 3 tangents to ellipse arc (at points P1, P2 and P3). The 3 normal lines and the hypothetical reflections, starting from point E (in black).

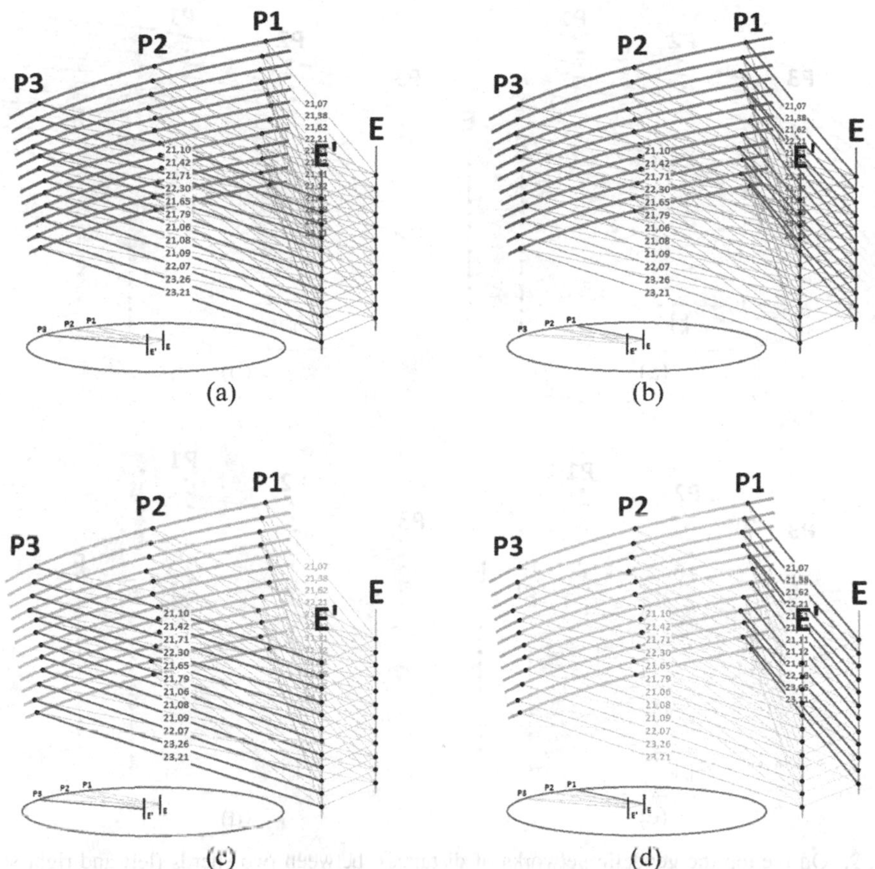

Fig. 8. On the top the geodetic networks of distances (left and right side of sherd). On the bottom the two consecutive number sequences, which represent the distance measurements.

However, as the already created reference system in the "*guide*" sherd, is unknown to the second sherd, a different way to achieve the second sherd alignment, to the original reference system, by creating a common coordinate system. Starting from the fact that to define an ellipse on a plane, we need 3 points (see Fig. 5), the two fixed focus points (E, E′) and a "*moving point*" P, which creates a locus of points for which hold the relation (PE) + (PE′) = (constant length, greater than EE′), we conclude, that the process of creating an additional grid of distances for the next sherd, will be repeated as many times, as there are successive measurements of lateral distances of the first "*guide*" sherd. Due to the necessity to operate on a common reference system, the algorithm turns into an exhaustive search procedure that examines all possible combinations. The process will be repeated for the other side of the "*guide*" sherd (the second sequence of successive measurements of lateral distances).

Moreover, the second sherd will be turned upside-down (relative to the "*guide*" sherd) and the process will be repeated again, as many times as there are consecutive lateral

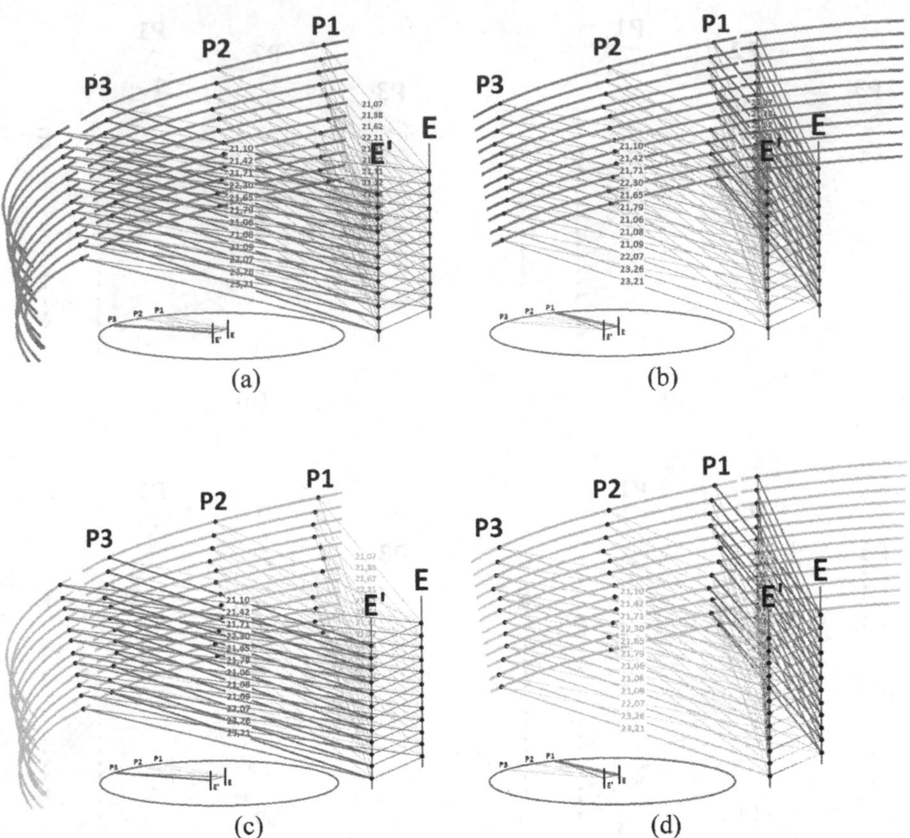

Fig. 9. On the top the geodetic networks of distances, between two sherds (left and right side of combination). On the bottom the two pair of consecutive number sequences (one sequence in bold-blue and the other, in bold-red). On the bottom-left (c), the left side of combination, on the bottom-right (d), the right side of combination.

distance measurements of the "*guide*" sherd (for both left and right sides). In the case of the schematic example seen in Fig. 9, the second sherd will give a total of 48 nets (12 from left, 12 from right, 12 from left upside-down and 12 from right upside-down).

These 48 networks will produce corresponding sequences of length measurements, which will be compared to the sequence of length measurements of the first sherd. The final aim is to gradually discard any false matches and progressively approach to a possible match. This process of successive comparisons, rejections, and matches looks like, "*dragging*" small sequences of distances into larger ones (see Fig. 9/c and 9/d). An optimal fitting can be achieved solely when the numerical sequence of the distances of a small sherd totally fits to a part of those related to a large fragment. However, an exact fitting could be feasible only in an ideal situation and not with real data. Thus, the method is actually seeking an optimum "*score*". Formally, optimum "*score*" means the minimum sum of the absolute values of the subtractions remainders between the distances of any two tested sherds. Besides, the method relies more on the abundance of distance measurements rather than on their precision. At the point where the best comparison is present, then we can conclude that we have a match.

The above methodology is inspired from an a similar one followed in the *Thickness Profile method*, which uses thickness measurements for the digital reassembly of fragmented potteries [17, 18].

3 Conclusions

In this paper we presented a methodology that can contribute to the digital reassembly of fragmented pottery. The procedure described, are applied to high-precision 3D digital models of ceramic sherds, that previously obtained with photogrammetry and macrophotography techniques. Using geodetic methods, we search and we determine, with geometric mainly quantities, coordinate points, by creating small local networks of distances and through suitable computational procedures, we manage to "*arrange, geodetically*" conjoined sherds and arrange them to their proper relative position.

We intend to use the proposed method in conjunction with the *Thickness Profile method*, which is based on the use of thickness measurements on sherds and which we have already presented, assisting the work of reassembling broken ceramic pottery of archaeological interest.

References

1. Gomarasca, M.A.: Geomatics. In: Gomarasca, M.A. (ed.) Basics of Geomatics, pp. 1–17. Springer, Dordrecht (2009). https://doi.org/10.1007/978-1-4020-9014-1_1
2. Deakin, R., Hunter, M.: Geometric Geodesy Part A. School of Mathematical and Geospatial Sciences. RMIT University, Melbourne, Australia (2013)
3. Deakin, R., Hunter, M.: Geometric Geodesy Part B. School of Mathematical and Geospatial Sciences. RMIT University, Melbourne, Australia (2010)
4. Toby, S.: Athenian Vase Construction A Potter's Analysis. The J. Paul Getty Museum, California (1999)
5. Orton, C., Tyers, P., Vince, A.: Pottery in Archaeology. Cambridge Manuals in Archaeology. Cambridge University Press, Cambridge (1993)
6. Samaan, M., Heno, R., Pierrot-Deseilligny, M.: Close-range photogrammetric tools for small 3D archeological objects. In: International Archives of the Photogrammetry, Remote Sensing and Spatial Information Sciences, XXIV International CIPA Symposium, Strasbourg, France, vol. XL-5/W2 (2013)
7. Yanagi, H., Chikatsu, H.: 3D modeling of small objects using macro lens in digital very close range photogrammetry. In: International Archives of Photogrammetry, Remote Sensing and Spatial Information Sciences, Part 5 Commission V Symposium, Newcastle upon Tyne, UK, vol. XXXVIII (2010)
8. Quattrini, R., Nespeca, R., Ruggeri, L.: Digital photogrammetry for archaeological artefacts acquisition. In: IMEKO International Conference on Metrology for Archaeology and Cultural Heritage, Lecce, Italy (2017)
9. Mara, H.: Documentation of rotationally symmetric archaeological finds by 3D shape estimation. Pattern Recognition and Image Processing Group, Institute of Computer Aided Automation, Vienna University of Technology, Technical Report, Vienna, Austria (2006)

10. Kampel, M., Sablatnig, R., Mara, H.: Robust 3D reconstruction of archaeological pottery based on concentric circular rills. In: Magnenat-Thalmann, N., Rindel, J.H. (eds.) Proceeding of the 6th International Workshop on Image Analysis for Multimedia Interactive Services, Montreux, Switzerland, pp. 14–20 (2005)
11. Kampel, M., Sablatnig, R.: Profile-based pottery reconstruction. In: IEEE Proceedings of Conference on Computer Vision and Pattern Recognition Workshop, Wisconsin, USA, pp. 1–6 (2003)
12. Kampel, M., Melero, F.J.: Virtual vessel reconstruction from a fragment profile. In: 4th International Symposium on Virtual Reality, Archaeology & Intelligent Cultural Heritage, VAST 2003, Brighton, UK (2003)
13. Kampel, M., Sablatnig, R., Mara, H.: Automated documentation system for pottery. In: 1st International Workshop on 3D Virtual Heritage, Geneva, Switzerland (2002)
14. Kampel, M., Mara, H., Sablatnig, R.: Automated investigation of archaeological vessels. In: 14th European Signal Processing Conference, EUSIPCO 2006, Florence, Italy (2006)
15. Lockwood, E.H.: A Book of Curves. Cambridge University Press, Cambridge (1961). https://doi.org/10.1017/CBO9780511569340
16. Stamatopoulos, M.I., Anagnostopoulos, C.-N.: Digital modeling of ceramic sherds by means of photogrammetry and macrophotography: uncertainty calculations and measurement errors. In: 3rd International Conference on Transdisciplinary Multispectral Modelling and Cooperation for the Preservation of Cultural Heritage – TMM_CH 2023, Athens, Greece (2023)
17. Stamatopoulos, M.I., Anagnostopoulos, C.-N.: A totally new digital 3D approach for reassembling fractured archaeological potteries using thickness measurements. Acta IMEKO **6**(3), 18–28 (2017)
18. Stamatopoulos, M.I., Anagnostopoulos, C.-N.: Simulation of an archaeological disaster: reassembling a fragmented amphora using the thickness profile method. In: Ioannides, M., et al. (eds.) EuroMed 2018. LNCS, vol. 11196, pp. 162–173. Springer, Cham (2018). https://doi.org/10.1007/978-3-030-01762-0_14

Advanced Digitization Methods for the 3D Visualization and Interpretation of Cultural Heritage: The Sphinx of the Naxians at Delphi

Athanasia Psalti[1], Marilena Tsakoumaki[1], Christina Mamaloukaki[1], Michael Xinogalos[2], Nikolaos Bolanakis[4], Christos Kavallaris[3], Andreas Polychronakis[3], Katerina Mania[3], and Emmanuel Maravelakis[4](✉)

[1] Ephorate of Antiquities of Phocis, Ministry of Culture and Sports of Greece, Athens, Greece
psaltinan@yahoo.gr

[2] Astrolabe Engineering, Nea Erithrea, Greece

[3] Department of Electrical and Computer Engineering, Technical University of Crete, Chania, Greece

[4] Department of Electronic Engineering, Hellenic Mediterranean University, Chania, Greece
marvel@hmu.gr

Abstract. Creating a 3D model for a Cultural Heritage (CH) asset is a rather time-consuming and complicated process. Latest-generation sensors in the field of cultural heritage and new photogrammetry algorithms have simplified the 3D modelling process reducing the cost of 3D scanning. In this work, the 3D model of the Sphinx of the Naxians, located in the Archeological Museum of Delphi, Greece, was created using UaV Photogrammetry. A Delphi Augmented Reality (AR) application was developed in order to allow users to virtually explore and learn about the Delphi's monuments in a way that is interactive and engaging, while walking around the archeological site viewing 3D models superimposed on real-world surroundings via a mobile phone. The AR visualization employs the 3D model of the Sphinx introducing the concept of archeological uncertainty regarding the initial orientation of the monument.

Keywords: Sphinx of the Naxians · Delphi · 3D Modeling · AR · Archaeological Uncertainty

1 Introduction

3D modeling for Cultural Heritage (CH) is widely used in archaeological museums, often in interactive exhibits. 3D models for CH can be employed for documentation, protection, reconstruction, conservation, dissemination and promotion of CH exhibits and monuments [1, 2]. Latest generation sensors in the field of cultural heritage and new photogrammetry algorithms have simplified the 3D modelling process and reduced the cost of 3D scanning [3]. User requirements in relation to the documentation and exploitation of the 3D model as well as environmental conditions should be considered, in order to define the optimal 3D scanning strategy for the creation of the final 3D model [4].

A. Moropoulou et al. (Eds.): TMM_CH 2023, CCIS 1889, pp. 55–64, 2023.
https://doi.org/10.1007/978-3-031-42300-0_5

An archaeologist's level of confidence in an interpretation derived from archaeological data is defined as uncertainty [5]. Multiple levels of uncertainty, related to how an archaeological structure may have existed in the past, can be visualized through Augmented Reality (AR) bringing the uncertainty element of the archaeological expert into the visualization. Augmented Reality is a technology that allows users to superimpose digital content onto the real world, creating a layer of information that enhances and expands upon the physical world. AR has the potential to revolutionize the way we interact with and experience the world around us, by providing a new level of digital augmentation of our surroundings and engagement with digital experiences. In a single 3D archaeological reconstruction, we can now differentiate through varying visualization the reconstructed parts for which there is strong evidence that they existed as visualized, as opposed to those for which there is less evidence and knowledge in relation to their former form [6].

In this work, the 3D model of the Sphinx of the Naxians was created using UaV Photogrammetry. We aim to employ this model to visualize the different options regarding the initial orientation of the monument, by providing varied interpretations based in historical evidence viewed by the visitor on-site.

We also put forward the Delphi AR application, through which we can visualize digitized monuments superimposed onto real-world surroundings via a mobile phone (Mobile Augmented Reality – MAR). Such monuments are often deployed in museums, sometimes being the integral part of interactive exhibits in the museum environment. The proposed AR visualization, for the first time, introduces the concept of archeological uncertainty to the user, while navigating the real-world surroundings of a historical site. Delphi AR is set up by a host or a museum curator and used by a visitor. The host of the AR application can walk through the historical site and place anchors at the potential locations of various monuments in the past, ensuring their correct placement, size and orientation on-site. A description of the monuments can also be provided, explaining their history and significance. Visitors of the Delphi archeological site can then use the AR application while walking around the site, selecting 3d monuments' reconstruction and viewing these in 3D through their phone camera simply by pointing their camera at the desired location. The AR application utilizes markerless tracking, e.g., it does not require any special markers or targets to function, allowing users to experience the 3D digitized monument from any angle, as superimposed on the real-world.

2 Description of the Monument

One of the most renowned monuments of Delphi, dominating Apollo's sanctuary, is the colossal marble statue of a Sphinx placed on the top of a 9.9-m-high Ionic column. It was discovered in 1861 by the French archaeologist Paul Foucart at a two meters distance from the Temple of Apollo, along with the initial carved rock used as the surface for its base. The statue stood on a large marble base near the terrace of the temple of Apollo and it was erected around 560 BC, as a votive offering of the island of Naxos. It constitutes the earliest Ionic architectural element found in the sanctuary of Delphi and its colossal dimensions and commanding position express the political and artistic supremacy of Naxos during the Archaic period [7]. The Sphinx is a hybrid creature with the head of a woman, the body of a lion and its majestic wings form an eastern influence assimilated by ancient Greek art forming a particularly popular motif in Archaic Greece [8]. The Sphinx is associated with the Delphic sanctuary on account of the story of king Oedipus, who encountered the creature upon his return from the oracle in his effort to avoid his god-ordained destiny. His tragic end is associated with the central ordain of the Delphic theology, "Know thyself", that commands that a person must lead a virtuous life irrespective of the knowledge of his predetermined by the Gods fate. On the political aspect the votive offering as testified by a decree inscription on the base of the statue da-ting in 328–327 BC bestowed the Naxians with the right to Promanteia, that is priority to the Delphic oracle [9].

3 The 3D Modelling Process

The "Sphinx of Naxians" has a height of 2.22 m and it is placed in the Archeological Museum of Delphi. 3D modelling with laser or structured-light 3D scanners was not applicable due to museum restrictions for placing a ladder or a scaffold near the statue. For this reason, 3D scanning with UaV photogrammetry was selected. This technique uses multiple overlapping photographs and advanced algorithms for producing an accurate 3D model of the CH asset [10, 11].

A Mavic Air 2 s drone was selected due to its small size and maneuverability. This drone uses a 1-inch camera sensor and has the ability to capture 4K video. Five different flights were conducted in a low speed around and on top the statue, capturing video with 4K resolution at 30 fps (Fig. 1). Using this video and with a ratio of 1 frame per second, 1812 oblique and top-down photographs were extracted (Fig. 2). The Reality

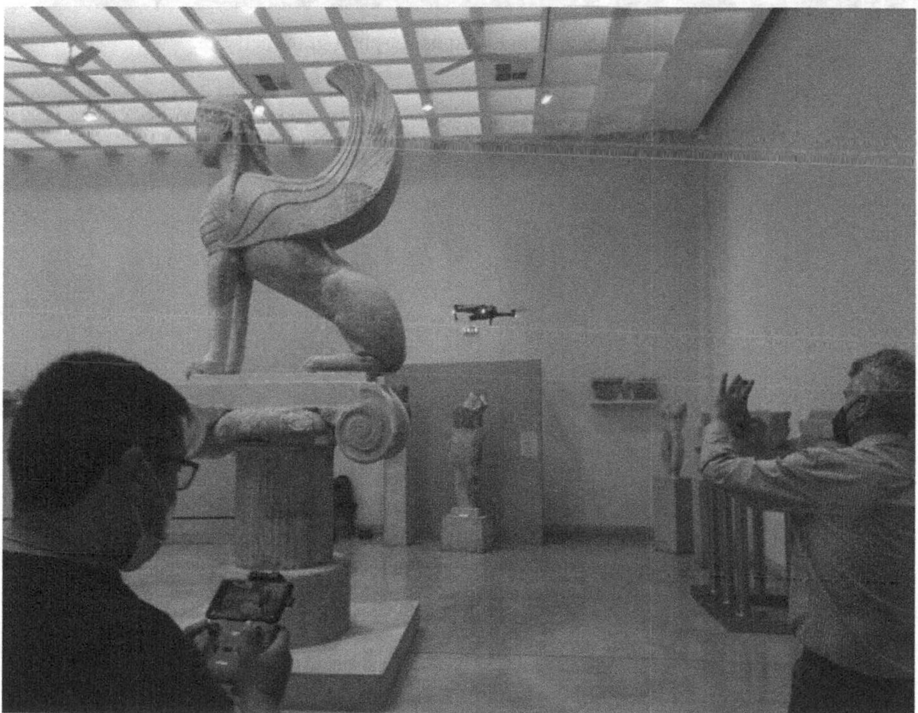

Fig. 1. The use of UaV for 4K video capture in the Museum

Capture software was then utilised in order to produce the final 3D model of the Sphinx of Naxians, consisting of 1.2 M triangles and 587 K vertices (Fig. 3). The scketcfab platform was used for publishing on-line the 3D model (https://skfb.ly/oxrzB). The 3D model of the Sphinx was 3D printed and painted and now it is exhibited in the exhibition hall reserved for the project (hall XIV of the Archaeological Museum of Delphi) (Fig. 4).

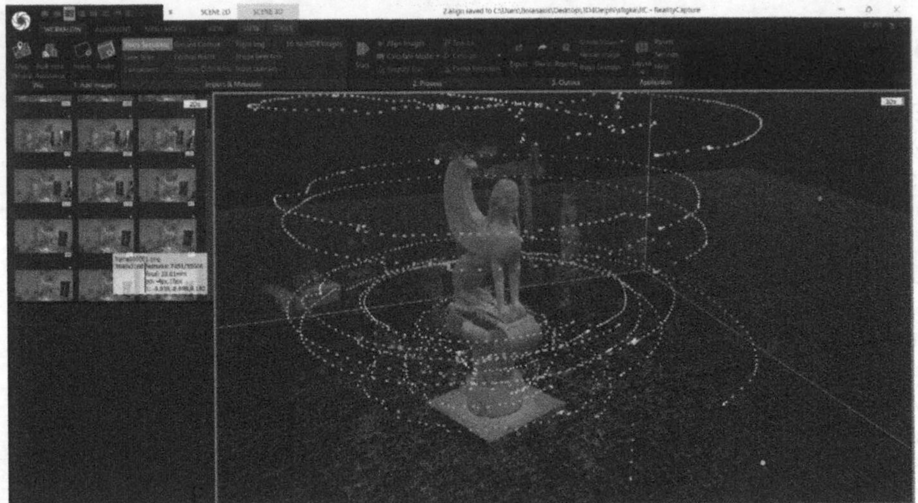

Fig. 2. Extracted photographs for photogrammetry.

Fig. 3. The 3D model of the Sphinx

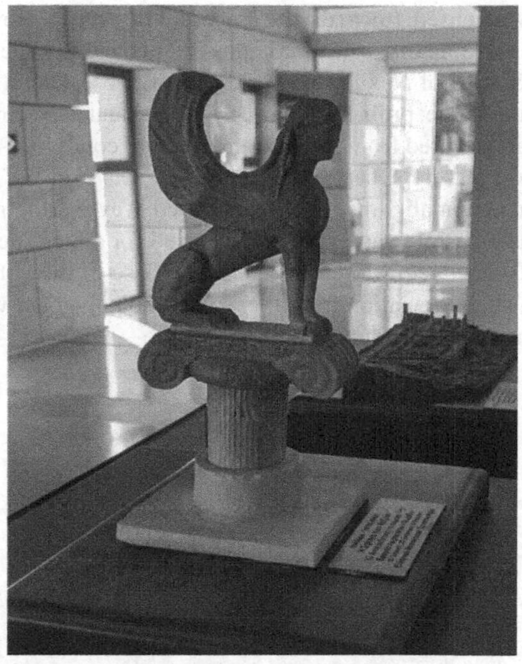

Fig. 4. 3D print of the Sphinx of the Naxians exhibited in the exhibition hall reserved for the project (hall XIV of the Archaeological Museum of Delphi)

4 Case Study Analysis

Although the position of the Naxian votive is certain, the orientation of the statue of the Sphinx remains unknown. Literary sources and the archaeological data indicate the following two most likely versions:

a) **The sphinx was oriented towards the temple of Apollo (NW).** Since its discovery during la the Great excavation at the end of the 19th century and according to the literary sources, the Sphinx was associated with Dionysos, whosc tomb was in the main part (Sekos) of the temple of Apollo and for this reason the Sphinx was facing the temple. In this case, the mythical creature formed a chthonic divinity with ferocious strength, which would assume the role of the guardian of the tomb [12]. Known from Aegean art of the Bronze Age, as well as Egypt and the Near East, this fabulous creature, relating to the death demons Keres, assumes a funerary and votive form and function. It was often present in funerary steles or formed a central decorative motif on sarcophagi from the later Mycenaean period, or as votive statues, mounted on Ionic columns, flanking the entrances to temples in an apotropaic sense, during the archaic period [13]. The first archaeologist to have supported this orientation associating the Sphinx with early funerary monuments in the Cyclades was Bernard Holtzmann [14].

b) **The sphinx was oriented towards the Sacred Way (NE).** However, the French archaeologist Pierre Amandry, who thoroughly examined the statue in the early 1950s, claimed that the Sphinx of Naxians was oriented NE, observing a mild deterioration at the left part of the statue, probably caused by its constant exposure to rain and wind, while the right part suffered from more severe weather conditions (Fig. 5). However, in the axonometric plan representing the votive he sets it in the E-SE axis, as this direction is orientated in alignment with the Sacred Way. Furthermore, he describes this orientation as plausible and expressed the need for a more detailed observation on the surface of the statue. Moreover, the actual base of the votive still preserved in situ presents a slight deviation from the axis of the polygonal wall of the Temple of Apollo diverging towards the Sacred Way.

Fig. 5. The Sphinx of Naxians in front of the Apollo Temple diverging towards the Sacred Way [7]

The Sphinx's face presents a different pattern of damages (dotted) on the right side of its face and on the hair, while the surface is clearly better preserved on the left part [**Fig. 6**]. Respectively, the wings and the rear part of the statue in general are more corroded on the right, than on the left. Furthermore, the front left part of the capital's spiral seemed to have a mild homogeneous deterioration, while the front right has been severely damaged. This conclusion could be verified by a study of the damage caused to marble by the winter rains, reinforced by the SW wind, and the summer storms precipitated into tempest by the North wind [9]. This theory also explains the observation of the archeologist Pierre de la Coste Messelière who found a slight asymmetry between the two sides of the face of the Sphinx. Recently, also Jean-Luc Martinez in his review of the Statue supports the aspect of damage due to climatic changes [14].

Fig. 6. Right and left part (respectively) comparison

5 Augmented Reality Visualization

The main use case for the Delphi AR application is to allow users to virtually explore and learn about the Delphi's monuments in a way that is interactive and engaging. Most importantly, the AR visualization aims to introduce the concept of archeological uncertainty, in relation to monuments and their past form, often neglected in 3D reconstructions which often communicate only one version of the past. The MAR Delphi application can be used by visitors or students as an educational tool, or simply by those interested in experiencing the monument in a new and innovative way while walking around the archeological site. It allows them to see the monuments in their true size and scale on-site, superimposed onto the real-world and to learn more about their history, cultural significance based on varied interpretations of their past as well as position and form. It also allows for a more personalized and flexible experience, as guests can select which monuments they would like to view and explore at their own pace [Fig. 7].

Historical sites and monuments often have incomplete or conflicting information about monuments' original appearance and layout. Therefore, the notion of archeological uncertainty is introduced, for the first time, embedded in the AR visualization. Regarding the Sphinx monument, the user can select and preview in real-time the different possible orientations of the monument and thus, better understand and consider varied historical hypotheses or theories. Overall, the markerless visualization of the monuments is a prime example of the potential of AR to enrich and enhance our understanding and appreciation of the world around us. By providing a new level of immersion and engagement, AR has the power to change the way we see and experience the world, and to enhance our appreciation of the world's history and cultural heritage.

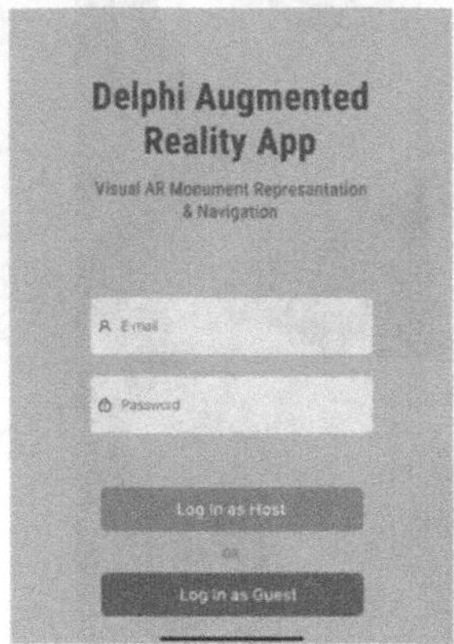

Fig. 7. Login Initial Screen (Host/Guest)

Fig. 8. Guest Model Selection to view onsite

Fig. 9. Guest's AR View (Camera disabled)

The Delphi MAR application is based around cloud anchors and a shared real-time database that can be accessed by the users. Cloud Anchors are virtual points that enable us to map real world locations and have them identified by the application, in order to superimpose the monuments on them. A real-time database holds the positional information in relation to the placement of the monument, as well as any relevant info that will be displayed to the user. The host of the guided tour has to, beforehand, scan the surrounding environment of the Sphinx using the device's built-in camera and correctly place a cloud anchor point that will then be used as a reference to spawn the Sphinx's 3D model.

After successfully mapping the environment and defining the anchor point, the host is asked to accurately rotate as well as scale the Sphinx's 3D model so that it can be seamlessly superimposed onto the Delphi Archeological site and confirm the changes. This information is then automatically synched onto the database and can be accessed by the visitors' companion app (Figs. 8 and 9). During the placement of monument, geolocation coordinates are also saved during this process and will then be used to guide the visitors around the archeological site and assist them in accurately pointing their device towards the desired location to view the AR experience. They will have the chance to view the Sphinx's possible orientations, thus, view varied scenarios regarding the monument's archeological uncertainty.

Finally, a sandbox-like mode has also been implemented, which enables the visitor to freely move as well as scale the Sphinx's model in real-time [Fig. 10]. Through this, visitors can experiment with it, bringing it closer in view on the mobile phone's screen, so as to examine geometric details such as materials used, or a specific aspect of the monument and overall have an engaging and informative experience.

Fig. 10. Visualization of the Sphinx's AR View.

6 Conclusions

Since the great excavation of Delphi, in the late 19th century, the emblematic monuments that were brought to light never ceased to be in the centre of archaeological research creating an ongoing debate of great interest for the scientific community. Many of them still present today several archaeological uncertainties, regarding their history, the reconstruction of their initial form, the nature of their function and the final process of deconstruction or destruction, resulting as such into different reconstruction approaches depending on the historical period assessed. The 3D4Delphi project aims at the development of alternative reconstructions of a specific chronological phase of a monument, based on the available scientific evidence, providing varied 3D reconstruction models within the frame of archaeological uncertainty, and finally assessing the degree of certainty of each alternative case by modelling uncertainty with Bayesian logic. In the case of the Sphinx, new evidence derived from the 3D scanning of the sculpture revealed its potential original orientation but also additional hypotheses, opening the discussion related to the contextual meaning of the famous Naxian votive at a new level of investigation through an interdisciplinary approach. In this sense, assessment of the archaeological data is incorporated in the scientific process integrating advanced

3D visualization as well as mathematical modelling of uncertainty with state of the art scanning technology.

Acknowledgements. This research forms part of the project **3D4DELPHI,** co-financed by the European Union and Greek funds through the Operational Program Competitiveness, Entrepreneurship, and Innovation, under the call 'Specific Actions, Open Innovation for Culture' (project code: Τ6ΥΒΠ-00190).

References

1. Skublewska-Paszkowska, M., Milosz, M., Powroznik, P., Lukasik, E.: 3D technologies for intangible cultural heritage preservation—Literature review for selected databases. Heritage Sci. **10**(1), 1–24 (2022)
2. Axaridou, A., et al.: 3D-SYSTEK: recording and exploiting the production workflow of 3D-models in Cultural Heritage. In: IISA 2014, The 5th International Conference on Information, Intelligence, Systems and Applications, pp. 51–56. IEEE (2014)
3. Pepe, M., Alfio, V.S., Costantino, D., Herban, S.: Rapid and accurate production of 3D point cloud via latest-generation sensors in the field of cultural heritage: a comparison between SLAM and spherical videogrammetry. Heritage **5**, 1910–1928 (2022)
4. Maravelakis, E., Konstantaras, A., Kritsotaki, A., Angelakis, D., Xinogalos, M.: Analysing user needs for a unified 3D metadata recording and exploitation of cultural heritage monuments system. In: Bebis, G., et al. (eds.) Advances in Visual Computing, pp. 138–147. Springer Berlin Heidelberg, Berlin, Heidelberg (2013). https://doi.org/10.1007/978-3-642-41939-3_14
5. Mania, K., et al.: Combining 3D surveying with archaeological uncertainty: the metopes of the athenian treasury at Delphi. In: 2021 12th International Conference on Information, Intelligence, Systems and Applications (IISA), pp. 1–4. IEEE (2021)
6. Sifniotis, M., Jackson, B., Mania, K., Vlassis, N., Watten, P.L., White, M.: 3D visualization of archaeological uncertainty. In: Proceedings of the 7th Symposium on Applied Perception in Graphics and Visualization, p. 162 (2010)
7. Bommelaer, J.-F., Laroche, D.: Guide de Delphes, Le site, École française d'Athènes, Coll. Sites et monuments – VII, Éd. De Boccard (2015)
8. Lexicon Iconographicum Mythologiae Classicae: vol. VIII, 1, L. « Sphinx », Artemis Verlag, Zurich, Dusseldorf (1997)
9. Amandry, P.: La Colonne des Naxiens et le Portique des Athéniens. In: Fouilles de Delphes, vol. II, Topographie et Architecture, Ed. De Boccard, Paris (1953)
10. Rahaman, H., Champion, E.: To 3D or not 3D: choosing a photogrammetry workflow for cultural heritage groups. Heritage **2**(3), 1835–1851 (2019)
11. Mulahusić, A., et al.: Integration of UAV and Terrestrial Photogrammetry for Cultural and Historical Heritage Recording and 3D Modelling: A Case Study of the 'Sebilj'Fountain in Sarajevo, Bosnia and Herzegovina. In: New Technologies, Development and Application V. Cham: Springer International Publishing (2022). https://doi.org/10.1007/978-3-031-05230-9_108
12. Homolle, T.: Ex-voto trouvé à Delphes. La colonne de Naxos. Bulletin de correspondance hellénique **21**(1), 585–588 (1897)
13. Tsiafakis, D.: Fabulous Creatures and/or Demons of Death? Centaur's Smile. In: Padgett, J. (ed.) Princeton (2003)
14. Martinez, J.-L.: Un âge d'or du marbre, la sculpture en pierre à Delphes dans l'Antiquité, sous la direction de Jean – Luc Martinez, Fouilles de Delphes, tome IV, Monuments figurés: Sculpture 8, vol.1, Ecole française d'Athènes, pp. 70–75 (2021)

Different Geodetic Approaches for the Creation of a HBIM

Tsilimantou Elisavet[1,2](✉), Pagouni Chara[3], Iliodromitis Athanasios[1], Anastasiou Dimitrios[4], and Pagounis Vasileios[1]

[1] Department of Surveying and Geoinformatics Engineering, School of Engineering, University of West Attica, Egaleo Park Campus, 28, Ag. Spyridonos Street, 12243 Athens, Greece
{etsilimantou,a.iliodromitis,pagounis}@uniwa.gr, eltsilim@mail.ntua.gr

[2] School of Chemical Engineering, National Technical University of Athens, 9 Iroon Polytechniou Street, 15773 Athens, Greece

[3] School of Architecture, National Technical University of Athens, 42-35 28is Oktovriou Street, 106 82 Athens, Greece

[4] School of Rural, Surveying and Geoinformatics Engineering, National Technical University of Athens, 9 Iroon Polytechniou Street, 15773 Athens, Greece
danastasiou@mail.ntua.gr

Abstract. This paper presents a comparative study of digitization and modeling of a heritage building with a terrestrial laser scanner and a wearable mobile laser system (WMLS). A procedure is applied for the processing and the development of three BIM models in regards to the resulting point clouds. A comparative analysis is described by means of time, accuracy and quality of the generated 3d point clouds for both the interior and the exterior of the heritage building as well as the generated BIM models. The results obtained corroborate with the accuracy and the digitization process, considering the generation of a BIM model that includes information regarding a restoration plan (structural elements, degradation, deformations, etc.). For this work, focus is given on one specific heritage example that is the first brewery in Greece operated in Heraklion, Attica. This brewery owned by brewer Johann Fuchs is believed to be the first that operated on a professional scale in Greece. It is located in Palaio Irakleio (Arakli), Athens, Greece. The case study of this paper is to create BIM 3D models with the usage of different point clouds, to investigate their properties and to finally extract comparative results.

Keywords: Documentation · Cultural Heritage · Point cloud · TLS · Mobile Laser System · Surveying techniques · BIM modeling · Heritage Building

1 Introduction

Documentation process of built heritage has increased over the last decade, especially since the documentation process has acquired advanced instruments that facilitate a rapid and accurate survey of an asset. Regardless the complexity, noninvasive and close-range sensing – based practices of three-dimensional (3d) documentation enables capturing of

A. Moropoulou et al. (Eds.): TMM_CH 2023, CCIS 1889, pp. 65–81, 2023.
https://doi.org/10.1007/978-3-031-42300-0_6

the assets' geometry, it's current state of preservation and if necessary, its surrounding environment [1–3]. Nevertheless, it is very important to consider the quality of the acquired data and also the usability of such. In addition, other parameters to consider are the accessibility of the heritage asset under study as well as the duration of the field work in conjunction with the accuracy and precision of the acquired data.

Several studies also focus on the development of 3d models deriving from 3d point clouds acquired by terrestrial laser scanning, conventional surveying, photogrammetry, hand-held scanners or Lidar scanner drones [4–6]. The development of 3d models for the documentation, visualization, management and evaluation of the built heritage is an increasing subject of interest especially since it focuses on the monitoring of the assets' state of preservation and consequently aid towards a restoration plan [7–9]. More specifically, the digitization of cultural heritage assets has become a prerequisite for restoration works.

In addition to the 3d documentation process, a holistic approach includes an integration of the digitized data within an Information System (IS), spatial fusion data and multidisciplinary data. An IS, where a holistic approach can be obtained, can be a Building Information Modeling (BIM) and more specifically in the case of built heritage an HBIM (Heritage or Historic) [10–13]. A HBIM creation of a heritage asset, can include spatial information that derives from 3d point clouds, incorporating multilateral information [14–20]. Particularly, the heritage assets' components are created and mapped to the survey data for the creation of a BIM model. The spatial elements (walls, openings, etc.) as well as their state of preservation are integrated within a HBIM, considering the quality of the documented features. Special attention should be given to the optimum level of detail (LoD) and level of development (LoD) that should be reached for the developed HBIM, in regards to the spatial and descriptive data of each documented building [21].

However, it should be noted that efficiency is another very important issue in terms of asset documentation and subsequently restoration or rehabilitation. Depending on the values and significances a heritage asset encompasses, different approaches are applied, regarding their documentation and restoration if necessary. Although the documentation of the built heritage should be approached in the same manner, this is not the case for the majority of heritage buildings that obtain common architectural and historical values.

In this paper, a study of a historic building is presented. Digital documentation is performed using three different types of sensors. The resulting point clouds are used for the development of three HBIM, under three pillars. Quality, Accuracy and Time are the pillars that determine the HBIM creation. In addition, the Spatial features in accordance with their quality and their state of preservation (Deformations, cracks, past restoration works), are used for the development of the three HBIM models and a comparative analysis is carried out. Comparative results are classified and documented leading to an optimum HBIM model.

1.1 Historical Information

After the arrival of King Otto (1833), the refugee issue and settlement became the main problems of the modern Greek State [22]. At the same time, the settlement of the Bavarian soldiers (came with King Otto) in open spaces was also planned in order to deal with the problem of paying their salaries, which was due to the loan of 60 million French francs the State had taken. Royal Decrees were signed for the creation of the "military settlement" in Arakli, Attica (finding and measuring the area, details for the properties etc.) [23].

Dozens of Bavarians came to Athens with King Otto in 1833 and subsequently founded Heraklion (Arakli) settlement. The center of the settlement was so-called Old Heraklion, better known among locals as Germanochori (Eng. German village) (Fig. 1) [24].

The legend says that Otto looked for an area for his country house and the settlement for families of his entourages. To select an optimal location, Otto ordered his courtiers to slaughter lambs and hang them on trees in various parts of Attica. He would choose the place where the lambs would rot later, since there would be less humidity and generally a better climate. Eventually, the lambs rotted with a longest delay in today's Othonos Square in Old Heraklion. Nevertheless, the altitude and the morphology of the terrain allowed the area to be approached by air currents from Evripos -Evia and to create a very good climate in the whole region.

Fig. 1. Plan of the surrounding area of the "Old - Heraklion" region (highlighted in green)

Thus, in 1837, Otto founded – with his first commander Christopher Nezer – the Bavarian Military Colony of Heraklion. About 33 persons, courtiers and mercenaries, settled at the place that represents the yeast of today's Heraklion community. According to the 1838 census, Heraklion had 42 inhabitants, majority of which were the Catholics [25]. One of the first settlers was Johann Adam Fix, born in Munich in 1797. He belonged to the "scientific staff" who came with King Otto, a mining engineer, who worked in Kymi-Evia and Lavrio- Attica from 1834 until 1851 where he was finally murdered by common criminals, probably in the area of Nea Ionia. According to Maltezos and Mavrideros, Fix first brewed beer in Kymi and then in Old Heraklion from 1840. His son was Ioannis Fix, who studied brewing in Munich. Ioannis Fix came to Greece to stay with his family in 1851 (Fig. 2). He married Maria-Eva Amerein in 1852 and they had five children. Ludovico, Lisa (later Mamou's wife), Guilielmo, Anna and Karl.

Fig. 2. The members of the Fix family who set up the first brewery in Old Heraklion

In 1854 the settler Petros Scheffler donated to Ioannis Fix a two-room house with storerooms and a stall as well as other properties totaling 160 acres in the wider area of Old Heraklion. In 1860 the house was transferred to the Athens land registry office in the ownership of Ioannis Fix [26]. This is the property that is located southwest of the church of Saint Luke and was bordered to the east by a road (Heraklion Avenue), to the west by Chalkidos Street, to the north by a parcel owned by Ekaterini Kerner and to the south by property Kellmeyer. From 1854, in this house and in its yard, measuring 1800 square meters, where Ioannis Fix lives with his family, he set up his first brewery [27].

This can be witnessed by the Kaupert's map from 1878 where the St. Luke church was shown probably for the first time. Namely, German topographer Johann August Kaupert, famous for land-surveying in Athens and the work "Atlas of Athens", represented the whole Attica in 1:25,000 scale maps. In the specific map (Fig. 3), one can see the St. Luke church (Kirche) with a few nearby houses.

The first map that depicts the heritage building is a map that established the organized city structure of Palaio Heraklio in 1936. The wider area was not an organized city structure until 1936. With the royal decree of the 8th December 1936, which was published in the Government Gazette 549A/1936, city blocks were developed in the area (Fig. 4).

The building under study (Fig. 5) is currently deserted and is in a poor state of preservation. Some years ago, a fire occurred and the roof was destroyed and part of the wall suffered plaster and mortar exfoliation, cracks, deformations and, in some cases, building material detachment. Also, the surrounding area is full of vegetation.

The methodological research conducted in this paper focuses on four steps. The main work steps analyzed in the next sections are:

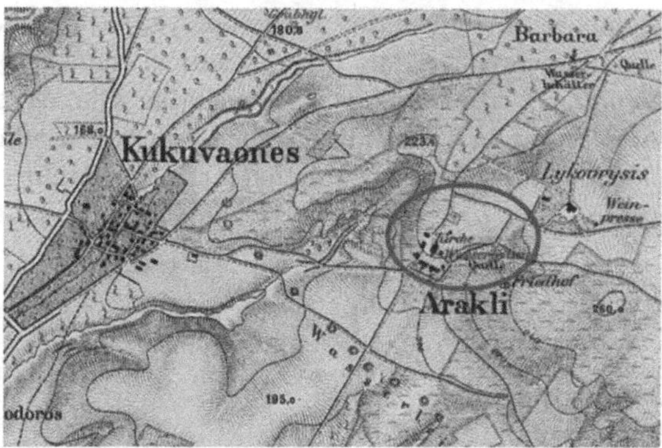

Fig. 3. First representation of the St. Luke Church on a scale map [adapted by Kaupert's "Atlas of Athens", in 1:25,000 scale map]

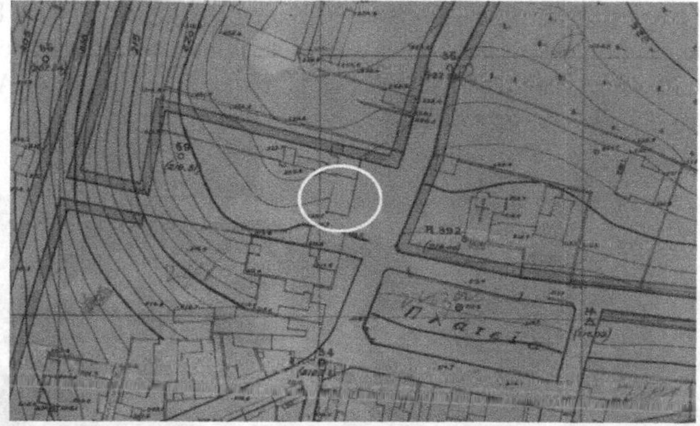

Fig. 4. First representation of the heritage building in a 1936 map of the royal decree of the 8th December 1936 (Government Gazette 549A/1936)

Fig. 5. The first brewery in Heraklion - Attica

i. Data collection.
ii. Data processing and creation of 3D models (for 3 sets of data).
iii. Development of the HBIM models.
iv. Comparative analysis of the resulting models.

In this study, geometric documentation was employed at the historic building in Old Heraklion, the first brewery, to obtain the geometrical characteristics of the asset, by using three different types of instruments. The resulting data, were used in order to evaluate the extent of information that can be acquired time and accuracy related for the creation of a BIM model incorporating information related to building materials' decay and state of preservation.

2 Materials and Methods

2.1 Field Work Data Acquisition

For the creation of the 3D models of the specific historic building, a series of technical procedures for data collection need to take place. Initially, the field work implements geodetic and surveying methodologies to set up the geodetic infrastructure for the geo-reference of the digital models and all the products in the HBIM. For the geodetic control of the project, a geodetic network comprising 3 reference points around the building was established. The coordinates of the points were determined using GNSS observations. The measurements were conducted using two dual frequency GPS-GLONASS geodetic receivers (Fig. 6).

Fig. 6. Geodetic network of three reference points around the building

The 3D data collection involved three different geodetic methodologies. A terrestrial laser scanning, a handheld imaging laser scanner and the tacheometry methodology were used in three different epochs for the geometric documentation of the external and internal parts of the building (Fig. 7).

Fig. 7. Geometric Documentation – (a) terrestrial laser scanning; (b) handheld imaging laser scanner; (c) tacheometry

2.2 Laser Scanning Measurements

The static scanning was performed using the Leica Geosystems BLK360 image laser scanner (https://leica-geosystems.com). All scans were performed with a 4 mm step and the distance between the object and the scanner was always less than 10 m. The percentage of the scan overlap ranged from 40 to 50%. Due to the lack of access to the entire building, a total of five scans were carried out, 3 external and 2 internal (Fig. 8a). Each scan took 6 min.

2.3 Hand-Held Scanner Measurements

For the dynamic scan a Leica Geosystems BLK2GO handheld scanner was used. The scanning was performed in such a way for best field of view. While the scanner was recording, a walk in a slow, steady pace with smooth turns and changes of direction was made, not only once, but twice in order to acquire better LiDAR coverage. Special attention was given on the distance from the walls, keeping at least 1 m distance from the walls and other features. Finally, the path of the documentation process began and ended at the same point for loop closure (Fig. 8b). The whole procedure took approximately 4 min.

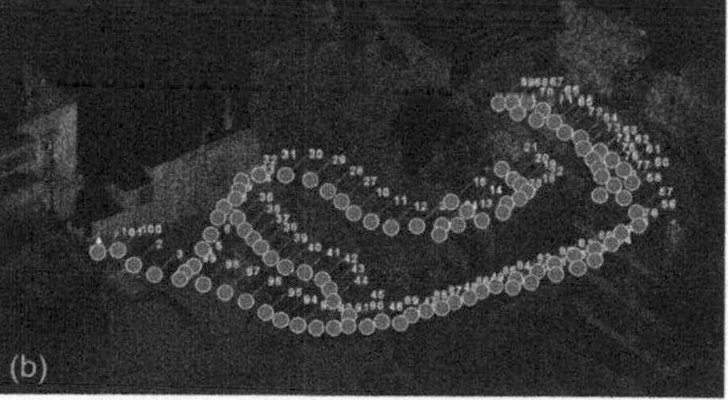

Fig. 8. Point Cloud Terrestrial Laser Scanner point cloud (a), Handheld Laser Scanner (b)

2.4 Tacheometric Methodology

For the tacheometric methodology a Topcon 3003LN (3″) Total Station was used. The data collection of the building was performed by three (3) station setups located in the west, south and southeast of the external facades of the building. A detailed sketch was prepared for the documentation process. The points measured were the groundlines, the exterior walls, the facades and the openings (Fig. 9). The whole procedure took approximately 70 min.

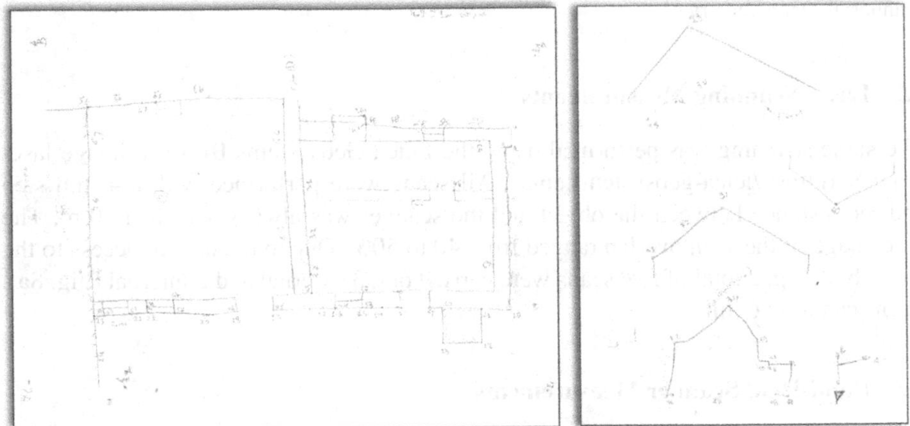

Fig. 9. Sketches of the measured points of the building

3 Results

3.1 Tacheometric Methodology Products

From the tacheometric methodology, a set of 3d points were measured and calculated. The exterior walls footprint, the openings (doors, windows), the groundline, as well as some characteristic detail points of the upper part of the walls where documented. The process time took about 1,5 h. The resulting data were then imported in a computer aided design software (CAD) and the plan of the heritage building was created (Fig. 10). Special attention was given to obtain the elevations of the characteristic points that were necessary for the model creation.

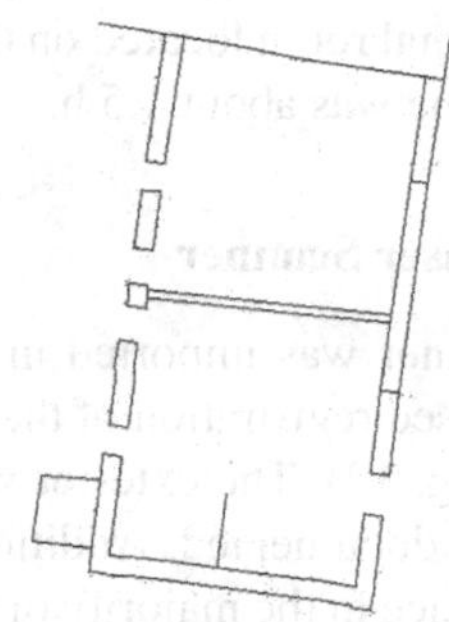

Fig. 10. Plan of the heritage building

3.2 Point Cloud of the Hand-Held Scanner

The export of the hand-held scanner was a point cloud of high-density. The point cloud was exported from the scanner and imported into a point cloud management software (Autodesk ReCAP) for manually cleaning (Fig. 11).

The areas located in the walk-though of the process where fully documented. The exterior and interior walls, the windows and openings, details of the composing walls (variation of structure) were visible through the developed point cloud. Deformations, cracks and building material detachment were also documented and the density of the point cloud allowed for a geospatial analysis. The only areas that did not provide a full coverage were those that had obstacles on their surface, such as vegetation and the areas

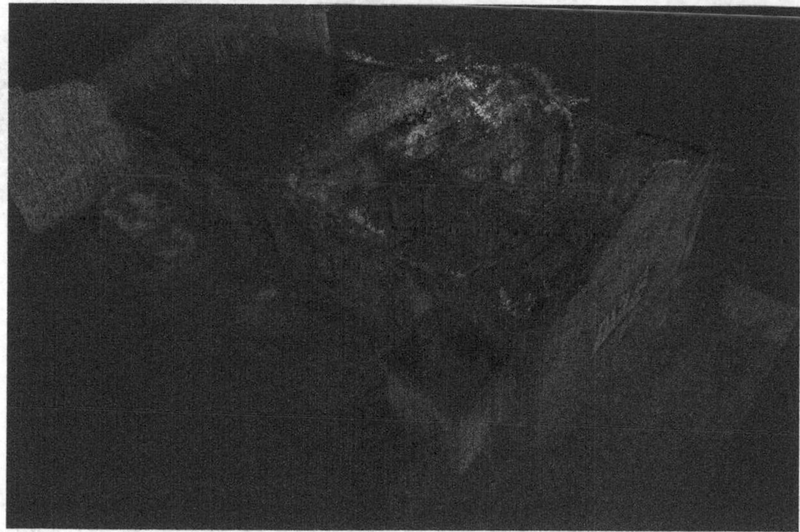

Fig. 11. 3d point cloud from the handheld documentation process

that were not accessible such as the internal room located on the north since it could not be walked through. The total process time was about 1,5 h.

3.3 Point Cloud of the Terrestrial Laser Scanner

The data from the terrestrial laser scanner was imported in a point cloud processing software (Leica Cyclone) for cloud – based registration of the five (5) scans. The resulting point cloud was of high density (Fig. 12). The exterior walls, windows, openings, architectural and structural details were documented. Additionally, the variation of the structure of the walls was also visible, since in the majority of them, the exterior layer of the plaster was exfoliated, and mortar and building materials could be observed. Plaster exfoliation was visible; cracks (capillary and side to side) as well as building material detachment were documented also.

Nevertheless, since it was not possible to enter the while building, the selected locations of the scans, did not permit for a complete documentation of the building, both external and internal. There is loss of information in specific areas of the building and more specifically, in the north part of the building, due to vast vegetation on the exterior wall, and in addition the lack of accessibility to the interior of the room, information regarding the complete documentation of the building is missing. Finally, the process time of the cloud-to-cloud registration as well as the cleaning process took approximately 2 h.

Fig. 12. Terrestrial Laser Scanner point cloud creation with a detailed documentation of the south wall of the building

4 Generating BIM Models

After the digitization process was completed the development of the BIM models was performed. Three models were generated, incorporating information from the different methods. Each process included only the information that could be exported from the 3d point clouds. The BIM development was made in Revit 2022 software.

4.1 BIM Model from the Tacheometric Documentation

For the BIM model of the tacheometric documentation, the 3d points and the surveying plan were imported in Revit. A basic model of the building was developed (Fig. 13), including data such as, wall creation, openings, levels and specific characteristic points with known elevation. The process time was 2 h.

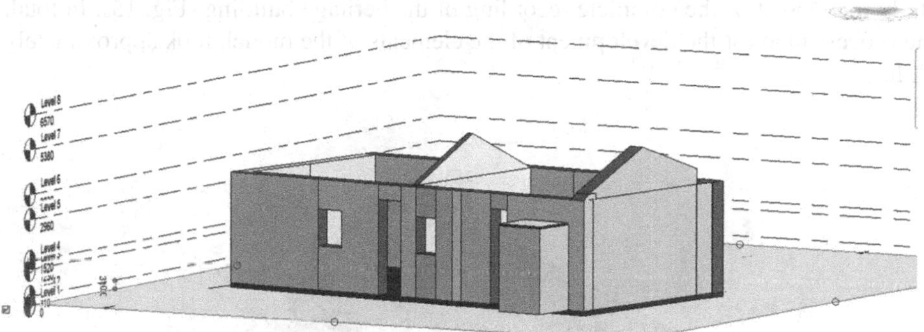

Fig. 13. BIM model creation the tacheometric documentation

4.2 BIM Model from the Hand-Held Scanner Point Cloud

Concerning the BIM creation from the hand-held scanner, the processed point cloud was imported in Revit and the components of the heritage building were developed. Parametric objects were created and modified including building material information, as well as incorporating information that depicted the current state of preservation (Fig. 14).

Fig. 14. HBIM model creation from the handheld laser scanner

Walls of different composition were created; windows and openings were modified and details of architectural value were added. In addition, building materials' composition were classified and enriched the wall objects and deformations were recorded, while observed past conservation interventions, visible in the point cloud, were recorded as new parametric objects.

Since, the acquisition process of this sensor included almost the whole entity of the heritage building, the developed BIM model and its components is considered in this study the closest of the complete recording of the heritage building (Fig. 15). In total, the process time for the development of the elements of the model, took approximately 16 h.

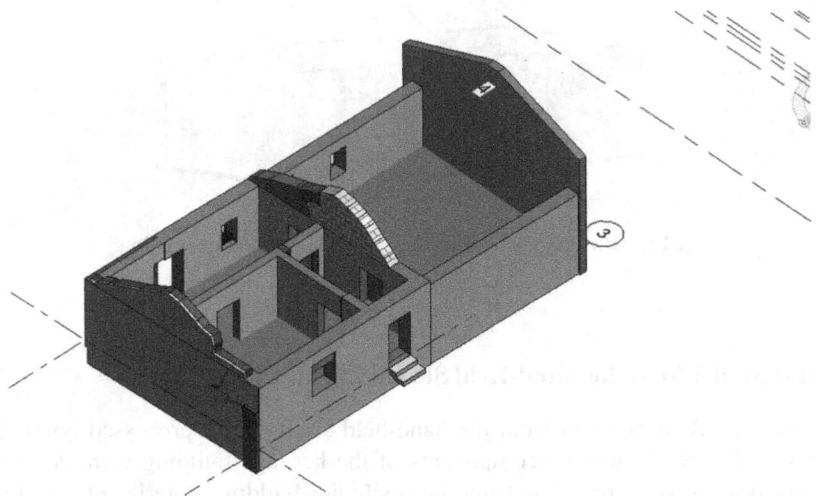

Fig. 15. HBIM model of the heritage building

4.3 BIM Model from the TLS Point Cloud

In the case of the BIM model deriving from the dense 3d point cloud of the terrestrial laser scanner, parametric objects were also created and modified including building material information, as well as incorporating information that depicted the current state of preservation. The current state of preservation of the heritage building was documented in a more detailed manner. The walls, openings, windows as well as architectural details were created and enriched by information that could derive from the observed dense point cloud. Building materials composition were classified and enriched the wall objects, cracks, voids and deformations were recorded, while plaster detachment and past conservation interventions, visible in the dense point cloud, were recorded as new parametric objects.

Nevertheless, lack of information deriving from the 3d point cloud could not provide a complete 3d model of the building to act as a blueprint for the development of the BIM model, since such data could not be acquired from narrow spaces in the interior of the building, as well as from areas with obstacles, (vegetation and lack of overlapping point cloud). The resulting HBIM of the heritage building did not include information for a room located in the north (Fig. 16). In total, the process time for the development of the elements of the model, took approximately 14 h.

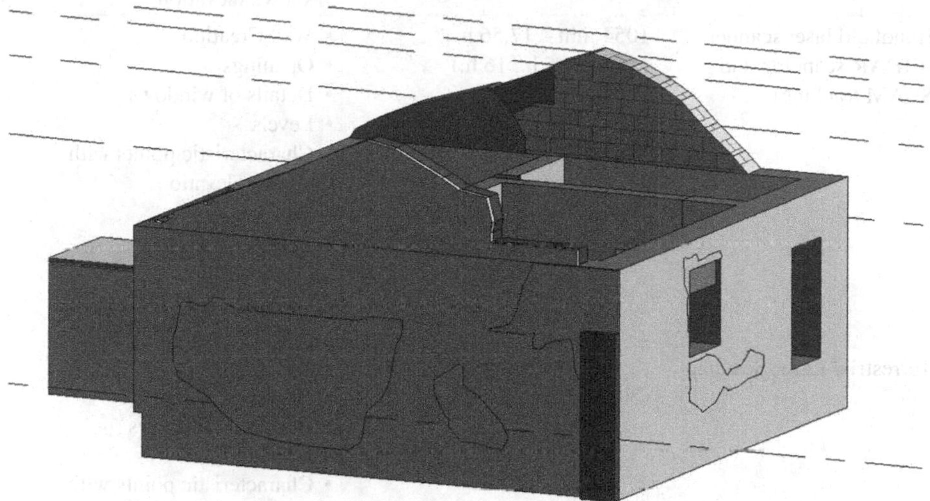

Fig. 16. HBIM of the heritage building from the TLS point cloud

5 Discussion – Comparative Analysis

A comparative analysis of the three developed models was conducted. The documentation process in conjunction with the total time related process and the information that was incorporated within each BIM model, are presented in the following table (Table 1). Tacheometric Methodology offered rapid and accurate results, 3d points, for the development of a BIM model. However, the LoD is low and does not include all the necessary information. The hand-held laser scanner offered rapid and accurate results, 3d point cloud, of high density and a complete recording of the asset was performed (apart from the interior of a room). However, in the developed BIM model, there are some details that could not be fully documented and the scan to BIM process was time consuming. The terrestrial laser scanner offered rapid and accurate results, 3d point cloud, of very high density. However, the heritage building could not be fully documented due to accessibility issues (the laser scanner could not be placed in the north part due to vegetation and the resulting point cloud could not with the other scans. Therefore, the developed BIM model did not include the complete asset since in cases such as the heritage building under study, where the deterioration is very progressed, it is not easy to perform a documentation process in spaces with limited access.

Table 1. Comparative analysis of the different documentation processes

Documentation Process	Total Time Related Process	BIM Model Information (LoD – LoD)
Conventional Topography – Total Station	280 min – 4,66 h (70 min, 1,5 h., 2 h.)	• Wall Creation • Openings • Levels • Characteristic points with known elevation
Handheld laser scanner (LIDAR scanning and SLAM tracking)	1054 min – 17,56 h (4 min, 1,5 h., 16 h.)	• Wall Creation • Openings • Details of windows • Levels • Characteristic points with known elevation • Deformations • Building material classification • Detachment of plaster, past conservation interventions
Terrestrial Laser Scanner	990 min – 16,50 h (30 min, 2 h., 14 h.)	• Wall Creation • Openings • Details of windows • Levels • Characteristic points with known elevation • Deformations • Building material classification • Detachment of plaster, past conservation interventions • Lack of information in narrow spaces (interior of the building) • Lack of information in spaces with noise from obstacles (vegetation through one room)

A diagram indicating the three pillars of the methodological framework is presented, where the accuracy of each of the three documentation practices is recorded, along with the total time process from the field observations. The results incorporated within the three BIM models are analyzed in conjunction with the level of detail and development of the BIM components (Fig. 17).

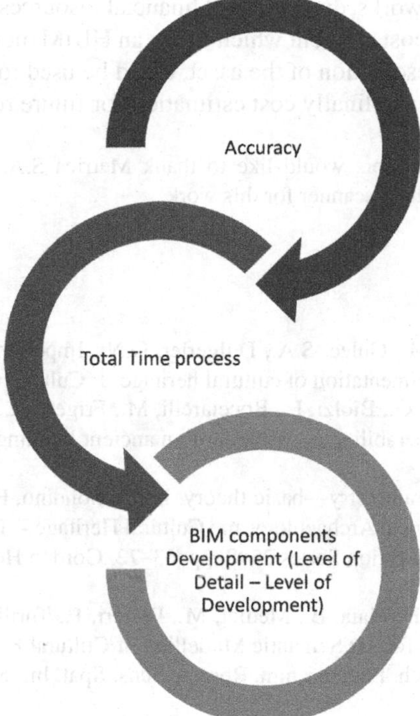

Fig. 17. Axes of the comparative analysis of the results towards BIM development

6 Conclusions

Geometric Documentation plays a pivotal role for the preservation of the values of a cultural heritage asset. As illustrated in this paper, various methods of geometric documentation can and should be used in order to ensure the complete recording of an asset at a specific time, considering the efficiency, accuracy and time of documentation. In general, geometric documentation data provides the basis for all associated technical analyses (architectural and structural) and therefore should be a prerequisite for each study that focuses on built heritage. Depending on the Level of Detail of an HBIM, and taking into account the demands and purpose it serves; additional tools should be tested and used, in order to optimize cost and time efficiency. Semiautomatic and automatic methods of HBIM creation could be utilized, in the case of a lower Level of Detail demand, for a rapid documentation process. On the other hand, other non-destructive techniques and studies could be applied and integrated within an HBIM model that could lead to an efficient restoration plan, including qualitative and quantitative data for this purpose.

Finally, for the specific heritage building, the use of a handheld laser scanner, the process of 3d point cloud creation time and accuracy related and finally the HBIM development serves as the optimum methodological process. It can therefore be concluded that for the majority of historic buildings that are deteriorating and are not yet considered suitable for rehabilitation works, due to lack of financial resources, or lack of governance, a process that is time and cost efficient which offers an HBIM model, that includes information for the state of preservation of the asset, could be used for optimization of other documentation processes and finally cost estimation for future restoration works.

Acknowledgements. The authors would like to thank Metrica S.A. for providing the Leica Geosystems BLK2GO handheld scanner for this work.

References

1. Yilmaz, H.M., Yakar, M., Gulec, S.A., Dulgerler, O.N.: Importance of digital close-range photogrammetry in documentation of cultural heritage. J. Cult. Herit. **8**, 428–433 (2007)
2. Fregonese, L., Barbieri, G., Biolzi, L., Bocciarelli, M., Frigeri, A., Taffurelli, L.: Surveying and monitoring for vulnerability assessment of an ancient building. Sensors **13**, 9747–9773 (2013)
3. Remondino, F.: Photogrammetry—basic theory. In: Remondino, F., Campana, S. (eds.) 3D Recording and Modelling in Archaeology and Cultural Heritage—Theory and Best Practices; Archaeopress BAR Publication Series 2598, pp. 63–72. Gordon House: Oxford, UK (2014). ISBN 9781407312309.
4. Di Giulio, R., Maietti, F., Piaia, E., Medici, M., Ferrari, F., Turillazzi, B.: Integrated Data Capturing requirements for 3D Semantic Modelling of Cultural Heritage: The INCEPTION protocol. ISPRS Int. Arch. Photogramm. Remote Sens. Spat. Inf. Sci. **XLII-2/W3**, 251–257 (2017)
5. Albano, R.: Investigation on roof segmentation for 3D building reconstruction from aerial LIDAR point clouds. Appl. Sci. **9**, 4674 (2019)
6. Georgopoulos, A.: Data acquisition for the geometric documentation of cultural heritage. In: Ioannides, M., Magnenat-Thalmann, N., Papagiannakis, G. (eds.) Mixed Reality and Gamification for Cultural Heritage, vol. 2, pp. 29–73. Springer International Publishing, Cham, Switzerland (2017)
7. Moropoulou, A., Labropoulos, K.C., Delegou, E.T., Karoglou, M., Bakolas, A.: Non-destructive techniques as a tool for the protection of built cultural heritage. Constr. Build. Mater. **48**, 1222–1239 (2013)
8. Bruno, N., Roncella, R.: A restoration oriented HBIM system for cultural heritage documentation: the case study of Parma Cathedral. Int. Arch. Photogramm. Remote Sens. Spat. Inf. Sci. **42**, 171–178 (2018)
9. Tsilimantou, E., Delegou, E.T., Nikitakos, I.A., Ioannidis, C., Moropoulou, A.: GIS and BIM as integrated digital environments for modeling and monitoring of historic buildings. Appl. Sci. **10**, 1078 (2020). https://doi.org/10.3390/app10031078
10. Murphy, M., McGovern, E., Pavia, S.: Historic building information modelling (HBIM). Struct. Surv. **27**, 311–327 (2009)
11. Barrile, V., Bernardo, E., Bilotta, G.: An experimental HBIM processing: innovative tool for 3D model reconstruction of morpho-typological phases for the cultural heritage. Remote Sens. **14**, 1288 (2022). https://doi.org/10.3390/rs14051288
12. Yang, X., Grussenmeyer, P., Koehl, M., Macher, H., Murtiyoso, A., Landes, T.: Review of built heritage modelling: integration of HBIM and other information techniques. J. Cult. Herit. **46**, 350–360 (2020)
13. Tommasi, C., Fiorillo, F., Jiménez Fernández-Palacios, B., Achille, C.: Access and web-sharing of 3D digital documentation of environmental and architectural heritage. Int. Arch. Photogramm. Remote Sens. Spat. Inf. Sci. **XLII-2/W9**, 707–714 (2019)

14. Costantino, D., Pepe, M., Restuccia, A.: Scan-to-HBIM for conservation and preservation of Cultural Heritage building: the case study of San Nicola in Montedoro church (Italy). Appl. Geomat. 1–15 (2021)
15. Sanseverino, A., Messina, B., Limongiello, M., Guida, C.G.: An HBIM methodology for the accurate and georeferenced reconstruction of urban contexts surveyed by UAV: the case of the castle of charles V. Remote Sens. **14**, 3688 (2022)
16. Klapa, P., Gawronek, P.: Synergy of geospatial data from TLS and UAV for heritage building information modeling (HBIM). Remote Sens. **15**, 128 (2023). https://doi.org/10.3390/rs15010128
17. Mellado, F., Wong, P.F., Amano, K., Johnson, C., Lou, W.C.E.: Digitisation of existing buildings to support building assessment schemes: viability of automated sustainability-led design scan-to-BIM process. Architectural Eng. Des. Manag. **16**(2), 84–99 (2020). https://doi.org/10.1080/17452007.2019.1674126
18. Brumana, R., et al.: SCAN to HBIM-post earthquake preservation: Informative model as sentinel at the crossroads of present, past, and future. In: Proceedings of the Euro-Mediterranean Conference, pp. 39–51. Limassol, Cyprus (2018)
19. Rodríguez-Moreno, C., Reinoso-Gordo, J.F., Rivas-López, E., Gómez-Blanco, A., Ariza-López, F.J., Ariza-López, I.: From point cloud to BIM: an integrated workflow for documentation, research and modelling of architectural heritage. Surv. Rev. **50**(360), 212–231 (2018). https://doi.org/10.1080/00396265.2016.1259719
20. Murphy, M., McGovern, E., Pavia, S.: Historic building information modelling-adding intelligence to laser and image-based surveys of European classical architecture. ISPRS J. Photogramm. Remote Sens. **76**, 89–102 (2013)
21. Brumana, R., Della Torre, S., Previtali, M., Barazzetti, L., Cantini, L., Oreni, D., Banfi, F.: Generative HBIM modelling to embody complexity (LOD, LOG, LOA, LOI): surveying, preservation, site intervention—The Basilica di Collemaggio (L'Aquila). Appl. Geomat. **10**, 545–567 (2018)
22. Fix, G.R.: The History of the FIX Family in Heraklio. From the Bavarian King Otto until today, Private Publisher, Heraklio (2005)
23. Maltezos, G.T.: The Chronicle of Heraklion – Attika. Publisher Anatolis, Athens (1970)
24. Konteris, T.: Research and Guide of Attica, Neon and Palaion Heraklio. Tilperiglou, N., Athens (1935)
25. Theodoropoulos, A.A.: Heraklio Attica (Ifistia – Ifaistia – Arakli 508 b.C.) Athens (1997)
26. Kounti, D.: Heraklio Attikis between legend and History. https://www.archaiologia.gr. Last accessed 25 Jan 2023
27. Anastasopoulos, A.G.: History of Hellenic industry 1840–1940, vol. A. Hellenic Publishing Company S.A. (1947). Mavrakis, G.: Zythopoiia Ioannou FIX, Industrial Reports. http://www.vidarchives.gr/reports/2018_06_25. Last accessed 26 Jan 2023

A New Low-Cost Rolling Ball Type Isolation Device for the Protection of Museum Collections

Alessia Di Martino[2(✉)], Francesco Cannizzaro[1], Giuseppe Cocuzza Avellino[1], and Nicola Impollonia[1]

[1] Università degli Studi di Catania, Piazza Università 2, 95131 Catania, Italy
{francesco.cannizzaro,nicola.impollonia}@unict.it
[2] Università Mediterranea di Reggio Calabria, Via dell'Università 25, 89124 Reggio Calabria, Italy
alessia.dimartino@unirc.it

Abstract. Recent seismic events highlighted the need to protect and preserve the cultural heritage for future generations. The International Council of Museums (ICOM) and the Italian guidelines for the safeguard of cultural heritage, indeed, stress the importance of protection policies from natural and human hazards. In particular, the preservation of artworks implies adopting measures to avoid any damage due to earthquakes. This research proposes a comprehensive approach for the mitigation of the seismic risk of art objects contained in confined environment. The study takes advantage of an interdisciplinary strategy for the evaluation of the seismic vulnerability of free-standing objects. According to this approach, a digital twin of the object is obtained by means of instrumentations such as Terrestrial Laser Scanner and Unmanned Aerial Vehicle, subsequently employed as geometry reference for the reconstruction of a scaled wooden physical specimen; a shaking table experimental campaign is finally conducted on the specimen. In this study, the mentioned approach is integrated by proposing a low-cost rolling ball anti-seismic device to mitigate the response of small-scale objects through base seismic isolation. The proposed device is characterised by a limited footprint and is obtained by flat wooden panels conveniently carved for the realization of the spherical caps with a milling machine. The study was applied to the Venere Landolina, the masterpiece preserved in the "Paolo Orsi" regional archaeological museum in Syracuse (Italy). The results of a preliminary shaking table experimental campaign, also in view of the adopted manufacturing technique and materials, shows the effectiveness of the proposed low-cost device. A first design procedure of the device is introduced and some considerations on the dissipation of energy associated to the seismic isolating device are provided.

Keywords: Cultural Heritage · Museum · Conservation · Seismic Vulnerability · Rolling ball isolator · Digital Twin · Shaking Table · Rigid Block Analysis

1 Introduction

Seismic assessment and protection represent a challenge for modern engineering not only for buildings but also for their content.

A. Moropoulou et al. (Eds.): TMM_CH 2023, CCIS 1889, pp. 82–93, 2023.
https://doi.org/10.1007/978-3-031-42300-0_7

The necessity to seismically protect small-scale objects is significant in two main cases: machinery located inside strategic buildings (e.g. medical devices, servers, control towers which have to guarantee their operability during the earthquake and in the aftermath) and artworks [1]. For the latter objects, the seismic assessment topic implies concerns for economic loss, and ethics connected to cultural loss. The seismic assessment and protection of building contents is a crucial topic in the artistic-monumental environment, mainly in countries such as Italy, where the cultural heritage is very large and spread all over the territory [1].

In the context of the seismic protection of artworks, their damage is mainly connected to their uplift and subsequent overturning. The crisis of the material is encountered only in a few cases, for which FE models are usually employed, mainly to study and interpret the presence of cracks in statues in static [2] and dynamic [3] conditions. For this reason, there is a broad literature aiming at proper modeling such systems in seismic conditions; most of these models are based on the rigid body motion assumptions [4, 5].

The interest in the seismic protection of artworks has been growing in the last decades. Some masterpieces, such as Michelangelo's David [2], the Bust of Francesco I D'Este [6], and the Bronzi di Riace, underwent detailed studies.

The present study integrates a novel interdisciplinary approach for the experimental assessment of statues involving survey, technology, and structural skills. The proposed methodology takes advantage of a previous study conducted on free-standing objects [7]. Starting from the analysis of the behavior of the artworks preserved in a confined environment, it aims at reducing their seismic vulnerability by an anti-seismic device. The approach includes different phases that, after the survey of the selected artworks, lead to the analysis of the overturning mechanisms of a scaled prototype, geometrically faithful to the original artworks, by means of a shaking table. The novel contribution here introduced is the study of the object when protected by a rolling-ball isolation device.

The proposed methodology is applied to the "Venere Landolina", a masterpiece preserved today at the *Paolo Orsi* Regional Archeological Museum in Syracuse (Italy).

2 Seismic Risk Mitigation of Museum Collections for the Preservation of History

The preservation and seismic protection of museum collections reflect the need to preserve our past and define the bases for a safe future [8].

Museums are responsible for the natural and cultural heritage which they preserve and they have to guarantee its preservation and enhancement [9], as defined in the Ethics Code of the ICOM – that is the international institution, which has been coordinating the museums of the world since 1948.

In the European context, the *Faro Convention* enshrines the fundamental role of the preservation of the cultural and artistic heritage which has as goal the human development. Highlighting the value of cultural heritage also means interpreting, protecting, and preserving the heritage itself [10].

The idea of reducing the effects of earthquakes on collections began in 1983 when the Paul Getty Museum in Los Angeles, California, carried out several studies that allowed the development of different methods for the mitigation of the seismic risk of small-scale museum assets by lowering the center of gravity. Alternatively, the use of clips was proposed to secure the objects by fixing them to the pedestals (although this contribution requires that the object has sufficient strength and rigidity). Finally, base isolation devices were suggested to limit the horizonal accelerations during the earthquake [11].

The Bronzi di Riace isolation system is a pioneering implementation of rolling-ball isolation devices realized by the ENEA following a project developed by Gerardo De Canio. The devices are semi-passive systems composed of two marble blocks in which the surfaces of the blocks are carved with an ellipsoid shape where four spheres, made by the same material of the blocks, can roll [12, 13].

A further example is represented by the seismic isolation system employed for the Bust of Francesco I D'Este and designed by FIP INDUSTRIALE in collaboration with the IUAV University of Venice [6].

It is worth to note that the studies carried out in this field and the achieved outcomes can find large-scale applications involving artworks with very different features.

3 Interdisciplinary Methodology for Small-scale Objects: the Venere Landolina

This study is applied to the most prestigious work of the "Paolo Orsi" Regional Archeological Museum in Syracuse [14], Italy: the Venere Landolina [15] (see Fig. 1), whose free-standing configuration and seismic behavior was previously investigated [7].

Fig. 1. The Venere Landolina statue.

The original devised procedure included three main phases: a *knowledge phase*, a *prototyping phase,* and the *experimental phase*. These three phases, based on a preliminary digital survey of the statue, allowed to create a digital twin and a subsequent physical model, which was finally tested on a shaking table considering spectrum compatible ground motions.

However, the subsequent step, that is the adoption of effective measures to seismically protect the statue, was not considered in the mentioned study. This work aims at integrating the previous study with a fourth phase, that is the *seismic protection phase*. (see Fig. 2).

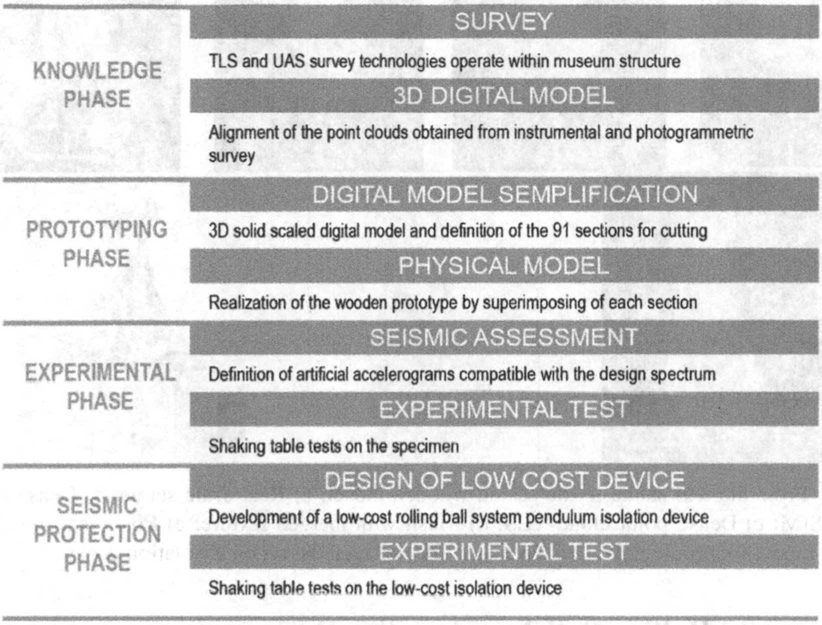

KNOWLEDGE PHASE

SURVEY

TLS and UAS survey technologies operate within museum structure

3D DIGITAL MODEL

Alignment of the point clouds obtained from instrumental and photogrammetric survey

PROTOTYPING PHASE

DIGITAL MODEL SEMPLIFICATION

3D solid scaled digital model and definition of the 91 sections for cutting

PHYSICAL MODEL

Realization of the wooden prototype by superimposing of each section

EXPERIMENTAL PHASE

SEISMIC ASSESSMENT

Definition of artificial accelerograms compatible with the design spectrum

EXPERIMENTAL TEST

Shaking table tests on the specimen

SEISMIC PROTECTION PHASE

DESIGN OF LOW COST DEVICE

Development of a low-cost rolling ball system pendulum isolation device

EXPERIMENTAL TEST

Shaking table tests on the low-cost isolation device

Fig. 2. The main phases of the proposed methodology.

The description of the first three phases falls outside the scope of this paper. A summary of all the considered steps of the study is reported in Fig. 3, which is here integrated with a final step that considers the application of an isolation device to protect the statue. In the free-standing configuration the spectrum-compatible ground motions led to the rocking of the statue without overturning. Although the specimen does not overturn, the rocking itself is dangerous for the statue due to multiple impacts; therefore, the design of a proper anti-seismic device able to significantly reduce the statue rocking under the design ground motion is a crucial aspect for its seismic protection. For the interested reader, all the data regarding the free-standing configuration of the statue can be found in [7, 16].

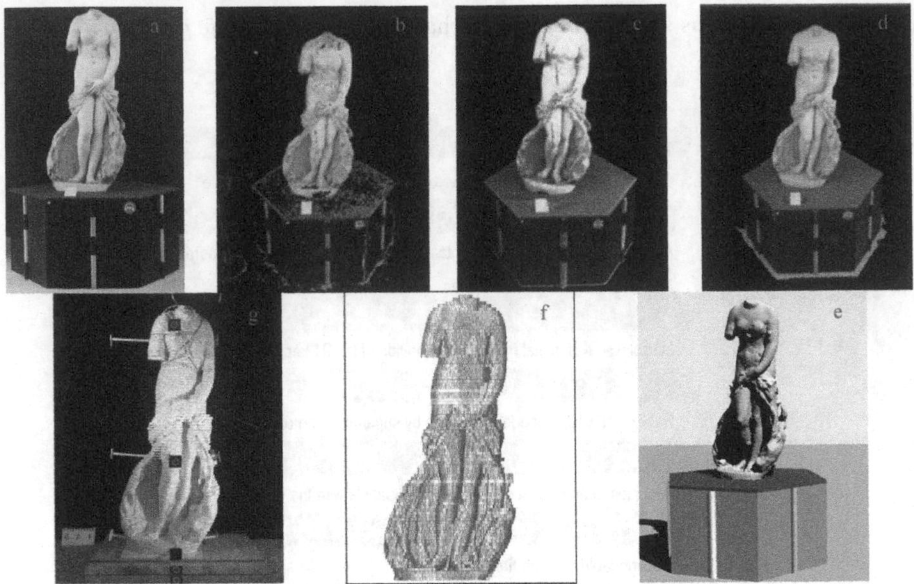

Fig. 3. From the real statue to the scaled wooden model: a) Real scale statue; b) Dense point cloud SfM; c) Dense point cloud TLS; d) Mesh with merged texture; e) Polygonal model; f) Scaled model for printing; g) Wooden scaled specimen on the seismic isolation device.

4 Low-cost Rolling Ball Type Isolation Device

The definition of a methodology for studying the seismic vulnerability of small-scale artworks contained in a confined environment constitutes a preparatory phase for the subsequent design and prototyping phase of an antiseismic device for artworks.

It was, indeed, developed the proposed low-cost rolling ball system pendulum isolating device, which consists of two beech wood plates carved with four spherical grooves, in which spheres can roll. This allows the decoupling of the bottom plate, subject to the seismic acceleration, and the top plate on which the object stands (see Fig. 4).

The main parameters to determine are: the overall geometry, the characteristics of the spheres, and the radius of curvature of the inner caps. They are related to the geometric and physical characteristics of the scaled model of the object to be seismically isolated.

Once the isolation period T_{is} is chosen, the following formula holds:

$$2\pi\sqrt{\frac{\widehat{R}}{g}} = T_{is} \tag{1}$$

where g is the gravity acceleration and $\hat{R} = 2(R - r)$, being R and r the radii of the caps and of the rolling spheres, respectively. Inversion of Eq. (1), considering r a given parameter associated to the availability of the size of the spheres, leads to infer the radius of curvature R of the caps.

The second step of the design procedure is the determination of the design displacement $d_{max} = 2R_c$ to be obtained according to the isolation period T_{is} and to the floor design spectrum in terms of displacement, and which determines the minimum footprint of the caps. It is important, indeed, that the combination of R and R_c must be compatible with the quantity of removable material, in order to avoid to compromise the efficiency of the device.

The third step is the design of the minimum distance between the caps to avoid the possible uplift and overturning of the top plate in seismic condition. The equilibrium, although assured in static conditions, must be verified during dynamic motion considering that the horizontal forces could be capable of tilting the top plate (see Fig. 4). In order to avoid such condition the distance between the grooves must be conveniently chosen. Enforcing the limit moment equilibrium with respect to point A, it is possible to determine a safe distance a between the vertical reaction and the resultant of the gravity loads (see Fig. 4):

$$a = \frac{\ddot{u}_{\max}}{g} l \tag{2}$$

where $\ddot{u}_{max}$ is the maximum expected horizontal acceleration of the top plate of the isolation device (to be evaluated according to T_{is} and to the floor spectrum), and l is the height of the centre of gravity of the system composed by the statue and the top plate with respect to the contact point with the rolling spheres. The admissible horizontal displacement d_{max}, can be related to the minimum distance of the spheres at rest $L_{c,min}$ as follows:

$$L_{c,\min} = d_{\max} + 2a \tag{3}$$

It is worth mentioning that in this preliminary procedure, both $\ddot{u}_{max}$ and d_{max} were evaluated without accounting for any energy dissipation associated to the presence of the anti-seismic device. For the latter reason, the design procedure could underestimate $\ddot{u}_{max}$ and overestimate d_{max}, respectively, with respect to the corresponding values experimentally evaluated.

5 Experimental Campaign

In this section the experimental response of the wooden scale model (scale factor 1:2) is reported for the seismically isolated configuration.

The experimental setup includes: i) a single degree of freedom shaking table LO.F.HI.S. series ND13014 (Low Frequency High Stroke and Velocity Shaker); ii) base acceleration selection; iii) a high frequency acquisition camera (DS-RX100 M5) for contactless displacement data acquisition method [17] – which allows a zeroing of measurement errors that could arise from the contact of the instrument during the measurement phase and which guarantees a more accurate evaluation of the motion. To this purpose, the video records are processed using the Tracker Video Analysis and Modeling Tool software ver. 5.0.7″ [18].

The design of the experimental campaign was performed considering seven compatible ground motion, chosen consistently to those adopted for the free-standing statue experimental campaign [7]. They were generated in according to the Artistic Limit State design spectrum (SLA) [19], following the Italian guidelines for artistic heritage [20], of the site where the Venere Landolina is located (Syracuse, Italy), considering a soil type C.

In agreement to the reference floor spectrum and the assumed design isolation period of the device set equal to 1,50 s, corresponding, according to Eq. (1), to $\hat{R} = 0{,}559$ m. By adopting a radius of the caps equal to 0,30 m (duly verified to be compatible with the wooden plates thickness 0,03 m) and radius of the spheres $r = 0{,}015$ m, the final analytical fundamental period of the isolated statue is $T_{is} = 1{,}53$ s. The design acceleration for the linearized isolation system is $\ddot{u}_{max} = 0{,}475$ m/s^2 which is slightly larger than the minimum uplift acceleration of the statue equal to 0,3924 m/s^2 obtained by means of simple tests [7], but low enough to avoid any significant rocking of the statue. The corresponding design displacement d_{max} is equal to 0,028 m.

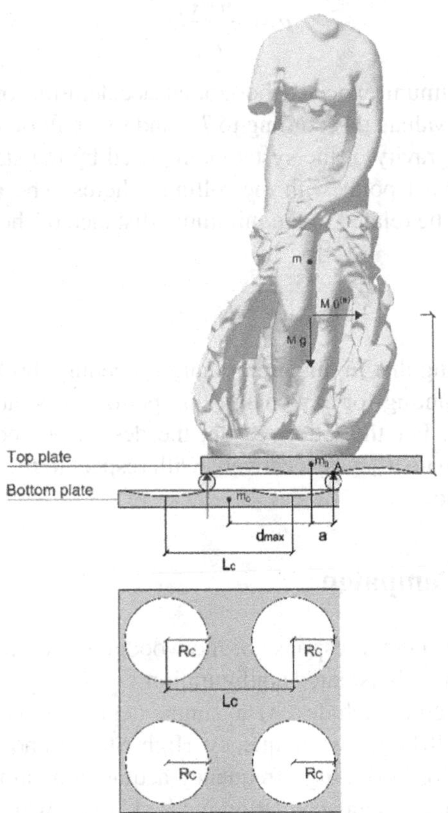

Fig. 4. Schemes of the designed device.

The distance l is obtained on the basis of the masses of the statue and of the top plate and is equal to 0,2849 m, thus leading, according to Eq. (2), to a safety distance $a = 0{,}0138$ m. The distance between the centres of the caps is finally obtained according to Eq. (3) and is equal to $L_{c,min} = 0{,}0556$ m. According to the described procedure it was possible to define all the geometric features of the isolating device (see Fig. 5), where R_C and L_C were assumed considerably larger than the minimum required in view of the approximated assumptions of the design procedure.

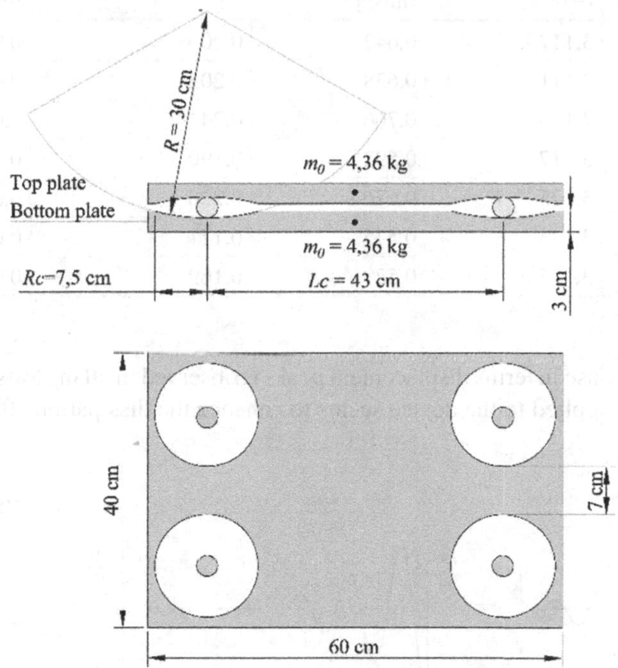

Fig. 5. Geometric layout of the isolating device designed for the Venere Landolina.

The efficiency of the seismic isolation system was evaluated conducting a set of test adopting the seven previously generated accelerograms. It was observed that the absolute acceleration of the top plate of the isolator is always significantly lower than the corresponding Peak Ground Acceleration (PGA).

The effectiveness of the isolation system was also measured by the ratio between the peak acceleration value related to the isolated system and the PGA, and by the maximum horizontal relative displacements of the two plates of the isolating device, reported in Table 1. The latter values are for all the tests lower than the design maximum displacements.

Discrepancies with respect to design spectral values are related to non-linear effects arising due imperfections and damped vibration induced by the mass of the statue. To this purpose, several free vibrations tests were carried out in order to characterize the dissipation provided by the device, evaluating the displacement decay of the response. For these tests spheres with $r = 0{,}0183$ m were employed.

It turned out that the dissipation is strictly related to the vertical load applied to the device. Figure 6 shows the horizontal relative displacement between the two plates for three free vibration tests associated to different values of the carried mass; a quasi-linear

Table 1. Efficacy of the isolation system based on the peak acceleration values related to the isolated and non-isolated system and their ratio for each generated accelerograms.

	PGA [m/s^2]	$\ddot{u}_{max}^{(iso)}$ [m/s^2]	$\ddot{u}_{max}^{(iso)}$/PGA [-]	$u_{max}^{(iso)}$ [m]
Acc_01	3,117	0,642	0,206	0,013
Acc_02	3,111	0,638	0,205	0,010
Acc_03	3,133	0,766	0,244	0,013
Acc_04	3,117	0,592	0,190	0,009
Acc_05	3,075	0,676	0,220	0,012
Acc_06	3,133	0,535	0,171	0,014
Acc_07	3,127	0,529	0,169	0,012

decay of the response in terms displacement peaks is observed in all the tests. In addition, the vertical load applied to the device seems to enhance the dissipation effect.

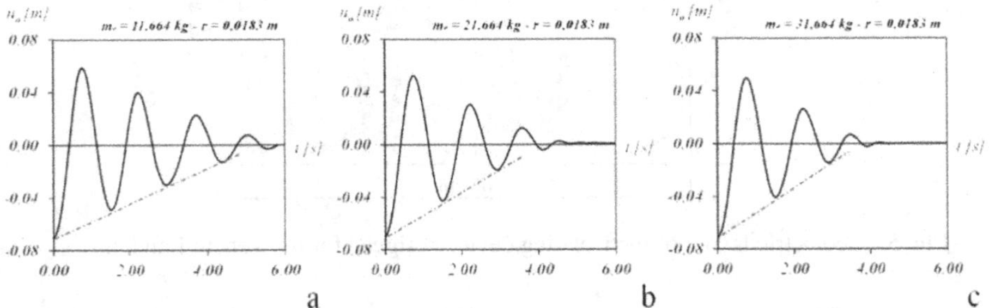

Fig. 6. Free vibration tests conducted on the anti-seismic with different vertical loads

In the case of the masterpiece of the Venere Landolina, the mass of the wooden prototype, located above the top plate of the design anti-seismic device, induces a considerable energy dissipation that justifies the difference between the experimental response and the design values in terms of peak acceleration and maximum displacement.

In Fig. 7 the design accelerogram (gray line), the absolute accelerations measured on the top plate during the experiment (black line) and the real uplift acceleration $\ddot{u}_R^{(e)}$ relative to the right edge of the statue (dashed line) are shown for one of the performed tests. In addition, for the same test (Acc_06) the response in terms of horizontal relative displacement between the two plates of the isolating device is also reported.

The first experimental results obtained have shown a limited variability in the response of the scaled model to the different ground motions, demonstrating a safe behavior of the statue thanks to the introduction of the proposed anti-seismic device.

Although neglecting the dissipation energy in the design procedure, which will be the object of further studies, these preliminary results are promising and suggest further investigations for an optimized design of an anti-seismic device to be rapidly adapted to the geometric and physical properties of the artwork to preserve, thus favoring large-scale applications.

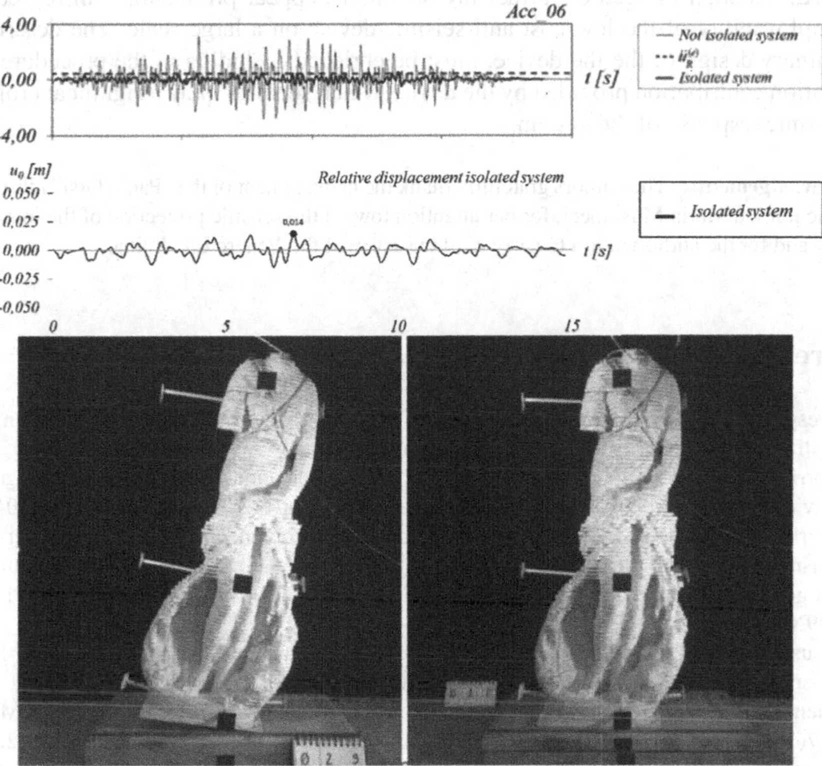

Fig. 7. Acceleration at the base of the statue with and without isolation system.

6 Conclusions

In this study a procedure for the protection of art objects from the risk connected seismic events, was defined. The interdisciplinary procedure includes the realization of scaled prototypes of statues based on a digital twin of the real statue, to be subsequently experimentally tested on a shaking table both in the free-standing and seismically isolated configurations.

The proposed methodology is here applied to the case of the Venere Landolina, the masterpiece of the Paolo Orsi Regional Archaeological Museum in Syracuse, Italy.

This methodology demonstrates the crucial importance of cooperation among the scientific fields and the knowledge integration to contribute to the scientific progress. The main advantage of the proposed procedure is the capability to perform experimental tests on the artworks (even though via a scaled replica) avoiding any direct contact with the real statue. A new low-cost rolling ball seismic device is introduced able to significantly limit the statue rocking when subjected to spectrum-compatible ground motions, thus completely preserving the statue from any damage. The anti-seismic device is described and some geometry design criteria are also presented. The preliminary results here reported, although in need of further investigations, appear promising with respect to the employability of the low-cost anti-seismic device on a large scale. The described preliminary design of the the device, must be enriched including in the procedure the dissipation contribution provided by the device which seems to play a significant role in the seismic response of the system.

Acknowledgements. The authors gratefully thank the management of the "Paolo Orsi" museum, in particular Dr. Maria Musumeci, for her attention toward the seismic protection of the museum content and for the authorization to carry out the survey of the Venere Landolina.

References

1. Crespellani, T.: Terremoto: "evento naturale" ed "evento sociale". In: Festival Scienza – L'alfabeto della Scienza – V Edizione, Cagliari (2012)
2. Borri, A., Grazini, A.: Diagnostic analysis of the lesions and stability of Michelangelo's David. J. Cult. Herit. **7**(4), 273–285 (2006). https://doi.org/10.1016/j.culher.2006.06.004
3. Cerri, G., Pirazzoli, G., Tanganelli, M., Verdiani, G., Rotunno, T., Pintucchi, B., Viti, S.: Seismic assessment of artefacts: the case of Juno's Fountain of The National Museum of Bargello. IOP Conf. Ser.: Mater. Sci. Eng. **364**, 012057 (2018). https://doi.org/10.1088/1757-899X/364/1/012057
4. Housner, G.W.: The behavior of inverted pendulum structures during earthquakes. Bull. Seismol. Soc. Am. **53**(2), 403–417 (1963). https://doi.org/10.1785/BSSA0530020403
5. Shenton, H.W., III., Jones, N.P.: Base excitation of rigid bodies. I: formulation. J. Eng. Mech. **117**(10), 2286–2306 (1991). https://doi.org/10.1061/(ASCE)0733-9399(1991)117:10(2286)
6. Baggio, S., Berto, L., Castellano, M.G., Rocca, I., Saetta, A.: Isolamento sismico del busto di Francesco I d'Este con isolatori a pendolo. Struct. Model. Magazine di ingegneri strutturale **19**, 22–31 (2018)
7. Cocuzza Avellino, G., et al.: Numerical and experimental response of free standing art objects subjected to ground motion. Int. J. Architectural Heritage **16**(11), 1666–1682 (2021). https://doi.org/10.1080/15583058.2021.1902019
8. Horizon Europe Homepage: https://horizoneurope.apre.it/. Last accessed 7 Jan 2023
9. ICOM Ethic Committee: ICOM Code of Ethics for Museums. https://icom.museum/en/resources/standards-guidelines/code-of-ethics/ (2004)
10. Council of Europe: Council of Europe Framework Convention on the Value of Cultural Heritage for Society. https://www.coe.int/en/web/culture-and-heritage/faro-convention (2005)
11. J. Paul Getty Museum: Protecting collections in the J. Paul Getty Museum from Earthquake Damage. WAAC Newslett. **29**(3), 16–23 (2007)
12. Jeong, M.Y., Lee, H., Kim, J.H., Yang, I.Y.: Chaotic behavior on rocking vibration of rigid body block structure under two-dimensional sinusoidal excitation (in the case of no sliding). KSME Int. J. **17**(9), 1249–1260 (2003). https://doi.org/10.1007/BF02982466
13. De Canio, G.: Basi antisismiche in marmo per i Bronzi di Riace. Archeomatica **2**(1), 6–9 (2011)

14. Museo Archeologico Regionale Paolo Orsi Homepage. https://www2.regione.sicilia.it/beniculturali/museopaoloorsi/. Last accessed 7 Jan 2023
15. Regione Siciliana Assessorato dei Beni culturali e dell'Identità siciliana Homepage. https://www2.regione.sicilia.it/beniculturali/dirbenicult/info/beniinamovibili/SrVenere-landolina.html. Last accessed 7 Jan 2023
16. Cocuzza Avellino, G.: Rigid body seismic vulnerability and protection by means of low-cost rolling ball system isolator: numerical and experimental analyses. University of Catania, Thesis for degree of Doctor of Philosophy. (2020)
17. Aicardi, I., Chiabrando, F., Grasso, N., Lingua, A.M., Noardo, F., Spanò, A.: UAV photogrammetry with oblique images: first analysis on data acquisition and processing. Int. Arch. Photogramm. Remote Sens. Spatial Inf. Sci. **XLI-B1**, 835–842 (2016). https://doi.org/10.5194/isprsarchives-XLI-B1-835-2016
18. Brown D., Wolfgang C.: Simulating what you see: combining computer modeling with video analysis. In: 8th International Conference on Hands on Science. Ljubljana (2011)
19. Ministero delle infrastrutture e dei trasporti: Decreto 17 gennaio 2018, Aggiornamento delle "Norme tecniche per le costruzioni" – NTC18 (2018)
20. Linee guida per la valutazione e la riduzione del rischio sismico del patrimonio culturale con riferimento alle Norme tecniche per le costruzioni di cui al decreto del Ministero delle Infrastrutture e dei trasporti del 14 gennaio 2008

Documentation of the Leprosarium of Chios

Athanasios Iliodromitis[1(✉)], George Pantazis[2], and Elena Konstantiniu[3]

[1] Department of Surveying and Geoinformatics Engineering, School of Engineering, University of West Attica, 12243 Egaleo, Greece
a.iliodromitis@uniwa.gr

[2] School of Rural, Surveying and Geoinformatics Engineering, National Technical University of Athens, 15780 Zografos, Athens, Greece
gpanta@central.ntua.gr

[3] School of Architecture, National Technical University of Athens, Athens, Greece
ekonstantinidou@arch.ntua.gr

Abstract. The documentation of an edifice can serve different purposes, such as restoration, renovation, repair, interventions, etc. When it comes to architectural heritage, documentation is the first step in the process of restoring a monument – the basic stage for its rescue and protection.

The evolution of technology has given an abundance of equipment and methods in order to use for reaching the desired precision and minimizing the measurements' time. The key factor, to the creation of a correct geometric diagram/plan, is the combination of these methods, especially when it comes to areas of historical importance.

Nevertheless, a substantial understanding of the historical building, a fundamental condition for any intervention, should include not only geometric documentation but also the recognition of the structure (i.e. the synthetic and functional composition) and its form (i.e. its building and construction characteristics). Also, the understanding of the historical and architectural knowledge it contains, the recording, analyzing, and interpreting as a tangible example of values.

In this paper the procedure of the documentation of the Leprosarium of Chios Island, is presented. First established in 1378, took its final form in 1933 and abandoned in 1959 is one of the longest-term health institutions of Greece. The very interesting building complex, in terms of historical and architectural value, was classified as a protected historical monument, in 2011. However, this was not enough for the protection of this important monument, as today it is completely abandoned.

The paper focuses on the geometric documentation of the Leprosarium, carried out with contemporary combined methods (e.g. conventional reflectorless total station, geodetic GNSS, close-range photogrammetry, aerial measuring methods, etc.).

It also attempts the overall recognition of the monument, based on the perspective of revealing, saving, and exploiting this unique historical monument of Chios.

Keywords: Documentation · Cultural Heritage · Leprosarium of Chios · Close-range photogrammetry · Aerial photogrammetry · Orthophoto/Rectified Image

A. Moropoulou et al. (Eds.): TMM_CH 2023, CCIS 1889, pp. 94–103, 2023.
https://doi.org/10.1007/978-3-031-42300-0_8

1 Introduction

Architectural Heritage, as a vital part of Cultural Heritage, is an expression of history and helps us to understand the relevance of the past to contemporary life. Constitutes a capital of irreplaceable spiritual, cultural, social, and economic value. An essential part of a community's identity that should be passed on to future generations as a part of the historical memory.

The issue of the protection and management of architectural heritage and the historic built environment nowadays is more topical than ever. The need to preserve important remains of the past and connect them with sustainable development policies, the functional activation of historical shells, and their integration into contemporary economic structures, alongside the need to directly connect the issue with the wider society.

Architectural Heritage is now treated as a single set of immovable cultural assets, part of the man-made as well as the natural environment, which must be globally protected, preserved as a non-renewable resource, and exploited through its integration into sustainable development, spatial and urban planning with the aim of producing social and economic surplus value.

The reuse of the Architecture of the past is an ancient practice that has greatly contributed to the preservation of historical structures, and to this day, it is an environmentally correct choice and offers great economic benefits. Reusing the past offers an invaluable experience, old spaces full of memories and values, which according to the prevailing ideology, must be preserved and highlighted in every way. By preserving historical structures communities can maintain their cultural heritage, provide educational and cultural opportunities, inspire new construction, and foster a sense of place and community identity.

Documentation is the basic tool, for the recording, analysis, and understanding of all kinds of constructions of the built environment. The first and necessary stage for the evaluation, restoration, preservation, and "comprehensive" protection of the architectural heritage in the present and in the future.

In this paper the procedure for the documentation of the Leprosarium of Chios Island is presented, a very interesting building complex in terms of historical and architectural value, today completely abandoned. The paper focuses on the geometric documentation of the complex, carried out with contemporary combined methods while it also attempts the overall recognition of the monument, based on the perspective of revealing, saving, and exploiting this unique historical monument of Chios.

2 The Leprosarium of Chios

The Leprosarium (or "Lovokomeio") of Chios is the first facility for the treatment leprosis, in Greece and one of the first in all Europe. It is located 1.5km north from the city of Chios (capital of the homonym island) and 2km far from the port of Chios. The area around the complex and the supportive facilities is about 15000 sq.m.

It was first established in 1378, by Genoese in the area of "Sifi" (today is called Kofinas), in the Valley of Ypakoi, which took its name from the church Panagia Ypakoi (it still stands near the complex). The aim was to prevent the spread of the disease to the general population and to provide care and treatment for those who were affected (Fig. 1) [1].

Fig. 1. The Leprosarium (or "Lovokomeio") of Chios.

During the prerevolutionary years the number of houses had reached 30 and accommodated up to 150 patients. In the massacre of Chios, in 1822, almost all the residents of the facility were slaughtered. Few years later, in 1931 the institution reopened, but during the catastrophic earthquake of 1881 it was completely destroyed. Its renovation started in 1885 with donations of wealthy locals but the conditions remained tragic and the institution was unable to meet its needs.

The first attempts for the full restoration started in 1909 with donations of Chians of the Diaspora, who were motivated by M. Kalvokoresis. With the designs of the engineer I. Veriketis, 16 antiseismic kiosks were built with 2 spacious rooms each, a covered outdoor space for the stay of patients, a small kitchen and a toilet. Each kiosk could accommodate 8 people. They were designed to accommodate both men and women, with separate quarters for each gender.

It took its final form in 1933. "Lovokomeio" by that time was a large complex of buildings, consisting, apart from the houses, of a chapel, a hospital and auxiliary facilities such as restaurant, laundry, recreation area and a sewerage network. There was also the possibility of hot water.

The materials were of excellent quality and many were imported from abroad, e.g. the iron poles for the roof from England, the tiles from France and the bricks from Asia. [2].

The chapel was an important part of the leprosarium and was used for religious services and other community gatherings. The hospital was equipped with modern medical facilities and was staffed by trained medical personnel. Patients were provided with medical treatment, including surgery, and were given the opportunity to participate in rehabilitation programs.

Despite its progressive design and purpose, life at the leprosarium was harsh and isolating. Patients were confined to the facility and were separated from their families and friends. They were subjected to strict quarantine measures and were not allowed to leave the facility or have visitors. This isolation was not only physically but also socially and emotionally damaging.

The colony shut its gates in 1957, leaving behind dilapidated ruins and memories of society's outcasts who inhabited the area for so long. [3].

In 2012 the complex was named as a modern monument from the Central Archaeological Council of the Ministry of Culture of Greece (decision ΥΑ ΥΠΠΟΤ/ΔΝΣΑΚ/99727/1801ΠΕ/5-3-2012, published in the Government Gazette 112ΑΑΡ/5-4-2012) [4].

Unfortunately, till today, the complex remains abandoned and fell into disrepair.

3 Documentation – Measuring Techniques

Geometric documentation is the action of acquiring, processing, presenting and recording the appropriate data for the determination of the position and the actual existing form, shape and size of an object in the three-dimensional space at a particular moment [5].

The process of geometric documentation involves the use of a variety of tools and techniques, including laser scanning, photogrammetry, and traditional surveying methods. These tools are used to create the drawing of the building or structure (e.g. topographic diagrams, elevations, floor plans, cross sections), which can then be used for further analysis and design work. From these data the

One of the key benefits of geometric documentation is that it provides an accurate and detailed representation of the building. This can be used to identify potential issues with the building's geometry and to ensure that it is built to the correct specifications. It can also be used to assess the structural stability of a building and to identify any potential safety risks.

Documentation is also useful for preserving the historical building. By capturing the details of a building's geometry, it is possible to create a digital archive of its design and construction. This can be used to inform future renovations or restoration work, and to ensure that the building is preserved for future generations [6–8].

The measuring techniques that were used in the specific case study and more or less can be used in almost every geometric documentation procedure are described below.

The duration of the measurement was 6 days combining conventional reflectorless total stations, geodetic GNSS, close-range photogrammetry, aerial measuring methods.

3.1 Conventional Surveying Methods

The conventional terrestrial surveying methods include the use of total stations and GNSS receivers for the calculation of the coordinates of specific points in a given reference system.

Depending on the accuracy and the size or geometry of the study area, the appropriate measuring method is chosen. The GNSS survey method can be used in an outdoor survey with clear horizon, but total station and its accessories can provide higher accuracy, which is necessary in documentation.

GNSS receivers were used to establish a geodetic network in the study area (static positioning) and to measure points in the perimeter of the study area (RTK technique). Total stations were used to establish a network of traverses along the building complex and to measure the points needed for the drawings.

3.2 Photogrammetry

Photogrammetry is a widely used documentation technique that involves the use of photographs to capture and analyze the geometry of a building or structure. This technique is particularly useful for capturing highly detailed and accurate information about complex shapes and structures that would otherwise be difficult to measure using traditional surveying methods.

Photogrammetry is based on the principle that photographs taken from different angles can be used to create a 3D model of the building or structure. To use photogrammetry, a series of photographs are taken from various positions. These photographs are then processed using photogrammetry software, which is used to extract information about the building's geometry.

One of the key advantages of photogrammetry is that it can be used to capture highly detailed and accurate information about a building or structure, even in difficult-to-reach locations.

Another advantage of photogrammetry is that it is a non-contact method, meaning that it does not require physical contact with the building or structure. This makes it ideal for the documentation of historic or delicate structures where direct contact could cause damage.

There are two main types of photogrammetry: aerial photogrammetry and close-range photogrammetry, both of which were used in the specific application,

Aerial photogrammetry was used to capture large-scale data, such as information about the topography of the landscape of the wider area. Moreover, it was used to capture the photographs just exactly above of the complex so that the orthophoto to be produced. Finally, it was used to take photographs from the facades.

For the needs of the application the DJI Mavic Mini was used. It is a light, compact and easy-to-use drone with a 12MP camera, suitable for close-range flights and applications.

Close-range photogrammetry is used to capture detailed information about smaller structures. The principle is the same as previous. It involves taking multiple overlapping photographs of the object with a handheld camera. It is a quick and cost-effective method (compared to other techniques), without the need for specialized equipment.

It the specific project was used to take photographs of the facades of the complex in order to produce the corresponding orthophotos.

4 Measurements – Final Products

One of the most important tasks in such projects is the preparation of the improvised sketches. The vast number of points that are going to be measured and the amount of information that is depicted on each sketch, impose the need for legible and clear sketches.

A proper and detailed sketch provides a visual representation of the features of the structure, giving a better understanding of it. It can also help in the decision of the shape of the geodetic network (traverses and station setups).

Finally, a sketch is a one-way in order to draw correctly the plans of the structure.

Different improvised sketches were prepared for the topographic plans, the floor plans (Fig. 2), facades (Fig. 3) and the cross-sections.

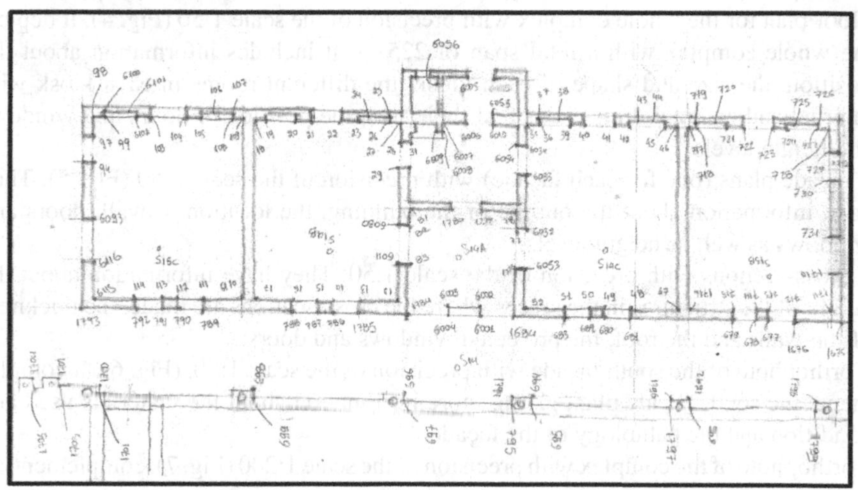

Fig. 2. Improvised sketch of the floor plan of a specific house block.

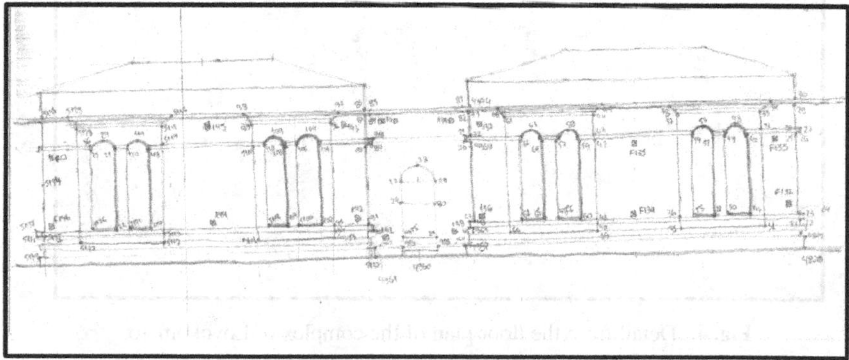

Fig. 3. Improvised sketch of the façade of a specific house block.

The network that was formed consisted of three (3) trigonometric points measured with GNSS static measurements and 95 station setups.

The points measured for the project were almost 1500 points for the topographic plan, 1400 point for the floor plan, 1200 point for the facades, 1000 point for the cross-sections.

For the creation of the orthophotos 80 photos were taken and 100 points were measured as GPSs.

The final products of the specific project were the all the drawings and orthophotos produced that describe the complex of Lovokomeio.

These include:

- Topographic plans of the wider area and the area of the complex in scale of 1:1000 and 1:200, respectively. They depict the building complex, the roads, the paths and the streams around it, the significant vegetation, height information (contours, and height points), cadastral information and information from the forest maps.
- Floor plan for the whole complex with precision of the scale 1:50 (Fig. 4). It depicts the whole complex with a total span of 225 m. It includes information about the position, the size and shape of each kiosk, the different rooms in each kiosk with internal and external dimensions and their area, the position of doors and windows and height levels
- 4 façade plans (one for each façade) with precision of the scale 1:50 (Fig. 5). They have information about the outline of the building, the location of wall, doors and windows as well as height levels.
- 3 cross-sections with precision of the scale 1:50. They have information about the height of the structures in the places where the cross-sections are made, the thickness of the walls and the roof, the projected windows and doors.
- 1 orthophoto of the south façade with precision of the scale 1:50. (Fig. 6). It complements the south façade plan, giving more information about the materials used and condition and the pathology of the façade.
- 1 orthophoto of the complex with precision of the scale 1:200 (Fig. 7), complementing the topographic plan.

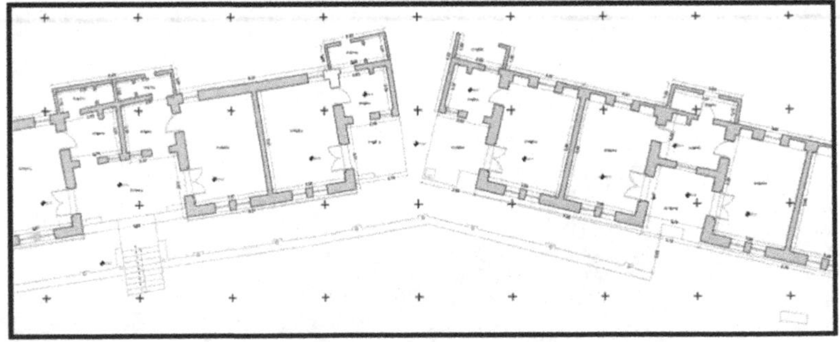

Fig. 4. Detail from the floor plan of the complex of Lovokomeio.

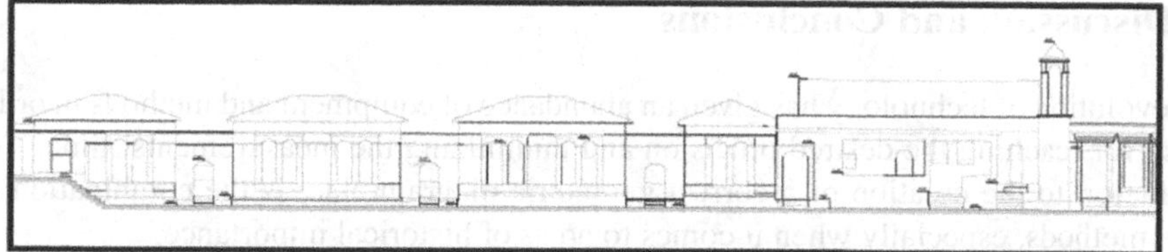

Fig. 5. Detail from the south façade of the complex of Lovokomeio.

Fig. 6. Orthophoto of the south façade

Fig. 7. Orthophoto of the complex

5 Discussion and Conclusions

The evolution of technology has given an abundance of equipment and methods in order to use for reaching the desired precision and minimizing the measurements' time. The key factor, to the creation of a correct geometric diagram/plan, is the combination of these methods, especially when it comes to areas of historical importance.

Nevertheless, a substantial understanding of the historical building, a fundamental condition for any intervention, should include not only geometric documentation but also the recognition of the structure (i.e. the synthetic and functional composition) and its form (i.e. its building and construction characteristics). Also, the understanding of the historical and architectural knowledge it contains, the recording, analyzing, and interpreting as a tangible example of values.

In this paper a complete case study of the combination of different terrestrial and aerial methodologies is described. The scope of the paper is to illustrate the basic advantages and possibilities of each of the different methods in order to conclude about the proper use of them in the documentation of the Leprosarium of Chios. It also attempts the overall recognition of the monument, based on the perspective of revealing, saving, and exploiting this unique historical monument of Chios.

Today, the Leprosarium of Chios is a testament to the history of public health in Greece and serves as a reminder of the challenges faced by people with leprosy in the past. It is a valuable cultural heritage site and could provide an opportunity for visitors to learn about the history of leprosy and its impact on society.

Finally, it should be noted that like the Leprosarium of Chios, many other monuments in Greece do not receive the respect or the attention they should. Geometric documentation is the step in the process of restoring a monument – the basic stage for its rescue and its protection so that, their history can be revealed and recognized by tourists or residents.

References

1. https://www.archaiologia.gr/. Last accessed 5 Feb 2023
2. Anastasaki, P.: The Leprosarium of Chios: Historical review, social options and future prospects of a local's history "silent witness". Diploma thesis. Hellenic Open University (2021)
3. https://www.atlasobscura.com/places/lovokomeio-chios-leper-colony. Last accessed 5 Feb 2023
4. https://www.arxaiologikoktimatologio.gov.gr/. Last accessed 5 Feb 2023
5. Stylianidis, E., Georgopoulos, A.: Digital surveying in cultural heritage: the image-based recording and documentation approaches. In: Ippolito, A., Cigola, M. (eds.) Handbook of research on emerging technologies for digital preservation and information modeling, pp. 119–149. IGI Global (2017)
6. Pantazis, G., Zafiris, V., et al.: The contribution of modern geodetic methods in the creation of geometric diagrams/plans for the management of historic centers. The Old & New Fortress of Corfu, Changing Cities V: Spatial, design, landscape, heritage and socio-economic dimensions, Corfu (2022)
7. George, G., Stefania, I., Nikolaos, K., George, P.: Documentation of cultural heritage monuments, by introducing new surveying technologies: implementation in Sarlitza Pallas, in Thermi Mytilene. In: Moropoulou, A., Georgopoulos, A., Doulamis, A., Ioannides, M., Ronchi, A.

(eds.) Trandisciplinary Multispectral Modelling and Cooperation for the Preservation of Cultural Heritage: Second International Conference, TMM_CH 2021, Athens, Greece, December 13–15, 2021, Revised Selected Papers, pp. 164–173. Springer International Publishing, Cham (2022). https://doi.org/10.1007/978-3-031-20253-7_14
8. Georgopoulos, A., et al.: Merging geometric documentation with materials characterization and analysis of the history of the Holy Aedicule in the church of the Holy Sepulchre in Jerusalem. Int. Arch. Photogramm. Remote Sens. Spatial Inf. Sci. **XLII-5/W1**, 487–494 (2017). https://doi.org/10.5194/isprs-archives-XLII-5-W1-487-2017

Digital Technologies for Heritage Conservation Labs Open to the Public. The Case of the CALLOS Project

Sophia Papida[1(✉)], Martha Athanasiadou[1], Kostas Petrakis[2], Lida Charami[2], Dimitris Angelakis[2], Chryssoula Bekiari[2], Kristalia Melessanaki[3], and Paraskevi Pouli[3]

[1] Ephorate of Antiquities of the City of Athens, Makrygianni 2-4, 11742 Athens, Greece
spapida@culture.gr

[2] Institute of Computer Science, Foundation for Research and Technology - Hellas, N. Plastira 100, 70013, Crete Heraklion, Greece

[3] Institute of Electronic Structure and Laser, Foundation for Research and Technology - Hellas, N. Plastira 100, 70013 Heraklion, Crete, Greece

Abstract. Attempts to preserve materials and constructions of the past are not new but the scientific aspect of cultural heritage (CH) conservation has emerged during the last two centuries. Today, conservation comprises all examinations, treatments and documentation work towards the life extension of antiquities and the engagement of audiences with CH. In museums, monuments and archaeological sites, conservation laboratories open for regular activities and educational programs to raise public awareness and create connections with their knowledge and interests. Digital technologies support open labs toward holistic documentation of all methods, materials and results while improving physical and digital access to CH through dissemination, reducing the gap between sciences and visitors via interdisciplinary, multimedia, fun and ultimately beneficial ways that enrich the CH narratives for all. In Greece, the first conservation lab open to peers and the public is implemented by the joint research project CALLOS for the Ephorate of Antiquities of the City of Athens (EACA). The article will discuss how a web-based platform and a portal for the management and dissemination of knowledge will support conservation science and openness of a chief lab equipped with innovative diagnostic and conservation tailored-made equipment.

Keywords: CALLOS project · conservation · cultural heritage interpretation · digital heritage · digital technologies · holistic documentation · open lab · public awareness · science communication

1 Introduction

Pausanias first described the beneficial effect of olive oil and water on the preservation of the ivory statues of the gods [1] but their perception as objects of CH emerged only during Renaissance [2]. The priority for their conservation was established after the

A. Moropoulou et al. (Eds.): TMM_CH 2023, CCIS 1889, pp. 104–113, 2023.
https://doi.org/10.1007/978-3-031-42300-0_9

wars and massive demolitions of the last three centuries and the progress of the sciences [3, 4]. Nowadays, preventive and remedial conservation are acknowledged to include all measures, examination, work and documentation that hold back the decay rate and prolong the life of CH's materiality and values for the benefit of future generations [5]. All diagnosis, treatments and control processes are implemented by qualified personnel, based on historical, quantitative and qualitative measurements, via minimum intervention [6, 7], interdisciplinary approach, advanced research and technological equipment [8, 9].

During the last decades, the multidimensional field of conservation has been argued to serve as an excellent means for learning about and being engaged with CH too [10] (See Fig. 1). This claim is based on the constructivist theory, which addresses learning as a contextual and active process that takes place as a social activity, as in museums or archaeological sites, where learners use prior knowledge and interests e.g. in history or the environment to learn how to learn, take time and follow their personal path [11].

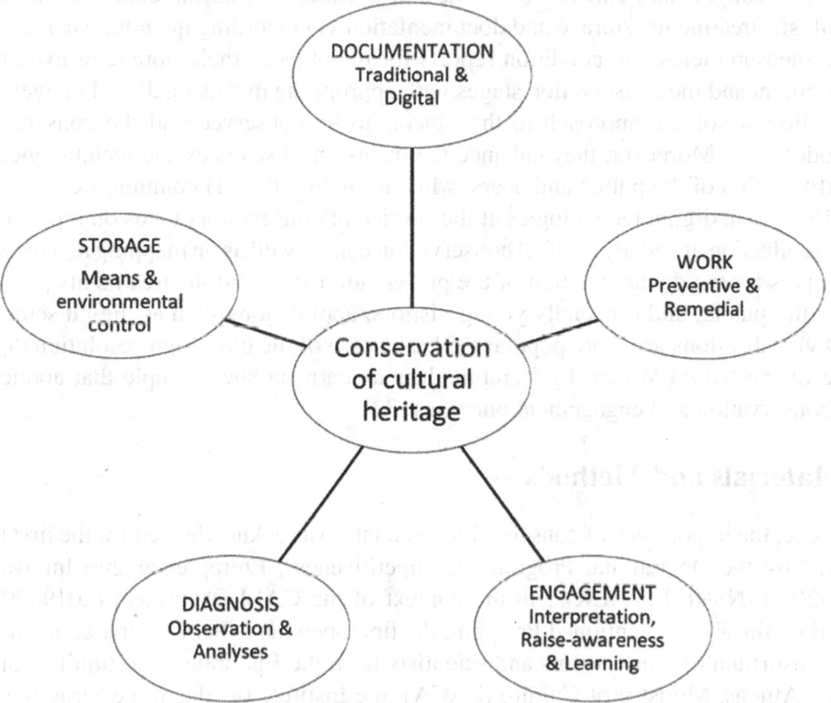

Fig. 1. The functions of conservation of CH

The multidisciplinary features of conservation are engaged with the understanding and interpretation of heritage through arts, history and all material sciences for analysis and diagnosis [12]. Conservation is connected to local topics too, such as the management and use of the collections by their communities of origin, or global issues such as climate change, illicit looting, or cutting-edge technology. Conservation combines all the components of modern pedagogy and visitors of all ages wish to learn more about it [13]. Rightly, in the last decade, conservation started to be increasingly used amongst the interpretation lines, in raising awareness campaigns and educational programs for school pupils e.o. by museums and CH organizations [14, 15] as "it offers the chance to be close to the real thing" [16] and connects beneficially people with different existential or social backgrounds with their heritage [17, 18].

Therefore, more and more museums and archaeological conservation laboratories open their doors with great appeal to the public. Some open labs invite guests during special occasions [19, 20] while in others, conservators are set on display while working through glass openings [21, 22] or in an open studio [23]. Many disseminate their work through blogs, podcasts, short films, webpages or social media too [24–27]. It cannot be ignored though that conservators first opened their labs in countries where art and CH are funded by stakeholders other than the state, thus making their work public was vital for their sustainability [28].

The progress of digital technologies increases the effect of all outcomes of open labs. They support and enhance all work that is conducted during conservation, such as analysis, treatments, storage and documentation via recording quantitative and qualitative measurements, the condition reports for the objects, their storage or exhibition environment and the conservation stages with appropriate metadata, digital images, etc. They allow a holistic approach to the objects to be conserved and the conservation methodologies. Moreover, they enhance the diffusion of sciences and technologies for the information of the public and peers, while affiliating the CH communities [29].

Most often, digital technologies at the service of conservators focus on repositories for the collection and analysis of all conservation data as well as on mapping and imaging techniques for the documentation of the preservation state and the treatments [30, 31]. As for the public, and especially young visitors, applications such as digital sculpting or 3D visualizations are more popular [32]. The case of the ultra-high-resolution digital image of the 'Night Watch' by Rembrandt is a characteristic example that applies to both conservation and engagement purposes [33].

2 Materials and Methods

In Greece, the importance of conservation open labs was acknowledged for the first time in 2017 by the Operational Program "Competitiveness, Entrepreneurship Innovation 2014–2020 (NSRF-EPAnEK)". In the context of the CALLOS project (2019–2023), funded by the above-mentioned Program, the first open lab is being prepared in Athens by a consortium of conservators and scientists from the Ephorate of Antiquities of the City of Athens, Ministry of Culture (EACA), the Institute of Electronic Structure and Laser, FORTH (IESL), the Institute of Computer Science, FORTH (ICS) and Raymetrics SA. The partners will convert a conventional conservation lab of EACA into a leading open lab with tailored-made innovative technological equipment for the diagnosis and conservation of antiquities and monuments of Athens.

The open lab will be perfectly qualified for physical demonstration and accessibility. A digital platform and a portal by ICS according to the needs of EACA, will serve effective management, communication and dissemination of data as acquired during all conservation stages and will make them digitally accessible to CH peers and the public.

2.1 The Platform

The platform designed is facilitated by the appropriate customization and extension of *Synthesis*, a Web-based system by ICS for the collaborative documentation of information and knowledge in the fields of cultural heritage and digital humanities [34]. *Synthesis* utilizes XML technology and a multi-layer architecture offering high flexibility and extensibility in terms of data structures, data types and sustainability. Each documented entity, such as an object, scientific examination, or conservation activity, is stored as an XML document, readable by humans and machines. Its database server is eXist-db5, a native XML database.

Synthesis is multilingual, supporting the parallel use of multiple languages for documentation and versioning of the documented information. The data model used is carefully designed for a given application domain (here the conservation and scientific examination procedures) particularly focused on semantic interoperability. This notion is defined as the ability of computer systems to exchange data with unambiguous and shared meaning. *Synthesis* achieves this by a) linking each element of its data model to a domain ontology, b) allowing users to add metadata about the data, and c) linking a term to a controlled (shared) vocabulary or thesaurus of terms.

Synthesis users create and document entities organized in entity types, each one of them having its data structure (schema). An XML-based schema contains a set of fields organized in a hierarchical (tree-like) structure. The leaves of the tree-like structure are the documentation fields filled by the users. Figure 2 shows a small part of the schema of the 'Conservation' entity, as configured for the CALLOS project.

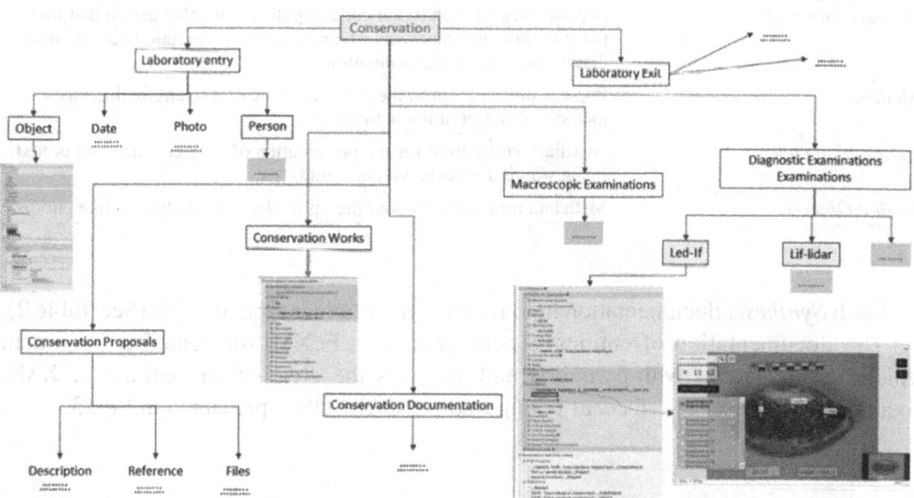

Fig. 2. A representation of CALLOS *Synthesis* tree-like structure of 'Conservation' entity. Down, an XML document of a specific conservation activity based on an XML schema

The schema of each entity type is fully compatible with CIDOC CRM[1] [35] and CIDOC CRM science model (CRMsci)[2]. Table 1 includes the CALLOS *Synthesis* entities.

Table 1. Entities of the Callos *Synthesis*

Entities	Description of documentation purpose
Objects	Administrative & scientific data used in the conservation department
Project	Projects of the conservation department
Examinations	Scientific examinations during diagnostic actions of a conservation activity e.g. LED-IF, LIBS, LIF-LIDAR
Conservation	Conservation activity
Intervention/ Restoration Works	An intervention/restoration action of a conservation activity
Preventative conservation works	Preventative conservation works action of a conservation activity
Laser cleaning	Laser cleaning action of a conservation activity
Samplings	Sampling action of a conservation activity
Samples	Samples taken during a sampling action
Devices	Devices for diagnosis & conservation actions of conservation activity
Persons	Personnel & collaborators involved in the various stages of a Project/conservation activity/actions/examination
Locations	Places where the diagnostic or conservation works took place
Bibliography	Information about bibliographic references related to all entities
Administrative documents	Official documents that are necessary for the activities/actions/works of the open Conservation laboratory
Conservation story	Popular presentation to the general public: a notable action that took place within the framework of a project or conservation activity or a diagnostic scientific examination
Methods	Popular presentation to the general public of a scientific diagnostic method or conservation action etc
Information Object	Auxiliary entity used for the presentation of subject consisting of text, images/digital objects, video, sounds, etc
Digital Objects	Metadata information about the up-loaded digital objects, like photos

Each *Synthesis* documentation field receives a particular type of value (See Table 2).

The documentation of entities is performed in a FeXML-dedicated environment which communicates with *Synthesis* and supports the creation and editing of XML documents. The user interface, as configured for CALLOS is presented in Fig. 3.

[1] CIDOC-CRM: high-level event-centric ontology for human activity, things and events happening in spacetime, providing definitions and a formal structure for describing the implicit and explicit concepts and relationships used in CH documentation (ISO 21127:2014- Information and documentation — A reference ontology for the interchange of cultural heritage information).

[2] CRMsci: Extension of CIDOC CRM to support scientific observation, Version 1.8, December 2022, https://cidoc-crm.org/crmsci/ModelVersion/version-1.8.

Table 2. Types of values for each documentation field of the CALLOS *Synthesis* platform

Documentation field	Type of value
Link to Entity	The user selects a different entity that is documented in the system, that can belong to one or more entity types
Link to vocabulary term	The user selects a term from a static or dynamic vocabulary
Link to Thesaurus Term	The user selects a term from a thesaurus of terms which is managed through the THEMAS[1] thesaurus management system
Unformatted free text	The user provides a small piece of text that cannot be formatted
Formatted free text	The user provides a longer piece of text that can be formatted
Number	The user provides a numeric value e.g., an integer number
Time expression	The user provides a date in an accepted format relevant to documentation of historical information e.g. decade of 1970, ca. 1920, 1500 BC, etc
Location coordinates	The user selects a point/polygon on a map; the field is automatically filled with corresponding coordinates. The system enables the user to query external geolocation services & get a unique ID & coordinates of the location
Digital file(s)	The user uploads digital files of a given type e.g. image or document

[1]THEMAS: Open source Web-based system for creating, managing and administering multi-faceted and multilingual thesauri according to ISO 25964-1 and ISO 25964-2 standards; it offers an API in order to connect with external applications.

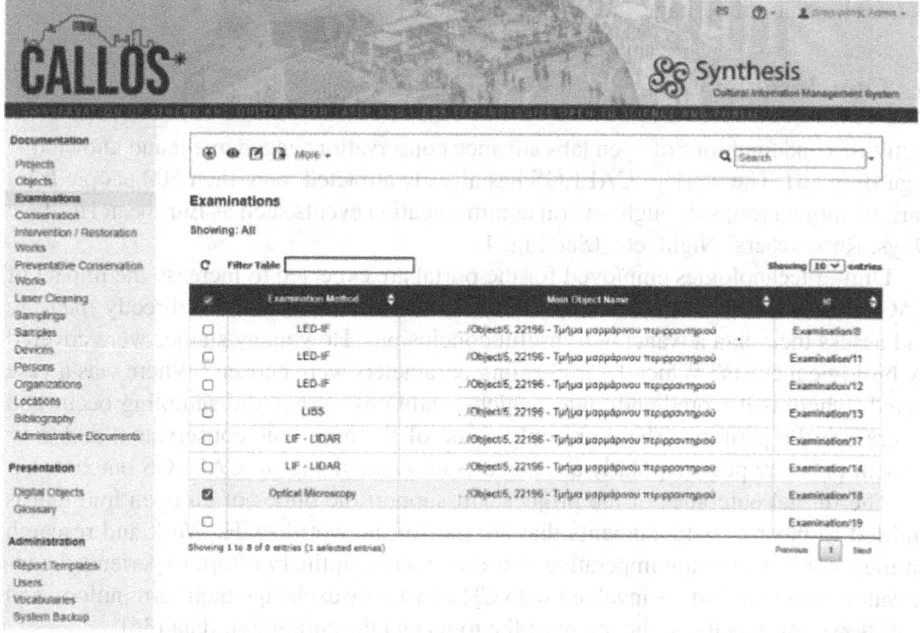

Fig. 3. The user interface of *Synthesis* for CALLOS project

2.2 The Portal

The CALLOS portal aims to disseminate knowledge of key issues and innovations and share information about conservation practices and applications of laser technologies to objects or monuments. Its design supports multiple dimensions of access and an effective presentation of an overview of the contents with a «semantic roadmap» to reach the point of interest shortly. The dimensions are phenomena of the object (elaboration, alteration, intervention), methods of diagnosis, imaging techniques, visual features, object context and history as employed in real conservation cases.

The portal will explain with example images the construction, decay and conservation of an object or monument. Concepts (terms) organized as a thesaurus of semantic poly-hierarchies allow retrieval from higher and narrower concepts. It will be populated by the conservation processes conducted in the Open Lab of EACA and will be used to improve access to information about state-of-the-art laser applications for the analysis and conservation of CH. To disseminate and exploit the knowledge produced, specialized entities have been designed to the CALLOS platform.

The CALLOS portal will be dynamic. XML-based entry sheets will allow users to define new content, verify the consistency of referred items and integrate new content consistently placed into the CALLOS Platform. Entry sheets will be populated by the conservators and will be exploited for the compilation of multimedia *Conservation Stories* or the design of a *Search the collection* interactive application to engage the users with cultural heritage and scientific issues.

3 Conclusions

Activities and functions of open labs advance conservation, engagement and knowledge regarding CH. The work of CALLOS has already attracted more than 500 people from various target groups through several communication events such as European Heritage Days, Researchers' Night, etc. (See Fig. 4).

Digital technologies employed for the portal are expected to increase the impact of EACA on the public while the platform will enable conservators to directly measure and assess their data advancing to useful conclusions. How many statues were covered by biological crusts? Which laser cleaning parameters were chosen? Where was a vase found, where is it stored and under which conditions? When did sampling occur and where are the permits? These are only some of the questions conservators and their present or future peers regularly ask and are answered thanks to CALLOS outcomes.

The digital outcomes of the project will support the duties of an open hub that is entitled to labor over monuments that are part of the world's CH. Work and research on their conservation are imperative. For this interdisciplinary effort, experienced conservators and IT scientists involved with CH constantly exchange their terminology and workflows towards the architecture of the tools and the curation of data [36].

But the use of digital technologies raises concerns too as it involves high costs, sets a framework for new work protocols and procedures and requires high expertise [37]. Conservators will replace traditional mapping with sophisticated digital mapping techniques and will upload all analyses and treatments, the content of paper registration forms and conservation reports as digital files into the platform entities. Moreover, they

Fig. 4. The CALLOS social media accounts effectively communicated dates and content of events and provided details for the participants, their interests and impressions

will be trained in data entry and management and will have to do so along with their previous routine. They will have to be precise when selecting decay and conservation terms from the thesaurus for their peers and at the same time, they will have to write *Conservation Stories* in plain language and host physically accessible public events.

The challenge is two-fold since public CH organizations have to keep up with the costs required for their hosting, updates and maintenance too. What is well understood is that open labs equipped with digital technologies are addressed to more heritage stakeholders and new work mentalities, workflows and CH policies are required.

Acknowledgments. The project CALLOS (Conservation of Athens antiquities with Laser & Lidar technologies Open to Science and public) (Τ6ΥΒΠ-0099, MIS-5056208) is implemented by EACA, FORTH (IESL, ICS) and RAYMETRICS S.A. in context of the "Open Innovation in Culture" action co-funded by ERDF and national resources through the O.P. "Competitiveness, Entrepreneurship Innovation 2014–2020 (NSRF-EPAnEK Greece)".

References

1. Pausanias: Description of Greece, § 5.11.1–5.11.11. Harvard University Press, Cambridge, MA; William Heinemann Ltd., London (1918)
2. Jokilehto, J.: A history of architectural conservation. D. Phil. Thesis, The University of York, England (1986)
3. Marijnissen, R.: Degradation, Conservation, and Restoration of Works of Art: Historical Overview, *CeROArt.* http://journals.openedition.org/ceroart/4785. Last accessed 1 Jan 2023
4. Mehr, S.Y.: Analysis of 19th and 20th century conservation key theories in relation to contemporary adaptive reuse of heritage buildings. Heritage **2**, 920–937 (2019)
5. Papadopoulou, M., Bouzaki, A.-A., Koupadi, K., et al.: Re-excavating' findings in storage: the refurbishment of the old acropolis museum in Athens. Museum Int. **73**(1–2), 42–51 (2021)

6. Perkel, J.M.: Museum laboratories: where art meets science. Biotechniques **48**(2), 95–99 (2018)
7. UNESCO Homepage, https://uis.unesco.org/node/3080254. Last accessed 1 Jan 2023
8. ICOM Homepage: https://icom.museum/wp-content/uploads/2018/07/ICOM-code-En-web.pdf. Last accessed 1 Jan 2023
9. ICOMOS Homepage: https://www.icomos.org/images/DOCUMENTS/Charters/structures_e.pdf. Last accessed 1 Jan 2023
10. Papida, S.: Conservation, communication and educational programs: Conservation work as a tool for the familiarization of the public and school groups with cultural heritage conservation issues. In: Conference of PACA (2012). (in greek)
11. Hein G. E. The constructivist museum. Hooper-Greenhill, E. The Educational Role of the Museum. Routledge, London, UK (1999)
12. SMK Homepage. https://www.smk.dk/en/article/projects-in-conservation-and-science/. Last accessed 1 Jan 2023
13. Papida, S.: Communicating Conservation: The informal communication of Conservation… communication system. MA Thesis, University of Leicester (2009). https://www.researchgate.net/publication/321874962_Communicating_Conservation_The_informal_communication_of_Conservation_to_the_visitors_of_the_three_most_appointed_Athenian_cultural_heritage_museums_Suggestions_towards_its_intentional_use_amongst_the. Last accessed 15 Aug 2023
14. The Metropolitan Museum of Art Homepage: https://www.metmuseum.org/~/media/Files/Learn/Family%20Map%20and%20Guides/MuseumKids/What%20is%20Art%20Conservation.pdf. Last accessed 15 Aug 2023
15. National Gallery of Art Homepage: https://www.nga.gov/calendar/lectures/celebrating-conservation.html. Last accessed 1 Jan 2023
16. Fabrikant, G.: Preserving the Past for Museum Visitors of the Future. The New York Times (2019)
17. Johnson, J.S., Cobb, C.K., Lione, B.M.: The role of conservation education in reconciliation: the example of the Iraqi Institute for the Conservation of Antiquities and Heritage Chapter. In: Peters, R.F., et al. (eds.) Heritage Conservation and Social Engagement, pp. 46–65. UCL Press, London (2020)
18. Wafula, G.K.: Cultural heritage conservation and public benefits: effectiveness of Kenya's legal and administrative framework. In: Peters, R.F., et al. (eds.) Heritage Conservation and Social Engagement, pp. 125–140. UCL Press, London (2020)
19. European Heritage Days Homepage: https://www.europeanheritagedays.com/search?keywords=conservation&type=All&ccode=All&month_datepicker_from=&month_datepicker_to=. Last accessed 15 Aug 2023
20. Heritage Malta Homepage: https://heritagemalta.mt/news/conservation-labs-open-day-the-importance-of-restoration-and-conservation-explored/. Last accessed 1 Jan 2023
21. Penn Museum Homepage: https://www.penn.museum/blog/tag/in-the-artifact-lab/. Last accessed 15 Aug 2023
22. Smithsonian American Art Museum Homepage: https://americanart.si.edu/art/conservation. Last accessed 1 Jan 2023
23. Leica Microsystems Homepage: https://www.leica-microsystems.com/applications/industrial-applications/art-conservation/. Last accessed 15 Aug 2023
24. Benaki Museum Homepage: https://benakiconservation.com/. Last accessed 1 Jan 2023
25. Podcast History Homepage: https://podcast.history.org/2010/04/05/conservation-where-art-and-science-meet/. Last accessed 1 Jan 2023
26. MFA Boston Homepage: https://www.youtube.com/playlist?list=PLlaGkbYsw6cckda-IC01XUj-s4wD7Tvw6. Last accessed 1 Jan 2023

27. Vimeo Homepage: https://vimeo.com/user22387042?embedded=true&source=owner_name&owner=22387042. Last accessed 1 Jan 2023
28. Crutcher, M.: Engaging visitors with conservation: the key to museum sustainability. In: The 6th Annual Graduate Student Research Symposium (2019)
29. Giglitto, D., Ciolfi, L., Bosswick, W.: Building a bridge: opportunities and challenges for intangible cultural heritage at the intersection of institutions, civic society, and migrant communities. Int. J. Herit. Stud. **28**(1), 74–91 (2021)
30. Naoumidou, N., Chatzidaki, M., Alexopoulou, A.: "ARIADNE" Conservation documentation system: Conceptual design and projection on the CIDOC CRM. Framework and limits. In: Annual Conference of CIDOC, Athens (2008)
31. Platia, N., Chatzidakis, M., Doerr, C., et al.: "POLYGNOSIS": the development of a thesaurus in an Educational Web Platform on optical and laser-based investigation methods for cultural heritage analysis and diagnosis. Heritage Sci. **5**(50), 1–17 (2017). https://doi.org/10.1186/s40494-017-0163-0
32. Chen, W.W.: Digital heritage and innovative collaborations workshop. In: SIGGRAPH Asia Workshops. Association for Computing Machinery, NY, Article 2, pp. 1–2 (2017)
33. Rijksmuseum Homepage: https://www.rijksmuseum.nl/en/stories/operation-night-watch/story/ultra-high-resolution-image-of-the-night-watch. Last accessed 1 Jan 2023
34. Bekiari, C., Doerr, M., Agelakis D., et al.: Building comprehensive management systems for cultural – historical information. In: Giligny, F. (ed.) Proceedings of 42nd Annual Conference on Computer Applications and Quantitative Methods in Archaeology. CAA, Paris (2014)
35. Bekiari C., Bruseker, G., Doerr, M., et al.: Definition of the CIDOC Conceptual Reference Model, v.7.1.1 (2021). https://cidoc-crm.org/sites/default/files/cidoc_crm_v.7.1.1_0.pdf. Last accessed 1 Jan 2023
36. Harrison, L.K.: A roadmap to applied digital heritage: introduction to the special issue on digital heritage technologies, applications and impacts. Stud. Dig. Heritage **3**(1), 40–45 (2019)
37. Huggett, J.: Challenging digital archaeology. Open Archaeol. **1**(1), 79–85 (2015)

Evaluating the Effectiveness of Unsupervised and Supervised Techniques for Identifying Deteriorations on Cultural Heritage Monuments Using Hyper-spectral Imagery

Nikolaos Chrysogonos, Kyriakos Lampropoulos, Ioannis N. Tzortzis, Charalampos Zafeiropoulos, Anastasios Doulamis(✉), and Nikolaos Doulamis

Department of Rural Surveying Engineering and Geoinformatics Engineering, National Technical University of Athens, 157 80 Athens, Greece
adoulam@cs.ntua.gr
https://www.survey.ntua.gr/en/

Abstract. In this paper, we investigate the potential usefulness of unsupervised and supervised Artificial Intelligence techniques on identifying and classifying material defects on Cultural Heritage monuments. Since hyper-spectral imagery is commonly used in such applications, we exploit spectral information aiming to enhance the training procedure and, accordingly, extend the learning ability of the utilized Machine Learning models. For the supervised monitoring approach we utilize CNN(Convolutional Neural Networks)-based models like the state-of-the-art VGG-16, while for the unsupervised approach we propose clustering solutions like K-means and DBSCAN. Additionally, in an effort to assess the importance of spatial information provided by the hyper-spectral images, we evaluate the aforementioned techniques by designing proper experimentation for the simple RGB images and the corresponding enhanced hyper-spectral images. According to the experimental results, the proposed supervised solutions can achieve as high F1-score as 88–90% on RGB images and almost 95% when utilizing the whole spectral information. On the contrary, unsupervised techniques can hardly achieve a F1-score of 60% in both cases. The outcomes of our work can be summarized in the following points; a) the proposed supervised Deep Learning techniques could be considered as proper solutions for monitoring defects on Cultural Heritage monuments, especially when exploiting hyper-spectral images - b) even though clustering techniques do not perform well, they can be used as auxiliary tools for highlighting some wider regions of interest for further processing by the proposed supervised techniques.

This work has been supported by the European Union's Horizon 2020 research and innovation programme from the YADES project (Grant Agreement No. 872931).

A. Moropoulou et al. (Eds.): TMM_CH 2023, CCIS 1889, pp. 114–124, 2023.
https://doi.org/10.1007/978-3-031-42300-0_10

Keywords: Cultural heritage · Deterioration · Defects · Machine learning · Computer vision · Hyper-spectral imagery · Supervised learning · Unsupervised learning · Clustering

1 Introduction

Since Cultural Heritage monuments suffer from man made hazards, bad weather conditions, air pollution and other extraneous factors, the regular inspections appears to be not only essential but, at the same time, indispensable [1]. The Structural Health Monitoring (SHM) [2] is the monitoring and the analysis of a structural system over time through the collection of dynamic diagnostic tools. The most techniques, that belong in the SHM, refer to measurement of forces, which require the installation of conduct sensors like accelerometers, voltage meters, optical fiber sensors, etc.

Due to the development of the state-of-the-art sensors, like digital cameras and cameras with high frames-per-second rate, unmanned vehicles, mobile sensors etc., there is an increasing interest regarding remote sensing techniques [3] for the detection and identification of structural integrity. Such techniques are applied in a more convenient way since they require less installation effort, lower cost and can acquire information for buildings through spatial and temporal high quality data. In contrast to the conventional sensors, the remote sensing tools collect images and video streams that require novel ideas in the fields of robotics, image processing, Computer Vision and Deep Learning. Thus, the remote sensing techniques regarding the structural integrity [4] is considered to be in an elementary stage. So, this new area in research and development appears to offer opportunity for experimentation.

2 Related Work

Even though, the application of Machine Learning techniques on remote sensing fields regarding the structural integrity is a new research area, as mentioned above, there are some worthy studies.

The authors in [5], exploit reflectance imaging spectral data in the visible or near IR range in an aim to study the layer structure in X-ray Fluorescence elemental maps of paintings.

In study [6], the authors propose an integrated framework that include advanced signal processing and machine learning techniques for the assistance of the artwork authentication procedure.

An advanced deep learning technique is adopted in study [1] for the detection and identification of different types of deterioration on ancient walls.

Additionally, the authors in [7] focus on the exploitation and integration of 3D and hyper-spectral data in order to assess Cultural Heritage monuments monitoring for preventing degradation.

The major problems in the aforementioned proposals are the a) the huge amount of data needed for the training of the Deep Learning models and b)

the complicated architectures. In this paper, we investigate the potential high efficiency of simple architectures and pre-trained models on the remote sensing application for the detection and identification of deterioration.

3 Methodology

3.1 The Dataset

The Machine Learning algorithms were applied on hyper-spectral images depicting parts of the Saint Nikolas ancient fortress, a historical monument of Rhodes in Greece. Due to its seaside location, the building is exposed to wind and salty water which are the major cause of serious deterioration types on the walls of the fortress.

The hyper-spectral images include 41 spectral bands, each one of them represents a part of the electromagnetic radiation spectrum. A double-cameras system was utilized to collect the aforementioned images; the first camera was used for the RGB image, while the second one was used for the Near-Infrared (NIR). By utilizing the pansharpening procedure, the outputs of the two cameras were combined for the construction of the final hyper-spectral image.

The dataset include 11 hyper-spectral images in total. Though, only for 6 of them the corresponding ground truth information was provided. In Fig. 1, two sample images are presented along with the corresponding annotations. Thus, the annotated images were used for the training procedure of the supervised ML model and the rest of them was used for the validation process. For the unsupervised approach there is no need for such annotations.

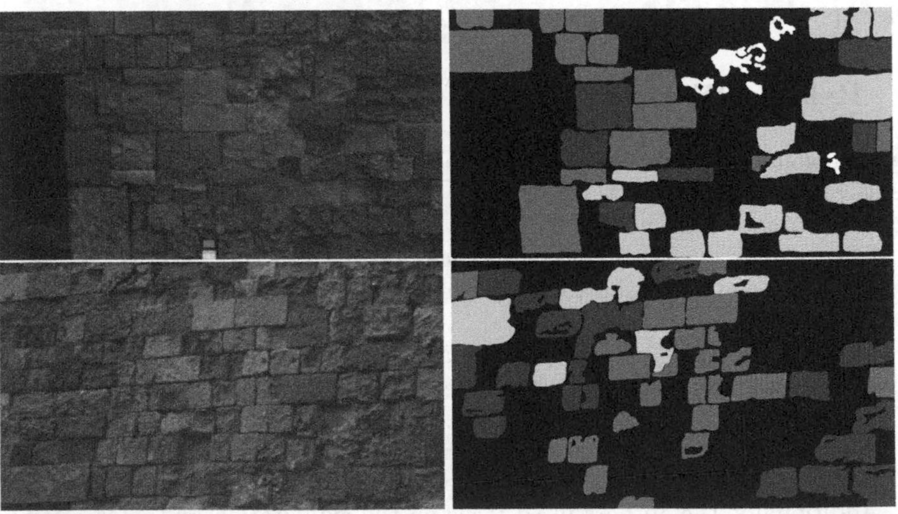

Fig. 1. The images in the left are two sample images from the dataset, while the right ones depict the corresponding ground truth.

3.2 The Supervised Approach

For the supervised approach regarding the detection and the identification of the input images, the state-of-the-art (SoA) ML model VGG-16 [8] was employed. It consists of 16 layers, 13 of them are convolutional with 3×3 filter size and the rest 3 of them are fully connected. The convolutional layers are divided into 5 groups, each one of them leads to a softmax layer. The model receives as input an image of size 224×224 pixels and provides as output a volume containing 512 map characteristics of size 7×7 pixels. This volume is converted to a single characteristics vector through the process of flattening. At the last step, this vector is forwarded to the fully connected layers, which generate the final vector which can be used by a softmax layer for the classification purposes. The detailed architecture of the VGG-16 model is shown in Fig. 2.

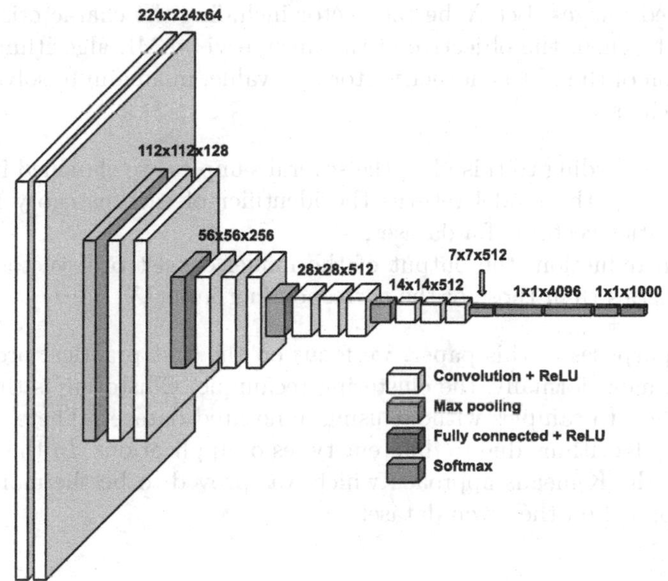

Fig. 2. The architecture of the state-of-the-art VGG-16 Machine Learning model.

3.3 Transfer Learning

The transfer learning [9] capacity is a benefit of Neural Network in contrast to the corresponding shallow ML models. According to this technique, the ML model is pre-trained on a specific set of data and then it gets adapted in order to generate proper predictions for another dataset. Normally, this new dataset represents a different application and occur from a divergent statistical distribution.

The main reason for the use of the transfer learning idea is the dependency of Deep Learning on huge amount of data with as similar distribution and characteristics form as possible. Such a construction of huge datasets is a complicated and time-consuming procedure. Thus, the exploitation of transfer learning technique could offer significant benefits.

Since the Deep Learning model is trained on a different dataset, it is necessary to apply some fine tuning and, often, make more significant changes regarding the architecture, aiming to make it more suitable for the new data. This intervention depends on the size of the new dataset and also on the degree of similarity between the two datasets. While working on similar datasets, the replacement of the final layer is sufficient and the new model behaves as a classifier. In other cases, it could be necessary to remove more layers and replace them with new ones.

3.4 The Unsupervised Approach

According to the unsupervised ML techniques [10], the dataset contains a set of non-annotated images. Let X be the vector including the characteristics of the given dataset. Then, the objective of the unsupervised ML algorithm would be the conversion of the X to another vector or a value, in an aim to solve practical problems such as:

- grouping; according to this idea, the several samples are classified in different categories and the model returns the identifier of each category for all the characteristics vectors of a dataset,
- dimension reduction; the output of the model consist of a vector with less characteristics than those of the corresponding input X.

For the purposes of this paper, we focus on the first practical problem, the grouping or, more formally, the clustering technique. Clustering is the problem of giving values to samples without using annotated dataset. There is plethora of clustering algorithms due to different types of applications. In this study, we present only the K-means approach which was proved to be the more effective technique applied on the given dataset.

4 Experimental Results

4.1 Evaluation Metrics

Aiming to evaluate the outcomes of the several pipelines we proposed, we employ some commonly used metrics that provide a more detailed view. Comparing the generated predictions with the provided ground truth images, we count the true positives (TP), true negatives (TN), false positives (FP) and false negatives (FN) [11]. Using these numbers, the evaluation metrics accuracy, precision, recall and f1 score [12] are calculated according to the mathematical Eqs. 1, 2, 3 and 4.

$$precision = \frac{TP}{TP + FP} \tag{1}$$

$$recall = \frac{TP}{TP + FN} \tag{2}$$

$$accuracy = \frac{TP + TN}{TP + TN + FP + FN} \tag{3}$$

$$F_1 = 2 * \frac{precision * recall}{precision + recall} \tag{4}$$

4.2 Results

In Figs. 3 and 4, we present the confusion matrix information of the VGG-16 model applied on the RGB and NIR images accordingly. As it is clear, the performance of the model on the NIR images seems to be higher since the FP and FN values are obviously less. Additionally, in Figs. 5 and 6 we present the evaluation metrics for the VGG-16 model applied on the RGB and NIR images accordingly. The scores appear to achieve higher values in the case of the NIR images utilization, offering more accurate and precise predictions. On the contrary, by observing the Figs. 7 and 8, it seems that the clustering approach does not perform so well even on the NIR images that include much more information than the RGB ones. In order to have a more tangible outcome, we compare the three different approaches using the accuracy and the f1 score as shown in Figs. 9 and 10.

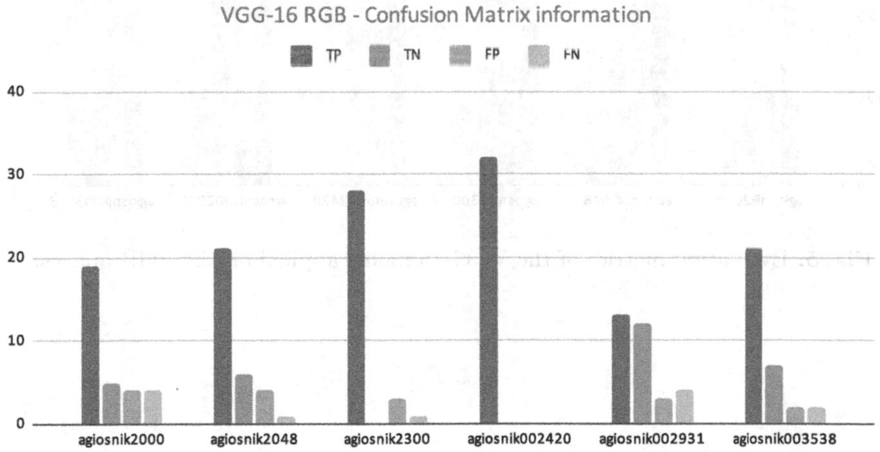

Fig. 3. Confusion matrix information of the VGG-16 model applied on the RGB images.

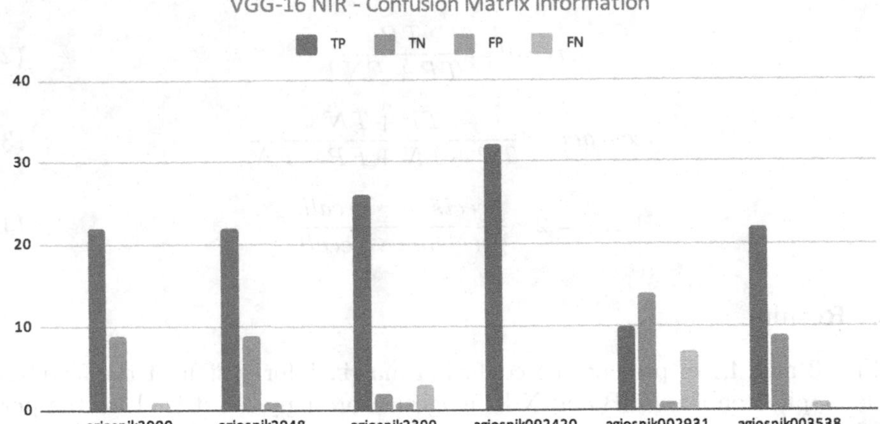

Fig. 4. Confusion matrix information of the VGG-16 model applied on the NIR images.

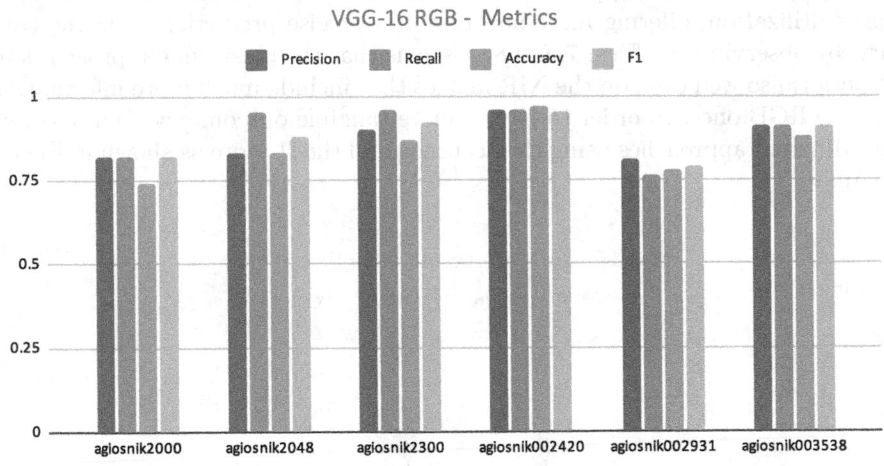

Fig. 5. Evaluation metrics of the VGG-16 model applied on the RGB images.

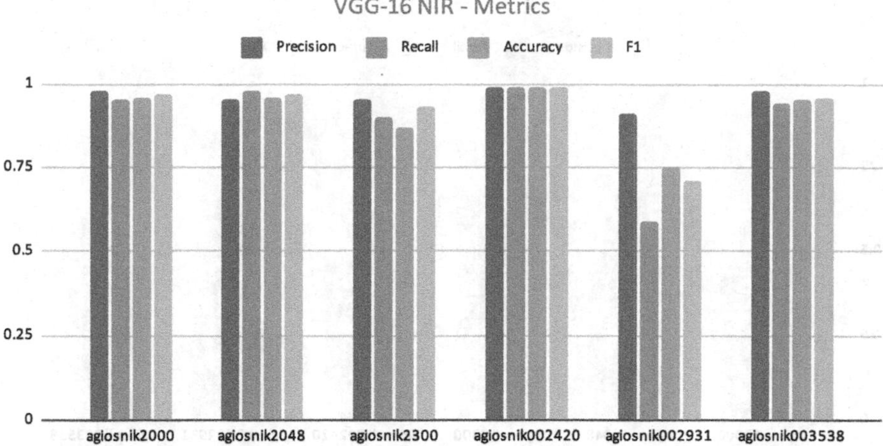

Fig. 6. Evaluation metrics of the VGG-16 model applied on the NIR images.

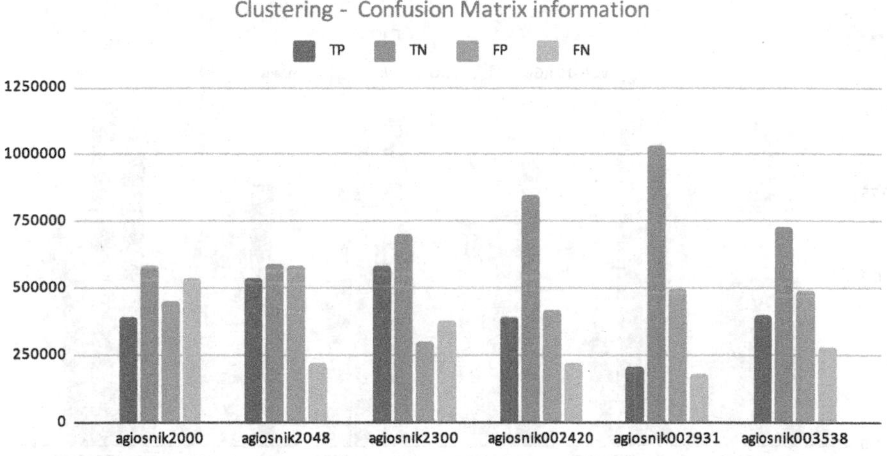

Fig. 7. Confusion matrix information of the K-means clustering algorithm applied on the NIR images.

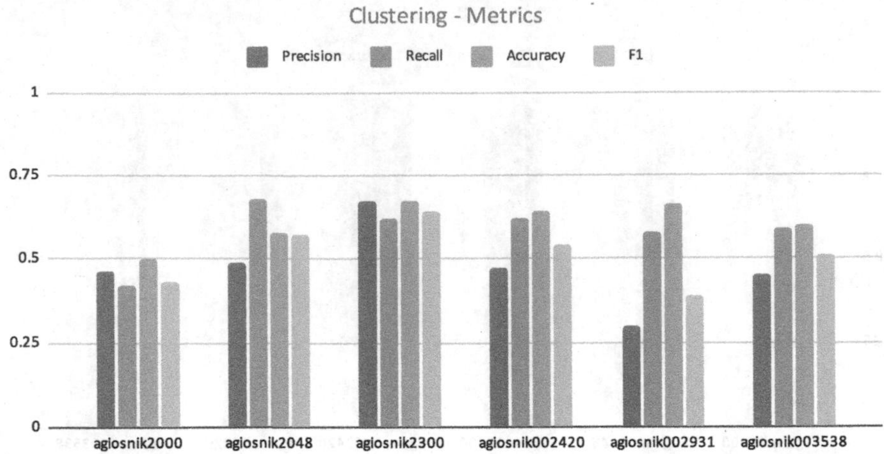

Fig. 8. Evaluation metrics of the K-means clustering algorithm applied on the NIR images.

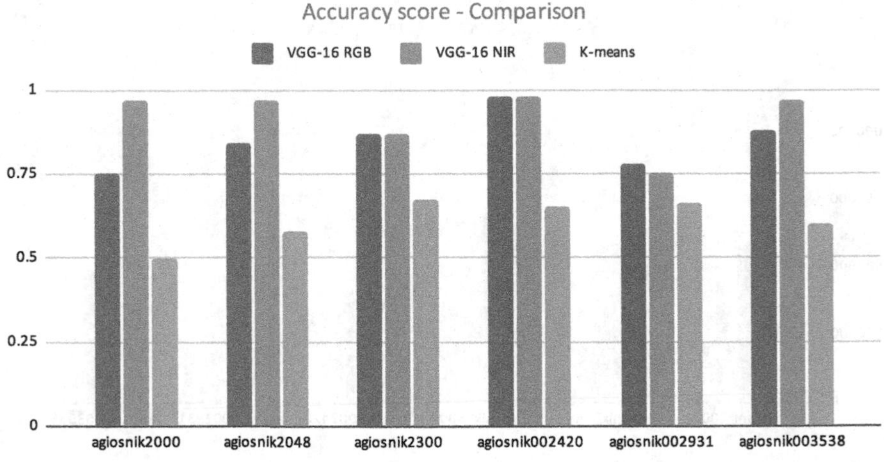

Fig. 9. Comparison among the three different approaches using the accuracy score.

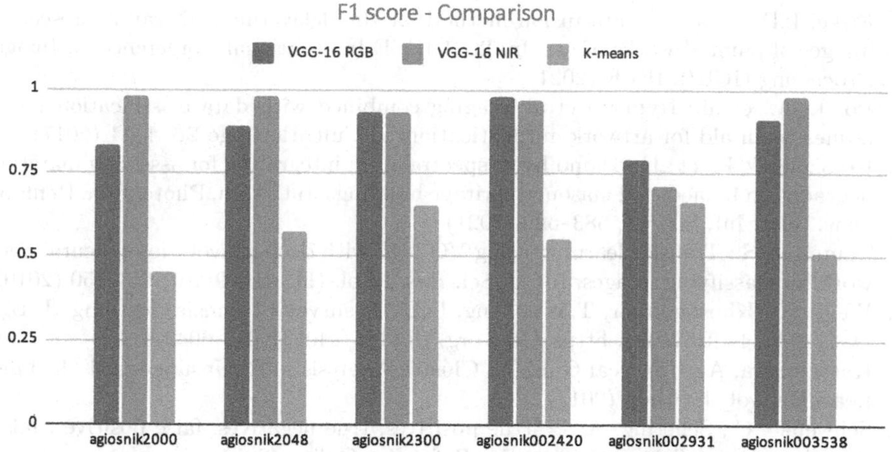

Fig. 10. Comparison among the three different approaches using the f1 score.

5 Conclusion

In this work, we study the behaviour of several different Machine Learning techniques while using them to detect and identify deteriorations on the walls of the ancient fortress of Saint Nikolas located in Rhodes, Greece. We followed two major ways; a) the supervised approach and b) the unsupervised one. Within the first approach, we employ the transfer learning capacity of the CNN based VGG-16 model which was applied on both the RGB and the NIR images. Within the alternative approach, we exploited the clustering approach on the NIR images with no additional annotation. According to the results, the supervised method performs much better than the supervised one, especially when the VGG-16 model is applied on the NIR images that include more detailed information. Thus, the proposed supervised approach could be considered as a proper framework for detecting and identifying deteriorations on walls. Additionally, even though the unsupervised technique does not perform sufficiently, it could be used as a primitive tool for achieving an initial detection of regions-of-interest.

References

1. Tzortzis, I.N., et al.: Automatic inspection of cultural monuments using deep and tensor-based learning on hyperspectral imagery. In: 2022 IEEE International Conference on Image Processing (ICIP). IEEE (2022)
2. Sohn, H., et al.: A review of structural health monitoring literature: 1996–2001, vol. 1, p. 16. Los Alamos National Laboratory, USA (2003)
3. Elachi, C., Van Zyl, J.J.: Introduction to the Physics and Techniques of Remote Sensing. Wiley, Hoboken (2021)
4. Alshehhi, R., et al.: Simultaneous extraction of roads and buildings in remote sensing imagery with convolutional neural networks. ISPRS J. Photogram. Remote Sens. **130**, 139–149 (2017)

5. Fiske, L.D., et al.: A data fusion method for the delayering of X-ray fluorescence images of painted works of art. In: 2021 IEEE International Conference on Image Processing (ICIP). IEEE (2021)
6. Polak, A., et al.: Hyperspectral imaging combined with data classification techniques as an aid for artwork authentication. J. Cult. Heritage **26**, 1–11 (2017)
7. Kolokoussis, P., et al.: 3D and hyperspectral data integration for assessing material degradation in medieval masonry heritage buildings. Int. Arch. Photogram. Remote Sens. Spat. Inf. Sci. **43**, 583–590 (2021)
8. Tammina, S.: Transfer learning using VGG-16 with deep convolutional neural network for classifying images. Int. J. Sci. Res. Publ. (IJSRP) **9**(10), 143–150 (2019)
9. Weiss, K., Khoshgoftaar, T.M., Wang, D.D.: A survey of transfer learning. J. Big Data **3**(1), 1–40 (2016). https://doi.org/10.1186/s40537-016-0043-6
10. Kassambara, A.: Practical Guide to Cluster Analysis in R: Unsupervised Machine Learning, vol. 1. Sthda (2017)
11. Schwenke, C., Schering, A.G.: True positives, true negatives, false positives, false negatives. Wiley StatsRef: Statistics Reference Online (2014)
12. Powers, D.M.W.: Evaluation: from precision, recall and F-measure to ROC, informedness, markedness and correlation. arXiv preprint arXiv:2010.16061 (2020)

Terrestrial Laser Scanning Coupled with UAVs Technologies: The Case of Old Navarino Castle in Pylos, Greece

A. Kompoti[1(✉)], A. Kazolias[1], M. Kylafi[2], V. Panagiotidis[1], and N. Zacharias[1]

[1] Laboratory of Archaeometry, Department of History, Archaeology and Cultural Resources Management, University of the Peloponnese, Old Camp, 24 133 Kalamata, Greece
akompoti@hotmail.com

[2] Ephorate of Antiquities of Messenia, Hellenic Ministry of Culture and Sports, 24133 Kalamata, Greece

Abstract. The archaeological site of Palaiokastro (Old Navarino castle), is located in Messenia on Koryfasio peninsula, at the southern end of the beach of Voidokoilia in the-Navarino Bay, SW Peloponnese. Palaiokastro was built during Frankish rule of the Peloponnese, in the 13th century, over the classical Acropolis of Pylos. The Castle as seen today is a result of additions made by other conquerors, such as the Venetians from 1423 to 1500 and the Ottomans from 1500 to 1686 [14].

The aim of this study is to present the methodology, challenges and outcomes of digital documentation in the remaining of the Palaiokastro castle using a combination of innovative technologies including terrestrial laser scanner (TLS) and aerial photogrammetry using unmanned aerial vehicles (UAVs). TLS and UAV photogrammetry were applied in an integrated design to rapidly facilitate the acquisition of the Main South gate, eliminating all possible obstacles. The TLS was exploited for the acquisition of the facades while the UAV was used to capture the top view of the castle gate. The recent improvement of the post-processing algorithms provides us with the ability to implement fusion methods of TLS and UAV models and also deliver an accurate 3D model of the whole gate.

The combination of photogrammetry from the UAV with the data of the terrestrial laser scanner was used in order to give us a multitude of products such as textured 3D model, orthophotos, 2D floor plans, elevations and sections which are necessary for the complete and accurate geometric documentation of the current situation of the Southwest gate of Palaiokastro in order to identify different construction phases.

Keywords: Terrestrial Lase Scanner · Point cloud · Pylos · Construction phases

1 Introduction

1.1 Historical Information

In the south west region of the Peloponnese Greece, the coastal area along the Ionian Sea surrounding the Bay of Navarino has been traditionally identified as the land that is described in Homer's Iliad and Odyssey as the land of the mythical king Nestor [4].

A. Moropoulou et al. (Eds.): TMM_CH 2023, CCIS 1889, pp. 125–136, 2023.
https://doi.org/10.1007/978-3-031-42300-0_11

Situated over the ridge of the Koryfasio hill at the northern end of Voidokoilia beach in the Navarino Bay is the fortification of the Medieval Castle known as Old Navarino. The Castle was constructed by the Franks during the 13th century (ADE1282/1289) over the remains of the classical fortification of Pylos. H. Schlieman in 1874 was the first for searching for Nestor's Pylos with no results (E. Schliemann, 1874). The 1970s the University of Minnesota under the program of the University of Minnesota Messenia Expedition (UMME)) and in early 1990s the University of Cincinnati under the program Pylos Regional Archaeological Project (P.R.A.P.) (Fig. 1).

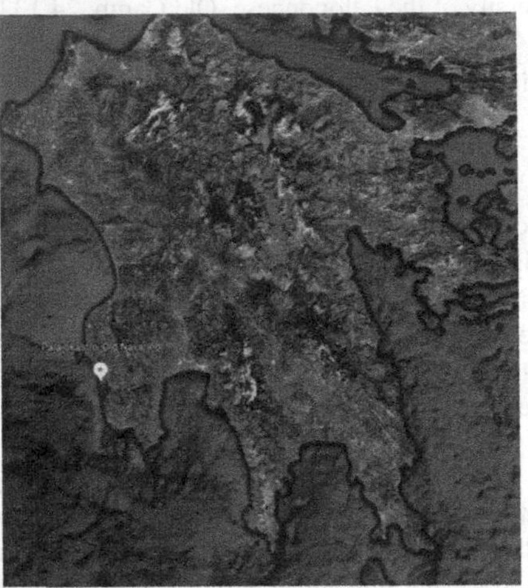

Fig. 1. Palaiokastro, Old Navarino (Google Earth)

The Navarino area according to archaeological findings was inhabited from the Neolithic to the Late Byzantine period (4500 BC-1453AD). Neolithic evidences (4500 – 3100BC) were found in the Cave of Nestor located on the north-east side of Koryfasio peninsula [17, 18] as well as on the northern arm of Voidokoilia Bay where the Tholos Tomb of Thrasymedes, (son of the mythical King Nestor) was built upon the Early and Middle Helladic settlement [15]. The Voidokoilia bay most probably was the palace harbor for the Mycenaean ships. The human activity decreased significantly but never disappeared in the periods followed the collapse of the Mycenean Palace of Ano Englianos under whose rule the whole area operated.[16].

During the late geometric period a new began with the Spartan rule over Messenia which continued until the establishment of the city of Messene (mid7th century BC – 369BC). During Spartan occupation Pylos occupied the Koryfasio peninsula, now dominated by the Frankish castle [16, 19].

Pylos gained its independence in 365BC and included in the territory of free Messenia (369BC). The city flourished during the Hellenistic and Roman period according to the numerous findings from the extended cemetery excavated along the sandbar that separates the Navarino bay from the Yalova lagoon and minted even its own coinage (ΠΥΛΙΩΝ AD 193-211) [12, 13].

The lack of significant findings in the area that can relate to the Byzantine period point to possible population movement towards the inland perhaps to avoid pirate attacks which was common during the period.

In the early 13th century, the Franks conquered and maintained rule over the Peloponnese peninsula (AD 1205 – 1453). Throughout Moreas, as the region was named by the western conquerors, citadel fortresses were built at strategic places in order to control the territory and the Castle of Navarino was one of them. The Palaiokastro was constructed over the remains of the classical Acropolis of Pylos. The medieval castle named 'Port de Junch' was built in 1282/1289 by the Flemish crusader Nicholas II of Saintomer and became one of the most important fortresses during the Frankish rule in the Morea. The castle was attacked on many occasions and changed a number of rulers – due to the strategic importance of its position. It underwent numerous significant structural interventions, modifications of uses and architectural changes, by the different conquerors, which altered its original physiognomy [1, 11, 21].

In the period of the first Venetian rule (1423–1500), during which the construction of the southern enclosure of the castle is attributed, walls were built only on the west and south sides. The east side facing the cliff is naturally fortified. The fortress consists of two enclosures, a smaller polygonal to the north and a larger quadrilateral to the south. The walls of the castle in their largest part are vertical and have been preserved up to the ramparts while they are interrupted by semicircular and rectangular towers (Fig. 2). The central gate on the south side of the castle as well as most of the semi-circular towers that reinforced the earlier walls have structural and morphological features such as the use of plinths and Islamic arches that can be attributed to the first Ottoman period (1500–1686) [1, 11, 22].

Fig. 2. The NW view of the fortification of Old Navarino (https://www.efames.gr/first_gr.html).

During this first Ottoman period a second fortress was built on the southern arm of the Navarino bay, Niokastro (new castle). Following Morozini's successful campaign against the Peloponnese the Palaiokastro fortress was surrendered to the Venetians and the Niokastro became of the four capitals of the Venetian Peloponnese during the second Venetian period (1686–1715). In 1715 the Ottomans reacquired the region and maintained their rule until the naval battle of Navarino,1827 that determined the outcome of the Greek Revolution (Fig. 3) [1].

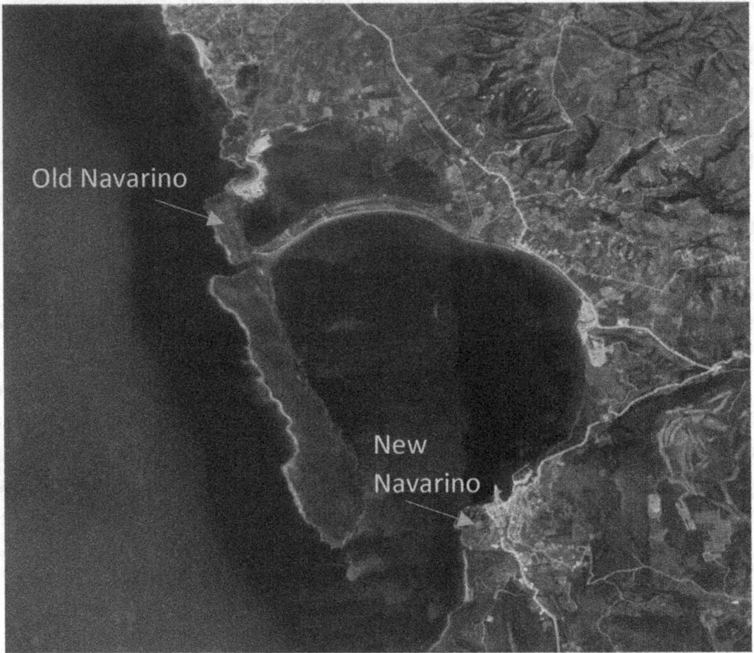

Fig. 3. Picture of New Navarino and Old Navarino proximity (Google Earth)

The several conquests of the fortress, are reflected in the interventions and additions to the initial erection. The Castle's layout of trapezoid shape includes two fortified enclosures, separated by a transverse wall which communicate with each other via a stone-paved path. It is considered that the inner enclosure, which covered the highest point of the northern part of the fortress, is located on the borders of the ancient acropolis and the Frankish castle of the 13th century, while the outer enclosure is the work of the Venetians of the 15th century and the Ottomans after the conquest of 1500 [11].

The Central South Gate of the Castle

The central South gate of the castle with its pointed arched roof is located on the ground floor of a rectangular tower that consists of a ground floor and the roof. The interior of the gate consists of a semi-cylindrical brick dome, which has been covered with brick, while traces of a retractable door are preserved from an earlier building phase. It was protected by a barricade, located on the south side of the enclosure. Access to this main entrance was served by a path, starting from the southernmost point of the Koryfasio peninsula. The fortress was built with mudstones and limestones, while partly use of bricks is seen after the 16th century. Internally preserved ruins of the buildings of the settlement have been identified in the Governor's quarters, houses, churches, wells, as well as large cisterns.

Three main building phases can be distinguished in the architectural structure of the fortification. The initial Frankish construction phase seems to use the engraving and the remains of the ancient fortification in several places. During the period of the Venetian occupation, the walls were repaired to adapt to the requirements of the new fortifications and a type of early cannon portholes were used with a circular opening on the outer side of the wall and a channel-like plan with a widening towards the inner side. At the same time, the enclosures are strengthened by the creation of a new zone of ramparts, which are rectangular with a dovetail ending. The Ottoman period which followed included extensive strengthening projects to the fortification such as raising the walls, construction of the central gate of the southern enclosure and the construction of two small semi-circular towers for cannons [16].

2 Methodology

The aim of this study is the documentation of the current situation of the medieval castle of Palaiokastro and initially the structural documentation of the South Gate applying innovative technology including terrestrial laser scanning (TLS) and aerial photogrammetry using unmanned aerial vehicles (UAVs). TLS and UAV photogrammetry has been used in an integrated design to rapidly facilitate the acquisition of the whole gate, eliminating all possible occlusions.

Initially a UAV was used to obtain the high-precision photos of the entire area of the Castle and its surrounding. The aerial pictures are processed using specialized photogrammetry software in order to produce a high resolution georeferenced basemap which in turn is used for planning the TLS scans (Fig. 4) [2, 20].

Following the aerial survey field inspection, the optimal route of the occupation points (OP) for the laser scanner were determined. Scan points were planned along a traverse path by setting the point from which to perform the scan ("Occupation point" or "OCC point") and from which to measure the previous scan point ("Backsight point" or "BS point"). In this way, each scan is automatically registered with the previous and the next one, in an operator-defined reference system, even without large overlapping areas. This is an important requirement for a site with many barriers and complex structures and in cases where standard approaches (scans with high percentages of overlap) are difficult to use. Optimal scan positions are selected by criterion of minimizing the number of scans while at the same time achieving maximum coverage and accuracy. Each OCC point was measured during the routing procedure in order to overcome logistical difficulties using the GR5 GNSS GPS by Topcon. The GR5 receiver uses Real Time Kinematic (RTK) method ensuring optimal accuracy of the geodetic measurements. The GPS receiver with absolute positioning moves along a path to the specific scan positions and directly calculates the coordinates (X, Y, Z) of each point. The GLS-2200 allows users to import scanner station coordinates before starting the process of scanning. Thus, each scan has known coordinates in the predefined reference system.

A total of 8 scan stations were placed on the perimeter of the castle surrounding the gate and inside the gate (Fig. 5). All scans acquired with the Topcon GLS2200 were

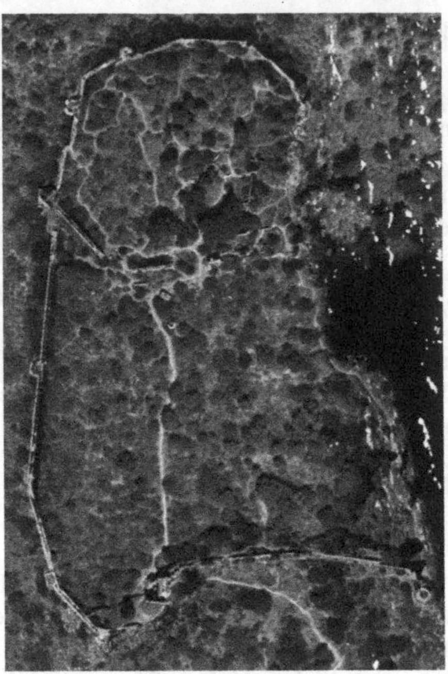

Fig. 4. Study areas orthophoto

carried out with a full dome field of views (360° in horizontal direction and 270 in vertical direction) and an average sampling step of 6 mm at 10m. Each scan lasted 10 min and the highest scan density was selected. Before starting each scan, high-resolution color panoramic (360°) photos were captured by TLS producing a colored point cloud with real RGB values [5].

The scans were transferred from the TLS to a computer and processed using Magnet Collage software to register and integrate the data of the generated point cloud files, so as to compose the integrated 3D model of the Old Navarino Gate. Magnet Collage is a software compatible with the GLS2200 scanner which enables users to process and manage the raw data of the scanner with automated procedures, such as the registration of already georeferenced point clouds, the possibility of removing unnecessary information (noise) and the data export in different formats, etc. As shown in Fig. 6, the overall workflow consists of the acquisition of the point cloud data on the Palaiokastro Gate using terrestrial laser scanning and the 3D modeling process.

The TLS survey of the Old Navarino Gate was carried out to document current situation of the whole Gate and the surrounding area. The TLS survey was carefully planned, taking into account several factors that characterize the morphology of the archaeological area [10].

The reference system used throughout the survey is the Greek Geodetic Reference System EGSA'87 carried out entering the three-dimensional coordinates of the scan positions. In this way, each cloud of points that is created, has its real coordinates from the beginning. All scans acquired along the traverse were automatically registered and a

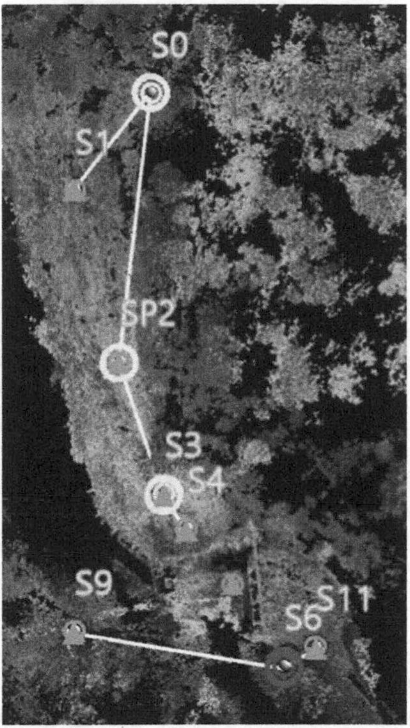

Fig. 5. The scheme of scan points inside and outside of Palaiokastro Gate

reference point cloud for the Gate about 13,500,000 points was achieved. Single GLS-2200 scans were also imported in Magnet Collage and registered with a cloud-to-cloud approach with the reference point cloud. The accuracy of the registration was verified on the scans points coordinates RMSE. Values are of about a few millimeters for east and north coordinates [3].

It is worth noting that the results and therefore the accuracy of the merging of the "singles" point clouds largely depend on the overlap percentage of the point clouds with each other, on the number and geometry of the homologous points. During the scanning process, all distances between the scanner and the object did not exceed 110 m, i.e. they are within the limits where the laser beam of the scanner has the minimum diameter to achieve the best possible accuracy. The 3D point cloud has its color information, enriching the scan data with the image from the camera that the laser scanner itself has taken. As a result of this process 2D drawings of sections and elevations were produced.

The aspect examined in this paper was the construction phases in Palaiokastro Gate. The study of historical sources as well as careful observation of the monument helped us to identify the historical phases of the monument. The different building phases of the gate, which obviously contain different materials and a different way of building, are presented with corresponding plans of views, sections of their representation.

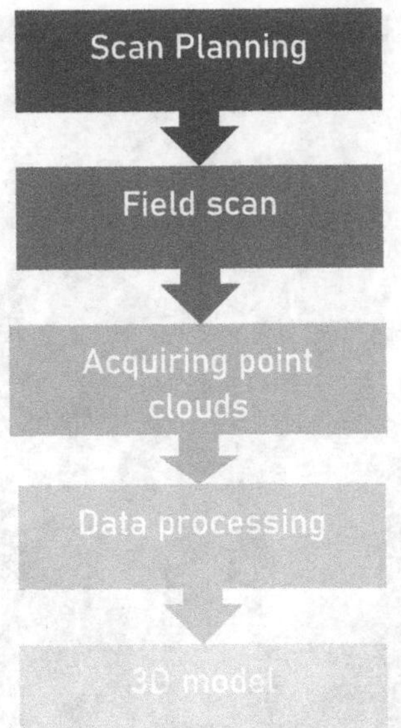

Fig. 6. Workflow of integrated 3D modeling using terrestrial laser scanning (TLS)

Zias and Kontogiannis (2004) give a description of the construction phases of the specific monument and specifically for the central south gate of the castle. Two construction phases are mentioned, which are chronologically placed as follows: A Construction Phase-Venetian (1423–1500), B Construction Phase – Ottomans (1500–1686).

The 3D Laser scanner is a very important tool for documentation cultural heritage due to its accuracy, speed and flexibility. It was used for the geometrical and visual documentation of the existing state of the gate.

The creation of a three-dimensional point cloud, which resulted from the merging of the individual clouds, provide us the geometric and color information of the object to be captured. The aligned point cloud is a three-dimensional representation that can be used to generate traditional two-dimensional drawings or orthoimages. The higher the density and resolution of point clouds, the greater the accuracy and detail orthoimages can provide [8].

Pointcab software was used for the 3D documentation of the Gate, due to its capability to create othophotos from the 3D point cloud. Taking advantage of the software's ability to create orthophotos of views and sections of the 3D point cloud, we respectively orient the axis parallel to the side we want, creating the appropriate views and sections. The images below show details (snippets) of parts of the 3D model, untextured and textured (Fig. 7) [7].

The observation of the arch's morphological elements of the inner building layer of the southern gate suggest that gate reinforcement works were done at the ottoman period. New masonry was added to the interior chamber of the gate that was covered by a barrel vault made completely out of brick. This masonry layer had niches and a small rectangular guard post inscribed in the walls, a reinforcement of the south door's frame with successive recessed arches (Fig. 8) [9].

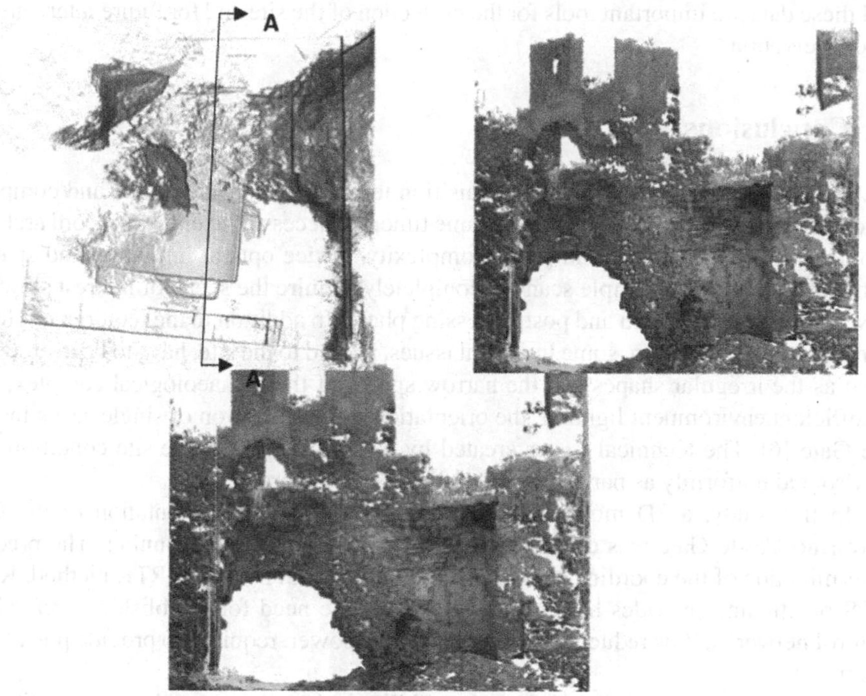

Fig. 7. Point cloud cross section (A-A) of the Gate

Fig. 8. Orthophoto from point cloud viewing the cross-section A-A with visibility to the interior of the Gate, including the Ottoman period construction phases (orange)

These facades are useful because it is possible in this way to control the preservation of the walls, to identify the different construction phases in order to create a phase map.

All these data are important tools for the protection of the site and for future intervention of conservation.

3 Conclusions

TLS technology is the fastest data acquisition technology for large scale and complex (archaeological) environments. At the same time, the necessity to entirely record archaeological sites, with spatial and shape complexity, device optical limitation and spatial constraints, requires multiple scans to completely acquire the scene of interest slowing down both the acquisition and postprocessing phase. In addition to the requirement for a complete documentation, some logistical issues, related to the site, have to be overcome, such as the irregular shapes and the narrow spaces of the archaeological complex, the insufficient environment lighting, the orientation and registration of single scans inside the Gate [6]. The technical issues created by the landscape and the site condition are confronted uniformly as part of the methodology of the project.

In this study, a 3D model and the associated digital documentation of the Old Navarino Castle Gate was established by using terrestrial laser scanning. The precise determination of the coordinates was ensured by using GPS and the RTK method. RTK GPS positioning provides high accuracy without the need for establishing local GPS control networks, thus reducing the time, and man power, required to provide positional control.

The use of the 3D model gave the possibility to examine the existing condition of the Gate from every necessary angle and focus in specific areas of interest. The removal of the texture layer provided the opportunity to examine a clearer model by showing only geometric data and focusing on the immediate relation of the monument and the surrounding landscape.

Terrestrial laser scanner survey produced very accurate geometrical data. The Magnet Collage software was used for processing the total datasets in order to integrate all scans. A complete 3D model of the whole Gate was achieved (Fig. 9). Using the coordinates of topographic points, the final 3D model was georeferenced.

The paper presents the results of the TLS survey carried out to document the remains of the archaeological site of Old Navarino Gate, known as Palaiokastro, which is located in Messenia Greece. This project is part of an overall attempt to digitally recreate the Old Navarino Castle in Koryfasio, the first digital surveying approach for the specific monument using TLS and aerial photogrammetry. The methodology highlights the application of new technologies in acquiring structural data in remote areas, here for the South Gate of the monument. Aerial photogrammetry assisted in planning the TLS survey of the surrounding area of interest. Using a topographic approach for scan registration; the scan acquisition process was optimized.

The produced 3D model can be used further creating a multitude of products such as orthophotos, 2D floor plans, elevations and sections which are necessary for the complete and accurate geometric documentation of the current situation of the Southwest gate of Palaiokastro.

Fig. 9. The exterior east side of Palaiokastro Gate, registered point cloud from Magnet Collage.

The significance of our study, it the fact that textured 3D models of archaeological sites are necessary tools for visualization, assisting archaeologists in identifying structural phases, construction techniques, sequences, restorations, etc. Additionally, in order to carry out further investigations of the site for conservation and preservation policies.

Acknowledgements. This project was implemented within the scope of the "Exceptional Laboratory Practices in Cultural Heritage: Upgrading Infrastructure and Extending Research Perspectives of the Laboratory of Archaeometry", a co-financed by Greece and the European Union project under the auspices of the program "Competitiveness, Entrepreneurship and Innovation" NSRF 2014–2020.

References

1. Andrews, K.: Castles of the Morea, Gennadeion Monographs IV. Princeton-New Jersey (1953)
2. Bilis, T., Kouimtzoglou, T., Magnisali, M., Tokmakidis, P.: The use of 3D scanning and photogrammetry techniques in the case study of the Roman theatre of Nikopolis. Surveying, virtual reconstruction and restoration study. In: The International Archives of the Photogrammetry, Remote Sensing and Spatial Information Sciences, vol. XLII-2/W3, pp. 97–103. 3D Virtual Reconstruction and Visualization of Complex Architectures, Nafplio, Greece (2017)
3. Chatzistamatis, S., et al.: Fusion of TLS and UAV photogrammetry data for post-earthquake 3d modeling of a cultural heritage church. In: The International Archives of the Photogrammetry, Remote Sensing and Spatial Information Sciences, vol. XLII-3/W4, pp. 143–150. GeoInformation for Disaster Management (Gi4DM), Istanbul, Turkey (2018)
4. Davis, J.: Sandy Pylos: An Archaeological History from Nestor to Navarino. University of Texas Press, Austin (TX) (1998)
5. Ebolese, D., Lo Brutto, M., Dardanelli, G.: 3D Reconstruction of the roman domus in the archaeological site of Lylibaeum (Marsala, Italy). In: International Archives of the Photogrammetry, Remote Sensing and Spatial Information Sciences, vol. XLII-2/W15, pp. 437–442. 27th CIPA International Symposium "Documenting the past for a better future", Ávila, Spain (2019)

6. Ebolese, D., Lo Brutto, M., Dardanelli, G.: The integrated 3D survey for underground archaeological environment. In: The International Archives of the Photogrammetry, Remote Sensing and Spatial Information Sciences, vol. XLII-2/W9, pp. 311–317. 8th International Workshop 3D-ARCH "3D Virtual Reconstruction and Visualization of Complex Architectures". Bergamo, Italy (2019)
7. Gonizzi Barsanti, S., Remondino, F., Visintini, D.: 3D surveying and modeling of archaeological sites – some critical issues –. In: ISPRS Annals of the Photogrammetry, Remote Sensing and Spatial Information Sciences, vol. II-5/W1, pp. 145–150. XXIV International CIPA Symposium, Strasbourg, France (2013)
8. Oleś, K., Kingsland, K.: Determining the stylistic origin of the Toledo Gate (La Puerta de Toledo) in Ciudad Real, La Mancha, Spain Using Terrestrial Laser Scanning. Peregrinations: J. Medieval Art Archit. **6**(4), 79–111 (2018)
9. Simou, X.: The Old Navarino fortification (Palaiokastro) at Pylos (Greece). Adaptation to early artillery. In: Defensive Architecture of the Mediterranean, vol XII, pp. 1401–1408, Navarro Palazón, García-Pulido (2020)
10. Wei, H., Yunfei, Q., Miaole, H.: The great wall 3D documentation and application based on multisource data fusion – A case study of No. 15 enemy tower of the new Guangwu great wall. In: The International Archives of the Photogrammetry, Remote Sensing and Spatial Information Sciences, volume XLIII-B2-2020, pp. 1465–1470, XXIV ISPRS Congress (2020)
11. Pylos: a Study in the Management and Enhancement of the Cultural Landscape of the Navarino Bay, (Master thesis), EKPA, University of Patras, University of the Aegean (2012). (in Greek)
12. Gialouris N.: Hellenistic cemetery at Gialova – Old Navarino, AD 20, Chronicles, pp. 204–205 (1965). (in Greek)
13. Gialouris, N.: Hellenistic cemetery at Gialova – Palaionavarino, AD 21, pp. 164–165 (1966). (in Greek)
14. Zias, N., Kontogiannis N.: Old Navarino Castle: Works and findings of the period 2001–2003. In: 24th Symposium of Byzantine and Post-Byzantine Archeology and Art. Athens, Athens: The Christian Archaeological Society, pp. 40–41 (2004)
15. Korres, G.: Messinia Historical and Archaeological Outline, Prehistoric Times, p. 427, 447 edn. Melissa. (in Greek)
16. Korres, G.: The problematic for the later use of the Mycenaean tombs of Messenia. In: Proceedings of the Second International Conference of Peloponnesian Studies, Peloponnesian Annexes 8, vol. II, pp. 363–450 (1981–1982). (in Greek)
17. Korres G., Sampson A., Katsarou S.: The Nestoros Cave in Voidokoilia Pylos, its research and the preliminary examination of the older and newer finds. In: Proceedings of the 4th Local Conference of Messinian Studies, pp. 49–50 Athen, (2014). (in Greek)
18. Marinatos, S.: Excavations in Pylos, PAE 1956, pp. 202–206. Athens (1961). (in Greek)
19. Marinatos S.: Excavation of Pylos: Korifassion, PAE 1958, pp. 184–187. Athens 1965 (1958). (in Greek)
20. Panagiotidis, V., Zacharias, N.: Digital Mystras: An approach towards understanding the use of an archaeological space. In: 2nd International Conference on Global Issues of Environment & Culture, Scientific Culture, vol. 8, no. 3, pp. 85–99 (2022)
21. Papathanasopoulos, G., Papathanasopoulos, T.: Pylos-Pylia-Travel in Space and Time, 2nd edn. Athens. T.A.P.A Publisher (2004). (in Greek)
22. Sfikopoulos I.T.: The Medieval Castles of Morea. Athens (1987). (in Greek)

A Contribution to Palaeocoastal and Beachrock Studies with the Application of Digital Technologies: The Case Study of Romanos Beach in Pylos

Evangelia Bilitsi(✉), Vayia V. Panagiotidis, Anastasios Kazolias, and Nikolaos Zacharias

Laboratory of Archaeometry, University of the Peloponnese, Old Camp, 24133 Kalamata, Greece
lillibilitsi16@gmail.com

Abstract. Science evolution encourages the collaboration of scientists of different disciplines accompanied in the last decades with the significant contribution of new technologies. This paper presents the methodology by which palaeoshores are surveyed, measured and calculated in relation to the beach formations visible along the coast. The purpose of the work is to highlight the specific methodology by which the application of digital technologies was used at Romanos beach, located on the West Messenia coast in south Greece. With the use of an Unmanned Aerial System (UAS) the coastal formations where documented and following photogrammetric processing studied further. For the first time, the specific formations of the area were captured through the application of photogrammetry with a tool of such high precision. In conclusion, based on the findings of the area during the field survey many different sediments and marine shell (fossils) and what was observed after the processing of the impression images, the formations of beachrocks arose from the old coast. From the above data new research directions and perspectives arise towards the holistic management of such environments; moreover, new data regarding the chronology of the rock's formations through sediments and the calculation of the position of the old coast, as well as evidences for sea-level changes over the past in the specific area.

Keywords: Beachrocks · Shorelines · Palaeocoasts · UAV Photogrammetry · Romanos Beach Pylos · Digital Applications · GIS · 3D Model

1 Introduction

The goal of the current investigation is to provide information concerning palaeocoast formation at a particular location that has not yet been studied, Romanos Beach in Pylos, Peloponnese, Greece, based on aerial surveying methods. Coastal systems have seen significant changes over the late Pleistocene period. Future changes can be predicted by examining these developments (Lambeck et al., 2001). The construction of the current

A. Moropoulou et al. (Eds.): TMM_CH 2023, CCIS 1889, pp. 137–145, 2023.
https://doi.org/10.1007/978-3-031-42300-0_12

coastal zone has been greatly influenced by global warming throughout the early and middle Holocene, as well as by the more than 100 m sea level increase. The fast rising of sea level slowed down over four thousand years ago. The Ionian Sea and the morphology of Navarino Bay underwent significant changes during the past 9000 years (Avramidis et al., 2014). Before 9500–8900 years, marine regression began. Sand was transported producing a sandy beach and dunes along the Ionian coastline. In summary, the geomorphological history of Yialova Lagoon can be divided into three distinct phases. The initial stage lasted between 6500 and 6100 BC and 6100–5800 years before today, the second phase. In its final stage, the area was a Mediterranean lagoon between 5800 and 3300 years before and still is to this day.

Investigations have been carried out in two locations next to the focus area mentioned in this work, one to the north and the other further south, locate Paleolithic installations. After dating sediments and studying artefacts from the sites it was concluded that they date to 28 + -5 ka and 8 + -1 ka. Since the sites were found on the coast, the strategic exploitation of the coast and the sea zone would have been very important to past inhabitants. This reason highlights even more the reasons that changes in the water level should be controlled.

Since beachrocks formations were created by carried sediments from subsequent coastal water movements, their presence is evidence of the presence of a palaeocoast. Beachrock formation can take several millennia, and they are thought to be a sign of the old ocean surface (Hopley, 1986). Due to their ability to preserve both the vertical and horizontal history of the shoreline, beachrocks serve as an important paleoenvironmental proxy.

Additionally, beachrocks are a sign of rising sea levels. This is because to the fact that the sediment deposition in them can reveal historical sea level phases and offer date information. Their mapping is typically done in shallow water or on the surface of the coastline. Only two research projects have used piloted aerial vehicles (UAVs) to map the rocks in the coastal zone, and there are relatively few studies on the utilization of various remote sensing data. The research located and documented a beach rock in northeastern Brazil (Chen et al., 2008) that served as a historic coastline 25 m below sea level using a Landsat TM photograph.

It was possible to identify beachrock in South Africa (Hastie et al., 2021) by processing aerial photos. Beaches and the greater coastline of Indonesia (Daryono et al., 2001) were mapped using a small commercial UAV and a compact camera. A coastal cliff in Syros, Greece, was mapped using a combination of data from a small commercial UAV, an unmanned surface vehicle, and measurements taken with a GNSS (Nikolakopoulos et al., 2018). The most relevant research to the subject of this work which has been done in the Greek area was conducted in Epirus, Western Greece and studied using UAV, GIS, and petrographic analysis for beachrock mapping and preliminary analysis in the compressional geotectonics settings. However, it is difficult to analyze coastal geomorphology because tectonic movements, eustatic sea level variations, anthropogenic impacts, and deposition or erosion interact in these habitats (Nikolakopoulos et al., 2022).

2 Case Study: Romanos Beach Pylos, Peloponnese

The area selected for study is located on the beach of Romanos, at the point where the facilities of the Westin Resort of Costa Navarino hotel complex are today (Fig. 1). Romanos beach presents a variety of coastal terrains, which help to study the factors involved in the formation and evolution of the coastline. The study area is located on the coastline where suitable materials for the formation of beach deposits have been found. The studied coastlines are formed between the shore and the beach (tidal zone), which is a more chemically active zone (mixing zone). Despite human interventions in the area and the beach in particular, the natural geomorphological landscape which concerns the beachrock formations do not show any destruction or damage. On site observations and field survey was conducted within a 3 day visit in the area.

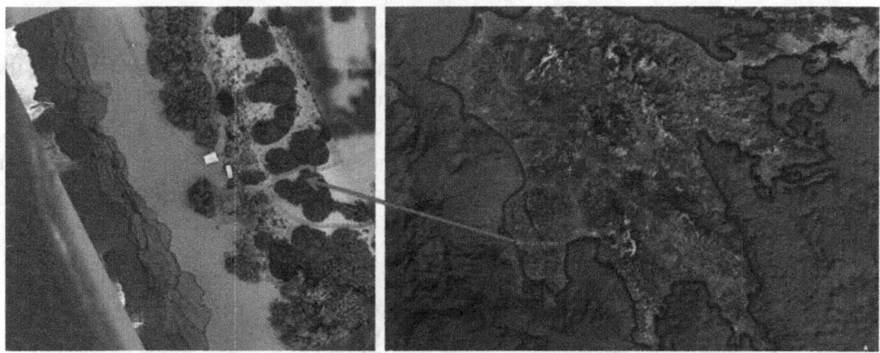

Fig. 1 Romanos Beach [left], Google Earth location [right]

The geomorphological formations (Fig. 2), which create the beachrocks, cover a slope with an incline ranging from under 9° to close to 80°. These formations create rocky steep terrain. The flora of this area is very intense. In particular, the large, tall and dense trees made research difficult in several places. The complete lack of pottery elements in the study area should be noted.

Macromorphologically, zones of consecutive layers reveal deposits created by the waves of various transported materials and sediments of marine origin. Marine fossils shells, were spotted sporadically at the study area (Fig. 3), providing evidence of the existence of an aquatic element in the area where the beachrock formations are today. Similarly, between the overlapping layers of beachrocks fossilized sections of shells were found. Marine shells (fossils) located between the layers contained solid parts, porous structure, white color and several damages and breaks. These findings can be identified as biotraces, i.e. traces of life left by an organism and which is imprinted in a geological layer but without leaving skeletal elements. It could be considered that the fossil has come from pericalcification. This type of fossilization occurs when an organism is completely covered by a layer of calcium carbonate. Such examples are often pine cones or river fish. The dissolved calcium carbonate contained in the water is deposited on their surface and as they flow from the current of the river their body is

Fig. 2 Photography from field research on beachrocks of Romanos Beach in Pylos

covered. This way the remains are enclosed in a crust of calcium carbonate and look like pebbles that contain the fossilized organism inside (Murphy and Hawboldt, 2018). It is true that in this particular specimen it is not a fossilization in the water. Nevertheless, when the fossil was created and closed in a chronologically earlier layer of the present surface, at that particular moment there was the presence of sea water.

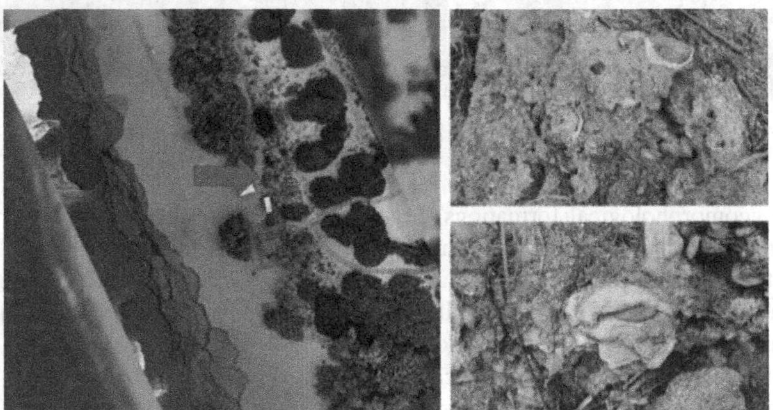

Fig. 3 Fossilized marine shells found within the beachrocks' formation

3 Definition of Palaeocoasts and Beachrocks

The most common indicators of the presence of seawater in the past in coastal areas that do not have water today are marine microorganisms and their accumulations which grow naturally as horizontal stratifications. In the countryside, the change in water level (the presence of water) can be perceived after comparing the current zones of living organisms with similar marine shells (fossils) of organisms that are now at different levels. In addition, there are characteristics that are produced by bio-erosion in the current and old sea levels (Liritzis, 2005).

Palaeoshorelines create discrete zones of seabed complexity, despite the fact that they developed hundreds of thousands of years ago and have endured the merciless assaults of tides and waves. In complex palaeoshoreline features, the community of algae and benthic (bottom-dwelling) organisms such as clams, sea sponges, and fish can be substantially different, and frequently more diversified, than nearby populations living on a flat, unstable seabed. Calcium carbonate banks that originated as near-surface coral reefs during times of lower sea level, for example, on the northern Greek shelf, sustain biodiversity "hot spots" when combined with other environmental factors.

This investigation of physical processes and responses in the coastal zone is frequently used in nature, but it also includes basic research to provide the underlying understanding needed to answer the pertinent questions. Beach erosion is a major coastal concern today and in the foreseeable future. Almost 70% of the world's sandy shorelines are eroding, according to estimates (Liritzis, 2005).

Beachrocks are typically formed by the quick blending of sand collected near the shoreline (Davidson-Arnot, 2010). Beachrocks are primarily cemented on the surface of the coastline and/or at a shallow depth in the subtidal zone in tropical and/or subtropical coastlines. Beachrocks are utilized as evidence of historical coastlines since they are formed in the equilibrium zone between inland and saltwater. Beachrock has been the subject of hundreds of research around the world because its presence is an indicator of sea-level rise or retreat (Leatherman et al., 1992).

Absolute dating methods, unlike relative dating methods, provide chronological estimations of the age of specific geological components associated with marine shells (fossils), as well as direct age measurements of the fossil itself. Researchers use a clock to calculate the date a rock or fossil was generated in order to ascertain its age. Radiometric dating methods, which are based on the natural radioactive decay of particular elements like potassium and carbon, are often used by geologists to date ancient events. Other methods, such as electron spin resonance and thermoluminescence, are used by geologists to assess the effects of radioactivity on the accumulation of electrons in imperfections, or "traps," in the crystal structure of a mineral.

In 2008, for the first time, Athanassas and Zacharias carried out detailed investigations of the area regarding the absolute dating with the OSL method for the uplifted marine sequences on the Southwest coast during the Upper Quaternary. Testing new laboratory protocols an advanced OSL technique (SAR) led to the following results: A stable pattern of uplift during the Pliocene and Pleistocene and subsidence in the early Pleistocene was identified. Based on SAR method, samples of stratified sand, mud and coastal sand from the specific area were dated. The dating indicated a period of total sea-level rise of about 300 Ka (Athanassas and Zacharias, 2008).

The researches of 2011, which have been mentioned in the previous paragraph, dated sediments, with the OSL method, from the two archaeological sites of the Paleolithic era that were found. The first site with Aliquot - Regenerated Dose and Thermally Transferred - OSL techniques dated the first site to around 28 Ka and the second site to ca. 8 Ka (Athanassas et al., 2011).

In 2013 the research continued using GIS and digital photography. Coastal deposits have been found from the middle to late Pleistocene. The ages resulted with the application of luminescence verified for chronological episodes that ascribe at OIS-5, OIS-7 and OIS-9 sediments. These ages were presented in the 3 warm stages of the Pleistocene. In the specific section being studied, sediments were dated which were dated to OIS -5, i.e. 125–75 Ka. Digital analysis of relief maps and field observations identified the existence of a sequence of five elevated platforms in the southwest of the Peloponnese, carved into the Quaternary beach. They concluded that each beach forms its creation independently and not as a single entity (Athanassas, 2013).

4 Methodology

Geomorphologically, the area under study consists of four parts: the sea, the coastal zone, the beach, and the slope on which the beachrocks' formations extend. Through mapping, the characteristics of these sections will be examined, as well as the extent of the beachrocks' relation to the current coast and the data available concerning the old coast in the wider area.

The DJI Mavic 2 Pro was used to photograph the research area (UAV). Ground Control Points (GCPs) were placed around the study region to help the model be georeferenced. A Top Con GR5 geodetic station was used to determine the exact coordinates of the GCPs. All data was gathered using the EGSA '87 Greek coordinate system. The UAV was flown at a relative altitude of 40 m from the launch point in the case of the Mavic 2 Pro to acquire images for the photographic overview of the study area. Each location was photographed separately, and the data was then aggregated (Panagiotidis and Zacharias, 2022). It should be noted that a single flight was performed in the wider area, achieving the correct adjustment of the relative altitude of the UAV to the ground and its stay at approx.40 m meters above the ground.

Following the survey, the photographic documentation and GCP coordinates are transmitted to a computer and processed using the photogrammetry program Agisoft Metashape (Agisoft, 2022). Image (camera) alignment, referencing system conversion, importing target coordinates (GCPs), generating the dense point cloud, classification, mesh construction, generating the DEM, and orthomosaic are all part of the processing operation (Fig. 4).

In this case it is normal to have small errors as well as the study area was quite hardy with dense flowering vegetation. The previous geomorphological conditions are understood to prevent the full accuracy of the point locations. To build the dense cloud certain specifications must be met. Furthermore, calculation of point colors and calculate point confidence are conducted in order to remove noise. Noise includes the details that prevent sufficient presentation of the object under study, in this case slope and sedimentary formations that have formed in the study area. Therefore, most of the foliage of the trees that hide the ground should be removed. In this case removing man-made structures also facilitates in the clearer depicture of the study area. In order to remove whatever noise is emitted from the sea during photography, water reflectance point cloud confidence is used. The cleaning process is done using point classification where the application recognizes objects and data in the model, in this case, ground, high

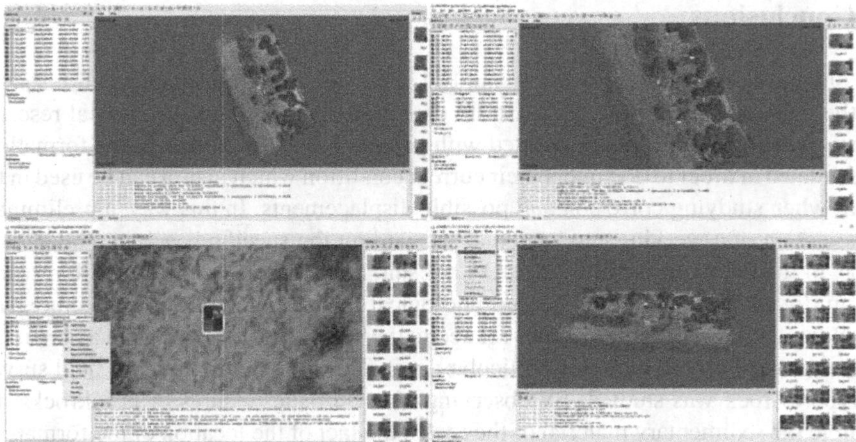

Fig. 4 Photograph processing (Agisoft Metashape)

vegetation, buildings, road surface and man-made object such as buildings, trees etc. (Fig. 5).

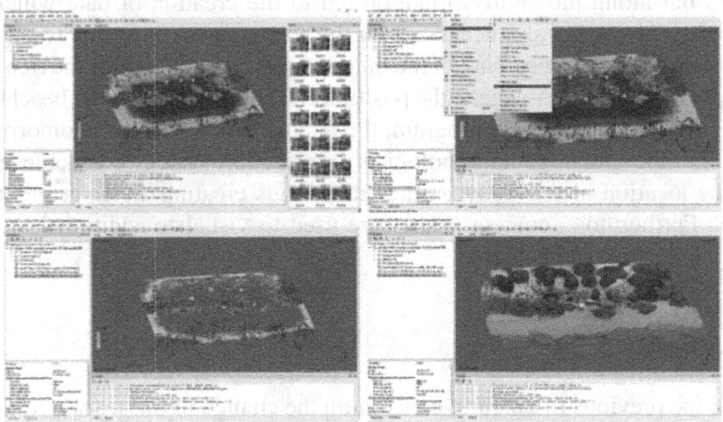

Fig. 5 Classification of point confidence

Selected data provided a pathway in order to successfully sort all the elements, classes, categories of data, created. This categorization helps in grouping items. After all the elements of the image have been categorized, the point cloud is filtered and only the elements required are maintained for the continuation of the work. Following class definition and filtering, the DEM - digital elevation model is generated. The DEM contains a color gradient of the altitude differences. An RGB gradation can be created from the blue color which characterizes the lowest mark to the red which characterizes the highest points.

5 Conclusions

The objectives of this work were to apply UAV technologies to map beachrocks and use the resulting imagery to demonstrate their contribution to archaeological research as they are shown to be interconnected with palaeoshores. 3D models of the formations were created in order to document their current condition which in turn can be used in the future when studying corrosion and possible displacements. In this way, a preliminary investigation of a working case was made regarding the specific beach in Romanos of Pylos, in the Peloponnese of Greece. As a result, a database was created with research data in digital form, regarding geomorphological features, georeferenced features and also elements of archaeological sites related to the area. This base will form a core in the development of research on this particular coast. Through the preliminary field survey, the type of rock was studied. By observing characteristic features of beachrocks, for example the sedimentary material of the rocks, the fact of the location of the formations which are parallel along the coast and the findings which are marine shells (fossils) of white seashells, it was concluded that the specific formation belongs to the category of beachrocks. Adding this formation to the category of beachrocks indicates its creation from transported sedimentary materials, which were transported by sea water to the coast.

The photogrammetric remote sensing with the unmanned UAV, with which a flight was carried out along the entire formation led to the creation of data which are not only useful in research but also necessary for the development of further research. More specifically, through the processing of the images taken, the removal of the rich flora was achieved, providing a clear image of the position and classification of the beachrocks. By inserting the image into the GIS program, the inclusion of a specific geomorphological formation into the global geomorphological information system was achieved, which specifies the location of the study on the "map" thus creating a clearer picture of the formations. Furthermore, contour lines were used to visualize additional information regarding their extent and heights.

6 Future Aims

The data of the previous researches, concerning the change of the sea water level in the wider area of the study, show intense changes of the water environment. It would be of scientific interest to compare the results of later surveys, as some beaches of these surveys are located on the same coastline as the beach of the present study. From the macroscopic observation of the location, size, shape and height of the beaches studied above, it is concluded that in the past the coast was several meters farther than it is today, and the water level is very likely to have drop quite a bit today by taking into account the altitude and steep slope formed by the rocks of the beach. Since the beach rocks provide an indication of an ancient coast, through our information they provide evidence for analyzes that assist dating of the site in local scale. Regarding the chronological sequences, in most similar cases the dating of sediment cores with biostratigraphic analysis of the sedimentary sequences is used. For absolute dating methods, the application of radiocarbon and luminescence analysis is usually found. Of outmost importance is the establishement of a model for sea-level changes in the scale of the site of interest with the aid to draw conclusions regarding human activities, trade routes and habitation patterns.

Acknowledgements. This project was implemented within the scope of the "Exceptional Laboratory Practices in Cultural Heritage: Upgrading Infrastructure and Extending Research Perspectives of the Laboratory of Archaeometry", a co-financed by Greece and the European Union project under the auspices of the program "Competitiveness, Entrepreneurship and Innovation" NSRF 2014-2020.

References

Athanassas, C.: Quaternary Neotectonic Configuration of the Southwestern Peloponnese, Greece, Based on Luminescence Ages of Marine Terraces. J. Earth Sci. **24**(3), 410–427 (2013)

Athanassas, C., Bassiakos, Y., Wagner, G.A., Timpso, M.: Exploring Paleogeographic Conditions at Two Paleolithic Sites in Navarino, Southwest Greece, Dated by Optically Stimulated Luminescence. WileyOnlineLibrary (2011)

Athanassas, C., Zacharias, N.: Recuperated-OSL dating of squartz from Aegean (South Greece) raised Pleistocene marine sediments: current results. Quaternary Geochronology (2008)

Avramidis, P., et al.: Depositional environments, sediment characteristics, palaeo-ecological analysis and environmental assessment of an internationally protected sha- llow Mediterranean lagoon, Gialova Lagoon – Navarino Bay, Greece. Earth and Environmental Science Transactions of the Royal Society of Edinburgh, pp. 189–206 (2014)

Chen, F., Fan, Y., Chun, X., Madsen, D., Oviatt, C.G.: Preliminary research on megalake jilantaihetaoin the arid areas of china during the late quaternary. Sci. Bull **53**, 1725–1739 (2008)

Daryono, L.R., Nakashima, K., Kawasaki, S., Titisa, A.: Shoreline mapping based on beachrocks identification in Krakal-Sadranan beach, Yogyakarta, Indonesia. Bull. Eng. Geol. Environ. **80**, 2825–2844 (2021)

Davidson-Arnot, R.: Coastal geomorphology. In: An Introduction to Coastal Processes and Geomorphology. Davidson Arnot (2010)

Hastie, W., Mthembu, A., Green, A.N.: Linking fracturing and rock mechanic properties to the erosion of a beachrock shore platform. Mar. Geol. **441**, 106616 (2021)

Hopley, D.: Beachrock as sea-level indicator, In Sea-Level Research: A Manual for the Collection and Evaluation of Data, pp. 157–173. Geo Books, Norwich, UK (1986)

Leatherman, S., Davison, A., Nicholls, R.: Environmental Science in the Coastal Zone, Issues for Further Research. National Academies, pp. 44–47 (1992)

Liritzis, I.: Μεταβολλές της στάθμης της θάλασσας, [Sea level changes]. Αρχαιολογία και Περιβάλλον, [Archaeology and Environment]. Kardamitsa, Athens (2005)

Murphy, J., Hawboldt, K.: Enzymatic processing of mussel shells to produce biorenewable calcium carbonate in seawater. Green Chemistry 12 (2018)

Nikolakopoulos, K., Lampropoulou, P., Fakris, E., Sardelianos, D., Papatheodorou, G.: Use of UAV and USV Dataand Petrographic Analyses for the Investigation of Beachrock Formations: A Case Study from Syros Island, Aegean Sea. Greece. Minerals **8**, 534 (2018)

Nikolakopoulos, K., Koukouvelas, I., Lampropoulou, P.: UAV, GIS, and petrographic analysis for beachrock mapping and preliminary analysis in the compressional geotectonic setting of epirus. Western Greece. Minerals **12**, 392 (2022)

Panagiotidis, V., Zacharias, N.: The Byzantine City of Mystras, The Byzantine Archaeological City of Mystras: The Hagia Sophia Monastery, CAA 2021-Digital Crossroads, Kalamata (2022)

Peppe, D.J., Deino, A.L.: Dating Rocks and Fossils Using Geologic Methods. Nature Education (2014)

The Digitization of Klissova Islet and the Church of Agia Triada in Mesologgi

A. Papoutsaki(✉), V. V. Panagiotidis, A. Kompoti, A. Kazolias, and N. Zacharias

Laboratory of Archaeometry, Department of History, Archaeology and Cultural Resources Management, University of the Peloponnese, Old Camp, 24133 Kalamata, Greece
anastasia.papoutsaki22@gmail.com

Abstract. The research portrayed in this paper aims to digitize the islet of Klissova and its monuments which consist of the church of Agia Triada and a memorial obelisk, in the Mesologgi region of Greece. The objectives of the digitization are the documentation, monitoring and the documentation of current preservation state of the islet and the monuments since they are highly endangered by the surrounding environment. The surrounding natural landscape is a lagoon ecosystem of high salinity which threatens the integrity of the cultural structures of the islet through rising water level, increased humidity and salinity. The development of a 3D model of the church and the islet stands as an essential tool for future sampling and restoration of the monuments. The digitization process was utilized with an Unmanned Aerial Vehicle, a GNSS receiver, and a Terrestrial Laser Scanner for high accuracy of the final model.

Keywords: Klissova · Photogrammetry · Cultural Heritage · 3D model · UAV · Agisoft Metashape

1 Introduction

Digital applications today are undeniably a part of everyday life. Cultural Heritage could not lag behind these developments making the application of new technologies for the documentation, restoration, and preservation of monuments a common practice [1, 2]. This paper focuses on the documentation of the Klissova islet and its monuments, using photogrammetry.

1.1 Location

The town of Mesologgi (38.3687° N, 21.4304° E) is located in western Greece and is the capital of the Aetolia-Akarnania regional unit (Fig. 1). The surrounding environment mainly consists of wetlands and river deposits [3, 4]. Klissova lagoon was formed by deposits of two rivers, Achelous and Evinos where the homonym uninhabited islet of Klissova is located (38°20′57.3"N 21°26′08.9"E) (Fig. 2). The perimeter of the islet is 280 m 2km from the city. The area has been included in the scientific catalog for protected areas, Natura 2000 by the European Commission [3, 5].

A. Moropoulou et al. (Eds.): TMM_CH 2023, CCIS 1889, pp. 146–154, 2023.
https://doi.org/10.1007/978-3-031-42300-0_13

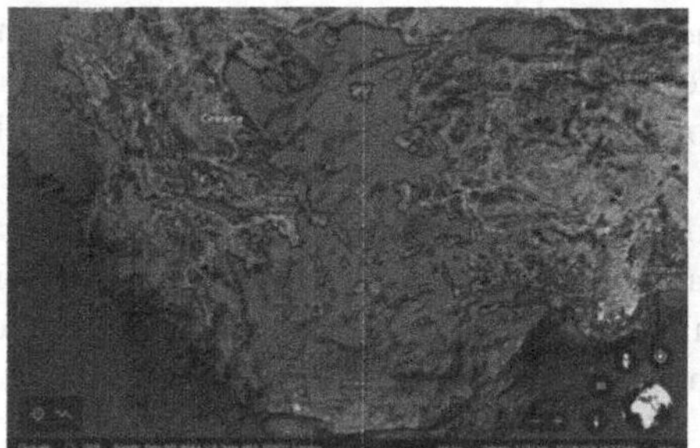
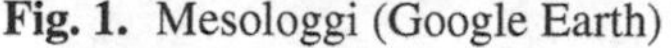

Fig. 1. Mesologgi (Google Earth)

Fig. 2. Klissova islet (Google Earth)

1.2 Historical Background

Greece was under Ottoman sovereignty for almost 400 years. In the year 1821, the Greek revolution started in the Peloponnese region, and it continued north, to Central Greece, freeing a number of cities and villages including Mesologgi. Mesologgi in western central Greece, was under the Ottoman siege from 1821 until 1826. Ottomans made three attempts to capture the city. After two failures (1822 and 1823) the Ottoman army returned in 1825, headed by Reşid Mehmed Pasha, also known as Kütahi, with the aid of Ibrahim Pasha of Egypt [6]. The third siege of Mesologgi which started on the 15th of April 1825 was the longest and most pressing one.

The Strategic Value of Klissova was already known from the previous sieges. Ottomans, after their victory in every islet of the lagoon, attacked Klissova, the last fortress. The number of Ottoman soldiers was disproportionate in comparison with the Greeks, 6.000 against 131 accordingly. Kutahi unsuccessfully attempted six attacks. On the 25th of March 1826, the last battle took place in the islet, which results in the victory of the Greeks. However, the successful defenses in Klissova do not entail victory in Mesologgi and on the 10th of April of the same year, the city felt. The church of Agia Triada was mentioned considerably in literature relevant to the war. Although the current church, and the site of interest of this study, is more recent and was built in 1848 at the foundations of the pre-existing one (2nd phase of the church) [7]. The 3rd phase of the church is in 1997 when there were some mortar additions as the inscription on the façade of the church signifies.

Every year for the memory of battle of Klissova, a reenactment takes place preserving the memory of the site alive. The commemorative events and the connection of the islet with local history have made Klissova a "living" historic place.

2 Materials and Methods

The documentation of Klissova islet is one of the major parts of the overall research concerning the estimation of the current state of preservation. Additional objectives of this research are the archaeometric study of materials regarding their production technology and the development of a conservation planning and finally the public awareness-raising. The 3D model that was created serves as an innovative interface for the visualization of the data produced during the study of the church and the surrounding environment. This 3D visual database will include architectural, material and archaeological data as a comprehensive digital repository that stores and presents information in a visually appealing and interactive format.

The database integrates data from various sources providing more sufficient organization schemes than those provided by traditional database design. The 3D modeling approach used to display the data as a virtual object can be viewed from different angles and perspectives allowing users to explore and analyze the information in a more intuitive and immersive way.

2.1 Equipment

For the data acquisition, an Unmanned Aerial Vehicle (UAV), the DJI Matrice 300 RTKwith the camera payload and the Topcon GR-5 GNSS receiver were transported by small boats to the islet for the survey. UAVs can provide high spatial resolution and high-quality images of buildings and areas that cannot be depicted by terrestrial photogrammetry [8]. The DJI Matrice 300 offers flexibility, long battery life (over 40 min of flight with the P1), high speed (max 23 m/s), and low cost, important features that make the Matrice widely used in the field of aerial photogrammetry [9, 10] and consequently it was chosen for the specific project. The DJI Zenmuse P1 camera's features are 45 MP Full-frame sensor, 35mm lens and stabilized Gimbal of 3-axis and is able to acquire image data in the visible spectrum. In addition, the UAVs RTK system can provide accuracy of 3cm horizontally and 5cm vertically [10]. However, the use of UAVs cannot stand alone in the capture of a site and the application of supplementary methods for the accurate georeference of the produced model is vital [11]. For the absolute positioning of the photos, a Global Navigation Satellite System (Topcon GR-5 GNSS receiver) was applied. A Terrestrial Laser Scanner (Topcon GLS 2200) was also utilized, and will be part of a future study.

For the caption of the islet, a specific flight plan was created with no significant difficulties since the islet has no elevation. Due to that fact, only one flight was necessary for the completion of the digitization process. Previous to the flight, a set of targets (GCPs) were placed on every side of the islet for the accurate georeference of the model (Fig. 3) [12]. The targets must be identifiable for the UAV, therefore they have a distinct size and specific design that is suggested by the photogrammetric software, Agisoft Metashape Pro. Later the software verifies the position of each GCP during the building of the point cloud for the georeference of the model. The UAV covered the entire area ($4.99e + 3m^2$) top-down (Fig. 4) with a photo overlapping of 80%. The flying altitude was 51 m. Additionally, the structures of interest (church and obelisk) were mapped with a 45o camera angle (Fig. 5) and from a lower altitude for higher accuracy and detailed end-product. The camera's specifications were F-stop f/4, exposure time 1/640 s and ISO-800. The UAV snapped 348 photos of the whole area, the islet, the monuments and the surrounding environment with an image resolution of 8192x5460 and pixel size 4.39x4.39 μm. Following the flight, the images taken from the UAV, that captured the islet and the monuments, are used as data input for Agisoft Metashape Pro to carry out the related processing.

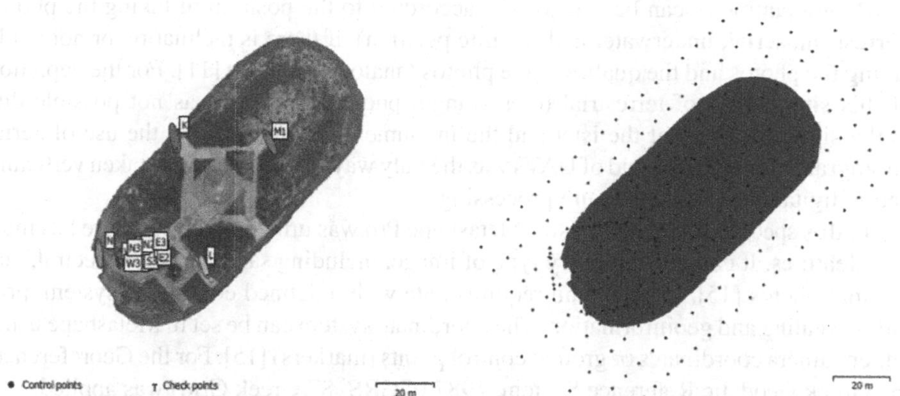

Fig. 3. Ground Control Points **Fig. 4.** Camera locations and image overlap

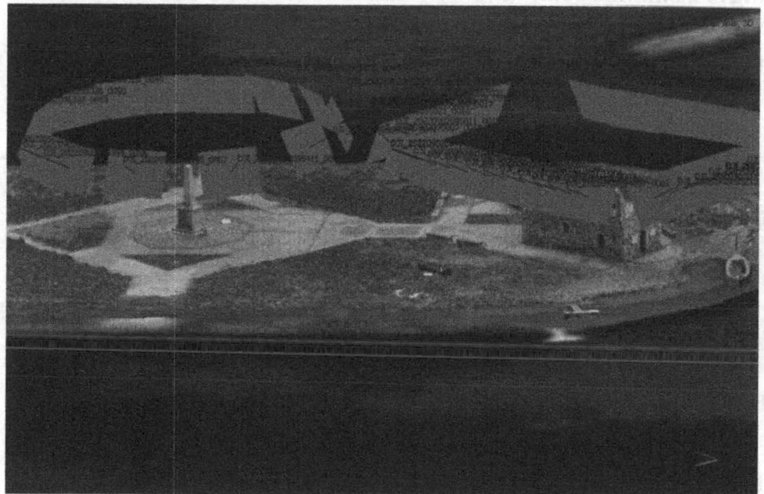

Fig. 5. Flight plan in the church and the obelisk

2.2 Photogrammetry

Digital photogrammetry is a measuring method that uses a series of digital photos to represent a three-dimensional (3D) object. To achieve this, certain images must be overlapped by changing camera positions and angles [13]. Photogrammetry can also determine the qualitative and quantitative characteristics of an object. Qualitative characteristics of an object can be the pattern, the shape, and the texture while quantitative characteristics can be considered the size, direction and position. Applications can vary and some examples are the measuring of coordinates, distances, heights, and the creation of topographic maps and orthophotos [14].

Photogrammetry can be categorized according to the position of taking the photos (terrestrial, aerial, underwater and satellite position), if there is inclination or not while taking the photos and the quality of the photos (analog or digital) [11]. For the depiction of this site the use of terrestrial (close-range) photogrammetry was not possible due to the significant size of the islet and the monuments. Consequently, the use of aerial photogrammetry with the aid of UAVs was the only way. The photos were taken vertically and indigitalform for their future processing.

In this specific research, Agisoft Metashape Pro was utilized. The software has multiple features. It can process every type of image, including satellite, multispectral, and thermal photos [15].The program requires data with a defined coordinate system, providing scaling and geoinformation. The coordinate system can be set in Metashape using either camera coordinates or ground control points (markers) [15]. For the Georeference, the Greek Geodetic Reference System, 1987 (GGRS_87/Greek Grid) was applied.

Using the photo alignment process, a sparse point cloud was generated, comprising of 153,808 tie points (Fig. 6), which was then followed by the creation of a dense cloud comprising of 24 million points (Fig. 7). A total of 16 markers were utilized, out of which 4 were placed on the ground of the islet for georeferencing of the 3D model, while 12 were installed on the facades of the church (3 on each side) to create the projected surfaces for planar orthomosaics.

Fig. 6. Sparse cloud - Tie points

Fig. 7. Dense point cloud

2.3 Side Views

Following the triangulation of the point cloud, the 3D model (mesh) was built. By using the georeferenced 3D model, the software can build the orthomosaics. Additionally, planar orthomosaics were extracted by utilizing the markers situated on the perimetrical walls of the church. Othomosaic is a high-resolution composite of individual images, corrected for any distortions caused by terrain relief or camera lens, resulting in a true-to-scale representation of the area. The planar orthomosaic of a building's facade is a 2D image generated by projecting the 3D model onto a single plane, resulting in an accurate representation of the facade in which precise measurements can be obtained. The creation of the side views of the church accurately presents its main characteristics such as its dimensions, textures and the different materials. Furthermore, the side views are vital for the upcoming research as they compose an important tool for the documentation of the two historic phases, the pathology and the sampling of the monument.

The first step was to establish markers and create the desired plane. After the first (origin) markers, the second one was set in a horizontal line and the third one must be vertical to the first one. Continuously, an orthomosaic was built and this process was repeated four times for each side of the church.

3 Results

Digitization of Klissova is a preliminary study of the site that aims at its future protection. This research started as a MSc thesis in Cultural Heritage Materials and Technologies program at the University of Peloponnese, Greece.

The digitization of the islet and its monuments using a UAV, GPS, and GCPs aims at the digital documentation of the current state of the site. The images from the UAV that were imported in the Agisoft Metashape Pro software, created a 3D model of the islet, the church, and the obelisk for the determination of the structural details such as the wall height, thickness, material, etc. In addition, the 3D model was created to be a reference point due to the lack of related research.

The need for a horizontal projection of the church for the depiction of its two phases (the historic phase and the restoration phase) and the types and variability of the structural materials (stones, ceramics, etc.) was achieved with the creation of orthomosaics in Agisoft. Additionally, the pathology of the church's materials (the material losses, the salts, the degradation of the mortar and stones, etc.) will be easily documented with the aid of the side views (Figs. 8, 9 and 10).

Fig. 8. 3D Model of the islet

Fig. 9. Agia Triada 3D Model

Fig. 10. Memorial obelisk 3D Model

In this versatile research, the archaeometric approach is vital. A considerable number of samples, mortars, and stones will be collected for the technological characterization of the materials. The orthomosaics will be implemented for the creation of digital maps from the sampling points.

The produced projected side views of each wall of the church can be measured with high accuracy. The facades of the church shown in Fig. 11, Fig. 12, Fig. 13 and Fig. 14, can be treated as scaled images and utilized by other software such as CAD or image recognition algorithms. This enables the use of these images for 2D design purposes, archaeological documentation and material recognition.

Fig. 11. West church façade

Fig. 12. South church facade

Fig. 13. East church facade

Fig. 14. North church facade

4 Conclusions and Future Research

The 3D model of the islet and the church is an undeniable tool for future research. The significance of digital documentation is the preservation of this historical site with great historic importance.

The site and the monuments are essential milestones of modern Greek history and for the local community. The place needs to be advertised and displayed beyond the local community to attract more visitors. This specific project can be the beginning of the creation of more digital applications like AR (Augmented Reality), VR (Virtual Reality), or Virtual tours of the area as a way of generally developing the region [16–18].

The 3D visual database generated for the overall project can be further applied for a wide range of applications, including research, education, and public outreach. Researchers can use the database to explore and analyze the data in a more holistic and comprehensive way, revealing new insights and relationships between different elements of the data. Educators can use the database to teach students about architecture, materials science, and archaeology in a more engaging and interactive way, while also providing them with hands-on experience with cutting-edge digital tools. Finally, the database can be used for public outreach and engagement, allowing members of the public to explore and learn about historical and cultural artifacts in a more accessible and inclusive way.

However, digital documentation and restoration cannot replace the actual monument and its need for conservation. They can however be useful tools for the actual conservation. The future steps include the creation of digital maps that depict the corrosion in the church and the sampling. In addition, analytical techniques will be applied for the production of a restoration plan.

Acknowledgements. This project was implemented within the scope of the "Exceptional Laboratory Practices in Cultural Heritage: Upgrading Infrastructure and Extending Research Perspectives of the Laboratory of Archaeometry", a co-financed by Greece and the European Union project under the auspices of the program "Competitiveness, Entrepreneurship and Innovation" NSRF 2014–2020.

Acknowledgments are appointed to the Ephorate of Antiquities of Aetoloacarnania and Lefkada, Ministry of Culture and Sports and the Mesologgi Municipality. Special thanks go to the members of the Archaeometry laboratory: Vasiliki Valantou and Elisavet Mantzana.

References

1. Ioannides, M., Fellner, D., Georgopoulos, A., Hadjimitsis, D.: Digital heritage. In: 3rd International Conference dedicated on Digital Heritage. Cyprus (2010)
2. Gonizzi Barsanti, S., Guidi, G., De Luca, L.: Segmentation of 3D models for cultural heritage structural analysis - Some critical issues. 26th International CIPA Symposium, Volume IV-2/W2 (2017)
3. Frouzi, A.: Lagoon of Messolonghi – Aetoliko. Department of Environment of Aegean University, Mytilene (2009). (in Greek)
4. Saranti, F.: Ancient settlement around lagoons of the Messolonghi area. The evolution of the landscape through mythological and historical references and geoarchaeological data, Ephorate of Antiquities of Aetoloacarnania and Lefkada (2021). (in Greek)

5. European Commission: Natura 2000 https://ec.europa.eu/environment/nature/natura2000/index_en.htm
6. Diakakis, A.: The city of Messolonghi during the Revolution of 1821: war, economy, politics, everyday life. Crete University (2017). (in Greek)
7. Kolomvas, N.A.: The epic battle in Klissova (1997). (in Greek)
8. Chatzistamatis, S., et al.: Fusion of TLS and UAV photogrammetry data for post-earthquake 3d modeling of a cultural heritage church. Int. Arch. Photogramm. Remote Sens. Spatial Inf. Sci. XLII-3/W4, 143–150 (2018). https://doi.org/10.5194/isprs-archives-XLII-3-W4-143-2018
9. Ulvi, A.: Documentation, Three-Dimensional (3D), Modelling and visualization of cultural heritage by using Unmanned Aerial Vehicle (UAV) photogrammetry and terrestrial laser scanners. Int. J. Remote Sens. (2021). https://doi.org/10.1080/01431161.2020.1834164
10. DJI: https://www.dji.com/gr/matrice-300, https://www.dji.com/gr/zenmuse-p1
11. Zacharias, N., Malaperdas, G., Panagiotidis, V., Kouri. M.: Cultural Heritage and New Technologies. Papazisis (2022). (in Greek)
12. Chapman, H.: GPS (Global Positioning System), The Encyclopedia of Archaeological Sciences. UK (2018). https://doi.org/10.1002/9781119188230.saseas0268
13. Barnes, A.: Digital Photogrammetry. The Encyclopedia of Archaeological Sciences, UK (2018). https://doi.org/10.1002/9781119188230.saseas0191
14. Aber, J.S., Marzolff, I., Ries, J.B.: Photogrammetry. Small-Format Aerial Photography (2010). https://doi.org/10.1016/B978-0-444-53260-2.10003-1
15. Agisoft Metashape User Manual: Professional Edition, Version 1.8. Agisoft LLC (2022). https://www.agisoft.com/downloads/installer/
16. Panagiotidis, V.: Imprints of Places, Virtual and Augmented Reality, Internet Applications for Culture in Zacharias Prefecture (ed.) Cultural Heritage and New Technologies. PAPAZISI Publications, Athens (2022). (in Greek)
17. Panagiotidis, V., Zacharias, N.: Digital Mystras: An approach towards understanding the use of an archaeological space. 2nd International Conference on Global Issues of Environment & Culture, Scientific Culture, Vol. 8, No. 3, pp. 85–99 (2022)
18. Panagiotidis, V., Zacharias N.: Digitizing Mystras: The Palace Complex, 2nd Transdisciplinary Multispectral Modeling and Cooperation for the Preservation of Cultural Heritage, Athens 13–15 (December 2021)

Digital Heritage a Holistic Approach

Crowdsourcing for 3D Digital Modelling: Ioannina City-Chairedin Pasha Sarai Case Study

Athina Chroni[1(✉)], Andreas Georgopoulos[2], and Pavlos-Stylianos Megalooikonomou[3]

[1] Hellenic Ministry of Education, Religious Affairs and Sports, Postdoctoral Research Associate-National Technical University of Athens, 20, Paramithias street, 10435 Athens, Greece
athina.chroni@gmail.com

[2] Laboratory of Photogrammetry, National Technical University of Athens, 9, Iroon Polytechniou street, 15780 Athens, Greece
drag@central.ntua.gr

[3] School of Applied Mathematical and Physical Sciences, National Technical University of Athens, 8, Granikou street, 10435 Athens, Greece
pmegalo@gmail.com

Abstract. Nowadays, billions of photographs are available on the internet, under an open-access/open-data status, thus forming the largest and most diverse collection of optical data ever assembled. These images can be easily recovered, and digitally processed for the photogrammetric restoration of monuments, partly or completely destroyed, thus rendering clear the effective contribution of crowdsourcing under the perspective of restoring our cultural past.

This is the case of the lost landmark of Chairedin Pasha Sarai in Ioannina city, Greece: the extensive scientific research on the building complex's location, form and dimensions aiming to the respective 3D digital model design and development, has been further creatively supported and supplemented by downloading from the internet and making use of several photographs depicting different aspects of the building, at various chronological periods, before its final complete destruction, thus allowing the visual 3D digital restoration of the landmark, as well as its interaction with the surrounding urban web and its successive alterations.

In this context, the crowdsourcing dimension might be considered as a basic element, a catalyst, for the restoration of cultural heritage, while the active participation of society in matters of culture, as is the contribution in monuments' documentation procedure, awakens the collective consciousness in the direction of the protection, preservation and highlighting of cultural heritage.

Keywords: Crowdsourcing · Cultural Heritage · Documentation · Digitization · GIS · Photogrammetry · 3D Modelling · Open Sources · Ioannina

1 Introduction

At the beginning of the 19th century urban lifestyle and urban architecture in Epirus reach full maturity. The architectural forms of the buildings' shells typologically and morphologically represent affinity and continuity with primary forms that developed in the Greek

A. Moropoulou et al. (Eds.): TMM_CH 2023, CCIS 1889, pp. 157–170, 2023.
https://doi.org/10.1007/978-3-031-42300-0_14

area during antiquity, as well as during the Byzantine and the Post-Byzantine/Ottoman periods. The afore-mentioned apply both to residence, involving the enclosed space of building complexes' "islets", and its correlation to the urban web, as well as to architectural ledges, openings to the street and the complexity and quality of semi-outdoor spaces. Moreover, the interior decoration does not lack eastern influences, originating, mainly, from Constantinople [15].

At the same time, the residence, as well as building shells of different uses, appears with a completely symmetrical and geometric organization of the constructed shell and its individual elements, such as openings or stairs, for example. All the afore-mentioned as resulted from the commercial contacts developed by long distance trade combined with the context of a general modernization trend of the Ottoman Empire [15], as expressed with the *Tanzimat Reforms,*[1] dating in the years 1839-1876, which will be the catalyst for the urban texture, and the reconfiguration of the cities across the Ottoman Empire, thus rendering the urban features more compatible with the ones of the modern cities of the western world [5].

In particular, Ioannina, a city of increased local importance, had been kept away from the great social, ideological and artistic movements that restructured the West in the period 1500-1900: the town is characterized by a traditional urban planning and structure although having also suffered, to a limited extent, the state modernization trends of the late Ottoman period, as afore-mentioned, especially after fires or road constructions. However, the defensive function of the urban space and the related organization in a closed internal layout are not completely lost. Since the composition of the population is multicultural (Christians, Muslims, Jews), the respective ethno[2]-religious groups of the urban area maintain the autonomous community organization, i.e., the units-neighbourhoods (*mahallades*) [15].

2 Selection of Chairedin Pasha Sarai Landmark-Reasoning

2.1 The Urban Web and Fabric of Ioannina in the 18th-19th c

In the central part of the city, functions are organized according to homogeneous activities, a fact which reflects the different "islets" of professionals (*guilds*). Thus, the built space acquires an organicity with variety in the relationship shell/street, as well as in the hierarchy of public/semi-public/private spaces; also, familiar combinations of volumes and shells arise. After all, the residence typically follows tried-and-tested standards, shaped by a long-term process of the needs of the extended type of family. [14, 15, 26] In this context, different morphological types of housing are developed; according to Loukakis; [26, 28] these typological differences are linked to the social class of their owners:

- The *folk* housing shells, which are stone-built on the ground floor and have a lightweight mixed construction wall, i.e., the *chiatma,* [18] on the first floor, when they do not border foreign properties. [15, 26]

[1] *Tanzimāt*, lit. 'Reorganization': a period of reform in the Ottoman Empire that began with the Gülhane Hatt-ı Şerif in 1839 and ended with the First Constitutional Era in 1876. [13]

[2] If we might call it so.

- The *household* houses are of the same construction as the *folk* houses, but they have, additionally, various decorative elements, such as arched lintels, for example. [15, 26]
- The *mansions* are built on large plots, with high perimetric walls enclosing the plot and imposing entrance gates. On the first level, i.e., the ground floor, they usually have vaulted spaces and arches to support the floor of the upper level which is accessed via an impressive double stone staircase, giving a monumental style to the facade of the building shell. [15, 26]

2.2 Chairedin Pasha Sarai

Glimpses of collective memory as invisible cracks in the modern urban fabric, formed the starting point for the research and deconstruction of the cultural palimpsest of the city of Ioannina. *Chairedin Pasha Sarai*, later on, *Ioannidis Mansion*, a contemporary urban legend, constituted until the second half of the 20th century one of the most characteristic landmarks of the city (Fig. 1).

adida
IASIS Postdoctoral Research Project.
School of Rural, Surveying and Geoinformatics Engineering-National Technical University of Athens.
Designed and developed by Athina Chroni. Supervised by Andreas Georgopoulos.

Fig. 1. Upper part of image: Chairedin Pasha Sarai in in the 1940s, before its destruction, in three photographs by Angelos Kalogeridis, [30] Lower part of image: Chairedin Pasha Sarai in the 2010s, after its destruction, in three photographs by Pavlos-Stylianos Megalooikonomou. [Source: Pavlos-Stylianos Megalooikonomou private collection] Lower part, middle photograph: detail from the preserved external entrance gate to the property, still surviving, in front of the modern multi-storey building with the glass façade. On the façade of the upper part of the entrance gate the stone relief depicts in relief the year 1263 A.H.[3]=1847 AD.

[3] *Anno Hegirae*: The year in which Muhammad, the Prophet of Islam, emigrated from Mecca to Medina, 622 CE. [1]

The Sarai/Mansion was an impressive building, located at the junction of the contemporary streets named Michael Angelou and Charilaou Trikoupi; it belonged to Chairedin Pasha, a descendant of Aslan Pasha. It is estimated that it was built around 1840, replacing an older building that had been destroyed in 1820, when the city had been set on fire in August of that year. Its basic characteristic feature was the wooden "bridge" that was expanded over Michael Angelou Street connecting the building with the opposite side, where the second garden of the mansion. The "bridge" was essentially a room, made of wood, with many elongated, arched, stained-glass windows, from where the women of the house had the chance to watch, unseen, the street. On the ground floor of the mansion the warehouses and on the first floor the main rooms were located. The stone double staircase was right on the axis of symmetry and ended in the center of the large room (*krevata*) overlooking the lush garden. A few years after the Liberation and the withdrawal of the Ottomans, the mansion passed to the ownership of Ioannidis family in 1923 [3].

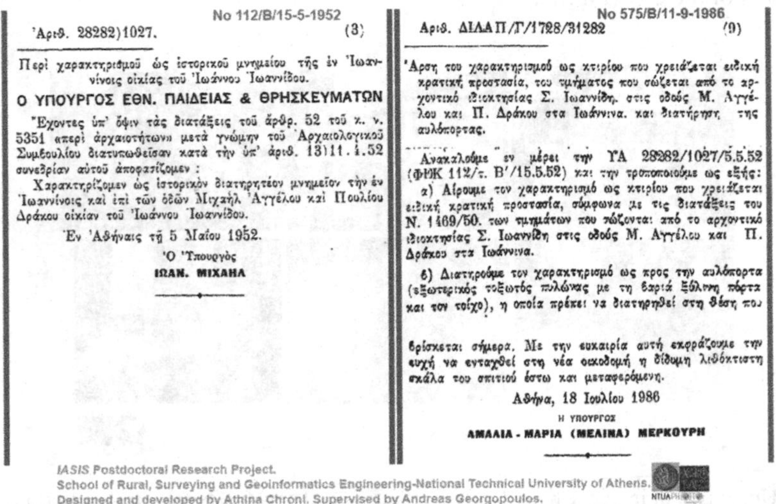

No 112/B/15-5-1952

'Αριθ. 28282)1027. (3)

Περὶ χαρακτηρισμοῦ ὡς ἱστορικοῦ μνημείου τῆς ἐν Ἰωαννίνοις οἰκίας τοῦ Ἰωάννου Ἰωαννίδου.

ΟΙ ΥΠΟΥΡΓΟΣ ΕΘΝ. ΠΑΙΔΕΙΑΣ & ΘΡΗΣΚΕΥΜΑΤΩΝ

Ἔχοντες ὑπ' ὄψιν τὰς διατάξεις τοῦ ἄρθρ. 52 τοῦ κ. ν. 5351 «περὶ ἀρχαιοτήτων» μετὰ γνώμην τοῦ Ἀρχαιολογικοῦ Συμβουλίου διατυπωθεῖσαν κατὰ τὴν ὑπ' ἀριθ. 13)11.4.52 συνεδρίαν αὐτοῦ ἀποφασίζομεν:

Χαρακτηρίζομεν ὡς ἱστορικὸν διατηρητέον μνημεῖον τὴν ἐν Ἰωαννίνοις καὶ ἐπὶ τῶν ὁδῶν Μιχαὴλ Ἀγγέλου καὶ Πουλίου Δράκου οἰκίαν τοῦ Ἰωάννου Ἰωαννίδου.

Ἐν Ἀθήναις τῇ 5 Μαΐου 1952.

Ὁ Ὑπουργὸς
ΙΩΑΝ. ΜΙΧΑΗΛ

No 575/B/11-9-1986

Αριθ. ΔΙΛΑΠ/Γ/1728/31282 (9)

Άρση του χαρακτηρισμού ως κτιρίου που χρειάζεται ειδική κρατική προστασία, του τμήματος που σώζεται από το αρχοντικό ιδιοκτησίας Σ. Ιωαννίδη στις οδούς Μ. Αγγέλου και Π. Δράκου στα Ιωάννινα, και διατήρηση της αυλόπορτας.

Ανακαλούμε εν μέρει την ΥΑ 28282/1027/5.5.52 (ΦΕΚ 112/τ. Β'/15.5.52) και την τροποποιούμε ως εξής:

α) Αίρουμε τον χαρακτηρισμό ως κτιρίου που χρειάζεται ειδική κρατική προστασία, σύμφωνα με τις διατάξεις του Ν. 1469/50, των τμημάτων που σώζονται από το αρχοντικό ιδιοκτησίας Σ. Ιωαννίδη στις οδούς Μ. Αγγέλου και Π. Δράκου στα Ιωάννινα.

β) Διατηρούμε τον χαρακτηρισμό ως προς την αυλόπορτα (εξωτερικός τοξωτός πυλώνας με τη βαριά ξύλινη πόρτα και τον τοίχο), η οποία πρέπει να διατηρηθεί στη θέση που βρίσκεται σήμερα. Με την ευκαιρία αυτή εκφράζουμε την ευχή να ενταχθεί στη νέα οικοδομή η δίδυμη λιθόκτιστη σκάλα του σπιτιού έστω και μεταφερόμενη.

Αθήνα, 18 Ιουλίου 1986

Η ΥΠΟΥΡΓΟΣ
ΑΜΑΛΙΑ - ΜΑΡΙΑ (ΜΕΛΙΝΑ) ΜΕΡΚΟΥΡΗ

IASIS Postdoctoral Research Project.
School of Rural, Surveying and Geoinformatics Engineering-National Technical University of Athens.
Designed and developed by Athina Chroni. Supervised by Andreas Georgopoulos.
NTUA

Fig. 2. Left: Screenshot from the Hellenic Government Gazette No 112/B/15-5-1952, p. 892, concerning Chairedin Pasha Sarai/Ioannidis mansion as a *listed monument*. Right: Screenshots from the Hellenic Government Gazette No 575/B/11-9-1986, pp. 5535-5536 concerning the landmark's declassification as a *listed monument*. [35, 36]

In 1952 it is characterized as a listed monument.[4] [5] In the 1960s, the Society for Epirotic Studies was housed in the mansion for some years. Afterwards, the mansion was turned into a youth hostel. Towards the end of its life, it was the residence of two or three families, as well as the laboratories of an advertising company. In 1968, footage

[4] Thus, constituting the second mansion of the city to be listed, after *Missios Mansion* on Asopiou street, also characterized as a listed monument.

[5] Classification as a listed monument according to the Hellenic Government Gazette No 112/B/15-5-1952, p. 892. [35]

of the movie "The lady and the tramp", was shot here. By the 1970s it was already in an advanced state of ruins, requiring costly repairs. [3]

In the afternoon of April 22, 1975, Ioannidis Mansion, was completely destroyed by fire. In 1986 it was declassified,[6] thus no longer being in a protected status as a listed monument. The classification of the listed monument remains only for the imposing external arched portal with the heavy wooden door, one of the two[7] architectural elements that escaped the fire and were integrated in the multi-storey building constructed in the 1990s, a business premises building with a glass facade. [3] (Fig. 2)

3 Methodology

GIS technology was applied in the context of the combined study of various geospatial data, [7] such as maps, urban plans, topographical diagrams, architectural plan views and remote sensing imagery[8] [9] of different dates, [6, 8, 12] in order:

- To achieve flexible management of said data through their organization at different levels of information.
- To enable their comparative study.
- To check their degree of reliability.
- To detect the changes in the urban fabric of the city of Ioannina, ensuring a high degree of reliability.
- To locate, identify and digitize the points of interest and, consequently, attribute georeference and spatial identity to the cultural asset processed.
- To enable the extraction of quantitative data.
- Subsequently to develop an online database, by editing an attribute table for each digitized point. Depending on the documentation available, quantitative (coordinates, sizes), qualitative (chronology, typology, brief description) and visual (photographs, visual representations) data have been integrated in the attribute table of each digitized point.

In the next stage of work, and under a subtractive choice of approach, a 3D digital model of the landmark processed,has been designed and developed [19, 20, 34].

3.1 Location and Size of the Lost Landmark

All the afore-mentioned data integrated in the GIS environment, have formed the springboard for locating the accurate site of the lost landmark and, also, for determining its exact size, in horizontal and vertical dimension. (Fig. 3)

6 According to the following Hellenic State act: Declassification as a listed monument according to the Hellenic Government Gazette No 575/B/11-9-1986, p. 5535-5536. [36]

7 The other one being the three-leafed stone staircase that gave access to the first floor of the house.

8 Aerial photographs and satellite imagery.

9 Geospatial data provided by the Directorate of Environment and Urban Planning-Municipality of Ioannina, [16] the Hellenic Military Geographical Service, [23] the former Hellenic Ministry of Environment, Urban Planning and Public Works of Greece, nowadays the Hellenic Ministry of Environment and Energy, [24] the Hellenic Cadastre [22] and the British School at Athens [2] contributing related data for free.

IASIS Postdoctoral Research Project.
School of Rural, Surveying and Geoinformatics Engineering-National Technical University of Athens.
Chairedin Pasha Sarai.
Designed and developed by Athina Chroni. Supervised by Andreas Georgopoulos.
NTUA

Fig. 3. Screenshots from the GIS and the 3D digital model developed for *IASIS* Postdoctoral Research Project. Starting from top: 1st image: air photograph, BSA No F30-4007, scale 1:26.000, date 18/08/1944. 2nd image: Layering of the Hellenic Cadastre ortho imagery, res. 50X50 cm, year 2015, with the air photograph, BSA No F30-4007. 3rd image: Layering of the air photograph, BSA No F30-4007 with Chairedin Pasha Sarai ground floor architectural plan view, by Loukakis P., 1960. 4th image: Layering of the Hellenic Cadastre ortho imagery, res. 50X50 cm, year 2015, with the air photograph, BSA No F30-4007 and Chairedin Pasha Sarai 3D digital model, designed and developed by Athina Chroni. ©For the air photograph: The British School at Athens. [2] ©For the ortho imagery: Hellenic Cadastre [22]

For the georeferencing of all the geospatial data, the ortho-image of the wider Ioannina area has been used. It has been provided free of charge by the Hellenic Cadastre [22] under a license of exclusive use in the framework of the specific Postdoctoral Research Project implementation. It consists of 132 sub-ortho-images, type LS025, dating in 2015, at a resolution of 50x50 cm, georeferenced at EPSG:2100-GGRS87/Greek Grid-Projected georeference system (Fig. 4).

IASIS Postdoctoral Research Project.
School of Rural, Surveying and Geoinformatics Engineering-National Technical University of Athens.
Chairedin Pasha Sarai.
Designed and developed by Athina Chroni. Supervised by Andreas Georgopoulos.

Fig. 4. Detail of Fig. 3. Screenshot from the GIS and the 3D digital model developed for *IASIS* Postdoctoral Research Project. Layering of the Hellenic Cadastre ortho imagery, res. 50X50 cm, year 2015, with the air photograph, BSA No F30-4007, scale 1:26.000, date 18/08/1944, and Chairedin Pasha Sarai 3D digital model, designed and developed by Athina Chroni. ©For the air photograph: The British School at Athens. [2] ©For the ortho imagery: Hellenic Cadastre [22]

The integration of the air photographs of the years 1943-1944, provided by the British School at Athens, [2] in the GIS renders more effective the procedure of photo interpreting the area of interest, given that, at this particular time, the urban construction remains limited.

More precisely, the following data have been integrated and processed in the GIS:

- Italo Bernasconi's city plan, dated in 1895, scaled 1:2000, proposing a new city planning. The original map is lost: an exact copy of it dated in 1904, according to an official note in the Ottoman language, certified with signatures and stamps, in the Greek and the Ottoman language, had been confirmed as accurately depicting the current state of the city by the Municipal Committee of the Hellenic State in 1916. [37]
- A map by unknown author, dated in 1905-1908, scaled 1:2000, in the French language, based on the afore-mentioned Bernasconi map of the city. [37]

- Melirrytos (& Christides[10]) urban plan, dated in 1916-1918, scaled 1:1000, in the Greek language, based on the afore-mentioned Bernasconi map of the city. [16]
- Hébrard's draft map, dated in 1919, scaled 1:4000, in the French language, confirming the road network of the afore-mentioned Bernasconi map of the city. [37]
- Air photographs of the years 1943 and 1944,[11] 1945,[12] 1960 and 1962.[13]
- Orthophotos of the years 1945 and 2015 provided by the Hellenic Cadastre. [22]
- Chairedin Pasha Sarai architectural plan view of the year 1960, by P. Loukakis. [28]

3.2 3D Digital Model of the Lost Landmark

The 3D digital representation of the Sarai/Mansion has formed the next step in the research procedure: it has been designed and developed by making use of the data extracted after the related processing in the GIS, already afore-mentioned. Under this perspective, composites of image products as derived from the GIS' multiple layers activation visibility,[14] have formed the background image for developing the respective landmark's 3D digital model. The volume of the 3D digital model has been chosen to be rendered in an abstractive way, focusing on its basic architectural elements. [7]

Final challenge, the exterior surfaces of the building, as well as of the perimetric wall enclosure that bounded both parts of the land property on either side of the current Michael Angelou street: under this perspective, photographs of the building complex, downloaded from the web, have been applied on the 3D digital model already developed.

In a final stage of work of the 3D digital modelling procedure, a virtual tour of the 3D-digital model has been implemented by producing an mp.4 digital file under the perspective of offering a more vivid experience to the visitor of the related website, developed as a *digital portal* for this research study, as well as for the related online virtual museum also designed and developed (Fig. 5).

---

[10] Christides D. cooperated in the first year of the urban plan's designing project, i.e., in 1916. Melirrytos P. was the one to fulfill the specific project for the Municipality of Ioannina. [37]

[11] Provided by the British School at Athens. [2]

[12] Provided by the Hellenic Military Geographical Service. [23]

[13] Provided by the former Ministry of the Environment, Urban Planning and Public Works of Greece, nowadays the Hellenic Ministry of Environment and Energy. [24]

[14] Keeping always visible a GIS layer representing the modern city, under the intention of rendering possible a continuous observation of the hypothetic interaction of the building complex with the modern urban web and, also, identifying the alterations of the urban texture. At the same time, a higher degree of perception of the aerial view of the city is achieved from the point of view of end users.

Fig. 5. Layering of Chairedin Pasha Sarai 3D digital model, designed and developed by Athina Chroni, on the BSA No F30-4007 air photograph, scale 1:26.000, date 18/08/1944. ©For the air photograph: The British School at Athens. [2]

4 Crowdsourcing for the 3D digital modelling

In the context of researching and crosschecking the documentation required, such as literary sources and visual data, the contribution of web-crowdsourcing and free-data[15] turned out to be valuable, given that the number of digital images that are freely available online today has reached unprecedented levels [7, 11, 27]

Crowdsourcing, a particularly rising trend nowadays, has proven to be highly effective in cases of widespread disasters, such as the case of the bridge of Plaka, in Epirus, Greece, destroyed by the rapid flow of the river waters combined with following heavy rains in the midst of severe weather conditions in the year 2015 [29] as well as the case of the National Museum of Brazil, completely destroyed by fire in the year 2018. [9] As part of the effort to collect data for the documentation of the destroyed bridge, in the first case, and the destroyed museum exhibits, in the second case, the scientific teams turn to the crowd and appeal to the public to send photos from their private collections. It is, perhaps, the first cases that the significant and decisive role of crowdsourcing in the field of culture and, in particular, in documentation, is highlighted with exceptional clarity. [9, 29]

Nowadays, there are billions of photos on the web, [11] making it the largest and most diverse collection of optical documentation ever assembled. These images can be recovered and digitally processed with software that has the ability to utilize this huge volume of imagery for the photogrammetric restoration of historical monuments. (Fig. 6)

[15] In the context of user licenses as specified on the respective websites where the related data are posted, respecting the regulatory framework within which these are provided by government bodies, private institutions or individuals [10].

In recent years, computer vision techniques such as *structure from motion* and *image-based reconstruction* have gained the lead in the field of computer graphics, known as *image-based modeling* [7, 27, 33].

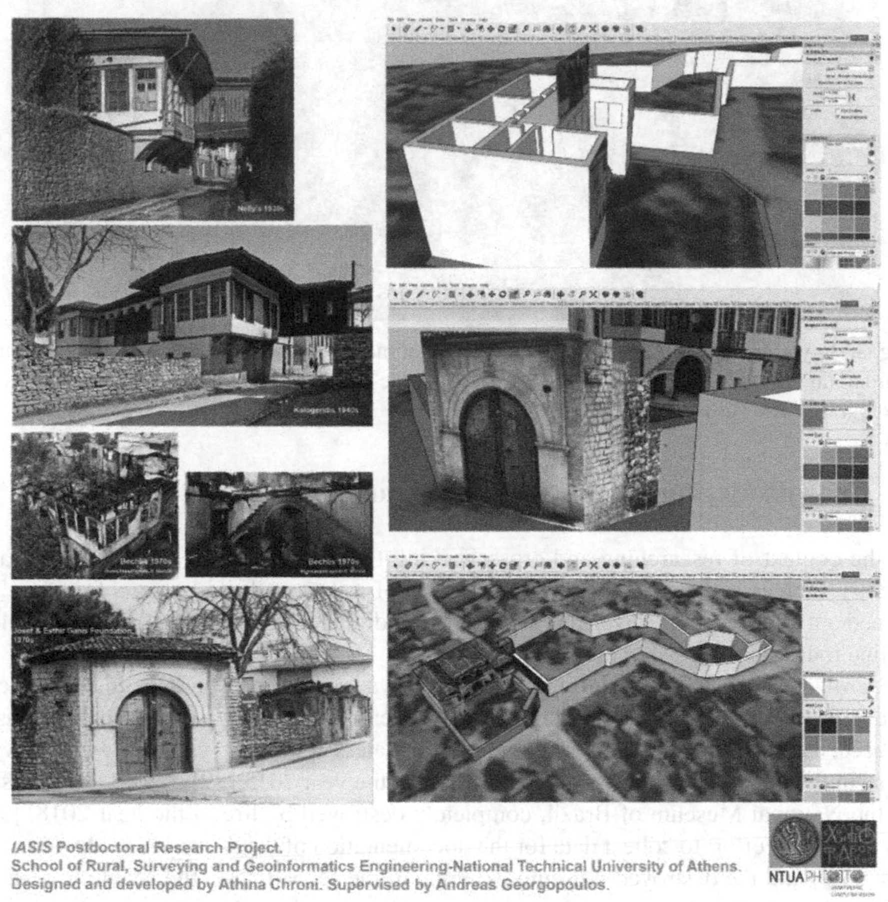

Kalogeridis, 1940s
IASIS Postdoctoral Research Project.
School of Rural, Surveying and Geoinformatics Engineering-National Technical University of Athens.
Designed and developed by Athina Chroni. Supervised by Andreas Georgopoulos.
NTUA

Fig. 6. Optical data documentation for Chairedin Pasha Sarai and related 3D digital modelling. Left, from top: 1st photograph by Nelly's, 1930s. 2nd photograph by Kalogeridis, 1940s. 3rd photograph by Bechlis, 1970s. 4th photograph by unknown photographer,[16] 1970s. Right: Screenshots from the successive work stages of the 3D digital modelling procedure of the lost landmark, designed and developed by Athina Chroni.

Considering the afore-mentioned, it becomes clear the creative contribution of crowdsourcing to the restoration of destroyed monuments and, therefore, to the reconstruction of the cultural past. The possibilities of photogrammetry can contribute decisively to the restoration of the form of monuments that have suffered large-scale disasters, and, at the same time, they function as an occasion for the activation of society in the

16 Source: Josef & Esthir Ganis Foundation. [25]

direction of providing relevant documentation and participating in cultural processes. (Fig. 7) A typical example is the photogrammetric restoration of Buddha statues in Afghanistan [21].

Fig. 7. Screenshot from Chairedin Pasha Sarai 3D digital model. Detail of the entrance gate. 3D digital model designed and developed, by Athina Chroni.

The imprint of time sometimes imposes terrible consequences on cultural heritage; as a result, it often becomes necessary to not only recover the memory of original features of historical buildings, urban and landscape environments, but also understand their likely evolution. [7, 32] Under this reasoning, the horizons of the 3D digital restoration of the cultural past become broadened, if we integrate the dimension of time, thus acquiring the 4th dimension, i.e., the evolution of the processed/represented cultural asset over time, or even the 5th dimension, if we decide to integrate additional semantic metadata information, to the original 3D digital model, thus acquiring a 4D and 5D digital model respectively. [7, 17]

5 Conclusion

Ioannina is a city with a high dynamic; it constitutes a neuralgic node for the wider region, both in the past as well as in contemporary times. Nowadays, a large part of the population, which is related to the University of Ioannina, i.e., students and staff, is constantly changing, having, in fact, noted an increase, due to the creation of new Schools already, such as the School of Architecture of Ioannina, founded in 2019. At the same time, there is an increasing trend in the city's commercial activity, as well as in tourism. The afore-mentioned cause pressing needs for short-term or long-term housing, an element that entails an increased risk for the historical buildings, still existing, which, due to their size and layout, do not meet current needs, while at the same time they occupy high-value plots within the urban web. Although the legislative framework seems to protect their preservation, it is not always effective: typical case the one of Chairedin Pasha Sarai with its successive initial designation, in 1952, as a listed monument and, then, its declassification in 1986; final act, its complete demolition, in order to construct a multi-storey commercial building.

Nowadays, achieving good practice and sustainable workflows for the management of heterogeneous cultural heritage data has been made possible by the exponential growth of digital tools for receiving/acquiring, registering and managing data, tools necessary at every work stage for monitoring, protecting and preserving cultural assets. [31] In this context, *crowdsourcing* is considered as an essential component for an integrated management of cultural heritage, i.e., monitoring-protecting-preserving-restoring-highlighting, taking into consideration that the active participation of society in a classified model of cultural assets management, via contribution to documentation issues as in this case, awakens the *collective consciousness* in the direction of cultural heritage protection and preservation, strengthening at the same time the notion of *collective memory*. The active participation of society, more precisely, of the local community in matters of culture, constitutes another rising trend of our times, which is gaining more and more ground, as its creative contribution to the preservation of cultural heritage is finally recognized, a fact which, in turn, might form an element for the sustainable development of a place. [9]

In fact, under this perspective, the *Buildings at risk* section, already developed and posted at *IASIS* website, [4] is aiming to activate and accelerate the registration-documentation-monitoring of historic buildings still existing, constituting a dynamic effort for the protection and "survival" of the said cultural heritage assets and awakening the collective consciousness in the direction of cultural heritage protection.

Crowdsourcing open call, *Buildings at risk* cultural interactive procedure, *open-data/open-access* mentality, *educational seminars* at different levels of the educational sector, *open workshops* for people of various backgrounds are practices applied in the framework of *IASIS* Postdoctoral Research Project for young people, community and non-traditional audiences' engagement, such as elder people or refugees hosted in the city. The society's active involvement in the procedure contributes in raising the feeling of "belonging", "sharing", "feeling useful and creative".

Acknowledgements. *Chairedin Pasha Sarai* case study has been implemented by Athina Chroni, Dr. Archaeologist, and supervised by Professor Andreas Georgopoulos, Laboratory of Photogrammetry-National Technical University of Athens, in the framework of the related Postdoctoral Research Project titled *IASIS*-National Technical University of Athens.

References

1. Britannica. https://www.britannica.com/topic/anno-Hegirae, last accessed 15 November 2023
2. British School at Athens-BSA, https://www.bsa.ac.uk/, last accessed 15 November 2023
3. Chroni A.: *IASIS* Postdoctoral Research Project, https://athinachroni.wixsite.com/my-site-1/chairentin-pasha-mansion, last accessed 15 November 2023
4. Chroni, A.: *IASIS* Postdoctoral Research Project, Buildings at risk. https://athinachroni.wixsite.com/my-site-1/buildings-at-risk

5. Chroni, A., Georgopoulos, A.: Reflections of the Tanzimat Reforms on the urban fabric. In: Archaeological Institute of America 124th AIA-SCS Joint Annual Meeting, January 5-8. New Orleans, Louisiana, U.S.A. (2023)
6. Chroni, A., Georgopoulos, A.: Perceptions of cultural heritage in post-covid times: *IASIS* integrated CH management system case study. 28th Annual Meeting of the European Association of Archaeologists-[RE]INTEGRATION. Budapest, Hungary (2022)
7. Chroni, A., Georgopoulos, A.: *IASIS*-Integrated Cultural Heritage Management System: A Christian Monastery, a Muslim Mosque and a Contemporary State Administrative Building, Ioannina: Digital Approach. In: Moropoulou, A., Georgopoulos, A., Doulamis, A., Ioannides, M., Ronchi, A. (eds.) Trandisciplinary Multispectral Modelling and Cooperation for the Preservation of Cultural Heritage. TMM_CH 2021. Communications in Computer and Information Science, vol 1574. Springer, Cham (2022). https://doi.org/10.1007/978-3-031-20253-7_8
8. Chroni, A., Georgopoulos, A.: Integrated Cultural Heritage Management: 3-D Digital rendering and web data base development for part of the city of Ioannina during the Ottoman period. 26th EAA Annual Meeting in Budapest. European Association of Archaeologists, Budapest, Hungary (2020)
9. Chroni, A.: *Syros Virtual Museum*: the tangible and the intangible element-Integrated cultural heritage management and new museological approaches-Standard data models and controlled vocabularies for cultural goods documentation. Master's Thesis. University of Piraeus-School of Information and Communication Technologies-Department of Informatics, Athens (2019)
10. Chroni, A.: Cultural Heritage Digitization & Copyright Issues. Proceedings of the 7th International Euro-Mediterranean Conference-EuroMed 2018 on Digital Heritage: Progress in Cultural Heritage. Documentation, Preservation, and Protection, October 29–November 3, 2018, Nicosia, Cyprus, (2018) Editors M. Ioannides et al., © Springer Nature Switzerland AG, ISSN 0302-9743, ISSN 1611-3349 (electronic), Lecture Notes in Computer Science ISBN 978-3-030-01761-3, ISBN 978-3-030-01762-0 (eBook) (2018)
11. Chroni, A.: Postcards-Contribution in the research of our cultural past. Study area: Ioannina city. Proceedings of the 2nd Panhellenic Conference on Digitization of Cultural Heritage-Euromed 2017. Volos, Greece (2017)
12. Chroni, A.: Applications of Photointerpretation and Remote Sensing in Archaeology. Doctoral Thesis, National Technical University of Athens, School of Rural and Surveying Engineering, Department of Topography, Laboratory of Remote Sensing, Athens, Greece (2012)
13. Cleveland, W.-L., Bunton, M.: A history of the modern Middle East, 6th ed., Routledge-Taylor & Francis Group, New York-London, ISBN 978-0-8133-4833-9 (2020)
14. Datsi, E.: Our esnaf, the reigned ones. Benaki Museum-Gavrielidis Publications, Athens (2006)
15. Dimitriadis, E.: The Vilayet of Ioannina during the 19th century. Kyriakidis Brothers Publishing House SA, Thessaloniki (1993)
16. Directorate of Environment and Urban Planning-Municipality of Ioannina, https://www.ioannina.gr/, last accessed 15 November 2023
17. Doulamis, A., et al.: 5D Modelling: An Efficient Approach For Creating Spatio-temporal Predictive 3d Maps Of Large-Scale Cultural Resources. ISPRS Annals of the Photogrammetry, Remote Sensing and Spatial Information Sciences, Volume II-5/W3, Taipei, Taiwan, pp. 61–68 (2015)
18. Filippides, D.: (Curator): Greek traditional architecture, Volumes 1–8. Melissa Publications, Athens (1991)
19. Georgopoulos, A.: Modern Technologies for Heritage Documentation. Proceedings of 1st International Conference on the Documentation of Natural and Cultural Heritage, Tehran, Iran (2018)

20. Georgopoulos, A.: Digital Technologies at the Service of Cultural Heritage: The Case of the Byzantine Churches of Troodos. Proceedings of the 1st Panhellenic Conference on Digitization of Cultural Heritage-Euromed 2015. Volos, Greece (2015)
21. Grün, A., Remondino, F., Zhang, L.I.: Photogrammetric reconstruction of the great buddha of Bamiyan, Afghanistan. Photogrammetric Record **19**(107) (2004)
22. Hellenic Cadastre, www.ktimatologio.gr, last accessed 15 November 2023
23. Hellenic Military Geographical Service-HMGS: https://www.gys.gr/, last accessed 15 November 2023
24. Hellenic Ministry of Environment and Energy, https://ypen.gov.gr/, last accessed 15 November 2023
25. Joseph and Esther Ganis Foundation. https://www.facebook.com/, last accessed 15 November 2023
26. Kanetakis, G.: The Castle: contribution to the urban planning history of Ioannina. Published by the Technical Chamber of Greece, Athens (1994)
27. Kyriakaki, G., et al.: 4D reconstruction of tangible cultural heritage objects from web-retrieved images. Int. J. Herit. Digi. Era **3**(2), 431–451 (2014)
28. Loukakis, P.: The Ioannite house. In: Michelis, PA: The Greek folk house. National Technical University of Athens-Chair of Architectural Morphology and Rhythmology, Teaching Papers 1. National Technical University of Athens Editions, Athens 194-228 (1960)
29. National Technical University of Athens Interdisciplinary Scientific Group: The bridge of Plaka: The NTUA scientific project for its restoration. Scientific Supervisor Golias Ioannis-Rector of NTUA. National Technical University of Athens, Athens (2018). ISBN 978-618-82612-4-2
30. Papastavros, A.: Ioannina. Olkos Publications/Rizarion Foundation, Athens (1996)
31. Pierdicca, R., Malinverni, E.S., Tassetti, A.N., Mancini, A., Bozzi, C.A., Clini, P., Nespeca, R.: Development of a GIS environment for archaeological multipurpose applications. The Fano Historic Centre, Aversa, Capri (2013)
32. Rodríguez-Gonzálvez, P., et al.: 4D reconstruction and visualization of cultural heritage: analyzing our legacy through time. The International Archives of the Photogrammetry, Remote Sensing and Spatial Information Sciences, Volume XLII-2/W3. Nafplio (2017)
33. Snavely, N., Seitz, S.M., Szeliski, R.: Modeling the world from Internet photo collections. Int. J. Comp. Vision **80**(2) (2008)
34. Stathopoulou, E.K., Georgopoulos, A., Panagiotopoulos, G., Kaliampakos, D.: 3D Visualisation of Lost Cultural Heritage Objects Using Crowdsourcing. The International Archives of the Photogrammetry, Remote Sensing and Spatial Information Sciences, Volume XL-5/W7, 2015 25th International CIPA Symposium 2015, 31 August – 04 September 2015. Taipei, Taiwan (2015)
35. The Hellenic Government Gazette No 112/B/15-5-1952, https://www.et.gr/SearchFek, last accessed 15 November 2023
36. The Hellenic Government Gazette No 575/B/11-9-1986, https://www.et.gr/SearchFek, last accessed 15 November 2023
37. Zygouris, T.: From Bernasconi to Hébrard-"Known" and Unknown urban maps of Ioannina. Municipality of Ioannina-Zosimaia Public Library of Ioannina, Ioannina (2019)

A Digital Cultural Landscape: Interpretations on Multisensory Projections

Eleni Maistrou, Konstantinos Moraitis, Yanis Maistros, Katerina Boulougoura, Amalia-Maria Konidi(✉), Karolina Moretti, and Margarita Skamantzari

National Technical University of Athens, Patision 42, 10682 Athens, Greece
boulougoura.k@gmail.com, amkonidi@gmail.com, kanel8car@yahoo.com

Abstract. InterArch is an ongoing research project, aiming at proposing a design of a site-based digital application, enhancing the cultural identity of archaeological sites. The city of Ancient Messene, considered as one of the most important archaeological sites in Greece is used as the research case study.

Digital technology is used to decisively vitalize interactive experience. Integrating the real-world environment with the endless realm of digital data facilitates the implementation of multisensory narratives in real time, engaging a multidimensional approach.

Non-linear narratives, both in terms of conceptual context and types of data are generated to highlight mnemonic and intangible references of the archaeological site. They thus reveal the complexity of ideological and imaginary frameworks and invigorate personal process of producing differentiated semantic interpretations and interrelations, in an extended number of possible multilingual and trans-cultural approaches.

This research proposes a design interactive process, in which visitors' physical presence on site, implementing GPS locators, is considered as a pivotal issue. Useful insight, concerning the way visitors engage and interact with their surroundings, may be positively applied in an analogous way, to similar archaeological sites.

Keywords: cultural heritage · digital data · landscape · archaeological sites · visitors' itineraries

1 Introduction

InterArch is a research project that aims at the design of a site-based digital application for archaeological visits and guided tours, supporting Virtual and Augmented Reality (VR, AR) technology. The proposal was designed by an NTUA research team, with the contribution of the Ephorate of Antiquities of Messenia, the Society of Messenian Archaeological Studies and the IT applications development company Diadrasis. The program is co-financed by the European Union and Greek national funds, through the Operational Program Competitiveness, Entrepreneurship and Innovation, under the call RESEARCH – CREATE – INNOVATE (project code: T2EΔK-01659). The case study of the research is the archaeological site of Ancient Messene, one of the most important archaeological sites in Greece where a unique landscape with monumental

A. Moropoulou et al. (Eds.): TMM_CH 2023, CCIS 1889, pp. 171–187, 2023.
https://doi.org/10.1007/978-3-031-42300-0_15

public buildings and structures of an ancient city have been revealed by the Society of Messinian Archaeological Studies in collaboration with the Ephorate of Antiquities of Messenia. Apart from the natural environment and the archaeological findings, the cultural value and the identity of the archaeological site is consisting not only of material elements, but also immaterial, intangible mnemonic references and more complex ideological frameworks. Digitized cultural content and data management using IT applications technologies, can emphasize the multiplicity of cultural interpretations (Fig. 1).

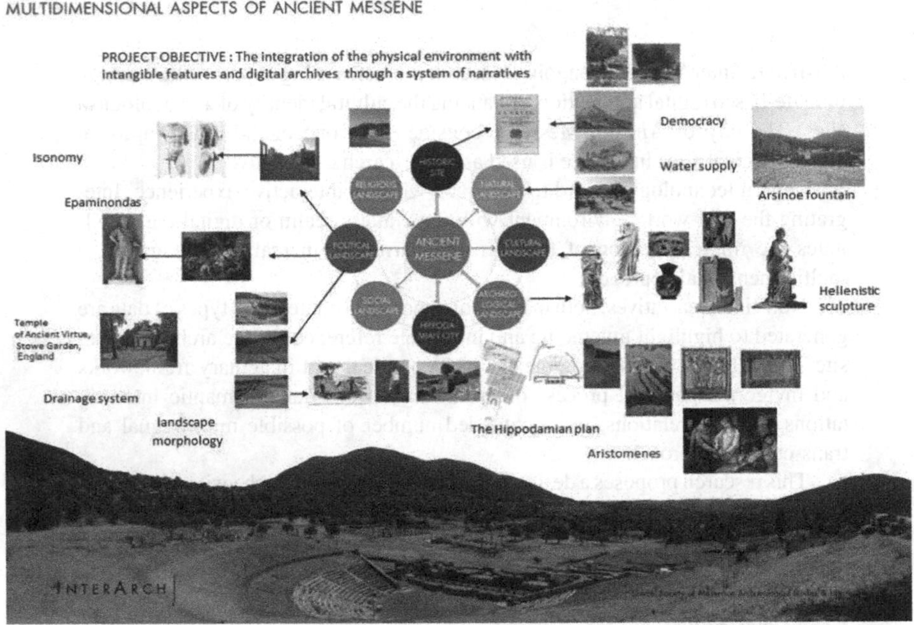

Fig. 1. Multidimensional aspects of Ancient Messene's cultural landscape.

Research Objective. The aim of the research is to enhance the real environment with the digital space of archaeological and cultural data, highlighting the way in which historical descriptions are presented and re-imprinted in the collective identity. Different data typologies such as oral speech, texts, drawings, sounds, photos, videos, are integrated within the spatial environment of the archaeological site. Furthermore, digital 3D modeling techniques combing image-based (photogrammetry) and laser scanning methods have been applied, providing additional data. Aligning with contemporary representational technologies, three dimensional recontractions of selected monuments, artifacts and landscape sceneries facilitate the integration of more sophisticated information, in specific locations, for the elaboration of multiple user scenarios and storytelling processes.

However, in-situ implementation of narrative associations using technologies like GPS locators, smartphones and augmented reality techniques should take into consideration the experience of physical presence. In order to explore ideas about the factors that affect the identity of such an expansive landscape, a vital field survey carried out. Visitors' walking itineraries throughout the archaeological site were recorded using GPS locators and a mobile application designed as part of the project by Diadrasis, so as to analyze the visitors' behavior in the open area. Spatial and temporal data, illustrate the ways in which visitors engage with archaeological finds, provide our project with a spatial assessment framework, useful for tracing the different instances through which historical and cultural descriptions could emerge. As visitors move around, interactions with the surroundings can indicate how the information may be linked to the archeological findings, providing narrative networks that emerge from the natural environment.

A characteristic feature of Ancient Messene is the configuration of the archaeological site in three distinct levels with great difference in altitude where visitors encounter clearly structured monuments or areas scattered with archaeological findings. This sort of site configuration generates different typologies in space, affecting visitors' physical wandering in actual place.

Site's specific typologies are:

- areas with perspective oversighted view where dynamic transitions can be proposed, both physically and cognitively.
- wide flat areas where there are many possible routes, so visitors' movement can be redefined constantly.
- highlighted spots that indicate a different scale of interest and perception compared to the broadness of archeological site (Fig. 2).

Fig. 2. Perspective views of the site (01–03), undefined areas (04, 05) and highlighted spots (06–08).

2 Materials and Methods

Field research concerning the archaeological site, was carried out between the 6th of July and the 6th of November 2021. The archaeological site was approached by selecting 20 monuments, the outlines of which were defined based on the visible excavated findings. These monuments were located both centrally and peripherally in relation to the archaeological site. The selection includes monuments of various sizes, which are more or less recognizable, such as the Ancient Theatre and the Asklepion Complex, but also the Sanctuary of Demeter and the Dioscuri. In addition, some of the monuments are typologically defined, while some others are not clearly outlined and seem randomly dispersed within the archaeological site, such as the Sanctuaries of the Agora and the cemeteries on the eastern side of the Asklepion. Archaeologists' open workplace was also selected, both as a possible point of interest and as a shading point.

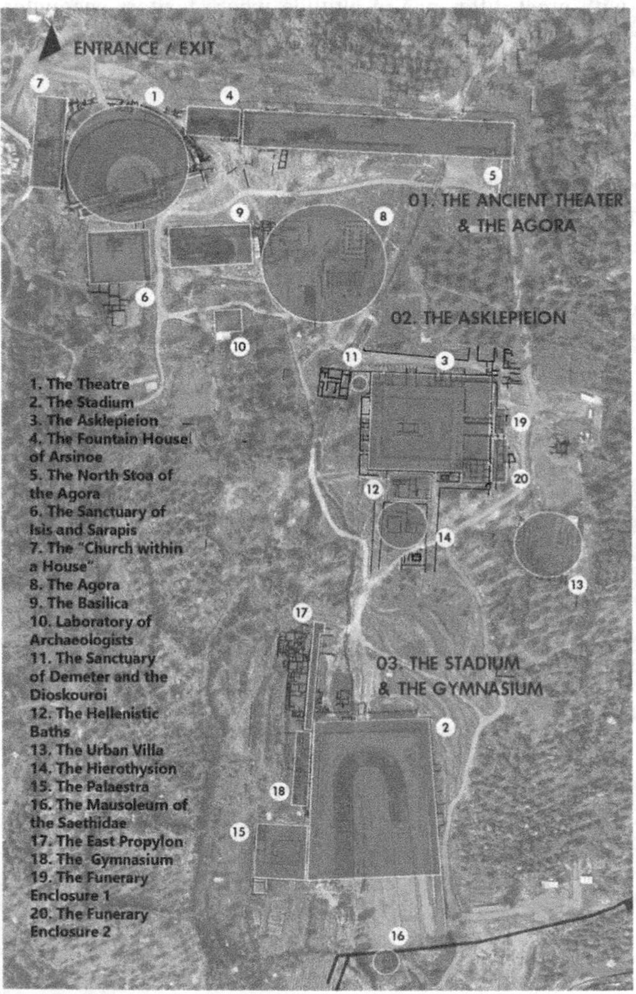

Fig. 3. Selected areas of interest – monuments (20) of Ancient Messene.

At this scale, the outlines are not defined spatially in an absolute way. Methodologically, extracting more precise data would require a more strictly defined correlation of the actual site and material remains with the visual access to them, at any given time and the level of conceptual completeness that the findings indicate for each monument. Therefore, the percentages and numbers reported in this survey just indicate trends of diffusion and presence in the site (Fig. 3).

The data collected involves several types of information. The application tracked the location of each visitor every 10 m. It also recorded the duration of time spent at each spot. In total, 235 paths were recorded and 144 of them were considered accurate, with no spatial discontinuities. Two different criteria were applied in order to distinguish the 144 routes, considered complete. Each visitor must be registered at the entrance of the archaeological site both at the beginning and at the end of each itinerary. In addition, it was checked that the points recorded were not more than 10 m apart.

The archaeological site is a particularly large area and has an altitude difference of 60 m from the upper to the lower level. Shaded areas are limited and consist mainly of existing trees with a resting area added. For these reasons, classification on seasonal criteria was initially considered necessary to investigate the impact of high temperature during hot summer days and the changes recorded on visitors' behavior, during daylight hours. Throughout the recording 78 of the archives retrieved, covered a time span of two months until the 31st of August and 66 archives covered a time span from September to the beginning of November (Fig. 4).

Fig. 4. Aspects of the archaeological site at different times of the year

Additionally, because of the inclination of the site and lengthwise setup of the archaeological findings, the visit trail is divided into two parallel routes with different directions and characteristics. The first one involves the transition across the archaeological site and the second one involves the uphill return towards the exit. The minimum latitude of each

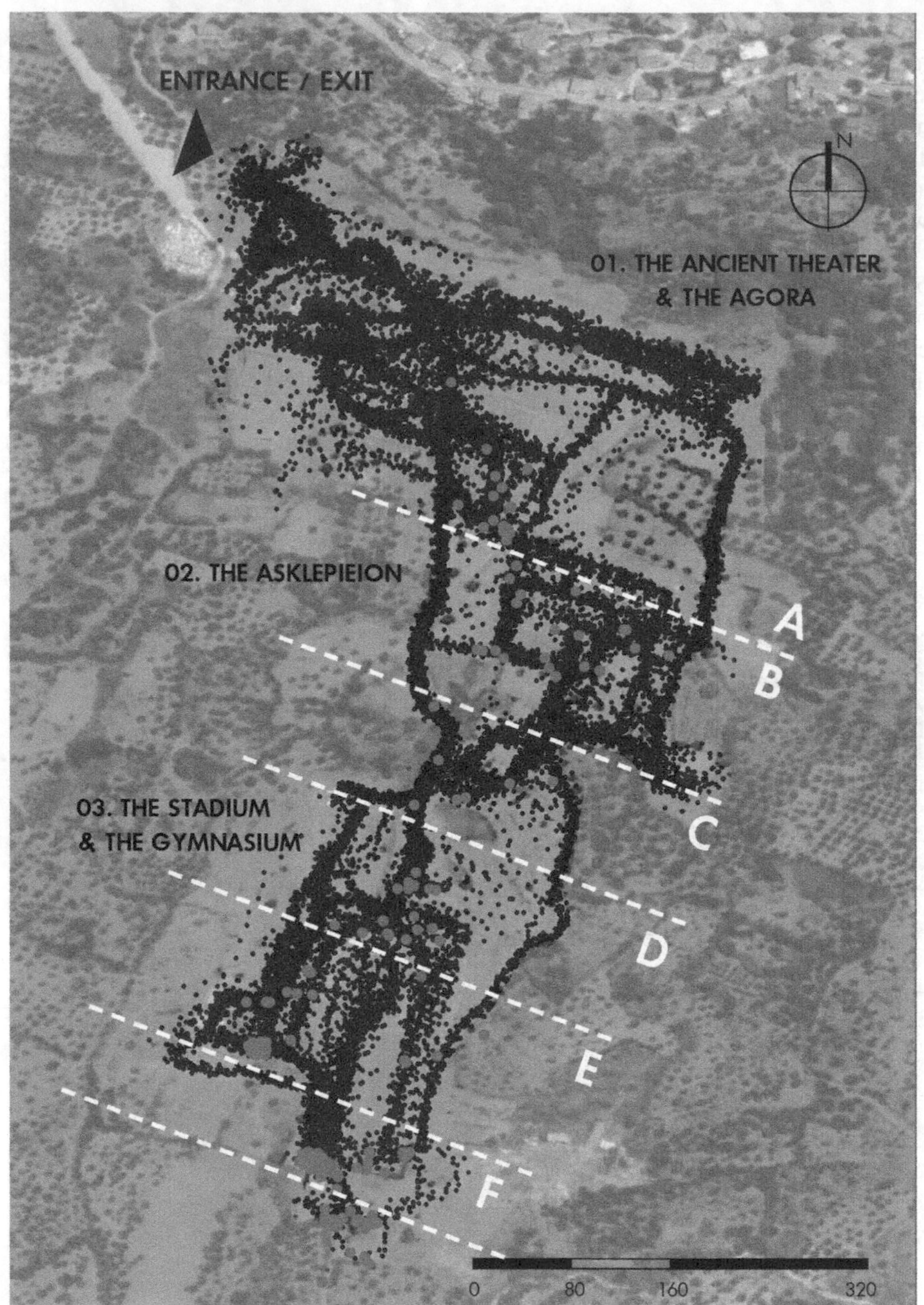

Fig. 5. Minimum latitude points of visitors' itineraries.

trail was identified, so as to indicate the furthest point reached by each visitor from the gate entrance. Each route was divided into two parts, encompassing both transitions and returns. It is already obvious that groups of visitors finish their route without reaching the most remote levels of the site (Fig. 5).

3 Results and Discussion

Identifying Most Visited Place. Initially, visits to the 20 sites surveyed were accounted without taking into consideration as a double presence the cases where a visitor crossed them on the way of transition or during their return.

The largest and most distinctly structured monuments were the most visited areas. The Theater attracted the 100% of the visitors, while the Northern Stoa of the Agora, the Asklepion and the Stadium around an 80% of visitors. The Agora, although not strictly outlined holds over a 90% of visitors, due to its central location and the density of its variety of findings (Fig. 6).

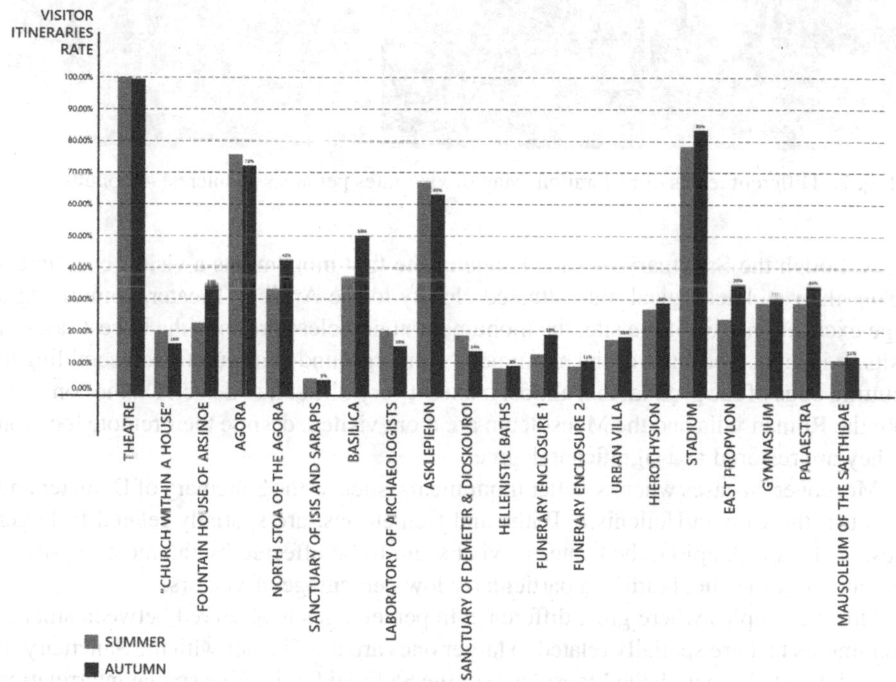

Fig. 6. Chart of visit rates per areas of interest – monuments.

In general, it has been observed that the visit rates of the centrally located and large scaled monuments are higher, such as the Theatre, the Agora, the Basilica, the North Stoa, the Asklepion and the Stadium, compared to those of smaller monuments, like the Roman Villa, the Mausoleum of the Sathidai family, the residential quarter of the

Theater and the Sanctuary of Isis and Sarapis. These monuments are situated on the periphery of the archaeological remains, and present different characteristics related to their location in the archaeological tour and the degree of restoration (Fig. 7).

Fig. 7. Different levels of restoration. Map of visit rates per areas of interest – monuments.

Although the Sanctuary of Isida is one of the first monuments a visitor encounters during their archaeological tour, situated closely to the Ancient Theater, comprising a large excavation area of the site, the monument nonetheless presents the lowest rates of visits. It is in fact, because of the monument's underground configuration, resembling to a cutting edge of the ground, that almost makes it very difficult to detect. On the contrary, both the Roman villa and the Mausoleum are more visited, despite their remote location as they are restored at a significant degree.

Moreover, in cases where smaller monuments, such as the Sanctuary of Demeter and Dioscuri, the Roman/Hellenistic Baths and Cemeteries, are spatially related to larger ones, such as Asklepion, their rates of visit seem to be affected by the most important monument of the site, holding a particularly low percentage of visitors.

Other examples where great difference in percentages is observed between smaller monuments that are spatially related to larger ones are the Theater with the Sanctuary of Isis and the Stadium with the Mausoleum of the Sathidai family. The spatial interrelation is formed both through proximity of the monuments and through visual correlation.

The duration of visit is recorded on average, by 1 h and 36 min during the summer period and by 1 h and 40 min during the autumn period. It is noteworthy that no great difference has been observed between seasons. However, the most remote locations of the archaeological site, are affected by seasonal changes and seem to have more visitors during the autumn period when the temperature is lower. This has also been observed,

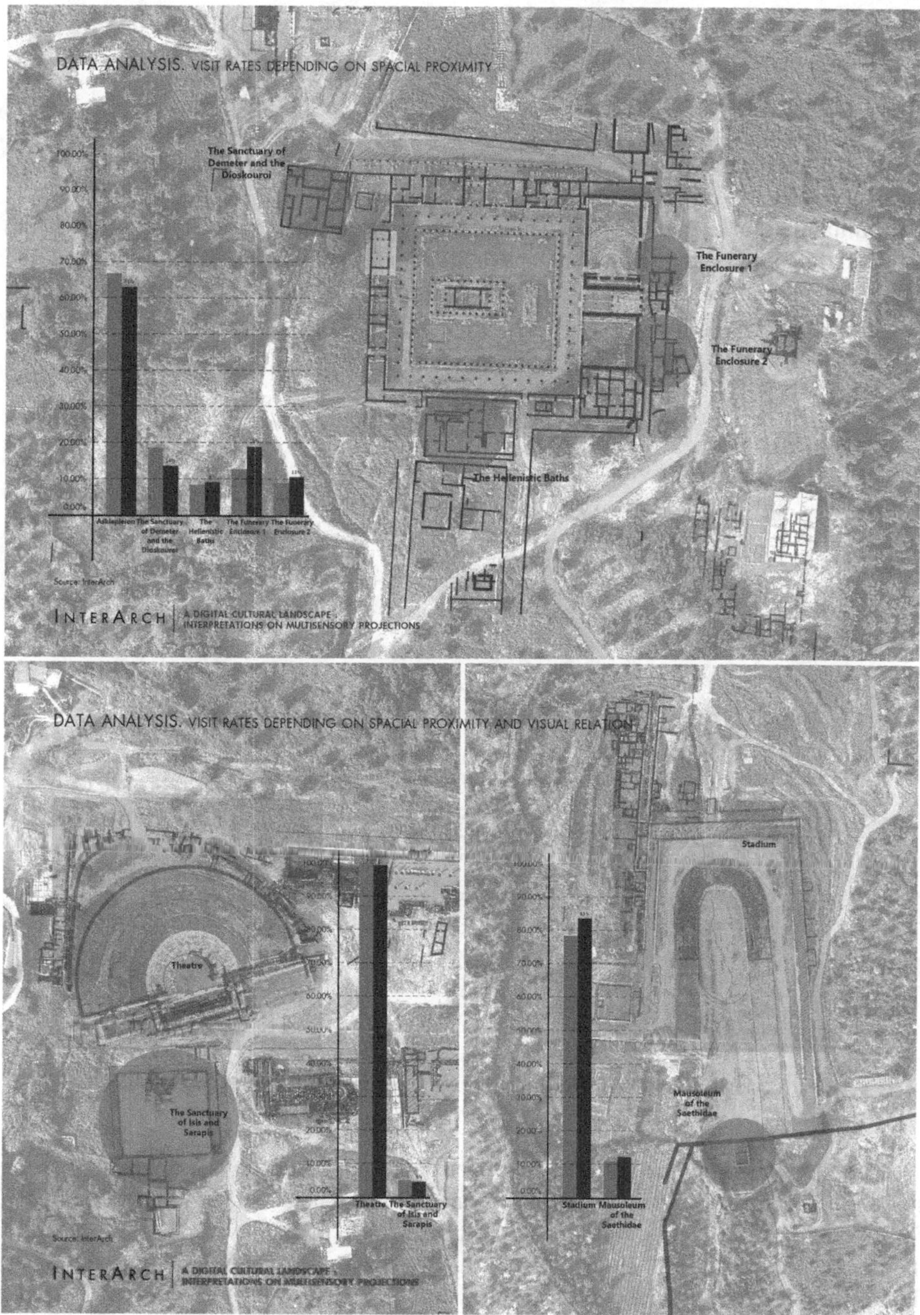

Fig. 8. Visit rates and spatial interrelations depending on proximity and visual correlation.

even in monuments that are extensively restored, such as the Palaestra, the Propylon and the Stoa of the Gymnasium which are more visited during the autumn period (Fig. 8).

Identifying Main Directions. The visitor's records are subsequently classified according to the direction of route in the part of the transition towards the archaeological site and in the other part of the way of return. According to this classification, monuments that are visited most often during the transition were identified, such as the Asklepion, the fountain Arsinoe, the northern Stoa of the Agora etc., as well as monuments that are visited mainly on the return, such as the Agora. In addition, it is noticeable that the smaller monuments are visited mainly during the transition process (Fig. 9).

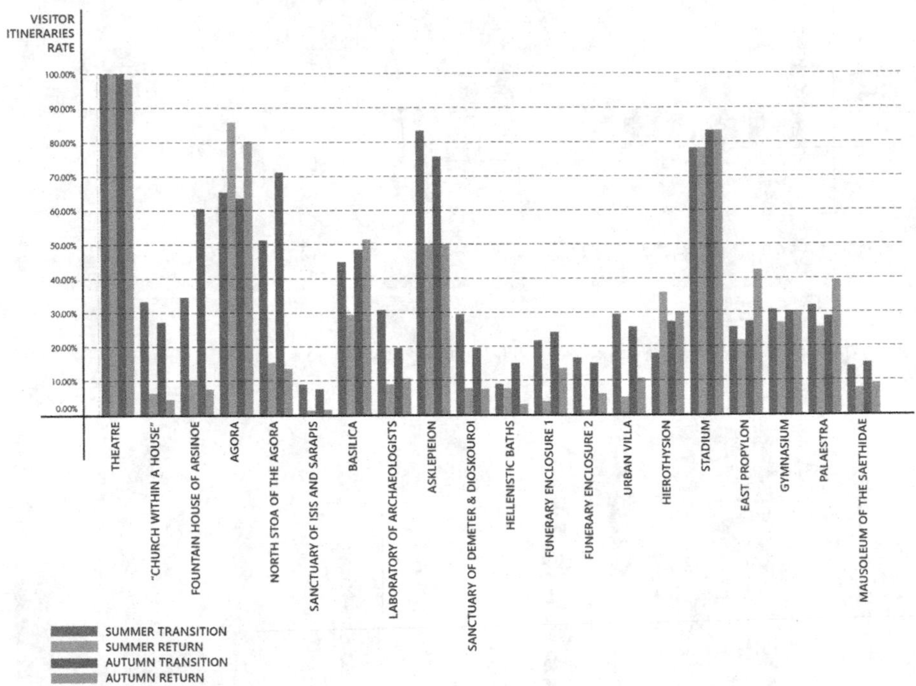

Fig. 9. Chart of visit rates divided in transitions and returns per areas of interest- monuments.

The maps showing the paths of transitions and returns during summer and autumn season indicate areas with a wide distribution of points where visitors move more freely, for example in the Agora area, in the north-east side of the Asklepion and between the area of the Stadium, the Palestra and the Gymnasium. At the same time, however, denser lines are formed, indicating specific routes through which the monuments of the archaeological site are approached. It is remarkable that there are no distinct differences between the paths followed in the summer season and those in the autumn season, either on the map of transitions or on the map of returns (Fig. 10, Fig. 11).

The movements depicted, lead from the Theatre, through the Agora and the Asklepion to the Roman villa and then passing through the Stadium or Palestra and end up in the

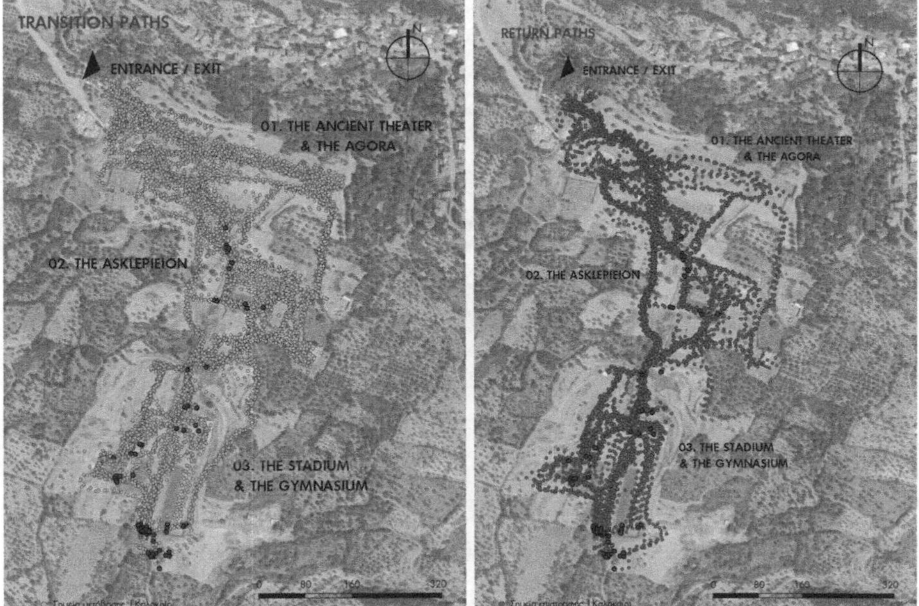

Fig. 10. Maps of visitors' itineraries divides in transitions and returns during summer period.

Mausoleum. On the return map, the density of dots forms a diagonal continuous line in a more specific way, indicating the main route to the exit.

A remarkable fact revealed by the fieldwork shows that a great number of visitors, 30% of them, choose to use a peripheral path at the endpoint of the North Stoa of the Agora, with no archaeological excavations, in order to reach the Asklepion and the Roman Villa, instead of passing through the main Agora area and the adjacent monuments. Even though this particular route is exposed to high temperatures, with no shaded areas and resting points along the way, the visitor's decision to use it, even on hot sunny days, seems irrelevant to seasonal criteria. Very few visitors use this route, on their way back from the archaeological tour. Then, one third of these visitors choose to access the Stadium from an upper level on the eastern side, reaching at the end of the monument and the Mausolium as well, through a peripheral path with no archaeological excavations but with great views that time (Fig. 12).

In addition, mapping of the itineraries illustrates the key intersections points where visitors have to choose how to continue their exploration. These key points are as follows:

- Point A, after leaving the upper part of the theatre with the first panoramic view, next to the Arsinoe Fountain, the visitor must choose whether to continue towards the Agora, to turn towards the Stoa or to visit the Orchestra of the Theatre. On the way back, everyone passes by this point towards the exit (Fig. 13).

- Point B relates to the decision whether or not to continue towards the Stadium without crossing the Asklepion. This point actually consists of two spatial points B1 and B2,

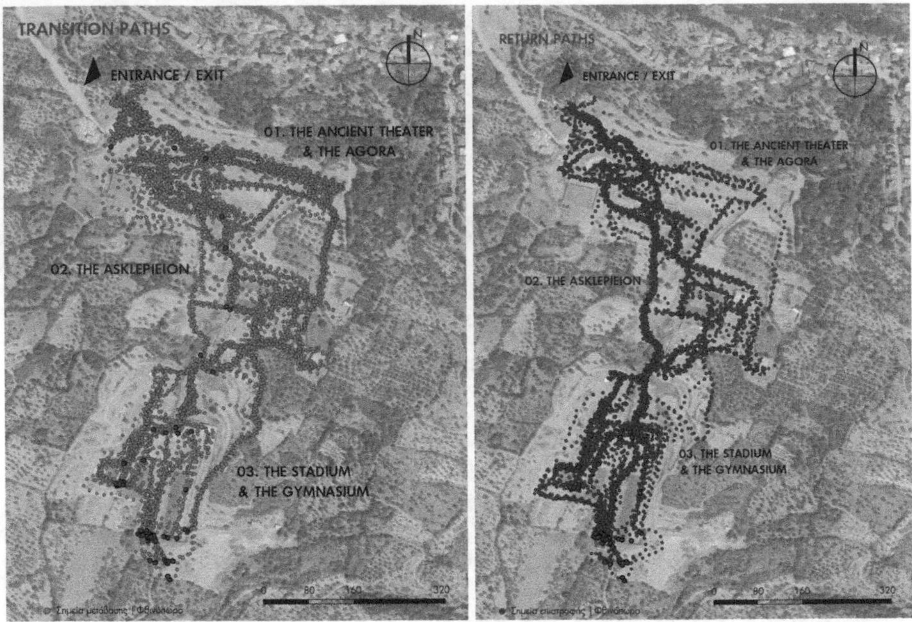

Fig. 11. Maps of visitors' itineraries divides in transitions and returns during autumn period.

as a secondary unofficial side entrance to the Asklepion is also recorded further to the south. This entrance is not relevant to the typology of the ancient building. On return, the division at this point relates either to crossing the Agora straight to the exit or reaching the sanctuaries of the Agora, the Basilica or the Orchestra of the Theatre. This indicates that it is not unusual to visit these monuments while returning.

- Point C, at the end of the North Stoa of the Agora, where visitors can choose to move towards the Asklepion and the Roman Villa via a peripheral path without archaeological finds or walk along the Agora site. In point C2, a more specific scenario can be investigated that determines whether or not someone will visit both the Asklepion and the Roman villa.
- Point D indicates the option of accessing the Stadium from an upper level on the eastern side, reaching the end of the monument.
- Point E, where visitors choose whether to enter the Stadium centrally or via Propylon road. On the way back, here, visitors choose whether to enter the Hierothesio and the Asklepion or to follow the diagonal route to the Agora or the exit.

Investigating the ways alternative routes are spatially organized through these points, led to several interesting observations:

Almost half of the visitors do not visit the Theatre Orchestra and about a 30% of the total do not cross the area of the Agora on the way of transition. Instead, they move along the North Stoa up to its endpoint and arrive peripherally at the Asklepion Complex and the Roman Villa. This 30% is part of those visitors who do not enter the Orchestra area. On the way back, 87% of the visitors who haven't passed through the Agora during the

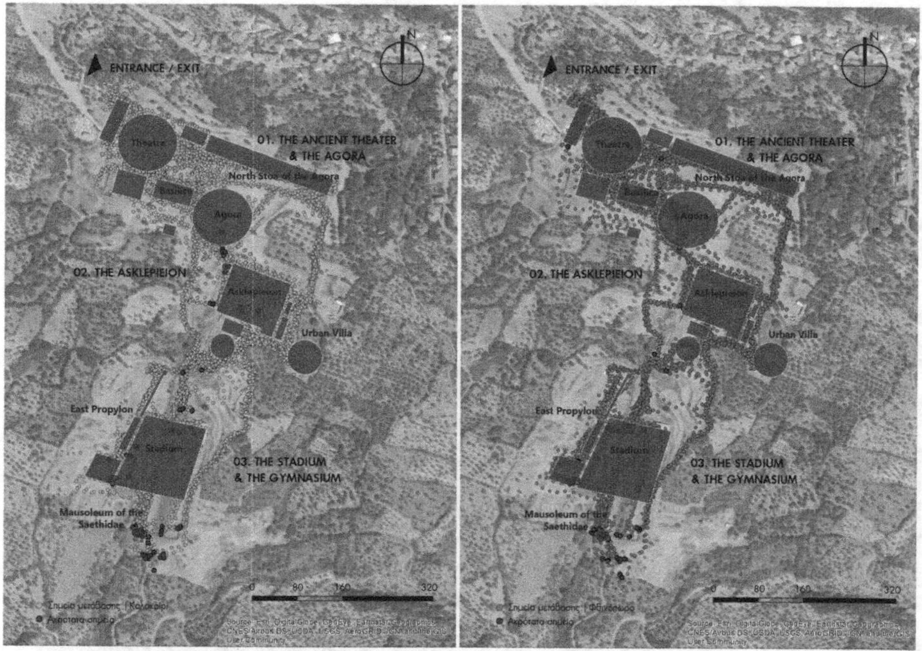

Fig. 12. Maps of visitors' itineraries in transitions during summer and autumn period with the 20 selected areas of interest – monuments.

transition, return through the Agora area. On average, it takes 19 min to visit the Agora during the transition and 12 min on the return.

It is obvious that there is a significant distinction regarding one's decision to visit or not the Theatre Orchestra. As far as Group I is concerned, the visitors' choice to see the Theatre Orchestra is simultaneously related to their choice of passing through the main Agora area. On the contrary, as far as Group II is concerned, visitors who choose to take the peripheral way to the Asklepion, the Orchestra and the Agora haven't been to the Orchestra or the Agora. There is also Group III that includes almost 13% of visitors who do not visit the Orchestra and continue straight to the Agora after passing through the Stoa. Finally, there is a Group IV depicting 10% of visitors who directly visit the main area of the Agora, showing no interest for the North Stoa or the Orchestra, and most of them end their tour at the level of Agora and return to the exit.

Further analyzing Group II, it is noted that 5% of visitors go straight to the Roman Villa without visiting at all the Asklepion Complex. The few visitors who choose to enter the Stadium from an upper level on the eastern side, reaching the southern end of the monument, is a part of Group II. In addition, if a visitor combines a visit to the Asklepion and the Roman Villa, it is possible to enter the Stadium not only centrally but also via the road that passes through the Propylon, otherwise if he chooses to visit only the Asklepion Complex, he will almost definitely reach the Stadium centrally. As for Group II, 86% choose to enter the Stadium centrally, 8% via Propylon Street and 6% choose the longest way from the upper level on the east side.

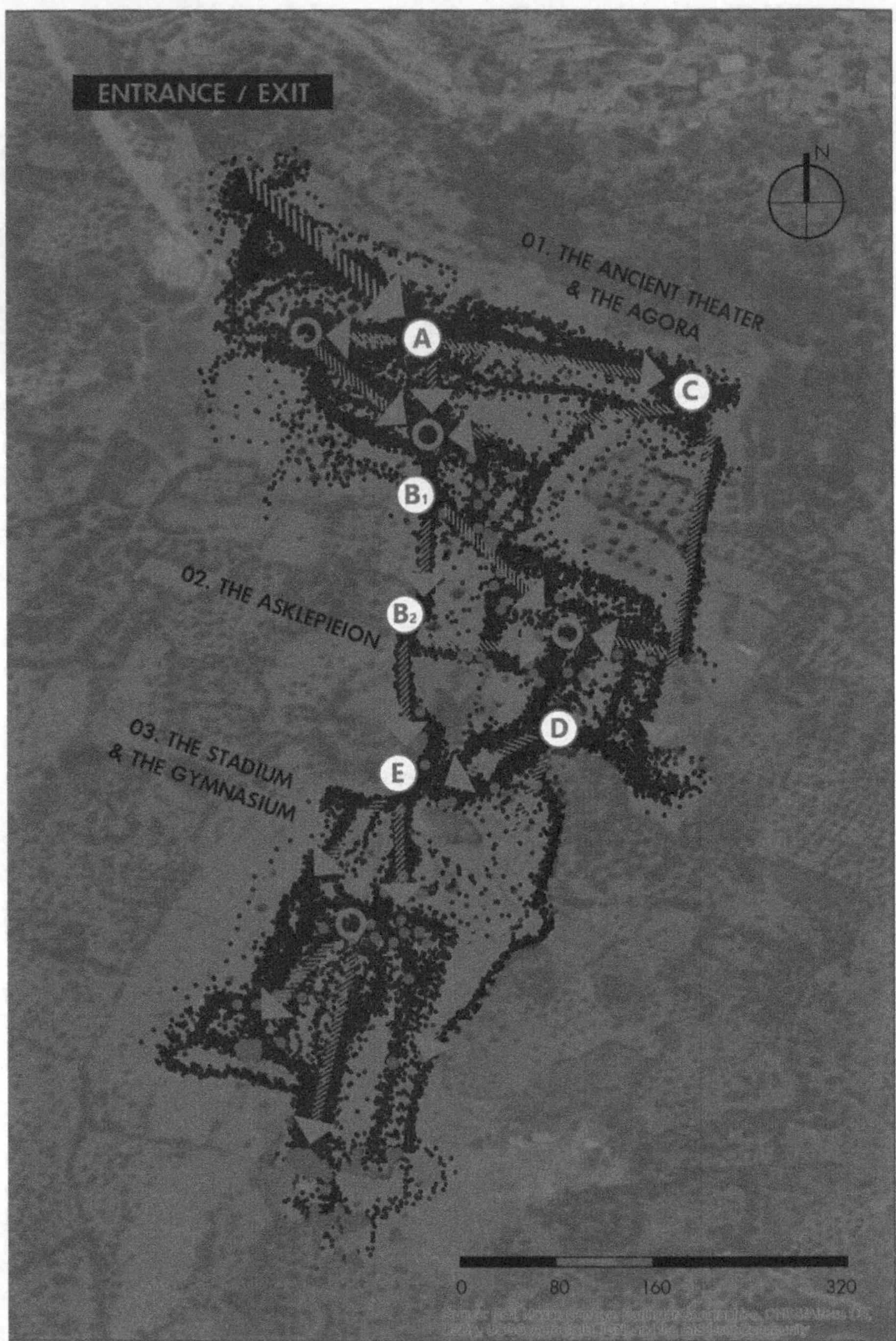

Fig. 13. Maps of visitors' itineraries, illustrating the key intersection points.

Group I includes 48% of all visitors and refers to those who visited the Theatre Orchestra and continued on to the Agora. Exploring further, the wider area, the Basilica has a high percentage of visitors with rates at 33%, and 9% of visitors also visit the Sanctuary of Isida. Regarding Group IV, very few visitors visit the Basilica and almost no one visits the Sanctuary of Isida. In addition, from Group III, no one visits the Basilica or the Sanctuary of Isida after having been to the North Stoa of Agora. However, even in Group I, there are few visitors who do not walk through the Agora but, after visiting the Basilica, head towards the Asklepion. Finally, contrary to Group II, it is noteworthy to mention that 19% – 13% of the visitors, depending on season, end their archaeological tour once they reach the Agora area or the Asklepion without ever reaching the Stadium. At the same time, there is not a great difference in the percentages of those who choose to walk centrally to the Stadium or pass through Propylon Street (Fig. 14).

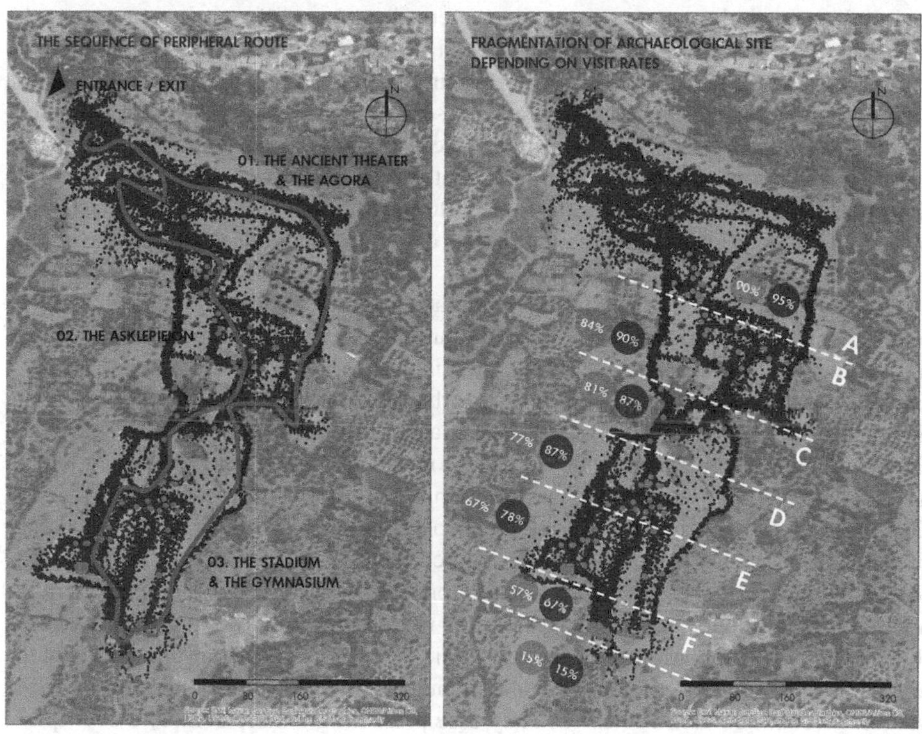

Fig. 14. The sequence of the circular route. Fragmentation of archaeological site depending on visit rates.

4 Conclusions

Activating the Narrations. The visit rates of the monuments as expected, depends on their size and their restoration level, factors that are crucial to relate findings with a recognizable typology and function. For this reason, monuments such as the Theatre, the Basilica, the Northern Stoa of Agora, the Asklepion and the Stadium are the most visited monuments, articulating the main axis of the visit tour. However, these monuments are spatially related to smaller ones that have particularly low visitor rates, in cases like:

- the theatre with the "church within a house" and the sanctuary of Isis and Sarapis, and the Basilica.
- the Asklepieion with the Sanctuary of Demeter and the Dioskouroi, the Roman/Hellenistic baths and the funerary enclosures.
- the Stadium with the Mausoleum of the Saethidae.

Therefore, developing a network of narratives motivated from instances of the popular monuments can draw attention to the characteristics of less-known monuments.

Furthermore, the investigation of the intersection points and the behaviour of the visitors' groups indicates two distinctive patterns based on different perceptions of the landscape. The first case of visitors focuses on a spatially limited area, with no inclined terrain, starting from the Orchestra area, focusing on the findings-rich areas of the Agora and Asklepion. On the contrary, the second case of visitors seems to be more 'attracted' by the wide-open landscape, they skip the Orchestra and the Agora at first, continuing so as to wander around the archaeological site as much as possible. In this case, the morphology of the natural environment seems to be important, in developing for example a route at a higher level of the Stadium, at its east side, where one can only have great panoramic views.

These cases illustrate two opposite approaches to the archaeological site. The first one indicates the minimum tour of the site and the second one shows the version of a circular route that can include all the monuments in a row, as described: Theatre – Fountain House of Arsinoe – North Stoa of the Agora – Funerary Enclosure – Urban Roman Villa – Stadium – Mausoleum of the Saethidae – Palaestra – Gymnasium – East Propylon – the resting area at the entrance of the Stadium where the only fountain at the area is located – Hierothysion – Hellenistic Bath – Asklepieion – Sanctuary of Demeter and the Dioskouroi – Agora – archaeologists' laboratory – Basilica – sanctuary of Isis and Sarapis – theatre orchestra "church within a house" – exit, providing the research with a sequence that can be used for proposing a scenario of a holistic narrative approach. Additionally, it is obvious that many visitors stop their routes without reaching the most remote levels of the site. The narration system can connect the upper level of the archaeological site with the most remote monuments and locations either by inspiring visitors to continue their routes or in any case presenting a more complete description of the cultural features of the site at the upper levels.

The implementation of narrative networks that present intangible features and cultural references, while creating associations, not only with archaeological findings but also with the spatial characteristics of the landscape, can be useful in the management, connection and promotion of an expansive archaeological site. However, at the same time, the integration of the natural environment instances in the rhythm of suggested narrations can further enhance a multidimensional structure of the information provided, a goal that is also critical for the ongoing research.

Acknowledgements. Warm thanks to P. Themelis for his rich and constructive cooperation, but above all, for his contribution to our country and the global culture related to the now excavated Ancient Messene.

This research has been co-financed by the European Union and Greek national funds through the Operational Program Competitiveness, Entrepreneurship and Innovation, under the call RESEARCH – CREATE – INNOVATE (Project code: T1EDK: 68144600).

Co-Financed by Greece and the European Union

References

1. Society of Messenian Archaeological Studies: Monument restoration (2007). https://www.snf.org/en/grants/grantees/s/society-of-messenian-archaeological-studies/monument-restoration/. Last accessed 22 Oct 2022
2. Themelis, P.: Ancient Messene. Kapon Edition, Athens (2019)
3. Foth, M.: Handbook of Research on Urban Informatics: The Practice and Promise of the Real-Time. Queensland University of Technology, Australia (2009)
4. Bilandzic, M., Venable, J.: Towards participatory action design research: adapting action research and design science research methods for urban informatics. J. Community Informat. Special Issue: Research in Action: Linking Communities and Universities **7**(3)
5. Georgopoulos, A., Tapinaki, S., Makris, G.N., Stefanakis, M.I.: Innovative methods for digital heritage documentation: the archaeological landscape of Kymissala in Rhodes. In: ICOMOS General Assembly and International Symposium, Florence, November (2014). http://openarchive.icomos.org/id/eprint/2020/
6. Evgenikou, V., Georgopoulos, A.: Investigating 3d reconstruction methods for small artifacts. In: ISPRS Archives, vol. XL-5/W4, pp. 101–108. WG V/4, CIPA -3D-Arch (2015). http://www.int-arch-photogramm-remote-sens-spatial-inf-sci.net/XL-5-W4/101/2015/isprsarchives-XL-5-W4-101-2015.pdf. Last accessed 6 Oct 2021
7. Doulamis, A., et al.: 5D modelling: an efficient approach for creating spatiotemporal predictive 3D maps of large-scale cultural resources. In: ISPRS Annals of the Photogrammetry, Remote Sensing and Spatial Information Sciences (2015). https://www.researchgate.net/publication/282521303_5D_Modelling_An_Efficient_Approach_for_Creating_Spatiotemporal_Predictive_3D_Maps_of_Large-Scale_Cultural_Resources

Smart City and Open-Air Museum: A Digital Application for the Promotion of the Old Town of Chania

Hippocrates Manoudakis[1(✉)], Ioulia Pentazou[1], and Maria Bakatsaki[2]

[1] Department of Culture, Creative Media and Industries, University of Thessaly, Argonafton & Filellinon, 38221 Volos, Greece
{imanoudakis,pentazou}@uth.gr

[2] School of Production Engineering and Management, Technical University of Crete, University Campus, Kounoupidiana, 73100 Chania, Greece
mbakatsaki@tuc.gr

Abstract. The framework of an Open-Air Museum, which includes institutionalized historical routes exploiting the functional features of a "smart city", could become a holistic approach to the management of a historical urban space. Furthermore, by producing Public History, an Open-Air Museum can reduce social isolation and more effectively strengthen a sense of identity, the collective identity, social cohesion, and therefore the sustainable development of a community. This paper presents a digital multimedia application, which serves as an enhanced digital guide that includes the institutionalized historical routes of the old town of Chania, transforming the specific urban area to a 'smart' tourist destination. The old town of Chania was chosen mainly due to its long uninterrupted human presence since the prehistoric era, whose remaining traces are retained in very good condition in today's times, especially the periods dating back to the Minoans, the Byzantines, the Venetians, the Ottomans and the Cretan State. In the era of digital technologies, 3D printing, simulation and virtual reality, the implementation of digital innovations can reach audiences not yet being reached by other means, increasing the attractiveness of historical sites and visitors' participation. Consequently, it can have a more powerful impact on the sustainable development of the local community.

Keywords: Digital Cultural Heritage · Open-Air Museum · Smart City

1 Introduction

In recent years, there has been a rapid development and implementation of e-government policies in Greece, specifically in terms of "smart city" applications, and an increasing spread of digital applications that focus on Public History. Furthermore, the devastating impact of the COVID-19 pandemic on the cultural sector led to UNESCO intervening in 2022 by calling for a reshaping of the ways in which culture is valued, arguing that it is fundamental to a more inclusive, ethical and sustainable future [1].

A. Moropoulou et al. (Eds.): TMM_CH 2023, CCIS 1889, pp. 188–201, 2023.
https://doi.org/10.1007/978-3-031-42300-0_16

The article presents the design and implementation of the digital application *Chania History Walk*, which helps the visitor in the evocative environment of the old town of Chania to choose and be led through suggested historical routes. These routes include monuments from various historical periods; they may also be themed, and they all take advantage of the smart city advantages offered by the Municipality of Chania. The broader project under study is part of the museum genre of Open-Air Museums and seeks to highlight the old town of Chania as an open-air museum in itself, using digital technology. Then, the cultural destination becomes safer and more attractive for the public, as they are not limited to closed spaces.

2 Smart City and Open-Air Museum

2.1 Smart City

The economic, technological and social developments of the last decades have shaped urban areas into cores of technological development and innovation, at the same time ascribing new features to the form of today's social life. In the urban centers where the aforementioned processes take place, citizens acquire an interactive relationship with the infrastructure, its complex transportation networks, communications, developmental structures and access to knowledge. These processes are supported by the corresponding economic activities carried out in modern urban centers, resulting in the development of the region and society. However, this development is often not synchronized with all the other features of an urban center, resulting in the emergence of a series of problems, such as traffic congestion, the inability to expand the urban fabric, a heavy environmental burden, the inability to manage a large amount of waste and the emergence of social inequalities [2]. In essence, what is required is an intelligent and sustainable management of all the above factors in order to achieve a durable design. Such problems, in connection with the rapid development of Information and Communication Technologies (ICT), have led to the creation of the concept of the *smart city* [3].

The smart city concept belongs to those categories of concepts that have more than one interpretation. Smart city concepts share common notions of planning and exploitation of ICT in innovative and productive ways to solve urban issues and problems, in order to acquire features that give them a competitive edge and create active citizens who will participate in the decision-making processes that concern them [4].

The features that must prevail in a city in order to be characterized as "smart" are a combination of the following five important factors [5, 6]:

- Fast-speed broadband
- A knowledge-intensive workforce
- Innovation
- Digital inclusion
- Marketing

One consequence of the features that make up the concept of a smart city is the emergence of new concepts that refer to social and economic activities, which also concern the tourism industry [7].

2.2 Open-Air Museum

Since the beginning of the 20th century, there have been various actions, at an institutional and non-institutional level, concerning the establishment and development of open-air museums. Some of these bodies are active to this day and the definitions of open-air museums are often derived from the purposes of their establishment as stipulated in their terms and conditions. An example is AEOM (Association of European Open-Air Museums), which is connected to ICOM (International Council of Museums), whose goal is to promote scientific and organizational experiences, with the main focus being on the activities of open-air museums. According to AEOM: *"Open air museums are defined as scientific collections in the open air of various types of structures, which, as constructional and functional entities, illustrate settlement patterns, dwellings, economy and technology"* [8].

Another organization is *EXARC* (European Exchange of Archaeological Research and Communication), which includes open-air museums within its research interests. It defines an Open-Air Archaeological Museum as follows: *"An archaeological open-air museum is a non-profit permanent institution with outdoor true to scale architectural reconstructions primarily based on archaeological sources. It holds collections of intangible heritage resources and provides an interpretation of how people lived and acted in the past; this is accomplished according to sound scientific methods for the purposes of education, study and enjoyment of its visitors"* [8].

In conclusion, a general definition of an open-air museum is that it offers representations of the past, a progressive archaeological perspective, an educational experience and an entertainment proposal. It is an institution of a modern society that connects today's world with historical periods.

Open-air museums are usually found in areas that have had continuous human activity from the past to the present. The main goal of such museums is to enact a representation of the everyday life of a society in a specific period. In order to achieve this, renovations, restorations and maintenance of the monuments or buildings of that time are required - not only externally, but also internally with the placement of authentic elements - including objects of a utilitarian or decorative nature, and/or architectural elements. In other words, the final visitor's experience can be a result of the combination of authenticity and representation. At the same time, the historical experience offered by an open-air museum is a result of the historical narrative that contains references to the present and is a result of the evolutionary course of a space within its historical context [9].

Open-Air Museums are referred to as a "*four-dimensional experience*", with these dimensions being defined by breadth, height, thoughts and the time period in the past. These dimensions offer a historical narrative to the visitor in two ways: First, through a sensory experience (sight, hearing, smell, taste and touch), and second, through thoughts and speech. Sensations activate feelings and these in turn create knowledge. Knowledge using thoughts and logic then proceeds to actions. This is how an open-air museum interacts: by combining emotions, insights, theories and practices. By applying multiple methods, it simultaneously conveys multiple messages to visitors through their active participation, which replaces passive browsing [9].

The new technologies that make up the concept of the smart city provide information and public access to points of historical and cultural interest, enhancing in this way the characteristics and properties of an open-air museum. By selecting the historical points of interest, and then constituting the historical routes, we can design and create a cultural product that can offer an integrated historical and educational experience, simultaneously highlighting the city as a touristic leisure destination which brings together a large number of people through shared cultural experiences in an engaging and entertaining way [10].

2.3 Historical Routes

The term "historical route" - or "cultural route" - defines the assembled points of interest with similar characteristics or properties, which have a central theme and are located in a specific area [11]. Points of interest are usually elements that have some special architectural or historical features, landscapes with natural beauty, buildings or monuments. A version of historical/cultural routes that is emerging today is the interconnection of the past of a historic urban center or an entire city with its present.

Historical routes, in accordance with international and European practices, constitute integrated tourist destination proposals that aim to cover as much as possible the desires and requirements of the modern visitor [12].

The points of historical interest which are to be integrated into the planned historical route, and which form a specific new cultural footprint, can be distinguished as: *Institutionalized points of interest*, *Crowdsourcing points of interest* and *Points of special interest* [11].

Institutionalized points of interest are places that are protected and promoted by state bodies, as well as being legally protected by state or interstate agreements [13].

The definition of *Crowdsourcing points of interest* was based on the modern English term "crowdsourcing" which, in Greek, is a compound word derived from the notions of 'many people' and 'sources'. Crowdsourcing is a form of collective mobilization with the help of the Internet: it is proposed to a group of people with diverse interests, knowledge and population size, following the initiative of an individual, institution, non-profit organization or company; people *"use and manage geographic information and its tools according to their interests, without taking into account the rules and techniques of mapping"* [13].

Points of special interest define a route, which could also be characterized as thematic, since the subject matter of the points is commonly known and is usually predetermined (religious, culinary, sports-related, etc.) [11].

2.4 Digital Heritage: A Holistic Approach and Sustainable Development

The definition for sustainable development given in 1987 by the UN-sponsored World Commission on Environment and Development (WCED), led by Gro Harlem Brundtland, is *"development that meets the needs of the present without compromising the ability of future generations to meet their own needs"* [14]. In 2011, ACTION IS1007, a study by the European Cooperation in Science and Technology (COST) identified three possible roles of culture within sustainable development: *"Culture in, for and as sustainable development. The first role ('in') sees culture standing as a fourth autonomous pillar of sustainable development; the second ('for') advocates a mediating role of culture between the three pillars; the third ('as') "defines culture as the necessary overall foundation and structure for achieving the aims of sustainable development"* [15].

Particular importance is given to the concept of heritage in relation to culture and the future of humanity, because it signals the *"cultural potential and characteristics"* of modern societies, contributes to the continuous re-evaluation of cultural identities, and comprises a vehicle for the transmission of experiences, skills and knowledge between generations [16].

Although cultural heritage assets differ from ordinary buildings, since they must be preserved for future generations, the concept of sustainability cannot be perceived in the narrow environmental context of buildings' preservation. It is an issue of how cultural heritage is perceived as a lever for the enhancement of a society's identity [17] and how culture can become the fourth pillar of sustainable development alongside the social, environmental, and economic pillars of sustainable development [18]. Studies have shown that cultural and heritage institutions are considered among the most trusted public institutions [19]; therefore, museums and cultural heritage professionals should think global and act local, constantly reviewing their ability to contribute to the improvement of social cohesion and development. Museums and monuments could promote human memory; hence, they are key to community resilience, as people seek to engage with the past, understand the present and plan for a meaningful future [20].

By producing public history, an Open-Air Museum can reduce social isolation, and more effectively strengthen a sense of identity, the collective identity, social cohesion, and in turn, the sustainable development of a community.

The evolution of ICT has created a separate category of digital applications, namely digital cultural heritage applications, which have strengthened the contact of culture with society and the life quality. Digital culture, both in theory and in practice -due to the possibilities offered by new technological data in terms of preservation and conservation, for the presentation and promotion of cultural assets- is increasingly being accepted by traditional cultural institutions, such as museums, archaeological sites, protected areas of natural beauty, archival bodies and communities [12].

The framework of an Open-Air Museum, which includes institutionalized historical routes by exploiting the functional features of a "smart city", could become a holistic approach to the management of a historical urban space. Holistic management should include the preservation, maintenance, accessibility, and emergence of historical places; it should promote these sites as an integrated tourist cultural destination and interconnect them with the local community and entrepreneurship. Museums that are integrated into society should co-create cultural capital to improve the quality of life, holistically, for both current and future generations [21, 22].

3 Materials and Methods

3.1 Case Study: The Town of Chania

The selection of the old historical town of Chania for the design and implementation of a digital application, which will contribute to the promotion of the old town as an open-air museum, was made because this place meets all the aforementioned criteria regarding a smart city, an Open-Air Museum and historical routes.

The old town of Chania features all the characteristics that can place it within the concept of an Open-Air Museum. Contained in an area of approximately 1 km^2, it is founded on the traces of the ancient settlement of Minoan Kydonia. It bears signs of uninterrupted human presence from the Neolithic era to the present day, with intensely appearance from the Minoan, Roman, Byzantine, Venetian and Ottoman periods, as well as the period of the Cretan State. These signs appear in various forms: monuments, buildings, architecture, houses, roads, water supply works, multicultural spaces (e.g. distinct Jewish, Catholic, Ottoman, Orthodox quarters) and fortifications. Collectively, they create representations of the past, educational experiences, and scientific knowledge (developing archaeological excavations and restorations of monuments), with the overall image of the old town - in combination with modern infrastructure and tourist businesses - being projected as a proposal for entertainment and leisure [23].

Within the above framework created by various elements of the Municipality of Chania as a smart city, in combination with the cultural heritage of the old town of Chania, the design of one or more historical routes constituted an excellent opportunity to create a branded cultural tourist product for the following reasons:

- it has a central and coherent theme (the evolutionary route of the current site from the Minoan era to the present);
- it covers a geographically defined area (the old town of Chania, within the Venetian walls);
- it extends the tourist season throughout the year, and
- with the help of local entrepreneurship, it will be a driver of development, contributing to the sustainability of the overall proposal of an open-air museum, as well as to the broader social, economic and environmental development of the region.

3.2 Digital Documentation

The documentation of the multimodal text and photographs was based on bibliographic and photographic sources from the publications of the Archaeological Service of Chania, the Historical Archives of Crete, scientific publications from the Municipality of Chania, publications from the Eleftherios Venizelos Foundation, and publications from the Municipal Library of Chania. The reason for using the so-called institutional sources of historical memory (libraries, archives, foundations, etc.) was to ensure access to scientifically documented information, using primary archival material, in order to avoid collecting material from social media, personal websites, and, generally speaking, from sources that do not follow any scientific ethics.

3.3 Methodological Approach for the Development of the Digital Application

As "digital design" of the application is defined the *"organization of information in such a way that it produces a conceptual and open narrative, which 'translates' and transforms the information into digital material through visualization"* [24]. Based on the fact that the information to be produced must be "*consumable*" by the users [24], some creative and innovative features have been incorporated. The first stage in digital design includes the organizational documentation of the digital material and the design of the functions, with a focus on the search function and the way the most important information will be presented on the screen, as well as the ways in which this information will be presented to the public.

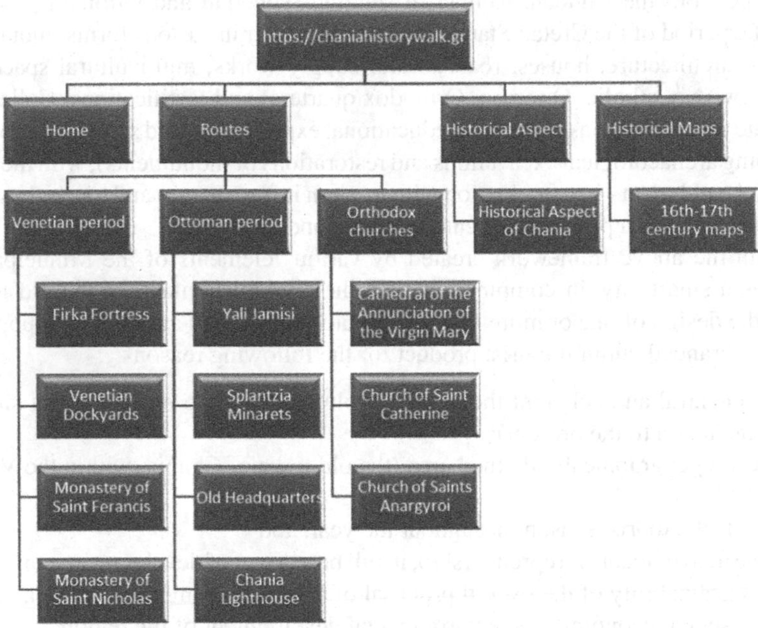

Fig. 1. Flowchart representing the structure of the organisation of the information contained in the website.

In the second stage, the analytical organization of the information about the historical point is captured and organized (Fig. 1) in such a way as to produce meaning and to present the implementation goals of *"substantial materiality"* for the public [24].

The information has been organized with the aim of being directly accessible to the user, with the multimodal text keeping to sharing essential information in a brief/concise way. The digital experience should be user friendly, instantly comprehensible and perceivable by the user, and it immediately familiarizes him/her with all those cognitive navigation elements that will "challenge" the visitor to explore the application [25].

Wordpress 6.0, a freeware popular software, was used to create the application and develop the user interaction.

In order to provide support for the interactive maps, the Google Maps application is used; it has the ability to display satellite images, aerial photos, street maps and panoramic images (Street View) in a website. The integration of an Application Programming Interface (API) allows our application to access Google Maps features [26].

The ResponsiveVoice API has been used, which provides the functional feature of text narration in 51 languages; it is also compatible with all known web browsers and has the option of a female or male voice.

4 Results and Discussion

4.1 The Chania History Walk Digital Platform - Brief Description

The digital platform *Chania History Walk* highlights 'monumental exhibits' with the support of scientifically documented text and visual material, offering a complete museum experience. It provides information for the public before and during their visit, as well as for anyone interested who will not have the possibility of physically visiting Chania town. A dynamic relationship between visitors and the application is developed through functional features such as the use of a cartographic application for the geolocation of the historical points, the drawing of the selected route on a digital map, and user navigation to get to the selected point, with feedback given by previous visitors, as well as multilingual support for the texts and narrative. Furthermore, the application supports the Open-Air Museum as a space for practicing public history, and it emerges as a tool for promoting the city as a smart tourist destination.

The page that hosts the online application was given the domain name https://chaniahistorywalk.gr/, which immediately reveals both the identity of the application and its recognizability, given the globally established extension "...historywalk.com" that has been adopted informally for corresponding routes.

The application presents the points of interest through the visualized transfer of information and narrative, which documents the physical and digital exhibit/point of interest. The texts describe the physical object/exhibit; images and photographs present the point of interest as it may have been in different periods, and/or its interior, as well as its geographical representation on the digital map.

The functional core of the application is the interactive maps, which depict the historical points that make up the historical routes, simultaneously providing the historical information, as well as photos of the exhibit from past periods. The purpose of this, is so that the provided information and the interactive material that accompanies each point will 'compose' a 'story', and through these 'stories', the Open-Air Museum will be presented spatially as a single integrated place.

The implemented application in this case incorporates all the functional features of a smart city, as well as those that classify it in applications for smart cultural tourism.

The home page of the digital platform *Chania History Walk* (Fig. 2) gives direct access to the main object of the application with a main options menu which includes "Routes", "Historical Aspect" and "Historical Maps"; each of these contains informational content that functions as supports for the "Routes" choice, including the ability to select the language used (on the right hand side in the basic options menu).

Fig. 2. Website home page Selecting "Routes"

Selecting "Routes" (Fig. 3) takes the user to the suggested routes mentioned in the application, which are thematically based around the "Venetian period", "Ottoman period", and "Orthodox churches". There is also an "All" option which includes all the proposed routes in the application, and gives the user the possibility to select more than one route; the visitor may also create a new (individualised) route that will include more points.

The "Venetian period" option (Fig. 4) contains the historical points of interest: "Firka Fortress", "Venetian Dockyards (Neoria)", "Monastery of Saint Francis" and "Monastery of Saint Nicholas", with corresponding multimodal texts, photographs and text narratives. The "Ottoman period" route is made up of the points "Yali Jamisi", "Splantzia Minarets", "Old Headquarters" and "Chania Lighthouse". The third route, "Orthodox churches", which is characterized as thematic, includes the "Church of Saint Catherine", the "Church of Saints Anargyroi" and the "Cathedral of the Annunciation of the Virgin Mary".

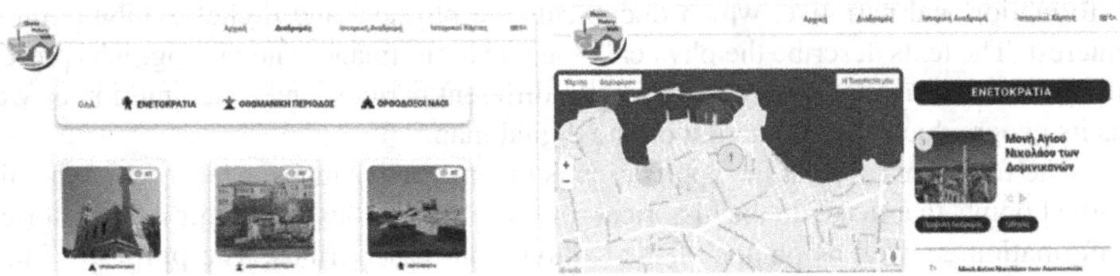

Fig. 3. Routes **Fig. 4.** Selected route: Venetian period

When a route is selected, the user sees a screen that is divided into three information points. In the upper horizontal frame, the basic options menu is always fixed, so that the user always has direct access to it. The rest of the screen is divided in two parts: the interactive Google Maps application on the left, and the supporting multimodal text of the historical point on the right (Fig. 5).

At the end of the multimodal text, there is an electronic form which the visitor/user can use to submit comments, observations, evaluations and their own photos (Fig. 6, Fig. 7).

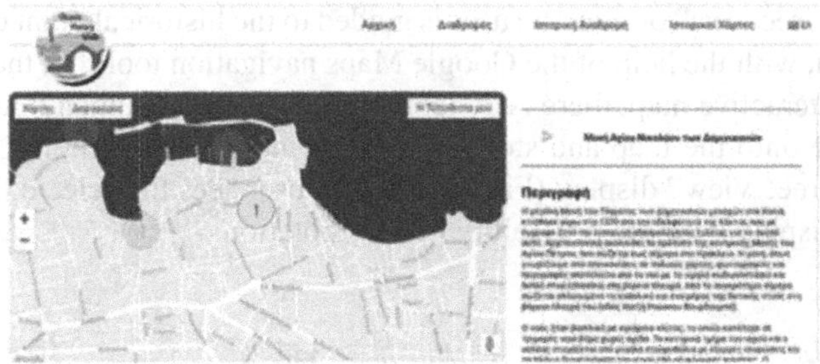

Fig. 5. Description of the route

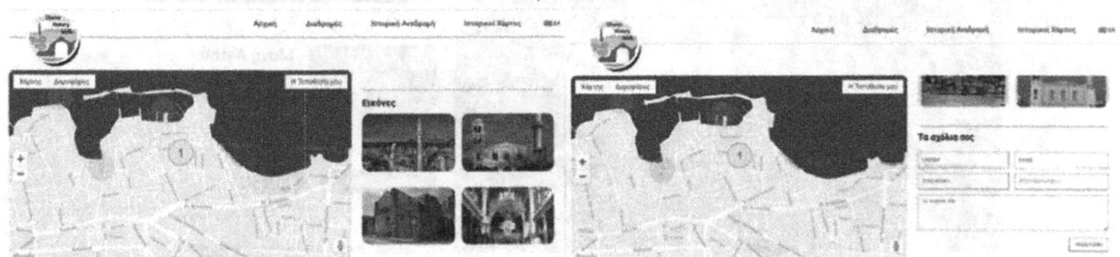

Fig. 6. Images from the route

Fig. 7. Guest feedback form

When using Google Maps (Fig. 8), if the user selects the option "My location", the application asks the user to allow access to his/her smart device (phone, tablet) in order to initially locate the visitor's geographical point (location).

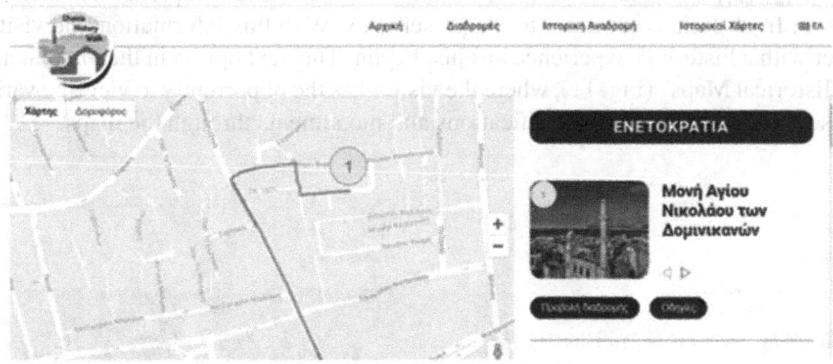

Fig. 8. Navigation of the route

With the "Directions" option, the user is guided to the historical point of interest that s/he has chosen, with the help of the Google Maps navigation tools. At the bottom right of the digital interactive map, there is an icon in the shape of a human figure. If the user drags the figure onto the map and stops it at the point of his/her choice, then the map turns into a "Street View" display (Fig. 9); i.e., the user sees the selected point in a 3D photographic display with the possibility of 360° rotation.

Fig. 9. Street view aspect

All points of interest have narratives, which makes it easier for the visitor and possibly their company to listen to the description of the point, without having to read text from the small screen of a portable smart device.

From the "Home" page, the user can also find a button for the "Historical Aspect" option (Fig. 10), which introduces the visitor to a concise and comprehensive history of the town, from prehistoric times to the present day. With this information, the visitor's contact with a historical experience has just begun. The next option in the main menu is the "Historical Maps" (Fig. 11), where the visitor has the opportunity to view the various phases of some of the town's fortifications and monuments through the maps.

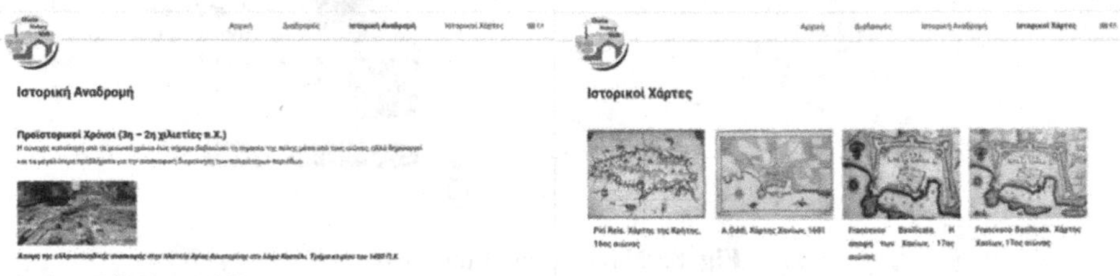

Fig. 10. Historical Aspect

Fig. 11. Historical maps

Fig. 12. QR Code

In terms of the promotion of the application and its direct access, it is proposed to place plexiglass signs measuring 40 cm × 40 cm with a QR (Quick Response) Code at each point of interest, at the entrances to the city (airport, harbours, bus stations), and also at central points in the town. The QR barcode has the main advantage of immediate readability of the code, providing a swift connection for the user to access the relevant website, which has been encoded in the QR Code [27].

More specifically, with the help of the QR Code reader application (Fig. 12), which is usually integrated in all modern mobile devices (smartphones, tablets), the user "reads" the code with the camera on their smart device and is immediately connected to the website. It is a relatively inexpensive way to promote the application and inform the visitor about the available app.

4.2 Limitations and Future Perspectives

Although the application includes 12 out of 44 existing historical routes in Chania, as described in the Master thesis that this paper is based on, many other routes can also be added [28]. Of crucial importance for the viability of the project is the establishment of an institutional administrational organization, which could scientifically support the content and functional operation of the application. The application also has the flexibility to be connected with many other digital applications of the Municipality of Chania, and to become the core functional element of an Open-Air Museum, enabling the transformation of the specific urban area of Chania to a 'smart' tourist destination.

The viability of such an application requires the establishment of the proposed institutional management body of the Open-Air Museum of the Old Town of Chania. Only an institutional body can ensure the sustainability of the historical routes, provide support and management of the digital application, maintain the scientific accuracy of its content, connect it with the information services of the Municipality of Chania and the other municipal infrastructure, and finally, support and complement it with additional historical and/or thematic routes. In this way, such an application forms an important tool for promoting the city as a tourist destination.

5 Conclusions

The paper introduces the *Chania History Walks* digital application, designed and developed with the purpose of showcasing the old town of Chania as an Open-Air Museum. This initiative makes use of the smart city infrastructure offered by the Municipality of Chania. The application's foundation lies in the theoretical underpinnings of cultural heritage and cultural tourism, which serve as wellsprings for fostering creativity and driving innovation. By amalgamating these concepts with smart city principles and harnessing the potential of information and communication technology (ICT), the city can cultivate distinct attributes that confer it with a competitive edge, thereby contributing to the realization of a sustainable future.

The historical routes lead the visitors to the discovery of the cultural heritage and the past, as it has remained so far in the town of Chania and enhance their learning process. In this way, the city of the present time can function as an Open-Air Museum. New ways of communication and contact emerge, which create new perceptions, imparting features of intimacy between the exhibits/monuments and the meanings/notions they convey. Historical routes are transformed into production spaces for a variety of different experiences, which strengthen individual memory and individual experiences, thus creating new historical narratives that lead to a deeper understanding of local history. Open-Air Museums that are integrated into urban spaces should co-create cultural capital to improve the quality of life, holistically, for both current and future generations.

Acknowledgment.

Co-funded by the ERASMUS+ Programme of the European Union" (Contract number: 101004049 — EURECA-PRO — EAC-A02-2019 / EAC-A02-2019-1).

References

1. UNESCO United Arab Emirates. Department of Culture and Tourism: Culture in Times of COVID-19: resilience, recovery and revival UNESCO, Abu Dhabi (2022)
2. Panagiotopoulou, M., Stratigea, A., Somarakis, G.: Smart cities and sustainable urban development - examples from the Mediterranean and Greek experience. In: Greek Section of the European Regional Science Association, 12th Scientific Conference on Urban and Regional Development: Contemporary Challenges (2014). https://www.researchgate.net/publication/265160346_Exypnes_Poleis_kai_Biosime_Astike_Anaptyxe_-_Paradeigmata_apo_te_Mesogeiake_kai_ten_Ellenike_Empeiria. (in Greek)
3. Toppeta, D.: The Smart City vision: How Innovation and ICT can build smart, "liveable", sustainable cities (2010).https://www.scribd.com/document/306968058/Toppeta-Report-005-2010
4. Harrison, C., Donnelly, I.A.: Theory of smart cities. In: Proceedings of the 55th Annual Meeting of the ISSS, vol. 55(1), Hull, UK (2011). https://journals.isss.org/index.php/proceedings55th/article/view/1703
5. Komninos, N.: The architecture of intelligent cities. In: Proceedings of the Conference on 'Intelligent Environments 06', Institution of Engineering and Technology, pp. 13–20 (2006). https://www.komninos.eu/wp-content/uploads/2014/01/2006-The-Architecture-of-Intel-Cities-IE06.pdf
6. Intelligent Community Forum (ICF): What is an intelligent Community? https://www.intelligentcommunity.org/what_is_an_intelligent_community
7. Buhalis, D., Amaranggana, A.: Smart tourism destinations. In: Xiang, Z., Tussyadiah, I. (eds.) Information and Communication Technologies in Tourism 2014, pp. 553–564. Springer, Cham (2013). https://doi.org/10.1007/978-3-319-03973-2_40
8. Paardekooper, R.: The value of an Archeological Open-Air Museum is in its use: Understanding Archeological Open-Air Museums and their Visitors. Sidestone Press, Leiden (2012)
9. Rentzhog, S.: Open air museums. The history and future of a visionary idea. Jamtli Forlag and Carlsson Bokforlag, Kristianstads (2007)
10. Richards, G., Bonink, C.: Marketing cultural tourism in Europe. J. Vacat. Mark. **1**(2), 172–180 (1995). https://doi.org/10.1177/135676679500100205

11. Andrakakou, M.: Online Web Map Application of Urban Routes of Cultural Heritage. NTUA, Athens (2017). (in Greek)
12. Hadžić, O.: Tourism and digitization of cultural heritage. In: Review of the National Center for Digitization, vol. 5, pp. 74–79. Faculty of Mathematics, Belgrade (2004). http://elib.mi.sanu.ac.rs/pages/browse_issue.php?db=ncd&rbr=5&start=10
13. Sylaiou, S.: Overview of applications of voluntary geographic information with emphasis on cultural heritage. Choro-grafies **3**(1), 15–22 (2012). (in Greek)
14. World Commission on Environment and Development (WCED): Report of the World Commission on Environment and Development: Our Common Future (1987). https://sustainabledevelopment.un.org/content/documents/5987our-common-future.pdf
15. Battaglini, E., et al.: Culture in, for and as sustainable development: conclusions from the COST Action IS1007 investigating cultural sustainability. In: Dessein, J., Soini, K., Fairclough, G., Horlings, L.: (eds.), University of Jyväskylä (2015)
16. Poulios, I.: Cultural management, local community and sustainable development. Kallipos, Open Academic Editions (2015). https://hdl.handle.net/11419/2396. (in Greek)
17. Moropoulou, A., Lampropoulos, K., Rallis, I., Doulamis, A.: Scientific architecture of the educational toolkit of the project EDICULA. In: Moropoulou, A., et al. (eds.): TMM_CH 2021, CCIS, vol. 1574, pp. 3–16. Springer, Cham (2022). https://doi.org/10.1007/978-3-031-20253-7_1
18. United Cities and Local Governments, Culture: Fourth Pillar of Sustainable Development. https://www.agenda21culture.net/sites/default/files/files/documents/multi/ag21_en.pdf
19. BritainThinks: Public perceptions of – and attitudes to - the purposes of museums in society. Report, Museums Association (2013). https://www.museumsassociation.org/app/uploads/2020/06/03042013-britain-thinks.pdf
20. Kosmopoulos, I., Siountri, K. and Anagnostopoulos, C-N: The use of deep learning in the classification of buildings at the post-revolutionary city of Athens. In: Moropoulou, A., et al. (eds.) TMM_CH 2021, CCIS, vol. 1574, pp. 110–124. Springer, Cham (2022). https://doi.org/10.1007/978-3-031-20253-7_10
21. Xydakis, N.: Museums for a Sustainable Society. Speech of the Deputy Minister of Culture at the event of the ICOM Greece for the celebration of the International Day of Museums (2015). https://www.culture.gov.gr/el/Information/SitePages/view.aspx?nID=1375. (in Greek)
22. Mavromati, E., Karatzani, A.: Sustainable management of cultural heritage. The science of conservation in the transition. Towards a global sustainable model. In: Moropoulou, A., et al. (Eds.): TMM_CH 2021, CCIS, vol. 1574, pp. 231–241. Springer, Cham (2022). https://doi.org/10.1007/978-3-031-20253-7_19
23. Tsivis, G.: Chania 1252–1940. EREISMA, Chania (2014). (in Greek)
24. Pentazou, I.: History in Exhibition. Digital Design Practices. Hellenic Open University Press, Athens (2019). (in Greek)
25. Drucker, J., Kim, D., Salehian, I., Bushong, A.: Introduction to digital humanities: concepts, methods, and tutorial for students and instructors. UCLA (2014)
26. Google Maps Platform: Build awesome apps with Google's knowledge of the real world. https://developers.google.com/maps/
27. Hung, S.-H., Yao, C.-Y., Fang, Y.-J., Tan, P., Lee, R.-R.: Micrography QR codes. IEEE Trans. Visual Comput. Graph. **9**(1), 2834–2847 (2020)
28. Manoudakis, H.: Smart city and Open Air Museum: A digital application for the promotion of the old town of Chania. M.Sc. Thesis, Hellenic Open University (2022). https://apothesis.eap.gr/handle/repo/55365. (in Greek)

Digitization of Industrial Heritage in Greece

Theodora Chatzi Rodopoulou(✉)

Quantitative Methods Laboratory, Department of Business Administration, University of the Aegean, 82100 Chios, Greece
dora.xr@gmail.com

Abstract. Since the late 20th century, the vestiges of industrialization have become an integral part of cultural heritage. Industrial heritage has been established worldwide as an outstanding historical resource that embodies a multitude of values while offering bright prospect for development. Key prerequisites for the efficient protection of this significant stock, its preservation and the exploitation of its potential is its documentation, the comprehension of its significance as well as the familiarization of local communities with it.

Contrary to the European practice, in Greece, the process of industrial heritage recording and documentation, as well as the training of local communities about its value and potential, have only recently started to be addressed in a systematic way. New technologies, offering enormous opportunities, have accelerated this ongoing process. The last two decades have seen an increasing trend of digitization of industrial heritage tangible and intangible elements in Greece, using novel technological means. New technological tools are also implemented for the interpretation and dissemination of the historic industrial stock significance.

The aim of this paper is to highlight modern approaches involving digital tools and technologies employed in the 21st century for the documentation of industrial heritage in Greece, its interpretation and the dissemination of its values to the public. Besides the overview of the achievements in relation to the digitization of industrial heritage in the country, the paper also discusses the opportunities opened by new technologies for industrial heritage protection, interpretation and care and provides suggestions for future action.

Keywords: Industrial Heritage · Digital Registry · Digital Platform · 3Dscanning · Photogrammetry · 3Dprinting · Industrial museums · Technology

1 Introduction

Industrial heritage has been recognized internationally as an invaluable cultural resource. The appreciation of the historic industrial stock in Greece and its establishment in the collective consciousness took longer in comparison to the north-western European countries and has only been achieved in the last couple of decades. Interest for industrial heritage was expressed for the first time in Greece in the late 1980s. During the last decade of the 20th century, research, survey and documentation initiatives of historic industrial sites were taken, revealing the significance and the potential of this new heritage group.

A. Moropoulou et al. (Eds.): TMM_CH 2023, CCIS 1889, pp. 202–212, 2023.
https://doi.org/10.1007/978-3-031-42300-0_17

Today, three decades later, the historic industrial stock is no longer considered an 'outsider' in the Greek cultural heritage context and has begun finding its place among the assets of Greek heritage. A factor that contributed to this development, greatly facilitating stakeholders in their quest to record and document industrial heritage, as well as disseminate its value and potential, was the use of new technologies.

This paper aims to review the digitization process of industrial heritage tangible and intangible elements in Greece, shedding light for the first time to this promising ongoing procedure. It does not seek to offer an exhaustive account of all industrial elements digitized but rather to showcase the multitude of technological means used for the digitization of industrial heritage, analyzing selected examples. Digital registries of historic industrial sites, surveys of industrial complexes, installations and machinery using photogrammetry or laser scanning, digital records of intangible dimensions of industrial heritage, as well as digital applications used in industrial museums for the interpretation of their collection will be discussed. The paper draws from the author's work in the last ten years as well as a wealth of cases including initiatives taken by: national and regional public bodies, industrial museums, researchers and research institutes, postgraduate students as well as volunteers. Data for those cases were collected using desktop research, literature review and the Delphi method.

This paper makes an important contribution to the growing area of research on digital cultural heritage, offering an overview of the achievements in relation to the digitization of industrial heritage in Greece so far, discussing the opportunities opened by new technologies for industrial heritage protection, interpretation and care as well as providing suggestions for future action.

2 Early Initiatives of Industrial Heritage Study, Protection and Interpretation

The first efforts for the protection of industrial heritage in Greece started in the 1980s with the action of public administration services, research and cultural organizations. The State assumed an active role in the protection of the Greek historic industrial stock in 1989, establishing the group 'Industrial Archaeology' in the Directorate of Folk Culture of the Hellenic Ministry of Culture. The group's aim was to introduce and coordinate the documentation, safeguarding, exploitation and conduct of reuse studies of industrial complexes and elements. The group in collaboration with the regional offices of Modern Monuments, launched the first systematic documentation program of industrial buildings that led to a series of listings. Furthermore, it compiled a specialized archive of industrial heritage assets including listed preindustrial and industrial buildings. Despite its impressive work, this initiative was restricted to its very first steps as the group was dissolved a year later without finding a successor. As a result, industrial monuments were incorporated in the general scope of the Directorate of Modern Monuments. Another important development of that era was the establishment of the Greek Section of TICCIH in 1992, which engaged and mobilized a large group of people and foundations advocating for the safeguarding of the Greek industrial legacy [1].

3 Recording Industrial Heritage

The growing interest in the relics of industrialization was manifested in the 1990s with the emergence of multiple targeted recordings by academic, scientific and research institutions, private bodies and individual researchers, either through research programs or during the creation process of local thematic museums and other reuse projects. Important targeted recordings were: the research program 'Historical industrial equipment in Greece' (National Hellenic Research Foundation - NTUA, 1998), the 'Preliminary Action for the Documentation of the Industrial Heritage in the Aegean Sea' (Ministry for the Aegean – Institute of Neohellenic Research of the National Hellenic Research Foundation, 2001–2004), as well as the documentation expeditions realized as part of the action of the Industrial Museum of Hermoupolis (National Hellenic Research Foundation, 1998–2001) and the Lavrion Technological Cultural Park (NTUA since 1994).

The abovementioned initiatives, gathered a wealth of data, using mainly manual card recording systems. Despite its undeniable value, this early recording approach presented multiple challenges, such as the establishment of common data standards, the use of geo-spatial referencing and the accessibility of the recorded data. Furthermore, those initiatives lacked the comprehensive scope of the national registries compiled in the same era abroad, synthesizing a fragmented and incomplete image of the Greek industrial heritage stock [1].

3.1 Digital Registries of Industrial Heritage

The first digital industrial heritage registries in Greece were compiled in the 2000s. The most prominent initiatives in that respect were taken by the public sector. In detail, the Ministry of Culture updated its digital registry Odysseus with a richer content including a thematic catalogue of listed industrial, technical monuments and workshops. Furthermore, in 2007 the Ministry of Environment launched a digital archive of traditional settlements and protected buildings. The archive, despite being generic, included various cases of protected industries. In the same period the National Hellenic Research Foundation launched the thematic registry: Industrial establishments and workshops in the Aegean. In parallel with those initiatives, the Greek Section TICCIH acknowledging the need for the creation of a comprehensive national registry of historic industrial assets, developed the 'Registry of the Greek Industrial Heritage'. The project started as an effort to collect and digitally index existing records, data originating from bibliography and various research programs and it was later combined with field research. By the end of the project the registry included 1.482 record sheets. The lack of resources however did not allow its continuation and the formulation of a functional database for the retrieval of the collected data by the public [1].

A decade later, in 2017, a small number of volunteers, noticing the lack of a single freely accessible registry for the Greek Industrial Heritage, formed the group 'Vault of Industrial Digital Archives' or VIDA (acronym for 'Industrial Records' in Greek). VIDA aimed to locate, gather and record information for digitizing the Greek industrial heritage, using internet applications and crowdsourcing. The selected free online tools that were originally used by the group to achieve its aims were: Facebook, Blogger,

Google Maps and YouTube. The information collected by an extended community of people and by the group members were formulated as records of a digital registry that was originally hosted in a blog (https://vida-omada.blogspot.com/), featuring an interactive map.

In 2020, VIDA created a new online platform (https://vidarchives.gr/) featuring multiple pages for disseminating its activities, including the digital registry (see Fig. 1). The new platform allowed the increase of the number of industrial categories, resulting in a more analytical map, while facilitating at the same time the process of information collection and the creation of industrial records for the users and the site administrators. VIDA was turned into an NGO in 2021 and continues its action to this day. Its growing digital registry counts 1676 record sheets, being the only open interactive database on the Greek industrial heritage [2].

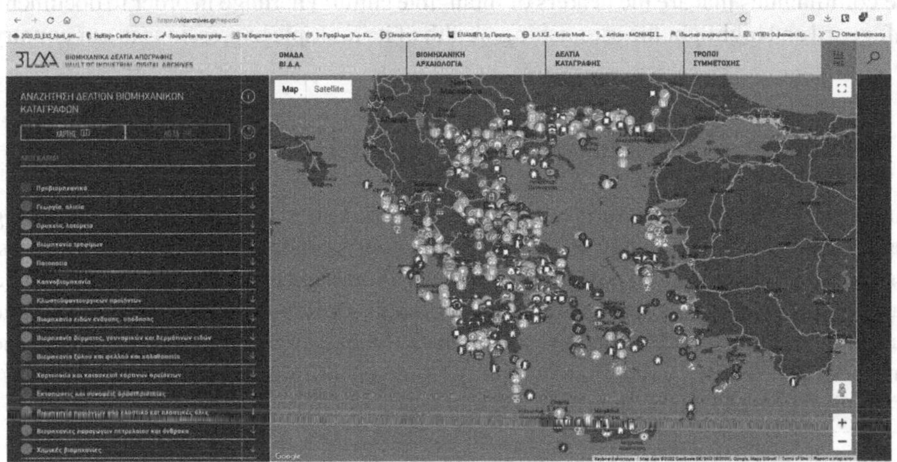

Fig. 1. The interactive map of VIDA featuring the industrial heritage elements that have been collectively documented (Source: https://vidarchives.gr/reports)

In 2018 another innovative online platform was launched, enabling the review of industrial heritage reuse practice in four European countries, including Greece. The website 'ReIH. Industrial Heritage Reuse in Europe' (https://reindustrialheritage.eu/) was the product of research, conducted within the framework of a PhD investigation titled "Control Shift. European Industrial Heritage Reuse in Review". Being more than a conventional database, it includes both an extended digital registry with more than 150 case studies of transformed industries across Europe as well as background information about the development of industrial heritage reuse practice in Britain, the Netherlands, Greece and Spain. An important feature of the website is its dynamic character, facilitating the processing and management of existing data while also allowing for the update and extension of the registry in a user-friendly way. This online knowledge platform aimed at the extensive recording of reused industrial sites, the dissemination of this information and with the familiarization of both specialists and the public on this significant, widely employed practice [3].

Records and data on the Greek preindustrial and industrial heritage can also be found in other digital registries and aggregators that have a wider scope. Movable industrial heritage assets and archival material for example, such as historic pictures of Greek industrial complexes and industrialists, old newspapers, journals, letters, reports can be found in the website SearchCulture.gr, developed in 2015 by the National Documentation Centre [4]. SearchCulture.gr is the Greek Aggregator for Cultural Content and National Provider for Europeana. The digital files available in the website are primarily photographs and other images, pdfs, 3D models and audio-visual material.

Information on intangible aspects of certain preindustrial and industrial sectors, such as the knowhow of key agro-industrial processes, preindustrial techniques and craftmanship, have been catalogued in the expanding digital National Inventory of intangible heritage. The registry was created by the Directorate of Modern Cultural Heritage of the Hellenic Ministry of Culture and Sports in the early 2010s, aiming to provide a voice to the communities that are the bearers of intangible cultural heritage in order to document, safeguard and highlight the astonishing wealth of its multiple expressions in our country [5].

4 Field Survey of Industrial Heritage Assets

Since the 1990s an increasing number of industrial sites have been surveyed using traditional survey techniques in the framework of conservation and transformation works, research projects as well as postgraduate studies. Prominent examples of hand measured based field surveys include the survey of the oil mills of Lesvos Island, the survey of the buildings and machinery turned into the industrial museum of Ermoupolis in Syros, the survey of the complex of the French mining Company of Lavrion, as well as the surveys of the lighthouses and the industrial loading jetties of Greece [1].

4.1 Industrial Sites Survey Using Modern Technology

The scale and complexity of industrial heritage sites, their state of conservation and the high likelihood of pollution renders surveys with the use of traditional survey techniques particularly challenging, time consuming and in many cases dangerous. Since the early 2000s, modern technological means have been progressively used facilitating and enhancing industrial heritage survey. Selected examples are presented below, illustrating different modern techniques adopted for surveying industrial sites.

A groundbreaking project in Greece in the field of industrial heritage conservation was the conservation study of the 19th century French loading jetty of Lavrio. The study was undertaken from 2018 to 2022 in the framework of a research project by the National Technical University of Athens, with the participation of seven laboratories specialized in different disciplines [6]. In order to establish the state of conservation and identify the level of damage of the historic structure, a survey of the loading jetty was carried out in two phases, using modern topographical and photogrammetric methods in combination with traditional measurement techniques.

In specific, in the first phase of the surveying process a geodetic network was established with permanent markings and measurements with geodetic rather that satellite methods, in GGRS '87, the Greek geodetic reference system 1987, for greater accuracy and with the minimum commitments, so that the distortion of the projection scale would not be introduced into it. Topographic measurements were taken, using high-resolution ground-based cameras as well as Unmanned Aerial Vehicles (UAV). Digital images were edited with the 'structure from motion' photogrammetric technique (SfM). Additional close-up detail photography of the jetty was conducted.

In the second phase, a precision imaging laser scanner was used for scanning the stone-masonry base of the structure. The scans were merged together by applying the ICP (cloud-to-cloud) algorithm. The merged cloud was georeferenced to the coordinate system of the previous survey by identifying a sufficient number of details, found in the older cloud that had been produced from low-altitude aerial photography and ground-based photography. The result of these processes was saved in a format that was editable in a digital design software.

Those means resulted in the production of an overall map of the wider area, a high-resolution overall map of the loading jetty and several sections and elevations of the stone-masonry base of the structure. A point cloud in color of the interior of the land part of the French loading jetty which had recently been excavated was produced as well as a point cloud, without color, of the land part of the French loading jetty, in the state that it was in 2018.

In 2022, three historic tanneries located in the town of Chios, were digitally mapped by the Cartography and Geoinformatics Laboratory, Department of Geography of the University of the Aegean. UAVs were used for the production of orthophoto maps and digital surface models of the buildings' envelope. GPS Real-Time Kinematic (RTK) technique was applied to measure about 20 ground control points (GCPs), in the GGRS '87, for georeferencing the photos taken from the UAVs. The produced models provide an accurate picture of the state of conservation of the buildings [7].

An architectural and technical survey of a significant railway heritage asset was carried out in the framework of an MSc study in the 'Protection of Monuments' Program of the National Technical University of Athens. The Roundhouse of the Lefka Railway complex in Piraeus was surveyed using a combination of photogrammetry and hand measuring. The photogrammetry method was used for the measurement of the building shell and the surrounding area (see Fig. 2). For placing the digital model in actual coordinate system and right alignment, a total of 45 marked points were measured on site with a geodetic station (Trimble M3 5″). Two georeferenced points were established, one in the exterior and one in the interior of the building. To Georeference the digital model in the GGRS '87 a GNSS geodetic receiver (Trimble R8) was used. The position of the two established standard points was determined through satellite observations applying the RTK technique.

Taking photos for the photogrammetric documentation was carried out in two phases: the first covered the ground shots of the interior of the shell and of its surrounding area, while the second covered the aerial shots, also in the interior and the exterior of the building, using an UAV. The photogrammetric processing was performed in the Structure from Motion (SfM) environment of the Agisoft MetaShape software. The main topographic plan was the result of the acquisition of photogrammetric stereoscopic images. The entire area of interest was captured by using an orthophoto derived from the drone.

Fig. 2. Digital elevation models of the Roundhouse of the Lefka were produced using photogrammetric techniques [8]

The design of the roundhouse was based both on conventional designing methods and procedural design. Through the production of 2D CAD drawings, it was possible to gain a deeper understanding of the unique structural and architectural elements of the roundhouse, its structural system and its pathology. The collected data, measurements and analyses were managed and displayed through Revit Architecture software, a platform for Building Information Modelling (BIM). The integration of photogrammetry in the BIM workflow offered a significant advantage in the study as scanned data contributed to the creation and design of specific elements-modules. During the scanning process of the structures on site, new relevant information emerged, resulting in the amendment of the initial design and the update of the project documentation. In the BIM environment a library of digital procedural elements was developed, making the entire design process controllable. The digital models were generated from a set of rules and parameters, being fully adjustable [8].

4.2 Mechanical Equipment Digital Documentation

A fundamental part of industrial heritage, that renders it challenging in every possible way, is the mechanical equipment. Machinery has, in almost every case, a complex geometry and it is exceptionally hard to document. Modern technological means have only recently started to be used for the survey of mechanical equipment in Greece.

A prominent example of mechanical equipment digital documentation is the survey of the content of the LIPTOL complex in Ptolemaida. The documentation was conducted in 2020 in the framework of the Public Power Company project: "Dismantling, removal and transportation of the historic mechanical equipment from the LIPTOL complex to the Steam Electric Power Station plant of Ptolemaida" [9]. The full range of the large scale and heavy weight lignite processing machinery of the complex was documented in situ, using two types of scanners. A mobile mapping system was used for the documentation of the general set-up of the equipment while handheld scanners were used for the documentation of machinery details. 3D scanning produced point clouds that were reversed engineered for the creation of 3D models.

During the disassembly phase the joint surfaces of the machines were scanned in a high resolution (accuracy 10 μm) in order to capture the adjacent surfaces and functional tolerances. The extraordinary accuracy of the produced models allows researchers to study the construction details of the machinery, identify missing parts of particularly small dimensions while providing at the same time the necessary information for the machinery reassembly.

5 Interpretation of Industrial Heritage in Industrial Museums

Technology has not only influenced the protection and the documentation of industrial heritage but it has also transformed the way the vestiges of industrialization are interpretated as well as the way their cultural significance is disseminated. Cultural organizations, such as industrial museums and visitor attractions in Greece have recently started using an array of technological applications including interactive multimedia applications and interactive games; 3D animation videos and virtual tours as well as 3D scanning and 3D printing technology. Selected examples provide a better view of this evolving process in the country.

A number of industrial museums, including the Naoussa Centre of Industrial Heritage - ERIA [10] and the majority of the Piraeus Bank Group Cultural Foundation industrial museums [11], offer virtual tours of their collection, providing their audience the opportunity to access them remotely. Sound installations can be found in various industrial museums including the Industrial Gas Museum in Athens while theatrical soundscapes have recently started to form part of exhibitions dedicated to industrial heritage (e.g. temporary exhibition 'People and Factories. Industrial Elefsina' organized in 2016) [12].

A small number of industrial museums' collections so far have adopted a combination of technological applications for the interpretation of their exhibits. An example of such a museum is the Matsopoulos industrial museum. In the framework of the transformation of the former flour mill central building to the Matsopoulos industrial museum in 2017, the building, machinery and the flour production process were digitally documented. The digitized information was used for the interpretation of the industrial environment, the form and the operation of the Mill.

In specific, the technological means used for the site's interpretation include interactive applications, active audio applications, 3D animation videos that reproduce the operation process of the main machines of the Mill's production line (see Fig. 3) as well as interactive games [13].

The last couple of decades have also seen the adoption of 3Dprinting and 3Dscanning technology from many cultural organizations for the documentation and promotion of their collections. Greek cultural organizations have only recently started to experiment with those novel technological means. In the framework of the action Aegean Digital Tourism Tank conducted as part of the program e-Aegean CulTour by the Quantitative Methods Laboratory and the Privacy Engineering and Social Informatics Laboratory of the University of the Aegean, the systematic production of cultural products and services using 3Dscanning and 3Dprinting technology is attempted. The project aims to contribute to the introduction of digital practices for cultural production and consumption and

Fig. 3. 3D animation video of the mechanical equipment operation of the Matsopoulos Mill (Source: https://www.youtube.com/watch?v=ncUv2Fbwb8c)

the evolution of the digital cultural innovation of the cultural organizations, promoting tourism in the islands of the North Aegean.

Exhibits from selected cultural and tourist organizations of the islands of the North Aegean Sea, including the Museum of industrial olive oil production of Lesvos and the Chios Mastic Museum, are scanned using 3Dscanners. Using different software packages and design tools the scans are turned to 3Dmodels, which can be printed on demand in 3Dprinters or can be downloaded by the visitors and personnel of the involved cultural organizations.

6 Discussion and Conclusions

The present paper reviewed the digitization process of industrial heritage in Greece from its beginning to this day, shedding light for the first time to this ongoing revolutionary procedure. An array of technological applications used for recording, surveying and interpreting industrial heritage were discussed, through multiple examples.

The analysis revealed the considerable advances made in recent years by the use of technology in the recording, surveying and interpreting of the Greek industrial heritage. In specific, the compilation of open access digital industrial registries which are available online allowed the wide dissemination of various aspects of the Greek industrial heritage to the national and international scientific community as well as the better familiarization of the public with this heritage category. Moreover, it was shown that modern digital registries stimulate the active engagement of the public, heightening awareness over the Greek industrial heritage, its significance and its unexploited potential. Another significant advantage of those registries is their dynamic character, facilitating the processing and management of existing data while also allowing for their update and extension in a user-friendly way. The compilation of such web-based registries of the Greek Industrial Heritage, opens the possibility for the realization of a much-needed evaluation and categorization of this material which can in turn lead to its informed management.

The paper also revealed the substantial advantages of industrial heritage surveying with the use of modern technological means. Photogrammetry and laser scanning have been proven faster, more efficient and in certain cases even safer methods of documenting industrial heritage sites and installations in comparison to traditional approaches. Both methods allow detailed documentation and more accurate reconstructions of elements that were almost impossible to document using traditional means.

In respect to the documentation of industrial machinery it is worth stressing the wide array of opportunities created by the use of new technological means. The 3D models produced by digital surveys make possible the full reconstruction of the machinery set-up, the illustration of the relationship of the intermediate products with the processing stages as well as the recreation of the means of the machinery interconnection. This not only facilitates the understanding of the production line but it also provides valuable information for the reassembly and the reoperation of the machinery if necessary. Moreover, the digital files can be used for the production of digital tours of both existing and demolished industrial sites, constituting an invaluable source of educational material.

The acquisition of dense data sampling with high accuracy in 3D digital data format which is made possible by modern techniques can play a significant role in the monitoring of historic industrial buildings, which ought to be the next step in cultural heritage care.

Finally, it should be stressed that the new technological means greatly facilitate the interpretation and the dissemination of industrial heritage cultural significance as well as the operation of industrial museums. The paper illustrated different applications and techniques currently used by industrial museums and visitor attractions that offer improved and more attractive experiences to their visitors, allowing them to extend their audience while making their collections more accessible and better understood. The use of AI as well as 3D printing and 3Dscanning, which have just started to gain momentum, can render industrial museums in the coming years more open, more inclusive and more accessible, contributing in the achievement of their 21st century mission.

The use of technology in the preservation and care of industrial heritage as well as in the public engagement that favors its better comprehension and appreciator are not limited to the topics discussed in this paper. Important issues that can be addressed in future studies are the digitization of industrial archives as well as the use of the world wide web and social media for engaging and educating a large audience and disseminating the cultural significance of industrial heritage further.

References

1. Chatzi Rodopoulou, T.: Control shift. European industrial heritage reuse in review. A+BE |Architecture and the Built Environment, [S.l.], no. 13, pp. 1-630, (2020). https://doi.org/10.7480/abe.2020.13.5195
2. Mavroidi, M.: VIDA, Reclaiming Industrial Heritage in Greece, TICCIH Bulletin, 2nd Quarter, no. 96, pp. 3–5 (2022)
3. Chatzi Rodopoulou, T., Floros, X.: ReIH: an online knowledge platform for industrial heritage reuse. In Rettig, J.M. (ed.) Proceedings of the XVII TICCIH Congress: Patrimonio Industrial. Entendiendo el pasado, hacienda el futuro sostenible. Santiago, Chile, 13–14 September, pp. 363–366 (2018)
4. SearchCulture.gr. https://www.searchculture.gr/aggregator/portal/?language=en. Accessed 23 Dec 2022
5. Intangible Cultural Heritage of Greece: National Registry. https://ayla.culture.gr/category/elements-inscribed-in-the-national-inventory-of-ich/. Accessed 23 Dec 2022

6. Sapountzakis, E. (P.I.), et al.: French loading jetty of the Lavrion mines. Research project preliminary study, NTUA- Municipality of Lavrion (2022)
7. Tataris, G.: Interview on the digital mapping of three historic tanneries in the town of Chios, by the cartography and geoinformatics Laboratory, Department of Geography, University of the Aegean (2022)
8. Farazis, G.: The Rotunda in the historic Piraeus Depot Complex: Documentation and Reuse Master's thesis, NTUA (2019)
9. Plytas, A.: Interview on the digitization of the mechanical equipment of historic industries in Greece (2022)
10. Naoussa Centre of Industrial Heritage – ERIA: Tour. https://erianaoussa.gr/vrtour/project.html. Accessed 23 Dec 2022
11. Piraeus Bank Group Cultural Foundation: 360° Experience. https://www.piop.gr/en/Experience.aspx. Accessed 23 Dec 2022
12. Koutsoudaki, E.: Interview on the technological applications in the Greek industrial museums (2022)
13. Adamidis, G., Amiridou, V., Tsoukalas, T., et al.: Matsopoulos industrial Museum in Trikala. The story of a flour mill. In: Restoration and Museological design of an Industrial Complex in Proceeding of the 2nd Panhellenic conference of cultural heritage digitization, Volos, pp.330–336 (2017)

Built Cultural Heritage and Digital Transition: The New Role of Data and Artificial Intelligence Applications in Administrative Procedures

Anna Maria Pentimalli Biscaretti di Ruffia(✉)

Politecnico di Milano (DABC), Via G. Ponzio 31, 20133 Milan, Italy
annamaria.pentimalli@polimi.it

Abstract. How is the approach to built cultural heritage conservation design project adapting to new IT tools? How can project data be crucial and what use can be made of artificial intelligence (A.I.) techniques to optimize information management? Starting from the research opportunity offered by the Phd project carried out by Politecnico di Milano ABC department on the topic of A.I. applications to Italian Public Administration (P.A.) digital procedures relevant to the Civil Code on Cultural and Landscape Heritage (legislative decree 42/2004) the paper outlines how a systemic use and a statistical view of design project data, according to the definition of automatically verifiable standard elements, could help guarantee a higher level of knowledge functional to the improvement of cultural assets protection. The overview of the Italian case study will lay the foundations for future developments regarding the important issue linked to the digital transition, which is affecting the entire building sector at various levels (administrative procedures, procurement procedures, project management, digital twins), looking into the potential and limits of the use of new technologies and data management systems (digital platforms) to improve conservation and enhancement of built cultural heritage.

Keywords: Conservation · public administration · digital procedures

1 Introduction

1.1 Public Administration and Digitization of Procedures: Where Are We at?

The contribution is part of the current scenario relating to the management of Public Administration (P.A.) information assets and to the progressive digitization of administrative procedures relevant to the Civil Code on Cultural and Landscape Heritage (legislative decree 42/2004). In particular the case study investigates the problem of heterogeneity of data managed by the Italian Ministry of Culture (MiC), both at national and local level, and the consequent difficulty of guaranteeing a uniform level of knowledge functional to the in-depth evaluation of built cultural heritage conservation projects. This aspect is also linked to the preliminary investigative phase of the design project, often limited or too generic due to the lack of a clear and uniform reference model for the submission of applications to the Fine Art Service (*Soprintendenze Archeologia Belle Arti e Paesaggio*) that is in charge of project evaluation [1].

A. Moropoulou et al. (Eds.): TMM_CH 2023, CCIS 1889, pp. 213–221, 2023.
https://doi.org/10.1007/978-3-031-42300-0_18

Indeed, mainly when working on historical pre-existences, it is knowledge that determines the quality of the intervention: the more in-depth the analysis is, the more evident will be the stratifications and the main elements that allow the history of the building to be recomposed and handed down over time [2]. Thus, during the planning and the submission of the applications for the design architects it becomes necessary to transfer to the public administration a cognitive framework relating both to the historical and constructive transformations that have affected the structure (analysis of the construction materials, of the structure, of the surfaces, of the decorative apparatus, technological contributions that have occurred over time) in order to demonstrate that they have understood the nature of the building and therefore are able to implement a respectful and careful design capable of enhancing historical structures and materials [3].

How to carry out a precise recognition of all this information and provide it efficiently to Public Administration? How to limit misunderstandings between the subjects involved in the protection processes? How to improve data flow efficiency?

The proposal follows this research line wondering what might be the most efficient way to increase the sharing and the quality of information digitizing the main procedures/user interfaces in order to provide increasingly high-performance and universally accessible services.

In recent years, public administrations both at national and local level have had the obligation to update their tools and operating practices to the increasingly innovative information and communication technologies (ICT) and to the new requirements imposed by the legislation on administrative procedures [4]. The goal, both at state and European level, is to create a new P.A. provider of services and reference center for users by improving the public service [5] and reducing costs and times through the adoption of technological and information models capable of guaranteeing e-government services.

The reference text on the matter is the Legislative Decree 7-3-2005, n. 82 or Digital Administration Code (CAD) that reorganize the IT legislation of the Public Administration and lay the foundations for the simplification of relations between the P.A. and private individuals and between different P.A. [6].

The interoperability of systems and the integration of service processes between administrations is instead regulated by guidelines issued by AgID (*Agenzia per l'Italia digitale*) which is linked to the Digital Administration Code and the main digital simplification tools at ministerial level are: the three-year plan for information technology in the public administration [7]; the 2025 Strategy for technological innovation and the digitization of the country [8]; digital platforms.

Between these, digital platforms are key since they represent the concrete tool used by P.A. to carry out its activities, allowing the digitization of procedures and the interaction between the various subjects involved in the processes [4]. In particular, among the main platforms governed by the CAD, the research is concerned with the National Digital Data Platform (*Piattaforma Digitale Nazionale Dati - PDND*), still under development, which aims to promote knowledge and use of the information assets held by public administrations, as well as data sharing, with a view to simplification of administrative tasks for citizens and businesses. The National Digital Data Platform is the technological infrastructure responsible for the interoperability of information systems and databases of public administrations and, at the same time, collects and stores information on accesses and activities. It aims to manage big data and administrative activities in cloud, implement the once only principle and ensure maximum interoperability between public administrations, citizens and businesses [9–12].

In dealing with the digitization process of the Public Administration, it is also necessary to mention the dematerialization of the related documents which plays an important role in the current management of incoming and outgoing communications from the deeds related to the authorization procedures which must necessarily be recorded electronically, as well as any type of document [13].

Therefore, the adoption of a document management computer system becomes mandatory (Art. 52 of Presidential Decree 445/2000) but the choice of the level of computerization to be adopted up to the individual Public Administration which, at present, should only guarantee the IT protocol [14, 15].

The IT system that manages administrative procedures regarding cultural heritage is just dealing with the digital protocol and document archiving but il does not allow direct contact between the various subjects involved in the conservation and enhancement process and does not systematically acquire data from other Public Administrations as the once only principle would require. Thus, the data that should already be in the possession of the various Public Administrations, as contained within the public information databases, are not yet collected and organized within a common virtual environment.

Furthermore, the requests submitted to the Fine Arts Service do not currently have reference models regarding the level of detail of the information content of the annexes and each of the 43 territorial offices chooses the information to provide to users in this regard. The result of this lack of unified management of the requests is the lack of a statistical analysis of the data submitted to P.A. In fact, the previous documentation relating to a specific building, complex of buildings or natural landscape is not provided in advance to the interested parties when drafting new projects and, likewise, the documentation produced as a result of a conservation and enhancement project is not included in a digitally accessible data environment.

In this context, what impact can the digital transition have on conservation strategies? How to improve existing telematics platforms for the digital management of requests of intervention on built cultural heritage in order to guarantee a unified system with a high information content throughout the national territory? How to improve the way public data is generated and managed? And finally, how to improve the institutions decision-making process which can often appear to be discretionary? (Fig. 1)

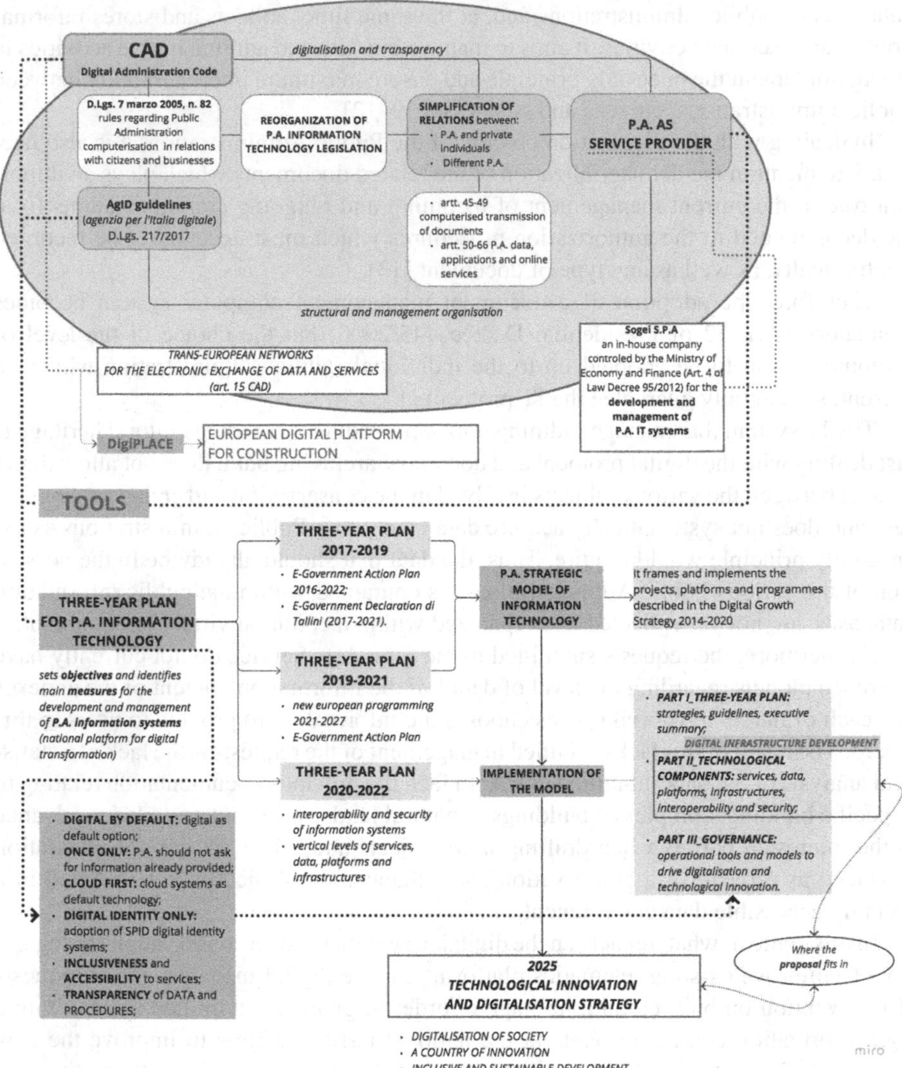

Fig. 1. Summary scheme of the state of the art useful for framing the topic addressed.

2 Materials and Methods

2.1 How to Innovate in the Management of Procedures? Challenges and Objectives

The research path develops and modifies to respond to the critical issues outlined in the state of the art and actively contribute to the valorization of P.A. data asset with a view to transparency and efficiency.

The most critical aspect concerns electronic document management that assume a strategic role, within the more general process of automated information systems, both to support the improvement of services, the transparency of administrative action, the containment of costs and, in this specific case, to effectively protect built cultural heritage.

The assumption is that the relevant legislations (T.U. 445/2000; Digtal Adiministration Code - *Codice dell'Amministrazione Digitale* D. Lgs. 82/2005; L. 241/90) would require P.A. to adopt a plan for the development of automated information systems aimed at achieving total automation of the phases of management, dissemination and use of their data, documents and procedures.

In addition, P.A. should deal with a progressive replacement of paper archives with computer archives [16]. The common goal to be achieved is to adopt a single electronic government system with which to manage the electronic processing of document flows and the automation of administrative procedures. Each P.A., according to its own organization and technological dimension, is gradually approaching this objective with a view to e-government.

Therefore, the proposal intends to help the Fine Arts Service to face digital transition suggesting the improvement of the currently used systems for protocol and computer flow management (G.I.A.D.A - *Sistema di protocollo informatico e di gestione documentale digitale*) thanks to the interoperability with a digital platform shaped for guarantee the statistical validation of data; the integration of data already held by P.A. according to the *"once only principle"* expressed in the Three Year Plan for P.A. information technology [7]; hence enabling direct dialogue between the various parties involved in the process of cultural heritage protection. This tool should ensure the strategic management of information relating to the building as well as a high level of preliminary knowledge thus allowing greater control of the project.

Furthermore, the platform could be considered as the starting point for a common data environment in which to relate the data regarding previous interventions with state of the art data and post intervention data, thus laying the foundations for its planned conservation.

What can be the role played by A.I. in the improvement of management processes and in the greater efficiency of administrative procedures? The new artificial intelligence software can be structured to make the workflows of each administrative procedure clear and transparent, improve the management of connected data by speeding up the preliminary activities and therefore making the administrative action more efficient [17] (Fig. 2).

2.2 Methodological Proposal for Digitizing an Administrative Procedure

The methodology hypothesized to implement the digitization of administrative procedures relevant to the Civil Code on Cultural and Landscape Heritage (legislative decree 42/2004) addresses three main elements: data analysis, development of the digital tool (platform) and network management.

Starting from the data analysis, the administrative procedure to be digitized was first defined within the Civil Code on Cultural and Landscape Heritage (legislative decree 42/2004) that is Art.21 d.lgs 42/2004 "interventions of any kind on cultural heritage". Then the most significant document for the procedure was chosen which summarized all the most important information relating to the architectural project and which was

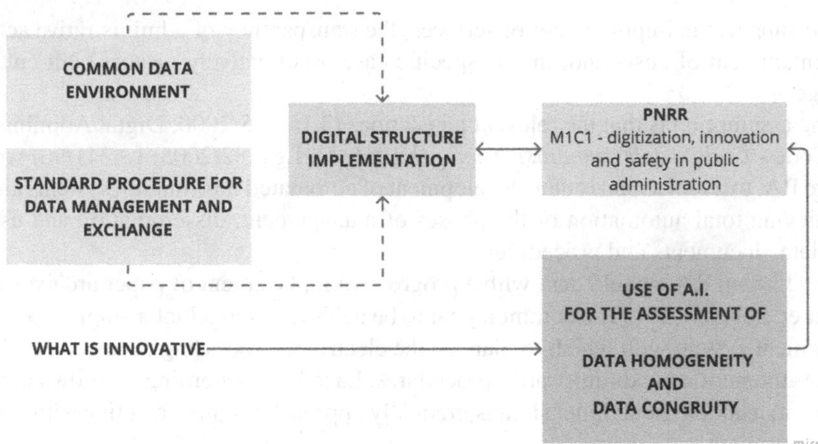

Fig. 2. The diagram shows the interaction between the proposed objectives.

relevant for the decision-making process: the technical report. The document is textual in nature in order to be able to define "domains", descriptive of the most relevant components of a conservation project, which can be managed through algorithms of Natural Language Processes use to quickly locate the most essential words and phrases. This technology could be used for checking if the submitted document is compliant with a defined reference standard for each class of intervention.

As already mentioned, one of the problems that architects have to face while submitting a request for interventions is defining the level of knowledge and the information content of the attachments in relation to the typology of intervention they intend to carry out.

Actually the rule, including "interventions of any kind on cultural heritage", by it's very nature leaves ample room for interpretation both in submitting and requesting the documents considered to be the most exhaustive for a specific case study.

At present the regulatory guideline refers to a ministerial annex that includes a list of documents which architects can check to organize the documents to be submitted to the Fine Arts Service and the rule leaves ample room for interpretation both in submitting and requesting the documents considered to be the most exhaustive for a specific case study.

How to better frame the minimum contents necessary for the project, in order to reduce discretionary margins and timing? Starting from the relationship between possible intervention classes and the existing and innovative construction components involved in the project, development of the digital tool includes the construction of an IT structure capable of linking the intervention class to the type and quantity of data necessary to achieve the minimum knowledge level necessary for the validation of the design choices described in the project.

However, the issue of identifying standard parameters for cultural heritage design projects is still much debated at both methodological and information level, as also proved by lack of guidelines established by law in Art. 29, paragraph 5 of d.lgs 42/2004 regarding the methodologies of intervention on cultural heritage. Therefore, the starting point is the standardization of the information level and the methodology of presentation and exchange of project data.

The analysis of inconsistencies will take place through the use of artificial intelligence technologies: his operation is defined as "Labeling" that is the identification of formulas and recurrent parameters in the question/answer query model. It is crucial for the construction of the algorithm that should determine which are the most requested data depending on similar interventions and which ones are the most taken into consideration.

The hypothesized IT tool for the consistent submission of documents could be part of a common data environment ad the interactions with other Public administrations should be possible exchanging information not only between the public and private sectors but also between different public authorities. Both tasks necessarily have to be supported and coordinated by the reference network at ministerial and academic level.

The experimental phase has begun with the identification of some possible classes of intervention that can refer to the authorization art. 21 Legislative Decree 42/2004 - *interventions of all kinds on cultural heritage*: 1. Variation in the floor-plan; 2. Change of use; 3. Coloring of the external elevations; 4. Preservation of decorated painted surfaces; 5. Excavations and preliminary investigations for demolitions; 6. Consolidation; 7. Seismic improvement; 8. Building services engineering; 9. Energy efficiency; 10. Safety systems; 11. Accessibility.

At the same time, starting from the UNI8290 standard, the standard that provides the classification and articulation of the technological units and technical elements that make up the "building" technological system, the existing and newly built construction components involved in the project were defined. For each class of intervention, existing and innovative constructive components, a database (under development) relating to the necessary documents has been associated, dividing into two categories A) General knowledge documents B) Project documents.

From the intersection of intervention classes and existing and innovative construction components involved in the project, the minimum documents to be presented will emerge. The parameters contained in the submitted documents should be verifiable by the IT tool and the relative link with the reference standard are currently being defined.

3 Results and Discussion

3.1 Benefits of Progress According to the Hypothesized Trajectory

It is now increasingly clear how much our society is data driven. Data are the real asset: the higher the information content, the better the outcome will be thanks to a simultaneous general and detailed view of the project ensured by the correlation of previous, current and future project data. In this context, technological development is fundamental for the optimal and efficient management of information flows which, of course, become more and more difficult to handle with time. The proposed articulation of a digital platform for built cultural heritage administrative procedure management could help defining clear project parameters and the interoperability of all the information that should be taken into consideration.

The proposed strategy will provide considerable support to the digital transformation of Public Administration in accordance with the provisions of the National Recovery and

Resilience Plan (PNRR) at point M1C1 - digitization, innovation and safety in public administration [8]. In particular, the development of a common data environment and of a standard procedure for the exchange and management of data related to interventions on cultural heritage will contribute to the implementation of the digital infrastructure envisaged in Part II - Technological components - of the P.A. Strategic Model or information technology.

Furthermore, the innovative character of the proposal consists in addressing, with an architectural technical vision and with the help of innovative A.I. techniques, issues traditionally addressed only from a legal point of view. Actually, in this specific field of research, the technological approach based on Machine Learning Techniques has not yet been used and will allow to identify the recurring parameters considered by Public Administration in formulating the protection provisions in order to ensure an objective and transparent control over conservation works.

4 Conclusion

In the light of the analytical description conducted through the present contribution, it emerges how the need to digitize the administrative procedures relevant to the Civil Code on Cultural and Landscape Heritage (legislative decree 42/2004), even though marked by initial operational difficulties, offers in itself a great opportunity to review the administrative procedures with a view to greater speed and efficiency.

The current limits to complete digitization as advocated concern, in addition to the adjustments in terms of technological resources of the offices on the Ministry of Culture and the transfer of technical skills of a technological nature to the subjects involved in the procedure, are substantially attributable to the lack of guidelines established by law in Art. 29, paragraph 5 of legislative decree 42/2004 regarding the methodologies of intervention on cultural heritage. Indeed, in order to express at best of their potential, IT systems need to refer to clear workflows framed within pre-established paths which therefore need to be defined first at a regulatory level and then translated into a digital tool.

However, the advantages deriving from the interoperability of public data and from the automation of the decision-making process of the administration through the use of a computerized procedure are unquestionably functional in improving the objective and transparent control over conservation works and in this way promoting a new strategy for the protection of built cultural heritage.

References

1. Della Torre, S., Petraroia, P.: Integration of maintenance and management activities with authorization procedures for listed architectural heritage. In: Proceedings Maintenance Management. Third International Conference on Maintenance and Facility Management, Roma (2007)
2. Pesenti, S.: Dal progetto di restauro al progetto di conservazione. Note sull'evoluzione del dibattito disciplinare. In: Pesenti, S., Il progetto di conservazione: linee metodologiche per le analisi preliminari, l'intervento, il controllo di efficacia, pp. 40–53. Alinea, Firenze (2001)

3. Della Torre, S.: Preventiva, integrata, programmata: le logiche coevolutive della conservazione. In: Biscontin, G., Driussi, G. (eds.), Pensare la prevenzione. Manufatti, usi, ambienti, pp. 67–76. Arcadia Ricerche, Venezia (2010)
4. Banfi, A.: La digitalizzazione delle pubbliche amministrazioni. Osservatorio sui Conti Pubblici Italiani **6**(1), 9 (2020)
5. Canonico, P., Tomo, A., Hinna, A., Giusino, L.: La digitalizzazione nella Pubblica Amministrazione. Egea Milano (2020)
6. Belisario, E., Ricciulli, F., Pagnotta, S.: Amministrazione Digitale. Guida ragionata agli strumenti. Maggioli Editore, Rimini (2020)
7. Piano Triennale per l'informatica nella Pubblica Amministrazione. https://pianotriennale-ict.italia.it/. Accessed 21 Dec 2022
8. Relazione al Parlamento sullo stato di attuazione del Piano Nazionale di Ripresa e Resilienza, 5 October 2022
9. European Commission, (2017) EU-wide digital Once-Only Principle for citizens and businesses – Policy options and their impacts, Directorate-General of Communications Networks, Content & Technology
10. Linee Guida sull'infrastruttura tecnologica della Piattaforma Digitale Nazionale Dati per l'interoperabilità dei sistemi informativi e delle basi di dati del 10.12.2021
11. Maesano, A.: Dati digitali e Piattaforma Digitale Nazionale Dati (PDND). https://www.diritto.it/dati-digitali-e-piattaforma-digitale-nazionale-dati-pdnd/. Accessed 12 Dec 2022
12. Santulli, A.: Lo Stato digitale pubblico e privato nelle infrastrutture digitali nazionali strategiche. in Rivista Trimestrale di Diritto Pubblico, Giuffrè Editore, Torino (2021)
13. Otranto, P.: Decisione amministrativa e digitalizzazione della p.a.. Online journal federalismi.it, 2 17 January 2018
14. Martines, F.: La digitalizzazione della pubblica amministrazione. Rivista di diritto dei media, no. 2/2018, p. 3 (2018)
15. Strategia per l'innovazione tecnologica e la digitalizzazione del Paese 2025. https://docs.italia.it/italia/mid/piano-nazionale-innovazione-2025-docs/it/stabile/index.html. Accessed 21 Dec 2022
16. Faraci, S.: Pubblica Amministrazione 2.0: i nuovi processi di digitalizzazione. https://www.diritto.it/pubblica-amministrazione-2-0-i-nuovi-processi-di-digitalizzazione/. Accessed 21 Dec 2022
17. Masi, I.: L'intelligenza artificiale al servizio della pubblica amministrazione 2.0. https://www.diritto.it/lintelligenza-artificiale-al-servizio-della-pubblica-amministrazione-2-0/. Accessed 9 Jan 2023

Design of a VR Environment Optimized for Cultural Heritage Sites and Objects: The Use Case of Its Kale, Ioannina, Greece

Christos Bellos[1](✉), Dafni Patelou[1], Konstantinos Stefanou[1], Georgios Stergios[1], Angeliki Kita[3], Persefoni Ntoulia[3], Vasileios Nitsiakos[2], and Ioannis Fudos[2]

[1] Lime Technology IKE, Ioannina, Greece
cbellos@uoi.gr, info@lime-technology.gr
[2] University of Ioannina, Ioannina, Greece
{bnitsiak,fudos}@uoi.gr
[3] Public Central Library of Konitsa, Konitsa, Greece

Abstract. We report on the processes and techniques used to create 3D objects and characters, their composition into scenes and the development of an interactive VR application optimized for cultural heritage sites and objects. To this end, technologies and methods are presented to achieve these objectives and some key decisions for the smoothest possible functionality of the produced applications are analyzed. The process of conversion of characters, objects, and platforms to integrate seamlessly in the context of specific historical eras with distinct cultural heritage characteristics is discussed in detail. A user study is presented, where the final VR platform is evaluated by a group of users via the System Usability Scale (SUS) and the Technology Acceptance Model (TAM). The VR platform is deployed on three devices: HTC VIVE Cosmos Elite, HTC VIVE Focus 3 and Oculus Quest 2.

Keywords: Cultural Heritage · VR · 3D objects · buildings reconstruction

1 Introduction

Virtual reality (VR) and the development of virtual environments have a tremendous progress during the last few years [1, 2]. For the creation of a VR environment and its individual structural elements, various technologies are being available and widely used, the most important being three free or open-source software suites: Blender, Unity 3D and MakeHuman. Blender software is a free and open-source 3D object creation platform. Blender provides tools for all steps of 3D object creation from modeling, rigging and animation to rendering [3, 4]. Unity is a graphics engine that runs on multiple operating systems and is used to develop games on desktop platforms, consoles, and mobile devices [5]. MakeHuman is a free and open-source software used to create digital humanoids. It is a specialized tool to build characters, which can be used for cartoons, animations, art renders, and more [6].

However, there are several issues that require attention during the design, development, and testing of such solutions.

A. Moropoulou et al. (Eds.): TMM_CH 2023, CCIS 1889, pp. 222–230, 2023.
https://doi.org/10.1007/978-3-031-42300-0_19

User Specifications and Experience. Before starting any development procedure, the scenarios that will be implemented and the user specifications should be studied to enhance the experience of the user. This process requires a holistic view of the product that is much more detailed than a simple reference and the goal is the complete immersion of the user. This is even more important when developing a cultural heritage scenario and implementing characters and avatars, as discussed in Sect. 2. For example, representing a historical figure with a 3D avatar, based on a painting is not enough, since details such as clothing, hair, and skin complexion may not be detectable in a painting.

VR Device Testing and UX. VR technology depends on specialized hardware. The only way to ensure the proper functioning of these products is by adapting the UX on each specific device. It is important to test that the devices work flawlessly, fit the body of the target demographic and provide an immersive user experience.

Accessibility Testing. The use of VR products can bring about significant physical effects. Headache, migraine, motion sickness [7], dry eye and other physical problems are some of the worst-case scenarios that the testers will pay close attention to [8]. Although complete immersion is the goal, it is nevertheless very important to set limits so as to alleviate the unpleasant effects mentioned above.

Compatibility Testing. Strict compatibility testing helps test teams to ensure that the product that arrives in the market does not encounter failures. Compatibility testing in the application helps to measure the performance of the application when it is used by devices with lower system specifications or a device for which it is not optimized. It can also help prevent non-functional problems, such as overheating.

2 Materials and Methods

This section describes all the steps that were followed to develop the VR platform for a working paradigm based on a historical scenario, that takes place at Its Kale (citadel) of Ioannina castle, Greece during the Ali Pasha period (1788–1822). Several steps are taken to optimize the objects and characters according to the cultural and natural heritage characteristics and context of that era, while the final VR platform is deployed on three devices: HTC VIVE Cosmos Elite, HTC VIVE Focus 3 and Oculus Quest 2.

2.1 3D Models and Characters

Through the open-source software MakeHuman, models of people were created according to the specifications that were provided by literature (i.e., age, morphological, clothing, etc.). For the characters representing historical figures (Ali Pasha, Hamko, Vasiliki, Kyra Frosini) additional material, mainly sketches and descriptions, were used as a reference to render as accurately as possible the characteristics and the morphology of each character.

For all models we start from a default generic humanoid model that is neutral in terms of gender, age, and cultural background. Then, all characteristics are realized incrementally according to the sources of reference.

An important part of the process was the creation of appropriate clothing according to the specific time period and the origin of each character. Ioannina during the time of Ali Pasha is a multicultural place that comprises three main social groups with different clothing. Blender software was used for this step as well as various websites with 3D models (Sketchfab, CGTrader, TurboSquid). Due to the peculiarity of the garments, it was necessary to accurately combine and manipulate off the shelf models of clothes, shoes, etc., with custom-made models and textures. For this purpose, several of the tools and capabilities offered by Blender have been exploited. Most importantly, the action of sculpting which allows the mesh of models to be properly edited using a large collection of tools. In this way, clothes can be adapted to the body of any human model regardless of body type. Also, the modifier cloth in combination with shape keys, give the ability to draw clothes from scratch and fit them automatically to the body of the character. This process was followed mainly for skirts and dresses.

Another central issue for the proper creation of the characters was the choice of suitable materials for clothing. For example, Ali Pasha and his family wear more expensive, luxurious fabrics, unlike other characters of urban middle class. To this end, we have used PBR (Physically Based Rendering) and adjusted the PBR parameters so as to model a specific fabric. After creating the appropriate attire for each character, the clothes were edited to fit the body type of the character.

2.2 Reconstruction of Historical Buildings

To obtain a faithful and realistic representation of the environment in which the scenarios take place, it was necessary to reconstruct landmark buildings, such as the buildings located in the citadel of the castle of Ioannina (Its Kale). For this process, architectural reference sources were utilized, so as to reconstruct them as correctly as possible.

For buildings that have been preserved until today like the Fethiye Mosque at Its Kale and the tomb of Ali Pasha we have used photogrammetry on collections of photos shot by drones or manually. Those photos are stored on a server of the Computer Graphics Research Group that is located at the department of Computer Science and Engineering at the University of Ioannina and can be provided to researchers upon request.

For building the 3D models of the buildings that have not been preserved until today or have undergone significant alterations during history we have used blender tools. Initially for each building its basic shape was created and then the appropriate protrusions were made for doors and windows and extrusions or more advanced operations were used for other parts. Then detailed models for the doors, windows, roofs and so on were added. Specifically, for the roofs of the buildings, the construction process was as follows: initially its general shape was created with a combination of planes for the rectangular and cones for the circular ones. Then, different textures of tiles and slabs were used placed in the way described in architectural drafts of references. Then, using height maps that correspond to each texture, the roofs became 3D. To be able to capture the details indicated by the height maps, the mesh needs to have a very large resolution (face count), so after the process of conversion to 3D it was necessary to simplify and optimize the mesh of the roofs. Finally, details were added to each building that make it recognizable, such as arches, turrets, plaster decorations, etc., which were also entirely created in Blender with a similar methodology.

For the model of the Fethiye Mosque and the tomb of Ali Pasha that were reconstructed using aerial photos and special software we have postprocessed the models to remove defects and to decrease the number of polygons used.

2.3 Scene Creation and Interaction Among Scenes

After developing the different objects, characters and buildings, the scene should be developed by placing everything in a global coordinate system. Then, the extra models such as trees, shrubs, rocks, etc. and finally the characters were added to the scene.

An important point is the custom process of creating the terrain, which differs from scene to scene. Specifically, for some of the scenes the ground is a 3D model developed in Blender. For others, a feature offered by Unity has been used to create the terrain. In this case, the ground is a mesh which is formed using altitude information and materials within Unity. This technique was used in scenes where the terrain is a large area and details in geomorphology were needed.

Fig. 1. A panoramic image produced by rendering the Its Kale scene and its terrain including the 3d buildings

A special case is the terrain for the scene of Its Kale (Fig. 1). In that case, the altitudes were implemented through an add-on of Blender, BlenderGIS, which uses satellite data and produces a 3D model. Then this model was imported to Unity and converted into a terrain object to be further processed. Then additional details were added to the terrain to achieve a more realistic result. In addition, various features (grass, soil, rocks) were introduced for the shake of realism.

The rest of the scenes were introduced into this project in the format of a timeline view, as depicted in Fig. 2. This was developed to achieve the main objective that was the optimization of the VR environment according to the cultural heritage specifications. Thus, the experience of the user was enhanced, and the visitor can navigate across time and better understand the cultural assets of the specific historical period.

The implementation of this process involves several steps and can be slightly different depending on the peculiarities of each scene. Initially the scene itself is introduced into the project. Then all the assets included in the scene need to be imported. These consist of prefabs, 3D models, scripts, audio clips, images for the menus (sprites), image files for

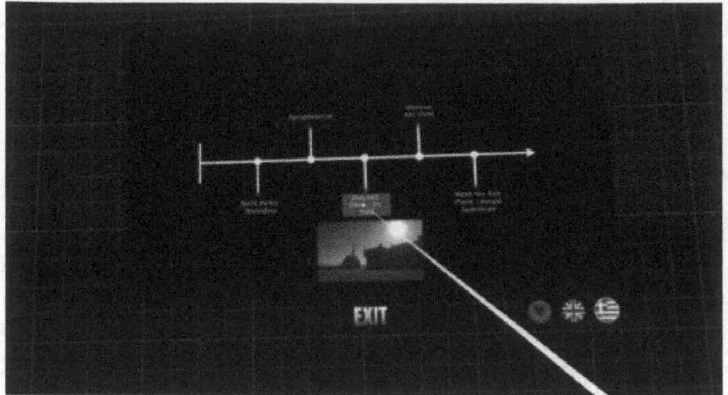

Fig. 2. A timeline view with teleporting capabilities

the materials (textures and maps) and the material properties of the models. Assets with the same name had to undergo a renaming process to derive persistent distinct naming scheme.

2.4 Animations

To create animations for the 3D models we have started from the basic movement, namely the skeletal animation. The way of implementation of the animation differs depending on the desired result. More specifically, for generic movement of characters the Mixamo software was utilized.

For the models that the animation was made in Blender, the model should be properly rigged. Then the procedure followed is the creation of the basic keyframes with the most representative poses of the movement, as depicted in the workflow of Fig. 3. For this reason, the appropriate bones are moved and rotated and when they are in the right position then this position is stored as a keyframe in the timeline.

2.5 Render Pipeline

A Render Pipeline performs several tasks to capture the contents of a scene on the screen. For applications that become a Build for Android, Universal RP was used, because it has a good tradeoff between quality and computational power. High-Definition RP was used for the deployment to the HTC Vive Cosmos Elite, while high-definition RP was used for the deployment to the HTC Vive Cosmos Elite. Applications that run on the computer have more room for computational costs, so there is also the possibility for better resolution. DRP is the most powerful unity has to offer in the field of graphics. It uses physically based lighting and materials and supports forward and deferred rendering.

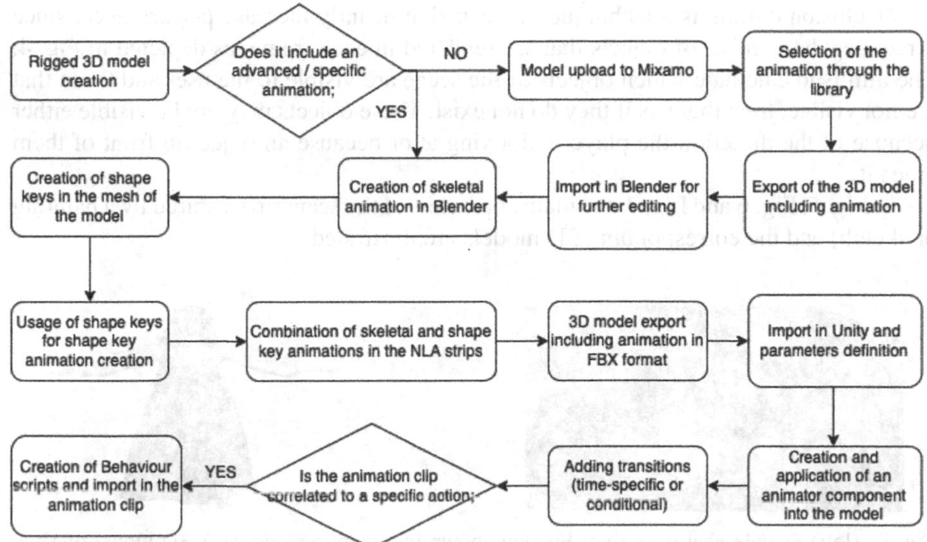

Fig. 3. Workflow indicating the process of developing and adding animation

3 Results

To deploy the VR scenarios on standalone VR Android devices (e.g. HTC VIVE Focus 3 and Oculus Quest 2) we need to carefully adjust the Unity settings during export. Usually, the volume of images used for realistic projects with multiple scenes is quite large, so their proper management can make a big difference in the performance of the application. The best choice in terms of performance is compression using the ASTC (Adaptable Scalable Texture Compression) format, which uses variable-sized blocks during compression. Textures used for terrains are excluded from this option.

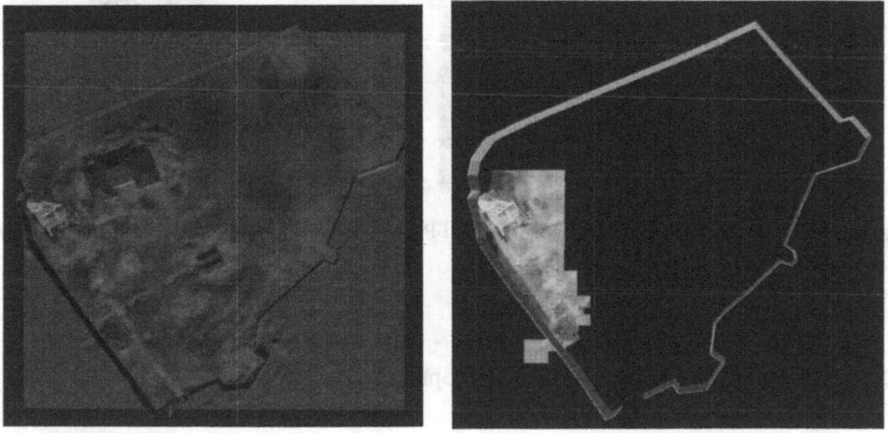

Fig. 4. A scene without occlusion culling (left) and with occlusion culling (right)

Occlusion culling is a technique that can significantly increase performance, since it reduces the number of objects that are rendered in each frame, as depicted in Fig. 4. The aim is to calculate which objects of the scene are visible to the user and those that are not visible, treat them as if they do not exist. These objects may not be visible either because of the direction the player is looking at or because an object in front of them hides it.

In Fig. 5, Fig. 6 and Fig. 7, the main characters of the scenario (inspired by a painting or sketch) and the corresponding 3D models are illustrated.

Fig. 5. (left) Female character Kyra Frosyni shown in a painting. (right) A 3D model of Kyra Frosyni.

Fig. 6. (left) Female character Kyra Vasiliki (Ali Pasha's wife) shown in a painting. (right) A 3D model of Kyra Vasiliki

Figure 8 depicts several screenshots of the developed scenes in the VR platform, including characters, objects and buildings optimized according to the characteristics of the specific era.

Fig. 7. (left) Male character Ali Pasha shown in a painting. (right) A 3D model of Ali Pasha

Fig. 8. Screenshots of the developed scenario

4 User Study and Evaluation

A VR hall has been set up in the Public Central Library of Konitsa, where visitors can use the VR devices to familiarize with the castle of Ioannina (Its Kale) and the Ali Pasha era (approx. 1787–1822). There are installed 8 Oculus Quest 2 devices, 2 VIVE Focus 3 and 2 VIVE Cosmos Elite.

To evaluate the VR platform according to usability and acceptance of the core services from the users, the SUS and TAM scales have been used, accordingly. One group of 15 pupils (aged 15–17 years old) and a group of 15 tourists (aged 40–50 years old) have used the devices, reporting a 85 score in SUS and 88% in TAM.

5 Conclusion

The goal of this work is to deliver a VR platform with a case study, in which the citadel of Ioannina (Its Kale) during the Ali Pasha era was revived into an immersive, interactive tour, including key characters (i.e., Ali Pasha, Kyra Frosyni, Kyra Vassiliki) and key objects. The key technical objective that is achieved with this study, is to optimize the reconstructed objects, building and characters (mainly clothing and facial expressions) according to a specific historical era and according to specific cultural heritage requirements.

Acknowledgements. This study has been co-financed by the European Union (European Regional Development Fund- ERDF) and Greek national funds through the Interreg Greece-Albania 2014–2020 Program "VirtuaLand".

References

1. Anthes, C., García-Hernández, R.J., Wiedemann, M., Kranzlmüller, D.: State of the art of virtual reality technology. In: IEEE Aerospace Conference, pp. 1–19 (2016). https://doi.org/10.1109/AERO.2016.7500674
2. Gandhi, R.D., Patel, D.S.: Virtual reality–opportunities and challenges. Virtual Reality **5**(01), 2714–2724 (2018)
3. Rohe, D.P., Jones, E.M.C.: Generation of synthetic digital image correlation images using the open-source blender software. Exp. Tech. **46**, 615–631 (2021). https://doi.org/10.1007/s40799-021-00491-z
4. Dovramadjiev, T.: Modern accessible application of the system blender in 3D design practice. Int. Sci. On-line J. SCI. TECHNOL. Publ. House Union Sci.-Stara Zagora (2015). ISSN1314–4111
5. Foxman, M.: United we stand: platforms, tools and innovation with the unity game engine. Soc. Media + Soc. (2019). https://doi.org/10.1177/2056305119880177
6. Gunther, P., Scataglini, S.: Open-source software to create a kinematic model in digital human modeling. In: DHM and Posturography, Chap. 17, pp. 201–213. Academic Press (2019). https://doi.org/10.1016/B978-0-12-816713-7.00017-9
7. Chattha, U.A., Janjua, U.I., Anwar, F., Madni, T.M., Cheema, M.F., Janjua, S.I.: Motion sickness in virtual reality: an empirical evaluation. IEEE Access **8**, 130486–130499 (2020). https://doi.org/10.1109/ACCESS.2020.3007076
8. Chang, E., Kim, H.T., Yoo, B.: Virtual reality sickness: a review of causes and measurements. Int. J. Hum.-Comput. Interact. **36**(17), 1658–1682 (2020). https://doi.org/10.1080/10447318.2020.1778351

When Technology Meets Heritage

Jenny Pange[1,2(✉)], Alina Degteva[1], and Vasiliki Manglara[1]

[1] Laboratory of New Technologies and Distance Learning, University of Ioannina, 451 10 Ioannina, Greece
{jpagge,a.degteva,v.magglara}@uoi.gr

[2] Institute of Humanities and Social Studies, University of Ioannina, 451 10 Ioannina, Greece

Abstract. Museum digitalization is not a new idea, but digital materials are actively introduced into museums worldwide. Information Computer Technologies are supporting the digitalization of museums. The digitalization of museums is connected with the preservation and presentation of objects of cultural heritage. The use of ICT affects positively the interaction between visitors and collections. This is in alliance with the primary outcomes of digital curation. Recent studies confirm that the digitalization of exhibits in museums improves the visitors' experience. Among the digital tools used in museums are QR codes. QR codes are a new way to upgrade visitors' experience in museums. It is an easy and fast-paced solution to inform visitors about the museum's objects. QR codes are attached to the exhibits of the museum and visitors receive information about them. Additionally, QR codes can be used in museums to help visitors learn the history of a country interactively and act as tools for e-learning. This study aims to present the development and application of QR codes in a museum of contemporary art in the city of Ioannina to help visitors understand better the history of the exhibits in the museum. We developed the QR codes for the exhibits of this museum, according to its needs. For the application of QR codes in the museum we used the ADDIE (Analysis, Design, Development, Implementation, and Evaluation) model. According to our findings, digital material offers an excellent alternative for visitors to understand the local history with the aim of QR codes.

Keywords: Digital Heritage · Digital Material · QR Codes

1 Introduction

Nowadays, communities have to be ready to adapt to many changes because they have many problems like the covid-19 pandemic, wars, and climate change, and at the same time they have to take care of the preservation of our cultural heritage [1].

Cultural and historical heritage is a unique and precious asset for every place in the world. Every society is responsible for preserving its cultural heritage and passing it on to the next generations. Information Computer Technologies (ICTs) are the main tools for supporting the preservation of historical and cultural heritage [2].

The main aim of preserving the cultural and historical heritage is that through it we exchange knowledge and ideas. The idea of preserving heritage for the next generations

A. Moropoulou et al. (Eds.): TMM_CH 2023, CCIS 1889, pp. 231–240, 2023.
https://doi.org/10.1007/978-3-031-42300-0_20

plays an important role in the need of the digitization of museums and there are many ways to digitalize a museum. Moreover, the use of digital technology facilitates the interaction between visitors and collections and supports promotion through media [3].

Museums collect rare objects, and at the same time, they offer non-formal education to visitors [4]. Museums offer interactive material, sounds, and colors that take visitors on a dynamic and informative journey [5].

One of the most common innovations in museums nowadays is the use of Quick Response (QR) codes to communicate all the data and information about an object in detail about exhibited items [6]. A QR code contains any digital information such as a website, video, or audio data, according to the creator's intent. Access to digital information about an object can be obtained by scanning its' QR code through a smartphone [7].

Recent studies show that visitors consider QR codes as an interesting and useful tool for museums. There are many other benefits for visitors to use QR codes in a museum. QR codes deliver text, audio, image, and video information about the objects exhibited in museums and they are part of non-formal learning [8, 9]. They create a pleasant experience for visitors in a museum, and at the same time educate and motivate the users of QR codes [9]. Some researchers emphasize that QR codes allow visitors, including also people with disabilities, to choose their own way to visit the exhibitions in a museum, according to their experience and individual needs [10–12].

Other researchers highlight the effectiveness of the learning process through the ADDIE model and its contribution to museums, including non-formal education and education using technology [13, 14]. The ADDIE model is also applicable to users of QR codes and this model is widely used by many instructional designers and training programmers to develop projects, courses, and training programs [13, 15, 16]. Especially, the ADDIE model has a flexible structure that allows it to be applied to different learning environments, including the museum environment [13–15]. The name of ADDIE model is an acronym for the five stages it defines for building training and performance support tools [13, 15, 16]: Analysis, Design, Development, Implementation, and Evaluation. In the analysis stage, the instructional problem is clarified, the instructional goals and objectives are established and the learning environment and learner's existing knowledge and skills are identified. The design stage deals with content, its structure, and assessment tool selection. The development stage is concerned with the production of educational material and testing of the content created during the design stage. During the implementation stage, an instructor tests the functionality of the created material. The evaluation stage consists of two parts: formative and summative; formative evaluation is present in each stage of the ADDIE process, while summative evaluation consists of assessment tools (e.g., questionnaires, interviews) that provide feedback from users [16].

This study aims to present the design, development, implementation, and evaluation of QR codes in a local museum of contemporary art "Theodoros Papagiannis" in the city of Ioannina, Greece, to help visitors sightsee the exhibits of this museum, which contains sculptures, paintings, and handmade coins. Today the "Theodoros Papagiannis" museum of contemporary art offers visitors limited use of technology in the museum, represented by audio tour systems. The objects of this museum combine the cultural and historical heritage of Epirus, Greece, with some objects for the main protection and conservation of the environment [17].

2 Materials and Methods

In this study, we used a mixed-methods research design, which combines both quantitative and qualitative research methods. This type of research design allows for a more comprehensive understanding of the use of QR codes for the topic being studied by combining different types of data.

The quantitative part of this study involved one randomly self-selected selecting group of visitors. For the needs of the study, an anonymous questionnaire was given to visitors of the 'Theodoros Papagiannis" museum of contemporary art. The questionnaire included:

- Demographic questions to design the visitors' profile.
- Questions that are related to the general experience of visiting museums.
- Questions that are related to the experience of visiting the "Theodoros Papagiannis" museum of contemporary art.

A self-selected group of forty-two (42) visitors answered the questionnaire anonymously and we used descriptive statistics to analyze the data.

Then we designed and created the QR codes using the Taplink platform (https://taplink.at/en/). Taplink website builder allows the creation of digital information without special skills in programming and designing. The templates of Taplink meet developer needs and requirements of the contemporary web pages. They include text, images, audio material, multilink, and forms of feedback. This platform has free and paid features. With the assistance of the manager of the museum, we implemented all these QR codes in the main areas and selected objects.

The qualitative part of this study included interviews with a randomly selected group of visitors. We interviewed twenty (20) visitors to evaluate their satisfaction with the QR codes. As a result, we collected 20 of their answers, described them, and grouped them into 5 categories.

3 Results and Discussion

3.1 Characteristics of Study Participants

Visitors of the "Theodoros Papagiannis" museum of contemporary art of different age groups took part in this study. Tables 1 and 2 summarize data by gender and age groups. According to our data, 69% of the participants were women and 26.2% were men. The participants were between 16 and 70 y.o.

Table 1. Gender of participants in this study.

Male		Female		No answer	
frequency	%	frequency	%	frequency	%
11	26.2	29	69	2	4.8

Table 2. Age of participants in this study.

Age	frequency	%
16–18 y.o.	4	9.5
19–29 y.o.	9	21.4
30–39 y.o.	11	26.2
40–49 y.o.	8	19
50–59 y.o.	7	16.7
60–70 y.o.	2	4.8
No answer	1	2.4
Total	42	100

The educational level of participants in this study, according to the International Standard Classification of Education [18], also varied. The largest group was made up of participants with upper secondary education (Level 3) (45.5%). There were also participants who graduated from bachelor's or equivalent (Level 6), master's or equivalent (Level 7), or doctorate or equivalent (Level 8) studies (Table 3).

Table 3. Level of education of participants in this study.

Level	frequency	%
Level 3	19	45.5
Level 6	3	7.1
Level 7	2	4.8
Level 8	1	2.4
Total	25	59.8

More than half of the participants were employed (52.4%). High school and university students (26.2%) and unemployed participants (14.3%) also took part in this study. Table 4 summarizes the data. We know also from the questionnaires that 9.5% of participants work in the private sector, the same number of the participants came from universities, and 2.4% of participants work in the public sector.

Table 4. Occupation of participants in this study.

Occupation	frequency	%
Students	11	26.2
Employed	22	52.4
Unemployed	6	14.3
Total	39	92.9

Half of the participants (50%) live in Ioannina, and participants from other cities in Greece were also included (Table 5).

Table 5. Places of residence of participants in this study.

Place	frequency	%
Ioannina	21	50
Thessaloniki	5	11.9
Athens	2	4.8
Patras	2	4.8
Arta	1	2.4
Veria	1	2.4
Chalcis	1	2.4
Total	33	78.6

In this study, we asked participants how often they visit museums. Twenty-five of the participants (60%) do not visit museums more than 4 times a year (Table 6).

Table 6. How often participants in this study visit museums.

Times a year	frequency	%
1–2 times a year	15	35.7
3–4 times a year	10	23.8
5–7 times a year	5	11.9
Over 8 times a year	6	14.3
Total	36	85.7

Most of the participants in this study shared the opinion that when they visit museums, they expect to see ICTs that will help them navigate museum exhibits (81.1%). Only

16.7% of the participants in this study preferred to explore museums without any ICT technology.

There is no correlation between the educational level of the participants in this study and their interest in technology and found that the chi-square statistic is 0.503, and the p-value is .478188.

Half of the participants (45.5%) when visiting museums had previous experience of using QR codes, while 52.4% of them did not know how to use QR codes when visiting museums or have not ever used them. Some participants, which had the experience of using the QR codes commented that *"the QR codes may be very useful when visiting exhibitions independently"* as well as that *"the QR codes give interesting and comprehensive information about the museums' objects which are not highlighted during the excursions"*.

Among the visitors of the "Theodoros Papagiannis" museum of contemporary art, 23.8% visited it for first time. Some participants visited the museum for second time (19%) or third time (16.7%), and some visited the museum more than three times (7.1%) (Table 7).

Many of the participants in this study replied that they heard about this museum from friends/relatives or colleagues (45.5%); 23.8% of the participants in this study learned about this museum from social networks; another 19% of the participants in this study were informed about the museum from its website.

Table 7. Number of visits to the "Theodoros Papagiannis" museum of contemporary art by participants in this study.

Number of visits	frequency	%
First visit	10	23.8
Second visit	8	19
Third visit	7	16.7
More than 3 visits	3	7.1
Total	28	66.6

Almost all participants of the questionnaire were interested in the use of technology in the museum, and most of them (74%) named QR codes as necessary for the "Theodoros Papagiannis" museum of contemporary art ICT tool.

3.2 Application of the ADDIE Model

The designing procedure for the application and evaluation of the QR codes was following the ADDIE model (ADDIE). With the participation of the manager of the "Theodoros Papagiannis" museum of contemporary art, we decided to create six QR codes for the most important museum exhibits and areas of the museum, according to the opinion of the museum manager. QR codes created with Taplink contained information in the form of web pages with imagines (slide show), text, and feedback forms (see Fig. 1). When creating digital materials, we used museum manuals and their website (https://theodoros-papagiannis.gr/en/node/1258).

Fig. 1. Screenshots of web pages accessed by visitors via QR codes at the "Theodoros Papagiannis" museum of contemporary art.

This digital material was developed (ADDIE) according to the needs of the museum and pursued the aims of promotion and education. The implementation of the QR codes (ADDIE) was in accordance with the science and the opinion of the museum manager. Six QR codes were put in the selected exhibits and areas of the museum. They could be accessed by smartphones and PCs (see Fig. 2).

For the next step of the ADDIE model, which is the evaluation of the QR codes (ADDIE) we applied at the "Theodoros Papagiannis" museum of contemporary art, we interviewed a random sample of visitors and asked their opinion about the helpfulness of these QR codes. We got 20 replies which were grouped into 5 different categories.

According to the first category, we found that ICTs were useful in the museum. Especially, one of the museum visitors (a female doctoral student), who visited the museum for the third time, said about the use of ICTs at the museum: *"The technology helps very much in the work of the museum. Its introduction is an excellent proposal for the future of the museum".*

The second category included answers that promote the use of technology, in particular, QR codes but subject to the application of activities that make it possible for senior people to use these QR codes. One of the museum visitors (a female bachelor student), who visited the museum for the first time mentioned that: *"For young visitors of the museum the QR codes and the audio tour systems were of particular interest since these ICT tools contained information in a comprehensive form as well as interesting and sometimes insignificant details".* And she also added that *"for the senior people*

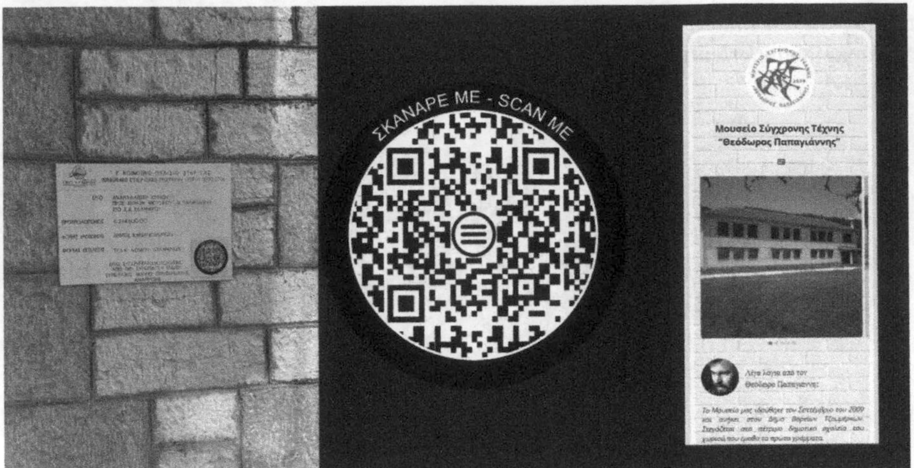

Fig. 2. QR code for the outdoor area of the "Theodoros Papagiannis" museum of contemporary art.

it might be often difficult to deal with new technology and for that reason, it was not worth making a full transfer immediately <...>; the combination of ICT with an "alive" contact with the museum objects was the best solution".

The third category included answers that promote the use of technology in combination with human effort. Additionally, another visitor (a female bachelor student) visiting the museum for the first time said, *"The technology helps but does not replace the human's presence and effort".*

In the fourth category, visitors focused on the benefits of QR codes for the "Theodoros Papagiannis" museum of contemporary art. One visitor (a male private sector employer) described in his interview the advantages of the QR codes and he said: *"the QR code ensures the freedom of movement and the independent viewing".* It should be noted that this visitor has visited the museum more than 5 times.

In the fifth category visitors discussed the problems of implementing the QR codes. One of the museum visitors (a female public sector employer), a frequent visitor to the museum (more than 3 times) said that: *"The QR codes were an interesting idea and I was in favor of their implementation concerning the most important objects of the museum. Anyway, I want to emphasize the importance of putting the QR code where it will be visible and protected from harmful effects".*

4 Conclusions

This study has shown that the use of technology, specifically QR codes, was very important for the visitor's experience at the "Theodoros Papagiannis" museum of contemporary art. The ADDIE model supported the idea of the feasibility of introducing the QR codes into the structure of the museum as part of the complex of the "alive" guided contact – technology". The QR codes were a solution for giving visitors information on the subject of interest to them.

According to the interviews and the data, obtained from the visitors, we found that digital material can improve the interaction with the collections and enhance the overall experience. However, this study has some limitations due to the small number of participants in the first questionnaire and the limited number of QR codes used. For a future study, we plan to add more QR codes to other museums to find out how useful they are.

Acknowledgements. We thank the owner of the "Theodoros Papagiannis" museum of contemporary art, Mr. Theodoros Papagiannis, and the manager, Mrs. Niki Giannatsi for the support of the study, interest, and comprehensive help.

References

1. Holtorf, C.: 3 steps to heritage conservation in a changing world. https://is.gd/lqO8wQ. Accessed 19 Jan 2023
2. Poriki, V., Tse, E., Panakoulias, K., Toki, E., Pange, J.: Digital games as tools for preserving and transmitting cultural and historical heritage: a case study. In: Plakitsi, K., Kolokouri, E., Kornelaki, A-C. (eds.) ISCAR 2019 "Crisis in Contexts", e-Proceedings, pp. 355–369. University of Ioannina, School of Education, Early Childhood Education Department, Ioannina (2019)
3. Li, Y.-C., Liew, A., Su, W.-P.: The digital museum: challenges and solution. In: 8th International Conference on Information Science and Digital Content Technology (ICIDT2012), pp. 646–649. IEEE, Jeju (2012)
4. Sheng, C.-W., Chen, M.-C.: A study of experience expectations of museum visitors. Tour. Manage. **33**, 53–60 (2012)
5. Elgammal, I., Ferretti, M., Risitano, M., Sorrentino, A.: Does digital technology improve the visitor experience? A comparative study in the museum context. Int. J. Tour. Policy **10**(1), 47–67 (2020)
6. Aguilera, F.J.G., Franco Caballero, P.D.: Evaluation for QR codes in environmental museums. Glob. J. Inf. Technol.: Emerg. Technol. **9**(2), 29–32 (2019)
7. How to use QR codes in museums and art exhibitions. https://www.qrcode-tiger.com/how-to-use-qr-codes-in-museums-and-art-exhibitions. Accessed 18 Jan 2023
8. Octavia, T., Handojo, A., Kusuma, W.T., Yunanto, T.Ch., Thiosdor, R.L.: Museum interactive edutainment using mobile phone and QR code. In: International Workshop on Computer Science and Engineering (WCSE 2019), Hong Kong, pp. 815–819 (2019)
9. Ovallos-Gazabon, D., Meléndez-Pertuz, F., Collazos-Morales, C., Zamora-Musa, R., Cardenas, C.A., González, R.E.R.: Innovation, technology and user experience in museums: insights from scientific literature. In: Gervasi, O., et al. (eds.) ICCSA 2020. LNCS, vol. 12249, pp. 819–832. Springer, Cham (2020). https://doi.org/10.1007/978-3-030-58799-4_59
10. Rouby, I.: The adoption of "QR codes" in the tourism sector: the case of Egyptian tourism students. J. Tour. Res. **23**, 110–125 (2019)
11. Khudaybergenov, T.: Perspectives of using of OWC in digital storytelling content delivering in museums. In: 2021 International Conference on Information Science and Communications Technologies (ICISCT), pp. 1–3. IEEE, Tashkent (2021)
12. Schultz, M.K.: A case study on the appropriateness of using quick response (QR) codes in libraries and museums. Libr. Inf. Sci. Res. **35**, 207–215 (2013)
13. Spatioti, A.G., Kazanidis, I., Pange, J.: A comparative study of the ADDIE instructional design model in distance education. Information **13**(9), 402 (2022)

14. Papadopoulou, M., Pange, J., Tsolakidis, C.: Archives, museums and libraries: dynamic systems for co-operation in distance education, through collection and dissemination of qualitative information. Stat. Educ. Res. J. **1**(2), 601–606 (2003)
15. ADDIE Model Wikipedia. https://en.wikipedia.org/wiki/ADDIE_Model. Accessed 18 Jan 2023
16. Instructional Design Models. ADDIE Model. http://www.instructionaldesign.org/models/addie/. Accessed 20 Feb 2023
17. Papagiannis, T.: Papagiannis museum. Foreword. https://theodoros-papagiannis.gr/en/node/1258. Accessed 19 Jan 2023
18. International Standard Classification of Education Wikipedia. https://en.wikipedia.org/wiki/International_Standard_Classification_of_Education. Accessed 24 Jan 2023

Preservation, Reuse and Reveal of Cultural Heritage through Sustainable Building and Land Management, Rural and Urban Development to Recapture the World in Crisis through Culture

AAGIS: An Archaeoastronomical Approach Using Geographic Information Systems

George Malaperdas[1](✉), Dimitris Sinachopoulos[2], and Eleni Valianatou[3]

[1] Laboratory of Archaeometry, University of the Peloponnese, Tripoli, Greece
envcart@yahoo.gr

[2] IAASARS, National Observatory of Athens, Athens, Greece

[3] Department of History, Archaeology and Cultural Resources Management, University of the Peloponnese, Tripoli, Greece

Abstract. ArchaeoAstroGIS (AAGIS) is a research project integrating archaeoastronomical orientations of archaeological sites and monuments using geodetic and GIS methods. Even though the compass, astrogeodetic approach, and, more recently, Google Earth are the most popular monument orientation methods, another unique method based on GIS and topography was applied here. Nowadays, archaeoastronomy's usage of GIS has yielded a slew of impressive discoveries, including novel techniques and answers to spatial analytic difficulties. Our measurements were taken using GPS technology. The key reason GPS technology was chosen was because, on the one hand, it's in situ accuracy of a few millimeters is more than sufficient for our needs, and on the other hand, the entire process is completed considerably fast. All of the data from the DGPS was imported into a GIS environment in our scenario. The points were tested for correctness against the topography at first. The test was carried out using satellite images of the research area, and the results were extremely positive. Usually, seven measurements were made for each tomb. We started measuring the first point at the most prominent north-northeast point of the tomb and proceeded towards its northwestern end. Through this process, a visual panorama was created that provided the first clear image of the orientation of the tomb. As a result, the entire project has helped a lot in both, the accuracy and management of information, as well as the visualization and clarification of the data, by using the data obtained from GPS and integrating it into the GIS system.

Keywords: AAGIS · Archaeoastronomy · Digital Heritage · Messenia

1 Introduction

The present case study focuses on Ancient Thouria Late Helladic chamber tombs, Messenia, Greece. Although these Mycenaean tombs are almost thousand years older than Messene's establishment in 369 B.C., Ancient Thouria became the most important city in eastern Messenia and the second in power city after Messene (Fig. 1). The ancient

A. Moropoulou et al. (Eds.): TMM_CH 2023, CCIS 1889, pp. 243–254, 2023.
https://doi.org/10.1007/978-3-031-42300-0_21

city's ruins are located on an elongated ridge running north-south, about 10 km north-west of Kalamata, on the right side of the Kalamata-Tripolis highway, and about 2.5 km north of the modern town of Thouria. There is a colony of 25 highly spectacular visible Late Helladic chamber tombs on the top slopes of Ellinika hill, on its eastern side, not far from its summit. Even though the majority of the 16 freshly found tombs had been looted, anyone can still see their huge size and remarkable dromoi and stomia. The present study focused on these 16 freshly found tombs as well as the only tholos tomb found in the area. Out of these 16 tombs, only one was built in the western side of the Ellinika hill, which proves that, at least, chamber tombs of this region and period were constructed to be oriented (dromoi and stomia) "to the East" with some few of them to be oriented exact to the East with azimuth ninety degrees.

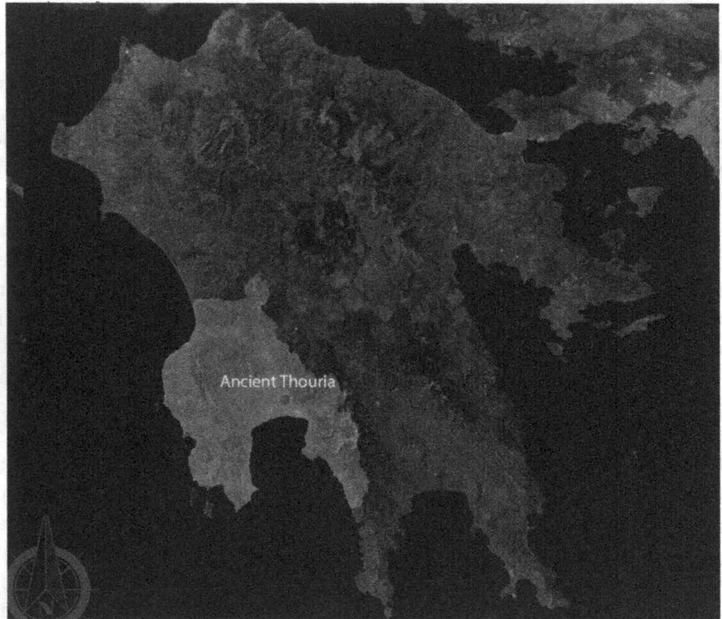

Fig. 1. The study area located in Messenia Prefecture, Peloponnese, Greece.

Although it might be a strange coincidence, one has to remark that local population still calls the hill "Hill of the Greeks" (Ellinika), which may reflect a special importance of the tomb region for the feeling of cultural heritage for the local population even three thousand years after the establishment of this Mycenaean cemetery (Fig. 2).

Fig. 2. Sample photos from the Necropolis of Ellinika, Thouria.

1.1 Messenian Burial Preferences: Tholos and Chamber Tholos Burials

Greek burial practices from Middle Helladic period (c.2200–1680 BC) onward can be divided into two groups: chamber tombs (being established but not widely use in Late Helladic I), and cist and pit burials that continue from Early MH period. In LH II, chamber and tholos tombs can be found across the mainland; after LH II, pits and cists, with the exception of child burials, are relatively uncommon, though they can be found in chamber tombs (Button 2007, 77). It is argued that chamber tombs were the most common type of burial and that pits and cists were not used separately for poor burials. In LH IIIC, chamber tombs are still common, but cists and pits are once again popular due to cremation practices and simpler requirements (Murphy 2020, 38).

Beginning in early Mycenaean times, there was a tremendous increase in the means to acquire movable wealth of the kind the Mycenaeans treasured in life and death, as the burial offerings suggest. Cemeteries of chamber tombs probably belonged to these royal relatives, and perhaps to the most prosperous commoners, as often a grave could occupy successive burials for several generations and even centuries (Bailey 2000, 25). Tholoi have been viewed as *"forms of corporate burial reflecting in groups linked together in a community*[1]*"*, *"grave constructions above ground as symbols of personal or family status, or as some type of territorial marker*[2]*"*, and *"objects in graves as clues to changes in social organization*[3]*"*.

The identification and location of burial sites in Messenia, began in the western side of the region in 1952, by Marinatos that has carried on an almost annual program of excavation, mainly of burial mounds, tholoi, and chamber tombs (McDonald and Simpson

[1] See also Dabney and Wright 2008, 49.
[2] Nordquist 1990, 35.
[3] Graziadio 1991, 403.

1972, 120). After Professor Marinatos' studies[4], special attention has been directed by UMME (Minnesota Messenia Expedition) and later PRAP (the Pylos Regional Archaeological Project) with a focus to the rest of west Messenia. The Alpheios-Kladheos nucleus was surveyed and characterized as more heavily occupied in LH in the north than it had been earlier. The current evidence is largely based on burial discoveries, including in some cases large chamber tomb cemeteries but not in so much consecration the north side (McDonald and Simpson 1972, 140).

Cavanagh and Mee, in their study on the distribution of Mycenaean tombs, came to the conclusion that there doesn't seem to have been a single main factor that determined the position of tombs within a territory (Dickinson 1983, 61). Preferable geological formations and burial conditions, particularly for the construction of specific types of tombs, like the rock-cut chamber tombs, certainly were preferred and defined in a way the position of the tomb (Cavanagh and Laxton 1981, 132–133). Other than the role of geology, the most important factor must be tradition and customs. The positioning of tombs has been explained by a number of theories, ranging from traditional and eschatological beliefs to territorial or social claims (Cavanagh and Mee 1990, 225). Ancestor cults established at prehistoric tombs may have served in historical times to legitimize the control of land, but we still have little reliable evidence from early Mycenaean times (in Messenia or elsewhere) about the dwellings of kings, courtiers, and commoners so that might be also the case in Messenia (McDonald and Simpson 1972, 138).

Overall, we should try to evaluate tombs and cemeteries in the context of their own social, geographic, and historical record. Location seems to have a very important role and in no case is accidental or unimportant especially for important burial monuments. This is due to the unique position tombs have taken in the socio-political, natural, or even eschatological landscape. In this respect location and associations rather than physical prominence may have been more important for the individuals that commissioned and interacted with these tombs.

1.2 The Cemetery of Ellinika in Ancient Thouria and Its Characteristics

The Andhrousa ridge on the west and the Ellinika (Thouria) ridge on the east, are the two natural barriers of the Pamisos region, which also overlook the central river crossings and control the north-south route corridors. This makes the site of Ellinika great political and military importance as both sides are naturally defended (Lukermann 1972, 161). The archaeological site of ancient Thouria is located at the top of Ellinika. At the southernmost and lowest end of the ridge, an extensive prehistoric settlement has been attested from the early Bronze Age (Early Helladic period 2750-2250/2200 BC) and mainly from the Mycenaean times (Late Helladic period 1680-1060 BC)[5], while on the eastern side, an extensive cemetery with monumental, Mycenaean chamber tombs have been identified and partially investigated (Arapogianni 2000, 279, Arapogianni 2017, 25).

[4] Marinatos has also published wider syntheses suggesting connections between the Late Bronze Age sites in Messenia and the rest of the contemporary Mediterranean world, as well as between the known Late Bronze Age situation and conditions described in the Homeric poems.

[5] In the same period as the construction of Nestor's palace (until 1200 BC when it was destroyed).

Two early Middle Helladic period mounds with elaborately decorated graves have been explored a short distance east of the Mycenaean cemetery (Morgan 2010, 49–50). Sixteen chamber tombs carved into the rock's natural surface form the cemetery and at least 25 chamber tombs have been found at the location on the Ellinika hill's eastern side, though not all of them have been excavated[6]. The graves are arranged into two nearly parallel rows, with the two roads on the E side, and are oriented from E to W. They can be distinguished by their large, imposing chambers and smaller, poorly constructed ones, which have narrow dromos[7] and chambers with collapsed ceilings. Their construction follows the well-known Mycenaean architecture of tombs and consists of an elongated dromos that ends in an imposing door. The stomio[8] of the entrance is deep and leads to one (or on some cases more) chamber where the dead were buried directly on the ground, in pits. The chamber of the tombs has a flat roof, and some are provided with a carved low table on one side for storage of the offerings (mainly pottery) that accompanied the dead. The burials, which were of family members, reflect the time period's economic and social standing (Arapogianni 2017, 25–26).

2 Materials and Methods

Even though the compass (Boutsikas, 2008), the astrogeodetic method (Pantazis et al., 2004), and, more recently, the Google Earth method (Sinachopoulos, 2019) are popular monument orientation methods, another innovative method utilizing Geographical Information Systems and Spatial Analysis was used here. Nowadays, the use of GIS in archaeoastronomy has yielded a number of excellent results, including novel approaches and solutions to spatial analysis problems (Mejuto et al., 2012; Higginbottom and Clay, 2016; Magli, 2017; Malaperdas and Panoskaltsis 2022). A GIS system is not just a tool for accurately simulating geomorphological features, but it also has the capability of analyzing geospatial data in an easily changing projection system (Malaperdas and Zacharias, 2019; Malaperdas et al, 2022).

As a result, databases are precisely combined with spatial information, which is extremely useful when managing a large number of either similar monuments (as in our case) or points of interest of varying nature (Wheatley and Gillings, 2002; Ardissone et al., 2005, Mafredas et al., 2021).

In our case, all of the DGPS data was managed to enter into a GIS environment. The points were initially checked for accuracy in relation to the topography. The test was carried out using satellite images of the study area, and the results were extremely satisfactory.

This process also resulted in the creation of a visual panorama, which provided us with our first clear picture of the tombs' orientation. As a result, we can conclude that the use and integration of GPS data in a GIS system assisted greatly in the overall project,

[6] Two other graves were investigated within the neighboring property of "Koutrafouris", on the western side of the hill, with its road to the SW, within the "Skartsilis" property (Arapogianni 2017, 25).

[7] The wide entryway leading to the main chamber was known as a dromos.

[8] The doorway into burial chamber.

both in terms of reliability and data management, as well as visualization techniques and data clarification.

3 Results and Discussion

It has already been argued that neither tholos nor chamber tholos tombs follow a specific pattern of burial orientation, but in some cases, some cemeteries seem to follow specific patterns: natural characteristics of the landscape, religious landmarks, delimit of habitation site, eschatological phenomena (Gallou 2005, 59). On Crete, Early Minoan tholoi of the Mesara have precise orientations northeast towards the summer-solstice sunrise and southeast towards the winter-solstice sunrise, as the peak sanctuaries (Branigan 1970, 105). A number of significant Minoan peak sanctuaries provide views of sunrises or sunsets behind especially notable mountain peaks (Blakolmer 2014, 121). Another important example of northeast to west orientation was noted in the Late Minoan III cemetery of Armeni located outside Rethymno at Crete. The cemetery has over 200 chamber tombs and one tholos tomb, all oriented towards northeast at the Mt. Vryssinas (east-west), which was at one time the site of a peak sanctuary. The chamber tombs were dug to the ground, known locally as kouskouras rock and remained well preserved. The tombs contained many dead, probably relatives (elite?) who were deposited either on the ground or in graves.

However, a spatial analysis of the relationship between Mycenaean cemeteries and settlements on the mainland of Greece reveals that there is no set pattern dictating the positioning and orientation of funerary architecture (Cavanagh and Mee 1998, 41–43; Malaperdas and Zacharias, 2018). Some Mycenaean cemeteries are located west of settlements, towards sunset, but others are not. Examples from other places in the Peloponnese might give the answer. Preliminary investigation of notable tholos tombs built in the Argolid indicates that the dromoi of many of them are (Georgiadis and Gallou 2006–2007, 171), like the Vapheio tholos (c. 1500 to 1450 BC), oriented to solstice or equinox events, as the sun rises or sets over hills and mountains on the horizon (Laskar 1986, 68). These examples must include tholoi such as the Dendra tholos (c. 1500 and 1180 BC) which is oriented to the winter solstice sunset; the Treasury of Atreus at Mycenae (c. 1350 and 1250 BC) oriented to the spring and fall equinox sunrise; the Tomb of the Genii at Mycenae (ca. 1400-1300 BC) oriented to the summer solstice sunset; the Kato Phournos tholos at Mycenae (ca. 1500-1400 BC) connected to the spring and fall equinox sunset and Tholos 1 at Tiryns (c. 16th BC) which faces the winter solstice sunset (Chapin et al. 2012, 150).

Other tholoi, however, point in different directions, and placement of these tombs may have also been influenced by practical factors, such as adapting to the topography of the area or orienting toward roads and palace monuments (Mason 2007, 37). All things considered, the data does not support the claim that the positioning and orientation of Mycenaean cemeteries and tombs were dictated by a widely held burial belief or ideology, instead, the norm is defined by diversity and variation (Cavanagh and Mee 1990, 56). This indicates that a decision was made by an individual or a (family?) group depending on the style of tomb created and its location and orientation. According to this, the positioning of some graves in relation to solstices or equinoxes likely reflects the beliefs of the tomb builders themselves (Chapin et al. 2012, 150).

Ano Englianos' Palace of Nestor is a significant for its connection to burial architecture (Nelson 2001, 48). The fact that the elaborate entranceway to the north-eastern sector of this circuit is aligned directly on the stomion of the tholos IV is significant because it highlights how certain individuals at Englianos may have chosen to associate the settlement closely with funerary monumentality and at the same time delimit the site of habitation. The Vagenas tomb stood prominently on the last ascent to the acropolis, while tholos IV was possibly the first significant building to be noticed by the passer-by arriving from the NE. Their locations also seem to follow the natural NE-SW contours of the ground. The Vagenas tomb had a magnificent view of the Bay of Navarino, the island of Sphacteria, and the regions southwest of it, i.e., the regions that would eventually become a part of Pylos' rule. These two tholoi may have served as territorial markers enclosing the settlement because they are not located on the top of the hill but rather lie on lower ground, one on either side of the ridge top. However, the position of tombs in the landscape may have already changed starting with LH I, becoming a means of displaying a new cultural rhetoric as well as a set of social and ideological practises that were imitated by numerous groups in the Pylos area and beyond. This later pattern is in no case restricted to Messenia; there's the example of Thorikos in Attica, Mycenae, in the Argolid and Knossos in Crete (Davis 2005, 428; Holmberg 1983, 53).

The building and re-negotiation of power relations took place as part of larger, more complicated strategies that included tombs (architecture and burial rituals). Important graves were located close to the main routes leading to and from the villages, which may have helped to create mnemonic landscapes and, in some cases, almost certainly marked the limits of individual settlements; thus, creating landmarks that shaped relationships between people and their natural and social environment (Galanakis 2008, 44, Galanakis 2012, 219). Monuments from the past were typically either forgotten or reconfigured to meet the requirements and goals of the new, emerging elites.

In our case study, we determined the azimuths of sixteen chamber-tombs dromoi using the method described by Sinachopoulos et al. (2023) in detail. Seven measurements per chamber-tomb dromos were usually done. We started measuring each tomb taking the first point at its most northeast NE visible point and proceeding towards its NW end. Adding two more measurements to the northern side of the tomb dromos. A fourth point was added in the middle of its north-western side, followed by adding three more measurement points of the tomb dromos southern side. Sometimes the access to a tomb was difficult and we had to reduce our measurements to five, two to each side and one to the tomb head.

Table 1 contains the azimuths of the tombs. Column one contains an identification of the tombs, given by a number, where Tomb No 1 is the most southern one. This number increases as we proceed to the north, so that tomb No 15 is the most northern of the tombs. Finally, tomb No 16[9] is the one separated from all other tombs, to the west of tomb No 15. In the second column the table contains the azimuth of each tomb.

[9] The tomb No 16 is oriented E-W, with the entrance to the West.

Table 1. The azimuth of the sixteen tombs in degrees.

Tomb Number	Azimuth (degrees)[a]
1	94
2	111
3	112
4	108
5	108
6	107
7	107
8	106
9	105
10	97
11	93
12	78
13	57
14	53
15	54
16	210

[a] Due to the bad shape of the tomb's *dromoi,* the dromos limits are often corroded by rainfalls, winds, or digging problems during excavations. Therefore, the accuracy of the tombs azimuths is limited to be between 2 and 3°.

4 Conclusions

In our conclusions, we must first take into account that geomorphologically, both the slopes of the ground and the geological formation of limestone rock, located in the specific point of Ellinika hill, provide the ideal conditions for the establishment of a Mycenaean cemetery. Furthermore, the tombs were carved with a vertical orientation to its axis spine and adapt to the slope of the two cheeks, resulting in them seeing towards the exact opposite points of the horizon.

Figure 3 shows the hill with its 16 chamber-tombs of our sample, as seen from the East, using Google Earth images. The white circles show the positions of each tomb on the hill, identified by its number, so that T1 denotes chamber-tomb No 1 etc. Five red lines correspond to contour lines for 130, 132.5, 135, 137.5, and 140 m.

Fig. 3. The hill with its 16 chamber-tombs. White circles show the positions of each tomb on the hill, identified by its number, so that T1 denotes chamber-tomb No 1 etc. Five red lines correspond to contour lines for 130, 132.5, 135, 137.5, and 140 m.

Apart of chamber-tomb No 16, which was built to the West slope of the hill, all other tombs were built to its Easter slope. So, practically all tombs are oriented "to the East", following the well-known pattern of earlier results, discussed earlier in this paper. An Eastern orientation is often related to the rising point of the Sun, or the Moon, or a planet, or even a very bright star. Although the Sun is often the preferable target of tomb orientation, this cannot be the case for tombs 13, 14, and 15, since their azimuth corresponds to orientations to the north of the Summer solstice.

But the remaining 12 chamber-tombs are oriented between the Winter-Summer solstices limits and can therefore be argued that they are oriented towards Sunrise points deliberately. This is remarkable because 75% of our sample chamber-tombs are oriented towards the rising Sun.

Back to chamber-tombs 13, 14, and 15 we remark with the aid of the altitude contour lines that although it was feasible to orient them also inside the Winter-Summer solstice limits -if they wanted-, they preferred a more to the North, but still Eastern, orientation, because the inclination of the slope of the hill made such an orientation more convenient.

It is possible a scenario according to which the oldest chamber-tombs were first built in the places of the hill, which were best suited for orientations inside the yearly solar path on the local horizon. Once the best places on the slope were taken by older-built tombs, newer tombs were then built to the North of the old ones, in non-taken places where the local hill slope made easier the tomb construction, in case that chamber-tomb dromoi were oriented more to the North, but still remaining oriented to the "East". In any case Myceneans took all efforts to have chamber-tomb dromoi oriented to the "East". Further investigation is carried out on the significance of Tomb No 16, which seems to be the only one that has been uncovered with its road facing the opposite direction from all the rest tombs.

Acknowledgements. This project was implemented within the scope of the "Exceptional Laboratory Practices in Cultural Heritage: Upgrading Infrastructure and Extending Research Perspectives of the Laboratory of Archaeometry", a co-financed by Greece and the European Union project under the auspices of the program "Competitiveness, Entrepreneurship and Innovation" NSRF 2014–2020.

References

Alcock, S.E.: Archaeologies of the Greek Past: Landscape, Monuments, and Memories. Cambridge (2002)

Arapogianni, X.: The asclepion. Archives (2017)

Ardissone, P., Rinaudo, F: A GIS for the management of historical and archaeological data. Paper Presented at the CIPA 2005 XX International Symposium 26 September–1 October 2005, Torino, Italy (2005)

Bailey D.: The archaeology of burial mounds. Theory and interpretation. In: Lungu, V. (ed.) Pratiques funéraires dans l'Europe des xiiie-xive s. av. J.-C. Actes du IIIe Colloque International d'archéologie funéraire, Tulcea 1997, Tulcea, pp. 23–28 (2000)

Blakolmer, F.P: Meaningful landscapes: Minoan "landscape rooms" and peak sanctuaries. Physis: L'environnement naturel et la relation homme-milieu dans le monde égéen protohistorique. Actes de la 14e Rencontre égéenne internationale, Paris, Institut National d'Histoire de l'Art (INHA), 11–14 décembre 2012, pp. 121–128 (2014)

Boutsikas, E.: Placing Greek temples: an archaeoastronomical study of the orientation of ancient Greek religious structures. Archaeoastronomy **21**, 4–19 (2008)

Branigan, K.: The tombs of Mesara. A study of funerary architecture and ritual in Southern Crete, 2800-1700 BC. Antiquaries J. (1970)

Button, S.: Mortuary studies, memory and the Mycenaean polity. In: Yoffee, N. (ed.) Negotiating the Past in the Past. Identity, Memory, and Landscape in Archaeological Research, Tucson, pp. 76–103 (2007)

Cavanagh, W.G., Mee, C.B.: The location of Mycenaean chamber tombs in the Argolid. In: Hägg, R., Nordquist, G.C. (eds.) Celebrations of Death and Divinity in the Bronze Age Argolid. Proceedings of the Sixth International Symposium at the Swedish Institute at Athens, 11–13 June 1988, SkrAth, 4°, 40, Stockholm, pp. 55–64 (1990)

Cavanagh, W.G., Laxton, R.R.: The structural mechanics of the Mycenaean tholos tomb. Annu. Br. School Athens **76**, 109–140 (1981)

Cavanagh, W.G., Mee C.B.: A private place: death in prehistoric Greece. SIMA 125, Jonsered (1998)

Chapin, A., Davis, B., Hitchcock, L.A., Banou, E.: The Vapheio tholos tomb and the construction of a symbolic landscape in Laconia, Greece. In: PHYSIS. L'environnement naturel et la relation homme-milieu dans le monde égéen protohistorique, pp. 145–152 (2014)

Davis, J.L., Alcock, S.E., Bennet, J., Lolos, Y.G., Shelmerdine, C.W.: The pylos regional archaeological project. Part I: Overview and the archaeological survey. Hesperia **66**, 391–494 (2005)

Dickinson, O.T.P.K.: Cist graves and chamber tombs. Annu. Br. School Athens **78**, 55–67 (1983)

Galanakis, Y.: A study of late bronze age tholos tombs in the Aegean, 1700-1200 BC. Ph.D., University of Oxford (2008)

Galanakis, Y.: Mnemonic landscapes and monuments of the past: tumuli, tholos tombs and landscape associations in late middle bronze age and early late bronze age Messenia (Greece). In: Ancestral Landscape. Burial mounds in the Copper and Bronze Ages (Central and Eastern Europe - Balkans - Adriatic - Aegean, 4th-2nd millennium BC) Proceedings of the International Conference held in Udine, 15th–18th May 2008, pp. 219–229. Maison de l'Orient et de la Méditerranée Jean Pouilloux, Lyon (2012)

Gallou, Chr.: The Mycenaean Cult of the Dead. BAR Int. Series, vol. 1372. Oxford (2005)

Georgiadis, M., Gallou Chr.: The cemeteries of the Argolid and the south-eastern Aegean during the Mycenaean Period: a landscape and waterscape assessment, Op Ath 31–32, 171–182 (2007)

Graziadio, G.: The Process of social stratification at Mycenae in the shaft grave period: a comparative examination of the evidence. AJA **95**, 403–440 (1991)

Higginbottom, G., Clay, R.: Origins of standing stone astronomy in Britain: new quantitative techniques for the study of archaeoastronomy. J. Archaeol. Sci. Rep. **9**, 249–258 (2016)

Holmberg, E.J.: A Mycenaean Chamber tomb near Berbati. Goteborg (1983)

Korres, G.S.: Messenia and its commercial connections in the Bronze age. In: Zerner, C., Zerner, P., Winder, J. (eds) Wace and Blegen: Pottery as Evidence for Trade in the Aegean Bronze Age 1939–1989, Amsterdam, pp. 231–248 (1993)

Laskar, J.: Secular terms of classical planetary theories using the results of general relativity. Astron. Astrophys. **157**, 59–70 (1986)

Mafredas, T., Malaperdas, G.: Archaeological databases and GIS: working with databases. Eur. J. Inf. Technol. Comput. Sci. **1**(3), 1–6 (2021)

Magli, G.: Archaeoastronomy in the Khmer Heartland. SDH, 1, 1, Article 1 (2017)

Malaperdas, G., Zacharias, N.: A geospatial analysis of mycenaean habitation sites using a geocumulative versus habitation approach. J. Geosci. Environ. Protect. **6**, 111–131 (2018). https://doi.org/10.14445/23939206/IJGGSV6I1P101

Malaperdas, G., Zacharias, N.: The habitation model trend calculation (MTC): a new effective tool for predictive modeling in archaeology. Geo-spat. Inf. Sci. **22**(4), 314–331 (2019). https://doi.org/10.1080/10095020.2019.1634320

Malaperdas, G., Maggidis, C., Karantzali, E., Zacharias, N.: The habitation model trend calculation (MTC): ancient topography - the mycenaean spercheios valley case study. Interdiscip. Archaeol. **13**(1), 29–39 (2022). https://doi.org/10.24916/iansa.2022.1.3

Malaperdas, G., Panoskaltsis, D.: The naval base of navarino: mapping the fortifications of the Italians in Pylos. In: Moropoulou, A., Georgopoulos, A., Doulamis, A., Ioannides, M., Ronchi, A. (eds.) TMM_CH 2021. CCIS, vol. 1574, pp. 149–163. Springer, Cham (2022). https://doi.org/10.1007/978-3-031-20253-7_13

Mason, D.: The location of the treasury of Atreus. OJA **26**(1), 35–52 (2007)

Mejuto, J., Gómez Castaño, J., Rodríguez Caderot, G.: GIS techniques in archaeology: an archaeoastronomical approach. In: Castanyer, O. (ed.) Archaeology, New Approaches in Theory and Techniques, pp.118–132 (2012)

Mee, C.B., Cavanagh, W.G.: The spatial distribution of Mycenaean tombs. BSA **85**, 225–244 (1990)

Morgan, C.: Messenia. Archaeol. Rep. **56**, 48–51 (2010)

Murphy, J.M.A.: Death in Late Bronze Age Greece: Variations on a Theme. Oxford University Press, Oxford (2020)

Nelson, M.C.: The Architecture of Epano Englianos, Greece. Ph.D., University of Toronto (2001)

Pantazis, G., Sinachopoulos, D., Lambrou, E., Korakitis, R.: Astrogeodetic study of ancient and Byzantine monuments: methodology and first results. J. Astron. Hist. Heritage **7**, 74–81 (2004)

Sinachopoulos, D.: A further application of Google Earth in studying the orientation of ancient Greek monuments. J. Astron. Hist. Heritage **22**(2), 211–224 (2019)

Sinachopoulos, D., Malaperdas, G., Psychas, A., Maggidis, C., Karantzali, E.: The winter solstice orientation of the cemetery chamber-tombs founded during the Mycenaean era at the Prophitis Elias, Kompotades (Central Greece). J. Astron. Hist. Heritage (2023, submitted)

Wheatley, D., Gillings, M.: Spatial Technology and Archaeology. The Archaeological Applications of GIS. Taylor & Francis, London and New York (2002)

Wright J.C.: Changes in the form and function of the palace at Pylos. In: Palaima, T.G., Shelmerdine, C.W. (eds.) Pylos Comes Alive: Industry and Administration in a Mycenaean Palace, New York, pp. 19–29 (1984)

Wright, J.C., et al.: Nemea valley archaeological project, excavations at Barnavos: final report. Hesperia **77**, 607–654 (2008)

Zangger, E., Timpson, M.E., Yazvenko, S.B., Kuhnke, F., Knauss, J.: The Pylos regional archaeological project. Part II: landscape evolution and site preservation. Hesperia **66**, 549–641 (1997)

Approaching Climate Resilience in Greek Cultural Heritage Using Geodata and Geoinformatics Tools

Athanasios Dimou(✉) and Christos-Nikolaos Anagnostopoulos

Cultural Technology and Communication Department, University of Aegean, 81100 Mytilene, Lesvos, Greece

{a.dimou,canag}@aegean.gr

Abstract. The scientific community and policy makers recognize that adaptation and resilience measures and strategies are needed to minimize the impacts of climate change. The incorporation of such strategies into mapping tools will help communities, authorities and stakeholders to manage extreme situations and emergency phenomena such as floods, winds, landslides, sea level rise, etc. Since spatial information is a key factor for any aspect of resilience to climate change and in order to enhance the resilience of cultural assets, it is necessary to adopt a multidimensional approach centered around geospatial information.

The modern tools of Geoinformatics (such as Geographical Information Systems, Satellite Remote Sensing, Photogrammetry, Spatial analysis, etc.) are a solution and utility in modern societies for the development of these systems either at a local, regional or global level. They are a complete solution, as they can combine geo-information, including data from the past, from the present and eventually become an approach - predicting model for the future, with many applications and at different scales.

Therefore, approaching and modeling the resilience quantitatively, can be defined using appropriate geodata sets (such as Digital Elevation Models - DEMs, hydrological network datasets, meteorological datasets, precision satellite datasets, etc.) combined with the use of Geoinformatics tools and Geographical Information Systems (GIS providing accurate and realistic belief-based estimations and better analysis of resilience indicators (sensitivity, recovery, adaptation, risk).

An attempt will be made to study monuments and sites, which are located in special geophysical, soil and climatic areas of the territory and at the same time not so well-known compared to other areas of Greece. A special broader area for specific cultural and archaeological sites is the Volcanic Arc. The area includes the Volcanoes at Sousaki, Methana, Santorini, Milos and Nisyros (of which 3 are active Volcanoes with past eruptions).

Along the arc there are important cultural and archaeological sites that need protection and attention mainly because they are exposed to island complexes and coastal areas of particular natural beauty and area.

Keywords: Climate Resilience · Geoiformatics · Geodata · Culture Heritage

A. Moropoulou et al. (Eds.): TMM_CH 2023, CCIS 1889, pp. 255–265, 2023.
https://doi.org/10.1007/978-3-031-42300-0_22

1 Climate Change

Climate change is a complex problem that interacts with human and natural existence. It affects and is affected by global issues such as poverty, economic development, population growth, sustainable development, resource management, etc.

The definition of climate change, according to the United Nations Framework Convention on Climate Change [1], is: "a change in climate that is directly or indirectly caused by human activity and alters the composition of the global atmosphere in addition to the natural climate variability observed over comparable time periods".

The Intergovernmental Panel on Climate Change [11] in its report states that global warming is indisputable, a large percentage of radiation enters the upper atmosphere of the earth than it leaves, with the result that since 1970 changes such as:

- Increase in the average temperature around the world, in land areas but also in oceans
- Strong changes in rainfall (increase in wet and decrease in dry areas)
- Reduction of snowfall and snow cover
- Frequent, increasing occurrence of extreme weather events (heat waves, extreme rainfall, etc.)
- Melting of glaciers in high altitude areas and in the Arctic Sea level rise

According to a report by the World Bank [2], the effects of global warming due to climate change have been recorded. As can be seen in the table below, in several countries around the world, we are witnessing records of rising temperatures, drought, heavy rainfall, etc. Unfortunately, the effects are even also intense and with several effects in our country as well (Table 1).

Table 1. Impacts of climate change by country and year

Region (year)	Event	Impact, Cost
England and Wales (2000)	Wettest autumn on record since 1766	~1.3 billion pounds
Europe (2003)	Hottest summer in at least 500 years	Death toll >70,000
Southern Europe (2007)	Hottest summer on record in Greece since 1891	Devastating wildfires
Easter Mediterranean. Middle-East (2008)	Dries winter since 1902	Substantial damage to cereal production
Western Europe (2011)	Hottest and driest spring on record in France since 1880	Grain harvest down by ~12%

1.1 International Agreements and EU on Climate Change

In 1992, governments adopted the United Nations Framework Convention on Climate Change [3] within the framework of the UN, also known as the Rio Summit. The aim of the Treaty is to stabilize the concentrations of greenhouse gases in the atmosphere.

The Kyoto Protocol in 1997 [4] is known for setting binding targets for many developed countries regarding the limitation of their emissions. According to Dessai et al. [25], developing countries should initially reduce their emissions since they contributed more to the accumulation of gases.

In 2015, the 21st meeting of the parties to the UN Framework Convention on Climate Change [5], the Paris Agreement took place. The aim of the agreement was to balance the temperature of the planet well below 2 °C with efforts to reach 1.5 °C.

In 2015, at the 3rd UN World Conference, Sendai Framework, 7 goals and 4 priorities for action were set to reduce the risk of natural disasters in the period 2015–2030. It is a voluntary, non-binding agreement. It also recognizes cultural property as a key factor in disaster risk reduction and states that heritage must be protected in order to improve resilience.

The 2030 Agenda [6] of the U.N. for sustainable development was approved in 2015 by the world leaders of the U.N. countries. Similarly, the approach of the EU with its member states, including our country, was set in the global framework for sustainable development with 17 development goals. Among the 17 goals, there are sub-goals (11b., 13.1, 13.2, 13.3, 13.a, 13b and others) that emphasize holistic management and disaster risk reduction, as well as resilience and adaptation to the risks that result from climate change (Fig. 1).

Fig. 1. UN Sustainable Development Goals

In 2013, the European Commission issued guidelines for the development of climate change adaptation strategies with steps and recommendations of the Adaptation Support Tool of Climate-ADAPT [7], the European Platform on Adaptation to Climate Change. Te guidelines were created by the collaboration between the European Commission and the European Environment Agency.

At the 43rd session of the World Heritage Committee in 2019, with the report from the International Union of Monuments and Sites ICOMOS entitled 'Future of Our Pasts: Engaging Cultural Heritage in Climate Action', proposed actions to manage and address climate change with interdisciplinary approach to cultural heritage. To achieve this better recognition of the cultural dimensions of climate change and adaptation of the objectives and methodologies of heritage practice is required [28].

2 Resilience

Climate change (including natural disasters but also the effects of ecosystems) interconnect and coexist with Resilience, Adaptation and Vulnerability (Fig. 2).

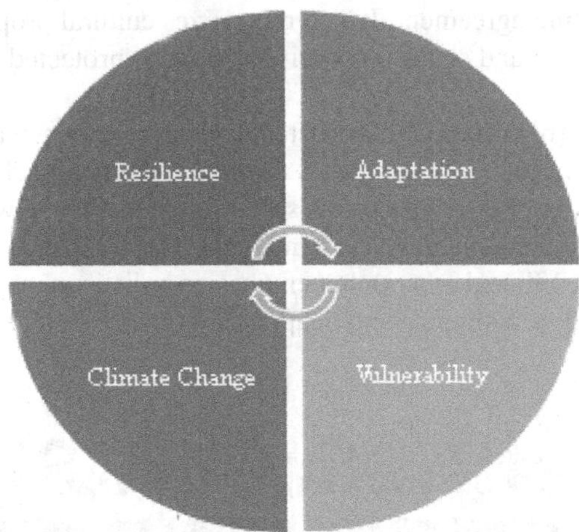

Fig. 2. Relationship of climate change, Resilience, Adaptation and Vulnerability

Resilience is defined as the ability of a social-ecological system to respond to climate change, to adapt and improve the sustainability of the system to be better prepared for future impacts of climate change [8, 9]. Both international and national actors are aware of the effects of climate change so that climate resilience is an important goal.

The term resilience was originally introduced by psychologist E. Werner [12], after he documented individual age-related growth over 40 years for 698 Hawaiian children. The most important finding was that some of the children recovered more from similar traumas and adverse situations (eg, poverty) than others. These kids were characterized as "resilient".

A key part of climate resilience is addressing the climate vulnerability that communities, states and countries have today to the consequences of climate change. In recent years, a large number of resilience measurement tools have emerged, offering ways to monitor and measure resilience at a range of scales – from individuals and households to communities and nations [13].

In a recent survey in 2019, the key components of resilience based on a large number of research articles and reviews were categorized and explained [14], as follows:

- Resilience and adaptability to climate-related stresses and shocks
- Evaluation and monitoring: resilience as a process
- Scale (Country, Regions, Cities, Neighborhoods, Individuals)

- Interdisciplinarity: resilience as an umbrella for various fields
- Learning and innovation
- Information and transparency: resilience as a tool for participation
- Environment (natural and built)
- Networked systems and agencies (multi-level governance)
- Ability to transform after disturbances but maintain self-organization
- Equity and Fairness: resilience metrics should not exclude others.

3 Cultural Heritage and Climate Change

Climate change affects monuments and archaeological sites due to increased drought (which increases fuel and forest fire risk), soil erosion, rising sea levels that can lead to coastal flooding, and the occurrence of extreme weather events and phenomena.

According to Cassar, M. [15], climate impacts on cultural heritage include:

- Rainfalls: they are not able to manage in many places heavy rains and it is difficult to access immediately and to maintain the spaces but also to adapt.
- Floods of fluids: subsidence of the ground due to water and as a result can damage the cultural heritage.
- Coastal flooding and storm surges: loss of coastal areas and risk from wind blowing of ruined buildings and archaeological excavations.
- Temperature: important for guest comfort. Deterioration of materials and contents because higher temperature would increase the rate of chemical reactions.
- Relative humidity: changes in relative humidity could lead to new insect species infesting collections.
- Table water and chemistry: the change may result from a drop in the height of the water table or from seawater intrusion. A change in moisture damage pattern may be observed in some areas.

According to [16] UNESCO World Heritage Sites (WHS) located in coastal areas are increasingly at risk of coastal hazards due to sea level rise. The risk of coastal flooding and erosion was studied with 4 scenarios of sea level rise up to the year 2100. The results were that of the 49 monuments and sites, 37 are at risk of flooding with an increase of 50% by 2100 while coastal erosion is at risk 42. Sounding the bell for adaptation and policy making with further studies and research at the local scale.

3.1 Cultural Heritage and Climate Change in Greece

Devastating forest fires broke out in the area of Ancient Olympia, due to the increase in temperature with over 150,000 hectares of forest and arable land burned.This led to new studies on proper vegetation selection and more advanced ones on fire suppression mechanisms [18].

The medieval city of Rhodes was threatened by a complex combination of natural factors of decay (marine atmosphere, salt decomposition, increasing humidity) artificial deterioration factors (tourism, air pollution due to traffic and increasing temperature and humidity), the sensitivity of local building materials (porous sandstone) and an inefficient city development planning system (problems of building stability, underground facilities, etc.) [17].

According to E. Korka [18], the famous archaeological site of Delos with its location near the sea in the middle of the Aegean is exposed to threats and dangers to the ruins. All ancient structures or outdoor sculptures are exposed to various environmental factors such as: winds, rising sea and groundwater levels and many others.

An interdisciplinary research project called CLIMASCAPE is underway, where it attempts to contribute to the protection of 8 archaeological sites included in the UNESCO World Heritage List from the dangers of climate change [23].

Indicative Objectives of the project are:

- the prediction of changes, in the light of climate parameters in places of cultural and touristic interest, especially in archaeological sites, with the use of climate models of high spatial resolution
- the assessment of the pressures and general effects exerted on the archaeological site due to tourism
- the assessment of the sensitivity and adaptability of the archaeological site
- the synthetic assessment of the vulnerability of the archaeological site
- the evaluation and categorization of risks per archaeological site.

4 Geoinformatics - Data and Tools

According to the Encyclopedia of Information Science and Technology (3rd edition) [26], Geoinformatics is academically referred to as the career of working with Geo-data to better understand and interpret human interaction with the Earth's surface.Geoinformatics refers to two words. "Geo" and "Informatics", "Geo" refers to Geospatial - Geography, "Informatics" refers to the multidisciplinary science of Information Technology (eg computer science, software engineering, computer vision, mobile and game technology, intelligent system etc.).

Geographical Information Systems are known around the world as GIS are developed by the ¨father of GIS¨ British scientist Roger Tomlinson in 1960. They have a rapid development and acceptance in our era, following the 4th industrial revolution and the development of of Information Technology and Artificial Intelligence. From 1960 until today, depending on on each scientific field, there was extensive cooperation and development with different definitions were set. However according to Goodchild [27], Geographical Information Systems is an integrated system of collecting, storing, managing, analyzing and displaying information related to issues of a geographical nature.

QGIS open source software used.

QGIS is open source GIS software, licensed under the GNU General Public License, by the Open Source Geospatial Foundation (OSGeo). The first version was released in 2009 and to this day volunteer developers around the world as well as GIS enthusiasts support the effort for a competitive and functional GIS software for the needs of citizens, researchers and professionals. The abundance of spatial analysis tools will be a forerunner for data management [24].

4.1 Geodata

The data will be drawn from global, European but also national and local agencies and organizations where they will be categorized according to use and region.An indicative list of data to be collected according to related literature, which are suitable for the calculation of resilience and climate change is as follows:

- Data of administrative boundaries (Regions, Municipalities etc.)
- Physicogeographical data (DEM., slopes, orientation, altitude, coastal erosion, etc.)
- Architectural - topographical data
- Urban planning data (land cover, land uses, zones, settlement boundaries, seafront & coastline, etc.)
- Spatial data (tourist areas, routes of natural and cultural interest etc.)
- Infrastructure Data (Road & Rail network, airports, ports, etc.)
- Demographic Data (population, visitors)
- Economic development data (employment, GDP)
- Environmental data (Natura2000, Rasmar etc.)
- Climatic data (temperature, Rain, Drought, Frost, Winds etc.)
- Satellite Data (Copernicus, Landsat, NOAA etc.)

As far as satellite data is concerned, Copernicus is a European Union Earth observation program coordinated and managed by the European Commission in cooperation with the European Space Agency (ESA), the EU Member States and EU organizations. One of the benefits of the Copernicus program is that the data and information produced under Copernicus are freely available to all users and the public, thus enabling the development of downstream services.

The services and data offered by the Copernicus program cover six main interconnected modules: Atmospheric data, marine & terrestrial data, climate change data, emergency and security data. The data are collected by special satellites called Sentinel (Sentinel family) which are classified according to the unit they represent.

A wealth of data concerns and illustrates metrics for cultural heritage. According to the study of the European Commission "Copernicus services in support to cultural heritage" which aims to assess the possibility of starting an institutional action to promote the use of Copernicus data for the preservation, monitoring and management of Cultural Heritage. The Copernicus program is one of Europe's flagship programmes, providing free and open data and information based on satellite images, models and on-the-ground data.

5 Study Area

Our case study focusses on the South Aegean Volcanic Arc, which is a "chain" of volcanoes in the South Aegean Sea. The literature states that the specific volcanic arc shows intense activity and was created due to the convergence of the two lithospheric plates in the Aegean region. The area includes the volcanoes at Sousaki, Methana, Santorini, Milos and Nisyros, from which three of them are active with past eruptions.

South Aegean Volcanic Arc extends over approximately 600 km, from Saronic Gulf to the islands of Kos and Nisyros up to Minor Asia coast. It is defined by the volcanic centers of Sousaki, Aegina, Methana, Poros, Milos-Antimilos, Santorini, Kolumbo, Kos, Yali, and Nisyros, starting from the northwestern part down to the southeastern part. It belongs to the Hellenic Orogenic Arc, which is formed along the convergent plate boundary of the northwards subducting African plate underneath the active margin of the European plate [20].

Along the arc there are important cultural and archaeological sites that need protection and attention mainly because they are exposed to island complexes with coastal areas of particular natural beauty and area (Table 2).

Table 2. Volcanoes in South Aegean volcanic arc

Name	Elevation (m)	Last Eruption
Aegina		Pleistocene
Gyali	180	Holocene
Kos	430	Pleistocene
Methana	760	258 BC
Milos	751	140 AD
Nisyros	698	1888
Poros	80	Pliocene
Santorini (Kolumbo)	−18	1650
Santorini (Nea Kameni)	130	1950
Sousaki		Quaternary

The scope of our research is to collect, process, analyze and manage appropriate geodata through geoinformatics tools for visualization purposes and better understanding.

The maps in Fig. 3 below show geodata of the volcanic arc area. Specifically, in Fig. 3 and the upper left map, average temperature in the periods 2010–2023 is depicted. Point data were extracted from the Hellenic Meteorological Service from the 47 stations out of a total of 538 in the country. Inverse distance weighting (IDW) was used, to estimate unknown values with specifying search distance, closest points, power setting and barriers. IDW is a type of deterministic method for multivariate interpolation [22], when only a set of scattered points is known.

In the respective map, bright red pixels display the highest values and as can be seen in a large part of the islands of the volcanic arc, the highest temperature is displayed.

In the upper right map of Fig. 3 the digital terrain model (DEM) from Copernicus satellite images with a pixel accuracy of 25 m and the Digital Bottom Model (DTM) of Greece is depicted. The map has a resolution of 15″ degrees (463 m), data from the Hydrographic Service of the Hellenic Navy. Through the DEM, additional contour maps, slope maps, aspect maps have been produced which will help to understand the terrain of the area.

Finally, the coastline of the entire study area was created with the digitization tools against the background of the orthophotomaps of the Hellenic Land Registry for the period 2015–2017. The coastline will be the limit for the unearthed archaeological sites and monuments of the area. It is also a basic geodata for the study of sea level rise.

In the bottom map of Fig. 3 all the approved archaeological sites and monuments located in the wider study area are identified. The geodata was downloaded from the Archaeological Land Registry of the Ministry of Culture as open geodata shapefiles. The monuments and archaeological sites that are located nearby the coast, in combination with the increased temperature of the area, are emphasized.

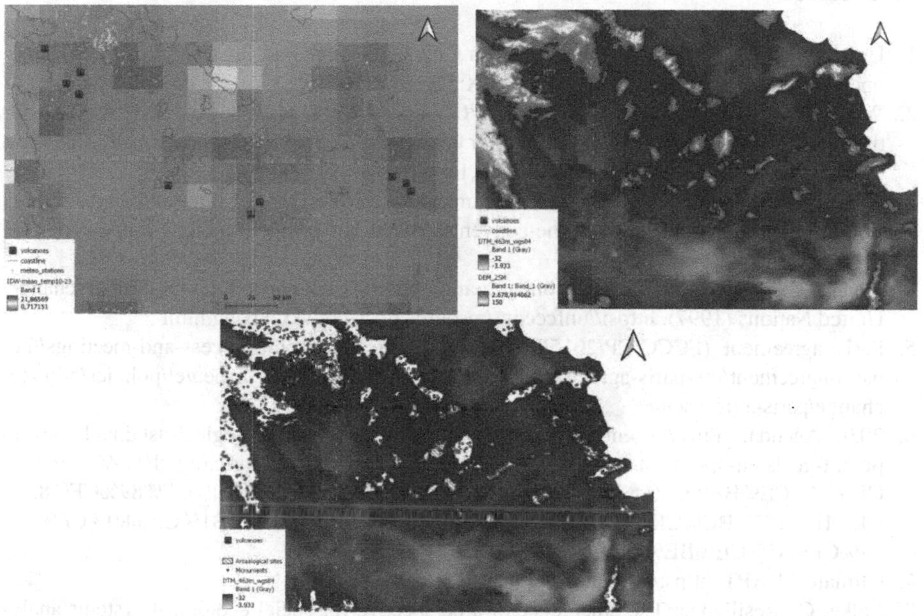

Fig. 3. Thematic maps for the volcano arc area

6 Conclusions

This paper proposes the creation and processing of appropriate geodata in combination with related quantitative and qualitative descriptive features of the areas under consideration (volcanic arc) to create models of resilience indicators for the prediction and protection of selected archaeological sites and monuments.

A major innovative contribution to the scientific literature on climate change is the application and use of innovative tools of Geoinformatics science. Geographical Information Systems, remote sensing tools (processing and analysis of satellite images), Photogrammetry tools (processing and analysis of aerial photographs), and appropriate precision geodata of the region are modern tools and a precursor for a different approach to climate change for our country with the rich cultural heritage.

It should be noted that, in the literature, resilience is approached mainly theoretically. In practical terms, it is tackled mainly creating and calculating mathematical models, but not in a holistic way, thus it is performed subjectively for each study case. Therefore, further study and analysis of resilience indicators for cultural heritage are needed in technical terms and and above theoretical approaches, with the implementation of innovative Geoinformatics and analysis tools. Those tools may becomes extremely valuable for making important decisions and political initiatives for the protection of our cultural heritage.

References

1. United Nations Framework Convention on Climate Change - UNFCCC. https://eur-lex.europa.eu/legal-content/EL/TXT/?uri=CELEX:52009DC0667
2. World Bank: Turn down the heat: why a 4°C Warmer World Must be Avoided? A report for the World Bank by the Potsdam Institute for Climate Impact Research and Climate Analytics, Washington, DC (2012). https://doi.org/10.1596/978-0-8213-9568-4
3. UNFCCC: What is the United Nations Framework Convention on Climate Change? https://unfccc.int/process-and-meetings/the-convention/what-is-the-united-nations-framework-convention-on-climate-change
4. UNFCCC: Kyoto protocol to the united nations framework convention on climate change. United Nations (1997). https://unfccc.int/resource/docs/convkp/kpeng.html
5. Paris agreement (FCCC/CP/2015/L.9/Rev.1). https://unfccc.int/process-and-meetings/the-paris-agreement/the-paris-agreement, https://www.consilium.europa.eu/el/policies/climate-change/paris-agreement/
6. 2030 Agenda. https://ec.europa.eu/info/strategy/international-strategies/sustainable-development-goals/eu-approach-sustainable-development_el, https://unric.org/el/17-%CF%83%CF%84%CE%BF%CF%87%CE%BF%CE%B9-%CE%B2%CE%B9%CF%89%CF%83%CE%B9%CE%BC%CE%B7%CF%83-%CE%B1%CE%BD%CE%B1%CF%80%CF%84%CF%85%CE%BE%CE%B7%CF%83/
7. Climate ADAPT. https://climate-adapt.eea.europa.eu/
8. Folke, C.: Resilience: The emergence of a perspective for social-ecological systems analyses. Glob. Environ. Change **16**(3), 253–267 (2006). https://doi.org/10.1016/j.gloenvcha.2006.04.002
9. Nelson, D.R., Adger, W.N., Brown, K.: Adaptation to environmental change: contributions of a resilience framework. Annu. Rev. Environ. Resour. **32**, 395–419 (2007). https://doi.org/10.1146/annurev.energy.32.051807.090348
10. Füssel, H.-M.: Vulnerability in climate change research: a comprehensive conceptual framework (2005). https://escholarship.org/uc/item/8993z6nm
11. IPCC (2007). https://www.ipcc.ch/site/assets/uploads/2018/03/ar4_wg2_full_report.pdf
12. Werner, E.E., Bierman, J.M., French, F.E.: The children of Kauai. A longitudinal Study from the Prenatal Period to Age Ten. University of Hawaii Press, Honolulu (1971). ISBN 0870228609
13. Schipper, L.: A comparative overview of resilience measurement frameworks analysing indicators and approaches. Overseas Development Institute (2015). https://odi.org/documents/4886/9754.pdf
14. Schaefer, M., Thinh, N.X., Greiving, S.: How can climate resilience be measured and visualized? Assessing a vague concept using gis-based fuzzy logic (2020). https://doi.org/10.3390/su12020635

15. Cassar, M.: Climate change and the historic environment, centre for sustainable heritage (2005). https://www.researchgate.net/publication/32886503_Climate_Change_and_the_Historic_Environment
16. Reimann, L., Vafeidis, A.T., Brown, S., Hinkel, J., Tol, R.S.J.: Mediterranean UNESCO world heritage at risk from coastal flooding and erosion due to sea-level rise. Nat. Commun. **9**, Article number: 4161 (2018). https://doi.org/10.1038/s41467-018-06645-9
17. Korka, E.: Cultural heritage facing climate change: experiences and ideas for resilience and adaptation. Natural Disasters and Risks in World Heritage Monuments of Greece. Lessons Learnt (2018)
18. Kanefusa, M. (ed.): Case study on the monastery of Daphni and archaeological site of Olympia. In: Research Report on International Cooperation in the Recovery Process of Disaster-affected Cultural Heritage, Greece, pp. 17–32. Ritsumeikan-Global Innovation Research Organization, Ritsumeikan University (2009)
19. Moropoulou, A.I., Labropoulos, K.C.: Non-destructive testing for assessing structural damage and interventions effectiveness for built cultural heritage protection. In: Handbook of Research on Seismic Assessment and Rehabilitation of Historic Structures, pp. 448–499 (2015). http://dx.doi.org/10.4018/978-1-4666-8286-3.ch015
20. Nomikou, P., Papanikolaou, D., Alexandri, M., Sakellariou, D., Rousakis, G.: Submarine volcanoes along the Aegean volcanic arc. Tectonophysics (2013). https://doi.org/10.1016/j.tecto.2012.10.001
21. Siebert, L., Simkin, T.: Volcanoes of the world: an illustrated catalog of holocene volcanoes and their eruptions. Smithsonian Institution. Global Volcanism Program Digital Information Series, GVP-3 (2002). http://www.volcano.si.edu
22. Shepard, D.: A two-dimensional interpolation function for irregularly-spaced data. In: Proceedings of the 1968 ACM National Conference, pp. 517–524 (1968). https://doi.org/10.1145/800186.810616
23. CLIMASCAPE. http://climascape.prd.uth.gr/
24. QGIS Official page. https://qgis.org/en/site/
25. Dessai, S., Hulme, M.: Climatic implications of revised IPCC emission scenarios, the Kyoto protocol and quantification of uncertainties. Integr. Assess. **2**, 159–170 (2001). https://doi.org/10.1023/A:1013300520580
26. Ayanlade, A., Jegede, M.O., Borisade, P.B.: Encyclopedia of Information Science and Technology. Geoinformatics in Eco-Climatic Studies, 3rd edn., pp. 3136–3144 (2015). https://doi.org/10.4018/978-1-4666-5888-2.ch307
27. Goodchild, M.F.: Geographie information systems in undergraduate geography: a contemporary dilemma. Oper. Geogr. **8**, 34–38 (1985)
28. Climate Change and Cultural Heritage Working Group International. The Future of Our Pasts: Engaging cultural heritage in climate action Outline of Climate Change and Cultural Heritage. Technical Report. International Council on Monuments and Sites - ICOMOS, ICOMOS Paris, 62p. (2019). http://openarchive.icomos.org/id/eprint/2459/

Salamis Island in the Challenge of a Digital Storytelling

Delazanou Maria(✉)

Department of Interior Architecture, University of West Attica, Athens, Greece
mdelazanou@uniwa.gr

Abstract. This paper is focused on a main question as "In what ways can digital technology contribute to promoting the cultural heritage of a place?" The aim of research in this paper has been the creation of a digital collection that records and promotes part of the tangible and intangible heritage of the island of Salamis. The choice of Salamis, as the object of research of the present paper, becomes necessary, as there no systematic researches and literature related to the cultural reserve of the island. As part of the research, fifty (50) items have been registered, which are photographs recording the cultural wealth of Salamis, such as historical buildings, monasteries, well-known place names, museums, etc. The digital material has been deposited in the digital repository Omeka.net. The project "Salamina: a digital tour to past and present" started as a vision for the protection and digitization of the culture of Salamis. The objective of the research has been to create a platform which will serve as a "virtual" guide through the main elements of the culture of Salamis, making use of new technologies. Its purpose will be to raise public and private cultural institutions, both at a local and national level, as well as to attract visitors and to enhance tourism. The success of this project will depend on its interaction with the users of the digital platform.

Keywords: Salamis · Omeka · digital collection · cultural heritage digitization

1 Introduction

Going through the century of the 4th Industrial Revolution, it is becoming more and more obvious that the application of new technologies and methods in the preservation and dissemination of a region's cultural heritage has a direct impact on society, on the tourism sector and the economic development of cultural industry of an entire country.

The 21st century is characterized by the rapid development of technology, creating the suitable conditions for a constant acquisition of information on the Internet and the incessant use of mobile phones and other digital media, so the user is simultaneously in an environment both digital and analog, being everywhere at any time receiving information through social media and email. Thus, these developments have influenced the way in which cultural institutions reach out their visitors by applying innovative methods of communicating the cultural reserve, with the aim at increasing the possibilities of accessibility [1].

A. Moropoulou et al. (Eds.): TMM_CH 2023, CCIS 1889, pp. 266–275, 2023.
https://doi.org/10.1007/978-3-031-42300-0_23

The use of new technologies concerning the digital documentation, restoration and visualization of cultural objects in order to create digital exhibitions and collections, contributes to preserving, managing and promoting cultural heritage, while at the same time it is made easier for the general public, to access the cultural wealth, that each country owns, through the internet [2].

The present paper was based on the research question: "In what ways can digital technology contribute to promoting the cultural heritage of the island of Salamis?". The choice of the place was based on the fact that to this day, Salamis remains for many, an unknown and indifferent island[1]. The officially recorded history of the island begins and ends with its famous Naval Battle[2]. Therefore, a digital collection was designed on an opensource platform, aspiring to guide internet users to the known and at the same time unknown Salamis. The vision of this venture is to raise awareness among public and private bodies, so that Salamis becomes a deserving tourist destination. The website, <https://salamina.omeka.net>, is the vehicle of touristic communication and promotion of Salamis to the domestic and international travelers.

2 The Case Study of the Island of Salamis

Salamis is the largest Greek island in the Saronic Gulf and the closest to the shores of Attica. Administratively it belongs to the Prefecture of Attica and more specifically to the district of Piraeus [6]. According to the results of the first digital census in Greece conducted by EL.STAT.[3] in 2021, its population reaches 37,175 inhabitants [7].

2.1 SWOT Analysis

Table 1 summarizes the advantages and disadvantages for the tourism promotion of the island of Salamis, with the help of the SWOT Analysis tool.

2.2 Planning a Digital Journey to Salamis

According to Alexandros Tsatsarounos, planning for the "post-coronavirus era" should not awkwardly follow the developments, but create them [8]. Under the current conditions of the pandemic, a prerequisite for the promotion of the destination, is the "digital"

[1] Haris Koutelakis and Amanda Foskolou, in the preface to their article, in the magazine "Historical Topics", state that the past of Salamis remains essentially unknown and mysterious [3].

[2] The naval battle probably took place on September 28 or 29, 480 BC., which ended with the victory of the Greeks against the Persians. The importance of this victory was great and decisive, because it created the foundations of Western civilization [4]. Nikos Kazantzakis, had said, that this victory "led humanity from chaos to the Parthenon… The highest achievement of human struggle", and it is no exaggeration to say that it led to the Democracy and Freedom for later generations [4]. Many internationally recognized historians consider that the two most important battles for the salvation of Europe from the dangers from the east, were the naval battle of Salamis and the battle of Poitiers where Charles Martel in 732 AD. Defeated the Arabs [5]. In September 2020 had exactly passed 2,500 years since the world-famous naval battle.

[3] Hellenic Statistical Authority.

Table 1. SWOT Analysis of the cultural and touristic development of Salamis.

Strengths	Weaknesses
• Easy accessibility • Diverse natural environment • Archaeological, historical, architectural and cultural heritage • Local gastronomy • Various cultural events • Within walking distance: Municipal Library, Folklore and Archaeological Museum	• Unexploited archaeological sites • Lack of official and valid literature of the history of the island after the Naval Battle • Poor and disorderly reconstruction • Degradation of Salamis as a tourist destination • Introversion of the local society • Lack of uniform neighborhood character
Opportunities	**Threats**
• Business activity related to culture Finding sponsors • Strengthening voluntary work • Utilization of national and European development programs (for example PA[a]) • Attractive social media exposure • Ideal destination based on alternative tourism	• Economic crisis • Covid 19 • Unemployment • Inability to take cultural risk due to present economic conditions • Risk of degradation for the natural and marine environment • Indifference

[a] Partnership Agreement for the Development Framework.

enrichment of the tourist product, including various technological applications for computers, tablets and smartphones, online workshops and seminars, virtual tours as well as tours on thematic routes. As Paris Tsartas states, the travel destination experience for the millennials generation is more demanding and absolutely intertwined with new technologies [9].

2.3 Related Work: The Digital Past of Salamis

The digital identity of the island actually starts in 2020, with the preparations for the 2,500th anniversary since the historic Battle of Salamis, with actions as the following:

- The digital exhibition "ἱστορίης ἀπόδεξις"[4] dedicated to the Greco-Persian wars, was designed by the Department of Exhibitions of the Directorate of Archaeological Museums, Exhibitions and Educational Programs of the Ministry of Culture and Sports [10].
- The virtual museum "The trireme and the naval battle of Salamis", of the Eugenides Foundation [11].
- The digital exhibition: "Salamis 480 BC – Visual Resonance 2020", which was organized by the Hellenic Maritime Museum of Greece with twenty-two contemporary visual works related to the historical naval battle [12].
- The "Trip to Salamis" website is an organized digital tour of the island of Salamis, a project funded by the Regional Development Fund of Attica [13].

[4] Meaning "Historical Research", a phrase of the ancient Greek historian Herodotus (484BC-425BC), found in the preface to Book 1 (Kleio) of his work Historiai [14].

2.4 Creating a Digital Storytelling

In this paper, digital storytelling is achieved through geolocation, enabling users to interact live during a visit, recording their journey thanks to GPS technology and relating other digital media such as videos, images and texts with comments. This is a "Mobile/Locative storytelling", a type of digital storytelling based on the combination between the use of portable digital devices (tablets, smartphones) and applications (GPS, compass, accelerometer, data connection, camera) [15, 16].This type of storytelling essentially bridges geographic location with social media, permitting an online communication among the users of the digital collection, where the place itself, in this case the island of Salamis, is the center of reference and the common denominator of an online discussion. As a consequence, an enriched space is produced which merges the physical with the digital space[5].

2.5 Challenges

Designing the promotion of the cultural heritage of Salamis on a digital level, is an innovative product and aspires to:

- create relationships between the users of the platform, through an online link which will unite them in a digital community of "friends" of Salamis
- collect experiences and feedback from users and visitors to continuously improve the collection's digital experience
- allow the future visitor to experience a cultural destination, through a rich digital collection of cultural objects in order to understand the place and the people of Salamis
- improve the travel experience.

2.6 Target Market

The digital collection is addressed to students and researchers, tourists, the local authorities, the residents and businessmen of the island, the tourist agents and managers of cultural institutions.

3 Methodology

Data collection is the result of qualitative research. The content of the collection consists of photographs which outline the history and culture of the island. They have been collected from the personal archive of the researcher, the official websites of museums as well as other entities, for which a hyperlink and a bibliographic reference have been created. Decoding all this material also defined the thematic sections of the collection, so that users' browsing is clearer. The "Omeka.net" digital platform is a tool for displaying the digital collection on the internet. The choice of this specific platform was based on the following:

[5] As Hadi Saba Ayon states: "Geolocation associates territories and networks, the material and the immaterial, analog and digital". Using the internet, a whole new space is created, a space with a digital identity, a space with a mental representation of the physical space [17].

- easily accessible
- organizing collection objects according to the popular Dublin Core metadata standard
- the exchange of data via the Internet and applications for mobile phones that allows the sharing of photos or videos and interactive mapping using the plugin: "Geolocation"
- the ability to publish files and collections on mobile phones, tablets and computers/"desktops"
- supporting all file types of images, videos, audio and texts
- the creation of interactive digital exhibitions, where the narrative text is combined with digital media in order to give a rich interpretation of the proposed collections (plugins: "ExhibitBuilder", "Geolocation", "Contribution", "Html5Media"). Figure 1 shows the use of "ExhibitBuilder" plugin.
- the flexible design of a digital environment, modifying the navigation and homepage of the website, choosing and configuring a theme, depending on the subscription plan

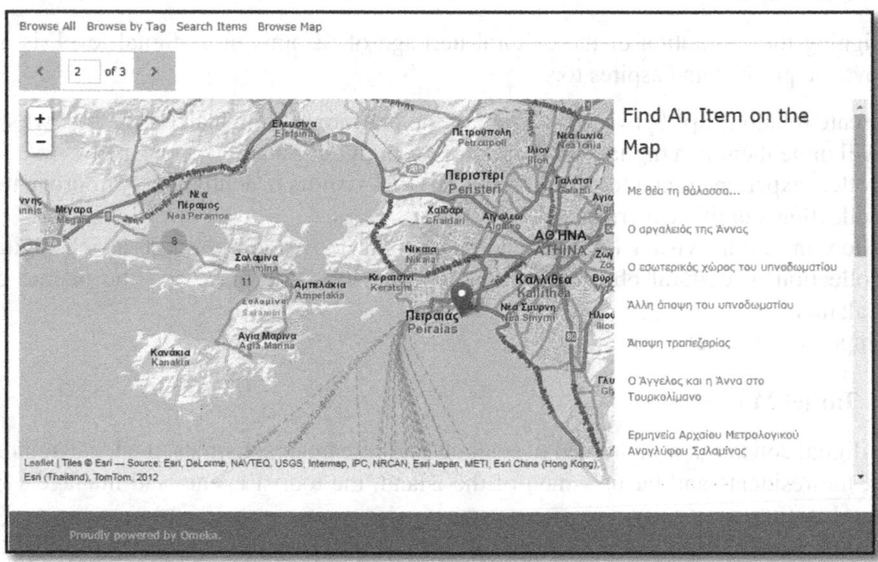

Fig. 1. The map of Salamis with the geographical identification of the items, with the use of the "ExhibitBuilder" plugin.

For the needs of the research, the "Silver Plan", which is a subscription plan, was chosen mainly to cover the file capacity of the digital items.

4 Presentation of the Repository

A website was developed with the link <salamina.omeka.net>, gathering in a digital repository fifty (50) items of the cultural heritage of Salamis. The items are structured into eight (8) thematic collections and five (5) thematic exhibitions, which create an attractive presentation framework (Fig. 2). The description of the items is bilingual

(Greek/English), with easy-to-use navigation and dynamic content, making use of the available audio-visual possibilities. The logo design was inspired by the olive tree of Orsa[6], which dates back to the Battle of Salamis, connecting the past with the present (Fig. 3). In the Dashboard, the overall structure of the repository is displayed, with the addition of the items, collections, exhibits, tags and plugins (Fig. 4).

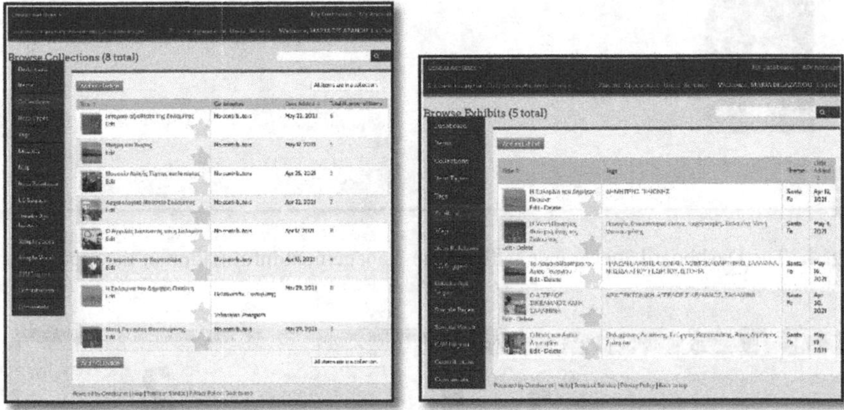

Fig. 2. The structure of the repository's thematic Collections and Exhibits

Fig. 3. The website's logo design

The Omeka.net digital platform enables the prospective user to navigate in three ways (Fig. 5):

1. Selecting the index "tags", which separate the database according to the subject of the "items" (Browse items by Tag)
2. Locating the collection items on the map (Browse items on the Map)
3. Searching with keywords that describe the objects in the collection (Search)

[6] Orsa's Olive Tree is the only living organism from the naval battle of Salamis and was planted by the Greek tyrant Peisistratus [18].

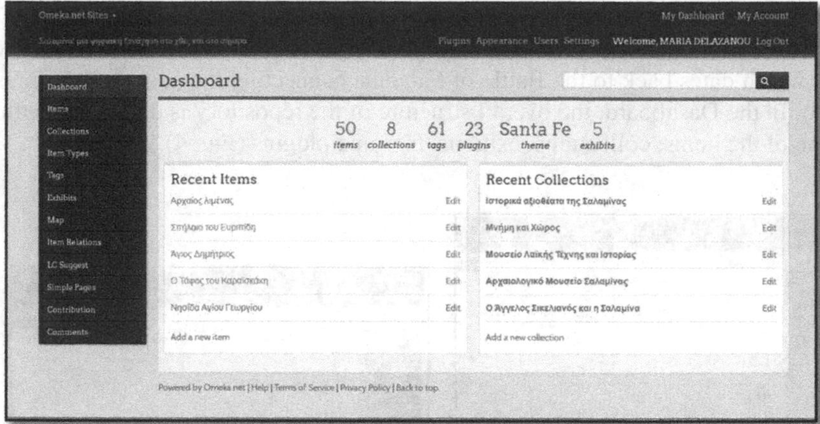

Fig. 4. The Dashboard appearance with all the management information of the repository

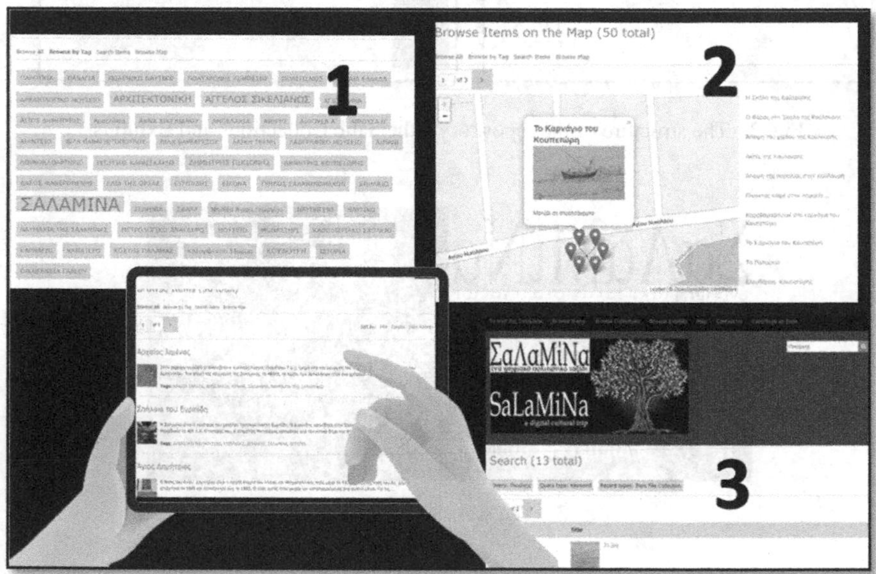

Fig. 5. Navigation options

4.1 Website's Structure in Collections and Exhibitions

Twenty (20) of the fifty-five (55) proposed Dublin Core metadata fields are used in the Omeka.net platform and twelve (12) plugins. For the purpose of indexing, fifty-one (51) keywords or tags have been used, in order to classify the objects into thematic sections such as: location, history, important personalities, religion, architecture, folk art. Table 2 shows the structure of the website. Fifty (50) items have been registered which are grouped into eight (8) thematic collections and five (5) thematic exhibits.

Each collection comprises different items. Each exhibit consists an introduction (initial) page and subsequent web pages, which are composed of related items.

Table 2. Subdomain: salamina.omeka.net

Salamina: a digital tour to past and present		
(8) Collections	Monastery of Panagia Faneromeni	**3**
	Salamis by Dimitris Pikionis	**11**
	Koupetori' s Shipyard	**4**
	Aggelos Sikelianos and Salamis	**11**
	Archaeological Museum of Salamis	**7**
	Museum of Folk Art and History	**3**
	Memory and Space	**5**
	Historical Sights of Salamis	**6**
	Total (50) items	
(5) Exhibits	Exhibits	
	Initial Page	Subsequent Pages
	Salamis by Dimitris Pikionis	Dimitris Pikionis The beach of Koulouri Koupetori's Shipyard ("Carnagio") Palukia Mountain landscapes of Koulouri
	The Monastery of Panagia Faneromeni of Salamis	The frescoes of the Faneromeni Monastery The landscape at Faneromeni Monastery
	The Lasarett of Agios Georgios	The ruins of the islet of Agios Georgios The church of Agios Georgios
	Aggelos Sikelianos and Salamis	The life and work of Aggelos Sikelianos The house of Angelos Sikelianos in Salamis Aggelos Sikelianos memorial site
	The Church of Agios Dimitrios	Georgios Karaiskakis Polychronis Lembesis (1848–1913)

4.2 Limitations of the Research

- The conditions of movement restriction, the suspension of the operation of museums and libraries in order to prevent the spread of the SARS - COVID-2 coronavirus, made the course of the research difficult.
- The introversion of the local society did not cultivate the appropriate conditions for the dissemination and cultivation of information concerning each item.
- The maintenance, management and operation of the repository requires constant financial support, as it is necessary to be supported by specialized technical staff skillful in software processing and web design for the enrichment of the collections and the successful sharing of the documents in social networks.

5 Conclusions

The challenge of this research project was to create a virtual place through digital tools in order to give voice to the known and unknown aspects of the cultural heritage of Salamis. The newly created site is focused on the cultural heritage of Salamis, aiming at retrieving from "oblivion" the Historical and Architectural wealth of the island, which unfortunately remains unexploited till now, as well as, at sparking the imagination of the digital tourists, so that they may get acquainted with the known sides of Salamis and, eventually, pave the way for the economic development and sustainability of the area. It presents evidence from ancient and modern history, architecture, religion and important personalities related to the place. In addition, it has a personal style and gives users the opportunity to participate in a different travel experience. Since there is nothing equivalent that provides a systematic record of the culture of Salamis and at the same time enables the interaction of online users, the repository "Salamina: a digital tour to past and present" is an innovative project. The recommended site acts as a tool aimed at preserving cultural heritage and history, as well as for the protection of historic buildings that tend to disappear. Future plans include the integration of the overall architectural landscape of Salamis with an emphasis on the neoclassical buildings through the period 1830–1950.

Acknowledgements. This paper was funded by the Special Account for Research Grants (ELKE) of the University of West Attica, in Greece. Special thanks to Zoe Georgiadou (Department of Interior Architecture, University of West Attica) who is the mentor and supervising professor of the author's Doctoral Thesis with the title: "The Architectural Heritage of Salamis with an emphasis on its neoclassical buildings (time period 1830–1950). Acknowledgements are also attributed to Konstantinos Kyprianos (Department of Archival, Library and Information Studies, University of West Attica), for his value contribution to creating media-rich online exhibits through the Omeka platform. Last but not least, thanks are given to Panagiotis Veltanissian (folklorist) for his continuous help and the excellent collaboration.

References

1. Ferla, K., Lampada, D., Tzedopoulos, G., Kamara, A.: Digital content, communication and cultural heritage: towards a global concept of the cultural reserve in the digital age. In: 2nd Greek Conference for Digitization of Cultural Heritage Proceedings- EuroMed 2017, pp. 355–361. Perrevia net, Volos (2017)
2. Chios, Th.: No photos please! Digitizing cultural heritage: the public sector under persecution? In: 1st Greek Conference for Digitization of Cultural Heritage Proceedings- EuroMed 2015, pp. 399–404. Palmos, Volos (2015)
3. Koutelakis, H., Foskolou, A.: Salamis: the unknown history of an island. Hist. Issues (35) (2004). https://salamina.gr/0/files/documents/salamina1645.pdf. Accessed 11 Dec 2022
4. Mitsakis, A.: The Naval Battle of Salamis. Naval Inspect. **176**(596), 24–41 (2016)
5. Kechagias, P.: Anniversary tribute of 2.500 years: the naval battle of salamis according to Aeschylus – Herodotus (2020). https://www.horc.gr/Images/Public/H_NAYMAXIA_THS_SALAMINAS.pdf. Accessed 11 Dec 2022
6. Salamina Municipality: Presentation of the Municipality. https://www.salamina.gr/en/presentation-of-the-municipality/. Accessed 25 Nov 2022
7. ELSTAT (Hellenic Statistical Authority): Census Results of Population and Residences- ELSTAT 2021, https://elstat-outsourcers.statistics.gr/Census2022_GR.pdf. Accessed 01 Dec 2022
8. Tsatsarounos, A.: Destination Management, Experience Tourism and Culture (2021). https://money-tourism.gr/diacheirisi-proorismon-toyrismos-empeirias-politismos-toyrismos/. Accessed 09 Dec 2022
9. Tsartas, P.: Questioning the role of tourism in the economy (2020). https://www.kathimerini.gr/economy/561169273/i-amfisvitisi-toy-roloy-toy-toyrismoy-stin-oikonomia/. Accesed 09 Dec 2022
10. Hellenic Republic- Ministry of Culture and Sports. https://digitalculture.gov.gr/2021/01/%E1%BC%B1storiis-%E1%BC%80podexis-i-diadiktiaki-ekthesi-gia-tous-ellinopersikous-polemous/. Accessed 11 Dec 2022
11. Eugenides Foundation, https://www.eef.edu.gr/el/to-idryma/eyropaika-programmata/nays/i-triiris-kai-i-naymahia-tis-salaminas/. Accessed 11 Dec 2022
12. Hellenic Maritime Museum. https://www.hmmuseum.gr/. Accessed 11 Dec 2022
13. ArcGIS StoryMaps. https://storymaps.arcgis.com/stories/96edb3819ed34e21bd7a37161085cc6b. Accessed 11 Dec 2022
14. Stefos, A., Stergioulis, E., Charitidou, G.: History of Ancient Greek Writing (A, B, C Grade of High School). Diofantos Institute of Computer Technology and Publications, Patra (2012)
15. Gibbons, A.: The mobile story: narrative practices with locative media (edited by James Farman). Gramma: J. Theory Criticism **23**, 167–168 (2016). https://ejournals.lib.auth.gr/gramma/article/view/5411/5305. Accessed 11 Feb 2023
16. Jones, A., Gyori, B., Hargood, C., Charles, F., Green, D.: Shelley's heart: experiences in designing a multi-reader locative narrative. In: NHT 2018, Baltimore (USA) (2018). https://core.ac.uk/download/pdf/157768448.pdf. Accessed 11 Feb 2023
17. Saba Ayon, H.: The relationship with space in the digital era: a reinvention of the identity and the environment. Interact **6**(1), 1–13 (2016). https://www.researchgate.net/publication/331568151_The_relationship_with_space_in_the_digital_era_a_reinvention_of_the_identity_and_the_environment. Accessed 11 Feb 2023
18. Boutsi, M.: The "Orsa's Olive Tree" 2530 years old. https://www.salamina.gr/en/presentation-of-the-municipality/. Accessed 01 Dec 2022

Planning to Live Longer: A Model for the Maintenance-Focused Heritage Building Conservation

Arturo Cruz[1(✉)], Vaughan Coffey[2], and Tommy H. T. Chan[2]

[1] Allister Property Detailing P/L, Caboolture, QLD 4510, Australia
art.cruz@hdr.qut.edu.au

[2] Queensland University of Technology, Brisbane, QLD 4000, Australia

Abstract. Maintenance neglect can cause major problems to heritage structures, to the point where a building is deemed uninhabitable. This poses a grave threat to heritage buildings, even more so than age, since abandoning the occupancy actually speeds up the building's deterioration. In the case of recently restored, or reconstructed, heritage buildings, a lengthening of their life cannot be guaranteed if post-restoration monitoring and continued maintenance are not implemented. Maintenance-focused conservation management planning and implementation are the key processes to increase or preserve the longevity of any building, and this is especially the case for heritage structures. Several charters dedicated to heritage conservation around the globe advocate taking necessary actions to keep these heritage buildings useable; however, changes should be kept to a minimum so that the cultural essence and significance is maintained. The model established by this research for use in ongoing and future heritage building conservation systems specifically focus on maintenance, and are designed to sustain the continued preservation and existence of Australian architectural legacies for the enjoyment and education of the current and future generations. This research examines in depth the requirements and constraints of managing and maintaining a heritage building. It also investigates the importance of monitoring the condition of buildings on a regular basis, and in a comprehensive manner, as mandated by the Burra Charter. Previously, and currently, this is often neglected as an integral part of conservation management planning.

Keywords: Heritage buildings · conservation management plan · building restoration · modern heritage buildings

1 Introduction

With the growing interest in, and awareness of, the importance of heritage buildings, there is an increasing demand to search for more innovative ways to retain the heritage fabric of such structures that involve minimal intervention, while maintaining structural integrity. Since this social pressure exists to keep heritage buildings from becoming derelict and being demolished, it is a critical juncture to develop an effective conservation

A. Moropoulou et al. (Eds.): TMM_CH 2023, CCIS 1889, pp. 276–286, 2023.
https://doi.org/10.1007/978-3-031-42300-0_24

strategy to retain such crucial buildings. Over the years, the extant literature reveals that maintenance operations have been fairly insignificant in the traditional Conservation Management Plan (CMP) approaches as promoted in the Burra Charter. This appears to be due to the traditional CMP usually being a history-laden document that often does not contain any distinguishable specific Action Plan. Often, the Action Plan (even if included within the CMP), offers conservation options based on undertaking major repairs, restoration and reconstruction. At least in the Australia context, this view was supported from both the conducted in interviews and focus group discussion [1].

For a substantial period, proper maintenance and monitoring have been known factors affecting service life and longevity for elderly buildings, especially for heritage structures. Maintenance neglect often causes major issues that increase the rate at which a building reaches the point where it is deemed uninhabitable. This is more serious than the mere natural aging of the building, since abandonment of occupancy speeds up a building's deterioration. With recently restored heritage structures, applied post-monitoring and maintenance processes help to ensure a longer and more sustained service life. Moreover, the survival of any building is importantly underpinned by regular maintenance [2, 3]. Many examples of existing heritage policies and guidelines for heritage conservation do not actually emphasize the critical importance of a maintenance component, which, most often takes the backseat of many conservation plans. In Brisbane, the Myer Centre features extensive façadism of several 19th century buildings. There are also numerous post-2000 CBD apartment/office blocks in Australian cities where a small portion of the façade of the original building has been retained and preserved, while the main structure has been largely demolished to make way for a new high-rise block. Another great example of façadism was the restoration of the State Capitol in California have failed to retain the authentic fabric of the architectural legacies of buildings under restoration because maintenance has been overlooked [4–6]. Often, conservation is only called for when the damage is already existing in the fabric of buildings being repaired and often previous major repairs are patently apparent; further, restoration, or reconstruction, efforts have sometimes resulted in loss of authenticity, and economic unsustainability among other social and environmental impacts [7–10].

In Australia, there are many discrepancies in the rapidly evolving local building codes and standards, and these are often at variance with the current policies and guidelines for heritage protection (see Fig. 1). In addition, there is the durability issue of modern heritage materials; these collectively and inevitably pose potential challenges for both conservation practitioners and stakeholders. The mismatch between the strict requirements of the current building regulations, the delicateness of building materiality and the rigidity of conservation policies are often causing building operators, engineers and realtors to shy away from involvement in heritage buildings [11]. In a climate of professional accountability, and responsibility for negative outcomes from heritage building repair work, many designers and building operators are not keen to risk their licenses because of risk and uncertainty [12].

While the most current update of the National Construction Code (NCC) establishes constraints regarding health, safety and sustainability, the Burra Charter promotes 'minimal intervention' as the prime consideration for any heritage buildings [13, 14]. Normandin and Macdonald [11] posit that the current building code requirements and

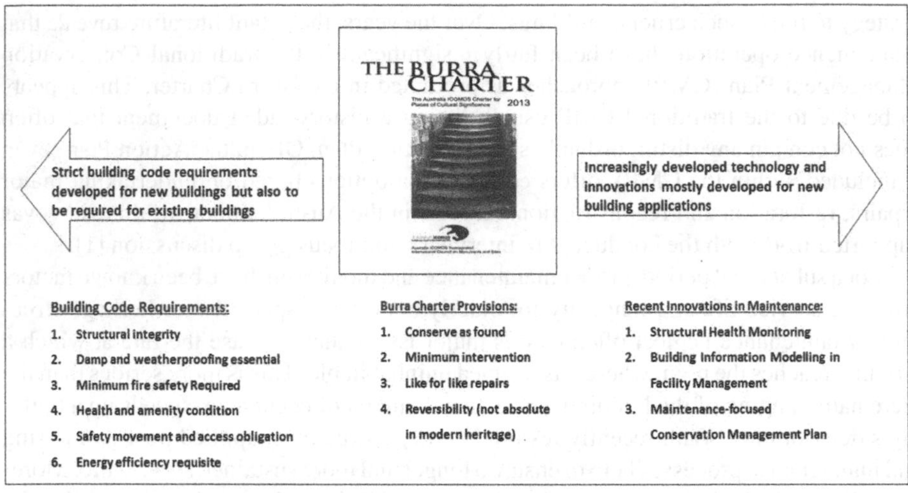

Fig. 1. Statutory constraints in conservation [13, 14]

the terms in the heritage building conservation charter are very demanding and often incompatible such as the NCC and the Burra Charter related to some of their provisions.

Further, despite the fact that current technologies are now so advanced in terms of their design, at the same time building construction is not flexible enough in relation to repairs and maintenance to cater for the compliance needs of heritage buildings as mentioned earlier. Whilst new digital and graphic design tools such as Building Information Modeling (BIM), Structural Health Monitoring (SHM), Building Codes and Standards are rapidly evolving, they are more often dedicated to use on newer structures rather than on heritage buildings [15]. Their application to heritage buildings is often cumbersome and, so far, mostly only experimental. It is often more convenient to use traditional methods for heritage and traditional buildings which only a relatively small number of professionals and contractors are accustomed to, or experienced with, and they are decreasing in numbers [16].

In Australia, heritage buildings are often outside the scope of most of the current Building Codes of Australia and the Australian/New Zealand Standards [5, 17]. For example, in the case of the Brisbane City Hall restoration completed in 2013, the compressive strength of the structural concrete was already far below the limits indicated by the standards in the pertinent Building Code for concrete structures at that time [18]. The engineers and architects who were engaged to undertake the design and supervision of the repair and restoration works were obligated by their professional ethical standards to bring the building up to the minimum safety requirements of the current Building Code. They thus had to evolve different operational methods beyond the traditional code of practice of that time. The engineers and architects of the Brisbane City Hall project needed to employ an independent consultant who was conversant with both innovative and traditional methods of repair and restoration, and the calculations and operational methodologies also needed to be checked and verified by an independent Structural Engineer and a specialist in the relevant faculty of the University of Queensland [6].

Along with satisfying the structural requirements of the NCC, there were several other prerequisites to fulfil in order for the Brisbane City Hall to be brought back to a usable condition. These included essential damp and weatherproofing, minimum fire safety, health and amenity conditions, safety movement and access obligations, and energy efficiency requisites [18–22]. These individual standards compliance requirements were far more challenging to address because of the restrictions imposed by other policies and guidelines, together with the Burra Charter requirements in Australia.

As time has moved-on, more innovative and compatible repairs are being evolved, and there has also been some relaxation of standards, improvements to policies and guidelines that are all more applicable to heritage buildings. While operators and stakeholders involved in modern heritage development and maintenance projects await new policies and guidelines to be developed, it becomes clear that an appropriate and effective model for maintenance-focused Conservation Management Plans (CMPs) and monitoring needs developing to fill this vacuum. Such a model would greatly help to ease the current burden to all stakeholders of conserving modern heritage buildings. Maintenance-focused conservation at this juncture would allow more buildings to be retained and preserved, whilst retaining most of the original features and fabric of such buildings.

2 Maintenance Versus Repair and Restoration

There is a general lack of maintenance because it is time-consuming, costly, and involves constant and frequent physical inspection. It was perceived to be an expensive option because it involves a large amount of labour and requires many man-hours to achieve successful outcomes. However, this notion could be reversed by understanding that it is cheaper to maintain a heritage building than waiting for the failures to happen and then taking action. Unfortunately, in today's construction industry climate, maintenance is less preferred than repair and restoration and is certainly less interesting to owners than sensitive forensic reconstruction.

The choice of solely using an approach-based on restoration or reconstruction, and executing major repairs when damage already exists, has consequentially resulted in loss of authenticity and economic unsustainability, among other social and environmental impacts. Many modern heritage repair projects have experienced abject failure in retaining the authentic fabric of these architectural legacies, and maintenance remains neglected and overlooked.

While this trend results in a worrying condition of eventual heritage loss, it also presents a justification to create a comprehensive maintenance-focused model that is integrated with normal cyclical conservation and has a monitoring component. Thus, maintenance was purposely placed as the central focus of this model to emphasise its importance as a priority element of conservation.

2.1 Introducing the Maintenance-Focused Conservation Framework

The model shown in Fig. 2 presents a detailed description of the component parts and its relationship to the major elements. It describes how the model can work and examines the potential benefits it can contribute. The parameters represented by oval shapes are the essential components in conservation, while the words linked by the arrows are the drivers that will enable the model for maintenance-focused conservation to function.

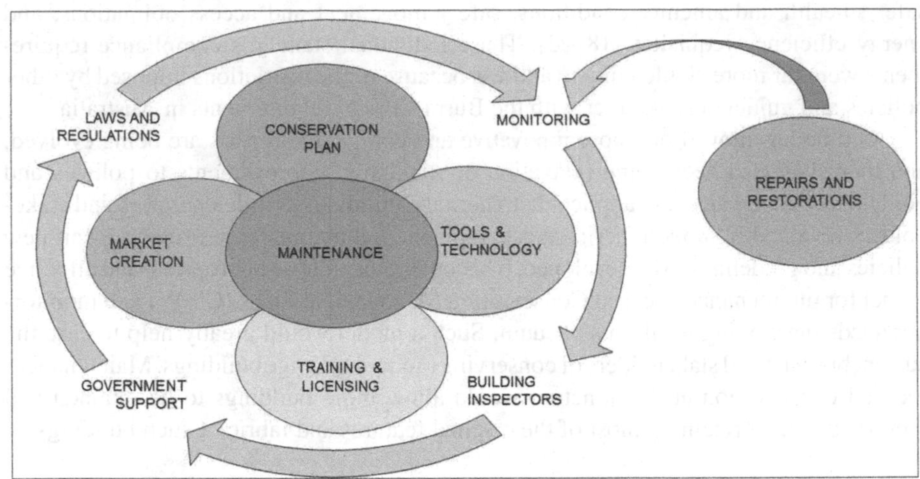

Fig. 2. Maintenance-focused heritage building conservation model

The maintenance-focused conservation drivers and parameters are: (a) Monitoring, using the advantages of the current available tools and technology; (b) Building Inspectors, produced through Training as well as Licensing to adapt with the current requirements of heritage buildings; (c) Government Support – in order to kick-start the Creation of Market for the Maintenance-focused approach in heritage conservation' and (d) Laws and Regulations – in the forms of building codes, standards and heritage charters to address the preparation of a conservation management plan prioritising maintenance other than repairs and restoration.

It is important to note that the terminology about repair and maintenance has evolved over the years; "conservative repair" borne out of the SPAB manifesto of 1877 now refers to as "maintenance". In Australia, the definition of 'maintenance' has also evolved and has been adapted for application to heritage buildings. Standards Australia [23] defines maintenance as '… continuous protective care of the fabric and setting of a place'. ICOMOS Australia [13], through the *Burra Charter*, adopted this definition and further suggested that maintenance should be a priority for heritage buildings and must be properly distinguished from repair. Repair often involves restoration or reconstruction. The distinctions can be further explained, for example, in relation to roof gutters: maintenance is the 'regular inspection and cleaning of gutters', while repair involves restoration ('returning of dislodged gutters') or may involve reconstruction ('replacing decayed gutters') [7].

There is a difference between repairs and restoration approach, and a maintenance approach. Repairs and restoration comprise the processes undertaken when failure occurs, while maintenance is what is undertaken for the failure not to occur. So, if maintenance is properly taken care of, then the repairs and restoration will not be such a relevant section in the conservation management plan, and will be diminished significantly (Fig. 3).

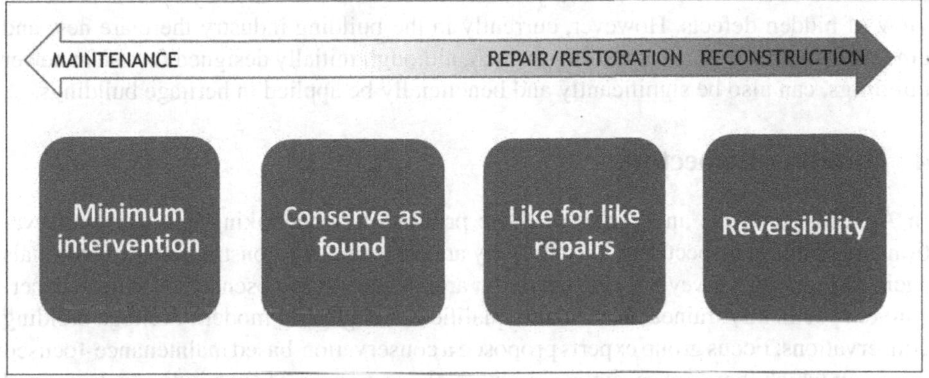

Fig. 3. Maintenance, repair/restoration and reconstruction vs. maxims of conservation

This is a model that promotes minimum intervention – doing as much as possible and as little as necessary: conserve as you find a building – this means no alterations to the size, dimensions and form of the building; like-for-like repairs – whatever is repaired can only be replaced with the same materials; reversibility –any intervention should be carried out in a way that will allow removal of repaired elements and substitute if ever a new and better solution comes along (Fig. 4). Conversely, the best form of conservation is based on a maintenance approach.

The degree of conservation can vary from a proactive conservative maintenance approach to a more reactive repair and restoration including reconstruction. As this degree is adjusted, the needs to conform with the maxims of conservation still stand, such as, minimum intervention, conserve as found, like for like repairs, and reversibility. Conservation that is opting for a repair and restoration approach finds it hard to conform with all the maxims of conservation, especially reversibility.

Each aspect of the maintenance-focused conservation model shown in Fig. 2 discussed below expounding on each significance as a part of the model.

3 Monitoring

Conservation efforts were usually deemed useless without subsequent follow-through, and stringent and rigorous, monitoring. In a restored building, it is critical to undertake post-construction/post-repair forensic examination and complete careful monitoring to ensure the efficacy of the fabric and structure and especially of any works already undertaken.

Amongst other assurances of work adequacy, it is absolutely critical to find out if the works and processes applied have eradicated the concrete cancer (such as in the case of the Brisbane City Hall restoration), or if there are any side effects of the works. Along with the maintenance-focused conservation system, there needs to be a more vigilant monitoring effort to anticipate issues before these become a trigger for another major repair project.

In building inspections, which are the heart of building monitoring, often the results are limited due to the poor visibility of any damage to the naked eye prevents a clear view of hidden defects. However, currently in the building industry there are new and emerging innovations in monitoring, which, although initially designed for use in newer buildings, can also be significantly and beneficially be applied in heritage buildings.

4 Building Inspectors

In Australia, there is an overlap of those professions undertaking heritage conservation and building inspections. Usually, they are performed by construction professionals such as building surveyors, engineers, or architects in the absence of dedicated personnel specifically trained, skilled and qualified to engage in modern heritage building conservations. Focus group experts proposed a conservation-based maintenance-focused model in which there are specialised individuals, or a group of such individuals, trained in conservation-based heritage building inspection, maintenance and monitoring.

4.1 Training and Licensing

The literature review indicated that there are many experts in conservation philosophy, theory and approaches to conservation, but these are not also experts in actual repair and maintenance work. Similarly, there are people who are experts in repairs and maintenance and are highly experienced in the nature of materiality and types of construction of modern heritage buildings, but are not experts in the principles of conservation [12]. Hence, data from interviews and focus group discussion revealed that training and licensing schemes are required for both sets of 'experts', but these will require extensive support from owners, professional institutes, tertiary education sources and from the government to kick-start such learning and certification.

Data reveals that regular inspections and maintenance have been shown to play a key role in prolonging the life of any structures, whether new, old or heritage. Most often, these important practical aspects were neglected, causing more damage to important buildings and structures than had ever been anticipated. The main reasons for this, aside from operators being somewhat complacent after the constructions or the repairs, were that often there were no dedicated personnel, nor instruments to monitor the post-construction or after-repair situation of these buildings. The added expenses for that contingency – namely, regular inspections and maintenance – were, most of the time, overlooked and ignored.

5 Government Support

There is a lack of a sustainable market in maintenance works and operations. This is due to the fact that currently there is a strong culture of dispose and replace in the building industry when major repairs, restorations and reconstructions are done, rather than any maintenance-type of conservation. Currently, there are two kinds of maintenance operations existing in Australia. The first one is operated by employing a traditional in-house facilities manager (or FM team).

While this setup is beneficial, especially in establishing a thorough familiarisation and specialisation in a particular heritage building, this is not as economically effective, since there is a wide range of heritage buildings across Australia. Most of their owners cannot afford to hire a dedicated facility manager for each and every building. However, to manage the maintenance and building operations on a high-profile modern heritage building, such as the Sydney Opera House, requires an experienced facilities manager and an extensive trained team of operational staff. There are many other heritage buildings of a lower profile registered within the local council, where budgets are much lower than for prestige buildings such as the Opera House, that do not employ facility managers to oversee maintenance and monitoring.

5.1 Market Creation

Market creation for maintenance-focused conservation system can be kicked-start in forms of government initiatives and incentives. There are two types of incentives: either the owner will not pay, or the owners get paid. The government could provide a new system to assist heritage preservation efforts at a much lower cost than through providing substantial repair grants. Such new systems from the government could operate on a similar basis to the Medicare structure currently used by medical practitioners where there is a pool of money and resources that can be allocated to patients in need of medical services.

Since modern heritage – in fact, all heritage – buildings are listed on either local, state, federal or national registers, and are assets of the listing body, it is these bodies that should pay the heritage operators for engaging the services of accredited building maintenance operators, if the owners make an order for a maintenance check-up. The listing body will pay for the maintenance check-up, equivalent to cyclical maintenance inspection, and for the heritage 'doctors' (experts) or inspectors.

6 Laws and Regulations

In Australia, a Conservation Management Plan (CMP) need to be submitted before any assessable developments are allowed to take place – whether the repairs proposed are embedded in reconstruction, restoration, adaptive re-use, conversion, refurbishment or any other type of projects or contracts [24–26]. But what about maintenance-only conservation? In practice, as this approach does not produce an assessable development, it does not require any form of formal CMP. Thus, the need for any formal maintenance plan relies solely on the decision of the owner, or the custodian, of the building, and more often than not, such a plan does not exist.

It is also suggested that a detailed Action Plan is incorporated into CMPs. The preparation of a robust and well-informed CMP should have the embedded proposals for implementation based on the research findings regarding the proper methodologies for the conservation of heritage buildings particular to Australia, since this is where the focus of this research is based. It must importantly be noted that the CMP detailed in this research would also be required to accord with the policy and guidelines outlined in the *Burra Charter* (2013) as the main statutory government document that guides the policies and principles of conservation.

7 Conclusions

Like any piece of equipment, a building should be maintained in a reasonable condition if it is to continue its function. Old buildings, particularly heritage buildings, should be protected through the application of preventative maintenance and monitoring rather than executing major repairs, restoration even reconstruction. That is because maintenance and monitoring can preserve better the authenticity of the building plus it is environmentally sustainable and more economical in the long run than the popular major repairs, restoration and reconstruction. However, because of the rarity of skill people, absence of some basic tools and lacking government support, it is very seldom that a building will properly be maintained and monitored.

The model presented on Fig. 2, representing maintenance-focused conservation management systems, is intended to provide new knowledge that can contribute to the debate regarding the ongoing and future conservation of modern heritage buildings. In Australia, most heritage buildings were built during the early 20th century, in the Modernist Period. The country also has some post-modern buildings, such as the Sydney Opera House. Likewise, while there are many examples of neo-classical modern heritage buildings made of synthetic materials, such as the Brisbane City Hall, there are also many modern heritage examples of buildings, such as the Royal Exhibition Building in Melbourne, as well as the many convict goals all over Australia, that are also part of the modern period; however, these latter buildings were made of more natural materials such as masonry, bricks and timber. The commonality among these modern and post-modern buildings is the minimalist approach used; that is, minimum materials for maximum heights, spans, and/or maximum savings, or profits, for the builder.

The advantage of model presented in Fig. 2 is that it espouses a highly appropriate approach for the most vulnerable modern heritage and post-modern heritage buildings that are all made of synthetic materials, and it is completely applicable to modern heritage examples that are not made of natural materials. The model can even be applicable and consistent to the conservation of ancient heritage structures and buildings that were made entirely of natural materials, such as stone and bricks, and where the scale of construction was massive compared with the minimalist approach of modern buildings.

What this model is trying to achieve is to encourage conservationists and other involved stakeholders to be more vigilant in maintenance and monitoring when undertaking work on modern heritage buildings. Currently, there is an obvious neglect for the maintenance-based approach, which could be because there is no new knowledge in the current literature, or there is simply an intentional neglect in maintaining heritage buildings in order to concentrate on more exciting and profitable forms of conservation, such as repair, restoration, or even replacement. Adoption of these latter approaches means that owners can enjoy new brand-new buildings, or additions, and the operators can have the opportunity to put their signature on this new or refurbished work.

8 Recommendations

The model in Fig. 2 recognises that there are so many parameters and variables prevalent in most heritage projects, and associated with current heritage buildings, that remain outside of current policy and guidelines, including the current version of the *Burra Charter*. It is recommended that these need to be considered and brought back into the focus of consideration as a missing part of the guidelines, plans and documentation currently controlling heritage works, and, once integrated, making them work. A flowchart diagram representation of the process suggested in this research is shown in Fig. 4.

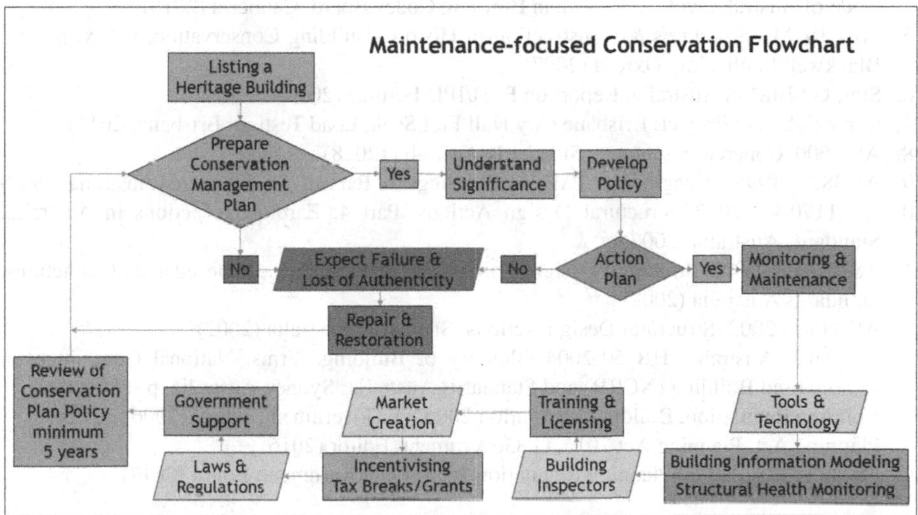

Fig. 4. Flowchart to introduced maintenance-focused conservation

References

1. Cruz, A.: Developing a model for maintenance-focused heritage building conservation (2020)
2. Armitage, L., Irons, J.: The values of built heritage. Prop. Manag. **31**(3), 246–259 (2013)
3. Forster, A.M., Kayan, B.: Maintenance for historic buildings: a current perspective. Struct. Surv. **27**(3), 210–229 (2009)
4. Worsley, J., et al.: Structural upgrading: managing construction on the California capitol. Assoc. Preserv. Technol. Bull. **20**(1), 17–26 (1988)
5. Cartwright, D., Belperio, R.: Saving Brisbane City hall. In: Australian Structural Engineering Conference, Perth Western, Australia (2012)
6. Cruz, A.: Re-strengthening Brisbane City Hall: A Case Study of Heritage Engineering (2013)
7. Wood, B.: Building Maintenance, vol. xii, p. 311. Wiley-Blackwell, Chichester (2009)
8. Levitt, J.: Facilities Management: Managing Maintenance for Buildings and Facilities, vol. xviii, p. 235. Momentum Press, New York (2013)
9. Chanter, B., Swallow, P.: Building Maintenance Management, 2nd edn., vol. xiv, p. 317. Blackwell, Oxford (2007)

10. Atkin, B., Brooks, A.: Total Facilities Management, 3rd edn., vol. xvii, p. 305 (2009)
11. Normandin, K., Macdonald, S.: A Colloquium to Advance the Practice of Conserving Modern Architecture (2013). http://www.getty.edu/conservation/our_projects/field_projects/cmai/cmai_colloquium.html. Accessed 26 Jan 2015
12. Custance-Baker, A., Macdonald, S.: Conserving Concrete Heritage - Experts Meeting (2014). http://www.getty.edu/conservation/our_projects/field_projects/cmai/pdf/Conserving_Concrete_Heritage_Experts_Meeting.pdf
13. ICOMOS Australia. The Burra Charter: The Australia ICOMOS Charter for Places of Cultural Significance (2013). http://australia.icomos.org/wp-content/uploads/The-Burra-Charter-2013-Adopted-31.10.2013.pdf. Accessed 27 Mar 2014
14. Australian Building Codes Board. NCC 2019: National Construction Code 2019. Building Code of Australia, vol. 3. Australian Building Codes Board, Canberra (2016)
15. Forsyth, M.: Structures & Construction in Historic Building Conservation, vol. x, p. 238. Blackwell Publishing, Oxford (2007)
16. Star, G.: BIM in Australia, Report on BIM/IPD Forums (2010)
17. Cartwright, D.: Project: Brisbane City Hall Full Scale Load Testing. Brisbane (2011)
18. AS 3600. Concrete Structures. Standards Australia (2018)
19. AS 3826 - 1998. Strengthening Existing Buildings for Earthquake. Standards Australia (1998)
20. AS 1170.4 - 2007. Structural Design Actions. Part 4: Earthquake actions in Australia. Standards Australia (2007)
21. AS 1170.1 - 2002. Structural Design Actions. Part 1: Permanent, imposed and other actions. Standards Australia (2002)
22. AS 1170 - 2002. Structural Design Actions. Standards Australia (2002)
23. Standards Australia. HB 50-2004 Glossary of Building Terms. National Committee on Rationalised Building (NCRB) and Standards Australia: Sydney Australia, p. 164 (2004)
24. Building Regulation. Building Regulation 2006, Q. Government, Editor (2006)
25. Planning Act. Planning Act 2016, Q. Government, Editor (2016)
26. Planning Regulation. Planning Regulation 2017, Q. Government, Editor (2017)

A Review of Heritage Building Information Modelling: Classification of HBIM through the Utilization of Different Dimensions (3D to 7D)

Efstratios Koutros(✉) and Christos-Nikolaos Anagnostopoulos

Intelligent Systems Lab., Department of Cultural Technology and Communication, University of Aegean, University Hill, 81100 Mytilene, Greece
cti22001@ct.aegean.gr, canag@aegean.gr

Abstract. The adoption of Building Information Modelling (BIM) as it is known today started in the early 2000s but it wasn't until the beginning of the previous decade the technology began to spread and appealed among historic buildings and monuments (Historic Building Information Modelling/HBIM). The first attempts were focused on the documentation of monuments through the utilization of libraries with architectural elements. The following years, most research efforts focused on generating HBIMs with accurate geometry that represents the reality, as identical as possible. Along with these efforts classifications of the HBIM geometry and information came up, to help the stakeholders comprehend the richness of the model. In recent years intentness have been given in creating HBIM that 7 can be used as integrated tools for the management of historic buildings. Depending on the type of information and the scope of the project, different dimensions grant an additional delineation of the HBIM. This particular review demonstrates the subject matters of HBIM case studies and research projects based on their dimension. To achieve this, it was necessary to classify every case study in the corresponding dimension. Through this classification, it was possible to correlate the different dimensions and therefore the corresponding thematic fields. Finally, the necessity of classifying a HBIM project according to its dimension is pointed out.

Keywords: Building Information Modeling · Cultural Heritage · Dimensions · Classification · Management · Review

1 Introduction

During the last decade the utilization of Building Information Modelling (BIM) technologies have become widespread among monuments and historical sites. Since its first introduction by Murphy et al. [1] in 2009 and the appliance of BIM as a modelling tool, Heritage or Historic Building Information Modelling (HBIM) is considered a collaborative methodology revolved around advanced technologies capable to associate the 3D geometry and the cultural context of a monument throughout its lifecycle [2]. In

A. Moropoulou et al. (Eds.): TMM_CH 2023, CCIS 1889, pp. 287–297, 2023.
https://doi.org/10.1007/978-3-031-42300-0_25

recent years the scientific community, dealing with the management of cultural heritage, focused on transforming HBIM to an integrated tool able to manage the multifactoriality of historical buildings.

An appropriate appliance is able to incorporate essential information for a historic building such as material and decay data, structural methods, environmental assets etc. Taking advantage of this, it is possible to carry out different studies and operations using the same informational system [3]. Furthermore, due to the interoperability of BIM platforms, stakeholders, engineers, responsible authorities, advisors and contractors are able to collaborate and communicate efficiently, overcoming complications and data lose arising from traditional design approaches.

1.1 HBIM Classification

Alongside with the spread of HBIM regarding managing cultural context, such as in the modern construction industry, the need for classifying a model depending on its geometry, details and information complexity came up. In the case of a modern building construction, a solid and linear procedure has been established, in order to enhance the Level of Geometry and Information (LoG & LoI) during the lifecycle of the settlement, from its design phase till its demolition. Every construction element is treated according to the Level of Development required for its planning, development and management [4]. However, because HBIM contains more complex entities, similar classifications came up to meet and complement the needs of the existing historical buildings. The previews concept of LoD and LoI are enriched with a more practical approach that enhances the process offering the benefit of classifying complex objects and data while giving, at the same time, traces about their modeling technique [5].

So far, Grade of Generation and Grade of Information (GoG & GoI) [6], in combination with the established, from the AEC, concepts, have offered a great deal in determining the requirements of a HBIM project both in matters of data collection and processing as much as in the effortless and direct transmission of the model's development. Stakeholders can be constantly aware of the amount and detail of information that are enveloped in the model. In this sense further studies can be focused in fulfilling deficiencies, additionally it is possible to utilize the model as a sustainability tool that can be used from cadets stakeholders at future time.

1.2 The Dimensions of HBIM

As far as the details, the amount and even the quality of information is concerned, standards have been set to serve the needs of HBIM projects and the requirements of unique specialized approaches. Similar efforts were carried out in order to apply the dimension classification for Historical BIM projects (see Fig. 1). In contrast to LoD and LoI, matching the dimension of a BIM for a modern contraction to the ones of a historical monument is not a direct process. For the most of these classes some differences arise imposing certain conversions [7]. Thus, the exact equivalence has not yet become clear, nonetheless, there is, for the time being, a common acceptance concerning dimension 3D to 7D.

The generation of a high detailed, in terms of architecture, model is common both in modern construction and existing buildings. The latest trends in documentation heritage buildings through BIM, although they are using high accuracy technologies to capture reality, focus on exploiting dense point clouds to achieve deep perception of the historical structure. Putting in use all this information the 3D of an HBIM is consisted of the meaningful geometrical elements in a conceptual way, sparing energy and time during the modeling process [8, 9].

The parameter of time in HBIM project, as it happens with modern constructions, is expressed with the fourth dimension (4D). Through this dimension the stratigraphy of the historical building can be captured, including phases that are not still preserved 'in situ' [10]. In this sense, historical analysts can interpret the construction process [11, 12] or events that affected the state of the monument, while engineers and constructors are able to scheduled restoration activities within this dimension.

The cost management for the construction of a modern building is concluded within 5D. For a new construction these costs respond to materials costs, land value, labor, construction machinery etc. Suchlike this dimension for heritage building corresponds to the cost of a restoration or a conversation operation and their parameters [13]. In such cases, intervention studies are conducted in a sustainable way preserving and promoting the cultural assets. Expanding the concept of cost around cultural heritage, 5D may include expenses for the dissemination of the cultural values of a historic building such as special lighting, occasional culture exhibitions or even operating costs (energy consumption, employees etc.).

The interaction of new buildings, with the physical aspects and the adjoining environment in general, is attributed through 6D. As it happens in modern facilities the environmental conditions affect directly a historical building [5]. Whether a building with a beneficial use or not is concerned, the state of preservation depends on natural mechanisms which, may cause critical damage to architectural parts and authentic material. If a historical building is still in use (original or alternative use), it is important for the stakeholders to incorporate within the HBIM all the physical aspects that affect the structure or the operation of the building [14, 15]. Nevertheless, just as the environment affects a historical building thus the second influences the first, it is essentially a relation based on interaction. In this sense, 6D correlates a historic building to the conditions that have been formed in the related area because of it. This becomes more understandable, when significant monuments are taken into consideration, due to which specific urban conditions and circular economies [16] have been established. These conditions may not necessarily correspond to the present, but perhaps they are referred to specific historical phases of the monument [17].

For the time being the correspondence of dimensions between BIM and Historical BIM reaches the seventh dimension (7D). Within this dimension, stakeholders enrich HBIM with all the necessary studies, information and data for the sustainable management of a historical building and its cultural values [18]. Such information may be conservancy status [19], decay, corrosion and decomposition data [20, 21], interoperability matters [22], activities for dissemination the cultural values [17, 23] and virtual reconstructions of collapsed monuments [24]. Moreover, having all this critical information attached to the same model, decision-making process is facilitated and managers reach optimal conclusions and solutions [25].

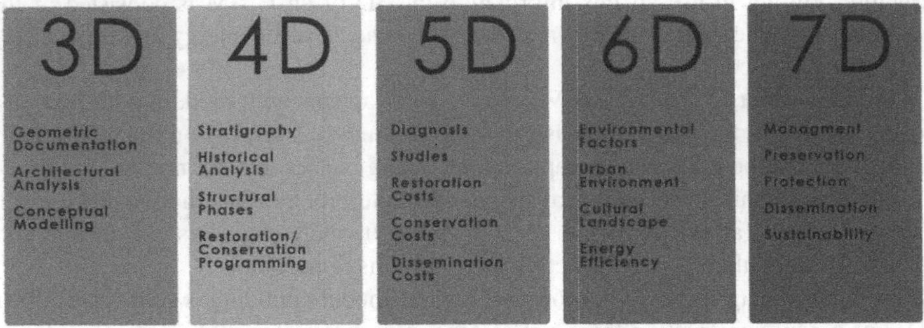

Fig. 1. Dimensions classification expressed with HBIM terminology.

1.3 Research Objectives

The purpose of this review is the gathering, the analyzing and the classification of a representative sample of HBIM studies related to historical buildings and cultural heritage management in general. The classifications concern the dimensions 3D to 7D of HBIMs, according to the information attached to them and the object of their subject.

This research was chosen to be conducted in order to fill in the gap detected within the scientific literature. Several analyses have been conducted concerning optimally workflows, open software, special classifications, efficiency of BIM among diagnostic and management issues, spread of HBIM over the years within other information systems, research of the latest trends around HBIM etc. [2, 6, 26–31]. Nonetheless, there are some missing points concerning the subject matter of HBIM projects over time and also the dimension classification of the projects which is not mentioned. This review aims to cover the bibliographical gaps, while at the same time, to confirm the importance of HBIM dimensions and their application to the efficient and sustainable management of cultural heritage.

2 Research Methodology

2.1 Data Collection and Coordination

In order for the review to be representative, seventy-tow (72) conference and scientific journal articles were selected, which they correspond to the research, projects and trends over the years and around the world. Every article or paper concerns a case study, either for a specific monument or for a set of historical buildings and a HBIM had been established for each of them. At first place, every case study was listed according on its publication date (year), the main author's name and affiliation details (country, university or agency). Also, for every one of them, a brief description was drafted for easy and rapid access to the key content. Furthermore, for convenience in analysis of the data a unique ID was assigned to each case study (see Fig. 2).

The second part of the data coordination, dealt with the correspondence of every HBIM dimension to each case study. According to the prevailing interpretation of the dimensions (as explained above), five categories were created (3D, 4D, 5D, 6D and 7D). For each case, the dimensions corresponded to the HBIM were marked. As a result, a list that connects every case study is created, to the dimensions it develops and all the necessary information, suited for the specific analysis as it presented in Fig. 2.

Case Study ID	Date (Year)	Country of origin	Institution/ Organization	Short Description	First Author	3D	4D	5D	6D	7D
1	2016	Spain	University of Sevilla	Η απόδοση στο HI	Juan E. Nieto	✓	✗	✓	✗	✗
2	2018	Poland	Military University of Technology in Warsaw	Ακριβήω μοντελοπ	Anna Fryskowska	✓	✗	✗	✗	✗
3	2018	Italy	University of L' Aquila	Αναπτύσει διαφορ	S. Brusaporci	✓	✗	✗	✗	✓
4	2018	Italy	Univerity of Salerno, Univerity of Napoli	Τεκμηρίωση της υ	Angela Bosco	✓	✗	✗	✗	✓
5	2020	Spain, Italy	University of Salamanca, University of Madrid, University of Torino	Αισθητήρες που τ	Rocio Mora	✓	✗	✗	✓	✓
6	2019	Spain, United Kingdom	University of Valencia, University of Huddersfield	HBIM πλατφόρμα	Isabel J. Palomar	✓	✓	✗	✗	✓
7	2020	Italy	University of Milano	Μέθοδος χαρακτη	Mattia Previtali	✓	✗	✗	✗	✓
8	2019	England	Trinity College in Dublin	Η πλατφόρμα του	Maurice Murphy	✓	✗	✗	✓	✓

Fig. 2. A part of listing and management of the necessary data from each case study.

2.2 Data Analysis

Prevalence of HBIM Dimensions. At first glance, it is obvious that most case studies concerning HBIMs have to do with the geometric documentation of the object and its overall management. As it is shown in Fig. 3 3D and 7D appear to be the most common dimensions.

As far as the 3D is concerned the geometrical documentation of the historical building is necessary, similarly to the case of setting up a HBIM. Furthermore, according to the data collected, it is noticed that during the first years of the past decade most of the research efforts focused on establishing a workflow for the modelling process utilizing laser scanner and photogrammetry documentation techniques. Contrariwise, in recent years, these research approaches have been minimized, as previous efforts paid off. In most of the case studies, Scan-to-BIM methods are applied, approaching the geometry of the object in a more conceptual way. In any case the deviation is checked depending on the projects' demands.

Almost in one out of three cases within the HBIM project the parameter of time, i.e. 4D, is included. The most frequently usage of 4D is related to the stratigraphy and the historical/structural phases of the monuments. There are also cases where the parameter of time participates in operations planning [32] or as information for the dissemination of the monuments' historical values [17]. However, despite the fact that the results were efficient, such applications were limited.

The dimension that was developed less among the case studies was 5D. One of the reasons related with this fact is that HBIM is not still a methodology applied widely for the execution progress. As a result, there is no need for estimating costs for the restoration tasks. Unless the stakeholders and managers put this new approach (HBIM) into practice there will be no change regarding this fact.

As in the previous case, 6D is a dimension that is not often included in the management process. In most case studies, 6D concerns the environmental parameters that have noticeable affects to a monument, while in fewer projects it is presented the relation between the monument and the urban environment [33]. However, the sustainability of cultural heritage is a major issue while the environmental factors are perhaps the most important aspect especially for recent monuments that are still in use [14]. In this sense, it is expected that 6D will be an integral part of the management process.

From the early ages that BIM technologies were applied within cultural heritage till the time being (December 2022), the main ambition was a methodology for the interoperable and integrated management of cultural heritage. In other words, 7D is a dimension appeared in most of the cases whether it concerns the preservation planning, the presentation of the cultural values or the management of a monument in general. During the past decade the research community examined the enrichment of a 7D HBIM with various parameters aiming to amplify the efficacy of cultural management not only within BIM platforms but other subprofessional applications due to the interoperability of BIM.

Dimensions Over Time. The utilization of HBIM dimensions depends on the usage of BIM techniques for heritage issues. Over time the use of such methods have increased impressively, especially during the last years. In general, it is marked that all dimensions (3D-7D) appear an increasing rate of appliance that is more intense during the last two years (2021 and 2022) (see Fig. 4). This incising rate is expected to continue, while the appliance of all dimensions will be balanced equally as HBIM systems are evolved to be an integrated management process.

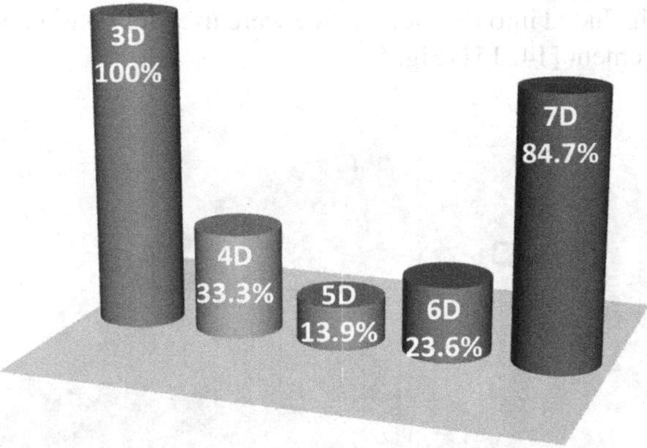

Fig. 3. Frequency of HBIM dimensions among the case studies (expressed in percentage).

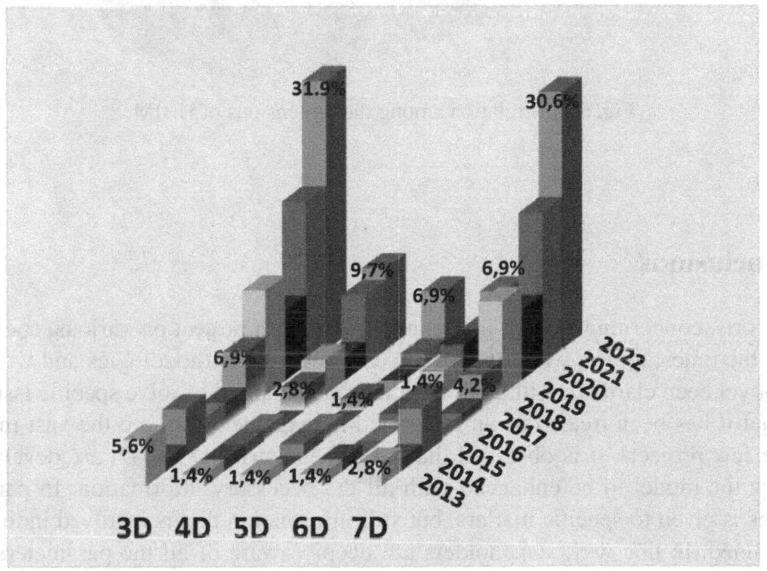

Fig. 4. Temporal evolution of the appliance of dimensions within HBIM projects.

Dimensions Correlation. The cases that all dimensions have been developed in a single project are few [34], but still embody the efficiency and benefits of using BIM techniques as an integrated tool for the management of a monument. High correlation is observed between 4D and 7D, since in many cases the historical and structural evolution of a monument is necessary and takes place before other management tasks. This way, the stakeholders are able to understand the monument and incorporate the appropriate parameters within the 7D. Another frequently occurring interconnection is the one between 6D and 7D. This is due to the fact that, in most cases, the environmental parameters were included into the model, they were used for conservation, preservation issues and management [14, 15] (Fig. 5).

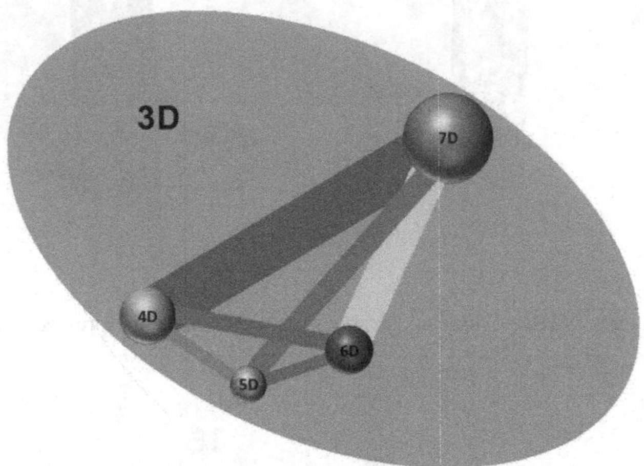

Fig. 5. Correlation among the dimensions of HBIM

3 Conclusions

Most efforts, concerning HBIM, are related to research project on various, specialized most of the times, topics, while in specific cases certain methodologies and workflows have not yet been clarified. Although BIM has been applied to solve specific issues, the cases that it has been treated as an integrated management tool are the vast minority. In these few projects, it is observed that all dimensions (3D to 7D) are developed in order for the model to be enhanced with all the necessary information. In particular, emphasis is given to specific matters, but still information that is involved indirectly is not sidelined. In this way, stakeholders are deeply aware of all the parameters of the monument, resulting in optimal decisions and more effective solutions.

The HBIM of a monument is not just about dealing with a specific situation or issue, instead it constitutes a depositor of information and data for the monument and if treated appropriate it can compose an integrated tool for the management of the monument. If the information and the geometry are being transformed accordingly to the changes that happen to the monument in reality, the HBIM can be turned into a digital twin. In this sense, the HBIM of a monument is a management tool that is meant to be for a long time after its development as it escorts the monument in every step of its life cycle. Therefore, just like it happens with the other classifications (LoD, LoI, GoG, GoI), it is necessary for the dimensions of a HBIM to be defined from an early stage. In this manner the stakeholders, especially the new ones, may be aware of the subject matter of the HBIM. This is a great help for other relevant specialists that have no experience is such matters.

In conclusion, dimension classification is characterized as essential for a HBIM. Through this particular research, utilizing this classification, it was made possible to study and analyze the subject matter of HBIM over the years. It seems that BIM techniques, concerning cultural heritage, are evolving impressively to a dynamic management tool. This modern approach, regarding historical buildings, has gone through evolutionary stages and has become a solid solution in the hands of the specialists. During the last two years, the appliance of BIM techniques has revealed a huge impact regarding the management of cultural heritage, while this fact is expected to be continued in the future more intensely.

References

1. Murphy, M., McGovern, E., Pavia, S.: Historic building information modelling – adding intelligence to laser and image-based surveys of European classical architecture. J. Photogrammetry Remote Sens. ISPRS **76**, 89–102 (2013). https://doi.org/10.1016/j.isprsjprs.2012.11.006
2. Zhang, Z., Zou, Y.: Research hotspots and trends in heritage building information modeling: a review based on CiteSpace analysis. Hum. Soc. Sci. Commun. **9**, 394 (2022). https://doi.org/10.1057/s41599-022-01414-y
3. Mora, R., Sanchez-Aparicio, L.J.: An historical building information modelling approach for the preventive conservation of historical constructions: Application to the Historical Library of Salamanca. Autom. Constr. **121**, 103449 (2020). https://doi.org/10.1016/j.autcon.2020.103449
4. Brumana, R., Ioannides, M., Pevitali, M.: Holistic Heritage building information modelling (HHBIM): from nodes to hub networking, vocabularies and repositories. In: Brumana, R., et al. (eds.) 2019 The International Archives of the Photogrammetry, Remote Sensing and Spatial Information Sciences. 2nd International Conference of Geomatics and Restoration, 8–10 May, Milan, Italy, vol. XLII-2/W11, pp. 309–316. Copernicus GmbH, Gottingen (2019). https://doi.org/10.5194/isprs-archives-XLII-2-W11-309-2019
5. Brumana, R., Oreni, D., Barazzetti, L., Cuca, B., Previtali, M., Banfi, F.: Survey and scan to BIM model for the knowledge of built heritage and the management of conservation activities. In: Daniotti, B., Gianinetto, M., Della Torre, S. (eds.) Digital Transformation of the Design, Construction and Management Processes of the Built Environment. RD, pp. 391–400. Springer, Cham (2020). https://doi.org/10.1007/978-3-030-33570-0_35
6. Banfi, F.: BIM orientation: grades of generation and information for different type of analysis and management process. In: Hayes, J., Ouimet, C., Quintero, M.S., Fai, S., Smith, L. (eds.) The International Archives of the Photogrammetry, Remote Sensing and Spatial Information Sciences. 26th International CIPA Symposium, 28 August-01 September, Ottawa, Canada, vol. XLII-2/W5, pp. 57–64. IRIS, Politecnico Di Milano (2017). https://doi.org/10.5194/isprs-archives-XLII-2-W5-57-2017
7. Carrasco, A.C., Lombillo, I., Sanchez-Espeso, J.M., Balbas, F.J.: Quantitative and qualitative analysis on the integration of geographic information systems and building information modeling for the generation and management of 3D models. Buildings **12**(10), 1672 (2022). https://doi.org/10.3390/buildings12101672
8. Martinelli, L., Calcerano, F., Gigliarelli, E.: Methodology for an HBIM workflow focused on the representation of construction systems of built heritage. J. Cult. Herit. **55**, 277–289 (2022). https://doi.org/10.1016/j.culher.2022.03.016

9. Georgopoulos, A., Brumana, R., Bregianni, A., Oreni, D., Barazzetti, L.: A HBIM for documentation, dissemination and management of built heritage. The case study of St. Maria in Scaria d'Intelvi. Int. J. of Heritage Digital Era **2**, 433–451 (2013). https://doi.org/10.1260/2047-4970.2.3.433
10. Bosco, A., D'Andrea, A., Nuzzolo, M.: A virtual reconstruction of the sun temple of Niuserra: from scans to ABIM. In: Matsumoto, M., Uleberg, E. (eds.) 2018. CAA2016: Oceans of Data, Proceedings of the 44th Conference on Computer Applications and Quantitative Methods in Archaeology, 30 March-3 April, Oslo, Norway, pp. 377–388. Archaeopress Publishing Ltd, Oxford (2016)
11. Beltramo, S., Diara, F., Rinaudo, F.: Evaluation of an integrative approach between HBIM and architecture history. In: Brumana, R., et al. (eds.) 2019 The International Archives of the Photogrammetry, Remote Sensing and Spatial Information Sciences. 2nd International Cenference of Geomatics and Restoration, 8–10 May, Milan, Italy, vol. XLII-2/W11, pp. 225–229. Copernicus GmbH, Gottingen (2019). https://doi.org/10.5194/isprs-archives-XLII-2-W11-225-2019
12. Diara, F., Rinaudo, F.: Building archeology documentation and analysis through open source HBIM solutions via NURBS modelling. In: The International Archives of the Photogrammetry, Remote Sensing and Spatial Information Sciences, pp. 1381–1388. Copernicus GmbH, Gottingen (2020). https://doi.org/10.5194/isprs-archives-XLIII-B2-2020-1381-2020
13. Del-Pozzo, D., Scala, B., Adami, A.: Geometry and information for the preservation of a roman mosaic through a HBIM approach. In: Dang, A., Hou. A.L., Yan, H. (eds.) 2021 The International Archives of the Photogrammetry, Remote Sensing and Spatial Information Sciences. 28th CIPA Symposium "Great Learning & Digital Emotion", 28 August-1 September, Beijing, China, vol. VIII-M-1–2021, pp. 73–79. Copernicus GmbH, Gottingen (2019). https://doi.org/10.5194/isprs-annals-VIII-M-1-2021-73-2021
14. Nieto-Julian, J., Lara, L., Moyano, J.: Implementation of a TeamWork-HBIM for the management and sustainably of architecture heritage. Sustainability **13**, 2161 (2021). https://doi.org/10.3390/su13042161
15. Gigliarelli, E., Calcerano, F., Cessari, L.: Numerical simulation and decision support system: an integrated approach for historical building retrofit. Energy Procedia **133**, 135–144 (2017). https://doi.org/10.1016/j.egypro.2017.09.379
16. Vythoulka, A., Delegou, E., Moropoulou, A.: Protection and revealing of traditional settlements and cultural assets, as a tool for sustainable development: the case of Kythera Island in Greece. Land **12**, 1324 (2021). https://doi.org/10.3390/land10121324
17. Mitchell, K., Murhpy, M.: Interactive timeline visualization with games engines and conceptual frameworks for disseminating historic architecture and archaeology (Preprint) (2019)
18. Castellano-Roman, M., Pinto-Puerto, F.: Dimensions and levels of knowledge in heritage building information modelling, HBIM: the model of the charterhouse of Jerez. Digit. Appl. Archaeol. Cul. Heritage **14**, e00110 (2019). https://doi.org/10.1016/j.daach.2019.e00110
19. Santos, D., Cabeleiro, M., Sousa, S.H., Branco, M.J.: Apparent and resistant section parametric modelling of timber structure in HBIM. J. Build. Eng. **49**, 103990 (2022). https://doi.org/10.1016/j.jobe.2022.103990
20. Garcia-Gago, J., Sanchez-Apericio, L.J., Soilan, M., Gonzalez-Aguilera, D.: HBIM for supporting the diagnosis of historical buildings: case study of the Master Gate of San Francisco in Portugal. Autom. Constr. **141**, 104453 (2022). https://doi.org/10.1016/j.autcon.2022.104453
21. Da Silva, F., Cuperschmid, A., Ceravolo, A., Fabricio, M.: A technological Prospect for a Diagnostic Model in HBIM. J. Comput. Cult. Heritage **15**(4), 1–24 (2022). https://doi.org/10.1145/3526091
22. Bruno, N., Roncella, R.: HBIM for Conservation: a new proposal for information modeling. Remote Sens. **11**(15), 1751 (2019). https://doi.org/10.3390/rs11151751

23. Murphy, M., Pavia, S., Cahill, J., Lenihan, S., Corns, A.: An initial design framework for virtual historic Dublin. In: Brumana, et al. (eds.) 2019 The International Archives of the Photogrammetry, Remote Sensing and Spatial Information Sciences. 2nd International Conference of Geomatics and Restoration, 8–10 May, Milan, Italy, vol. XLII-2/W11, pp. 309–316. Copernicus GmbH, Gottingen (2019). https://doi.org/10.5194/isprs-archives-XLII-2-W11-901-2019
24. Al-Muqdadi, F., Ahmed, A.: Applying heritage building information modelling (HBIM) to lost heritage in conflict zones: Al-Hadba in Mosul, Iraq. In: Yilmaz, A., Wegner, J.D., Remondino, Q.F., Fuse, T., Toschi, I. (eds.) 2022 The International Archives of the Photogrammetry, Remote Sensing and Spatial Information Sciences. XXIV ISPRS Congress “Imaging today, foreseeing tomorrow”, Commission II, 6–11 June, Nice, France, vol. XLIII-B2, pp. 753–760. Copernicus GmbH, Gottingen (2022). https://doi.org/10.5194/isprs-archives-XLIII-B2-2022-753-2022
25. Saricaoglu, T., Saygi, G.: Data-driven conservation actions of heritage places cured with HBIM. Virtual Archaeol. Rev. **13**(27), 17–32 (2022). https://doi.org/10.4995/var.2022.17370
26. Volk, A., Stengel, J., Schultmann, F.: Building information modeling (BIM) for existing buildings – literature review and future needs. Autom. Constr. **38**, 109–127 (2014). https://doi.org/10.1016/j.autcon.2013.10.023
27. Bruno, S., De-Fino, M., Fatiguso, F.: Historic Building Information modelling: performance assessment for diagnosis-aided information modelling and management. Autom. Constr. **86**, 256–276 (2018). https://doi.org/10.1016/j.autcon.2017.11.009
28. Brunott, N., Suprum, E., Stewart, R.A., Mostafa, S.: Guidance for implementing data capture and modelling techniques for managing heritage assets: vision for heritage BIM (HBIM) (2022)
29. Sciamma, A., Gaglio, G.F., La-Guardia, M.: HBIM Data management in historical and archaeological buildings. Archaeologia e Calcolatori **31**, 231–252 (2020). https://doi.org/10.19282/ac.31.1.2020.11
30. Yang, X., Grussenmeyer, P., Koehl, M., Macher, H., Murtiyoso, A., Landes, T.: Review of built heritage modelling: integration of HBIM and other information techniques. J. Cult. Herit. **46**, 350–360 (2020)
31. Diara, F., Rinuado, F.: Open source HBIM for cultural heritage: a project proposal. In: Remondino, F., Toschi, I., Fuse, T. (eds.) 2018 The International Archives of the Photogrammetry, Remote Sensing and Spatial Information Sciences. ISPRS TC II Mid-term Symposium “Towards Photogrammetry 2020”, 4–7 June, Riva del Grada, Italy, vol. XLII-2, pp. 303–309. Copernicus GmbH, Gottingen (2018). https://doi.org/10.5194/isprs-archives-XLII-2-303-2018
32. Moyano, J., Carreno, E., Nieto-Junial, J.E., Gil-Arizon, I., Bruno, S.: Systematic approach to generate historic building information modelling (HBIM) in architectural restoration project. Autom. Constr. **143**, 104551 (2022). https://doi.org/10.1016/j.autcon.2022.104551
33. Plata, A.R.M.D.L., Franco, P.A.C., Franco, J.C., Gibello-Bravo V.: Protocol development for point clouds, triangulated meshes and parametric acquisition and integration in an HBIM workflow for change control and management in a UNESCO’s world heritage site. Sensors 21, 1083 (2021). https://doi.org/10.3390/s21041083
34. Brumana, R., et al.: Generative HBIM modelling to embody complexity (LOD, LOG, LOA, LOI): surveying, preservation, site intervention – the Basilica di Collemaggio (L’Aquila). Appl. Geomatics **10**, 545–567 (2018). https://doi.org/10.1007/s12518-018-0233-3

Environmental and Socioeconomic Pressures and Cultural Heritage Degradation. Evidence from Elounda, Crete Island

George Alexandrakis[1](✉), Stelios Petrakis[2], Nikolaos Rempis[1,3], Antonios Parasyris[1], and Nikolaos Kampanis[1]

[1] Foundation for Research and Technology-Hellas, Institute of Applied and Computational Mathematics (FORTH-IACM), N. Plastira 100, 70013 Heraklion, Greece
alexandrakis@iacm.forth.gr

[2] Institute of Oceanography, Hellenic Centre for Marine Research (HCMR), 46.7 Km Athens-Sounion, Athens, Greece

[3] Department of Geography, University of the Aegean, University Hill, 81100 Mytilene, Greece

Abstract. Areas of cultural heritage, apart from their pananthropic cultural value, also constitute a major, sensitive, and non-renewable factor of economic income for the stakeholders that exploit them. Most cultural and archaeological sites in the island of Crete, Greece, are settled in coastal or near-coastal areas. Thus, they are constantly subjected to climate change effects and anthropogenic expansion, structural degradation, corrosion of settlements etc. Furthermore, the areas surrounding the sites are also profit-generating, since the visitors of the sites use the tourism facilities (i.e., hotels, beaches, restaurants). The area under investigation is the bay of Elounda, which is a submerged archaeological site with many cultural heritage sites in its coastal zone, whose economy is based almost entirely on tourism. Most of the coastal site is under severe erosion due to various factors, which are not strictly related to climate change, resulting to loss of profit for the local population. Moreover, the growing need of land space for touristic facilities enhances the anthropogenic pressures on the cultural heritage sites in the bay. The main objective of this study is to compute the overall land loss during the last 72 years, and to estimate the impact due to the erosion and human expansion. The methodology includes the analysis of the erosion from aerial photos and satellite imagery to calculate the urban expansion and coastline evolution over the years. Five areas were selected for investigation, which included the mapping and calculation of socioeconomic vulnerability indices on the areas of interest using a GIS platform.

Keywords: Cultural heritage · Climate change · Socioeconomic impact · Elounda · Crete Island

1 Introduction

Areas of cultural heritage, apart from their pananthropic cultural value, also constitute a major, sensitive, and non-renewable factor of economic income for the stakeholders that exploit them. Most cultural and archaeological sites in the island of Crete, Greece,

A. Moropoulou et al. (Eds.): TMM_CH 2023, CCIS 1889, pp. 298–307, 2023.
https://doi.org/10.1007/978-3-031-42300-0_26

are settled in coastal or near-coastal areas. Thus, they are constantly subjected to climate change effects and anthropogenic expansion, structural degradation, corrosion of settlements etc. The coastal zones are of outmost importance worldwide on the aspect of their contribution in the national GTP, since they are considered among the most productive, exploitedand threatened areas (Agardy et al. 2005; Kiousopoulos 2008; Rempis et al. 2018). These zones have significant environmental, economic, social, and cultural importance (Rempis and Tsilimigkas 2021; Tsilimigkas and Rempis 2021). The significant and increased pressures in coastal areas are the result of: (a) the expansion of the existing traditional coastal activities and uses; (b) the emergence of new forms of activities and uses; and (c) environmental changes (Schultz-Zehden et al. 2008). Sociologically, the human inhabitation and urban sprawl in coastal zones has massively increased during the last 100 years, while tourism plays a significant role in the rapid expansion of built-up areas along the coasts (Kizos et al. 2017; Tsilimigkas and Rempis 2017, 2018, Tsilimigkas et al. 2020).

The economic importance of coastal tourism is indisputable as it represents one of the main sources of revenue for many countries and regions. This has resulted in creating major socio-cultural, economic, physical and environmental impacts in many coastal areas, which are particularly vulnerable to pressures associated with its growth (Alexandrakis et al. 2019)]. Tourism beyond the carrying capacity of a destination often creates many negative impacts on the environment as well as the local society. Massive tourism developments have altered the natural dynamics of near shore ecosystems, resulting in coastal erosion, loss of valuable habitats (such as sand dunes, coral reefs, wetlands and mangrove forests), and the degradation of the ecosystem (Jordan and Fröhle 2022). The lack of land-use planning and building regulations in many destinations has facilitated sprawling developments along coastlines, valleys and scenic routes for providing tourism facilities (Green and Hunter 1992; Razzaq et al. 2023). Archeological sites in such areas are also affected by the quick urbanization, huge construction projects etc. (Jarah et al. 2019).

2 Area

Elounda bay is located at the NE part of Crete Island, covering an area of about 10 km^2. Its coast is about 6 km long and is located at the Eastern part of the homonymous bay, at the Northern part of Mirabello Bay in E. Crete (Fig. 1). It is a semi-enclosed bay with an eastward-facing entrance on the north side. Its southern end consists of a tombolo formation, which connects the island of Crete with the Kolokitha peninsula. The shores of the study area consist mainly of low slope rock formations, while there are beaches with thick cobbles and small natural and artificial sandy beaches (Alexandrakis et al. 2014). The width of the beach differs, as about half of the shoreline length is coastal constructions (road network or coastal walls), leaving only a small percentage of uninterrupted beach, mostly at the northern part, where the beach width is about 15 m. Most of the small beaches consist of sand and gravelly sand, whereas the biggest beach of the area consists of cobbles. The underwater part of the coast consists mostly of sand and gravel. The relief of the surrounding area is rather low, apart from the central part. The economy of the area is based almost entirely on tourism. The touristic exploitation of the broader area is at a large scale, since numerous luxury hotels have been built in the Mirabello slopes (Petrakis et al. 2019). The coastal area hosts various sites of archaeological interest, such as ancient cities and facilities, dating from the Minoan era (27th–15th century B.C.) to the recent historical monuments of the early 20th century. Among them, the most important is the Spinalonga fortress, located on a small island at the centre of the gulf, which has recently been nominated as a UNESCO World Heritage site. The fortress was built on the island by the Venetians in 1579. Also, southern of that are located the submerged ruins of ancient Olous (2nd century AD) around Poros that connects the settlement of Elounda with the Kolokitha Peninsula, which extend into the sea and are clearly visible when the waters are calm, while in the SW part of the Kolokitha peninsula there are floor mosaics from that period. Additionally, the windmills located in the area "Kanali" were built at the beginning of the 20th Century, are considered representative samples of local architecture and have been designated as historical monuments along with their surroundings.

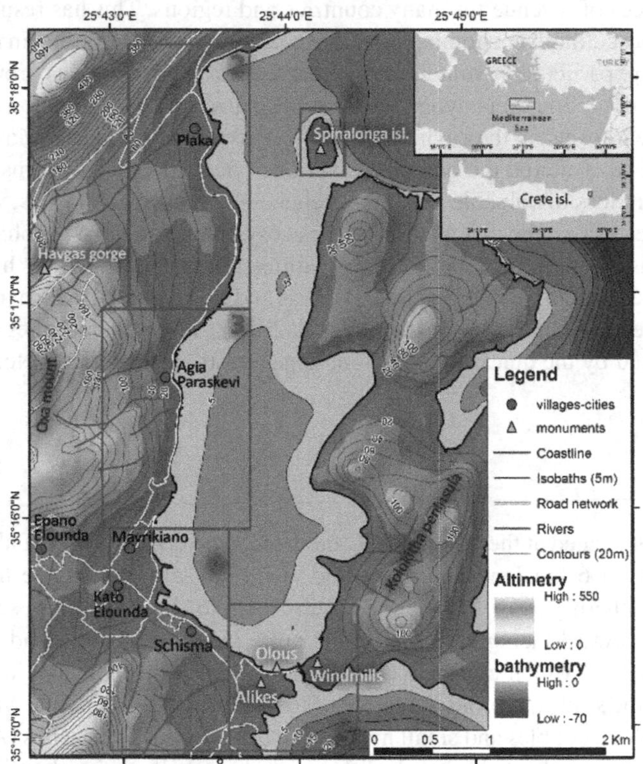

Fig. 1. Elounda study area.

3 Methodology

For the implementation of this research, in addition to the collection - evaluation of the published data and information, a series of field measurements were carried out concerning the terrestrial and submarine morphology (repeated measurements), the inter-seasonal coastal hydrodynamic regime (rippling, sea-state), morphology of the coastal area etc.

The collection of existing data concerns topographic maps and diagrams, orthophoto maps, aerial photographs, satellite images, hydrographic and geological maps, old photos of the coast, studies for coastal technical works as well as scientific publications and published data for the study area. The following is a summary of the data collected and considered during the preparation of the present study. Additionally, the legislative framework was considered, and the current provisions governing land use and permitted interventions in the area were collected. Also, regulatory frameworks and local decisions were considered.

Topographic maps were used with a scale of 1:50.000 and topographic diagrams on a scale of 1:5.000. Satellite images with 0.5 m resolution for the years 2002, 2003, 2010, 2013 from the QuickBird satellite receiver. Aerial photographs of 1945 and 1960 with a nominal scale of 1:30.000 and 1998 with a nominal scale of 1:40.000 and the geological map of I.G.M.E. for the area, on a scale of 1:50.000 were used.

To quantify the urban expansion at the coastal zone and the shoreline variations of the study areas, a series of aerial photographs and satellite images were used, covering a time-period of 77 years with collection years 1945, 1966, 1972, 1989, 1998, 2004, 2007, 2013, 2017, and 2022, acquired from the Hellenic Military Geographic Service (HMGS) and the Google Earth platform and were analyzed using a Geographic Information System (GIS). The various dates were digitized in polygons of constructed coverage for each date. The polygon areas were measured and summarized for each year, producing the total constructed study area in each of the cultural heritage sites under investigation, for the specific dates, during the last 77 years. Likewise, the coastlines of each date were digitized, and the overtopping of all coastlines revealed alterations, which were categorized in three conditions of the coast: (i) loss, (ii) gain and (iii) artificial gain, loss referring to coastal erosion, gain to accretion and artificial gain to man-made accretion through coastal constructions. Except for the coastline, the coastal works (e.g. coastal walls, ports, groynes, etc.) were also digitized, in order to correlate them to the urban fabric expansion through time.

3.1 Cultural Heritage Landmarks Areas Under Investigation

Five areas, related to nearby established cultural heritage areas, were selected for further investigation (Fig. 1), labelled with numbers 1 to 5 as shown in Fig. 1, and will be henceforth referred to as such. Those are: Area 1. Spinalonga islet. The study area includes the coastal area of the Kolokitha peninsula and the island of Spinalonga (Fig. 1). The length of the coastal front is about 14.3 km. The peninsula of Kolokitha has few buildings, because of its declaration as an archaeological site almost on its entirety, while on the island of Spinalonga the buildings have remained unchanged from 1945 to 2017, covering a built area of 11.893 m^2.

Area 2. The area of Plaka is on the NW side of the bay of Elounda (Fig. 1). It extends from the North side of Plaka beach to the north of the settlement of Agia Paraskevi. The length of the coastal front is about 2.5 km. Within the area is the settlement of Plaka and the hotel complexes Elounda Bay and Elounda Gulf Villas. On the north side of the area is the gorge of Havgas and some ephemeral torrents. The southern part of the area is the foot of Mount Oxa. Several coastal protection works have been constructed on the coastal front, as well as sediment nourishment projects.

Area 3. The area of Tsifliki (Fig. 1) has a length of about 3 km. Within the study area, from north to south, there are several hotel units. The area is located at the foot of Mount Oxa, crossed by a coastal road, with steep slopes and absence of large natural beaches. Many coastal protection and restoration projects are constructed along the coastal front, as well as sediment retention works, while an artificial beach has been created.

Area 4. Elounda, includes the settlements of Mavrikianos and the northern part of the settlement of Elounda, up to Schisma beach. A coastal road crosses the entire coastal front from the north to the beach of Schisma. The beach of Schisma has been created artificially, as vertical groynes of about 130 m in length have been built on both sides, between 1966 and 1972. In the area, the main alteration of the coastal area is the construction of the port of Elounda, which took place in various phases. From a small pier in 1945, between 1966 and 1972, a port was built, which acquired its current form since 1989. Almost the entire coastal area of Elounda has been constructed to protect the coastal area from erosion.

Area 5. Alikes include the area from the end of the urban fabric of Elounda in the east to the hotel complex of Elounda Island Villas in the Kolokitha peninsula in the west and includes the area of Alikes, the archeological site of Olounda and the canal that connects the area of Elounda with Kolokitha (Fig. 1). The length of the coastal front is about 1 km. The main characteristics of the study area are the existence of salt pans and the archeological site of Olous. The salt pans operated continuously from the 15th century until 1972, while the ancient city of Olous was active during the Roman years and nowadays a large part of it has sunk in the bay of Elounda.

4 Results and Discussion

Six coastal types have been identified in the area: Hard rocky coasts occupying 58.89% of the total shoreline length, soft rocky coasts (2.34%), beaches with length <100 m (2.75%), beaches with length between 100 and 1000 m (12.23%), and a very small percentage (0.39%) of beaches with length more than 1 km; the latter are very narrow, rarely exceeding 10 m in width. A significant percentage (23.41%) of the shoreline hosts man-made structures i.e., ports and fishing shelters, coastal walls and groynes. In addition, there are several hotels and other leisure facilities. In the surrounding areas, there are organized settlements and scattered farmhouses. The local transport network consists of a paved coastal road and some dirt roads that serve agricultural activities. The main road is of major importance, as it is the only road connecting the coastal town of Elounda with the inland villages, and it is supported by a coastal wall at most of its length.

The gulf of Elounda has undergone a significant change in land-use during the last 77 years. Areas of sclerophyllous and natural vegetation have turned progressively into urban areas, mostly due to the construction of large-scale touristic settlements (see Fig. 2). The urban expansion begins during the 60's and is mostly noted after 1990 where an exponential increase in mostly touristic settlements of large scale is observed. Thus, the area cover with settlements in Elounda Bay after 1989 has doubled, more intensively during the period 2004–2007, with a total area of settlements measuring about 0.57 km^2, eight times larger than that of 1945 (see Table 1 and Fig. 2).

Table 1. Urban fabric expansion (by covered area and %) during the last 77 years.

Year	km^2	period	%
1945	0.070	–	–
1966	0.072	1945–1966	2.8
1972	0.113	1966–1972	57.3
1989	0.243	1972–1989	115.2
1998	0.329	1989–1998	35.8

As seen in Fig. 2, most of the established inland cultural heritage areas at the western side of the gulf have been covered with new constructions, whereas the Kolokitha Peninsula (all of which is an established cultural heritage area) remains still without any development projects.

Beach area from 1945 to 2022 was decreased by 14011 m^2 due to erosional factors. About 13551 m^2 of beach has been added to the coastal area, all of it due to coastal constructions. About 35541 m^2 of artificial area has been added to the coastal area through constructions (Fig. 3).

In the specific areas, Spinalonga islet and Kolokitha have a total coastal land loss of 212 m^2 and no further expansion of urban area. The area of Plaka has a total land loss of 1240 m^2. There are some small-scale coastal protection works and a construction of a small port during the 90's. Severe slope instability has been observed at the northern part of Plaka during the last 15 years. The significant expansion of urban fabric was triggered after 1970. The area of Tsifliki has a total land loss of 2258 m^2 and beach retraction has been found to be 6 m on average. Small-scale coastal protection works and construction of large-scale touristic facilities are built, almost 80% of which are dated after 2004. Half of the facilities are built within the cultural heritage area, most of them dating after 2007, covering approximately 25% of its area. Also, the main developments in the last decade are found there. Elounda's Port shows no significant land loss. The expansion of the port was made during two faces (~1970 and ~1985) and the coastal road was constructed around 1970. There is a significant expansion of urban fabric after 1970. The established cultural heritage area is covered of facilities by about 30%, most of it built after 1995. In Alikes, the total land loss is 7291 m^2, most of it at the area of the salt pans. Small-scale coastal protection works were made before 1950. Significant expansion of urban fabric was found after 1990, due to the expansion of the city of Elounda towards the East. About 20% of the established cultural heritage area is covered by facilities, mostly built after 1990.

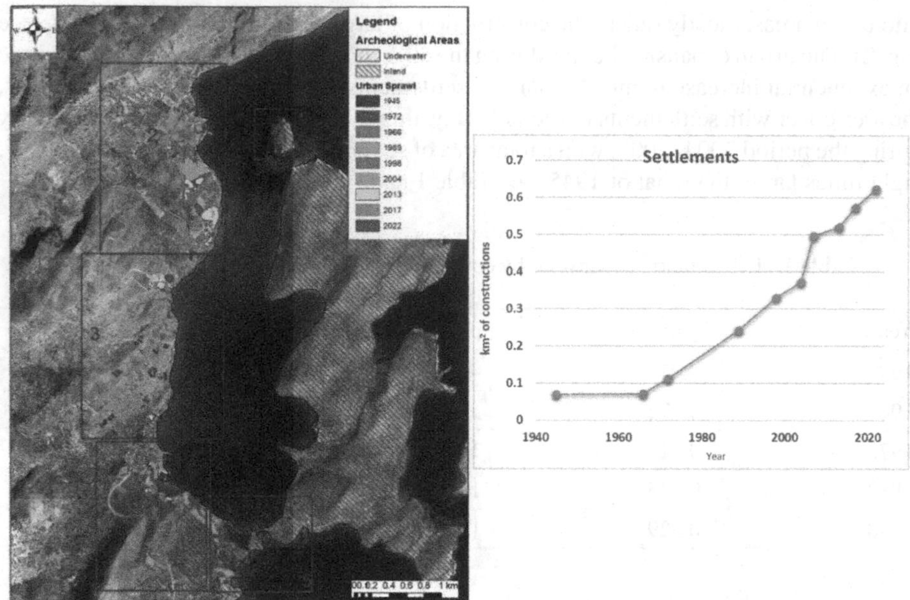

Fig. 2. Urban fabric expansion, related to cultural heritage areas urban fabric expansion during the last 77 years

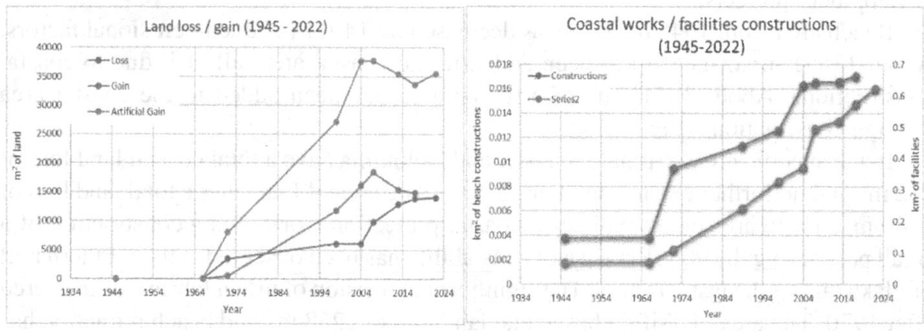

Fig. 3. Total land loss and gain (natural & artificial) during the last 77 years, progression of area covered with artificial constructions, comparison of facilities/coastal works for the last 77 years.

The coastal area, as a general picture, is in a state of erosion, which is more intense in the northern and central part. Specifically, in the northern part, where erosion is most intense, the recession of the coastline reaches about 10 m on average, in the last 77 years. At certain points, the setback reaches up to 20 m, while it is obvious that the construction of coastal protection projects did not bring the desired outcomes. Near the settlement of Elounda, there is a land reclamation of the coastal area to create parking spaces. In terms of the spread of the residential fabric, the growth follows an increasing rate, mainly in areas 2 and 3. The whole study area, due to the rather shallow sea that surrounds it and the absence of a coastal wall, shows intense erosion in almost the entire coastal area, although along the coast there are transverse groynes to retain sediment. The total eroded surface is 7633 m^2, the surface that has been accreted is 825 m^2 and the artificially filled area is 625 m^2. Considering the nature of the surrounding area and its archaeological significance, the study area is found to be poorly structured. The buildings in the area are the saltwork facilities, the accompanying warehouses of the windmills and the hotel complex "Elounda Island Villas" which was built in the 80's. In 1945 the built-up area was 266 m^2, in 1998 it had increased to 3728 m^2 mainly due to the construction of salt processing areas from the salt pans that were made before 1966 and small scattered houses as well as the hotel complex. In 2014 the built-up area was 4542 m^2 and in 2017 the built-up area was increased to 5145 m^2.

The eroded surface in recent years is only 59.9 m^2, while approximately the same (47.4 m^2) is the surface where accretion is observed, while 17.126 m^2 is the surface covered by coastal works (groynes, coastal walls, etc.). The structured surface of the main urban fabric of Elounda increased exponentially during 1945–1998 (from 24.692 m^2 to 139.227 m^2) while since then the pace of construction has decreased (149.768 m^2 in 2004 and 159.725 m^2 in 2017).

5 Conclusions

The area under investigation is subjected to significant erosion. Since 1945 about 14.000 m^2 of coastal land has been lost, part of it due to human induced processes. The facilities and coastal constructions at the area increase significantly over time, especially during the last two decades (Fig. 2), and this tourism development has introduced additional pressures to an already sensitive coastal cultural heritage landscape. Most of the coastal front has been covered with constructions (coastal road, marinas/ports, groynes) though some constructions did not manage to reduce the erosion. All the established cultural heritage areas are located within 200 m from the coastline and are subjected to relatively low to medium vulnerability. A large part of the cultural heritage areas has now been covered by man-made interventions. These two factors, in some cases linked to each other, cause degradation of the cultural heritage environment, thus reducing their attractiveness. The restriction of the expansion of the man-made interventions and the implementation of specific coastal erosion mitigation techniques is suggested in order to decelerate that degradation, although further work is needed in order to propose specific mitigation strategies and scenarios. This works' objective to identify the scale of the erosion problem in the coastal area and to compute the overall land loss which is translated to a negative societal impact, is considered the first step towards the solution of this problem. If the issue of the degradation of the cultural heritage landmarks that is highlighted in this work stays unattended, it may affect the areas surrounding these sites which are profit-generating, since the visitors of the sites use the nearby tourism facilities and have a negative socioeconomic impact. In addition, coastal erosion creates the need for protection works within the bay of Elounda, a submerged archaeological site, thus creating even more pressure on the coastal area.

References

Agardy, T., et al.: Coastal systems (Chapter 19). In: Ecosystems and Human Well-Being: Current State and Trends, vol. 1. pp. 513–549 (2005)

Alexandrakis, G., Petrakis, S., Ghionis, G., Kampanis, N., Poulos, S.E.: Natural and human induced indicators in coastal vulnerability and risk assessment. In: 10th International Congress of the Hellenic Geographical Society, Thessaloniki, Greece, 22–24 October 2014, pp. 136–138 (2014)

Alexandrakis, G., Manasakis, C., Kampanis, N.A.: Economic and societal impacts on cultural heritage sites, resulting from natural effects and climate change. Heritage **2**(1), 279–305 (2019). https://doi.org/10.3390/heritage2010019

Razzaq, A., Fatima, T., Murshed, M.: Asymmetric effects of tourism development and green innovation on economic growth and carbon emissions in top 10 GDP countries. J. Environ. Plan. Manag. **66**(3), 471–500 (2023). https://doi.org/10.1080/09640568.2021.1990029

EC (European Commission). Recommendation of the European Parliament and of the council of 30 May 2002 Concerning the Implementation of Integrated Coastal Zone Management in Europe (2002)

Green, H., Hunter, C.: The environmental impact assessment of tourism development. The environmental impact assessment of tourism development, pp. 29–47 (1992)

Jarah, S.H.A., Zhou, B., Abdullah, R.J., Lu, Y., Yu, W.: Urbanization and urban sprawl issues in city structure: a case of the Sulaymaniah Iraqi Kurdistan region. Sustainability **11**(2), 485 (2019). https://doi.org/10.3390/su11020485

Jordan, P., Fröhle, P.: Bridging the gap between coastal engineering and nature conservation?: a review of coastal ecosystems as nature-based solutions for coastal protection. J. Coast. Conserv. **26**(2), 4 (2022). https://doi.org/10.1007/s11852-021-00848-x

Kiousopoulos, J.: Methodological approach of coastal areas concerning typology and spatial indicators, in the context of integrated management and environmental assessment. J. Coast. Conserv. **12**(1), 19–22 (2008)

Kizos, T., Tsilimigkas, G., Karampela, S.: What drives built-up area expansion on Islands? Using soil sealing indicators to estimate built-up area patterns on Aegean Islands, Greece. Tijdschr. Econ. Soc. Geogr. **108**(6), 836–853 (2017). https://doi.org/10.1111/tesg.12244

Petrakis, S., Alexandrakis, G., Rempis, N., Kampanis, N.: Coastal geomorphological changes in a semi-enclosed bay, induced by recreational interventions. In: Proceedings 1st DMPCO, Athens, 8–11 May 2019 (2019)

Rempis, N., Tsilimigkas, G.: Marine spatial planning on Crete Island, Greece. Methodological and implementation issues. J. Spatial Sci. (2021). https://doi.org/10.1080/14498596.2021.1955025

Rempis, N., Alexandrakis, G., Tsilimigkas, G., Kampanis, N.: Coastal use synergies and conflicts evaluation in the framework of spatial, development and sectoral policies. Ocean Coast. Manag. **166**, 40–51 (2018). https://doi.org/10.1016/j.ocecoaman.2018.03.009

Schultz-Zehden, A., Gee, K., Scibior, K.: HANDBOOK on Integrated Maritime Spatial Planning. INTERREG III B CADSES. PlanCoast Project. Sustainable Projects, Berlin (2008)

Tsilimigkas, G., Rempis, N.: Maritime spatial planning and spatial planning: synergy issues and incompatibilities. Evidence from Crete Island Greece. Ocean Coast. Manag. **139**, 33–41 (2017). https://doi.org/10.1016/j.ocecoaman.2017.02.001

Tsilimigkas, G., Rempis, N.: Marine uses, synergies and conflicts. evidence from Crete Island, Greece. J. Coast. Conserv. **22**(2), 235–245 (2018). https://doi.org/10.1007/s11852-017-0568-7

Tsilimigkas, G., Rempis, N.: Spatial planning framework, a challenge for marine tourism development: location of diving parks on Rhodes Island, Greece. Environ. Dev. Sustain. **23**(10), 15240–15265 (2021). https://doi.org/10.1007/s10668-021-01296-1

Tsilimigkas, G., Rempis, N., Derdemezi, E.: Marine zoning and landscape management on Crete Island, Greece. J. Coast. Conserv. **24**(4), 43 (2020). https://doi.org/10.1007/s11852-020-00757-5

UN (United Nations) Conference on Environment and Development. In: Agenda 21, United Nations Conference on Environment & Development Rio de Janerio, Brazil, 3 to 14 June 1992 (1992)

Analysis Between Cultural Heritage, Human Settlements and Landscapes Using Earth Observation and Archaeological Data

George Alexandrakis[1(✉)], Georgios V. Kozyrakis[1], Nikos Paxakis[1], Antonios Parasyris[1], Anastasia Vythoulka[2], Nikolaos A. Kampanis[1], and Antonia Moropoulou[2]

[1] Coastal Research Lab, Institute of Applied and Computational Mathematics, Foundation for Research & Technology-Hellas, Heraklion, Greece
alexandrakis@iacm.forth.gr

[2] Lab of Materials Science and Engineering, School of Chemical Engineering, National Technical University of Athens, Athens, Greece

Abstract. Geological and environmental conditions that influence local topography also affect indirectly the location of human settlement dynamics. Understanding those relationships plays an important role in environmental and cultural heritage research related to the evolution of settlement dynamics. This work aims to present preliminary results of a study of the patterns of human settlements, based on known archaeological sites at four small islands of Dodecanese, Greece, and to generate hypotheses about the relations of cultural heritage patterns with the landscape. To that end, a Web-GIS database was created, which was fed with topographic, geomorphological data and Earth Observation data. Geomorphological analysis, derived from earth observation products, can provide useful estimations into the processes that shape landscapes and insight into the location and evolution of settlements. The analysis includes a series of different data correlation, from geomorphologic to socioeconomic, integrated by an indicator analysis. A series of thematic maps were developed to interpret why areas were selected to host settlements. Using the database, a set of indexes have been applied, that included exposure and vulnerability indices for the inland and coastal areas for specific sites. The areas under investigation present different characteristics in their geomorphological but also their societal evolution. Geomorphological data was further analysed in a ternary diagram that indicated the relative influence of each of the parameters in each area. From the diagram it is seen that the locations of human activities are strongly affected by environmental factors.

Keywords: Index approach · Earth Observation · vulnerability · Cultural Heritage

A. Moropoulou et al. (Eds.): TMM_CH 2023, CCIS 1889, pp. 308–320, 2023.
https://doi.org/10.1007/978-3-031-42300-0_27

1 Introduction

Vulnerability is the state of susceptibility to damage from exposure to environmental and social factors, as well as a lack of adaptability (Adger, 2006), while in related natural hazards the term refers to the potential impacts of a particular event (Marzocchi et al., 2009). In general, vulnerability must consider economic, social, geographic, demographic, cultural, institutional, governance and environmental factors (UNISDR, 2009; IPCC, 2012). Spatial analysis and spatial data integration are important tools for vulnerability to natural and climate change hazards. The United Nations Environment Program (UNEP) considers vulnerability measurement and mapping to be a top priority to support decision-making in planning and protection (PROVIA, 2013). Spatial vulnerability assessment methods differ depending on the topic and scope of study, but in general, they are used to identify areas of potentially high risk for natural hazards and climate impacts (UNISDR, 2009). Natural hazards (e.g. earthquakes, landslides, volcanic activity, soil and coastal erosion, floods) can pose a threat to various natural and social entities. Natural hazards are strongly determined by geomorphology (Scheidegger, 1994). In this sense, geomorphological hazards can be classified as endogenous such as neotectonics, and exogenous such as flooding, rockfalls or landslides, erosion, sedimentation, etc. (Slaymaker, 1996). The dual character of natural disasters needs to be addressed by considering not only their natural characteristics but also the social and economic environment (Alexander, 1993). Geomorphology has contributed to the assessment of natural hazard vulnerability with different methods. All geomorphological processes influence the preservation of the archaeological sites (Canuti et al., 2000) which constitute one of the most important datasets for the development of human settlements and paleoecological processes in Mediterranean areas (Mercuri and Sadori, 2014).

The main objective of most existing indices is to classify the country into areas with similar attributes or characteristics; the majority use multidisciplinary data on natural processes. The need to include socioeconomic variables was also recognized by Gornitz et al. (1993) who noted that omitting socioeconomic variables from their Coastal Vulnerability Index could potentially limit the assessment of vulnerable areas. Likewise, the indices reviewed by Cooper and McLaughlin (1998) indicate a general need to include socioeconomic variables in the classification process (McLaughlin et al., 2002). This has led to criticism of vulnerability studies and the separation of the physical from the socio-economic aspects in vulnerability studies (e.g. IPCC, 2001; Nicholls and Small, 2002). In the past, socioeconomic variables were excluded due to the difficulty in obtaining and classifying the data. In addition, socioeconomic data may change over time (e.g., new homes and roads being built, etc.) and perceptions of threats and appropriate responses may also change over time (Carter, 1993).

Nowadays, these procedures are simpler and may be updated in the future. The fact that socioeconomic indicators are time-limited also complicates their use (McLaughlin et. al., 2002), although they can also be more difficult to categorize as it is not easy to assign an economic value to an attribute. The indicator-based approach proposed by Kaiser (2006) has been recognized as one of the most appropriate approaches for intangible elements that have no physical form. Despite these difficulties, the inclusion of socioeconomic variables is of great importance in developing valid vulnerability indices for risk mitigation and adaptation to environmental and climate change (OBrien et al., 2006). However, vulnerability assessment involves various practical challenges, the complexity of the problem, and our poor understanding of the issues involved, regardless of the significance of the results (Patt et al., 2009). Some vulnerability studies have attempted a more integrative assessment approach, combining both physical and socioeconomic vulnerability with a general vulnerability index system (Boruff et al., 2005; Preston et al., 2008). The present investigation proposes a methodology for the examination of vulnerability in four small Dodecanese islands, with the introduction of socioeconomic indicators into a GIS-based Socio-economic Vulnerability Index, and presents preliminery results.

2 Study Area

As case study areas, four small Islands of the Dodecanese Island chain are considered. Firstly, Symi is located about 41 km north-northwest of Rhodes and has 58.1 km^2 of mountainous terrain. It has small valleys, and its coastline alternates between rocky cliffs and beaches, and isolated coves. Its main town, located on the northeast coast, is also named Symi where the port is located. The island has 2,580 inhabitants, mostly engaged in tourism, fishing, and trade. Next, Chalki is located 9 km west of Rhodes with an area of 28 km^2 and it is the smallest population in the Dodecanese with 330 permanent population. The third location is Kastellorizo that lies almost 2 km off the south coast of Turkey, and 125 km east of Rhodes. It represents a small archipelago where Megisti with 11.98 km^2 is the larger one. The Kastellorizo archipelago comprises several islands and islets. The island is mountainous, with high and steep coastlines. Lastly, Kasos lies southwest of Karpathos, and eastward of the island of Crete, with an area of 49 km^2 and it is very mountainous. In all four islands (Fig. 1), there are many historical sites and history that have been -evolving continuously through different eras, which attract tourism and increase the visitor population during the summer period.

3 Methodology

For the estimation of the island's vulnerability, three different indices were used following a modified methodology from Alexandrakis et al. (2019). The Geomorphological Characteristics index (GC) is related to the resistance of the island to erosion, the Natural Forcing index (NF) quantifies the forcing variables, and the Socio-Economic index (SE) quantifies the vulnerability of existing societal activities and infrastructure. The Geomorphological Characteristics sub-index (GC), which is related to the type of Landforms (Lf), Lithology (Li), Slope gradient (Sg), Slope Aspect (AS), and Drainage System density (DS), is calculated employing the following Eq. (1).

$$GC = \sqrt{\frac{Lf \cdot Li \cdot Sg \cdot DS \cdot AS}{5}} \tag{1}$$

The Natural factors Forcing sub-index, which includes the indicators of Structural stability of the geological formations (Ss), Vegetation coverage (Vg), Soil Erosivity

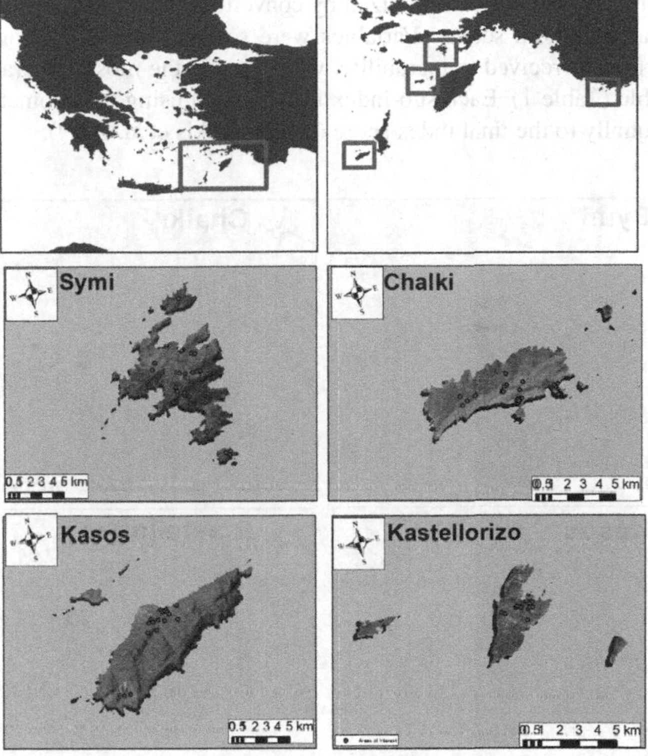

Fig. 1. Case study areas.

(SER), Soil Thickness (ST), Landslide Type (LT), and Land cover (LC), is given by Eq. (2):

$$NF = \sqrt{\frac{Ss \cdot Vg \cdot SER \cdot ST \cdot LC}{6}} \tag{2}$$

The Socio-Economic sub-index includes the socio-economic indicators of the presence and size of Settlements (SET), Cultural Heritage sites (CH), the Transport Network (TN), Land Use (LU), and Economic activities (E) and is estimated by Eq. (3) that reads:

$$SE = \sqrt{\frac{SET \cdot CH \cdot TN \cdot LU \cdot E}{5}} \tag{3}$$

An example of the spatial distribution of the land cover variable can be seen in Fig. 2 bellow, where the historical sites are symbolized by dot marks, and demonstrates their plurality and high density in the study area.

Based on the ranking from the relative Table 1 gives the ranking of all variables. The final index for the inland part of the island is estimated by Eq. (4) bellow.

$$SVI = \frac{GC + NF + SE}{3} \tag{4}$$

The resulting scores were normalized by converting them to a range defined by the maximum and minimum scores. Variables were selected and ranked on a 1–5 scale according to their perceived vulnerability, with 5 being the most vulnerable and 1 the least vulnerable (Table 1). Each sub-index is calculated using the geometric mean and contributes equally to the final index score (Alexandrakis et al. 2019).

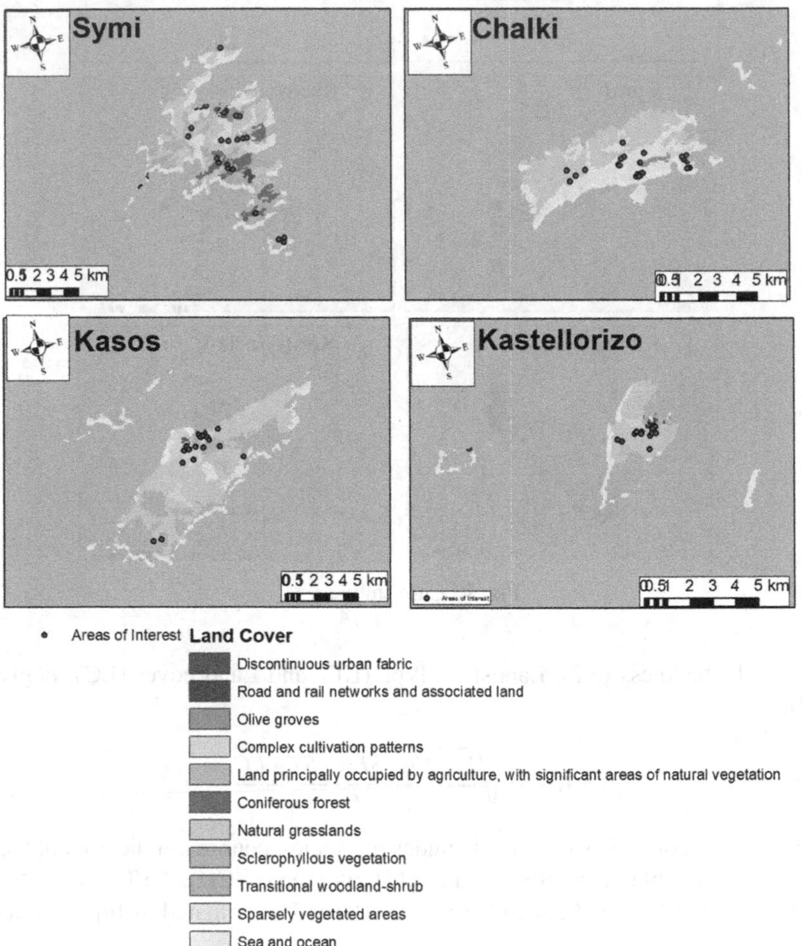

Fig. 2. Spatial distribution of land cover. The location of the historical sites are symbolized with dots.

Table 1. The vulnerability indices through ranking variables.

VARIABLES			Categories				
			1	2	3	4	5
			Very Low	Low	Moderate	High	Very High
Geomorphological Characteristics	Landforms	Lf	Beaches, Deltas	Terrace. Alluvial Plains	Low Cliffs	Medium Cliffs	High Cliff, landslides
	Slope (^{O})	Sg	10	10 – 25	25 - 30	30 - 45	< 45
	Aspect	AS	< 15	15–30	30–45	45–75	> 90
	Lithology	Li	Limestones, plutonics, metamorphics	Sandstones, tuffs, low grade metamorphics, conglomerate	Clays, low-cohesion sedimentary rocks	Non-cohesive materials, coarse and poorly sorted unconsolidated sediments	Debris, weathered material, fine unconsolidated sediments
	Drainage density (km/km^2)	Ds	< 1	1–1.5	1.5–2	2–2.5	> 2.5
Natural factors	Structural stability	Ss	none	Joints	Bedding Planes	Faults	Open cracks
	Vegetation coverage (%)	Vg	> 70	60–70	50–60	40–50	< 40
	Soil Erosivity	SER	0.15	0.15- 0.30	0.30–0.45	0.45- 055	> 0.55
	Soil thickness (m)	ST	> 10	5–10	1–5	0.5 - 1	< 1
	Landslide type	LT	None	Rock falls	Toppling	Debris/earth flow	Debris avalanche
	Land cover	LC	Bare rocks/water bodies	Artificial areas	Forest	Grasslands	Cultivated area
Socio-Economic	Settlement	SET	Absent	Village	Small Town	Large Town	City
	Cultural Heritage	CH	Absent	Local	Regional	National	Global
	Transport Network	TN	Absent	Secondary	National road	Ports	Highway
	Land Use	LU	Absent	Forest	Semi-rural	Agricultural	Urban, Industrial
	Economic activities	E	Absent	Industrial	Agricultural	Commercial	Tourism

4 Results

4.1 Ranking of Index Variables

The variables controlling all sub-indices were determined and assessed based on existing information, which was combined and spatially interrelated. An example of the spatial variation of the values can be seen in the next Fig. 3.

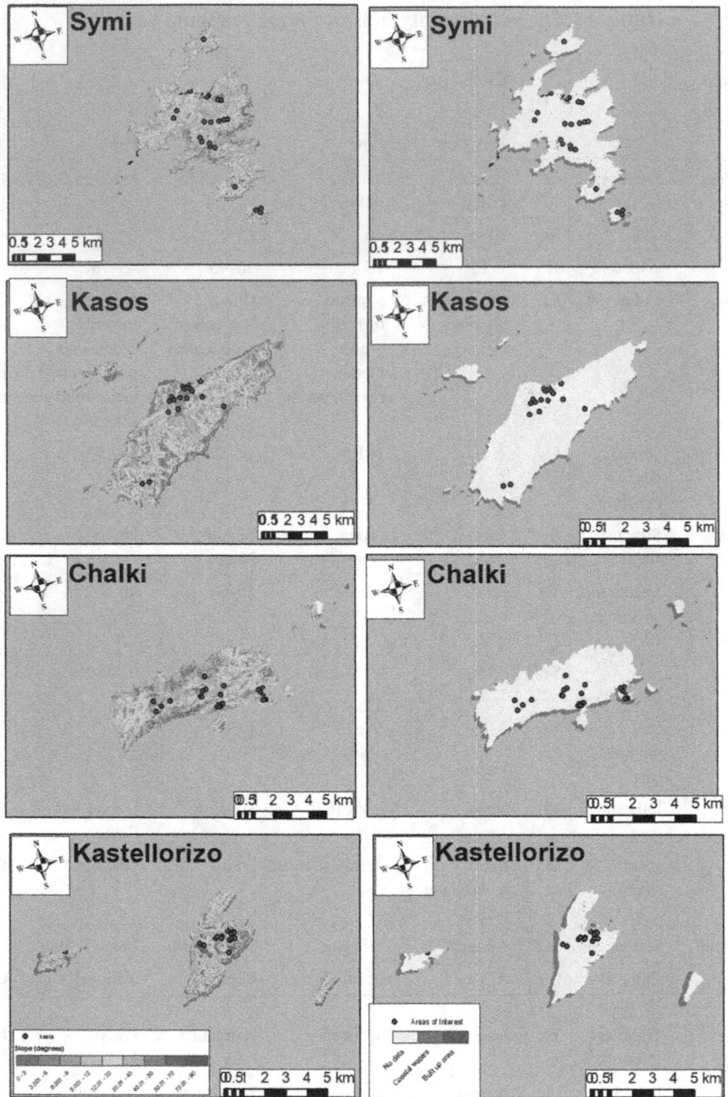

Fig. 3. Spatial distribution of the Geomorphological Characteristics sub-index variables of Slope (left) and Settlements (right). The dots symbolize the location of the historical sites.

A common charasteric of the all the islands is that the drainage density, Settlements and transport network variables are ranked as very low for the all the islands due to the almost complete absence of a drainage network, settlements and infrastracture. Additionally the aspect variable has similar values for all islands with the values for very low vulnerability range from 52.3% to 56.3%.

Concerning variables related to the Symi island's geomorphological characteristics, it was found that the Landforms variable is associated with almost 60% and 27.05% of high and very high vulnerability. The slope variable for Symi was found also to be more than 50% of high and very high vulnerability. Lithology variable for Symi ranks mostly at Very low and Low with a percentage more than (80%). Regarding variables that are related to natural factors for Symi, Structural stability has more than 85% in the very low and low vulnerability categories. The vegetation coverage variable lies mostly in the moderate and high category. Soil Erosivity has a very low ranking in 75.1% of the island, while the other classes make up the remaining 24.9%. Soil thickness is ranked mainly in the very high category (33.47%) and the second bigger percentage is found at the high category with 26.3%. A very low vulnerability for Landslide type variable was found in 86.2% of the area. Land cover has a 46.7% of high and very high vulnerability. Settlement and Transport variables were found mostly in the very low category since there are a few settlements and transport infrastructure there. For the Cultural Heritage variable, 87.2% of the area is ranked as very low. For the Land Use variable, 21.3% of the area is assigned to the very low category, and 66.86% to the medium category. For the Economic Activities variable the majority of the area (52.52%) belongs to the medium category. The cumulative ranking of the index variables for Symi island is presented in Fig. 4.

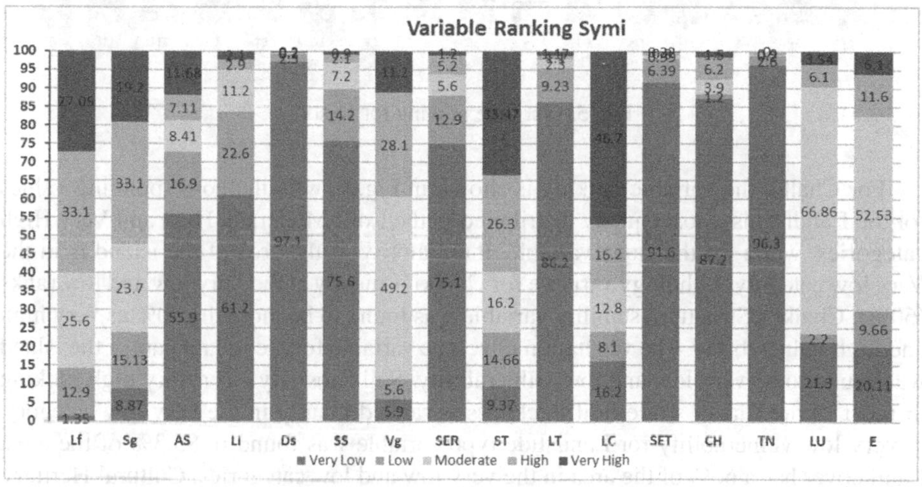

Fig. 4. Variable ranking for Symi.

For Kasos, we present the variable rankingsariable in Fig. 5. More specifically, the values of the Landforms variable are categorized more than 60% in the High and 27.7% in the Very High column. The slope variable is ranged in the Very low and Very High categories. Lithology for Kasos is ranked mainly in the very low (56.3%) and low (15.9%) categories. Structural stability is calculated to be mostly at very low and low vulnerability with more than 77.5%. The vegetation coverage variable for the inland part of the island was found to be very high (92.49%). Soil Erosivity has a very low ranking in 68.2% of the island, while Soil thickness is also ranked mainly in the very low category (60.85%). A very low vulnerability for Landslide type variable was found in 82.3% of the area.

Land cover has the majority of the island ranked in the very low and low categories. For the Cultural Heritage variable, 47.6% of the area is ranked as very low, the 20.3% as low, 15.3% as medium. For the Land Use variable, 25.3% of the area is assigned to the very low category and 65.01% to the medium category. Lastly, for the Economic Activities variable the majority of the area (56.4%) belongs to the medium category.

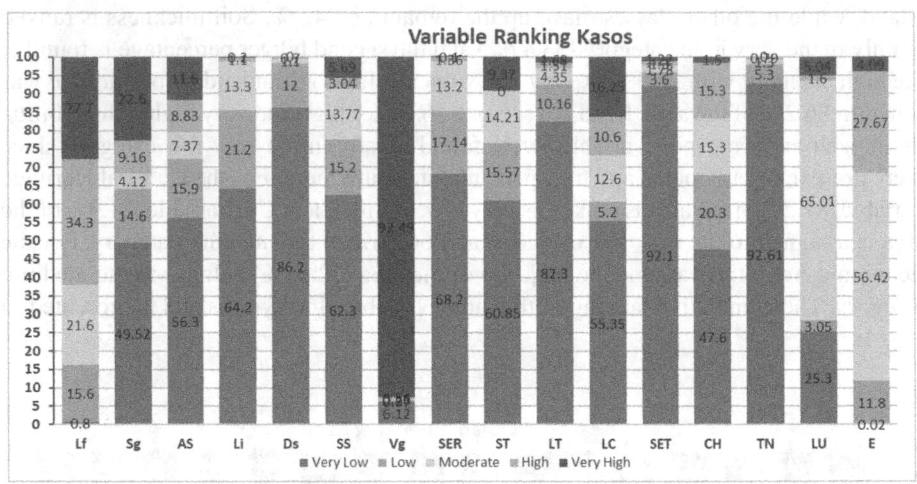

Fig. 5. Variable ranking for Kasos.

For Chalki, the variable ranking is shown in Fig. 6, with the corresponding values for the Landforms alsost equally distributed in the Low, Moderate, High and Very High categories, while for the slope variable, the majority of the area of the island is in the Very low category. Lithology variable for Chalki is mostly at the Very low and low ranks (60%). Chalki's Structural stability variable was found to be more tha 80% as very high and high vulnerability. The vegetation coverage variable for the inland part of the island was found to be very low and low vulnerability. Soil Erosivity has a very high ranking in most of the island, while Soil thickness is ranked mainly in the very low category. A very low vulnerability for Landslide type variable was found in 85.3% of the area. Land cover has a 60% of the area in the very low and low categories. Cultural Heritage variable exhibits low and very low vulnerability with more than 60%. For the Land Use variable, 29.04% of the area is assigned to the very low category and 54.2% to the medium category. Lastly, for the Economic Activities variable the majority of the area (33.36%) belongs to the medium category, and 25.49%of the area as high and very high since it is occupied by small-scale tourist activities.

Lastly, the analogous percentage calculations of the variable rankings for the island of Kastellorizo are cumulativelly presented in Fig. 7. More in depth, it is found that the Landforms variable is associated more than 50% in the Very low and Low categories,and the slope variable ranks more tha 60% of the area as Very low and Low vulnerability., Lithology is calculated at 50% in the High and Very High vulnerability scales. Structural stability variable is presented more than 70% in the very low and low vulnerability categories. The vegetation coverage variable for the inland part of the island was found

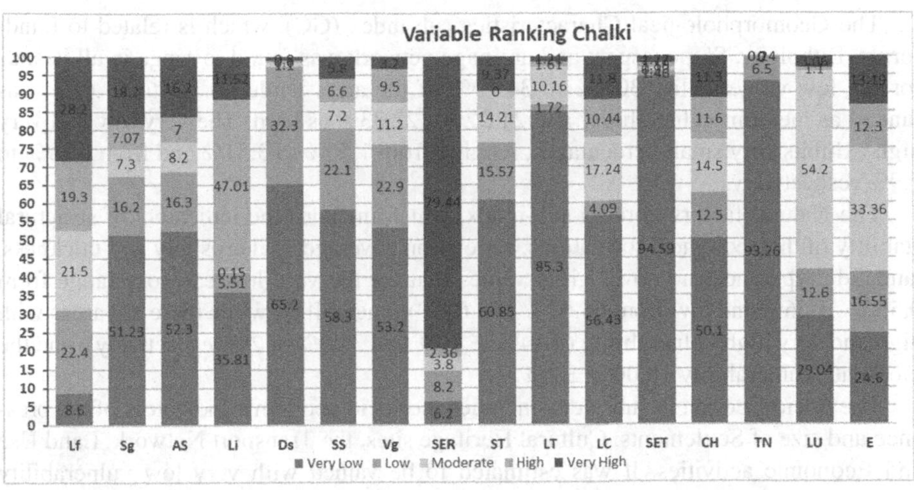

Fig. 6. Variable ranking for Chalki.

to be very high (92.49%). Soil Erosivity has a very high ranking in 91.76% of the island while Soil thickness is ranked mainly in the very low category (60.85%). A very low vulnerability for Landslide type variable was found in 85.3% of the area. Land cover has a more than 65% in the high and very high vulnerability categories. For the Cultural Heritage variable, 82.1% of the area is ranked as very high and the 11.09% as very low. For the Land Use variable, 28.1% of the area is assigned to the very low category, and 62.3% to the medium category. Lastly, for the Economic Activities variable the 22.3% belongs to the medium category, and 31.6% of the area as high and very high.

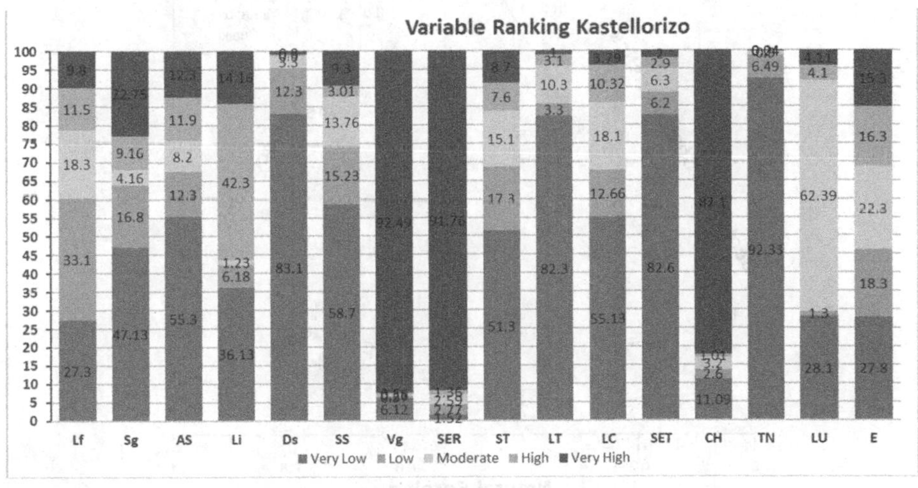

Fig. 7. Variable ranking for Kastellorizo.

The Geomorphological Characteristics sub-index (GC), which is related to Landforms, Lithology, Slope, aspect and drainage network was found to range in all islands for the low vulnerability 30.2% to 34.19% of the area, while 40.1% to 41.62% was ranked as medium vulnerability and 21.22% - 22.33% as high. The very low and very high exhibits very small percentages, ranging from 1.56% to 3.51% and from 0.29% to 1.9% respectively.

The Natural factors Forcing sub-index, which includes the indicators of structural stability of the geological formations, vegetation coverage, soil erosivity and thickness, landslide type and land cover gives values that for the very low category range from 0.55% - 1.66% and low from 65.62% - 69.63% vulnerability, while there are areas with high and very high vulnerability (8.14% ± 10% and 3.63% ± 2% respectively), and the moderate vulnerability 18.06% ± 5%.

The Socio-Economic sub-index includes the socio-economic indicators of the presence and size of Settlements, Cultural Heritage sites, the Transport Network, Land Use and Economic activities. It was estimated to be valued with very low vulnerability 37.53% ± 5% and low vulnerability at 59.08% ± 12%, while the medium 3.10% ± 1%, high 1.2% ± 0.3% and very high vulnerability around 0.5%

Moreover, for the inland area, a ternary diagram was used in order to present the relative influence of each of the three sub-indices in each area of interest (Fig. 8). The diagram shows a general tendency for the natural forcing and geological characteristics sub-indices to dominate the overall influence, with the socio-economic index having the least influence. The diagram also demonstrates that the overall index via its sub-indices does differentiate between areas. If all of the sites were clustered around the centre of

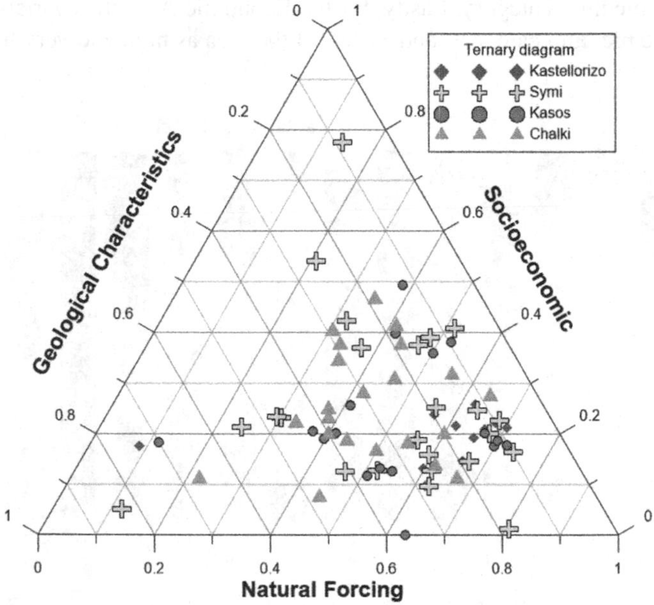

Fig. 8. Ternary diagram presenting the influence of each sub index to the overall score for the areas of interest.

the triangle then this would suggest that all areas studied were mostly impacted by the geological characteristics and the natural forcing variable and less impacted by their socio-economic attributes.

5 Conclusions

Vulnerability is a human value judgement, so ultimately the perceived estimates for coastal areas will strongly influence management decisions. Consequently, the socio-economic component of coastal vulnerability is at the very heart of management practice. The inclusion of socio-economic variables in vulnerability indices is extremely important as the inclusion of socio-economic variables in vulnerability assessment studies may prove to be a useful tool for making management decisions more focused on society's actual needs. The preliminery results of the analysis indicate that, for all four islands considered, the sites under investigation are strongly influenced by the natural forcing factorswith slope to be a high-risk factor. The analysis indicated that the main factors that influence a specific area can be identified. The consideration/implication of socio-economic variables to existing vulnerability indices that were based initially only on natural processes is of great importance, although the accurate quantification of most socio-economic variables remains a serious challenge. Moreover, the inclusion of socio-economic variables in vulnerability analysis can bring to a focus the actual society's needs.

Acknowledgement. «Acknowledgment: This research has been co-financed by the European Regional Development Fund of the European Union and Greek national funds through the Operational Program Competitiveness, Entrepreneurship and Innovation, under the call RESEARCH – CREATE – INNOVATE (project code:T2EDK-01278)».

References

Adger, W.N.: Vulnerability. Glob. Environ. Chang. **16**(3), 268–281 (2006). https://doi.org/10.1016/j.gloenvcha.2006.02.006

Alexander, D.: Natural Disasters, p. 656. Routledge, London (1993)

Alexandrakis, G., De Vita, S., Di Vito, M.: Preliminary risk assessment at Ustica based on indicators of natural and human processes Ann. Geophys. **61** (2019https://doi.org/10.4401/ag-7765

Boruff, B.J., Emrich, C., Cutter, S.L.: Erosion hazard vulnerability of US coastal counties. J. Coast. Res. **21**, 932–942 (2005)

Canuti, P., Casagli, N., Catani, F., Fanti, R.: Hydrogeological hazard and risk in archaeological sites: some case studies in Italy. J. Cult. Herit. **1**(2), 117–125 (2000)

Carter, B.: Retreat to the future. Nat. Trust Mag. **70**, 28–29 (1993)

Cooper, J.A.G., McLaughlin, S.: Contemporary multidisciplinary approaches to coastal classification and environmental risk analysis. J. Coastal Res. **14**(2), 512–524 (1998)

Gornitz, V., Daniels, R.C., White, T.W., Birdwell, K.R.: The development of a coastal risk assessment database: vulnerability to sea-level rise in the U.S. southeast. DE-AC05–84OR21400, U.S. Government Report, Oak Ridge National Laboratory, Tennessee (1993)

International Panel of Climate Change: Climate Change: The Third Assessment Report of the IPCC, Cambridge University Press, UK (2001)

International Panel of Climate Change: Managing the risks of extreme events and disasters to Advance climate change adaptation. A special report of working groups I and II of the intergovernmental Panel on climate change. In: Field, C.B., et al. (Eds.), Cambridge University Press, Cambridge, UK, and New York, NY, USA, p. 582 (2012)

Kaiser, G.: Risk and Vulnerability analysis to coastal hazards – an approach to integrated assessment, Christian-Albrechts-Universitat zu Keil, PhD Thesis (unpublished), vol. 253 (2006)

Marzocchi, W., Mastellone, M.L., Di Ruocco, A., Novelli, P., Romeo, E., Gasparini, P.: Principles of multi-risk assessment. Interaction amongst natural and man-induced risks. European Communities, 330 Brussels (2006)

McLaughlin, S., McKenna, J., Cooper, J.A.G.: Socio-economic data in coastal vulnerability indices: constraints and opportunities. J. Coast. Res. **1**(36), 487–497 (2002)

Mercuri, A.M., Sadori, L.: Mediterranean Culture and Climatic Change: Past Patterns and Future Trends. In: Goffredo, S., Dubinsky, Z. (eds.) The Mediterranean Sea, pp. 507–527. Springer, Dordrecht (2014). https://doi.org/10.1007/978-94-007-6704-1_30

Nicholls, R.J., Small, C.: Improved estimates of coastal population and exposure to hazards released. EOS Trans. **83**(2), 301–305 (2002)

O'Brien, G., O'Keefe, P., Rose, J., Wisner, B.: Climate change and disaster management. Disasters **30**, 64–80 (2009)

Patt, A.G., Dazé, A., Suarez, P.: Gender and climate change vulnerability: What's the problem, what's the solution? The Distributional Effects of Climate Change: Social and Economic Implications, eds RuthM, IbarraránM (Edward Elgar, Cheltenham, UK), pp 82–102 (2009)

Preston, B.L., et al.: Mapping Climate Change Vulnerability in the Sydney Coastal Council Group. Prepared for the Sydney Coastal Council Group and the Australian Government Department of Climate Change (2008)

PROVIA, 2013: PROVIA Guidance on Assessing Vulnerability, Impacts and Adaptation to Climate Change. Consultation document, United Nations Environment Programme, Nairobi, Kenya, p. 198 (2013)

Scheidegger, A.E.: Hazards: singularities in geomorphic systems. Geomorphology **10**, 19–25 (1994)

Slaymaker, O.: Introduction. In: Slaymaker, O. (ed.) Geomorphic Hazards, pp. 1–7. Wiley, Chichester (1996)

United Nations International Strategy for Disaster Reduction; Terminology: Basic Terms of Disaster Risk Reduction (2009). http://www.unisdr.org/we/inform/terminology. Accessed 19 Mar 2014

ICT and Semantic BIM Technologies for the Advanced Documentation and Condition Assessment of Cultural Heritage Sites

Marco Medici[1(✉)], Roberto Di Giulio[1], and Beatrice Turillazzi[2]

[1] Department of Architecture, University of Ferrara, Via Ghiara 36, Ferrara, Italy
{marco.medici,roberto.digiulio}@unife.it

[2] Department of Architecture, University of Bologna, Viale del Risorgimento 2, Bologna, Italy
beatrice.turillazzi@unibo.it

Abstract. The paper reports the results of a research project funded by the University of Ferrara (FIR 2020 Program) and aimed at developing and testing some achievements of the project "INCEPTION - Inclusive Cultural Heritage in Europe through 3D semantic modelling" (H2020 EC funded research project).

The tests carried out on the INCEPTION platform functions, outcome of the research project and subsequently implemented by the homonymous spin-off, have shown the potential of semantic-BIM technologies in the field of Cultural Heritage sites maintenance.

Novel and innovative applications grounded on the platform core functions include: tools and protocols for the management of inspection procedures supported by information and instructions provided by the platform; assessment, based on inspection data, of the condition of the site and/or individual parts based on a "condition scale"; access to constantly updated condition information, shown on the virtual model as linked to the objects of the BIM model; remote analysis and evaluation of site condition data through interaction, in a virtual environment, with 3D model "objects".

The paper presents the main elements of the ongoing experimentation: the matrixes for the automatic analysis of the detected data and the assignment of the "condition score", the structure of the ontology with which the semantic tools of the platform operate, the workflows for data loading phases such as: in situ inspections, remote monitoring, planning of interventions.

The tests on features and procedures reported in the paper have been carried out on the 3D model of the church of Santa Maria delle Vergini in Macerata, as part of a wider collaboration between the INCEPTION spin-off company and the ICCD (Istituto Centrale per il Catalogo e la Documentazione) of the MIC (Ministero della Cultura).

Keywords: Cultural Heritage · Conservative Maintenance · Condition Assessment · H-BIM

A. Moropoulou et al. (Eds.): TMM_CH 2023, CCIS 1889, pp. 321–334, 2023.
https://doi.org/10.1007/978-3-031-42300-0_28

1 Introduction

The digitisation of cultural heritage is accelerating rapidly due to recognising its strategic role as a new lever for value creation and as a tool for documentation and preservation. The effort is supported by the advancement of applied research and the development of ICTs and also involves the field of conservative maintenance of historical sites and buildings, offering unique opportunities (Di Giulio et al., 2020).

Preventive planned maintenance of artefacts is a well-established area of research and practice which finds in periodic inspections one of the main methods for identifying the state of conservation and promptly evaluating the major risks and vulnerabilities; direct cyclical controls also provide regular monitoring of the evolution of degradation phenomena thus aligning the maintenance plan itself.

The data acquired during the site inspections and through the - ever more frequent - digital sensor and monitoring systems installed, are quantitatively and qualitatively consistent and require effective and reliable repositories and databases capable of managing and updating heterogeneous information.

Planning the maintenance of cultural heritage has to tackle an additional challenge beyond the identification and monitoring of the condition of conservation: it has to be capable of recognising the historical and architectural value of the asset and assessing its physical consistency to knowledgeably indicate the most appropriate procedures for conservative intervention (Simeone et al., 2019).

In the field of modelling, management and interoperability of 3D digital models related to Cultural Heritage, the H2020 European research project INCEPTION (Inclusive Cultural Heritage in Europe through 3D semantic modelling), ended in 2019, achieved several innovative results which have been further exploited and developed by the start-up INCEPTION Srl, a University of Ferrara spin-off.

The core of the project is the Building Information Modelling (BIM) - and the conversion of data acquired through 3D Laser Scanner survey systems as its first implementation - whereas the main objective is the opportunity for other applications to interact with the generated three-dimensional models, hence necessarily interoperable. In these models, each 3D digital element is enriched with metadata, i.e. massive information describing features, properties, up to historical and documental data, of the corresponding real building element. The system is enabled by a semantic platform not intended to merely archive, but to search, interact, enrich, process and acquire the hosted models.

The development of novel functionalities of the INCEPTION platform, therefore, allows the creation of applications fully devoted to improving the tools and procedures for condition assessment and maintenance planning of historic buildings and sites (Di Giulio et al., 2019).

2 Toward the Use of ICT Tools in Condition-Based Maintenance

The tests carried out on the INCEPTION platform functions, had already shown the potential of semantic H-BIM technologies in the field of Cultural Heritage sites maintenance.

However, the tests were carried out using software for scheduling inspection and maintenance activities for buildings and civil infrastructures. It was then clear the limit resulting from the application of models and procedures that did not take into account the specificity of maintenance strategies for cultural heritage sites and buildings.

Working in the field of historical building it is necessary to take into account the specific data of each individual object on which you operate. Inspections and condition assessments of materials and components cannot be done "at random". Spot checks are required and, not infrequently, the checks must also be carried out on similar components or on different points of the same element. In a historical building there are often components and materials of different periods on which the degradation process, while acting on similar materials, can give rise to different defects and pathological phenomena.

On the other hand, there are very few scheduled maintenance interventions, carried out at fixed time intervals and based on standard protocols and procedures. They are configured, in most cases, as interventions of conservative maintenance if not as real restoration work.

The decision to launch this type of interventions, the deadlines for their execution, the specifications on products and technologies to be used, and the required specializations and skills of the workers who will have to carry them out, depend on decisions that must be based on the results of inspections or on the data from the monitoring systems.

It is therefore necessary to proceed according to "Condition Based Maintenance" models in which the evaluation of conditions is not a plan of routine checks aimed at optimizing the frequency of maintenance interventions, but a thorough campaign of inspections, monitoring and diagnostic investigations.

On the basis of these principles, the current research is developing a procedure to carry out controls and a tool to read and interpret the collected data enabling the operators involved in the management of the building to.

- operate remotely by interacting with the 3D H-BIM model (i.e. the digital twin) of the building;
- carry out the control activities in situ guided by information and data provided by the platform that hosts the 3D H-BIM model;
- upload to the platform, which then provides the continuous updating of the 3D H-BIM model, the data collected and have a continuously updated picture of the conditions of each part of the building.

3 Objectives and Methodology

The research objectives consist in extending the functionalities of the INCEPTION platform with tools for the management of inspections, monitoring and planning of "conservative maintenance" in cultural heritage sites and buildings.

These tools consist of a protocol for inspecting and assessing the condition of building components or parts, and applications to perform guided inspections, transfer the collected data to the platform, and later access that data by interacting directly with the building's digital twin.

The inspection and subsequent monitoring protocol is carried out in four steps:

1. analysis of the building decay supported by the data provided by the INCEPTION platform through which the inspector, interacting with the 3D H-BIM model (the building's digital twin) through a device connected to the platform, accesses all the technical information necessary to identify, interpret and report the defects of the component under examination;
2. the condition assessment of the component or elements it is made of, through the condition assessment methodology of the Dutch Standard NEN 2767 "Condition assessment built environment - Part 1: Methodology" based on a measurement expressed as a condition score on a scale from 1 (component "as new") to 6 (component in worst condition);
3. the uploading of the condition score and other possible remarks, photos, or technical documents on the platform that provides to associate all data, in form of metadata, to the component of the BIM model;
4. the remote monitoring of the building conditions through the inspection results analysis, the display of the decay levels reproduced on the 3D H-BIM model, and then the analysis of the defects found in every single component for the evaluation of when and how to perform the conservative maintenance interventions.

The tools required in the various steps of the procedure just described consist of a set of applications that integrate with those already present on the platform, in particular with those that allow to interact with the BIM model and to access data on the conditions of the building components through the semantic search tools. Items created and added to the INCEPTION toolbox include in particular:

- an application that allows to easily and quickly integrate the H-BIM model with the tools necessary to manage, for each single object, the metadata corresponding to the decay conditions;
- an automatic condition assessment system based on an application that calculates and assigns condition scores on the basis of the defects found by the inspector simplifying his task (he is therefore not required to have high levels of specialization): the inspection is limited to the identification of defects, guided by information and images provided by the platform, and to the input on the platform of data on their extension and intensity;
- the routines necessary to transfer data, in IFC format, from the H-BIM model to the platform and from the platform to the model (to keep it updated);
- a dashboard that allows to monitor and analyze data on the conditions of every single part of the building and and to interact in order to optimize the maintenance strategies.

Procedures and tools, detailed in the following paragraphs, has been tested on a portion of the H-BIM model of the church of Santa Maria delle Vergini, in Macerata (Italy), created by INCEPTION spin-off researchers in collaboration with the Istituto Centrale per il Catalogo e la Documentazione (ICCD) of the Ministry of Culture.

4 The Demontration Case

The church of Santa Maria delle Vergini is a majestic building with a Greek cross plan, surmounted by an octagonal dome erected on a drum, supported by four imposing pillars with a quadrangular base; the arms of the Greek cross end in semicircular apses, each with two cross-vaulted "scarsella" chapels (Canullo, 2016). A first plant of the church dates back to 1355 but the consecration of the current configuration of building took place in 1577. The facade, developed on two horizontal registers, does not correspond to the interior space, because it was later completed. The interior of the church has 11 chapels decorated between the late sixteenth and late eighteenth centuries. The church has also undergone the action of various seismic events: among the most recent and important we remember those of 1997 and 2016, with particular injuries to the drum supporting the dome, still under restoration (Fig. 1).

Fig. 1. Aerial photo of the church of Santa Maria delle Vergini in Macerata before the 2016 earthquake (on the left) and the dome damaged in 2016 (on the right).

For the survey of the church, the 3D acquisition has been developed by integrating different survey technologies: terrestrial laser scanner (Faro x330HDR), terrestrial and aerial photogrammetry (Dji Mavic Pro + Agisoft Metashape) and topographic survey by total station (Leica TCR1202+R100). Once the overall registration of the point cloud model has been done, data were imported in the Autodesk Recap software towards the creation of an H-BIM model. Thus, in the modeling procedure, we opted for the use of Autodesk Revit. Since the purpose of the modeling is the condition assessment, the most appropriate LOD according with the Italian regulation UNI 1137:2017 would have been LOD G. However, even if such LOD has been described, there are no technical specifications to develop it consistently. Consequently, it was decided to operate a modeling where the LOG (Level of geometric detail) and the LOI (Level of Information) would allow to accommodate the information of required for the condition assessment procedure later described. As far as possible, we proceeded to model using system families or local families within Revit, but considering the possibility of using free-form modeling elements with external tools when necessary. The model thus created was then exported in open IFC format, version 2 × 3, in order to be uploaded on the INCEPTION platform (Bonsma et al., 2016) for making use of the SOLID-ICE tool. In order to make the uploading procedure easier and the web navigation smoother, we applied preliminary geometric decimations to the IFC export, as well as optimizations and compressions of the standard file to make it as light as possible (Fig. 2).

Fig. 2. Scan-to-BIM procedure applied to Santa Maria delle Vergini. Visualization of the point cloud on the top and the resulting BIM model on the bottom.

SOLID-ICE is one of the tools grounded on the Inception Core Engine (ICE), which is based on a semantic approach. This consists in transforming all the geometries of a specific BIM model into semantic triples that connect one element to another using specific predicates, defined in a dedicated semantic ontology. All these triples are stored in a semantic triple store, accessed via HTTP through a dedicated Apache Fuseki SPARQL server. SOLID-ICE client is a web application provided with a 3D WebGL viewer giving access to all the functionalities. The platform allows users to enrich their models with new semantic metadata. Indeed, the web client allows you to enrich the models with new data (e.g., a date, a value, some textual remarks, see Fig. 3) as well as attachments (e.g., pictures, thermographic images, 3D models of specific details, videos, etc.), all of which are related to the CH site or a specific geometrical element (Bonsma et al., 2018).

The generality of this approach allows you to represent both tangible and non-tangible information. To give an example, a single element (e.g.: a brick) can be linked to a wall, as well as to one or more documents, or to some metadata, or even to external information on the web, using nothing but semantic triples (Iadanza et al., 2019). In Fig. 4 is shown how the building can be enriched with documents that can be either linked to the whole 3D model or to one or more specific parts.

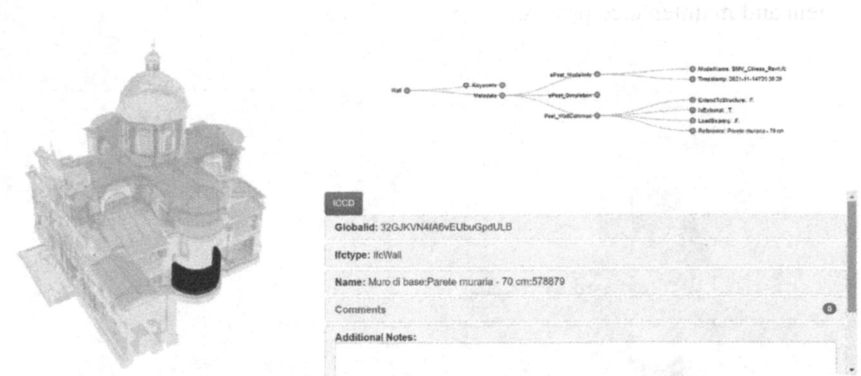

Fig. 3. Every element of the building can be used to perform a live SPARQL query that returns all the details for that element, according to the HBIM ontology. Each value can be updated via web, thanks to the SPARQL 1.1 Update functionalities.

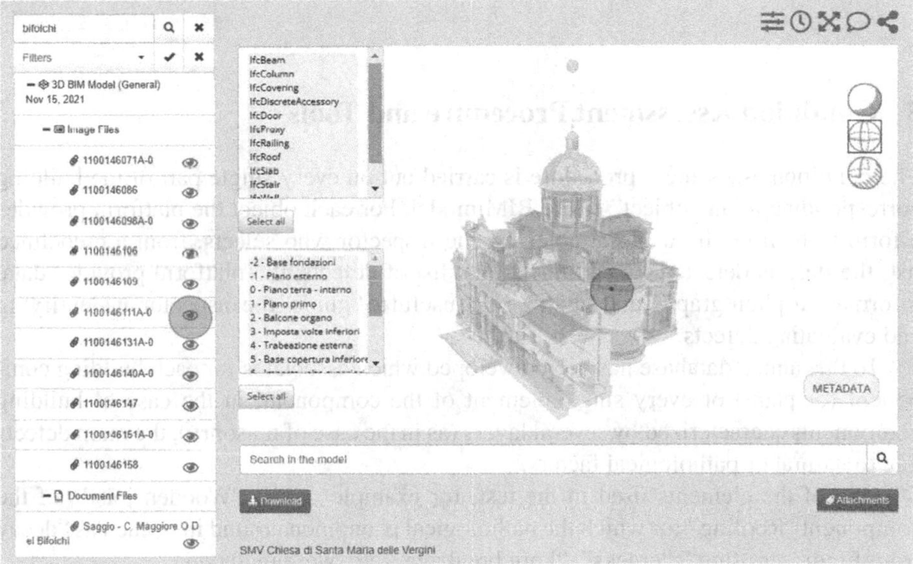

Fig. 4. The building can be enriched with documents that can be either linked to the whole 3D model or to one or more specific parts.

SOLID-ICE can be used advantageously for "Condition Based Maintenance", both for off-site and for on-site operations, allowing users to interact directly with the 3D model, also leveraging collaboration tools. As shown in Fig. 5, users can start a thread about one or more specific elements (as well as about the whole building). This functionality can be exploited for planning tasks and assigning roles in a collaborative way.

Media can be attached to elements, as well, to document the various steps of the condition assessment and maintenance process.

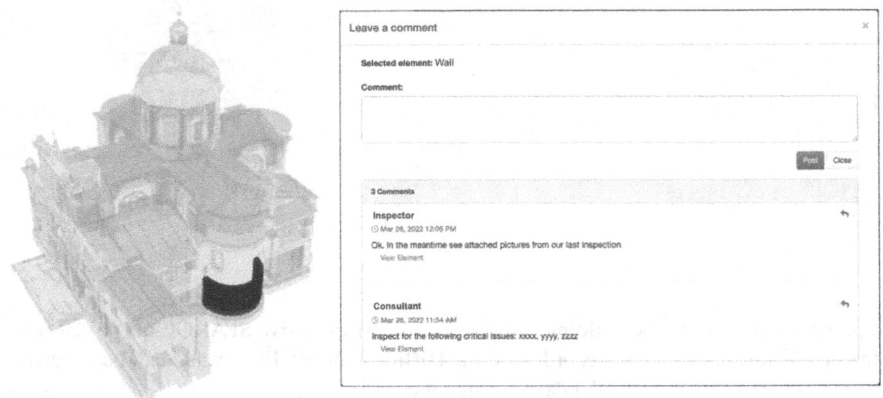

Fig. 5. Collaboration tools: users can start a thread about one or more specific elements

5 Condition Assessment Procedure and Tools

The condition assessment procedure is carried out on every single part of the building corresponding to an "object" of the BIM model. For each object the platform provides a form to be filled in, using a tablet, by the inspector who selects, from a predefined list, the defects detected. In addition to the list of defects, the platform provides data, information, photographs, and anything else useful to "guide" the inspector in identifying and evaluating defects.

To this aim, a database has been developed which associates for each building component (or plant) or every single element of the component, in the case of building components characterized by several layers (as in the case of masonry), the main defects due to natural or pathological factors.

One of the elements used in the test, for example, is the "Wooden joist", of the component "Roofing" for which the pathological phenomena found in it, such as "decay from fungi", "rotting", "cracks", "knot breakage", etc. were included.

The database, initially containing standard records relating to the standard building elements, is continuously updated with the addition of new technical elements and the corresponding lists of defects (themselves subject to additions and updates) each time the system is applied to a new building.

The above-mentioned database can be turned into a set of semantic triples, according to a specific semantic ontology, in keeping with the approach that underpins SOLID-ICE. There are numerous benefits of switching to a semantic solution. For example, using standard and open protocols makes the system intrinsically interoperable. It is worth recalling, here, that defining a dedicated ontology is much more than just defining a taxonomy (i.e., a tree of categories and subcategories). A semantic ontology, indeed, allows you to define properties and inference rules that link one category to another. Hence, the unique chance of enabling a real semantic reasoner, or "reasoning engine", based on these rules, able to extract new knowledge.

Based on the procedures indicated in the Dutch standard NEN 2767-1, each defect has been assigned a priori the characteristic of "Importance" (generally not subject to interpretation), while the evaluation of the "Intensity" and the "Extent" is left (but guided by a range of description or values) to the evaluation and the judgment of the inspector, as synthetically specified in the following tables.

The following Tables (1 – 2 - 3) are based on the Dutch standard and define criteria and advice to be used by the inspector to identify and evaluate the defects (Straub, 2003). Inspector is provided with specific information (detailed descriptions and explanations, photos, pictures, technical reports, etc.) available in the BIM model as metadata linked to each building element.

Table 1. Framework for defects (Source: NEN 2006)

Importance	Explanation
Critical	Critical defects harm directly the function of a building components
Serious	Serious defects mean degradation of a building component without directly harming its function
Minor	Minor defects do not harm the function of a building component

Table 2. Classification of Intensity of defects (Source: NEN 2006)

Intensity class	Name	Description
Intensity 1	Low	The defect is hardly visible
Intensity 2	Middle	The defect is progressing
Intensity 3	High	The defect cannot progress any further

Table 3. Classification of Extent of defects (Source NEN 2006)

Extent class	Percentage	Description
Extent 1	<2	The defect occurs incidentally
Extent 2	2–10	The defect occurs locally
Extent 3	10–30	The defect occurs regularly
Extent 4	30–70	The defect occurs frequently
Extent 5	>70	The defect occurs generally

"Extent" and "Intensity" of the defects lead to the condition assessment (from excellent to worst) using 3 different matrices corresponding to the 3 levels of "Importance" as shown below (Tables 4 and 5).

Table 4. Six-point scale Dutch standard for condition assessment of buildings - Source: NEN (2006)

Condition rating	1	2	3	4	5	6
General condition description	Excellent	Good	Fair	Poor	Bad	Very bad

Table 5. Matrix of resulting condition ratings for critical, serious and minor defects (Source: NEN 2006)

Critical	**Extent 1**	**Extent 2**	**Extent 3**	**Extent 4**	**Extent 5**
Intensity 1	1	1	2	3	4
Intensity 2	1	2	3	4	5
Intensity 3	2	3	4	5	6

Serious	**Extent 1**	**Extent 2**	**Extent 3**	**Extent 4**	**Extent 5**
Intensity 1	1	1	1	2	3
Intensity 2	1	1	2	3	4
Intensity 3	1	2	3	4	5

Minor	**Extent 1**	**Extent 2**	**Extent 3**	**Extent 4**	**Extent 5**
Intensity 1	1	1	1	1	2
Intensity 2	1	1	1	2	3
Intensity 3	1	1	2	3	4

In general, a component is made up of several building elements where different decay conditions can be assessed. The system assigns to the component as a whole the condition score corresponding to that of the element in the worst condition.

The example shown in Table 6 shows a condition assessment on wooden joists: the inspector, using the tables and matrices provided by the system, enters the defects detected and the data corresponding to "Intensity", and "Extent" ("Importance" is automatically assigned). Then the system calculates, interpolating the values, the resulting condition for each defect and the overall condition of the joists.

Inspections will concern, at least in the first phase, mainly the external visible surfaces of the elements. The system, therefore, assigns, to the components where the inspection concerns two different sides or surfaces (often different as in walls, floors, and roofs), two values: one corresponding to the condition of "surface A" (inside/intrados) and one to that of the "surface B" condition (external/extrados), corresponding to two different condition assessment forms. Once the forms are completed, the resulting scores are uploaded into the BIM model.

Table 6. Wooden joists condition assessment

Element	Defects	Importance	Intensity	Extent	Condition
Wooden joists	Alteration of surface finish	Minor	Middle	<2%	1
	Knots breakage	Serious	Low	>70%	3
	Cracks	Critical	High	10%-30%	4
Total					**4**

The demo case of the church of Santa Maria delle Vergini was developed, as previously stated, using Autodesk Revit (version 2022) and the demonstration was focused on four families of objects/components: walls, floors, roofs and columns. New specific parameters had to be created for individual element identification and subsequent condition assessment. The shared parameters created are:

- ID Revit, containing the identification code of the single element generated by the software
- Man_A_1-ID, containing the "surface identification code" A of the specific element
- Man_A_2-Condition, containing the "A surface condition" of the specific element
- Man_A_3-Priority, containing the level of priority for action based on the detected conditions
- Man_B_1/B_2/B_3 as the previous ones referred to B surface
- The "surface identification code" consists of a string that considers the following elements:
- "Revit ID"_"Revit Family"_" Basic Level/Constraint"_"Maintenance Surface (A or B)"

The use of such a string is due to the possibility, even without the visual contribution of the 3D model, to understand, thanks to the analysis of the Revit family (wall, floor, etc.) and to the basic level/constraint of the element itself, if the element actually inspected corresponds to the provide condition assessment form.

The introduction of the "priority" parameter makes it possible to diversify the planning of interventions on the basis of needs that may go beyond the specific conditions of the elements.

At the end of the inspection, the data on the conditions detected in the various components (i.e. the scores assigned by the system according to the defects found), are uploaded to the 3D model which, with a specific display option, gives each component a colouration corresponding to its condition.

Figure 6 shows the portion of the model used for the test in which the various components, once updated the metadata related to their condition, automatically take on a colouration that goes from light green (corresponding to condition 1) to bright red (corresponding to condition 6).

The system, that is still under development for what concern the user interface, is equipped with a dashboard of tools to interact with the model in two main ways:

- data acquisition (inspection reports, details and images of detected defects, data transmitted in real-time by sensors, etc.);
- data elaboration (entry or modification of intervention priority coefficients, entry of diagnostic data on defects and interventions to be carried out, data entry for the activation of maintenance interventions, etc.).

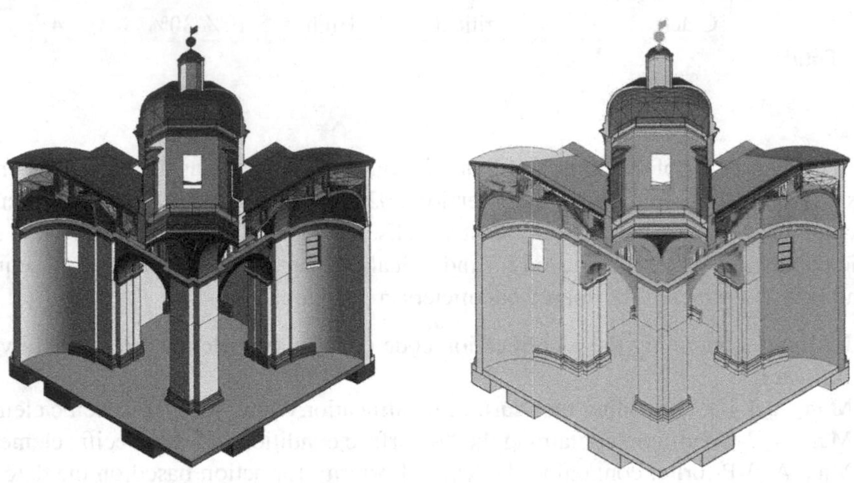

Fig. 6. Display of component conditions based on the 6 conditions scale after the inspection

The workflow and the steps of the inspection, the data upload procedure and the uploading/updating process (model to platform and vice versa) is shown in the following diagram (Fig. 7).

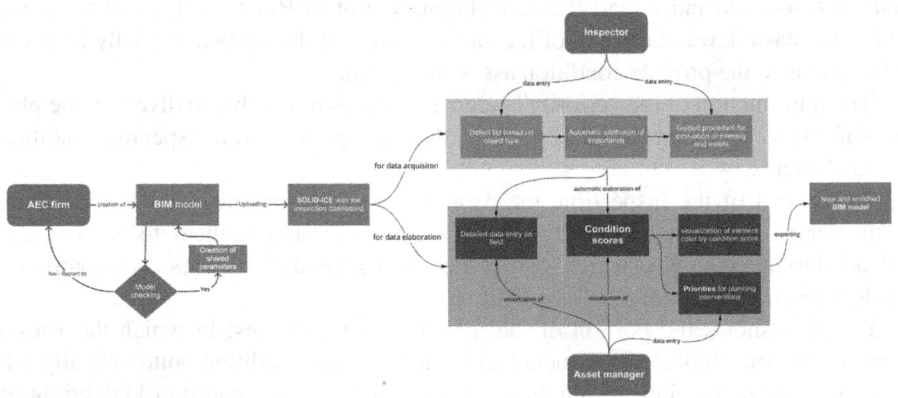

Fig. 7. Flowchart of the condition assessment process made possible by the use of SOLID-ICE equipped with the dedicated dashboard.

6 Conclusions and Further Developments

The positive results of the tests made on the case study of the church of Santa Maria delle Vergini, have confirmed the advantages of a procedure of condition assessment and remote evaluation of the data collected supported by the BIM model of the building and the tools developed on the INCEPTION platform.

However, it was remarked that:

- the procedure requires thorough inspections;
- only partial recourse can be made to "random" surveys;
- the procedures to be activated in the event of detected deterioration cannot be based on standard protocols.

The level of detail and the number of elements to be inspected shall be defined during the preparation of the BIM model. In this phase, the level of breakdown of the technical elements and of any single parts of the same technical element will have to be evaluated on the basis of the specific characteristics of the building (in the case, for example, of an intrados of a wooden floor with decorated joists, the single joists will have to be separated and the condition of each of them will have to be detected).

As for the diagnosis and planning phase of the maintenance or restoration intervention, the system can only provide some first recommendations based on the technical data that the BIM model transfers to the INCEPTION platform. These recommendations may be more detailed only after a first period of application of the system against data and technical reports on the interventions already performed. Also, in this case, the tools offered by the BIM model and the INCEPTION platform can help to optimize time and costs by operating as an effective Decision Support System.

The system developed in this first phase of research has focused on the optimization, both in terms of time and costs, of the condition assessment phase and, in particular:

- simplifying inspection procedures by means of tools to support their execution;
- calculation of condition scores by automatic interpolation of the values corresponding to the detected defects;
- transfer of inspection results into a digital twin providing a continuously updated overview of the building's condition and detailed data on the condition of individual elements.

The next steps of INCEPTION platform SOLID-ICE module development program will focus on dashboard improvements, in particular:

- completing the development of user interfaces for data acquisition activities: guided identification of defects, data and information consultation to define their intensity and extension, condition scores insertion;
- development of user interfaces for data elaboration activities: visualization of the model, remote reading of condition data, insertion of priority coefficients of interventions and specifications of interventions to be carried out;
- development of tools for scheduling maintenance work.

Funding. This research has been funded by the University of Ferrara under the programme FIR (Fondo per l'Incentivazione alla Ricerca) 2020.

References

Bonsma, P., et al.: Handling huge and complex 3D geometries with semantic web technology. In: IOP Conference Series: Materials Science and Engineering, vol. 364, no. 1, p. 012041. IOP Publishing (2018)

Bonsma, P., et al.: Inception standard for heritage BIM models. In: Ioannides, M., et al. (eds.) Digital Heritage. Progress in Cultural Heritage: Documentation, Preservation, and Protection. EuroMed 2016. LNCS, vol. 10058, pp. 590–599. Springer, Cham (2016). https://doi.org/10.1007/978-3-319-48496-9_4

Canullo, G.: I Bifolchi e l'eucarestia. La cappella maggiore della chiesa di Santa Maria delle Vergini a Macerata. In: Il capitale culturale, Studies on the value of cultural heritage. XIII (2016), pp. 37–78. EUM - Department of education, cultural heritage, and tourism. University of Macerata (2016)

Di Giulio, R., Maietti, F., Piaia, E.: Advanced 3D survey and modelling for enhancement and conservation of cultural heritage: the inception project. In: Moropoulou, A., Korres, M., Georgopoulos, A., Spyrakos, C., Mouzakis, C. (eds.) Transdisciplinary Multispectral Modeling and Cooperation for the Preservation of Cultural Heritage. TMM_CH 2018. CCIS, vol. 962, pp. 325–335. Springer, Cham (2019). https://doi.org/10.1007/978-3-030-12960-6_21

Di Giulio, R., Turillazzi, B., van Delft, A., Schippers-Trifan, O.: Innovative management tools of quality performance over time for historical and monumental buildings. TECHNE (20), 265–274 (2020)

Iadanza, E., et al.: Semantic web technologies meet BIM for accessing and understanding cultural heritage. Int. Arch. Photogramm. Remote Sens. Spat. Inf. Sci. **42**, 381–388 (2019)

EUROPEAN COMMISSION (2021). Commission Recommendation of 10.11.2021 on a common European data space for cultural heritage

Simeone, D., Cursi, S., Acierno, M.: BIM semantic-enrichment for built heritage representation. Autom. Constr. (97), 122–137 (2019)

Straub, A.: Using a condition-dependent approach to maintenance to control costs and performances. J. Facil. Manag. **1**(4), 380–395 (2003)

Enhancing Heritage Management for Sustainable Development in Insular Areas Through Digital Documentation: The Case Study of the Historic Center of the Megisti Island (Kastellorizo)

Aspasia E. Fafouti[1], Anastasia Vythoulka[1], Ekaterini T. Delegou[1], Agapitos Xanthis[2], Antonios Giannikouris[2], Nikolaos Kampanis[3], Georgios Alexandrakis[3], and Antonia Moropoulou[1,4](✉)

[1] Lab of Materials Science and Engineering, National Technical University of Athens, Athens, Greece
amoropul@central.ntua.gr

[2] Technical Chamber of Greece-Department of Dodecanese, Athens, Greece

[3] Institute of Applied and Computational Mathematics Foundation for Research and Technology - Hellas (ITE), Athens, Greece

[4] Member of the Executive Committee – Technical Chamber of Greece, Athens, Greece

Abstract. Protection and promotion of cultural and environmental heritage could be a key factor of an area's integrated sustainable development plan, while presenting social, environmental, cultural, and economic benefits. In remote areas, sustainable development usually depends on external economies, such as tourism. This study focuses on the Megisti Complex and the historic center of Kastellorizo, aiming to propose an applicable, innovative approach for their sustainable development. Through analysis and documentation of the cultural and environmental assets of the area, a data base of important information was created. Integrated heritage management is one of the main challenges in areas such as Kastellorizo. Involving a diverse set of stakeholders, including users, owners, experts, public agencies, and the private sector was crucial to achieve a holistic approach based in interdisciplinarity. The study's proposals are based on ensuring appropriate infrastructure to enhance the quality of life in local communities and promoting Cultural, Responsible Tourism. Additionally, the study emphasizes on the role of local communities that are considered as the leading stakeholders in the planning, development, and operation of these procedures. The main purpose of this study, focused on Kastellorizo, is to enhance the island's cultural and environmental assets through strategic sustainable planning and the use of Information and Communications Technologies (ICTs). The final goal is to promote the island's international recognition as a significant national border of great geopolitical importance with a unique Aegean cultural identity.

Keywords: Sustainable Heritage Management · Island Development · Digital Documentation · Kastellorizo

A. Moropoulou et al. (Eds.): TMM_CH 2023, CCIS 1889, pp. 335–352, 2023.
https://doi.org/10.1007/978-3-031-42300-0_29

1 Introduction

1.1 Cultural Heritage as a Driver of Sustainable Development to Mitigate Insularity

Sustainability, which first brought to the attention of the international community at the United Nations (UN) Stockholm Conference on the Human Environment in 1972 [1], continues to serve as a fundamental basis for international development and collaboration. In the literature, the most widely recognized definition of sustainable development is that proposed by Rutland, which posits that "Sustainable development is development that meets the needs of the resent without compromising the ability of future generations to meet their own needs" [2]. In recent years, the 17 Sustainable Development Goals (SDGs) of 2030 Agenda for Sustainable Development, that first adopted in September 2015 by all United Nations Member States, have 169 specific targets that nations are striving to achieve by 2030 [3, 4]. These specific objectives focus on regional and global stability, ensuring the health and prosperity of the planet, fair and resilient societies, and prosperous economies [5].

Sustainability is widely regarded as possessing three interrelated dimensions, which referred to as the environmental, economic, and social pillars [6]. However, in his work "The Fourth Pillar of Sustainability," [7] Hawkes argues that culture must be recognized as the fourth pillar of sustainable development, alongside the economy, society, and environment. According to literature, advancement in the integration of culture in sustainable development can be accomplished through the cultivation of the cultural sector, including heritage, creativity, cultural industries, cultural tourism, and crafts, as well as through the allocation of appropriate consideration for culture within all policies, particularly regarding education, economics, science, communication, environment, social cohesion, and international cooperation [8].

Islands, with their well-defined limits and discernible flow patterns, provide ideal "laboratories" for the assessment of sustainability [9, 10]. Based on the "Europe 2000+: Cooperation for spatial planning in Europe" report by the European Commission [11], the specificities of island regions must be recognized and addressed through differentiated development measures. The priorities for these regions include:

- Improving and modernizing road and maritime transportation systems.
- Enhancing passenger and freight transport infrastructure (airports and ports).
- Diversifying the production base.
- Developing human resources.
- Promoting the natural and cultural heritage.
- Facilitating interregional cooperation within the EU.

Moreover, the European Parliament's report on the preservation of European natural and architectural heritage in rural and island regions highlights the necessity of dedicating special attention to the safeguarding and improvement of the natural and cultural heritage in Europe's island areas [12]. The principles that must be considered in implementing intervention measures in both rural and island areas are:

- a sustainable balance between population and the environment
- the integrated approach of traditional rural areas
- the participation of local populations in the formulation and implementation of policies and the alignment of their views with central planning.
- Continuous dialogue with civil society organizations and voluntary organizations active in the field of cultural heritage.

Recognizing the significant impact of culture on the sustainable development of islands [13], as highlighted by existing literature, the developing plans for the management and preservation of cultural heritage in insular communities can be linked to the promotion, protection, and enhancement through cultural tourism, cultural reserves, and environmental conservation [14]. It is also imperative to acknowledge the significance of empowering the local communities' involvement in the formulation and execution of islands' sustainable development strategies, as they possess the most intimate knowledge of their community's requirements and priorities [15, 16].

1.2 ICTs in Cultural Heritage Management

In recent years, the management and promotion of cultural heritage has become increasingly challenging due to the multiple evolving parameters that need to be considered for effective action planning [17]. According to A. Giannakidis [18], digital tools can be divided into two categories for the use of local communities and cultural organizations: Digital Documentation and Digital Communication. Digital Documentation tools are essential for scientific interpretation, conservation, digitization, and management of cultural heritage, such as a database or a Geographical Information System (GIS).

Digital Communication tools are crucial for disseminating cultural heritage and increasing public access to it. In any case, these digital tools can significantly aid cultural heritage protection bodies and aid in the sustainable management of cultural resources [19, 20]. According to literature, Information, and communication technologies (ICTs) play a critical role in cultural heritage management of isolated islands [21]. ICTs provide a range of tools and platforms that can help address some of the challenges posed by insularity in these regions [22, 23]. Some of the ways that ICTs can contribute to cultural heritage management in isolated island contexts are [24–33]:

- Creating digital records and documentation of cultural heritage sites, which can be used to preserve and protect these sites in the long term.
- Increasing the accessibility of cultural heritage sites, both physically and digitally, by providing virtual tours, online databases, and other interactive resources that can be accessed by a wider audience.
- Educating and raising awareness about the cultural heritage of isolated islands, by providing information and resources to local communities and other stakeholders.
- Facilitating networking and collaboration among cultural heritage stakeholders, including researchers, practitioners, and local communities.

Monitoring and evaluating the impact of cultural heritage management initiatives, by providing real-time data and insights into the state of cultural heritage sites and the effectiveness of conservation and management strategies.

Also, academic research has extensively documented the intricate relationship between tourism and technology, highlighting their interdependence [34, 35]. The growth and widespread use of ICT has had a profound impact on the tourism industry, with far-reaching implications of achieving sustainability, fostering better partnerships with stakeholders, and engaging in meaningful dialogue with the community [36]. Although, the literature highlights the need for further investigation into the potential of using Information and Communication Technology (ICT) to reduce the negative effects of tourism and enhance its positive impact, particularly in conjunction with the promotion and preservation of natural and cultural heritage [37]. In this study, using ICT applications to create data bases, will help the development management of an insular area. ICT applications can also be used for data integration and mapping to provide management organizations and local authorities with a clearer picture of conditions at the destination for better decision-making [38].

2 Materials and Methods

The case study of the historic center of Megisti (Kastellorizo) was examined according to the methodology as follows:

- Axis I: Analysis, documentation, modeling, and management of the Cultural and Environmental assets.
- Axis II: Utilization of innovative ICT applications
- Axes III: Design and creation of new products for touristic local development
- Axis IV: Circular economy and social cohesion.

The methodology employed in the analysis of Kastellorizo was based on a comprehensive bibliographic review of relevant data pertaining to the island's natural environment, historical background, architectural and cultural heritage, and social organization. This holistic approach was necessary to thoroughly comprehend the interactions between these factors and their impact on the sustainable development of Kastellorizo. The bibliographic review aimed to provide a detailed and holistic assessment of the island, capturing the full range of its physical, cultural, and social attributes. An active engagement with local entities, such as the Municipality of Megisti as well as with members of the community and relevant stakeholders, was requisite for the purposes of conducting an in-depth analysis. The information collected was combined with the findings of the bibliographic review to describe an accurate representation of the current state of Kastellorizo. The results of this procedure -organized into data sheets, along with the local community's aspirations for sustainable development and the preservation of cultural and environmental assets of Kastellorizo, led to the proposals for the sustainable tourism and energy efficiency initiatives on the island.

3 Results and Discussion

3.1 Analysis of the Study Area – The Case Study of the Historic Center of Megisti Island (Kastellorizo)

Megisti (Kastellorizo) is a Greek island of the Dodecanese Island complex in the south-eastern Aegean Sea (Fig. 1a & 1b.). Megisti is the largest island (area 9, 1 sq.km. Coastline 19,5 km.) of a cluster called Megisti or Kastellorizo complex and includes 13 islets. The most well-known of them are the islets Ro and Strongyli. Strongyli is the easternmost tip of Greek territory and was the easternmost tip of the European Union until Cyprus joined. Located just 1.25 nautical miles from the southwest coast of Asia Minor of Turkey, 72 nautical miles from Rhodes and 328 nautical miles from the port of Piraeus, [39] Megisti constitutes a significant national border of great geopolitical importance and possesses a unique Aegean cultural identity.

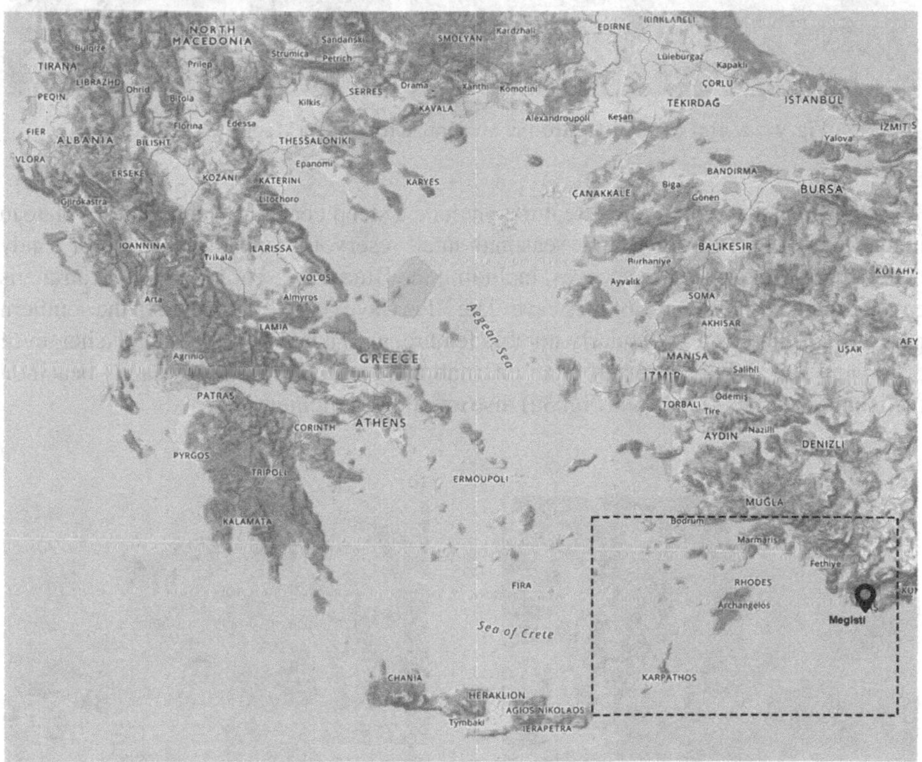

Fig. 1. a. Megisti in the map of Greece

Megisti is connected to the mainland through ferry services from Piraeus and more frequently from Rhodes. The Port Station of Megisti, which is part of the Port Fund of Southern Dodecanese, covers port and sea activities and has Customs services. Despite its small size, Megisti has an airport –4 km from the port- with connections to Athens and Rhodes, with more frequent flights during the summer and can be reached via the island's only asphalt road. Public transportation on the island includes taxi and summer-only bus services, with boats also available for reaching the caves and beaches of the complex's islets.

The island of Megisti is characterized by its predominantly rocky terrain, with the highest point being Vigla at an elevation of 273 m. The island is notable for the presence of Paleokastro (Fig. 2a), the ancient acropolis that was inhabited until the early 20th century and is located on the highest point of the island, Vigla [40].

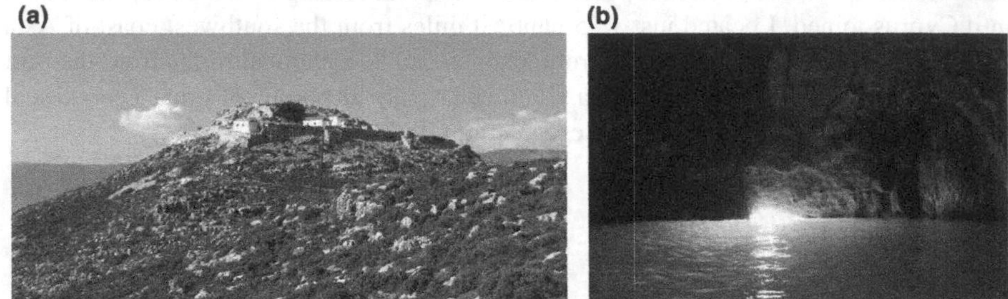

Fig. 2. a. and b. Palaiokastro-the ancient Acropolis of Megisti & Blue Cave

The island's morphological features include a steep coastline that creates a plateau in the largest part of the island, seasonal small reservoirs, and the absence of sandy beaches, as well as a few sea caves, including the Blue Cave, Parastas Hole, Katranztis cave, Arnaoutis cave, and Colones cave. The Blue Cave (Fig. 2b), located in the southern part of the island, is a particularly notable feature, with a length of 75 m and a height of 35 m, and is widely recognized as an international landmark. The only sandy beach on the island is in the Mandraki (Fig. 3a) district of the settlement [41].

Fig. 3. a. and b. Mandraki & Historic center of Megisti

Archaeological evidence suggests that Kastellorizo was inhabited as early as the Neolithic period, and during the Mycenaean and Minoan eras, it was considered a "merchant" of Crete, with commercial relations with the Minoans. The port served as an intermediary station in transactions with Cyprus. During the Byzantine era, Kastellorizo, along with the other islands near Rhodes, belonged to the provincial insular, and later became part of the Kibyrraeots. During World War II, Kastellorizo was a crucial military base and was used as a supply station by the British after the capitulation of Italy in 1943. However, on October 17, German fighters began bombing the island, leading to widespread destruction, and forcing its inhabitants to evacuate. The bombings ended with the fire on July 6, 1944. Kastellorizo officially became part of Greece in 1948.[42] In the first half of the 20th century, political instability and successive occupations by European states prompted mass immigration from Kastellorizo. Most of the permanent population immigrated to Australia, where they established a thriving Greek community. Today, the population of Megisti reaches 492 inhabitants according to the 2011 census of ELSTAT.

The settlement of Megisti has an amphitheatrical layout and its history -as aforementioned- is reflected in its current form. The urban gaps from the bombings of the war are distinctive, and the houses have neoclassical elements (Fig. 3b.) due to the area's 19th century economic development. The street plan is irregular, and roads were developed based on property lines rather than a plan, following the port's relief and form. The plateaus of the settlement are of interest. Megisti's settlement (Fig. 4) is characterized as a pre-existing settlement as of 1923 according to Greek legislation, and is considered traditional, with a 1,000-m protection zone established to preserve its character. The whole island is declared as an archaeological site and as an area in need of special protection under the Presidential Decree 10-5-2002, which defines the restrictions and special building conditions in the off-plan and out-of-settlement areas of the island.

Fig. 4. The Historic center of Megisti (National Cadastre)

The cultural reserve of Megisti (Fig. 5) includes ancient monuments such as the Lycian tomb, the castle of Agios Nikolaos, the Paleokastro, and the acropolis on Mount Vigla. Significant Christian monuments include St. George of the Well, St. Mercury, St. George the Sandrape, St. George of the Mountain, and the Holy Church of Constantine and Helen. More recent monuments include the municipal market building, the Santrapia urban school, and the old mosque with the historical collection of Kastellorizo.

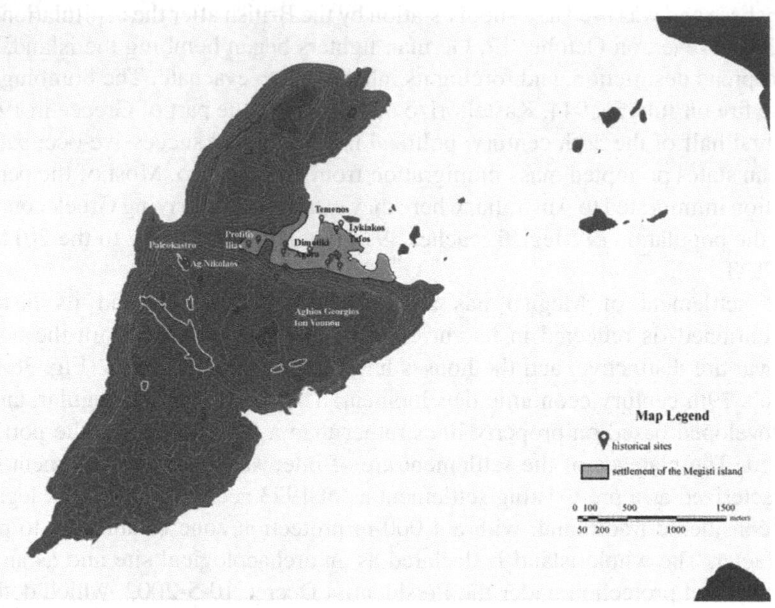

Fig. 5. Megisti complex's cultural reserve

As far as infrastructure concerned, the island a has a Kindergarten and a school for primary education, and a Gymnasium for secondary education. A regional clinic with telemedicine and laboratory capabilities also serves the island.

Megisti is an arid island with no springs, so drinking water is transported from Rhodes through an aquifer and stored in a 1000 sq. m tank in Profitis Ilias. The island has a desalination plant in Mandraki that produces 60 sq. m of water per hour. A small portion of the desalinated water is stored in the Prophet Elias tank for drinking, while the rest is used for other purposes. Moreover, the island has a small reservoir with a capacity of 82,500 cubic meters located at Kolia, intended to collect rainwater from the airport and surrounding watersheds for the island's water supply needs. The few crops on the island, mainly family vegetable gardens, have minimal irrigation needs. The reservoir project was completed in 2001, but it has never been filled due to sealing issues. The island's energy infrastructure is mainly the electricity grid, which is supplied by a PPC autonomous station. Renewable energy sources, such as solar energy for domestic water heating, are limited.

Due to the arid and rocky terrain of the island, there is limited development in the primary sector. The only agricultural activity is mainly limited to fodder cultivation for hay, family vegetable gardens, and olive groves for family consumption [43]. There are 14 professional fishermen on the island with 11 small-sized fishing vessels, but the inhabitants' involvement in fishing is limited. Past attempts to establish a tuna farm failed. There is no fishing shelter on the island and both professional and amateur boats use the central commercial port. In the secondary sector, besides a bakery, there are no processing units or craft enterprises related to primary sector products. The tertiary sector is the most developed production sector on Megisti Island, with a thriving tourism industry. The island gained worldwide recognition due to the Oscar-winning Italian film "Mediterraneo" shot there in 1991 [44] and the spectacular total solar eclipse in 2006, attracting visitors from around the world. The annual Kastellorizo documentary festival "Beyond Borders" (Fig. 6) is also a significant contributor to the island's prominence and takes place on the Aegean border between West and East. The festival celebrates culture and cinematography and is accompanied by parallel cultural activities, such as art and photography exhibitions, training programs, and workshops, attracting both the local and international community [45].

Fig. 6. "Beyond borders"-The international Documentary Film Festival of Megisti

3.2 Sustainable Development Initiatives in the Historic Center of Megisti

Within the framework of the National Development Program (NDP), the regional development program (RDP) for the southern Aegean 2021–2025 is being prepared. The South Aegean Region is the planning authority and the Special Service for the Management of the Operational Program (OP) of the Aegean Region is the implementing body. The RDP focuses on the insular character and geographical isolation of the region and has five pillars: Smart Development, Green Development, Social Development, Infrastructure Development, and Extroversion. Effective administration support is essential for the success of the mentioned development goals [46].

Moreover, the Ministry of Environment and Energy, the Natural Environment and Climate Change Organization, and the Municipality of Megisti signed a memorandum to fund a study on the comprehensive network mapping (Fig. 7) of 30 km of hiking trails (1.the route of the settlement; 2. Megisti-Plakes- Agios Stefanos; 3. Megisti-Mounta-Kastreli-Agios Stefanos; 4. Moni Agias Triadas- Cape Pounentis; 5. Megisti – Palaiokastro; 6. Moni Agias Triadas-Agios Ioannis-Connectio with French Trail; 6A. Connecting Leg of Routes 6,7,8; 7.Megisti- Moni Aghios Georgios tou Vounou; 8. Megisti-Avlonia-Moni Aghios Georgios tou Vounou; 9. Megisti – Cape Niftis – Avlonia; 10. The French Trail; 11. View Trail; 12; Charoupias' Trail) [47].

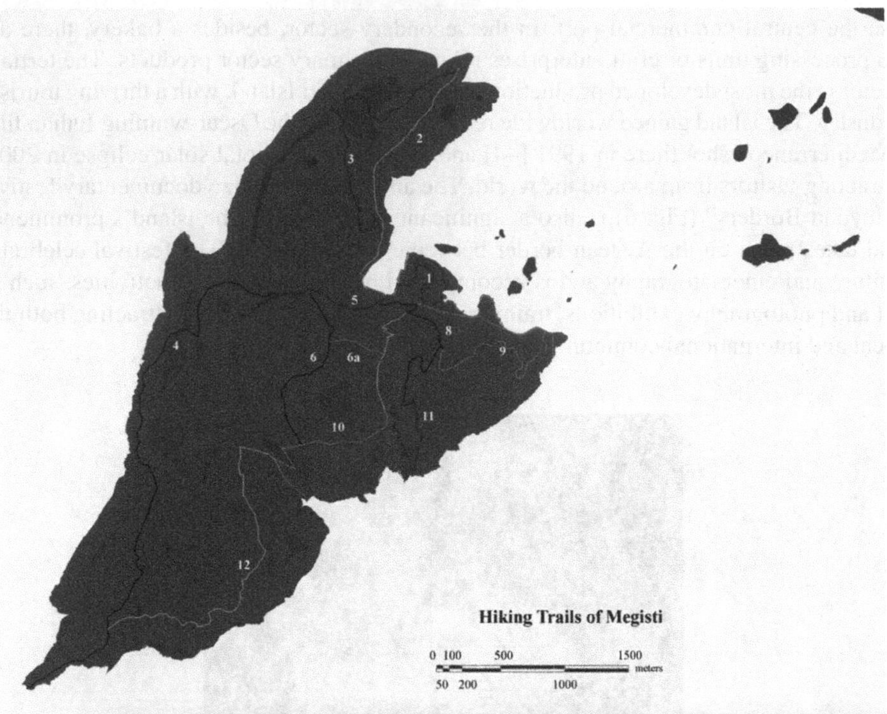

Fig. 7. Megisti's proposed trails (according to the study of the Ministry of Environment and Energy, the Natural Environment and Climate Change Organization, and the Municipality of Megisti)

These initiatives are crucial and could led to Megisti's sustainable development through actions that utilize the cultural and environmental reserve. The trails will serve as a bridge towards green development and preserve the environmental identity of the island. In addition,

3.3 Utilizing Megisti's Cultural and Environmental Heritage for Sustainable Development: Proposals for the Island

A cooperative effort was undertaken with the Technical Chamber of Dodecanese and local government to address the challenges faced by the Megisti island. Proposals were formed after engaging with local stakeholders and integrating their aspirations into the proposed sustainable development policy. During study area analysis, the cultural reserve of Megisti was documented in sheets that identify the key elements of each monument, including its name, administrative affiliation, location, type, architectural style, construction period, historical background, current and original use, protection status, conservation status, building materials, damage, restoration efforts, photographs or drawings, its spatial location, and its financing. Additionally, all the trails, natural heritage, and the analyzed information were organized in data bases using ICTs applications, to make efficient decisions on the sustainable management of Megisti island.

The proposed system aims to promote the cultural heritage and natural environment of the island within the context of sustainable development and circular economy. The major challenges faced by the island include limited infrastructure, such as transport, connectivity, and communication, and limited access to basic services like healthcare and education. To address these challenges, interventions are divided into four categories: improving living conditions, upgrading the environment and daily life in deprived areas, attracting alternative and sustainable tourism models, and safeguarding the island's geographical integrity.

Enhancement of Infrastructure

In the Megisti area, proposals for the development and promotion of the cultural and environmental reserve necessitate appropriate infrastructure. This includes completing and extending the ring road to reach Diakouri and Plakes, securing and protecting the recently implemented desalination project with road access to the settlement, and establishing road connectivity between the historic center and Mandraki. To promote sustainable and green development, the island's public transportation system is proposed to be upgraded with electric municipal buses. This will not only protect the settlement but also enhance the living conditions for the permanent population.

In the context of infrastructure, the proposal for the redeployment of port facilities is crucial for the historic center of Megisti to become a destination for visitors and protect its historical form. According to the Foundation for Research and Technology – Hellas (FORTH), the current port has limited capabilities with a narrow opening of 158 m and a vertical distance to the entrance of 365 m. Additionally, the depths in the old port are less than 20 m., making it challenging for larger ships to dock (Fig. 8).

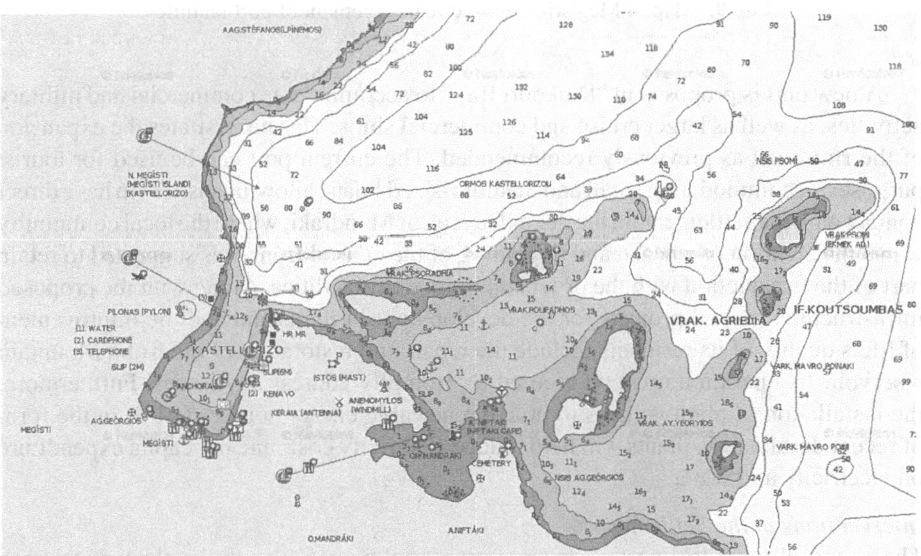

Fig. 8. Port isobaths

Additionally, the infrastructure of the existing port platform needs restoration to prevent failures from increasing traffic. For the above reasons, but also after contacting the local authorities, the following port rearrangement is proposed as follows (Fig. 9).

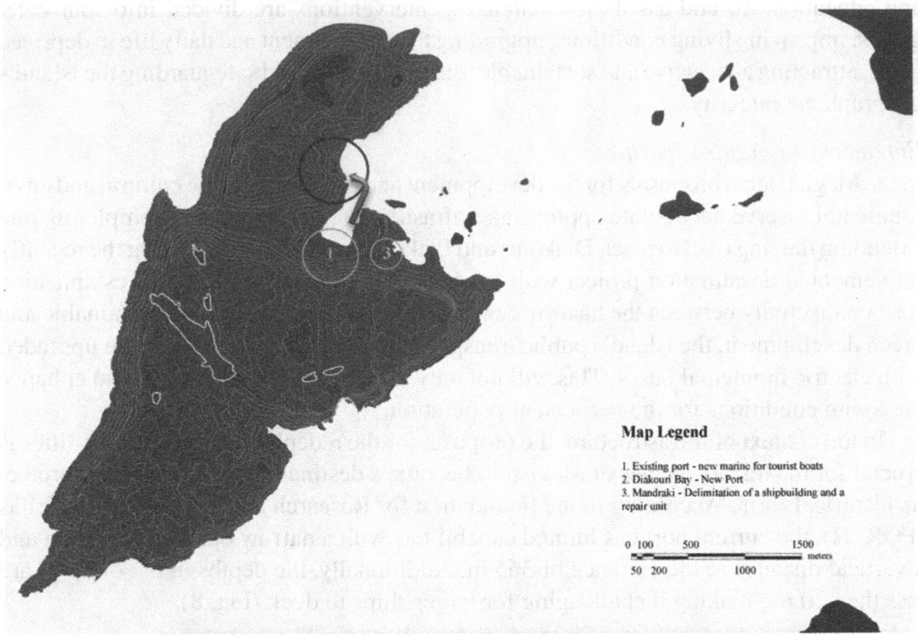

Fig. 9. Map of Megisti-Proposed rearrangement of port facilities

A new port is proposed in "Diakouri Bay" to accommodate commercial and military activities, as well as larger cruise and commercial ships. This necessitates the expansion of the ring road as previously recommended. The current port can be used for tourist purposes, accommodating small and medium-sized boats, allowing visitors to have direct contact with the settlement. In the degraded area of Mandraki, where the local community wants the creation of a beach and upgrading of the coastal front, it is suggested to retain part of the fish auction with the provision of modern facilities. Along with the proposed infrastructure, crucial projects for the development of the island and the improvement of life's quality of its residents include the repair and restoration of the Kolia Mountain reservoir. Its operation must be secured to promptly address any issues. Furthermore, the installation of photovoltaics to utilize renewable energy sources (RES) in the form of recent desalination plants will help reduce electricity costs and per capita expenditure on electricity and water.

Interventions in the Settlement
The proposal aims to improve and preserve public spaces in the settlement through renovations, starting with the redevelopment of the Kordoni of the Port. The project has been submitted to the Ministry of Infrastructure, Transport and Networks, but further studies are necessary to confirm the compatibility of the settlement's aesthetics (such as

benches, lighting, garbage bins, and public configurations) with the architecture, and to restore the structural stability of the port's quay to prevent coastal failures. A connection of the settlement's plateaus is proposed (Fig. 10) to highlight its history and create an attractive route for visitors beyond the seaside. The configuration of public spaces as part of a comprehensive redevelopment plan of the settlement would further emphasize the interventions of the historical building stock. The selected plateaus, including the Plateau of Aghios Georgios tou Pigadiou, the Museum plateau, the Documentary Film Festival plateau, the Mandraki Pier, and the Municipal Market, are key points of social activity in the settlement.

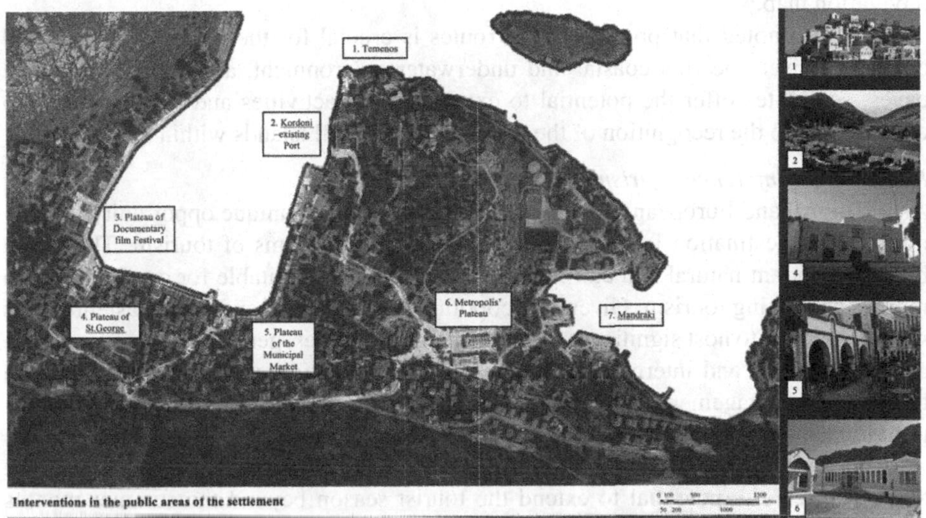

Fig. 10. Map of Interventions in the historic center of Megisti

The plateau of the Metropolis holds the island's most important public buildings, including the metropolitan church of Constantine & Helen, the Church of Agios Nikolaos, and the Church of St. George of Lucca. The Sandrapeia School, a miniature of the University of Athens, and the Girls' School are also noteworthy. The pebbled floor of the square is of special aesthetic interest and should be highlighted.

In the degraded area of Mandraki, which served as the second port of Kastellorizo until the 19th century as a ship repair zone, a proposal for its compatible revival and restoration on the left side of the bay is proposed. The area, located near the Metropolis plateau, could host a naval technology exhibition, including outdoor exhibitions and cultural events during the summer months, either outdoors at the pier of Mandraki or indoors at the Girls' School. The creation of a tourist shelter near the pier is also proposed, without affecting existing or proposed functions of the area. In response to the residents' request for a developed coastal front and accessible beach, a beach can be created on the right side of the bay near the cemetery area. Finally, a critical issue for the region of the island complex is the resolution of the settlement's borders and the proclamation of a General Urban Plan.

Cultural and Sea Routes in the Island Complex of Megisti
The study of trails, as aforementioned, plays a crucial role in enhancing the promotion of cultural and environmental heritage. The study provides a comprehensive analysis of the technical and qualitative aspects of twelve trails, spanning a total length of thirty kilometers. The proposed network of trails can incorporate markers of declared monuments through the utilization of QR Codes and smart applications. The information is organized in an integrated database and can be used to facilitate the visitors. Furthermore, at the Municipal Market square, visitors can access a QR Code through an app to obtain information on the trails, including length, degree of difficulty, estimated time, and points of cultural and environmental interest. This enables the creation of a digital navigation map.

It is also noted that promoting sea routes is crucial for the entire Megisti Island complex. Given the rich coastal and underwater environment, as well as the unique caves, sea routes offer the potential to expand tourist activities and visits, while also contributing to the recognition of the national space in all islands within the complex.

Promoting Conference Tourism
As a national and European border, Kastellorizo presents a unique opportunity for promotion as a destination for conferences and alternative forms of tourism. The island boasts important natural and cultural resources, making it suitable for combining with marine and hiking tourism. Given its geopolitical significance and size, Kastellorizo is well-positioned to host significant conferences and speeches, generating increased interest from visitors and international attention. This projection can be achieved through the effective engagement of delegates who are well-respected and financially well-off individuals, without incurring significant expenses.

The promotion of Kastellorizo as a destination for conferences and alternative tourism offers the potential to extend the tourist season beyond the summer months and bring economic benefits to the local population through high tourist spending. The establishment of conference facilities and visitor services is essential for the effective organization of conferences and can lead to the creation of new employment opportunities. The improvement of the island's infrastructure and connectivity with the mainland is a prerequisite. The traditional Stamatiou School building, which is owned by the Municipality of Megistis and was originally established in 1903 as a kindergarten, is proposed as the primary conference venue. The building, located on the plateau of Aghios Georgios tou Pigadiou, was converted into a Cultural Center in 1999, but was unfortunately destroyed in a fire in 2016. In 2018, the Stavros Niarchos Foundation donated for the study of restoration and reuse of the Cultural Center in Kastellorizo.

4 Conclusions

Megisti Island possesses a unique potential to serve as a model for sustainable development design, practices, and innovation in insular areas. The integration of digital documentation and ICTs, along with the involvement of international educational and research institutions, holds great promise for the protection and promotion of the island's environmental and cultural heritage, and the development of new tourism models. The ongoing investment and growth in tourism, despite the challenges posed by the pandemic, further underscores the dynamic nature of the tourism sector in insular regions. The main objective of the proposals formulated was the creation of sustainable tourist activities that respect the environmental and cultural resources and the establishment of conditions necessary for new job creation and potentially attracting a permanent population.

The crucial role of ICT applications in documentation was one of the key conclusions drawn, with the creation of efficient databases serving as a crucial tool for local governments in making decisions towards sustainable development.

The success of sustainable development on an island is closely linked to the well-being of its residents. The participation of local communities and leadership in discussions about the sustainable development of Megisti was therefore deemed vital. The proposals prioritize the involvement and awareness of the island's residents in preserving their cultural heritage and emphasize the importance of empowering the local community and supporting cultural initiatives as the foundation of any efforts to promote the island.

Acknowledgements. This research has been co-financed by the European Regional Development Fund of the European Union and Greek national funds through the Operational Program Competitiveness, Entrepreneurship, and Innovation, under the call RESEARCH – CREATE – INNOVATE (project code: T2EDK-01278).

References

1. Nurse, K.: Culture as the fourth pillar of sustainable development. J. Small States Econ. Rev. Basic Stat. **11**, 24–40 (2006). https://scholar.google.com/citations?view_op=view_citation&hl=en&user=UNmsD1gAAAAJ&citation_for_view=UNmsD1gAAAAJ:u-x6o8ySG0sC
2. Brundtland, G.H.: Our Common Future: Report of the World Commission on Environment and Development. Geneva, UN-Dokument A/42/427 (1987)
3. The 17 Sustainable Development Goals, United Nations page. https://sdgs.un.org/goals. Accessed 14 Jan 2023
4. International Institute for Sustainable Development. https://www.iisd.org/
5. EUR-Lex, Communication from the Commission to the European Parliament, the Council, the European Economic and Social Committee and the Committee of the Regions: Next steps for a sustainable European future European action for sustainability. https://eur-lex.europa.eu/legal-content/EN/TXT/?uri=COM%3A2016%3A739%3AFIN. Accessed 28 Jan 2023
6. Purvis, B., Mao, Y., Robinson, D.: Three pillars of sustainability: in search of conceptual origins. Sustain. Sci. **14**(3), 681–695 (2019). https://doi.org/10.1007/s11625-018-0627-5
7. Hawkens, J.: The fourth pillar of Sustainability: culture's essential role in public planning, pp. 48–55, Humanities.com (2001). https://books.google.gr/books?id=NHITl2xmw3EC&pg=PR4&hl=el&source=gbs_selected_pages&cad=2#v=onepage&q&f=false
8. Astara, O.H.: Culture as the fourth pillar of sustainable development. J. Sustainable Dev. Cult. Tradit. **1a, 2a**, 93–102 (2014). http://sdct-journal.com/index.php/2015-10-18-22-23-19/2014-volume-2-a/351-culture-as-the-fourth-pillar-of-sustainable
9. McElroy, J.L., de Albuquerque, K.: Tourism penetration index for the small-Island Caribbean. Ann. Tour. Res. **28**, 145–168 (1992). https://www.sciencedirect.com/science/article/abs/pii/S0160738397000686?via%3Dihub
10. Spilanis, I., Kizos, T., Koulouri, M., Kondyli, J., Vakoufaris, H., Gatsis, I.: Monitoring sustainability in insular areas. Ecol. Indicators **9**(1), 179–187 (2009). https://doi.org/10.1016/j.ecolind.2008.03.003

11. CORDIS. https://cordis.europa.eu/article/id/4496-europe-2000-cooperation-for-european-territorial-development. Accessed 27 Nov 2022
12. Legislative Observatory, European Parliament. https://oeil.secure.europarl.europa.eu/oeil/popups/ficheprocedure.do?lang=en&reference=2006/2050(INI). Accessed 24 Dec 2022
13. Castanho, R.A., Behradfar, A., Vulevic, A., Naranjo Gómez, J.: Analyzing transportation sustainability in the Canary Islands archipelago. Infrastructures **5**, 58 (2020). https://doi.org/10.3390/infrastructures5070058
14. Nocca, F.: The role of cultural heritage in sustainable development: multidimensional indicators as decision-making tool. Sustainability **9**, 1882 (2017). https://doi.org/10.3390/su9101882
15. Rodriguez Diaz, M., Espino Rodriguez, T.F.: Determining the sustainability factors and performances of a tourism destination from the stakeholders' perspective. Sustainability **8**, 951 (2016). https://doi.org/10.3390/su8090951
16. Sheldon, P.J.: The challenges to sustainability in island tourism. School of Travel Industry Management, University of Hawai'i. Occasional Paper 2005-01, October 2005. https://lib.icimod.org/record/11965
17. UNESCO. https://www.unesco.org/en/cultural-heritage-7-successes-unescos-preservation-work?TSPD_101_R0=080713870fab200041af9e6a5d592767b34ce000b85385e6e24caade8a11be317af320d775cfd57108a6dfe522143000c8e6536df7bbbf8b3763f14a792dd6154470955d01cf5a48655fd8a05b51dc2459272c93f6c86b1ebc05d141213c5166. Accessed 2022
18. Poulios, I., et al.: Cultural Management, Local Community and Sustainable Development [Undergraduate textbook]. Kallipos, Open Academic Editions (2015). https://hdl.handle.net/11419/2392. Accessed 06 Dec 2022
19. Mudge, M., Ashley, M., Schroer, C.: A digital future for cultural heritage. In: XXI International CIPA Symposium, Athens, vol. 10. no. 1, p. 222 (2007). https://www.isprs.org/PROCEEDINGS/XXXVI/5-C53/papers/FP104.pdf
20. Arnold, D., Kaminski, J.: Cultural heritage tourism and the digital future. Contemporary Issues in Cultural Heritage Tourism, pp. 289–310. Routledge (2013). https://www.taylorfrancis.com/chapters/edit/10.4324/9780203583685-31/cultural-heritage-tourism-digital-future-david-arnold-jaime-kaminski
21. Koutși, D., Stratigea, A.: Sustainable and resilient management of underwater cultural heritage (UCH) in remote Mediterranean islands: a methodological framework. Heritage **4**, 3469–3496 (2021). https://doi.org/10.3390/heritage4040192
22. Stratigea, A., Kyriakides, E., Nicolaides, C.: Smart Cities in the Mediterranean, pp. 47–49. Springer, Cham (2017). https://doi.org/10.1007/978-3-319-54558-5
23. Online book "Strengthening ICT and knowledge management capacity in support of the sustainable development of multi-island Caribbean" SIDS. https://repositorio.cepal.org/bitstream/handle/11362/45064/1/S1901146_en.pdf. Accessed 03 Feb 2023
24. Interreg Europe. https://www.interregeurope.eu/news-and-events/news/use-of-ict-in-protection-of-natural-and-cultural-heritage. Accessed 02 Feb 2023
25. Guccio, C., Martorana, M.F., Mazza, I., Rizzo, I.: Technology and public access to cultural heritage: the Italian experience on ICT for public historical archives. In: Borowiecki, K., Forbes, N., Fresa, A. (eds.) Cultural Heritage in a Changing World. Springer, Cham (2016). https://doi.org/10.1007/978-3-319-29544-2_4
26. Poulopoulos, V., Wallace, M.: Digital technologies, and the role of data in cultural heritage: the past, the present, and the future. Big Data Cognit. Comput. **2022**, 6, 73 (2022). https://doi.org/10.3390/bdcc6030073 Author, F., Author, S., Author, T.: Book title. 2nd edn. Publisher, Location (1999)

27. Brizard, T., Derde, W., Silberman, N.: Basic Guidelines for Cultural Heritage Professionals in the Use of Information Technologies. How can ICT support Cultural heritage? Tamara Brizard, Willem Derde, Neil Silberman & The Interactive Institute AB (2007). https://www.enamecenter.org/files/documents/Know-how%20book%20on%20Cultural%20Heritage%20and%20ICT.pdf
28. Liang, X., Lu, Y., Martin, J.: A review of the role of social media for the cultural heritage sustainability. Sustainability **13**, 1055 (2021). https://doi.org/10.3390/su13031055
29. Oikonomopoulou, E., Delegou, E., Sayas, J., Moropoulou, A.: An innovative approach to the protection of cultural heritage: the case of cultural routes in Chios Island, Greece. J. Archaeol. Sci. Rep. **14**, 742–757 (2017). https://www.sciencedirect.com/science/article/abs/pii/S2352409X16305922]
30. Masini, N., Soldovieri, F.: Cultural heritage sites and sustainable management strategies. In: Masini, N., Soldovieri, F. (eds.) Sensing the Past. Geotechnologies and the Environment, vol. 16. Springer, Cham (2017). https://doi.org/10.1007/978-3-319-50518-3_1
31. Moropoulou, A., Delegou, E.T.: Integrated Environmental Management for the Preservation of Historic Cities. Conference and Brokerage Event the Construction Aspects of Built Heritage Protection. European Construction Technology Platform, Dubrovnik, Croatia (2006)
32. Oikonomopoulou, E., Kioussi, A., Delegou, E.T., Tsilimantou, E., Moropoulou, A.: Innovative methods for the protection of cultural heritage. application on cultural and natural heritage site paths. Scienza e Beni Culturali Vol. XXIII. Publ. Arcadia Ricerche Editore, Padova, pp. 335–346 (2010)
33. Delegou, E.T., Tsilimantou, E., Oikonomopoulou, E., Kiousi, A., Sayas, J., Moropoulou, A.: Strategic planning of materials and conservation interventions for the damage rehabilitation of the Sarantapicho Acropolis and the Erimokastro Acropolis in Rhodes. In: Proceedings of the 8th International Symposium on the Conservation of Monuments in the Mediterranean Basin, Patras, Greece. Droj, G., 2010. Cultural heritage conservation by GIS (2010). http://www.geo.info.hu/gisopen/gisopen2010/eloadasok/pdf/droj.pdf. Accessed 28 June 2012
34. Navío-Marco, J., Ruiz-Gómez, L.M., Sevilla-Sevilla, C.: Progress in information technology and tourism management: 30 years on and 20 years after the internet-Revisiting Buhalis and Law's landmark study about eTourism. Tour. Manag. **69**, 460–470 (2018). https://www.sciencedirect.com/science/article/abs/pii/S0261517718301134?via%3Dihub
35. Ali, A., Frew, J.A.: ICT and sustainable tourism development: an innovative perspective. J. Hosp. Tour. Technol. **5**(1), 2–16 (2014). https://doi.org/10.1108/JHTT-12-2012-0034
36. Cole, S.: Information and empowerment: the keys to achieving sustainable tourism. J. Sustain. Tour. **14**, 629–644 (2006)
37. Ruggier, G., Calo, P.: ICT and tourism impacts in Islands. Ecocycles **4**(2), 4–11 (2018). https://doi.org/10.19040/ecocycles.v4i2.102
38. European Union. https://europa.eu/capacity4dev/eu-working-group-land-issues/documents/geographic-information-systems-gis-spatial-dimension-development-cooperation. Accessed 15 Jan 2023
39. Kastellorizo online. https://www.kastellorizo.online/en/services/information/. Accessed 03 Jan 2022
40. Alfa cert. https://certs-it.com/listing/kastellorizo/. Accessed 03 June 2022
41. Ragkousis M., Abdelali M.: New alien Mediterranean biodiversity records (October 2020). Mediterr. Mar. Sci. **21**(3), 631–652 (2020). https://doi.org/10.12681/mms.23673
42. Greece-Is. https://www.greece-is.com/the-long-history-of-kastellorizo-from-ancient-empires-to-modern-wars/. Accessed 05 June 2022
43. Energy Transition of the island of Kastellorizo, Study of the Institute of Energy Of Southeast Europe (IENE). https://www.iene.eu/articlefiles/kastellorizo%20executive%20final%20eng.pdf. Accessed 07 Aug 2022

44. Online Article about Kastellorizoo by Archyde. https://www.archyde.com/in-kastellorizo-the-island-of-the-film-mediterranean-winds-of-war-between-turkey-and-greece/. Accessed 06 June 2022
45. Beyond Borders festival homepage. https://beyondborders.gr/en/. Accessed 03 June 2022
46. South Aegean Regional Programme 2021–2027 homepage. https://pepna.gr/el/perifereiako-programma-notioy-aigaioy-2021-2027. Accessed 30 Jan 202
47. Official site of the Ministry of Energy. https://ypen.gov.gr/sto-kastellorizo-gia-ta-monopatia-o-yfypourgos-perivallontos-kai-energeias-giorgos-amyras/. Accessed 03 June 2022

Delivering Education on the Sustainable Aspects of Heritage

Stavroula Thravalou(✉) and Maria Philokyprou

Department of Architecture, University of Cyprus, Nicosia, Cyprus
thraval@ucy.ac.cy

Abstract. In response to the need for educational practices and approaches to be updated within the area of sustainable heritage, this paper presents the lessons and good practices derived from two European Erasmus Plus projects (HERSUS and Smart Rehabilitation 3.0). These projects strive to create an innovative new framework that integrates vital educational challenges in the field of sustainability in heritage. Among the prime concerns of these research projects are to challenge different problems related to heritage conservation, generate sustainable-based approaches, and finally, create a homogeneous curriculum for experts in rehabilitation and sustainability. The major research outcomes presented for the purpose of this paper are the creation of, a) an innovative integrated Master's course on heritage and sustainability, with new developed courses offered from five different European Universities; b) a series of remote-access Massive Online Courses (MOOCs); and c) a number of digital tools promoting open access in education, such as a sharing platform and an online database for technological innovations and best practices for sustainable conservation through case studies. The conclusions highlight the benefits of adopting innovative, integrated approaches and digital tools for teaching, contributing to the delivery of lifelong learning opportunities, while bridging the gap between sustainability and built heritage awareness.

Keywords: education · built heritage · sustainability · e-learning · Massive Online Course-MOOC

1 Introduction

Cultural heritage has vast potential to improve the quality of life for people, as well as to provide a sense of belonging, while at the same time shaping our future [1]. Today, heritage conservation studies that focus on the aspects of sustainability are becoming more relevant than ever [2]. Especially in light of an aging European housing stock and the growing issues of climate change; both of which trigger unprecedented social challenges. A greater understanding and awareness of the transformative nature of our cultural heritage can work to put societal changes into perspective, while reducing the stress experienced by people affected. However, the ever-changing nature of cultural heritage and its regenerative ability have not been thoroughly researched [3]. In response to this challenge, innovative efforts should be made to enhance the quality and relevance of human capital, and strengthen the knowledge triangle between education, research, and practice [3].

A. Moropoulou et al. (Eds.): TMM_CH 2023, CCIS 1889, pp. 353–363, 2023.
https://doi.org/10.1007/978-3-031-42300-0_30

2 State of Play Regarding Sustainability and Heritage Education

In recognition of the vital part education plays in creating more equitable and sustainable societies, the United Nations launched the 'Decade of Education for Sustainable Development (DESD)' in 2005. The objective of this initiative was to integrate the values and practices of sustainable development into education [4]. The concept of promoting high-quality, inclusive education was also emphasised in the Bonn Declaration (2009) [5] and the Gothenburg Declaration (2008) [6]. As expressed in the latter, there is a need for higher education institutions to become open educational centres and hubs, while universities should become more involved in bringing together local and global communities [6]. This refers to the capacity to address sustainability issues on a local scale, using global networks to take advantage of innovation and expertise around the world. A barrier against the implementation of a holistic concept of sustainability in the higher education sector, is the lack of interdisciplinarity in research development and administration. Emphasis is often placed solely on environmental or technical aspects, without considering the wider societal implications. As DESD suggests, emphasis should be placed on embracing the wider field of global social responsibility, embracing an interdisciplinary approach [7]. After all, sustainable development as defined at the World Commission on Environment and Development Report (1987), is a development "which meets the needs of the present without compromising the ability of future generations to meet their own needs" [8]. This reveals that the concept of sustainable development should not be limited to a few disciplines but is actually applicable on a global scale, both now and in the future. Therefore, the ability to work in an interdisciplinary manner is essential for educators and experts in the field.

According to the latest EU report on cultural heritage resilience [3], the concept of cultural heritage, as well as the relationship between cultural heritage and climate change are hardly addressed in European education systems. Overall, education on climate change focuses mainly on technical and financial aspects rather than socio-cultural ones. This is a missed opportunity, as heritage can be used as a way of raising awareness on climate change, as well as its impact on European cities and societies. This view is adopted by the New European Bauhaus initiative, which underlines the importance of built heritage reuse as a driver for sustainable cities and societies [9]. Furthermore, Sustainable Development Goals (SDG4) highlight that integrating cultural heritage aspects into climate change education offers many benefits [10]. A key aspect for adopting a more inclusive and holistic approach is to acknowledge that culture plays a vital role in embracing the concept of sustainability, "taking into account local conditions and culture, as well as building awareness of cultural expressions of heritage and their diversity" [10].

Furthermore, digital and e-learning tools promote life-long education, and have proven particularly effective during the recent pandemic [11, 12]. Online education offers the advantage of flexibility in terms of time and place, as well as greater accessibility achieved through the use of digital educational tools. However, the introduction of digital and e-learning tools in the higher education of cultural heritage conservation and sustainability seems to be limited [13]. In the field of architecture in particular, the challenges of online pedagogy refer to the lack of a collective studio environment which affects self-motivation and complicates communication between students and teachers. An additional challenge is the replacement of manual drawing by digital, and the substitution of physical models creation by three-dimensional modelling [14]. In order to change this, it is deemed essential to strengthen the use of new knowledge and technologies through training, upskilling and sharing expertise, while at the same time revitalising traditional, forgotten skills [3].

In response to the need to update educational practices and approaches in the field of sustainable heritage conservation, this paper presents the principal outcomes of recent research projects (namely HERSUS and Smart Rehabilitation 3.0) that strive to create an innovative educational framework that addresses vital educational challenges in the field of heritage and sustainability. The research objectives are to link scales of built heritage, challenge different problems related to heritage conservation, generate sustainable-based approaches, and finally, create a homogeneous interdisciplinary curriculum for experts in rehabilitation and sustainability. The purpose of this paper is to present the methodologies adopted for enhancing heritage sustainability awareness in education, as well as the main outcomes and tools developed through this process. The above-mentioned research projects offer a valuable overview of the different contexts, methods, materials and teaching experiences that are further discussed in this paper. The major research outcomes presented for the purposes of this paper are the creation of, a) an innovative integrated Master's course on heritage and sustainability, with newly developed courses offered by five different European Universities (HERSUS Project); b) remote-access Massive Online Courses (MOOCs) that address the needs of professionals, students or graduates who want to tap into the vast potential of connecting heritage and sustainability (Smart Rehabilitation 3.0 project); and c) various tools promoting open access in education, such as a digital sharing platform (HERSUS Sharing Platform), and an online database for technological innovations in heritage (Database no1 and Database no2 developed in the framework of Smart Rehabilitation 3.0). The conclusions highlight the benefits of adopting innovative, integrated approaches and digital tools for teaching, contributing to the delivery of lifelong learning opportunities, while bridging the gap between sustainability and built heritage awareness.

3 Methodology

3.1 Research Framework

The main objective of this paper is to present good practices and lessons learnt from recent research focusing on education around the sustainable aspects of heritage. The discussions and results of this work are based on two Erasmus + research programmes. The first is the Erasmus + programme entitled 'Enhancing of Heritage Awareness and Sustainability of Built Environment in Architectural and Urban Design Higher Education' (HERSUS), developed within the strategic partnerships for higher education action. The HERSUS project (https://hersus.org/) is a collaboration of five universities from Serbia, Italy, Cyprus, Greece, and Spain (University of Belgrade, Iuav University of Venice, University of Cyprus, Aristotle University of Thessaloniki and University of Seville - UNESCO Chair on Built Urban Heritage), in order to promote innovative teaching practices in the field of sustainability within built heritage. The main objective is to create a homogeneous curriculum for the training of conservation experts within the framework of higher education. The project strives to enhance the competence and motivation of educators to include curricula elements that will have tangible results in linking heritage studies and sustainability aspects.

The second Erasmus + research project, entitled 'Innovating Professional Skills for Existing Building Sector' (Smart Rehabilitation 3.0, https://smart-rehabilitation.eu/), aims to mitigate and bridge the gap between the educational offering and the social reality. Four European universities from Spain, Cyprus, Italy and Lithuania participate in this effort (Polytechnic University of Catalonia, University of Cyprus, University of Palermo and Kaunas University of Technology). A major contribution of this project is the creation of four Massive Online Courses (MOOCs), offering the potential for e-learning, as well as continuous access to education. The main objective is to support the development of learning-outcomes-oriented curricula, aligning students' needs with labour market requirements.

3.2 Development of a Common, Flexible, and Inclusive Graduate Programme for a Master's in Heritage and Sustainability

Capacity building was the first step towards drafting a targeted and effective education and training programme in the field of sustainability and cultural heritage. Partner countries participating in the project – Serbia, Italy, Cyprus, Greece, and Spain – conducted a comprehensive state-of-the-art analysis in a field of, a) pedagogical and educational models integrating the concepts of built environment sustainability and heritage awareness, b) successful built architectural and urban projects on sustainable conservation, and c) policies addressing the sustainability of heritage adopted in a local context. A questionnaire survey followed, involving professionals and experts in the field of conservation, as well as policy-makers and decision-makers. This survey shed light on the challenges of the field, opening the discussion with the academic community.

The next milestone for the development of a common, flexible, and inclusive syllabus was based on reaching a consensus regarding the fundamental group of terms perceived as engaging contents of learning. These are: Notions, Design Actions, Design Approaches, Heritage Types, and Tools. Finally, the common structure of the curriculum was decided among the partners. The specific syllabus aimed to train students and postgraduate professionals to learn new skills in rehabilitation and restoration, specifically addressing aspects of sustainability. The pillars for this development were the following thematic areas:

- Restoration – urban heritage revitalisation used to address urban scale challenges.
- Reuse – the process of reusing existing architectural heritage for a new purpose.
- Resilience – design of adaptable and transformable structures that can adjust to their environments and future challenges.

The international standards for quality in architectural education – set by UNESCO-UIA Validation Council for Architectural Education – were also respected [15].

3.3 Development of Online Training Courses (MOOCs)

The development of a series of online courses aim to attract a wide audience of varying backgrounds, such as practitioners or professionals engaged in heritage conservation who want to enrich their knowledge in the field of sustainability. In turn, attending this training could improve the participants' career opportunities, broaden their horizons and provide more cross-border relationships.

As a first step, the development of the MOOCs entailed the review of existing and readily available online courses related to sustainable aspects of heritage and innovation in the conservation sector. As a second step, the objectives, scope and target audience of each MOOC were defined, as well as the skills and competences for future experts in the field. Next the participating universities from Spain, Cyprus, Italy, and Lithuania reached a consensus regarding the thematic areas to be developed, as well as the development of a common structure. The latter consists of a short trailer introducing the module's specific contents and concepts, a didactic guide, theoretical and practical material, additional reading material and references, and lastly, self-assessment questionnaires. The relevant material was prepared and hosted by the leading institution – Polytechnic University of Catalonia – on a central interactive platform (https://mooc.upc.edu/). Finally, the MOOCs were released on a pilot basis in order to obtain feedback from a number of participants and proceed with final adjustments to the content.

3.4 Creation of Open-Source Digital Tools for Accessing Information and Dissemination

The implemented dissemination approach of both research programmes strives to raise academic and public awareness, as well as to encourage further relevant networking in order to enhance the impact on target audiences. The overall objective was to incorporate activities designed to ensure the continuing visibility, accessibility and use of the results, even after the end of the projects. Different types of exploitation activities were conceptualised in order to provide access to open educational material. These include the creation of the projects' website, visual identity and promo materials, national and international events, publications in scientific journals and international conferences, as well as digital databases and data sharing platforms.

4 Results and Discussion

4.1 An Integrated Master's Degree on Heritage and Sustainability

Establishing a Common Ground Among Participating Universities. The comparative analysis of 20 courses offered by the participating universities (five courses per country) demonstrated that most offer graduate programmes on conservation of historic buildings or landscape heritage, as well as programmes on Energy Efficiency, Environmental Architectural and/or Urban Design, that are interdisciplinary and interdepartmental. However, while environmental and social aspects of sustainability are more developed, especially in relation with heritage and conservation, financial aspects are less frequently addressed. Both theoretical and studio-based courses are offered, while various methodological/teaching tools are used, such as lectures, overview and case study analysis, student presentations, teamwork, design studio, site visits, discussions, workshops, laboratory work etc. [16].

A total of 766 students and 54 experts participated in the questionnaire study, in order to highlight the gaps between higher education and practice. Most practitioners and experts acknowledge a gap between the theoretical and practical subjects, and design skills. Furthermore, many experts suggest that interdisciplinarity should be further enhanced. In turn, most students consider the skills and knowledge acquired in the fields of both sustainability and cultural heritage to be important for their employability.

In total, 75 terms describing the relationship between design and sustainability of heritage were examined. The terms were clustered in five groups: a) Notions (e.g. Cultural and Collective Memory, Resilience, Heritage Genealogy etc.), b) Heritage Types (e.g. Modern, Vernacular, Tangible and Intangible, Archaeological, Natural, Religious etc.), c) Design Approaches (e.g. Environmentally Responsive and Passive or Active Design, Design for All, Acoustic/Thermal/Visual Comfort etc.), d) Design Actions (e.g. Preventive Conservation, Restoration, Adaptive Reuse, Rehabilitation, Heritage Management, Nature Based Solutions, Public Advocacy for Social Participation etc.), and e) Tools (3D Printing, Space Syntax, GIS, BIM, Thermal/Energy/Lighting Simulation, Collaborative Workshop etc.) [17]. Through this research, the acceptance of common terms of communication on heritage and sustainability issues was achieved, an important step towards the creation of a common curriculum in the field.

In conclusion, the capacity building contributed to the consideration of different landscapes, cultural contexts, and scales, providing new insight into the complexity of defining heritage in the contemporary context. Therefore, it was made evident that teaching sustainability and cultural heritage requires interdisciplinarity and the development of skills in the field of architectural and urban design through studio-based, theoretical, seminar, elective, and extracurricular courses. Studio courses and specialised intensive workshops should be further enhanced on academic curricula, to link academic education with professional practice. The outcomes of the capacity building phase are reported and made available online by the consortium [18–20] (see Fig. 1).

Development of the Common Syllabus. The integrated Master's programme that was drafted by the consortium of the HERSUS project extends through three academic semesters. Each semester focuses on one of the three pillars, i.e., Restoration, Reuse and Resilience. In the first semester, fundamental knowledge of the field is provided, as well as the concepts of heritage identity preservation, and general challenges related to the past. In the second semester, the focus is on Adaptive Reuse, i.e., heritage identity transformation, composition, revitalisation and challenges related to the present. Finally, in the third semester, the focus is on Resilience, i.e., research on hybrids, building identity and challenges related to the future of heritage.

As indicated through the results of the capacity building phase, particular attention is placed on the Design Studio. This is a strategy to empower the application of theoretically acquired knowledge in practice, dive into more practical aspects of conservation, and familiarise students with real field conditions.

The programme will consist of three semesters, each of which will involve a course on the fundamental aspects of heritage studies (Fundamental 1 – Linking heritage and sustainability, Fundamental 2 – Linking heritage, sustainability and people, Fundamental 3 – Linking heritage, sustainability, people and environment). Also included will be design studio courses, specialisation (electives) courses, workshops and a Master's thesis.

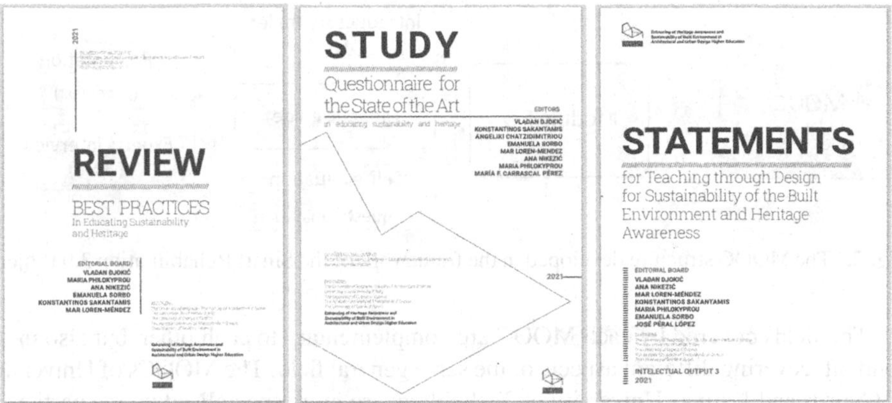

Fig. 1. Research reports of the HERSUS project regarding capacity building [18–20].

4.2 Open Access Online Courses (MOOCs)

Required Competences and Skills for an Expert in the Field of Heritage and Sustainability. The survey conducted on the general competences required for experts in sustainable heritage rehabilitation identified the following: forward-thinking; open-mindedness; ability for trans-cultural understanding and cooperation; participatory, planning and implementation competence; management, mediation and leadership skills; and ability to feel empathy and to motivate people [21]. Specific skills and competences to design/redesign and define/redefine urban spaces in a sustainable way concern the capacity to explore and understand the multifunctionality and layering of heritage. In this sense, it is essential to have a good understanding and involvement in all the stages of rehabilitation or restoration intervention. This includes the initial building survey and diagnosis of the conservation state, as well as the definition of the renovation/restoration project, the implementation and execution of the works, and the capitalisation of a restoration/rehabilitation project after its completion. Finally, the desired professional profile should also include competence in the use of up-to-date digital tools and software. More insight on the qualifications and skills for experts in the rehabilitation sector are published by the consortium of Smart Rehabilitation 3.0 project [22].

Development of MOOC Structure and Contents. In terms of structure, each MOOC comprises five to six modules, with the first one having an introductory character. More specifically, each module contains at least three different resources: a) audio-visual material e.g., video, animated photos, and/or verbal explanations of the basic contents of the module and concepts to be introduced; b) a detailed didactic guide in the form of power-point presentations or text documents, including theoretical references, examples, and links to relevant publications and websites to facilitate a deeper understanding of the subject; c) an assessment of the comprehension of the particular content, in the form of quizzes (self-evaluation practices) (see Fig. 2).

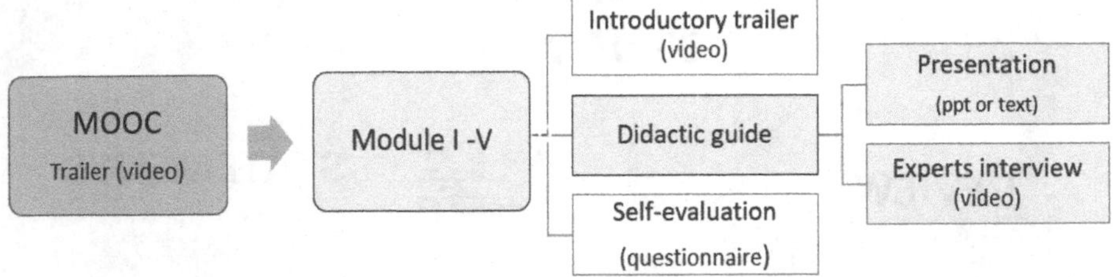

Fig. 2. The MOOC structure developed in the framework of the Smart Rehabilitation 3.0 Project.

The fields covered by each MOOC are complementary to each other, but also independent, covering different aspects of the same general field. The MOOCs of University of Cyprus and Kaunas University of Technology are more specialised in one particular thematic area, focusing on vernacular architecture and wooden constructions respectively. The other two MOOCs developed by University of Palermo and Polytechnic University of Catalonia, cover a wider spectrum of the subject of rehabilitation and renovation strategies (see Fig. 3).

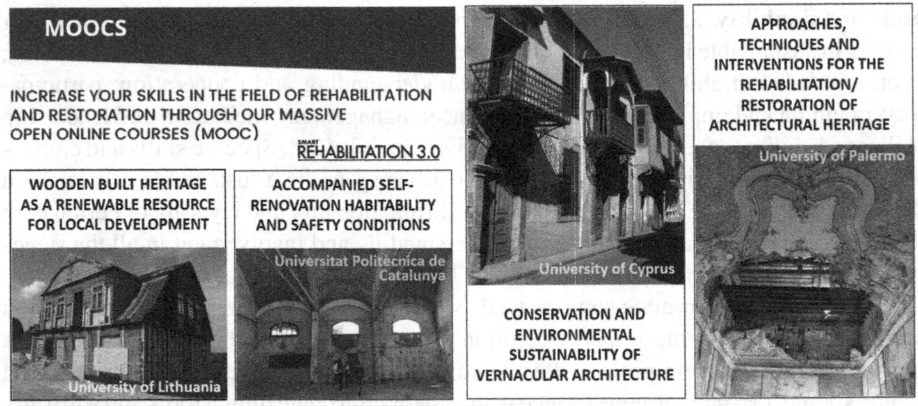

Fig. 3. The four MOOCs developed in the framework of the Smart Rehabilitation 3.0 Project.

4.3 Digital Repositories

Creating digital repositories and freely available online databases is in the spirit of sustainability and the digitisation of education. Such tools result in the creation of a knowledge base which will remain available to all interested parties, irrespective of a projects' duration. Two tools were developed in the framework of both projects: a) a sharing platform – HERSUS Sharing Platform (HSP) – targeted to the wider pubic, professionals and academic community; and b) two online databases for technological innovations regarding heritage (Database no1 and Database no2, developed in the framework of Smart Rehabilitation 3.0), which aim to offer insight into practical aspects of conservation, best practices and case-studies of restoration and rehabilitation.

The HSP (Accessible at: https://HERSUS-sharingplatform.org/) was designed as an innovative tool to enrich teaching and improve the learning experience, functioning as a backbone for open access strategy. The platform is organised into different specific open-access areas: a) open access area for international and inter-disciplinary collaboration and discussion. Here, a network of experts, academics, policy and decision-makers share their knowledge, experience and best practices related to the main topics of the HERSUS project; b) open access area for the dissemination of the project's outputs, studies, analysis and design outputs, etc. In addition, the platform hosts lectures and seminars (held by professors and field experts) on innovative approaches to the sustainability of built cultural heritage, as well as conservation theories and practices. The success of the platform is celebrated internationally, as it recently received the first prize at the 31st International Salon of Urban Planning Exhibition in the categories of: Digital techniques, design and production in urbanism and architecture; Media presentation of urbanism and architecture.

The digital library created in the framework of Smart Rehabilitation 3.0 contains two databases regarding, a) technological innovations, and b) innovative interventions in heritage building rehabilitation (Accessible at: https://smart-rehabilitation.eu/digital-library/). The first Database (no1), entitled 'Technological innovations for rehabilitation', organises the technological innovations according to various building parts, (e.g. foundations and underground structures, vertical structures, horizontal structures and vertical connections, roof and terraces, building façade, finishes and completion elements), integrated services, as well as general strategies for building recovery. Particular attention is placed on the practical aspects of conservation, e.g., the application of new materials, as well as innovative restoration techniques. The techniques hosted on the database are the outcome of valuable input from private companies working in the rehabilitation and restoration sector. The second Database (no2), entitled 'Innovative architectural intervention in rehabilitation', focuses on emblematic case study heritage buildings that have been either restored or rehabilitated. Thus, providing good examples of the integration of innovative approaches in the conservation of built heritage. Local stakeholders and architects involved in rehabilitation/restoration of heritage buildings also contributed to the creation of this database.

5 Conclusions

The work presented in this paper proposes the enhancement and testing of innovative teaching practices in the field of sustainability of built heritage. The results derive from two research projects which strive to bridge the gap between theoretical knowledge and practice in heritage and sustainability. Literature review and questionnaire-based analysis confirmed the increasing complexity of thinking about built heritage, representing a growing challenge for both researchers and educators to implement such topics in curricula. The strategy to address the identified gap between education and practice is through interdisciplinary education and the involvement of relevant stakeholders, institutions, and professionals in postgraduate studies. As far as the link between sustainability and heritage is concerned, a variety of theoretical and methodological approaches are proposed to enhance its importance in architectural and urban design education.

Among the tools developed in this direction are the four MOOCs that offer the potential of e-learning and provide participants with continuous access to education, even in a state of emergency (possibility for remote asynchronous attendance). In this way, a significant contribution to the lifelong learning of rehabilitation strategies and sustainable development is established. In the same direction is the creation of an online platform and open-access repositories for the exchange of information, resources and experience in education, practice, and regulation in the field of heritage protection.

The development of a new innovative graduate programme on heritage and sustainability is of great importance and was achieved with the contribution of the five European Universities. The multidisciplinary character of this programme lies within the involvement of professionals from different fields, as well as the incorporation of various types of courses introducing holistic methodological approaches. Research and design-based courses, workshops, theoretical and practical oriented courses are introduced in the curricula, in an attempt to develop a holistic and broad educational profile for graduates. In this way, education in the field of heritage and sustainability is promoted, preparing students and educators to become real actors in the protection of cultural heritage, safeguarding the environment.

Acknowledgements. HERSUS project was developed in cooperation with the University of Belgrade, Faculty of Architecture as a Lead organisation, Iuav Universita di Venezia, the University of Cyprus, the Aristotle University of Thessaloniki, and the University of Seville, UNESCO Chair on Built Urban Heritage CREhAR in the digital era, co-funded by the Erasmus+ Programme of the European Union (HERSUS.org). The creation of these resources was co-funded under grant no. 2020-1-RS01-KA203-065407 (funding period 2020–2023).

Smart rehabilitation 3.0 project was developed in cooperation with Association Rehabimed as a Lead organisation, Polytechnic University of Catalonia, University of Cyprus, University of Palermo and Kaunas University of Technology, Cesie and AEEBC, co-funded by Erasmus+ Programme of the European Union. Project Number: 2019-1-ES01-KA203-065657 (funding period 2019–2022).

References

1. Jan Borowiecki, K., Fresa, A., Forbes, N. (eds.): Cultural Heritage in a Changing World. Springer Nature, Cham, UK (2016). https://doi.org/10.1007/978-3-319-29544-2
2. UNESCO: Convention Concerning the Protection of the World Cultural and Natural Heritage. UNESCO, Paris (1972)
3. European Commission: Strengthening cultural heritage resilience for climate change: where the European Green Deal meets cultural heritage. Publications Office of the European Union (2022)
4. Carolee, B., Heather, C.: Shaping the future we want: UN Decade of Education for Sustainable Development; final report. UNESCO (2014)
5. Bonn Declaration. UNESCO World Conference on Education for Sustainable Development, 31 March–2 April 2009
6. Holmberg, J., Lotz-Sistka, H., Samuelsson, B., Wals, A.E.J., Wright, T.: Specific recommendations on integrating ESD in higher education. In: Samuelsson, B., Ottosson, P. (eds.) The Gothenburg Recommendations on Education for Sustainable Development. Gothenburg, Sweden

7. Wals, A.E.J.: Sustainability in higher education in the context of the UN DESD: a review of learning and institutionalization processes. J. Clean. Prod. **62**, 8–15 (2014). https://doi.org/10.1016/j.jclepro.2013.06.007
8. Report of the World Commission on Environment and Development : note/by the Secretary-General. (1987)
9. New European Bauhaus Concept Paper. https://europa.eu/neweuropean-bauhaus/system/files/2021-07/2021-06-30_New_European_Bauhaus_Concept_Paper_HLRT_FINAL.pdf#:~:text=The%20goal%20of%20the%20New,of%20the%20European%20Green%20Deal
10. United Nations Department of Economic and Social Affairs: SDG Good Practices: A compilation of success stories and lessons learned in SDG Implementation. UNDESA (2022)
11. Fauzi, M.A.: E-learning in higher education institutions during COVID-19 pandemic: current and future trends through bibliometric analysis. Heliyon **8**, e09433 (2022). https://doi.org/10.1016/j.heliyon.2022.e09433
12. Rapanta, C., Botturi, L., Goodyear, P., Guàrdia, L., Koole, M.: Balancing technology, pedagogy and the new normal: post-pandemic challenges for higher education. Postdigital Sci. Educ. **3**, 715–742 (2021). https://doi.org/10.1007/s42438-021-00249-1
13. Senevirathne, M., Amaratunga, D., Haigh, R., Kumer, D., Kaklauskas, A.: A common framework for MOOC curricular development in climate change education - findings and adaptations under the BECK project for higher education institutions in Europe and Asia. Prog. Disaster Sci. **14**, 100222 (2022). https://doi.org/10.1016/j.pdisas.2022.100222
14. Asfour, O.S., Alkharoubi, A.M.: Challenges and opportunities in online education in Architecture: Lessons learned for Post-Pandemic education. Ain Shams Eng. J. 102131 (2023). https://doi.org/10.1016/j.asej.2023.102131
15. International Union of Architects: UNESCO-UIA Validation Council for Architectural Education. UNESCO-UIA Validation System Procedures Manual for Study Programmes and Systems. , Paris, France, (2017)
16. Djokić, V., Milojevic, M., Milovanović, A.: Enhancing of Heritage Awareness and Sustainability of Built Environment in Architectural and Urban Design Higher Education: Review of Best Practices. Presented at the XI SCIENTIFIC AND PROFESSIONAL CONFERENCE, Cultural Heritage Preservation Insitute of Belgrade (2021)
17. Djordjevic, A., et al.: Developing methodological framework for addressing sustainability and heritage in architectural higher education—insights from HERSUS project. Sustainability **14**, 4597 (2022). https://doi.org/10.3390/su14084597
18. Djokić, V., Philokyprou, M., Nikezić, A., Sorbo, E., Sakantamis, K., Loren-Méndez, M. (eds.): REVIEW: Best Practices in Educating Sustainability and Heritage. University of Belgrade, Faculty of Architecture (2021)
19. Djokić, V., et al. (eds.): Questionnaire for the State of Art in educating sustainability and heritage. University of Belgrade, Faculty of Architecture (2021)
20. Djokić, V., et al. (eds.): STATEMENTS for Teaching through Design for Sustainability of the Built Environment and Heritage Awareness. University of Belgrade, Faculty of Architecture (2021)
21. Michelsen, G., Burandt, S.: Sustainable development as a guideline for higher education: an innovative concept for teaching and learning. In: decade of progress on education for sustainable development: reflections from the UNESCO Chairs Programme, pp. 38–47. UNDP United Nations Educational, Scientific andCultural Organization (2017)
22. Smart Rehabilitation 3.0: Building Rehabilitation Expert. Development of training programs for a new professional qualification. RehabiMed (2022)

Development of a Support System for Improved Resilience and Sustainable Urban Areas to Cope with Climate Change and Extreme Events Based on GEOSS and Advanced Modelling Tools

Charalampos Zafeiropoulos(✉), Ioannis N. Tzortzis, Ioannis Rallis, and Anastasios Doulamis

Institute of Communication and Computer Systems, Athens, Greece
{mpampiszafeiropoulos,itzortzis}@mail.ntua.gr, irallis@central.ntua.gr, adoulam@cs.ntua.gr

Abstract. The proposed framework focuses on developing integrated solutions for urban environments, based on the European needs of security, health, prosperity and wellbeing, with regards to the detrimental impact of Climate Change (CC). To achieve that, this research will combine multiple Earth Observation (EO) datasets, such as GEOSS and Copernicus datasets and services, with ensemble modelling, socio-economic and in-situ data at the spatial and temporal scales, at which interactions in the land and atmosphere ecosystems operate. Regarding to the Sustainable Urban Development, this work posits that use of EO is a crucial tool towards resilient cities and the assessment of urban footprints, to promote equity, welfare and shared prosperity for all. Next, the proposed framework will test modern Remote Sensing (RS) tools and 3D and 4D monitoring, Machine Learning (ML)/Deep Learning (DL), Artificial Intelligence (AI) techniques to develop a modular scalable data-driven multi-layer urban areas observation information knowledge base. Information about the local level of neighborhoods/building blocks will be provided by the use of Satellite data time series, spatial information and auxiliary data. The scope focuses on two pillars: a) Natural and manmade hazards intensified by CC: urban flooding, soil degradation and geo-hazards (landslides, earthquake and ground deformation) and b) Manmade hazards: heat islands, urban heat fluxes, Air Quality (AQ) and gas emissions (e.g., Green House Gas (GHG) emissions). Therefore, pollution and microclimatic monitoring strategy will be developed based on a combination of satellite observation technologies (including Unmanned Aerial Vehicles-UAV) acquisitions Near-Infrared (NIR) caption, multiband Synthetic Aperture Radar (SAR), high-resolution thermal IR imaging, optical and infrared radiometers, atmospheric composition monitoring, altimetry caption - and onsite meteorological-AQ monitoring systems. Last but not least, this research will not neglect the social and humanitarian aspects of resilience planning and will use crowdsourced data under GDPR rules which can give invaluable information with respect to citizens' lives.

Keywords: Earth Observation · Climate Change · Geo-hazards · Thermal IR imaging

A. Moropoulou et al. (Eds.): TMM_CH 2023, CCIS 1889, pp. 364–374, 2023.
https://doi.org/10.1007/978-3-031-42300-0_31

1 Introduction

The proposed platform will offer integrated AI and Decision Support System (DSS) solutions for Earth Observation (EO) researchers, AI specialists, policy makers, citizens and the wider audience to create and analyze valuable EO and non-EO big data. This platform will be developed with the fundamental principle to provide a interoperable ecosystem taking into consideration other initiatives and State of Art (SoA) solutions (i.e., DIAS, ONDA, GEOSS). This research employs AI tools on top of GEOSS and offers innovative solutions for risk management, damage prevention, protection from eco hazards and preparedness for potential future calamities. The majority of the adopted technologies are already mature providing cutting edge solutions (i.e., Hopswork, Elastic, Kibana, Granafa, TensorFlow). In the context of this project, the beneficiaries will focus to extend the capabilities of existing solutions in order to provide decision support tools for urban environments, tailored to the needs of European citizens and public stake-holders in domains of health, prosperity, security and overall well-being to address the detrimental impact of Climate Change (CC). This work integrates GEOSS urban and climate data with other local, regional and global datasets to develop applications that support adaptation and mitigation measures of the Paris Agreement for urban environments, in a state-of-the-art seamless "holistic solution".

Authorized members and data engineers will have access to both data and metadata from distributed EO and non-EU sources using download services acting as a Discovery and Access Broker (DAB). The GEO DAB implements the necessary mediation and harmonization services through APIs. These APIs allow data providers to share resources without having to make major changes to their technology or standards. Presently, GEOSS Platform brokers include more than 150 autonomous data catalogs and information systems, useful for the different GEO Societal Benefit Areas including data from: CAFF [1], Data.gov [2], EEA [3], GBIF [4], JRC Open Data catalog [5], NASA [6], NCAR [7], NOAA [8], OCHA HDX [9], RCMRD [10], UNEP [11], UNOSAT [12], USGS [13], WMO WIS [14] and many more. Data providers are constantly being added and brokered, according to user needs, the thematic and geographic balance of the data and the relevance of shared resources. Project's services, as well as the IRAP [15] applications will all make use of this GEOSS [16] brokerage. The processing, transformation, storage and retrieval of climate and georeferenced data that are collected from various heterogeneous sources is an essential task of the platform that aims to exploit AI and ML techniques for predictive modelling, accurate decision-making procedures and an eye-catching visualization interface considering access to multiple databases.

In the initial version, the platform will consider previous solutions and existing applications developed by the beneficiaries and or other EU funded projects (i.e., AI4EU, AI4Copernicus). In addition, at this stage all the appropriate open-source solutions will be scrutinized providing interoperable and secure interconnections among all submodules. Furthermore, the consortium will survey the adaptation of licensed software (i.e., Hopswork) or other services (i.e., VMs, AWS) that could provide added value to the ecosystem. This platform will ensure seamless communication among the sub-modules, components and third-party applications considering the minimization of complexity and computational costs. The platform will be upgraded periodically targeting on a more coupled integration optimizing dataflows, processing (meta)data among various sources and APIs, from data harmonization to the visualization.

2 Materials and Methods

2.1 Related Work

There are many indicative relevant projects and approaches whose results will be used within our framework. 7FP URBAN-API (ASDE) introduces advanced technologies for predicting results from different growth models of urban growth (under URBAN-API - 7th FP of the EU). The project provides urban planners with: a) The 3D Scenario Creator, b) The Mobility Explorer c) The Urban Development Simulator. BG-FR-BULGARISK (ASDE) presents integrated satellite images in operational procedures for risk management in Bulgaria. The project is a French-Bulgarian project, aiming to integrate satellite imageries in the operational procedures of risk management in Bulgaria. Led by Spot Image/Astrium and the State Agency for Information Technologies and Communications. The project developed operational capacities on satellite and in-situ data integration and interpretation, as well as fast track mapping, early warning procedures, simulation modeling on various nature risks – floods, forest fires, etc. EO4SEE (UVT) proposes pathfinder assessment for regional high volume data access, processing and information service delivery platforms – South Eastern Europe Region.

SEN4RUS (GSH, FORTH) develops indicators that effectively and efficiently exploit the information content provided by Copernicus Sentinels mass data streams in support of city and regional planning in Russia. INDESMUSA (GSH) offers integrated monitoring solutions constitute a prerequisite towards risk mitigation and urban planning policies against soil subsidence and seismic motion, providing valuable knowledge and data for investigating the corresponding physical mechanisms. FLOODIS (ALPHA) proposes exploitation of European satellite technologies to support populations affected by flood event in Europe and worldwide. To this extent, EO and GNSS technologies are combined to deliver alerts and interactive maps on flooding risk/ events and affected infrastructures to users in the field that are in the geographical area at risk. The developed methodologies for the exploitation strategy and socio-economic impact will be applied to this framework in the frame of the "Exploitation Activities, Route to the Market and Sustainability issues". I-REACT(ALPHA) focuses on developing a solution through the integration and modelling of data coming multiple sources. Information from European monitoring systems, EO, historical information and weather forecasts are combined. The developed methodologies for the exploitation strategy and socio-economic impact will be applied to this work. SHELTER's (ALPHA) purpose is to establish cross-scale, multidimensional, data-driven and community based operational knowledge framework for heritage-led and conservation-friendly resilience enhancement and sustainable reconstruction of Historic Areas to cope with CC and natural hazards. The developed methodologies for the exploitation strategy and socio-economic impact will be applied to this research in the frame of the "Exploitation Activities, Route to the Market and Sustainability issues".

URBANFLUXES (FORTH) proposes new methods for estimating the spatiotemporal distribution of urban heat fluxes in local scale by using Copernicus Sentinels data and exploiting their improved quality, coverage and revisit times. GEOURBAN

(FORTH) supports the development and on-line evaluation of satellite-based indicators for urban planning and management. CURE's (FORTH) goal is the development of Copernicus Services cross-cutting applications for urban resilience. DRM (CTI) proposes drone Rapid Mapping, support for Polish Crisis Information Centre, rapid processing of images acquired by drones. CREODIAS cloud infrastructure-based processing data sent by drone operators from the field resulting in fast automated geospatial products generation (vital support for emergency rescue teams' activities in disaster areas). ProGIreg(URBASOFIA-Piraeus) Productive Green Infrastructure for Post-Industrial Urban Regeneration. Lastly, RA-SOR (INGV) built an open access online platform for the rapid analysis of a number of natural risks.

2.2 The Project

This framework employs AI tools on top of GEOSS and offers innovative solutions for risk management, damage prevention, protection from eco-hazards and preparedness for potential future calamities. This work also streamlines the process of formulating long-term strategic approaches to adapt to CC and wield policy tools for economic resilience. This research aims to achieve that by introducing a research framework which downscales the created climate and atmospheric composition and the associated risk maps down to the building block - neighborhoods (urban site) scale, applying the suitable damage functions. Applying atmospheric modelling for specific CC scenarios at such refined spatial and temporal scales allows for an accurate quantitative and qualitative impact assessment of the estimated micro-climatic and atmospheric stressors. This project will perform combined damage assessment under normal (past) and changed (future) conditions (anthropogenic and/or natural disasters) for urban heat, geohazards [17], ecosystem damage and human health, based on the climatic zone, the micro-climate conditions and the environmental/physical characteristics of the surrounding environment. The data coming from the integrated monitoring system will be coupled with simulated data (under the IRAT environment) and will be further analysed through our data management system and support communities' participation and public awareness. The data from the monitoring system will support sustainable plans for the urban areas damages to the vulnerable assets. The system ends up to an enhanced visualization tool with improved 4D capabilities (3D + time) that can provide a simple and easy way for all relevant stakeholders to assess damage. The produced vulnerability map (based on the produced climate risk regional models) will be used by the local authorities to assess the threats of CC (and other natural hazards), visualize the built environment and urban landscape under future climate scenarios, model the effects of different adaptation strategies, and ultimately prioritize any rehabilitation actions to best allocate funds in both pre- and post-event environments (Fig. 1).

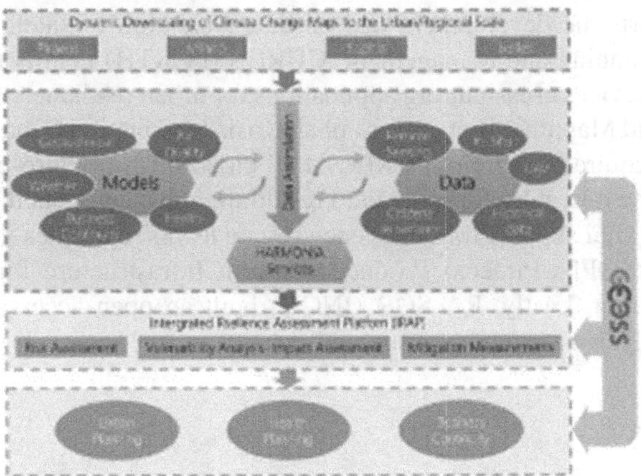

Fig. 1. Iterative Research Methodology For Each Research Step

3 Results Discussion

3.1 Strategic Objectives

First strategic objective refers to the reliable quantification of climatic, hydrological and atmospheric stressors. The proposed framework employs quality-assessed numerical modelling results for selected climate scenarios in city centres, covering processes and interactions from the short-term to the long-term (10 years-end of the century). These data will be used to estimate quantitative indicators for the potential impact of CC on urban areas, at scales ranging at neighborhood size. Changes in the average climate and the increase of climatic/weather events intensity and frequency will both be considered. A Land Surface Model will be used to account for the impact of climate and atmospheric composition on soil surface parameters (e.g., the presence of liquid water).

Second strategic objective is the reliable quantification of urban heat fluxes and their effects on air quality. This research enhances the scientific and operational exploitation of timely and reliable EO data from the Copernicus missions in combination with simple meteorological measurements to quantify the past and current state of the heat conditions in cities. These data will be used to estimate the urban heat emissions and the net flow of the heat stored in the urban canopy at local scale. The urban heat emission refers to the heat exchange between the urban surface and the atmosphere, namely the turbulent sensible heat flux. It is strongly modified by the specific properties of the urban surface, i.e., 3D geometry, high roughness, impervious surfaces, complex source/sink distribution and injections of heat and water into the urban atmosphere by human activities (traffic, heating, waste management, etc.). This research will implement the Aerodynamic Resistance Method4 to estimate it at local scale, following the most advanced methodologies for determining the aerodynamic resistance parameterization. The net low of the heat stored in urban canopy represents all the mechanisms of storage of energy within the volume, i.e., the air, on trees, in buildings constructed in the ground, etc. Among all the effects caused by the substitution of natural ecosystems by urban land-use, the most pronounced is the increase in the amount of energy stored in the urban canopy, which is approximately 2–6 times larger than in non-urban canopies. This research will use an updated version of the Objective Hysteresis Model to estimate heat storage at local scale. For the estimation of the urban heat fluxes, several urban surface cover and morphology products will be derived, as well as the urban surface temperature at local scale, using downscaling approaches. The SUEWS model will be used for urban heat fluxes simulations.

Next strategic objective refers to the reliable quantification of CC effects. Impact assessment of CC and atmospheric composition stressors on urban areas can be conducted with the proposed framework, by identifying and monitoring 20 specialized climate indicators, based on the catalogue of Essential Climate Variables (ECVs), using GEOSS data. At least 5 standardized, multi-hazard modules for vulnerability assessment will be selected and delivered. Downscaled impact maps will be used for potential damage assessment. This research uses two long-term climatic scenarios, those being Baseline and Worst Case. The impact maps and auxiliary data will be used to assess the relationship between the impacts resulting from CC and those due to local geohazards. Monitoring of local geohazards (based on EO and ground data) will be used to model long term hazard occurrence and impacts. The latter will be analysed within the evolving conditions set by macro- and micro-scale CC scenarios to simulate a number of multi-hazard impact scenarios of practical use in urban management. Main cause-effect relationships are expected between the hydrological effects of CC with ground deformation at different scales and rates, as for landslides, areal subsidence, sinkholes. Conversely, the effect of geohazards independent of CC, as earthquake ground shaking, can exacerbate the effects of CC impacts, and will be incorporated in worst case, multi-hazard scenarios.

Regarding the ecological Integrity Indexes - Essential Biodiversity Variables, this work will use the innate feature of the GEOSS platform which monitors the efficiency of policy indicators and directly checks if goals are met (and in which percentage), focusing on urban areas, where large housing concentrations are present, and measures need to be developed the most. The high concentration of impermeable materials such as concrete within urban environments leads to these areas having a disproportionate effect on hydrological flows. Integrating forecasts, measurements and planning rules into one system can help to improve these plans and possibly lead to adaptations of the hydrogeological network in these areas. Treating the planet as a complex but living organism, this project aims to install stations to monitor anthropization (the process of human action degrading terrain and soil), aided by meteorological monitoring satellite systems, a process which can massively contribute to the management of ecosystem components in an organic and homogenous way. Vegetation Fluorescence Mapping using airborne/UAV on site surveys will quantify photosynthetic activity in cities, assess the climate-alteration potential of emissions and estimate how the 'urban green to build environment' ratio might play into the carbon cycle and affect human health. Using these variables (Ecological Integrity indexes and Essential Biodiversity Variables), the proposed framework will reliably forecast the transformation of urban ecosystems, make estimations regarding ecological integrity and biodiversity, through a GIS-based environment with geospatial tool applications. The vast data set will be harmonized to ensure information clarity and transferability, with respect to cultural development and ethical diversities intrinsic to the study areas.

Another strategic objective is the multi-Hazard modelling. As CC aggravates environmental (temperature, humidity etc.) and hazardous (mudflow, landslide, flooding etc.) phenomena in urban areas, which are often afflicted by contemporaneous events, this research aims to provide thorough, exhaustive solutions that take all such factors into account. Through hydrological and seismic modelling, this work will be used to produce inundation maps, as well as seismic hazard maps (quantified in terms of peak ground acceleration, spectral estimates, and surface faulting deformations), and their spatiotemporal distribution for any given area by using stochastic modelling approaches (probabilistic seismic hazard analysis). Analysis of CC risk scenarios in 1D, 2D and 3D spatial resolution and assessment of CC impacts on acceleration of materials and elements degradation will also be monitored.

Another challenge rise through the environmental monitoring – state of the art identification and diagnosis. The proposed framework will be capable of producing a plethora of crucial data for damage assessment such as: a) smart wide-area damage assessment maps, degradation analysis, contour diagrams and temperature profiles, b) full 3D capabilities for the city and models, c) spatiotemporal 4D change detection maps assessing damages, taking changes in climate into account, d) construction of an environmental condition profile for urban sites (sea-level rise, ditch overflows, Urban heat fluxes). All this is possible through novel Computer Vision (CV), ML/DL algorithms, which utilize data from a vast array of sources, namely: i) Satellite, Airborne, “low cost” terrestrial sensors, such as unattended microclimate stations (wind-speed, air humidity, temperature, soil moisture and temperature), ii) smart tags (air humidity, temperature, vibrations), iii) information from active communities’ participation. All these allows the proposed framework to precisely describe urban sites and bolsters efforts to combat CC and geohazards.

Regarding the citizens - active communities, the strategy focuses on fully exploiting the potential of the ‘citizens as observatories’. The active participation of citizens using smartphones, armed with low-cost sensors (new mobile solutions for community science), will be encouraged. Customization of this equipment will be available, taking into account users’ expertise. The proposed framework strikes a balance between data quality and ease of measurability, tailored to non-technical agents. Thus, this research, also, serves an educational role, emboldening communities to involve themselves in environmental affairs and dutifully co-operate with institutional and scientific components.

Another challenge refers to the design of an Integrated Resilience Assessment Tool (IRAT), which supports communities’ participation. The proposed environment allows the integration of various analysis, modelling tools and damage/vulnerability functions, incorporating information from a plethora of sources (literature, surveys, census, satellite, etc.), including data collected from the’citizens-as-observatories’ initiative with different levels of granularity (building/block/ national level) accounting for the associated uncertainties. IRAT is a GIS-based cross-platform initiative, integrating existing open-source hazard assessment software and network simulators, together with socioeconomic impact analysis tools. The result is a comprehensive application capable of producing quantitative and qualitative estimations (such as loss estimations), used for the development of an end-to-end simulation platform, capable of running any number of different "what-if" scenarios. In effect, IRAT offers: i) Risk and impact assessment of geological, atmospheric and urban heat phenomena on the structural/non-structural components of the urban environment, ii) Testing and evaluation of risk management approaches, plans, strategies and countermeasures, iii) Resilience - Sensitivity appraisal of urban areas, regarding individual or cascading hazardous events, iv) Simulation of a disastrous event, to estimate damages and facilitate faster response times, v) Streamlining of the response strategies and contingency plans formulation process, vi) Maximum Acceptable Damage (MAD) evaluations of urban environments, vii) A community-based, participatory environment, with built-in APIs for social media. IRAT aims to integrate all the hazard and impact assessment tools and modelling data in order to support decisions at a strategic, tactical and operational level.

Next challenge includes the validation of results in Milano, Ixelles, Piraeus and Sofia. The main focus of this project will be on testing the project outcomes in real-scale, neighborhoods and in 4D. A comparison will be made between the proposed system versus manual, non-automated methods, measuring cost, benefit and incurred procedures. For the purposes of the initial demonstration, the platform will be integrated on-site in the cities of Milano, Ixelles, Piraeus and Sofia.

Last strategic objective refers to the provision of a Handbook to include: a) technical information on methodologies and AI tools for sustainable urban areas, b) proper response strategies for various CC and urban heat, air pollution and geo-hazards, c) post-disaster reconstruction examples, d) practical checklists and references to assist practitioners, field-workers, city authorities and other stakeholders in making the proper choices, e) recovery requirements identified for each business sector and operational area, and f) guides and techniques to encourage, facilitate, design and develop bespoke reciprocal agreements between same type of businesses so as to facilitate timely service/product provision recovery.

3.2 Measuring the Impact

The proposed framework will use the direct support of the adaptation and mitigation measures of the Paris Agreement, as well as the other GEO engagement priorities such as the Agenda for Sustainable Development, and the Sendai Framework for Disaster Risk Reduction 2015–2030; This project offers detailed, data-driven, sensor-informed modeling of urban areas, revealing an unprecedented resolution in time and space, and helps communities predict, assess and combat CC induced hazards focusing on urban flooding, soil degradation, buildings erosion, geohazards and urban heat and AQ. Through this research and IRAT, multi-hazard risk evaluation, improved preparation procedures and faster response times to these phenomena will be accomplished, though suitable adaptation and mitigation measures, in accordance with the Paris Agreement, the Agenda for Sustainable Development and the Sendai Framework for Disaster Risk Reduction 2015–2030. This work aims to enhance resilience and reduce vulnerability of urban areas to CC related hazards.

The proposed framework will measure the impact based on the European input to the GEO Work Programme post-2019 to address the climate change challenge cross-cutting all GEO Societal Benefit Areas (SBA) (e.g. for improved land use management); This project is a crucial tool for any urban community to pursue the mitigation of hazardous CC related phenomena. This operates in service of the SBAs (all of which relate to climate), around which the GEO Programme is exerting its efforts. This research will help communities, urban planners and policy makers to tackle Sustainable Urban Development, Disaster Resilience as well as Biodiversity and Ecosystem Sustainability and take the critical actions possible to address urgent environmental challenges. With respect to environmental integrity and resilience, this work will incentivize European communities to address CC and foster to EO data and AI use for urban planning.

Nowadays, Europe experiences an increasing capability to combine multiple EO data sets with models, socio-economic and in-situ data, based on a systematic exploitation of the GEOSS Platform; The proposed framework will develop, deploy and validate modern RS tools and systems to enhance the resilience of urban sites. The project aims to use satellite and auxiliary data available in EuroGEOSS, and other operational EU and international services like DIAS and urban TEP, GEP, in order to quantify CC effects on urban areas, seeing the lack of a dedicated process towards this goal. Hence, data, info and processed products (using current AI techniques) will be delivered faster (30%) than using exclusively COPERNICUS and TEP. ML/DL techniques help to develop a modular scalable data-driven multi-layer urban area observation information knowledge base. The timely, multi-modal data and geospatial information will be integrated with other data coming from airborne and existing on-situ sensors, as well as with statistical and socio- economic data for the pollution and microclimatic strategies. Enhanced CV and ML- DL algorithms will be used for improved and faster identifications of damages to diverse structures in near real time processing complexity.

Moreover, European observing systems have been developed for the monitoring of internationally recognised Essential Climate Variables (co); This project will conduct an impact assessment of CC, urban heat and atmospheric composition stressors on urban areas by identifying and monitoring 20 specialized climate indicators, according to the catalogue of ECVs, using GEOSS data, visualizing tools and onsite meteorological-AQ monitoring systems.

Another impact refers to new EuroGEOSS pilot applications to better understand climate change contributors and impacts, and minimise the degradation of the Earth system, support accountability towards long-term goals and inform climate services and decision making. The open-source suite of software developed under the project will be available to the e-shape Pilots to be incorporated into their services, leading to direct impact on European communities and promoted and developed as part of the e-shape project (GA 820852–See Section 1.3.1.3). The datasets and infrastructure developed in the proposed framework will be specifically useful to e—shape Showcase 6/Pilot 2: GEOSS for disaster management and Showcase 6/Pilot 3: Assessing Geohazard vulnerability of cities and critical infrastructure.

Last impact includes the mobilising the most dynamic actors of the European commercial sector, developing new EO-derived mass markets and increasing cross-domain exploitation of EO data, the proposed framework has been conceived to include since the very beginning dynamic actors of the European commercial sector, such as experienced SMEs and advanced research centres, all with a strong expertise on EO-based applications. These actors could register different impacts thanks to the project, considering that they could exploit this platform in different sectors. Moreover, they can, also, provide new EO-based services and solutions (for future development and adoption), e.g., from technological products to consultancy services, from marketing to commercial activities, from user involvement to communication actions with a cross-domain approach. In fact, the majority of these products and services could target different markets (e.g. from emergency management to precise agriculture), different industries (from urban planners to health departments units or insurance companies) and different geographies (European to a global dimension). In line with that, the project will reach and involve other relevant actors within the European commercial sector to enhance its potential impact towards institutional and private players, as well as professionals and mass-markets within different domains.

4 Conclusion

This work provided a short introduction to Harmonia; an EU funded project, which purpose is to combat climate change using all sorts of tools, methods, and policy commitments. To support the adaptation and mitigation measures of the Paris Agreement, the EU-funded project focus on a solution for climate applications. It tests modern remote sensing tools and 3D-4D monitoring. Specifically, the project leverage existing tools and services to deliver an integrated assessment platform working on top of Global Earth Observation System of Systems (GEOSS). Machine learning/deep learning techniques are also used to develop a modular, scalable, data-driven, multi-layer knowledge base of urban areas. The proposed framework considers the local ecosystems of European urban areas with extra attention to sustainable urban development goals. The project aims to deliver an integrated resilience assessment platform (IRAP).

Acknowledgement. This paper is supported by the European Union Funded project Harmonia "Development of a Support System for Improved Resilience and Sustainable Urban areas to cope with Climate Change and Extreme Events based on GEOSS and Advanced Modelling Tools" under the Horizon 2020 program H2020-EU.3.5.6., grant agreement No 101003517.

References

1. https://www.caff.is/
2. Lakhani, K.R., Austin, R.D., Yi, Y.: Data. Gov. Harvard Business School (2002)
3. https://www.eea.europa.eu/data-and-maps
4. Beck, J., et al.: Spatial bias in the GBIF database and its effect on modeling species' geographic distributions. Ecol. Inform. **19**, 10–15 (2014)
5. Friis-Christensen, A., et al.: The JRC multidisciplinary research data infrastructure. In: Proceedings of the 19th International Conference on Information Integration and Web-based Applications Services (2017)

6. Acker, J.G., Leptoukh, G.: Online analysis enhances use of NASA earth science data. Eos, Trans. Am. Geophys. Union **88**(2), 14–17 (2007)
7. Kripalani, R.H., Kulkarni, A., Sabade, S.S.: Western Himalayan snow cover and Indian monsoon rainfall: a re-examination with INSAT and NCEP/NCAR data. Theor. Appl. Climatol. **74**, 1–18 (2003)
8. Gruber, A., Krueger, A.F.: The status of the NOAA outgoing longwave radiation data set. Bull. Am. Meteorol. Soc. **65**(9), 958–962 (1984)
9. https://data.humdata.org/
10. https://www.rcmrd.org/about-us
11. Van Leeuwen, S.P.J., De Boer, J., Van Bavel, B.: First worldwide UNEP interlaboratory study on persistent organic pollutants (POPs), with data on polychlorinated biphenyls and organochlorine pesticides. TrAC, Trends Anal. Chem. **46**, 110–117 (2013)
12. Sean, M., Lorenzo, P. M.: Using the Grid for Satellite Imagery with UNOSAT. Internal UNOSAT-CERN report (2005)
13. https://www.usgs.gov/
14. https://public.wmo.int/en
15. Tzortzi, J.N., et al.: HARMONIA: strategy of an integrated resilience assessment platform (IRAP) with available tools and geospatial services. In: IOP Conference Series: Earth and Environmental Science, vol. 1122. no. 1. IOP Publishing (2022)
16. Roncella, R., et al.: Publishing NextGEOSS data on the GEOSS Platform. Big Earth Data, **7**(2), 413-427
17. Baumann, P., Rossi, A.P.:2016 IEEE International Geoscience and Remote Sensing Symposium: IGARSS Datacubes as a Service Paradigm, pp. 186–188 (2016)

Cultural Heritage Protection and Artificial Intelligence; The Future of Our Historical Past

Eugenia Giannini[1(✉)] and Evi Makri[2]

[1] National Technical University of Athens, Attorney at Law, Eugenia Giannini and Associates Law Firm, Athens, Greece
gianninimail.ntua.gr

[2] National Technical University of Athens, Athens, Greece
evimakri@mail.ntua.gr

Abstract. This paper aims to present the existing regulatory framework, both at the level of the European Union and at the level of Greece, regarding the protection of cultural goods and the wider cultural heritage. The paper is a comprehensive overview of the conventions, agreements and legal texts adopted, at the international and regional level, for the protection of cultural heritage.

In particular, the paper begins with the presentation of the main terminology aiming to give the concept of cultural heritage as it has been shaped over time and the elements that define it.

Therefore, in the first part, the paper presents the main definitions as set through the UNESCO Convention for the Protection of the World Cultural and Natural Heritage of 1972.

Then, the paper, in the second part, analyzes the existing regulatory protection framework as it applies in the European Union. First, the basic pieces of European legislation aiming at protecting cultural heritage, at all levels and by any means, are presented. Then, the corresponding framework established at the national level, in Greece, is analyzed in a similar way.

In the third part, the connection with Artificial Intelligence (Artificial Intelligence and henceforth AI) is attempted. The connection focuses on two main areas: the first concerns the possibilities that Artificial Intelligence provides in the protection of Cultural Heritage and the second the possibilities offered through AI in improving the accessibility of the individual to cultural goods. Finally, the approach of developing that regulatory framework that will delimit the possibilities of AI within the framework of Ethics and the reliability of Artificial Intelligence methods is attempted.

Keywords: Cultural Heritage · Monuments · Natural Heritage · Protection · Regulatory Framework · Cultural Goods · Artificial Intelligence · Ethics

A. Moropoulou et al. (Eds.): TMM_CH 2023, CCIS 1889, pp. 375–400, 2023.
https://doi.org/10.1007/978-3-031-42300-0_32

1 Introduction

1.1 The Notion of Cultural Heritage

A. Cultural heritage, as defined by UNESCO, is "the heritage of physical objects and intangible characteristics of a group or society that are inherited from past generations, preserved in the present and handed down for the benefit of future generations" [1][1].

In addition, the term is also defined by Article 1 of the 1972 Convention for the Protection of the World Cultural and Natural Heritage (World Heritage Convention), which considers the following types of natural artefacts and intangible features as "cultural heritage" [2][2]:

- monuments: architectural works, works of monumental sculpture and painting, elements or constructions of an archaeological nature, inscriptions, cave dwellings and combinations of features, which have outstanding global value from the point of view of history, art or science;
- groups of buildings: groups of separate or connected buildings which, because of their architecture, their homogeneity or their position in the landscape, have outstanding universal value from the point of view of history, art or science;
- sites: works of man or combined works of nature and man, as well as places, including archaeological sites, which have outstanding universal value from a historical, aesthetic, ethnological or anthropological point of view.

The World Heritage Convention, as it also covers the protection of Natural Heritage, proceeds by considering it as the set of those natural features formed by natural and biological formations or as the groups of various such formations of exceptional universal value from an aesthetic or scientific point of view. In addition, geological and physiographic formations and precisely demarcated areas that constitute the habitat of endangered species of animals and plants of exceptional universal value from the point of view of science, or the conservation of the natural environment, are also considered as Natural Heritage.

The convention then includes in the meaning of the term, natural sites or precisely defined natural areas of outstanding universal value in terms of science, conservation or natural beauty [2][3].

It is also observed that the vision of the protection of Cultural Heritage is further expanded after the adoption of the World Heritage Convention (1972). In particular with the 1980 Recommendation on the Safeguarding and Preservation of Moving Images, UNESCO recognizes the audiovisual Heritage as part of the Cultural Heritage. So the Moving Images are dynamically added to the protective network of the World Heritage.

---

[1] Magdalena Pasikowska-Schnass, Briefing on Cultural heritage in EU policies, PE 621.876–June 2018

[2] Article 1, Convention for the Protection of the World Cultural and Natural Heritage, Paris, November 1972

[3] Article 2, Convention for the Protection of the World Cultural and Natural Heritage, Paris, November 1972

In addition, the concept of Cultural Heritage was broadened once again with the adoption of the 2001 Convention on Underwater Heritage aimed at the protection of underwater areas and, subsequently, with the 2003 Convention aimed at safeguarding the Intangible Cultural Heritage, which added a new dimension to the term regarding the protection of human traditions and way of life.

Overall, taking into account the armed conflicts that threaten the preservation of cultural heritage, which is protected by The Hague Convention for the Protection of Cultural Property and its two Protocols, since 1954, UNESCO has categorized cultural inheritance to the following types:

- tangible heritage, which includes movable heritage such as sculptures, paintings, coins and manuscripts; immovable monuments, archaeological sites and others; and underwater cultural heritage such as shipwrecks, underwater ruins and cities;
- intangible heritage, such as oral traditions, performing arts, crafts and rituals;
- natural heritage, i.e. cultural landscapes, geological, biological and physical formations; and
- cultural heritage threatened by destruction and looting in armed conflicts.

Under this prism, the World Heritage List was sculpted, in which several sites and traditions are included.

B. Among the heritage included in the List, almost half of the sites and a quarter of the intangible cultural heritage are located in Europe and mainly in the EU [1]. This spatial designation is obviously not exclusive and definitive. On the contrary, it highlights the problem of recording the elements of the Cultural Heritage at a global level so that UNESCO can extend its safety net to these elements as well. However, at the European level, the European Union has developed the relevant regulatory framework in order to ensure the protection of Cultural Heritage within the territorial scope of the EU member states.

2 The Regulatory Framework on the Protection of Cultural Heritage

2.1 The Framework in the European Union

A. Multilateral Conventions

Considering the total amount of cultural heritage elements found in various forms in the area of the European Union, the action taken in the EU level towards the protection of it, has been shaped by several relevant Conventions and further developed within the Union's regulatory framework by specific regulatory acts. Apart from these, the importance of culture is highlighted under the Treaty of the Functioning of the European Union and more particularly the Article 167 of it. According to the provisions of the aforementioned, it is initially noted that the Union "shall contribute to the flowering of the cultures of the Member States, while respecting their national and regional diversity and at the same time bringing the common cultural heritage to the fore".

In addition, Article 167 sets the aim for the relevant action taken by the EU to encourage inter-Union cooperation and to support the Member States when their actions are related to i) improving the knowledge and dissemination of the culture and history of the European peoples; ii) conserving and protecting cultural heritage of European significance; iii) boosting artistic and literary creation, including in the audiovisual sector; and iv) conducting non-commercial cultural exchanges. Moreover, it is pointed out by the provisions of the present Article, that Member States are expected to enhance cooperation with third countries and the competent international organizations in the sector of culture, with particular emphasis being given on the Council of Europe. Furthermore, the EU is obliged to consider all the necessary cultural aspects when acting under the provisions of the Treaties, aiming to promote the diversity of its cultures and to boost respect towards them [3][4].

Finally, the TFEU foresees the need for the European institutions to act in specific ways in order to contribute to the success of the previous goals. More specifically, according to the same Article, the European Parliament and the Council shall act in accordance with all the legislative procedure and adopt any incentive measures, only after consulting the Committee of the Regions respectively. Excluded from such measures are those concerning any harmonization of the laws and regulations of the Member States. In addition, the Council, also acting in accordance with the relevant legislation, shall adopt recommendations, following the Commission's proposals [3][5].

Further, in 1985, the Council of Europe established, through the Granada Convention, which focuses on the protection of Architectural Heritage, the common principles of European coordination and cooperation on architectural conservation policies. Thus, contracting Parties of it undertake, inter alia, the tasks of taking statutory measures to protect the architectural heritage, within the framework of which and by means specific to each State or region, they also need to shape the provisions for the protection of monuments, groups of buildings and sites [4][6].

Following, with the 1992 Valetta Convention on the Protection of the Archaeological Heritage, the aim of protecting archaeological heritage from illegal excavations and major construction projects was set. To this end, Parties undertake to institute, in a proportionate way, a legislative system on the protection of the archaeological heritage, provisioning in particular the framework on the maintenance of an inventory of its archaeological heritage and the designation of protected monuments and areas; the creation of archaeological reserves, even where there are no visible remains on the ground or under water, for the preservation of material evidence to be studied by later generations, as well as the reporting, mandatorily, to the competent authorities by a finder of the chance discovery of elements of the archaeological heritage and setting them available for examination [5].

Further, Parties are expected to apply procedures for the authorization and supervision of excavation and other archaeological activities in such a way, so that to prevent any illicit excavation or removal of elements of the archaeological heritage

[4] Article 167, par. 2–4 , TFEU

[5] Article 167, par. 5, TFEU

[6] Article 2, Convention on the protection of Architectural Heritage, Granada, 1985

and ensure at the same time that archaeological excavations and prospecting are undertaken in a scientific manner. They are also expected to safeguard that excavations and other potentially destructive techniques are carried out only by qualified, specially authorized persons, using methods and equipment also properly authorized under the relevant domestic legislation [5][7].

A few years later, in 2001, the EU Convention on the Protection of the Audiovisual Heritage broadened the understanding of cultural heritage, by expanding it to audiovisual productions, under the provisions of which it was moreover introduced as a requirement the compulsory legal deposit of moving image material, such as films and videos [6][8].

Then, the Framework Convention on the Value of Cultural Heritage for Society that followed in 2005, emphasized in the social and economic benefits of preserving cultural heritage as a prerequisite for achieving sustainable development. Consequently, it defined the common European heritage as covering all forms of cultural heritage, in the context of a shared source of identity. The convention, throughout its provisions focused on the importance of the cultural heritage to the creativity and social cohesion, and to the ideals, principles and values deriving from previous experiences and current efforts to make progress. Finally, through the provisions of the Faro Convention the link between cultural heritage and the development of a peaceful society is presented, which is based on the constant respect for human rights and the rule of law [7].

Additionally, the Council of Europe Convention on Offences relating to Cultural Property aiming to prevent and combat the illicit trafficking and destruction of cultural property, in the framework of the Organization's action to fight terrorism and organized crime, stands as the sole international treaty, particularly dealing with the criminalization of the illicit trafficking of cultural property, establishes a number of criminal offences, covering cases of theft and other forms of unlawful appropriation; unlawful excavation and removal; illegal exportation and illegal importation; acquisition; placing on the market; falsification of documents; destruction and damage. The Convention sets the base for wide-reaching preventive measures, both at domestic and international level while it focuses on transnational co-operation to fight offences regarding cultural property [8].

B. European Regulations

Apart from the above, the European regulatory framework concerning the protection of the cultural heritage has seriously been based on the Regulation (EEC) No 3911/92 on the export of cultural goods, which had been amended by the Regulation (EEC) No 752/93 on laying down the provisions for its implementation and the Regulation (EC) No 974/2001, before its replacement by the Council Regulation (EC) No 116/2009 of 18 December 2008 on the export of cultural goods. Following this development, the Regulation (EEC) No 752/93 has accordingly been replaced by the Commission Implementing Regulation (EU) No 1081/2012 of 9 November 2012 for the purposes of Council Regulation (EC) No 116/2009 on the export of cultural goods[9]

[7] Article 8, Valetta Convention on the Protection of the Archaeological Heritage, Valetta, 1992

[8] Article 5, EU Convention on the Protection of the Audiovisual Heritage, Strasbourg, 2001

[9] See Appendix A.

In particular, the present Regulation, governing the export of cultural goods in the EU level initially lists the goods characterized as cultural in the Annex I and includes among them, indicatively:

a) Archaeological objects more than 100 years old which are the products of: excavations and finds on land or under water, archaeological sites or archaeological collections;
b) Elements forming an integral part of artistic, historical or religious monuments which have been dismembered, of an age exceeding 100 years;
c) Pictures and paintings, other than those included in categories 4 or 5, executed entirely by hand in any medium and on any material;
d) Mosaics in any material executed entirely by hand, other than those falling in categories 1 or 2, and drawings in any medium executed entirely by hand on any material;
e) Original sculptures or statuary and copies produced by the same process as the original, other than those in category 1;
f) Books more than 100 years old, singly or in collections and
g) Printed maps more than 200 years old [9][10].

In addition, the Regulation sets the procedure and the prerequisites on issuing the license for such exports, along with the provisions on the competent authorities, while highlighting the importance of administrative cooperation between the competent authorities of the Member States. Further, it is noted that Member States need to inform the Commission on the measures taken pursuant to this Regulation, which shall pass such information on the other Member States.

Then, the Commission is also expected to present a report every three years to the European Parliament, the Council and the European Economic and Social Committee, regarding the implementation of this Regulation [9][11]. The procedural details regarding the licensing of these exports are established by the Regulation (EU) No 1081/2012 of 9 November 2012 for the purposes of Council Regulation (EC) No 116/2009 on the export of cultural goods.

C. European Directives

Moreover, the framework regarding the protection of cultural heritage within the EU also includes the Directive 2014/60/EU of the European Parliament and of the Council of 15 May 2014 on the return of cultural objects unlawfully removed from the territory of a Member State, which has replaced the Council Directive 93/7/EEC of 15 March 1993 on the return of cultural objects unlawfully removed from the territory of a Member State, as amended by Directive 96/100/EC of the European Parliament and of the Council of 17 February 1997 and Directive 2001/38/EC of the European Parliament and of the Council of 5 June 2001[12].

In particular, the Directive 2014/60/EU governs the return of cultural objects classified or defined by a Member State as being among national treasures, which have

[10] Annex I,, Council Regulation (EC) No 116/2009 of 18 December 2008 on the export of cultural goods

[11] Articles 2, 3, 6 and 10, Council Regulation (EC) No 116/2009 of 18 December 2008 on the export of cultural goods

[12] See Appendix A.

been unlawfully removed from the territory of that Member State. Further, as 'cultural object' is considered an object which is classified or defined by a Member State, before or after its unlawful removal from the territory of that Member State, while as being among the 'national treasures possessing artistic, historic or archaeological value' under national legislation or administrative procedures within the meaning of Article 36 TFEU. Thus, the Directive provisions set that such objects that have been unlawfully removed from the territory of a Member State shall be returned in accordance with the procedure and in the circumstances provided by it. To that cause, the cooperation between the States' central authorities and the States' national competent authorities need to be highly promoted [10][13].

Additionally, the provisions of the Directive set the process each requesting Member State needs to follow in order to secure the return of such cultural objects [10][14], while following, in Article 8, it is stated that the Member States need to include in their legislation the provision that the return of objects under this Directive shall not take longer than three years since the date the competent local authority became aware of either its location or the possessor of it. Following, the procedure of the return, the expenses and thc necessary details on any related compensation the requesting Member State may be eligible to receive, are also established in next provisions of the Directive [10][15].

Finally, the Directive also foresees that Member States need to submit to the Commission a report on the application of this very Directive which will, in its turn, present a similar report to the European Parliament, the Council and the European Economic and Social Committee, reviewing the application and effectiveness of this Directive. The report shall, further be accompanied if necessary, by appropriate proposals [10][16].

Last but not least, the Regulation (EU) 2019/880 on the introduction and the import of cultural goods is similarly to the Regulation (EC) No 116/2009 on the export of cultural goods, important for the framework covering the protection of cultural heritage since it sets out the conditions that govern the introduction of cultural goods respectively.

In addition, it establishes the procedures regarding the import of cultural goods as well, in order to safeguard humanity's cultural heritage and to prevent the illicit trade in cultural goods, especially where such illicit trade could contribute to terrorist financing [11].

A list regarding the above mentioned regulatory framework is displayed in the Appendix A.

2.2 The National Framework in Greece

A. International Conventions and Agreements in the National Legislation

[13] Article 1–5, Directive 2014/60/EU of the European Parliament and of the Council of 15 May 2014 on the return of cultural objects unlawfully removed from the territory of a Member State

[14] Articles 6–7, Directive 2014/60/EU.

[15] Articles 8–10, Directive 2014/60/EU

[16] Article 17, Directive 2014/60/EU

Similarly to the European level, the protection of cultural heritage is of high importance within the national framework as well. In that sense, numerous parts of the legislation begin shaping the respective framework by ratifying several international or regional Conventions, or important bilateral agreements connected to aspects of cultural heritage and its protection.

The first one among them is Law 1103/1980 on the Ratification of the UNESCO Convention on the means of prohibiting and preventing the illicit import, export and transfer of ownership of cultural property (1970), followed by Law 1114/1981 with which the Convention for the Protection of Cultural Property in the Event of Armed Conflict (Hague Convention - UNESCO) and its Protocol were ratified.

In the same year, Law 1126/1981 ratified the UNESCO Convention on the Protection of the World Cultural and Natural Heritage (Paris, 1972), the primary goal of which was to set the initial base regarding the protection of both cultural and natural heritage after having the terms clearly defined first. Based on this Convention, the vision of the protection of cultural heritage, including the parts considered as natural heritage, was further developed and expanded in the process through significant texts. In the light of the above, important Conventions resulted within the Council of Europe work fame, such as the Conventions regarding the Protection of the Archaeological Heritage and the one concerning the Protection of the Architectural Heritage (Granada Convention), both ratified by the Law 1127/1981 and Law 2039/1992 respectively.

A few years later, the revised Convention concerning the protection of the Archaeological Heritage, known as the Valletta Convention was ratified by Law 3378/2005, while in parallel, Law 3317/2005 ratified the Second Protocol of the Convention for the Protection of Cultural Property in the Event of Armed Conflict (Hague Convention - UNESCO). In the meantime, the Council Directive 93/7/EEC on the return of cultural objects unlawfully removed from the territory of a Member State was ratified by the Presidential Decree 133/1998, along with its amending Directive 96/100/EC. The Presidential Decree had respectively been amended by the Presidential Decree 67/2003, before it got annulled and replaced by Law 4355/2015 on introducing the Directive 2014/60/EU on the return of cultural objects unlawfully removed from the territory of a Member State. Respectively, the latter, had priory replaced Directive 93/7/EEC in the European Union level.

In addition, bilateral agreements, important for the protection of cultural heritage for Greece, were signed and introduced in the national regulatory framework as Laws. Such an Agreement is the one between the Government of the Hellenic Republic and China on the prevention of theft, illegal excavation and illicit import and export of cultural property, which was written in law through L. 3914/2011, or the Agreement between the Federal Council of the Swiss Confederation and the Government of the Hellenic Republic on the import, transit and repatriation of cultural property, which was introduced by L. 3915/2011, as well. Then, another example is the Bilateral Agreement between the USA and Greece regarding imposing import restrictions of archaeological and Byzantine artifacts dating up to the 15th century AD, which was signed in July 2011 and introduced later that year by L. 4026/2011.

Further and most recently, another convention was ratified by law connected to the protection of cultural heritage and that one is the Council of Europe Convention on Offences relating to Cultural Property, (Nicosia 2017), ratified by Law 4744/2020[17]

B. Elements of the National Legislation on Cultural Heritage
Apart from the above, the main law particularly focused on issues related to the protection of antiquities and cultural heritage within the national legislation, is Law 3028/2002, as amended by Law 4744/2020 on the Ratification of the Convention on Offences relating to Cultural Property; and Law 4761/2020 on the Reorganization of the Fund for Archaeological Resources and Expropriations and its renaming to Organization for the Management and Development of Cultural Resources, promotion of the cultural heritage abroad, arrangements for the Historical Museum of Crete and other provisions. In particular, the context of the current law concerns protection provided by provisions that includes the cultural heritage of the country from the ancient times until today. The purpose of this protection is to preserve the historical memory for the sake of the present and future generations and to upgrade the cultural environment.

In addition, it is set that the cultural heritage of the Greece consists of the cultural goods located within the borders of the Greek territory, including the territorial waters, as well as within other maritime zones in which Greece exercises relevant jurisdiction in accordance with international law, while such cultural heritage also includes intangible cultural assets. What is more, in the framework of the rules of international law, the Greek State also takes care of the protection of cultural goods coming from the Greek territory whenever they are removed from it, while it also safeguards, in the context of international law, the protection of cultural goods that are historically associated with Greece wherever they are located [12][18].

Then, Law 3028/2002 governing antiquities defines several useful to its content acts, among which it distinguish cultural objects from monuments, defining the first ones as "testimonies of the existence and the individual and collective creativity of human kind" and the second one as "cultural objects which constitute material testimonies belonging to the cultural heritage of the country and which deserve special protection". These are stipulated by the provisions of the Law among the following categories: a) ancient monuments b) recent monuments c) immovable monuments d) movable monuments [12][19].

These categories are particularly described as such:

- Ancient Monuments or Antiquities are considered to be all cultural objects (artifacts and monuments) back to prehistoric, ancient, Byzantine and post-Byzantine times up to 1830. Among these, caves and paleontological remains, for which there is no evidence that they are related to human existence, are also included.
- Recent Monuments are defined as those cultural objects dating after 1830, which deserve protection due to their historical artistic or scientific significance.

[17] See Appendix B.

[18] Article 1, Law 3028/2002 (FEK A' 153/28.6.200)–[Main Law on Antiquities] - Law on the Protection of Antiquities and Cultural Heritage in General

[19] Article 2, Law 3028/2002 (FEK A' 153/28.6.200)–[Main Law on Antiquities]

- Immovable monuments means those monuments which have been connected with the ground and which remain on it or at the bottom of the sea or at the bottom of lakes or rivers, as well as monuments which are on the ground or at the bottom of the sea or at the bottom of lakes or rivers; it is not possible to move without damaging their value as testimonies.
- Immovable monuments include facilities, constructions and decorative and other elements that are an integral part of them, as well as their immediate environment.
- Then, Archaeological Sites are areas on land, at sea, in lakes or rivers that contain or there is evidence that they contain, ancient monuments, or which have constituted or there is evidence that have constituted monumental, urban or burial groups from ancient times up to 1830. Archaeological sites shall also include the necessary open space so as to allow the preserved monuments to be considered in a historical, aesthetic and functional unity.

Moreover, in the context of the current law, the protection of the cultural heritage of the country mainly consists of a) locating, searching recording and documenting and studying its data; b) preserving and preventing its destruction, deterioration and in general any direct or indirect damage to it; c) preventing illegal excavation, theft and illegal export; d) its maintenance and, where appropriate, necessary restoration; e) facilitating public access to and communication with it; f) its promotion and integration into modern social life; and g) education, aesthetic education and public awareness of cultural heritage [12][20]. In that sense, the protection of monuments, archeological sites and historical sites is included in the objectives of any level of spatial, developmental, environmental and urban planning or plans of equivalent effect or their substitutes.

In total, the provisions of the Law set the governing framework for the management and protection of immovable monuments and sites and any activities happening is these; the protection of movable monuments and the rights and obligations of the owners of them; the framework regarding archeological research and activities of monuments' preservation; and the framework governing the operation and accessibility of museums.

Furthermore, Law 3658/2008 on Measures for the Protection of Cultural Objects, as amended by Law 4761/2020, is also significant for the relevant framework in the country, since its provisions established within the Ministry of Culture, the service unit at the level of Management, entitled "Directorate of Documentation and Protection of Cultural Property", which reports to the General Directorate of Antiquities and Cultural Heritage. In particular, the purpose of the unit is the protection of cultural goods and the fight against antiquities, by searching, documenting the origin and movement and claiming movable monuments, within the meaning of Law 3028/2002, which are products of theft, embezzlement, illegal excavation or hoisting (from the seabed, lake or river) or have been smuggled in or out of the country. Following to these, the provisions of the current Law set the necessary details for the structure, responsibilities and operation of the Unit [13][21].

C. General Provisions on Culture

[20] Article 3, Law 3028/2002 (FEK A' 153/28.6.200)–[Main Law on Antiquities]

[21] Articles 1–3, Law 3658/2008 (FEK A'70/22.04.2008) - Law on Measures for the Protection of Cultural Objects

As far as the general framework on cultural issues is concerned, several provisions of laws and acts are relevant to the protection of cultural heritage in an indirect way. For instance, Article 10 "Regulations Related to the Ministry of Culture" of Law 3207/2003 regarding the Preparation for the Olympic Games is one of them, while Law 3323/2005 on the establishment of the Governmental Committee on Culture and Education and governing the operation of it, is an additional one. Similarly, Articles 17 and 21 on partnerships and archeological findings respectively, of Law 3389/2005 on Public-Private Partnerships, are indirectly connected to the protection of cultural heritage as well, since they include provisions on excavations during public construction works.

Finally, in an even broader sense, Law 3525/2007 on Cultural Sponsorship; Law 3691/2008 on the prevention and repression of legalization of income from criminal activities and financing of terrorism and other provisions, and more particularly the Article 3 of it, before its annulment; Law 3711/2008 on regulating the administrative issues related to the new Acropolis Museum; and the Presidential Decrees 85/2012 and 86/2012 on the establishment of the new "Ministry of Education, Religious Affairs, Culture and Sports" and appointment of the Ministers, Deputy Ministers and Deputy Ministers, as amended by PD 118/2013, along with the P.D. 96/2012 on the establishment of Secretariat of Culture, Ministry of Education, Culture and Sport are also among those parts of the national legislation that contribute indirectly into shaping the general framework on the protection of cultural heritage domestically.

A list regarding the above mentioned regulatory framework is displayed in the Appendix B.

3 The Use of Artificial Intelligence in the Cultural Heritage

3.1 Artificial Intelligence and the Use of Predictive Modeling for the Protection of Cultural Heritage

The development of the regulatory framework for the protection of cultural heritage highlights the importance of its preservation for present and future generations and their culture. At the same time, the world is undergoing a major digital transition, the media of which can play a critical role in preserving cultural heritage and developing ways to secure it. In this sense, research and work on the applications of Artificial Intelligence (AI) in the field of cultural heritage has been done by important actors coming from or collaborating with the field of advanced technology.

To begin with; it is important to explain particular terms. Thus, within the complex terminology of artificial intelligence, the use of the term "machine learning" means a set of algorithms that are capable of learning from data. Furthermore, "deep learning" is a form of prior machine learning that excels at solving high-dimensional problems. The results of training a machine learning algorithm are the development of a predictive "model" that can be used to provide additional metadata from a given piece of content. In addition, "data models" used in the field of cultural heritage, such as Europeana[22] - which aims to empower cultural heritage through its digital transition by developing

[22] The project's official website: https://pro.europeana.eu/about-us/mission.

expertise and tools to adopt digital progress and drive innovation - are mechanisms that support cultural heritage institutions to structure metadata about related objects. In this sense, when referring to an AI model it refers to an algorithm trained to carry out a specific task. Such a task could be, in a very simplified way, determining what an object is among certain choices. In this case, the algorithm will be trained to look for key features of specific objects and judge whether or not what is presented is accurate to any of them.

Besides, according to the text of the European Ethics guidelines for the development of Artificial Intelligence, that intelligence is defined as such, which refers to systems characterized by intelligent behavior, analyzing their environment and acting - with a certain degree of autonomy - to achieve specific goals. AI-powered systems can be purely software-based, acting in the virtual world (e.g. voice assistants, image analysis software, search engines, speech and facial recognition systems) or AI can be embedded in hardware devices (e.g. advanced robots, autonomous cars or Internet of Things applications) [14][23]

Following on from these, Artificial Intelligence has the potential to produce large amounts of data that can be used to enrich collections of cultural heritage objects, either by making them easier to explore, or by providing institutions with the ability to link many collections to others in different institutions, etc. Today, considering that a large part of cultural heritage has been digitized and includes a lot of data and materials, the quality of this data is of the utmost importance. For example, instead of picking 100,000 random paintings from the internet and training a model to recognize 'impressionist art', what could be done is to use heritage materials that will already be able to provide advice and guidance on accuracy. Similar applications of artificial intelligence extend far beyond painting, also to many areas of the cultural heritage sector in general.

More specifically regarding the use of artificial intelligence in the field of cultural heritage, multiple applications are already underway that support the preservation of important elements of both tangible and intangible cultural heritage, as defined at the beginning of this analysis.

Therefore, in addition to the above applications of artificial intelligence in the field of cultural heritage, the contribution to the preservation of other forms of cultural heritage, such as that of rarely spoken languages, is valuable. It is estimated that a language disappears every two weeks when its last speaker dies. Thus, technology can now be used to preserve and revive such endangered languages. One such example is the contribution of artificial intelligence to the preservation of the tereo Maori language in New Zealand, when experts worked with Microsoft to introduce their language into everyday use, launching it as a Microsoft Translator language and making it accessible to a new generation of speakers[24]

Together, technology and artificial intelligence can create the future of our historical past by providing all the necessary means to preserve the heritage of world culture. Through the use of advanced technology such as drones, 3D printing, virtual reality

[23] European Commission, Directorate-General for Communications Networks, Content and Technology, Ethics guidelines for trustworthy AI, Publications Office, 2019, https://data.europa.eu/doi/10.2759/346720.

[24] The project's official website: https://inculture.microsoft.com/arts/maori-language/.

applications and wider digitization, current and future generations can access detailed explanations of ancient languages, expanded restoration of ancient texts (through the use of deep learning), more accurate identification antiquities, while a further contribution of technology is in the field of art crime detection and the detection of fake works of art by specially designed algorithms.

Additionally, in light of the use of modern technologies for cultural heritage conservation, the use of GIS (Geographic Information System) and spatial analysis to develop predictive models in preventive archeology is of great importance. In particular, such tools are mutually important for the Decision Support System (SDS) for archaeological research, as well as for providing information necessary to minimize archaeological risks. In this sense, a number of predictive models have been developed, with differences found mainly in the methodological approaches and parameters used for the analysis. In general, predictive modeling is characterized as a technique used to predict archaeological sites in an area, based on either the observation of patterns or hypotheses about human behavior.

Over the years, the use of predictive modeling has contributed significantly to the field of archaeology, while today there are two main reasons for the use of predictive modeling, which are: the prediction of archaeological site positions, in the sense of management of archaeological heritage, in order to guide future developments in the contemporary landscape, as well as the possibility of gaining knowledge of past human behavior in a given landscape, in the sense of academic research.

Furthermore, as Archaeological Predictive Models were developed, there were two typical types of research under them: Qualitative Models, i.e. a mainly theoretical approach based on the observation of human-ecosystem relationships to determine habitat suitability but without a level of quantitative assessment of spatial areas, and the Quantitative Models, i.e. models based on the quantitative extrapolation of environmental variables and the creation of statistical estimates of known archaeological sites, for projection into unexplored areas.

In addition to these, another type of predictive model has been used, almost by the majority of experts in the field, and is the type of Informal (Intuitive) Models. In light of these models, the process involves designing strategic research based on the idea that one could distinguish suitable site areas according to simple rules, such as that people do not live on steep slopes, instead they will likely choose to live near permanent water sources etc. In this sense, archaeological sites are more likely to be found in places similar to where they have already been found before, while specific areas that have been destroyed since people lived there do not need to be investigated.

In general, predictive models are central to both archaeological research and cultural resource management. However, their application is often inadequate due to small training data sets and insufficient statistical techniques available, together with a lack of theoretical knowledge to explain the responses of past land uses to the predictor variables.

As a result, it becomes evident that greater use of AI feeds a greater range of information into predictive models and therefore predictions tend to be formulated at a more detailed level, drastically reducing the chances of prediction failure.

3.2 Artificial Intelligence and the Improvement of the Individual's Accessibility to Cultural Goods

Another aspect of the contribution of Artificial Intelligence to the Protection of Cultural Heritage manifests itself in the field of accessibility of cultural heritage by people who lack mobility, hearing or vision.

This field is the tip of the spear of the association of Cultural Heritage with Artificial intelligence: Cultural Heritage is given meaning through the fact that it contributes to the formation of the historical consciousness of the individual. Concomitantly, expanding the number of people who can have access to what is considered Cultural Heritage is also the underlying reason for its protection.

In this field, Artificial Intelligence opens a new era since the possibilities are multiple [15]. It is an area of Artificial Intelligence in which human-centered applications are created with the aim of enabling the individual to experience the Cultural Heritage object even in those cases where the individual cannot visit the archaeological site or the museum in situ. The possibility of access that can be ensured by artificial intelligence is developed through specific applications that create a virtual experience for the remote visitor which, however, is not static in nature but interactive. It becomes obvious that the specific applications acquire enormous importance, mainly of an educational nature, since now the learners (whether they are pupils or students) have the possibility to virtually tour places that are geographically or even health-wise (after the recent experience of the pandemic crisis) inaccessible.

In order to provide a complete experience of virtual access to different groups of visitors (different age groups and/or different linguistic and cultural backgrounds), Artificial Intelligence has integrated both data from the learning sciences and data from evolutionary psychology [15]. This is how the interaction between the Cultural Heritage asset and the virtual visitor is achieved and is analyzed in the following methods-technologies: Interaction with virtual reality and three-dimensional (3D) visualization, interaction on the websites of the respective cultural space, interaction with automated models (Robots) in remote visit. Especially for this last possibility, Robots are located inside the museum space and conduct a guided tour in the language chosen by the virtual visitor adapted to their age [15][25].

More specifically, Microsoft has recently entered into partnerships with the public sector in various places, including Greece, in order to implement the use of artificial intelligence to support and highlight important archaeological sites. Under this light, the Greek competent authority, the country's Ministry of Culture and Sports, created, in collaboration with Microsoft, the Common Grounds[26] project which is a revival project aimed at preserving and restoring pieces of human history that are precious, as well as empowering global audiences to embrace the idea of finding common ground through our widely shared history.

As part of this project, viewers have the opportunity to explore Ancient Olympia as it was in ancient times, through the use of artificial intelligence technology, allowing

[25] Relevant EU funded projects: TOURBOT and WEBFAIR

[26] The project's official website: https://inculture.microsoft.com/arts/ancient-olympia-common-grounds/.

history, sports and culture lovers to be part of a virtual interaction with the historic site. More specifically, the company collaborated with another technology company, specialized in the digitization of historical sites in 3D, in order to create a model of Ancient Olympia. Thanks to the use of ground cameras and drones simultaneously, thousands of photos were taken from the field, which were then processed by Microsoft AI to create accurate models, with a sense of photorealistic performance. The project was developed by facing various challenges and covered the extensive network of ancient ruins in the area by bringing these structures to life. Moreover, the work is unique for an additional reason, that it is accessible from anywhere in the world and not particularly by those who actually visit the site in person.

The penetration of Artificial Intelligence into the sensitive area of Cultural Heritage Protection presents two important challenges [16, 17]. One concerns the development of those applications that will ensure the diagnostic need to include those elements of Cultural Heritage that have not been included to date and therefore escape the protective regulatory framework of the relevant legislation. The second challenge concerns the development of reliable applications in order to achieve the optimal effect of accessibility in the experience of each cultural asset. For both of these challenges the need to come up with reliable AI applications and whose footprint remains within the ethical rules that delimit the possibilities of AI is now more than important. To the extent that our Cultural Heritage determines the historical reference of each individual, the violation of the above frameworks automatically means the cancellation of the history of the human race.

At this point, it would be expected that the European legislator had not been content with formulating guidelines. On the contrary, it would be expected to have dared to take the next step that would mark the first (worldwide) attempt to legislate Artificial Intelligence on the altar of preserving the history of the human race, but free from the risk of its alteration [18][27].

4 Artificial Intelligence; from Ethics to the Regulatory Framework

4.1 Basic Values and Principles

Under the prism of the worldwide increasing use of new technologies, data and methods of machine learning and deep learning, UNESCO issued recently a set of recommendation on the moral standards that should be kept in mind when using such artificial intelligence tools. This text manages to express the tendency on the field and provide a general insight on what the future framework on the use of AI systems could begin to look like.

The aim of the recommendation lies on providing the base to ensure that AI methods and systems shall be used for good purposes and in peaceful ways. In addition, its scope is to set a universally accepted framework on the use of AI which will include the factors of inclusiveness and environmental protection in it, as well as which will make the stakeholders involved to take shared responsibility on this.

[27] UNESCO has already published its text, Recommendations on the Ethics of Artificial Intelligence: https://en.unesco.org/courier/2018-3/ethical-risks-ai

Following, among the objectives [18] of the text the creation of a common values and principles framework is included, in order to guide the legislators of all states in shaping their AI related policies and regulatory frameworks accordingly. Additionally, among these objectives is also the goal of providing guidance to individuals or groups acting privately or through institutions, on absorbing such AI ethics in their processes throughout their life cycle activities. In parallel to these, one of the goals that the recommendation on AI ethics tries to achieve is the promotion of respect on human rights and freedoms and of the preservation of the natural environment while using AI systems or applications at any stage of their development and operation. To that cause, multidisciplinary discussions need to be done and supported on the moral issues arising from the use of AI. Last but not least, sufficient and fair accessibility on the developments in the sector of AI is being highlighted as necessary to be ensured.

In the light of the above, the international community tries setting commonly accepted values and principles [18]–that have been already met and implemented in the several other fields so far–for the development and use of AI systems and applications.

Such values include:

- the respect and protection of the human rights and liberties as well as of the human dignity;
- the protection and preservation of the natural environment and the broader ecosystem;
- the promotion and support of inclusiveness and diversity; and
- the safeguarding of a peaceful life within fair and interconnected societies.

In addition, among the fundamental principles proposed by the international community, through UNESCO's Recommendation on the Ethics of AI, on the morality of AI are:

- the promotion of the proportionality principle;
- the "do no harm" principle;
- the principle of fairness and non-discrimination;
- the principle of safety and security, in order for unwanted harms or vulnerabilities to attack to be avoided (safety and security risks);
- the sustainability;
- the protection of the privacy rights and data protection;
- the principle of transparency;
- the human oversight;
- the responsibility and accountability on the use of AI;
- the public awareness and literacy; and
- the adaptive governance and cooperation.

Furthermore, in parallel with the development of UNESCO's principles, the European Union also proceeded to issuing relevant guidelines on the trustworthy use of AI in a way that respects fundamental rights [19]. In that sense, the European Commission first released its definition proposal on AI [20] which is described as such:

"Artificial intelligence (AI) systems are software (and possibly also hardware) systems designed by humans that, given a complex goal, act in the physical or digital dimension by perceiving their environment through data acquisition, interpreting the collected structured or unstructured data, reasoning on the knowledge, or processing the information, derived from this data and deciding the best action(s) to take to achieve the given goal. AI systems can either use symbolic rules or learn a numeric model, and they can also adapt their behavior by analyzing how the environment is affected by their previous actions.

As a scientific discipline, AI includes several approaches and techniques, such as machine learning (of which deep learning and reinforcement learning are specific examples), machine reasoning (which includes planning, scheduling, knowledge representation and reasoning, search, and optimization), and robotics (which includes control, perception, sensors and actuators, as well as the integration of all other techniques into cyber-physical systems)." [19].

After having the AI defined as possible, the EU presents in its Ethics guidelines for trustworthy AI [19] the fundamental human rights that need to the basis on the framework governing the use of AI in a trustworthy way. These rights are - in the same spirit with the values included in UNESCO's guidelines:

- the respect on human dignity;
- the freedom of the individual to make decisions and express themselves;
- the respect for democracy, justice and the rule of law, in the sense that AI should be used to facilitate democratic procedures and maintain the respect on the numerous different values and choices of the individuals;
- the equality, non-discrimination and solidarity, which in the sense of AI use means that the system's administrators should not generate biased outputs, as well as that it should operate on with the necessary respect on vulnerable and marginalized people and groups;
- the citizens' rights, such as their right to vote, to good administration, to access to information and public documents and more, which need to be safeguarded and not negatively affected by the use of AI systems.

Following, based on the need to protect the above mentioned fundamental rights, the EU provides some key principles towards the development of the framework to be governing the use of AI in an ethically accepted manner. These are the principle of respect for human autonomy; the principle of prevention of harm; the principle of fairness and the principle of explicability. In particular, the principle of respect for human autonomy aims on protecting the ability of the individuals to effectively self-determine themselves when interacting with AI system. In addition, the principle of prevention of harm prioritizes the protection of human dignity and human mental and physical health against the potential malicious use of AI systems. Further, the principle of fairness aims on the protection of equality and justice in both the procedural and substantive dimensions. Then, the principle of explicability, completes the set of principles by highlighting the importance of transparency and clarity of the use and purpose of the AI systems to those directly or indirectly affected by these [20].

On the basis of the guidelines issued on the ethics of AI - both internationally and on the EU level - it is clearly shown that the further development and future use of AI systems include important risks on valuable elements of people's lives. Something that leads, consequently, to the necessity of shaping an adequate regulatory framework on the use of AI, adjusted to the needs and the rights of those interacting with it directly or not.

4.2 Artificial Intelligence Ethics on the Culture

Following the discussion on the connection between human rights and the development and use of AI, UNESCO took some further steps by suggesting the implementation of the relevant values of AI ethics on particular fields of the present operations. In that framework, UNESCO's recommendations try a division of the moral issues to be addressed among several of these fields, in eleven policy areas that include: ethical impact assessment; ethical governance and stewardship; data policy; development and international cooperation; environment and ecosystems; gender; culture; education and research; communication and information; economy and labor; as well as health and social well-being [18].

Under that prism, considering that the right to share the benefits of the common heritage of mankind belongs in the third generation of human rights, it makes sense that among the areas listed in UNESCO's recommendations is the policy area of culture, in a universally innovative initiative [21].

More particularly, in the area of culture UNESCO's text encourages States to use AI solutions under the principle of proportionality and when appropriate, in order to preserve or enrich or manage either the tangible or intangible cultural heritage including endangered parts of it such as rarely spoken languages and indigenous knowledges. Such use of AI solutions could be met in the form of educational programmes with a participatory character. In that framework, countries are supported to initiate - especially related to intangible cultural heritage - the examination of the cultural impact of AI systems, like the natural language processing applications on the nuances of human language and expression.

At the same time, states are also encouraged to move forward with AI education and digital training for professionals of art in order to maximize the suitability of AI applications in their fields of work, considering that AI can be used to create, distribute and consume a broad variety of cultural goods and services–always keeping into consideration in important role on preserving cultural heritage and freedom of arts. In that sense, states should also raise awareness and promote the evaluation of AI solutions among the smaller or bigger actors of local cultural industries.

Following that, tech companies should also be supported to get involved as stakeholders in the field of cultural heritage and its protection - as it has already happened in several examples, as mentioned earlier in this paper. This would lead to a diverse supply of cultural expressions enhancing the visibility of local content.

Further, emphasis needs to be given on the relation between AI and intellectual property (IP), especially when it concerns issues as to how to determine or protect the work created by means of AI systems. In parallel, what should also be examined under that prism, is the ways AI systems might affect the rights or the interests of intellectual property owners the work of whom might have been used to research and develop AI solutions.

Finally, states are seriously advised to support entities such as museums, libraries etc. to use AI technologies nationally, in order to promote their collections and to enrich their databases while increasing their accessibility as well.

What is being highlighted by the UNESCO recommendation for the states, before closing, is the need to implement concrete, well-structured and transparent procedures and mechanisms–nationally implemented–in order to monitor in a credible way and in accordance to their internal particularities and governing conditions, the implementation of the ethics on AI. Such mechanisms should consist of a combination of qualitative and quantitative methods in order to bring the most accurate and realistic results possible in each case.

4.3 Future Challenges to be Addressed

Under the prism of the potential of AI in the cultural sector and after having considered the main points of AI ethics related to it, it is important to focus on two crucial issues out of which important challenges might arise in absence of the necessary regulatory framework respectively.

To begin with, as it has already been mentioned, AI can be used in order to increase the accessibility of cultural sites through virtual tours and tools of virtual reality, providing this way access to a vast amount of monuments and historical sites to a great deal of people who might not be able to physically visit them in their lifetime. On top of that, AI can also be used to bring in the present the experience of important historical events, also through the use of virtual reality tools. In that sense, AI contributes to increasing the quality of human life by enriching it with easily accessible elements of humans' common history, while raising awareness on these elements for the younger generations of people to preserve [22].

However, apart from the challenge of the huge workload until this can be efficiently implemented, considering the huge amount of cultural elements in the world, it is important here to highlight the risk arising on the topic of data protection. More particularly, when using AI and virtual reality methods on facilitating the "visits" on cultural sites big amounts of data are produced along with the respective need for their protection. Indicatively, using AI and VR to facilitate people with physical disabilities to e-visit an archaeological or historic site not only their identity data are being produced and stored but also the very fact of their physical disabilities. Of course, such a sensitive detail of a person's identity needs to be secured and treated in the safest and most regulated way possible.

In addition to the above, further risks arising from the use of AI are related with the protection of the Intellectual Property rights of the individuals interacting with these systems. In the general sense, AI is designed to work similarly to the human brain. On top of that though, it is designed to continuously improving its system through the operation of the AI algorithms [23]. In that sense, initial creators of software, or even hardware at times, might lose their intellectual property entitlement on devices and systems they worked to develop in the first place. More specifically, a valid concern arises regarding copyright claims and IP rights on software coding which has been globally protected as work of literature and arts [24, 25].

Under the prism of the above, the developers of the coding and software have been considered to have the same rights over their creations as authors have over their writings. It is although noted that, such rights often vary according to the different jurisdictions but it is commonly accepted that in general they touch upon the reproduction, change and distribution of the systems. As a consequence, when parts of the AI systems and their software are being improved or developed by the very AI system itself, important issues arise of the ownership of these creation. Issues that are critical to be efficiently regulated and framed in the near future so that they can be adequately resolved once they arise.

5 Conclusions

In conclusion, it is a fact that cultural heritage and its preservation, in all its forms, is of utmost importance not only for a specific region and people but for the entire humanity on a global scale. Europe in particular, is undeniably a rich and diverse mosaic of cultural and creative expressions, which come as a legacy from the previous generations of people living on the continent and pass on to the next generations as a legacy.

A. Cultural heritage, worldwide, in Europe, the EU or in Greece in particular, includes natural, built and archaeological sites. Monuments; museums and works of art, including literary, musical and audiovisual works; in many cases certain historic cities as a whole and of course the knowledge, experiences, practices and traditions of previous generations of people. Thus, its protection is vital to the development of today's vibrant communities and actually enriches their individual lives, adding quality to them and acting as a driving forçe for the cultural and creative sectors to keep moving forward.

   In addition to these, cultural heritage is also important for supporting and strengthening European social capital, since it is, moreover, an important source of economic development, employment and social cohesion, offering, among other things, the possibility of revitalizing urban and rural areas and promotion of sustainable tourism.

B. Consequently, it appears, as expected, that the legislator, at all the above-mentioned levels, is particularly interested in the protection of cultural heritage and this can be seen from the moment the course of development of the relevant regulatory framework is observed, as it is reviewed in the context of this text.

C. Promoting the objectives of Cultural Heritage protection through Artificial Intelligence is obvious. Both in terms of protection per se, as well as in terms of the development of the individual's accessibility to cultural elements, it constitutes a cornerstone of the need for its protection.

   However, important legislative gaps arise:

- Although the global legislator demonstrates a maximalist attitude when defining the term "cultural heritage", it has not shown the corresponding dynamics in the adoption of those legislative texts that would limit the possibilities of Artificial Intelligence, especially in the direction of its development of reliable applications and within the framework of the ethical rules for Artificial Intelligence prescribed by UNESCO.
- In parallel, even though the legal framework on Data Protection and Intellectual Property are quite mature, till present, no attempt to interconnect them with the development and use of AI in a legal level has been done.

Appendix A

Protection of Cultural Heritage – EU Level

Treaty on the Functioning of the European Union (TFEU)	Consolidated version of the Treaty on the Functioning of the European Union; Title XIII, Culture, Article 167 (ex Article 151 TEC)
1985 Granada Convention	Convention for the Protection of the Architectural Heritage of Europe, Granada 03/10/1985
1992 Valetta Convention	European Convention on the Protection of the Archaeological Heritage (Revised), Valletta 16/01/1992
EU Audiovisual Heritage Convention, 2001	European Convention for the Protection of the Audiovisual Heritage, Strasbourg 08/11/2001
2005 Faro Convention	Council of Europe Framework Convention on the Value of Cultural Heritage for Society, Faro 27/10/2005
CoE Convention on Offences relating to Cultural Property, 2017	Council of Europe Convention on Offences relating to Cultural Property, Nicosia 19/05/2017
Regulation (EEC) No 3911/92, not in force. Replaced by Council Regulation (EC) No 116/2009 of 18 December 2008	Council Regulation (EEC) No 3911/92 of 9 December 1992 on the export of cultural goods: Amended by the Commission Regulation (EEC) No 752/93 of 30 March 1993 on laying down the provisions for the former's implementation; and Council Regulation (EC) No 974/2001 of 14 May 2001
Regulation (EEC) No 752/93, not in force. Replaced by Commission Implementing Regulation (EU) No 1081/2012 of 9 November 2012	Commission Regulation (EEC) No 752/93 of 30 March 1993 laying down provisions for the implementation of Council Regulation (EEC) No 3911/92 on the export of cultural goods
Regulation (EC) No 116/2009. In force	Council Regulation (EC) No 116/2009 of 18 December 2008 on the export of cultural goods
Regulation (EU) No 1081/2012. In force	Commission Implementing Regulation (EU) No 1081/2012 of 9 November 2012 for the purposes of Council Regulation (EC) No 116/2009 on the export of cultural goods

(*continued*)

(*continued*)

Directive 93/7/EEC, not in force. Replaced by Directive 2014/60/EU of the European Parliament and of the Council of 15 May 2014	Council Directive 93/7/EEC of 15 March 1993 on the return of cultural objects unlawfully removed from the territory of a Member State: Amended by Directive 96/100/EC of the European Parliament and of the Council of 17 February 1997; and Directive 2001/38/EC of the European Parliament and of the Council of 5 June 2001
Directive 2014/60/EU of the European Parliament and of the Council of 15 May 2014. In force	Directive 2014/60/EU of the European Parliament and of the Council of 15 May 2014 on the return of cultural objects unlawfully removed from the territory of a Member State and amending Regulation (EU) No 1024/2012 (Recast)
Regulation (EU) 2019/880 of the European Parliament and of the Council of 17 April 2019. In force	Regulation (EU) 2019/880 of the European Parliament and of the Council of 17 April 2019 on the introduction and the import of cultural goods

Appendix B

Protection of Cultural Heritage – National Level

Law 1103/1980	Law 1103/1980 (FEK 297 A'/19.12.1980) - Ratification of the UNESCO Convention on the means of prohibiting and preventing the illicit import, export and transfer of ownership of cultural property -Paris 1970
Law 1114/1981	Law 1114/1981 (FEK A' 6/08.01.1981) - Ratification of the Convention for the Protection of Cultural Property in the Event of Armed Conflict (Hague Convention - UNESCO) Ratification of the Protocol
Law 1126/1981	Law 1126/1981 (FEK A' 32/10.2.1981) - Ratification of the UNESCO Convention concerning the Protection of the World Cultural and Natural Heritage, Paris, 16 November 1972
Law 1127/1981	Law 1127/1981 (FEK A' 32/10.2.1981) - Ratification of the European Convention on the Protection of the Archaeological Heritage, CoE - London 1969

(*continued*)

(*continued*)

Law 2039/1992	Law 2039/1992 (FEK A' 61/13.4.1992) - Ratification of the Convention for the Protection of the Architectural Heritage - "Granada Convention" - CoE
Presidential Decree 133/1998, not in force. Replaced by Law 4355/2015	Presidential Decree 133/1998 (FEK A' 106/19.5.1998) - Presidential Decree conforming Greek laws to the Council Directive 93/7/EEC of 15 March 1993 and 96/100/EEC of 17 February 1997 on the return of cultural objects unlawfully removed from the territory of a Member State. - as amended by Presidential Decree 67/2003; Amendments and additions to Presidential Decree 133/1998 -
Law 3028/2002	Law 3028/2002 (FEK A' 153/28.6.200)–[Main Law on Antiquities] - Law on the Protection of Antiquities and Cultural Heritage in General, *as amended by* Law 4744/2020 on the Ratification of the Convention on Offences relating to Cultural Property; and Law 4761/2020 on the Reorganization of the Fund for Archaeological Resources and Expropriations and its renaming to Organization for the Management and Development of Cultural Resources, promotion of the cultural heritage abroad, arrangements for the Historical Museum of Crete and other provisions
Law 3207/2003, Art. 10	Law 3207/2003 (FEK A΄ 302/24.12.2003) - Preparation for the Olympic Games [Relevant Article 10: "Regulations Related to the Ministry of Culture"]
Law 3323/2005	Law 3323/2005 (FEK A' 61/7.3.2005) - Governmental Committee on Culture and Education
Law 3378/2005	Law 3378/2005 (FEK A' 203 / 19.8.2005) - Ratification of the European Convention for the protection of the Archaeological Heritage - "Valletta Convention" - CoE
Law 3317/2005	Law 3317/2005 (FEK A΄ 45/23.02.2005) - Ratification of the Second Protocol of the Convention for the Protection of Cultural Property in the Event of Armed Conflict (UNESCO)
Law 3389/2005, Art. 17 and 21	Law 3389/2005 (FEK A' 232/22.9.2005) - Public-Private Partnerships; Relevant articles 17 and 21: Regulations on excavations during public construction works

(*continued*)

(*continued*)

Law 3525/2007	Law 3525/2007 (FEK A' 16/26.01.2007) - Law on Cultural Sponsorship
Law 3658/2008	Law 3658/2008 (FEK A'70/22.04.2008) - Law on Measures for the Protection of Cultural Objects *as amended by* Law 4761/2020 on the Reorganization of the Fund for Archaeological Resources and Expropriations and its renaming to Organization for the Management and Development of Cultural Resources, promotion of the cultural heritage abroad, arrangements for the Historical Museum of Crete and other provisions
Law 3691/2008, Art. 3	Law 3691/2008 (FEK A' 166/5.8.2008) - Prevention and repression of legalization of income from criminal activities and financing of terrorism and other provisions; Relevant Article 3
Law 3711/2008	Law 3711/2008 (FEK A'/5.11.2008) - Law regulating the administrative issues related to the new Acropolis Museum
Law 3914/2011	Law 3914/2011 (FEK A' 19/16.02.2011) - Agreement between the Government of the Hellenic Republic and China on the prevention of theft, illegal excavation and illicit import and export of cultural property
Law 3915/2011	Law 3915/2011 (FEK A' 20 / 17.02.2011) - Agreement between the Federal Council of the Swiss Confederation and the Government of the Hellenic Republic on the import, transit and repatriation of cultural property
Law 4026/2011	Law 4026/2011 (FEK A' 231 / 3.11.2011) - Bilateral Agreement between USA and Greece signed in July 2011 on imposing import restrictions of archaeological and Byzantine artefacts dating up to the 15th century AD
Presidential Decree 85/2012 and 86/2012	Presidential Decree 85/2012 and 86/2012 (FEK A΄ 141/21.6.2012) - Establishment of the new "Ministry of Education, Religious Affairs, Culture and Sports" and Appointment of the Ministers, Deputy Ministers and Deputy Ministers, as amended by PD 118/2013 (FEK A'152/2013)
Presidential Decree 96/2012	Presidential Decree 96/2012 (FEK A' 154/24.7.2012) - Establishment of Secretariat of Culture, Ministry of Education, Culture and Sport

(*continued*)

(*continued*)

Law 4355/2015	Law 4355/2015 (FEK A' 178/18.12.2015) - Conforming Greek laws to Directive 2014/60/EU of the European Parliament and of the Council of 15 May 2014 on the return of cultural objects unlawfully removed from the territory of a Member State
Law 4744/2020	Law 4744/2020 (FEK A' 213/4.11.2020) - Ratification of the Convention on Offences relating to Cultural Property, CoE–Nicosia 2017
Law 4761/2020	Law 4761/2020 (FEK A' 248/13.12.2020) - Reorganization of the Fund for Archaeological Resources and Expropriations and its renaming to Organization for the Management and Development of Cultural Resources, promotion of the cultural heritage abroad, arrangements for the Historical Museum of Crete and other provisions

References

1. Pasikowska-Schnass, M.: Briefing on Cultural heritage in EU policies, PE 621.876, (2018)
2. "Convention Conserning the Protection of the World Cultural and Natural Heritage," Paris (1972)
3. Treaty of the Functioning of the European Union (2009)
4. Convention on the Protection of the Architectural Heritage of Europe, Granada (1985)
5. European Convention on the Protection of the Archaeological Heritage (Revised), Valleta, (1992)
6. European Convention for the Protection of the Audiovisual Heritage, Strasbourg (2001)
7. Council of Europe Framework Convention on the Value of Cultural Heritage for Society, Faro (2005)
8. Council of Europe Convention on Offences relating to Cultural Property, Nicosia (2017)
9. "Council Regulation (EC) No 116/2009 of 18 December 2008 on the export of cultural goods," 2009
10. Directive 2014/60/EU of the European Parliament and of the Council of 15 May 2014 on the return of cultural objects unlawfully removed from the territory of a Member State (2014)
11. Regulation (EU) 2019/880 of the European Parliament and of the Council of 17 April 2019 on the introduction and the import of cultural goods (2019)
12. Law 3028/2002 (FEK A' 153/28.6.200)–[Main Law on Antiquities] - Law on the Protection of Antiquities and Cultural Heritage in General, (2002)
13. Law 3658/2008 (FEK A'70/22.04.2008) - Law on Measures for the Protection of Cultural Objects, (2008)
14. Ethics guidelines for trustworthy AI, European Commission, Directorate-General for Communications Networks, Content and Technology, Publications Office (2019)
15. Pisoni, G., Díaz-Rodríguez, N., Gijlers, H., Tonolli, L.: Human-centered artificial intelligence for designing accessible cultural heritage. Appl. Sci. **11**(2), 870 (2021)

16. Perez-Higueras, R., Ramon-Vigo, R., Capitan, J., Caballero, F.: A navigation system in telepresence robots for elderly. In: Proceedings of the Workshop on International Conference on Social Robotics, Kansas City, MO,USA 1–3 (2016)
17. Charisi, V., Mainverni, L., Schaper, M., Rubegni, E.: Creating opportunities for children's critical reflections on AI, robotics and other intelligence technologies. In: Proceedings of the ACM Interaction Design and Children Conference: Extended Abstracts, London, UK (2020)
18. Recommendation on the Ethics of Artificial Intelligence, UNESCO (2022)
19. Hleg, A.: A definition of AI: Main capabilities and scientific disciplines, European Commission, Brussels (2019)
20. Hleg, A.: Ethics Guidelines for Trustworthy AI, European Commission, Brussels (2019)
21. Zieck, M.Y.A.: "The Concept of 'Generations' of Human Rights and the Right to Benefit from the Common Heritage of Mankind with Reference to Extraterrestrial Realms." Verfassung Und Recht in Übersee/Law and Politics in Africa, Asia and Latin America, vol. 25, no. no 2 (1992)
22. Setiawan, P.A.: Delivering cultural heritage and historical events to (2021)
23. Bublitz, J.C.: Might artificial intelligence become part of the person, and what are the key ethical and legal implications? (2022)
24. Berne Convention for the Protection of Literary and Artistic Works (1986)
25. WIPO Copyright Treaty, Article 4 (1996)

AegeanDigital Tourism Tank: Experiences and Products for Enhancing the Sustainable Preservation of Digital Heritage of Cultural Organizations of North Aegean

Dora Chatzi Rodopoulou[1], Athanasia Kadrefi[1], Christos Kalloniatis[2](✉), Angeliki Kitsiou[2](✉), Maria Koltsaki[1], Anna Kyriakaki[1], Katerina Mavroeidi[2], Evangelia Proiou[1], Maria Sideri[2], Stavros Simou[2], Stavros Stavridis[2], Katerina Vgena[2](✉), and Mania Mavri[1]

[1] Quantitative Methods Laboratory, Department of Business Administration, University of the Aegean, 82100 Chios, Greece

[2] Privacy Engineering and Social Informatics Laboratory, Department of Cultural Technology and Communication, University of the Aegean, 81100 Lesvos, Greece

{chkallon,a.kitsiou,kvgena}@aegean.gr

Abstract. Aiming at achieving cultural heritage digitization, 3D scanning, modelling and printing for cultural organizations are considered as innovative and effective practices for the restoration, presentation, and production of cultural goods, while offering a robust foundation for preserving the cultural heritage assets. Many approaches have been introduced in 3D area regarding intangible heritage, thus a lack of standards and proven methodologies has been indicated. In this regard, the AegeanDigital Tourism Tank research action intends to establish an expert-driven methodology for managing holistic and user-oriented 3D scanning, modelling and printing. The contribution of this holistic approach not only enhances the preservation of digital Heritage in the North Aegean, but also increases the scientific, economic and social impact of advanced services to the potential audiences of the cultural organizations of North Aegean.

Keywords: AegeanDigital Tourism Tank · 3D holistic approach · digital heritage

1 Introduction

Previous research highlights the future growth of the novel technological advances and applications deployed to the more and more complex cultural environments worldwide [1]. Since the current focus of the value of cultural heritage concerns its intangibility in order to be preserved [2], digitization is provided. Towards cultural heritage digitization, 3D scanning, modelling and printing offer a robust foundation for preserving the cultural heritage assets. 3D scanning is the process that converts physical objects into precise digital models, enabling the quick and accurate capture of an object's shape and geometry. The data collected by the 3D scan process is used to develop digital 3D models of

A. Moropoulou et al. (Eds.): TMM_CH 2023, CCIS 1889, pp. 401–410, 2023.
https://doi.org/10.1007/978-3-031-42300-0_33

real-world objects. A 3D scanner is an imaging device which analyses an object or environment to collect distance point measurements [3]. This information that is recorded as three-dimensional data points has been defined as a pointcloud [4]. Almost always, a single scan will not produce a complete model of the object. Multiple scans, from different directions are usually helpful to obtain information about all sides of the model. These scans have to be brought into a common reference system, a process that is usually called alignment or registration, and then merged to create a complete 3D model. This whole process, going from the single range map to the whole model, is usually known as the 3D scanning pipeline. 3D printing is an emerging technology in which a 3D model is converted from a digital file to a physical object. 3D printing as a process requires very little time to create objects, it enables the fast creation of prototypes aiming to increase the production of low-cost products immensely and minimize failures [5].

3D scanning, modelling and printing are being adopted as a technology by cultural heritage management and promotion organizations, such as museums, thanks to the ability to offer new ways of interacting with their exhibitions, collections, exhibits, and cultural assets as a whole [6]. For example, laser scanning and photogrammetry are effective methods of preserving and communicating archaeological exhibits and sites, as a 3D model is virtually accessible from anywhere [7]. Thus, this occurs fragmentally, following different techniques and standards and therefore a more holistic approach is needed.

Considering that, AegeanDigital Tourism Tank is a research action of the "Regional Excellence" Action of the Operational Program "Competitiveness, Entrepreneurship and Innovation", aiming at the digitization and creation of 3D models for the cultural organizations of North Aegean under unified procedures, so as the management of cultural digital information within these organizations to be represented and integrated in similar way, despite their different contexts. The aim of the paper is to present this unified methodology. The rest of the paper is organized as follows. Section 2 addresses previous works regarding 3D approaches for digital heritage. In Sect. 3, the AegeanDigital Tourism Tank holistic approach is outlined. Finally, Sect. 4 discusses the steps of the whole procedures and concludes the adopted methodology.

2 Related Work

2.1 3D Approaches for Digital Heritage

3D printing has been intensively used within the people involved in cultural heritage [8]. In the recent years, the specific technology has been used for the preservation, restoration and dissemination. Many museums and heritage organizations around the world have adopted this technology and the results are very promising and fascinating [9]. 3D printing has opened up new horizons in terms of both museum usability and cataloging and study [10].

Objects and relics as well as monuments and archeological sites due to their fragility/sensitivity but also their historical importance cannot be touched and are usually protected behind enclosed glass displays [9]. This, however, has begun to change with the production of replicas. Replicas have the advantage of being touched without destroying the state of preservation of the original object, and establishing a new way of interacting with it [10]. A typical example and well-known digital fabrication project is the replica of Tutankhamun's tomb in the Valley of the Kings in Egypt. The replica allows visitors to experience the inside of the King's tomb without slightest alteration to the original burial site [9]. 3D printing replicas can be accomplished in different ways. According to the American Society for Testing and Material (ASTM) standard, there are seven main types of 3D printing technology that 3D printers use today: Vat Polymerization that includes stereolithography (SLA), digital light processing (DLP), and masked stereolithography (MSLA), Material Extrusion that includes Fused deposition modeling (FDM), Powder Bed Fusion that includes Direct metal laser sintering (DMLS), Electron beam melting (EBM), Selective heat sintering (SHS), Selective laser melting (SLM) and Selective laser sintering (SLS), Material Jetting, Binder Jetting, Direct Energy Deposition, Sheet Lamination that includes ultrasonic additive manufacturing (UAM) and laminated object manufacturing (LOM).

In the last two categories, no case studies have been observed that have implemented 3D printing in the field of cultural heritage [11]. The most widespread categories in the printing of cultural products are: material extrusion, stereolithography, material jetting, and binder jetting. The Fused Deposition Modeling (FDM) process is considered and is the most widespread process due to its low cost and wide availability [11] as opposed to stereolithography and material jetting, which are considered reliable for aesthetic restorations. These two techniques produce prints with precision and detail. Finally, the binder jetting process is used due to the surface of the material, which resembles plaster or sand resulting in a resemblance to ceramic and stone objects [11]. Using and applying the methods of three-dimensional documentation, laser scanners and photogrammetry, people working on the cultural heritage can acquire the necessary data and produce highly accurate digital models [10]. 3D printing now covers a very wide range of cultural products in the field of protection, preservation and restoration of cultural heritage. Characteristic examples are recorded in the following areas: capturing and replicating archaeological sites in smaller sizes, creating accurate replicas of statues or relics, recreating objects, documenting and preserving works of art such as paintings, accessible and comprehensive education in cultural heritage, reproduction textiles, selling souvenirs/souvenirs, supporting people with visual impairments.

Archeological Sites

An integrated project that combines cutting-edge technologies such as digital media, 3D printing and audio-visual material, was conceived and realized in the context of an exhibition on the cultural heritage of Marseille, entitled Virtual journey through the history of Fort Saint Jean (VJ-FSJ). The exhibition was held at the Museum of European and Mediterranean Civilizations (MuCEM) in Marseilles. It was presented in a holistic way through video mapping, augmented reality effects and optical illusions and within real surfaces and virtual projections [8]. The 3D printing was created using different techniques, partly in polyurethane, partly in plaster in a scale 1:100 from the original. Four separate pieces were printed and assembled for the needs of the model and treated with primer and acrylic paint. Finally, special lighting was added to the model for better visibility.

The photogrammetry laboratory of the Iuav University of Venice in collaboration with a research institution in the area decided to implement an exhibition at the Doge's

Palace in Venice [12]. The exhibition objects included 3D printed models representing islets, complexes and building infrastructures in the Venetian lagoon. In this way, the historical development of the region was recounted in a realistic way [10]. The Chinese classical garden rockeries are part of China's cultural heritage. Their digitization was considered necessary for their preservation [13] and their protection from both natural factors such as solar radiation, erosion by rain, winds, etc. and the human factor such as tourists' climbing and unintentional or intentional detachment of pieces. Due to the above factors, the authorities were forced to prohibit access to the hills where the gardens are located, resulting in visitors not having the possibility of physical contact and guided tours of the sites. The 3D printing of the model at different scales was realized and exhibited to visitors throughout the year. The implementation of printing was carried out with stand-alone scanners as well as hand-held 3D laser scanners for better scanning angle of narrow paths. The 3D printing technology used for the model was a combination of Stereolithography (SLA) and Fuse Deposition Modeling (FDM).

Another imprint of an area of cultural interest is the Valley of five polish ponds, which covers a total area of 61.000 m^2 in Poland. The area was modeled using the Digital Elevation Model (DEM) and satellite photos [14]. The 3D model was printed using the incremental method that build objects layer by layer. The scale was decided to be 1:15000 due to printer limitations, which is why the model was divided into three parts. The pieces were then welded onto a 3D base, which was created using the FDM technique. On the model, the morphology and relief of the ground were accurately captured and the walking paths were created with different colors. The model was painted using a colorless acrylic primer for a smooth and waterproof surface. 3D printing of such surfaces can be used in a variety of ways, including ski trails, mapping relay tower locations, terrain understanding by the visually impaired, and for educational purposes.

Replication/Recreation of Statues and Relics

An important role in relation to 3D technology was the remodeling and replication of small relics/objects of cultural interest and statues. The specific categories, due to their small sizes and the 3D printer limitations (especially in the past) are easier to produce. The formation replicas of a couple of marble statues in the Baptistry of San Giovanni in Corte of Pistoia (Italy) is one of the many examples in the field of 3D printing. The Baptistry housed both the marble statues of St. Johan the Baptist and St. Jacopo. The statues, approximately one-meter-high, were modelled using both the structure from motion (SfM) technique that allow to quickly and automatically reconstruct the surfaces and offering, at the same time, excellent overall accuracy and the technique of photogrammetry [15]. Each statue was segmented into blocks by horizontal cutting planes and printed. All the printed blocks contained a hole in the middle, which fit into a rod with a metal base and were welded together with special resin and plaster their junctions where necessary. The scale of the replicas was 1:1 and fused deposition modeling (FDM) technique was used for printing them. A part of the original statue was missing on the lower right, which was reproduced in the replica. The basic differences between the replicas and the originals are focused on the assembly of the blocks, where the horizontal lines are somewhat distinguishable and on the surface details, where there is a smooth effect that implies a loss [15].

Another statue, the marble statue of Dionysus with Satyr (a Roman copy of the second half of the 2nd century B.C.) is exhibited in the National Archaeological Museum of Venice. The height of the statue reaches 2.17 m and mixed techniques were used to acquire data: triangulation-based laser scanning and digital photogrammetry. The "structure from motion" technique was also used for this model along with suitable software. Three models were printed: one with the laser technique and two with photogrammetry. The first technique had better results in the context of the details. The statues were printed with both the FDM technique and the SLA at a scale of 1:20 [10]. However, in both cases the accuracy of the replicas is not very good and is quite far from the original.The Roman statue Laocoön and His Sons (probably first century B.C.) is on display at the Uffizi Gallery Museum in Florence. The original size of the statue is 208cm × 163 cm × 112 cm. It is entirely made of marble and as part of the digitization of the gallery's works, a 3D digitized model of high resolution geometry and texture was created [16]. The statue was then printed in full color at a scale of 1:10. In addition to the model, a 3D print of the heads of Laocoön and his sons was created using the Colorjet sandstone printing. All the printed replicas were placed on a stand that was made to mimic the composition of the statue and to provide different possibilities of interaction between the physical 3D replicas and the users.

The archeological finding of the upper Paleolithic (11.600 B.C.), "Uomo barbuto di Vado all'Arancio" (Bearded Man of Vado all'Arancio) was used for the needs of 3D printing. The size of the object is very small (8.2 × 4.1 × 1.1 cm). On the main side shows (engraved) a bearded man, while on the opposite side there are traces of what could have been another human face. To reproduce the object, a triangulation-based laser scanner with high resolution is used in order to capture the outline of the faces (the signs of engraving), which are very difficult to be felt even by human touch [10]. It was then, 3D printing technology using the selective laser sintering (SLS) technique and four different copies in different colors were produced. The purpose of the copies was to be exhibited in museums where people with visual impairments will be able to access them. Because the surface shows engravings that are only visible to the human eye and cannot be felt by touch, it was decided to print an "augmented" printed model [10] with a texture guide for more depth.

3 Materials and Methods

3.1 3D Approaches Within the AegeanDigital Tourism Tank Case

Considering previous research, applications of 3D scanning, modelling and printing are broad regarding the digitization of cultural artifacts and heritage, while, there is a variety of 3D technologies with different capabilities and results and in each case, depending on the application and the quality required. However, a lack of standards and proven approaches, in 3D area regarding intangible heritage has been indicated, due to the limited applicability of 3Dmodels and related metadata [2]. In this regard, AegeanDigital Tourism Tank establishes an expert-driven methodology for managing holistic and user-oriented 3D scanning, modelling and printing in order for not only enhancing the preservation of digital Heritage, but also to increase the scientific, economic and social impact of advanced services to the potential audiences of the cultural organizations of North Aegean.

The AegeanDigital Tourism Tank holistic approach was structured in four stages:

1. Selection of cultural assets for digitization
2. 3Dscanning of cultural assets
3. Design/Post-scan enhancement of digital models
4. 3Dprinting of digital models

Selection of Cultural Assets for Digitization

Given the wealth and the diversity of the heritage assets belonging to the selected cultural organizations of the North Aegean, on the one hand and the complexities of the digitization process, on the other, a set of selection criteria was decided for choosing the most appropriate assets for digitization. In specific, a two-phase selection process was performed for ensuring the digitization of a representative sample base of cultural assets from the selected organizations. The set of criteria is defined as follows:

Selection Cultural Criteria - Phase 1

a) Cultural heritage: The objects selected represent different categories of the North Aegean cultural heritage, namely tangible and intangible heritage, movable, immovable and natural heritage [17].
b) Type of object: The selection ensures the representation of different types of objects such as machines, tools, finished products, statues of key personalities, works of art, crafts etc.
c) Time period: The objects selected belong to different historical periods and cover the entire historical spectrum of the Aegean culture, from prehistory and Byzantium to the 19th century and modern times.

Selection Technical Criteria - Phase 2

a) Freestanding objects: To ensure the quality and completeness of the final 3D scanned model, the selected object should be easily accessible from all its sides. As a result, only objects, that the scanner user could easily reach around, were selected.
b) Texture: Certain material textures and surfaces limit the ability to scan parts accurately and completely. Such textures include reflective or transparent materials that are impossible to scan without the use of special anti-glare scanning sprays. In order to avoid applying such sprays to the fragile surface of museum exhibits, objects made of reflective or transparent materials were avoided.
c) Color: Very dark colored objects absorb the light emitted from laser scanners rather than reflect it. To avoid complications in the creation of digital design files, very dark objects were avoided.
d) Controlled environment: Most of the cultural assets selected were located in a controlled environment that provided appropriate conditions of light, facilitating the scanning process [18].

3D Scanning of Cultural Assets

Two main methods of 3D scanning were used for the AegeanDigital Tourism Tank action;

photogrammetry and structured light scanning. Photogrammetry refers to the process of taking overlapping photographs of an object, structure, or space, and converting them into 2D or 3D digital models. Structured light scanners are devices that use a camera system and projected light patterns [19]. Their operation is based on the principle that projecting a narrow band of light onto a surface produces a line of illumination that appears distorted from other perspectives than that of the projector, and so it can be used for the representation of the geometric shape of this surface [20]. In this project, in order to decide which method is better for digitizing an object, the area size of the model and the accuracy level were the main factors to consider. When high accuracy measurement was needed, structured light scanner based on triangulation was chosen. On the other hand, photogrammetry was preferred when less accuracy with more visual photorealism was required. Concerning the equipment used for 3D scanning process, two different 3D scanners of structured light technology were applied; Shining3D Einscan H and Creality CR-Scan01. Each was chosen based on the level of accuracy and most importantly the size of the scan model. For more detailed models or larger objects, the Einscan H was more effective, while for smaller ones where less resolution was required, the Creality CR-Scan 01 was the most suitable device. In case of photogrammetry, state-of-the-art mobile phones with corresponding 3D scanning applications were selected. The 3D scanning applications installed and used were Trnio and Kiri engine both for Android and iOs operating systems. The final models were selected after a series of scan tests and process modifications.

Design/Post-scan Enhancement of Digital Models

Depending on the requirements for quality and accuracy, as well as the complexity of the model, different software packages and design tools are available for the post-process enhancement of the scan output. In the framework of this project, the digitized objects were edited with the use of Autodesk Meshmixer. This was a necessary stage for cleaning-up the digital models produced by the scanning process as well as for their alignment and preparation for 3D printing. In specific, Meshmixer served for repairing damaged mesh produced by scanning process, adding branching support structures beneath the models, analyzing the stability and thickness of the print, simplifying meshes as well as for automatically optimizing the print bed orientation, layout and packing.

Some objects that were considered highly important but were not meeting some of the selection criteria listed above (e.g., flat stencil plates) were photographed, measured by hand and designed in AutoCAD. Special cases of assets of natural heritage, such as the schinos and olive tree that are representative parts of the native flora of Chios and Lesvos islands, were photographed and turned into three-dimensional relief plates, using the lithophane software.

3D Printing of Digital Models

In order to print a model, 3D scanning, edit and design of the model must be done first. To have a successful 3D printing procedure some specific characteristics were taken for granted. Beginning with the technology used, among a wide variety, the FDM (Fused Deposition Modeling) was chosen to print the models of this project, being easy to learn and handle. The main material used was PLA (Polylactic acid). As for the types of the printers, Da Vinci MiniMaker, Da Vinci w+, and DaVinci Color from XYZ, Ender 3 Max from Creality and Sindoh 2X were used. Each of these printers was controlled by its own slicer program where the user could edit, preview, and slice the model into layers, before having the final model. All the digital content was in an STL format, as this is the most common file type used in 3D printers. Many printing tests were performed before the latest version of each model to check the printing quality, and to define the appropriate instructions for each model (nozzle and bed temperature, fan speed, dimensions etc.). The models were offered either in digital (stl file) or physical form (3D printed object).

4 Discussion-Conclusions

One of the main outcomes of the AegeanDigital Tourism Tank is the creation of digital 3D files and cultural assets, representing artifacts of the local cultural heritage in the North Aegean islands, where the University of the Aegean is located, while offering this experience to visitors and support tourism and culture organizations to provide this opportunity to their visitors. Following the above mentioned unified approach, the technologies of 3D allow users to get in touch with their history and culture regardless geographical boarders. With the 3D scanning technology in combination with 3D printing, visitors have the ability to interact with exact replicas of physical objects and their experienced is improved. Additionally, creating a digital collection of 3D models is an effective way of digitizing and documenting cultural heritage and thus contributing to its safeguarding. In the following Fig. 1, the whole process is summarized and presented through seven steps.

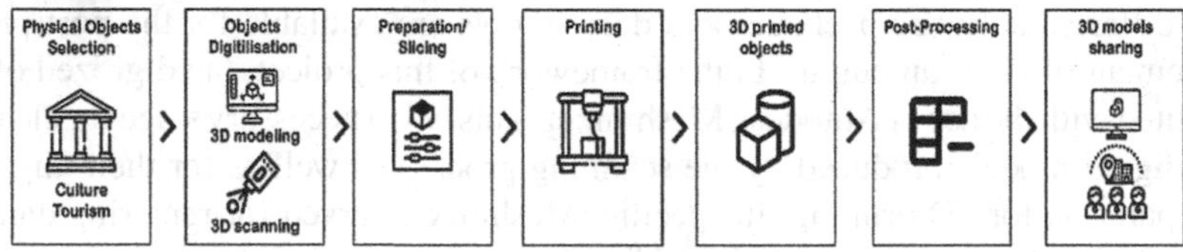

Fig. 1. The AegeanDigital Tourism Tank whole process

Step 1: The choose of the appropriate physical object/ for scanning or modeling from the organization. The physical object adheres to a specific specification, such as the surface of the physical object must not be black or shiny, or transparent.
Step 2: Regarding the complexity of the geometry of the physical object the appropriate technique between 3D modeling and scanning is chosen to transfer it to the digital world.
Step 3: The next phase concerns the settings for the printer such as infill density, layer height, support, and bed adhesion. These are set considering the need of the digital object. Then the digital object is compiled into a form that a printer can understand. The objects are sliced in many layers and the result is a g-code file.
Step 4: The g-code file is sent to the printer and the printing procedure is started. The nozzle of the printer, which is the part that melts the filament, starts to form the object layer by layer.
Step 5: When the printing process finishes the final result is a replica of the exhibit.

Step 6: After the removal of the object from the printer the post-process procedure is starting. The supports are removed and the surface of the object is smoothed.
Step 7: Finally, the 3D printed model is given to the visitors of the organization or the visitors can download the digital file and print it by themselves.

The innovation of this process lies a) at identifying the usefulness of digital technologies and additive manufacturing methods, satisfying the imperative need to integrate them into the production process and finally familiarizing the employees of the selected cultural organizations with the concept of digital transformation and b) in the scanning of both real-world objects and existing miniatures already produced by conventional production methods. Following this, the AegeanDigital Tourism Tank provides visitors with the opportunity to interact with replicas of valuable and/or sensitive exhibits due to the risk of alteration and high preservation cost for the cultural organizations themselves. Furthermore, the ability to change the scale of the objects enables the North Aegean cultural organizations moving and presenting them in different exhibitions, by also adapting them accordingly so that they are consistent with the specifications of each exhibition. It is also worth noting that since products can be manufactured on demand, the costs associated with inventory management and possible overproduction are significantly reduced.

Acknowledgments. This research was funded by the Research e-Infrastructure "[e-Aegean CulTour] Aegean Interregional Digital Transformation in Culture and Tourism" {Code Number MIS 5047046} which is implemented within the framework of the "Regional Excellence" Action of the Operational Program "Competitiveness, Entrepreneurship and Innovation". The action was co-funded by the European Regional Development Fund (ERDF) and the Greek State [Partnership Agreement 2014–2020].

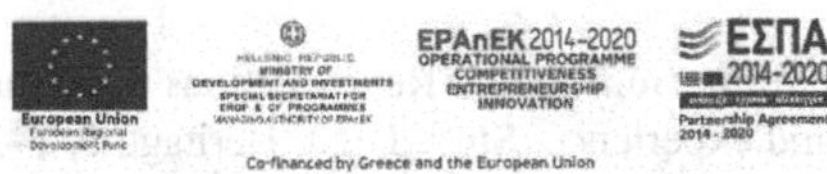

References

1. Batchelor, D., Schnabel, M.A., Dudding, M.: Smart heritage: defining the discourse. Heritage **4**, 1005–1015 (2021). https://doi.org/10.3390/heritage4020055
2. Ioannides, M., Davies, R.: Towards a holistic documentation and wider use of digital cultural heritage. In: Garoufallou, E., Sartori, F., Siatri, R., Zervas, M. (eds.) MTSR 2018. CCIS, vol. 846, pp. 76–88. Springer, Cham (2019). https://doi.org/10.1007/978-3-030-14401-2_7
3. Ebrahim, M.: 3d laser scanners: history, applications, and future (204).https://doi.org/10.13140/2.1.3331.3284
4. Little, C.: Mephisto's Final Days: 3D Modelling to Reveal WWI Secrets (2016). https://www.brisbanetimes.com.au/national/queensland/mephistos-final-days-3d-modelling-to-reveal-wwi-secrets-20160205-gmmx6e.html. Accessed 16 Dec 2022
5. Vardhan, G.H., Charan, G.H., Reddy, P.V.S., Kumar, K.S.: 3D printing: the dawn of a new era in manufacturing. Int. J. Recent Innovation Trends Comput. Commun. **2**, 2373–2376 (2014). https://doi.org/10.17762/ijritcc.v2i8.3713

6. Use of 3D Printing by Museums: Educational Exhibits, Artifact Education, and Artifact Restoration | 3D Printing and Additive Manufacturing. https://www.liebertpub.com/doi/abs/.https://doi.org/10.1089/3dp.2015.0030 Accessed 16 Dec 2022
7. Cooper, C.: You can handle it: 3D printing for museums. Adv. Archaeol. Pract. **7**, 443–447 (2019). https://doi.org/10.1017/aap.2019.39
8. Fatta, F., Fischnaller, F.: Enhancing cultural heritage exhibits in museum education: 3D printing technology : video mapping and 3D printed models merged into immersive audiovisual scenography (FSJ-V3D Printing+MM installation). In: 2018 3rd Digital Heritage International Congress (DigitalHERITAGE) held jointly with 2018 24th International Conference on Virtual Systems & Multimedia (VSMM 2018), pp. 1–4 (2018). https://doi.org/10.1109/DigitalHeritage.2018.8810056
9. Echavarria, K.R.., Samaroudi, M.: How 3D printing is transforming our relationship with cultural heritage (2019). http://theconversation.com/how-3d-printing-is-transforming-our-relationship-with-cultural-heritage-112642. Accessed 16 Dec 2022
10. Balletti, C., Ballarin, M.: an application of integrated 3d technologies for replicas in cultural heritage. ISPRS Int. J. Geo Inf. **8**, 285 (2019). https://doi.org/10.3390/ijgi8060285
11. Acke, L., De Vis, K., Verwulgen, S., Verlinden, J.: Survey and literature study to provide insights on the application of 3d technologies in objects conservation and restoration. J. Cultural Heritage **49**, 272–288 (2021). https://doi.org/10.1016/j.culher.2020.12.003
12. Galeazzo, L., Phillimore, J.F.: The Island of san secondo. In: Visualizing Venice; Routledge 2017 (2021). ISBN 978-1-315-10068-5 (2021)
13. Dong, Q., Zhang, Q., Zhu, L.: 3D scanning, modeling, and printing of Chinese classical garden rockeries: Zhanyuan's south rockery. Heritage Sci. **8**, 61 (2020). https://doi.org/10.1186/s40494-020-00405-z
14. Wabiński, J., Mościcka, A.: Natural heritage reconstruction using full-color 3D printing: a case study of the valley of five polish ponds. Sustainability **11**, 5907 (2019). https://doi.org/10.3390/su11215907
15. Bonora, V., Tucci, G., Meucci, A., Pagnini, B.: Photogrammetry and 3D printing for marble statues replicas: critical issues and assessment. Sustainability **13**, 680 (2021). https://doi.org/10.3390/su13020680
16. Malik, U.S., Tissen, L., Vermeeren, A.: 3D Reproductions of cultural heritage artifacts: evaluation of significance and experience. Stud. Digit. Heritage **5**, 1–29 (2021). https://doi.org/10.14434/sdh.v5i1.32323
17. UNESCO, Cultural Heritage. https://uis.unesco.org/en/glossary-term/cultural-heritage. Accessed 16 Dec 2022
18. Flynt, J.: A Troubleshooting Guide to Common 3D Scanning Issues. https://3dinsider.com/troubleshooting-guide-common-3d-scanning-issues/. Accessed 16 Dec 2022
19. Little, C., Patterson, D., Moyle, B., Bec, A.: Every footprint tells a story: 3D scanning of heritage artifacts as an interactive experience. In: Proceedings of the Proceedings of the Australasian Computer Science Week Multiconference; Association for Computing Machinery: New York, NY, USA, January 29, pp. 1–8 (2018)
20. Furht, B.: Encyclopedia of Multimedia, p. 222 Springer, New York (2008). ISBN 978–0–387–74724–8

‘Orphaned’ Monuments or Common Bicommunal Heritage? Conservation of four Gothic Churches in Famagusta Cyprus, Promoting Cultural Understanding, Exchange and Peace

Nasso Chrysochou(✉)

Associate Professor of Architecture, Frederick University, Nicosia, Cyprus
art.cn@frederick.ac.cy

Abstract. The paper concerns the process of the conservation of four Gothic churches, located in the former ‘Syrian sector’, at the north-western end of the walled medieval city of Famagusta, near the Martinengo bastion. They include the church of the Virgin of the Carmelites; the church of the Virgin Mary of the Armenians; the so-called Tanners’ Mosque, possibly a church of the Jacobite community of Famagusta; and the church of St Anne, originally a Latin church belonging to the Order of St. Benedict and later given to the Maronite community. All four monuments were built in the 14th century and were parts of greater monastic complexes the buildings of which have disappeared over time. Through the process of the historical and archival research and subsequent architectural documentation that was carried out in order to proceed with their conservation, some very interesting and complex matters emerged. The study of the churches’ “histories” and “stories” revealed an intriguing and complex interrelationship between the Latins, the Armenians, the Ottomans, the British colonials and the Turkish and Greek Cypriots which will be presented here, but also uncovered links with a far away, ancient past which remains to be explored further.

Keywords: Gothic architecture · Martinengo · Famagusta

1 An Introduction to the Martinengo Cluster

This paper will introduce the conservation of four Gothic churches in the medieval city of Famagusta, an undertaking that was both complex but also extremely transformational in promoting mutual understanding and bridging cultural divides. Since the 1974 division, this part of the island has been isolated diplomatically and economically from the rest of the world, but Famagusta has been recognized as an extremely important multi-cultural heritage site.

In 1192, Cyprus came under the control of a European crusader dynasty, the Lusignans, with a brief period of control by the Genoese until the Venetians took control of the island in 1489, investing in impressive fortifications, following the Renaissance

A. Moropoulou et al. (Eds.): TMM_CH 2023, CCIS 1889, pp. 411–424, 2023.
https://doi.org/10.1007/978-3-031-42300-0_34

standards of the time. The city of Famagusta was of outstanding importance, as it was the main port of the island with palaces, churches, and monasteries all imbued with art and wealth. In its northwest corner is located the Martinengo bastion and the former 'Syrian sector', where four Gothic churches lay abandoned for centuries. (See Fig. 1) They include the church of the Virgin of the Carmelites, the church of the Virgin Mary of the Armenians, St Anne and the so-called Tanners' Mosque, possibly a church of the Jacobite community of Famagusta. The construction of all four monuments dates to the 14th century, during the Lusignan dynasty. Among the rich cultural heritage of Cyprus, the four Gothic monuments are only a small sample of many others which lie unused and forsaken. Why does this Gothic heritage often receive the least attention among the many civilizations that have left their mark on the island?

Perhaps the answer lies in the relations of the Latins and the Greeks going back to the latter's occupation of the island. The French Latin Church, established on the island at the end of the 12th century, was unsuccessful in its initial plan to proselytize the Cypriot population to Catholicism, and this created enduring tensions between the two faiths which endured over the centuries. The strain only started to gradually ease after the large exodus of many of the Latin monastic orders following the 1426 Mameluke attack on the island [1]. As the Latin Church became less powerful on the island and more accepting of the Orthodox faith, by the late 15th and 16th centuries a more tolerant attitude emerged from both sides [2]. This, however, was interrupted by the Ottoman takeover of the island in 1571, allowing the Orthodox Church to reach a relatively innocuous if sometimes precarious relationship with the new occupiers. On the contrary, the Latin Church and the Catholic population were driven from the island or were forced to convert to the Ottoman faith, leaving many Gothic churches and monasteries with no ownership and no utilization [3–5].

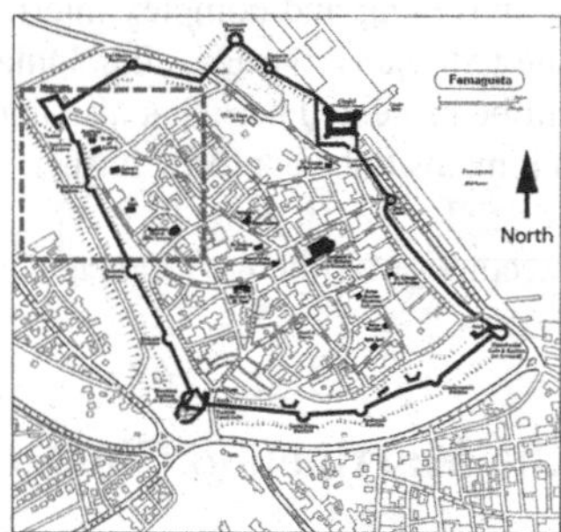

Fig. 1. The city of Famagusta with the four Gothic churches near the Martinengo bastion in the northwest part of the medieval walls.

The Gothic churches of the port city of Famagusta were especially vulnerable. The whole city, which was predominantly Latin, was during the Ottoman period underutilized to a large degree, and its monuments, apart from a few churches which were converted to mosques, left in ruinous state by the Ottomans. Thus abandoned, shunned by the Orthodox population and gradually deteriorating, they became quarries for building material which became an asset as, to a large degree, it was loaded on ships and exported to Egypt to build the Suez Canal and Port Said [6]. This continued into the British era (1878), until the British government passed the first law for their protection with the Famagusta Stones Law of 1891 and its Amendment of 1901 and, aided by enlightened architects and archaeologists and the new philosophical approach towards restoration, took an interest in the preservation of the past.

The first to take partake in the Gothic heritage of Cyprus were the French historians and archaeologists Charles-Jean-Melchior Vogüé and Baron Emmanuel Guillaume in 1860, as well as the British architects Edward I'Anson (1811–1888) and Sidney Vacher in 1882–1883 [7]. However, it was the French archaeologist and art historian Camille Enlart, who painstakingly documented most of the Gothic and Renaissance buildings on the island. When he visited Cyprus in 1896 he was delighted to find "pure" Gothic architecture, untouched by the restorers' efforts which had dramatically changed Gothic monuments in France [8]. (See Fig. 2).

The colonial British did not immediately acknowledge the importance of this rich heritage [9]. One person was who was instrumental in starting the campaign for their preservation was George H.E. Jeffery, the Curator of Ancient Monuments in Cyprus, who from 1903 until his death in 1935 restored ancient buildings as well as worked to declare some of the Famagusta churches as ancient monuments. His campaign to save the Gothic monuments, documented in the "Spectator" magazine in 1899, was so successful that by 1900 newspaper editorials criticised British colonial disrespect for Gothic and Mediaeval architecture [10].

Fig. 2. The four Gothic churches as recorded in 1896 by Camille Enlart.

In the 1930s and early 1940s the architect of the Department of Antiquities Theophilus Mogabgab carried out further conservation and repair works on all the monuments of the Martinengo area, which were again suffering from disrepair only thirty years after Jeffrey's conservations, as Mogabgab's photographic archives show[1]. What is apparent studying the archival pictures is that the first interventions during the British period were of a more consolidating nature, while later with the establishment of the

[1] Mogabgab's photographic archive is with the Famagusta Department of Antiquities. Access to it was gained by the Turkish Cypriot members of the team.

Department of Antiquities in 1935, more extensive works were carried out in a stylistic restoration approach replacing missing decorated parts with similar found in nearby churches. (See Fig. 3).

Fig. 3. The Armenian church as recorded in 1896 by Camille Enlart and after its restoration by Mogabgab in 1937–41, where a service was held there on 04.1945 (From Camile Enlart's and Mogabgab's photographic archives).

Unfortunately, all the conservation works came to a sudden halt in the aftermath of the island's independence in the year 1960. Following inter-communal riots between 1963–74, the medieval city of Famagusta became a shelter for Turkish Cypriots from various regions of Cyprus, who put the ready-made shells of the abandoned churches to use. Later, the wider area where the four churches under study are located was used as an army camp. With the unresolved political situation following the Turkish invasion and division of the island in 1974, many such edifices found themselves in a conflict zone, where international conservation aid and guidelines could not be applied [11].

2 The Histories and the Stories of the Monuments

In 1291, an influx of Christian refugees fleeing the downfall of Acre in Palestine settled into the small town of Famagusta and transformed it into a sea gateway to the Levant and one of the richest cities in Christendom [12]. In 1372 the city was seized by the Genoese and in 1489 by the Empire of Venice, which invested in impressive fortifications. By the mid-14th century, when the four churches were built, Famagusta was said to have the richest citizens in the world and was the main port of the island with fortifications, palaces, churches and monasteries of outstanding architecture and wealth.

Following the fall of Famagusta to the Ottomans in 1571, Greek Cypriots were banished from the walled city, while Turkish Anatolians were resettled there. Due to both the siege as well as a general disinterest in the state of Famagusta by its new residents, the city rapidly fell into decline. In an oil painting from the first years of British rule (1878), the poor condition of the four churches under study is visible [13].

Damage to the churches was caused both by cannon balls fired over the walls during the siege of 1571, but also most probably by the earthquakes that relentlessly and repeatedly devasted Famagusta in 1546, 1567, 1735 and 1741[2][14]. What remained of the building fabric suffered further, from abandonment and vandalism.

The largest monument, the church of our Lady of Carmelite, was part of a monastic complex established by Carmelite monks. Historical records show that it was famous for housing the tomb of Saint Peter Thomas, papal legate and Patriarch of Constantinople, thus allowing us to place its construction date between the years 1324 and 1366 [15].

St Mary of the Carmelites is a beautiful and simple building consisting of single nave with three bays and a semihexagonal apse. The most western bay contained pointed arched niches housing tombs that have now disappeared. The second bay is slightly enlarged in width with a barely protruding transept formed by two large, arched openings on the north and south walls. In the west are two turret shaped buttresses supporting the south and north corners. The southern one houses the remains of a stair that led to the roof. Indeed, the tracery screen in the western window is placed on the exterior of the facade, not for morphological reasons as has been suggested but due to the need to support the hidden stair exiting to the south of the window[3].

A three-story building with a wooden roof, traces of which are outlined on the church's wall, was attached to the southern wall of the church, at the eastern corner between the two large buttresses. (See Fig. 4).

Fig. 4. The southeastern aspect and interior pictures of the Virgin Mary of the Carmelites before the conservation works of 2015.

The southern part of the transept aisle appears to have also been possibly connected to the monastic buildings, as the wall that closes it from the south seems to have been built with material in reuse unlike the northern one. It is quite obvious that the arches for its construction, were opened after the completion of the church, possibly in the 16th century, as the foundations and plinth of the church continues under them. Whether this was ever completed seems to be an unlikely scenario.

2 The church of St Mary of the Carmelites appears on a map of 1571 but the fact that it was never used as a mosque indicates that it already had serious problems, if not a collapsed roof, already at the end of the 16th century.

3 M. Olympios, ref. [15], suggests that this was possibly a direct copy of the Essome Sur Marne church, the design carried over by Champagne-trained stone masons used to build the Nicosia cathedral.

The paintings in the church have sadly mostly disappeared[4] [16]. The fact that even traces of them survive to this day is thanks to the works of a British conservator, Mrs Monica Bardswell, who waxed the frescoes in the churches in the year 1934 [17]. Due to the severe problems that the Carmelite church faced quite early on, it probably fell into disuse after the 16th century.

The church of Saint Anna is a building with similarities to the Carmelite church and was probably influenced by its simplicity and lack of decoration. The church was originally Latin, probably belonging to the Order of St. Benedict but was given at a later date to the Maronite community. After 1571 it became a mosque but was later abandoned and had been used as a stable until 1907. An apsidal chapel, photographed by Camille Enlart in the 1890s and mentioned by Jeffrey, was located about twelve meters off the northwest corner of St. Anne's [18]. Unfortunately, this was destroyed under unknown circumstances.

After the 1974 war, the church was used by Turkish Cypriot refugees. Memories of the church, as related to the conservation team by a lady who during the 1974 war lived in the church with her family, are of a drafty, vast, dark space, lit by a hanging lamp which swung in the wind, casting dim light and dark shadows on the faces of the frescoed icon figures "who appeared to come to life in the semidarkness".

The church consists of a single nave with two bays with groin vaults, separated by transverse ribs. However, unlike the Tanners' mosque, in this case the vaults are supported directly onto the walls. The rib-vaulted choir terminates in a semi- hexagonal apse similarly to the Carmelite church. An element of architectural localism is the creation of a flat roof above the groin vaults instead of the wooden roofs found in Western Europe. In the east, on the external side of the apse is a staircase which cantilevers from the wall and which gave access to the roof from the second storey of the destroyed monastic building. On the roof is a small covered opening from which it has been suggested that the sacristan would lower a candled chandelier. (See Fig. 5).

Fig. 5. The church of St Anne. Floor plan and southern and western elevations

On the far west side of the south and north wall there are niches with pointed arches that were most likely used for a tomb, possibly incorporating now lost sarcophagus. Both of these niches had been bricked in during recent years, preserving behind them

4 When Enlart saw the church in the 18th c. there was a raised styllobate painted in black squares with the lion rampant of the Lusignans and Jerusalem quartering Lusignan. Above it was large painting of the crucifixion in the apse with the donors to the south being five kneeling women dressed in Western-style cloths, amongst them a Black lady.

medieval frescoes waiting to be revealed. Above the west entrance and the south facade is a row of beam holes and stone corbels that supported a porch. Similarly, a balcony must have existed on the western end used to access the double bells which hung in the two arches of the belfry. A cross is carved in relief on the west side of the north wall, which recent research suggests might represent the approval of the Greek community or indicates the presence of a relic of the True Cross housed inside [19].

The church as seen by Enlart in 1896 and described by Jeffery in 1917 appears to have been decorated with important paintings, now covered with whitewash or lost.

The third church of the project is the Virgin Mary of the Armenians, which was most likely built by Armenian refugees who fled to Famagusta after being expelled from Lajazzo, Armenia by the Ottomans. The use of the church by the Armenians is also linked to the siege of Nicosia when the Armenians possibly supported the Ottoman forces against their hated Latin overlords [20]. This church was built on a smaller, simpler scale and form than the other three. Historical records show that it was a Monastic church named St Marie de Vert and was completed by 1317 [21]. The church, as seen in a drawing by the architect Edmond Duthoit, appears not to have been in a bad state in 1862. The same sketch reveals a belfry in the west with two or three arched openings. However, photographs by Camille Enlart in 1896 and Lucien Roy in 1911 show a building greatly destroyed. (See Fig. 3).

Works to restore the church were undertaken by the British colonial architects such as Jeffery who followed a stylistic approach, taking some liberty with the new reconstructed parts. Also, minor excavations in the area revealing the monastic buildings and a small chapel [22]. The decision to undertake these works was directly linked to a rental agreement between the British government and the Armenian Church to grant them permission to use the church [23].

Following the repairs of the church by Mogabgab between 1937–41, a new window was added to the west façade as well as a truncated belfry. None of these appear in Enlart's sketch of 1900, advocating the point that stylistic restoration was still the norm in the first decades of the 20th century. Following these restorations works, the Armenian community returned and got permission to hold a service there in 1945 and, in a repeat of history, in 2015 after the conservation works.

The church consists of a single nave and apse, rather tall for its footprint as was common in Armenian churches. It is roofed by a square groin vault with short barrel vaults to the east and west, supported on the exterior by buttresses. Acoustical vases inserted in the vaults aided the sound as well as lightened the structure. Near the apse, holes in the roof indicate possibly the position of the ropes that lowered or lifted the chandeliers. There were three doors to the west and south and north but the last has been bricked in, probably to accommodate a mihrab when it was briefly converted to a mosque.

The interior floor still bears traces of a room that was added inside the church, possibly when it was used by Turkish Cypriot refugees after the 1974 war, with access to its roof by a staircase whose traces were still visible before the 2015 restoration. (See Fig. 6).

The last monument, the Tanners' Mosque,is located between the Carmelite and Saint Anna churches and is a curious combination of French, Gothic and Byzantine

Fig. 6. The church of The Virgin Mary of the Armenians. Floor plan and section showing interventions by refugees who used the space by adding divisions, a staircase and second floor and lastly a picture showing the 1974 residents' intervention in the space.

architecture. Enlart mentions that it was probably built in the 15th century and might have been built by Latins Greeks or Armenians[5]. It may have been a monastic church of the Jacobite community of Famagusta while it was later converted into a small mosque of the tanners, who worked in the caves near the neighbouring Carmelite church. By the end of the 19th century, it was obviously abandoned once more, and it was subsequently used as a grain warehouse by Evkaf in the 1880s and 1890s in order to protect the provisions against locusts [24].

Build with fine-cut ashlar stone it consists of two bays roofed with groin vaults and has a circular apse with a semi-dome. In the triangular spaces between the flat roof and the vault were embedded earthen jugs for acoustics. The low walls and the groin vault roof exert no real force on the wall, therefore buttresses were omitted. A monolithic stone stair runs through the thickness of the wall at the far northwest side and inside the western wall, giving access to the roof. A second opening on the western wall most likely gave access to an internal balcony used by the church keeper to ring the bells. The lack of buttresses and the weakening of the structure along the north and west caused the church roof to be severely damaged, as recorded by Enlart 's sketch. The cause was once more an earthquake that must have interrupted the original construction or severely damaged the newly built structure, causing major rebuilding of the roof at a later stage. This is supported by the fact that there appear to be different types of stones used in the vaults. The more whitish stones came from the Karpas region, indicating that quarrying in Famagusta had already ceased during the repairs and reconstructions.

This small church and subsequent mosque had lost both its congregation and, due to its dangerous condition, also a possible new use. After its conservation it now lies locked until a new community will reclaim it for its own purposes and use (See Fig. 7).

3 The Conservation Works as Vehicles of Healing a Past

Despite the animosity of the division of Cyprus, this bicommunal project in occupied Famagusta has managed to deal with the issue of the four abandoned and crumbling monuments in a successful way. The conservation of the four churches, financed by the United Nations Development Fund, served as a vehicle for the collaboration of a large interdisciplinary team of Turkish and Greek Cypriot architects, engineers, archaeologists, historians and conservators. The United Nations Development Program (UNDP)

[5] See ref. [9]

Fig. 7. The Tanners' (Tophane) mosque as seen from the northeast and from the interior looking eastwards.

on 25 August 2015, after a successful bid, commissioned the interdisciplinary and bi-communal team consisting of the architects Nasso Chrysochou, Natali Neophytou, Selia Ioakeim and Selen Avkan, the civil engineers Platon Stylianou, Alberto Farinola and Mehmet Onculay and the quantity surveyor Marino Demosthenous to provide services in relation to the study and supervision of a conservation plan for the churches. All four were until recently in a fenced area controlled by the Turkish troops and thus inaccessible to all. The main objective of the project was to assess their safety and to propose the minimum conservation measures that would prevent further damage, without altering their architectural character and monumental wealth.

After extensive historical and archival research, the team proceeded with the structural assessment, damage assessment, and came up with general actions for their preservation. Historical documentation has brought to light not only the histories and the stories of the churches but also the many earlier interventions which had to be documented and evaluated as historic phases. This was aided by the Turkish Cypriot members of the architectural team, who were allowed access to the Famagusta archives and who obtained the necessary permits for the use of sensitive electronic equipment such as drones used in the documentation process.

The architectural documentation also revealed many new elements concerning the wider area. From the cadastral map but also from the photographic archives of the British era, as well as existing underground cave spaces, it became obvious that the area around the four churches abounded with underground quarries and caves. This was confirmed after Geoteam Engineering Ltd, a Turkish Cypriot geotechnical engineering firm, prepared a study on behalf of UNDP. The findings indicated many caves and tunnels within the sandstone formation around the churches, some void, others filled with earth, and some showing human interference. These underground caves/quarries provide another link with the past, but one that might go as far back as the Hellenistic and Roman times. (See Fig. 8).

The painstaking documentation and the direct contact with the monuments, brought about a better knowledge of them and revealed particularities in their constructions. Under the surface of the ground, the foundations of monastic buildings meant that any works which required digging were prohibited.

At the same time, analysis was carried out by the laboratory of the Cyprus University, headed by Dr Ioannis Ioannou, on the stones, mortars and plasters to ascertain

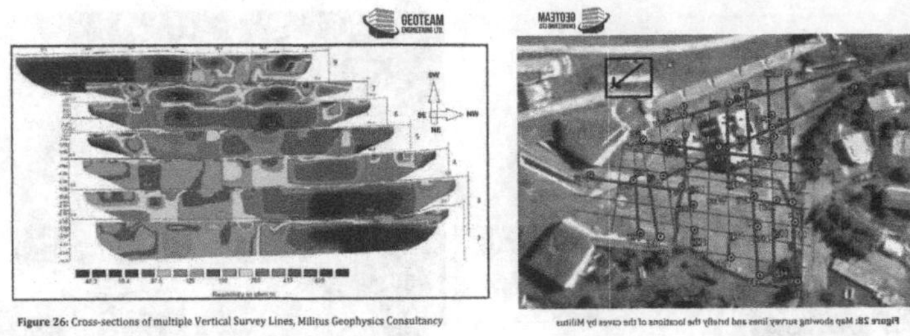

Fig. 8. The geological-geotechnical investigation report showing caves around the church of the Carmelites

their quality and condition. Over the centuries, the proximity to the marine environment and chronic neglect had brought the monuments to a state of desolation. The calcareous sandstone masonry showed alveolization and large loss of the stone parts, weathering crusts and plant growth as well as lichens. The inflow of rainwater from the roofs washed away the binding mortar, and the cycles of humidity and dryness brought about crystallization of the salts in the inner part of the vaults, resulting in great loss of their volume. (See Fig. 9).

Doors and windows were missing and in some cases were walled in to prevent further damage. These had to be replaced with ones that were of simple construction but good functionality allowing ventilation of the monuments when not in use.

Fig. 9. Documentation sample of the four churches with damage and pathology recorder with a devised index.

4 A Holistic Approach to the Monuments' Conservation

The requirements of the study were apart from the maintenance of the monuments with the minimum possible interventions, the assurance of their static adequacy, the preservation of the Carmelite church in the form of a ruin, accessibility for visitors to all the monuments, and the management of rainwater in the wider area. The resulting solutions that will be presented succeeded within the narrow margins set by the various committees to solve multiple problems and deliver a scientifically and aesthetically pleasing result.

Since the monuments belonged to a group and a specific area, they had to be treated as one unit, both as far as their maintenance was concerned, as well as the general management plan. The first decision was to make the four churches an archaeological site, open to visitors, which required solving the issues of visitor safety, surface rainwater, visitor routes, floors, ventilation, disabled access and more. Simultaneously, the solutions proposed needed not to endanger ancient foundations below the surface which were not recorded.

As an example of how this project bridged cultural divides, the conservation works were carried out by a Turkish Cypriot contractor whose family came from the south part of the island and therefore communication was carried out in English, Greek and Turkish.

The problem of the extensive and different deterioration of the stone bodies required a comparative evaluation criteria in order to judge their possible replacement or maintenance. Since the construction of all the churches is entirely of masonry, the ICOMOS "Illustrated glossary on stone deterioration patterns" [25] was used to code their deterioration and then consecutively replace or repair the stone parts. After the analysis of the stones and mortars, a search was made to find a quarry to supply suitable stones. Thus, stones with a loss of more than 75% of their mass were replaced, while at the other end of the spectrum, stones with wear of less than 15% remained as they were. For cracks, a classification was also made.

In all the churches it was decided to ensure the waterproofing of the roofs and at the same time, the restoration of ancient frescoes. All the churches also received reconstruction and reinstatement of their perimeter drainage channels as well as their downspouts and missing roof gutters constructed in a modern form. In the Tanners' mosque, due to the existing shallow and weak foundation, as well as signs of subsidence, micro pilings were made in places where it was indicated that there were no archaeological remains.

Faced with the many restoration of the past, the team needed to decide the approach towards them. Were Mogabgab's reconstructions stylistic restorations or life-saving interventions? Whatever our attitude towards the British era works, the fact is that these helped preserve the monuments and carried them forward into the 21st century. The decision of the team was to respect all historic rebuilding as historic phases and part of the history of the monuments, and conserve them in the overall plan.

The catholicon of the Carmelite Monastery presented the most structurally vulnerable structure, due to the absence of the roof. The amount of reconstruction needed to structurally consolidate the church was an issue that was discussed extensively with the conservation team and the UNDP's monument's committee. Any type of roof construction needed to protect the monument from the elements, was deemed by the committee to be too large an intervention. A minimum solution to this was the selected filling and static strengthening of the gaps (window and bell tower) and the construction of a drainage channel in the centre of the church to drain surface water, with the placing of the stone keys of the cross vaults in the corresponding positions on the floor in order to show in a minimum way the missing roof pattern. The engineering team of both Greek and Turkish Cypriots also worked on a special 3D analysis and parametric studies for the church.

In the church of the Virgin of the Armenians, the accessibility and possibility of use by the Armenian community presented an issue to be dealt with. Since the original floor of the church was not preserved and the existing one presented many anomalies, a new elevated one was built with wood. The good condition of the floor and the new windows and doors in St Anne's church, provided any possible future use for occasional services by the Maronite community.

The cast window frames similar to the original found on the church and possibly dating to the early 20th century, were reconstructed with integrated metal mesh to ensure the required ventilation and lighting. Similarly, the percentage of open but screened openings to guarantee ventilation against moisture build up, was calculated and implemented in all the other churches.

The management of the rainwater of the wider area of the complex, with limited interventions on the ground due to the archaeological site, was a challenge. The proposed solution implemented was surface water management with new levels created sloping gently away from the monuments, aiding the expulsion of surface rainwater away from them while drainage channels with pipes around their perimeter of the churches lead to absorption pits in selected places. The pipes were placed beneath raised, reversibly constructed pathways, (metal and crushed stone), which guided the visitors along a secure, designed access to all the four churches culminating in handicap access for them. Incorporated along the paths but also in the main points of interest was signage for the visitors, designed having integration and multiethnicity in mind. This is of different scales, the overall site information, the history of each monument and lastly small-scale information such as exits, etc. (See Fig. 10).

Fig. 10. The Armenian church after the conservation works.

Concluding, the scientific analysis and technological understanding of the building's techniques and vulnerabilities was a product of the bicommunal scientific team and manifested the unique localism in their design common to both cultures. The decision-making and the challenges faced for their conservation and future use, prompted a discovery and an understanding of a common culture and heritage, both tangible as well as intangible which expanded beyond the Greek and Turkish Cypriots to include the Maronite and Armenian communities. The contributions of the British restorers were extremely valuable in aiding the survival of the monuments to this day, as were the stories provided by members of the local Turkish Cypriot community.

The conservation and promotion of these monuments served as a stimulus for a cultural transition to new owners and stakeholders, protecting and honouring this unique architectural patrimony, while it also served to advance mutual protection and respect of the shared heritage between the Greek and Turkish Cypriot communities, the Armenians and the Maronites and further promoted collaboration between all of them.

References

1. Lusignano, S., Chorograffia et Breve Historia Universale Dell' Isola de Cipro, Bologna 1573
2. Schreiner, P.: Παρατηρήσεις στις πολιτιστικές σχέσεις Ελλήνων και Λατίνων στη μεσαιωνική Κύπρο', Πρακτικά του Β' Διεθνούς Κυπρολογικού Συνεδρίου, Λευκωσία, 20–25 Απριλίου, 77–82 (1969)
3. Παπαδόπουλος, Θ. (επιμ.): Ιστορία της Κύπρου, Τομ. Δ., Ίδρυμα Αρχιεπισκόπου Μακαρίου Γ', Λευκωσία (1995)
4. Olympios, M., Reminiscing about the crusader levant: royal architecture and memory in Lusignan Cyprus. In: Ingrid Baumgaertner, I., Vagnoni M., and Welton M. (eds) Representations of Power at the Mediterranean Borders of Europe (12th-14th Centuries), [mediEVI 6], pp. 139–158. Florence (2014)
5. Coureas, N: The Latin Church in Cyprus, 1195–1312. Routledge, Aldershot (1997)
6. Hoak-Doering, E: The ancient stones of Cyprus and the construction of the Suez canal. Cahiers du Centre d'Études Chypriotes **47**, 165–192 (2017)
7. Pilides, D., Jeffrey, G.: His diaries and the ancient monuments of Cyprus, vol.2, Department of Antiquities, Nicosia (2009)
8. Enlart, C., Dictionary of art historians. https://arthistorians.info/enlartc. Accessed 24 Oct 2023
9. Tumer, E.: Twentieth century restorations to the Medieval and renaissance monuments in Cyprus. In: Walsh, M., Edbury, P., Coureas, N. (eds.), Medieval & Renaissance Famagusta: Studies in Architecture, Art & History, pp 27–234, Ashgate (2012)
10. Konstantinidou, D.: "Ruined cities in Cyprus": how a three-hundred-word letter kick-started the preservation of Cyprus's medieval structure. J. East. Mediterr. Archaeol. Heritage Stud. **9**(4), 313–335 (2021)
11. Langdale, A., Welsh, M.: A short report on three newly accessible churches in the Syrian quarter of Famagusta. J. Cyprus Studies **13**, 105–123 (2007)
12. Jacoby, D.: Refugees from acre in Famagusta around 1300. In: Walsh M., Kiss, T., Coureas N., (eds) The Harbour of all this Sea and Realm Crusader to Venetian Famagusta, pp. 53–68. Department of Medieval Studies & Central European University Press Budapest · New York, Budapest (2014)
13. Σεβέρη, Ρ., Ταξιδιώτες ζωγράφοι στην Κύπρο 1700–1960, Ίδρυμα Κώστα και Ρίτας Σεβέρη, Λευκωσία (2003)
14. Geological Survey Department - Earthquakes - Historical Earthquakes, "historic earthquakes" (2015). http://www.moa.gov.cy/moa/gsd/gsd.nsf/dmlHistEarthquakes_gr/dmlHistEarthquakes_gr. Accessed 21 Jan 2023
15. Olympios, M.: Networks of contact in the architecture of the Latin east: the Carmelite church in Famagusta, Cyprus and the Cathedral of Rhodes. Br. Archeological Assoc. **162**, 29–66 (2009)
16. Enlart, C.: Gothic art and the renaissance in Cyprus. In: Hunt, D. (ed.), Trigraph, London (1989)
17. Kouymjian, D.: "Holy Mother of God Armenian church in Famagusta," with "Armenian Mss Colophons from Famagusta & Cyprus," & "Notes by M. Bardswell, 1937 (Apend. IV, V), Courtauld Institute," In: Walsh, M., Edbury, P., Coureas, N. (eds.), Medieval & Renaissance Famagusta: Studies in Architecture, Art & History, pp 133–146, Ashgate (2012)

18. Jeffrey, G.: The historical monuments of Cyprus Studies in the archaeology and architecture of the island, W.J. Archer, government printer at the G.P.O., Nicosia (1918)
19. Plagnieux, P., Soulard, T.: L'Eglise Sainte-Anne. In: Langdale, A., Walsh, M,. (eds.) L'Art Gothique en Chypre, Memoires de l' Academie des Inscriptions et Belles Lettres, Jean-Bernard de Vaivre and Philippe Plangnieux, vol 34,pp.261-265. Diffusion de Boccard, Paris (2006)
20. Gunnis R.: Historic Cyprus: A Guide to Its Towns and Villages, Monasteries and Castles. Methuen & Company Ltd, Nicosia (1936)
21. Langdale, A., Walsh, M.: The architecture, conservation history, and future of the Armenian church of Famagusta. Cyprus, CHRONOS Revue d'Histoire de l'Université de Balamand **19**, 7–31 (2009)
22. Kaffenberger, T.: The architecture of the Armenian church and convent, the Armenian church of Famagusta and the complexity of Cypriot Heritage. In: Prayers long Silent, Welsh M.J.K. (ed.), pp.143–168. Palgrave Maclillan (2017)
23. Λυμπουρή, Ε., Αποκαταστάσεις μνημείων στην Κύπρο. Από την ίδρυση του Τμήματος Αρχαιοτήτων το 1935 έως το 2005. Διδακτορική διατριβή, Αριστοτέλειο Πανεπιστήμιο Θεσσαλονίκης (2010)
24. Tuncer Bagiskan T.: Ottoman Islamic and Islamised monuments in Cyprus, T. Sinclair (Trans.) Cyprus Turkish education foundation, Nicosia (2009)
25. ICOMOS-ISCS Illustrated glossary on stone deterioration patterns / Glossaire illustré sur les formes d'altération de la pierre Coordination: V. Vergès-Belmin Publisher: ICOMOS 2008, 78 http://www.international.icomos.org/publications/monuments_and_sites/15/index.htm

Author Index

A
Achillas, Charisios 3
Alexandrakis, George 298, 308
Alexandrakis, Georgios 335
Anagnostopoulos, Christos-Nikolaos 43, 255, 287
Angelakis, Dimitris 104
Athanasiadou, Martha 104
Athanasios, Iliodromitis 65
Athanassiou, Athanassios 3

B
Bakatsaki, Maria 188
Bekiari, Chryssoula 104
Bellos, Christos 222
Bilitsi, Evangelia 137
Bochtis, Dionysis 3
Bolanakis, Nikolaos 55
Boulougoura, Katerina 171

C
Cannizzaro, Francesco 82
Chan, Tommy H. T. 276
Chara, Pagouni 65
Charami, Lida 104
Chatzi Rodopoulou, Theodora 202
Chroni, Athina 157
Chrysochou, Nasso 411
Chrysogonos, Nikolaos 114
Cocuzza Avellino, Giuseppe 82
Coffey, Vaughan 276
Cruz, Arturo 276

D
Darlas, Andreas 3
Degteva, Alina 231
Delegou, Ekaterini T. 335
Demosthenous, M. 23
Di Giulio, Roberto 321
Di Martino, Alessia 82
Dimitrios, Anastasiou 65
Dimou, Athanasios 255
Doulamis, Anastasios 114, 364
Doulamis, Nikolaos 114

E
Elisavet, Tsilimantou 65

F
Fafouti, Aspasia E. 335
Fellas, A. 23
Fudos, Ioannis 222

G
Georgopoulos, Andreas 157
Giannikouris, Antonios 335
Giannini, Eugenia 375

I
Iliodromitis, Athanasios 94
Impollonia, Nicola 82

K
Kadrefi, Athanasia 401
Kalloniatis, Christos 401
Kampanis, Nikolaos 298, 335
Kampanis, Nikolaos A. 308
Karagkounis, Dimitrios L. 13
Karkazi, Elli 3
Kavallaris, Christos 55
Kazolias, A. 125, 146
Kazolias, Anastasios 137
Kita, Angeliki 222
Kitsiou, Angeliki 401
Koltsaki, Maria 401
Kompoti, A. 125, 146
Konidi, Amalia-Maria 171
Konstantiniu, Elena 94

A. Moropoulou et al. (Eds.): TMM_CH 2023, CCIS 1889, pp. 425–426, 2023.
https://doi.org/10.1007/978-3-031-42300-0

Koutros, Efstratios 287
Kozyrakis, Georgios V. 308
Kylafi, M. 125
Kyriakaki, Anna 401

L
Lampropoulos, Kyriakos 114

M
Maistros, Yanis 171
Maistrou, Eleni 171
Makri, Evi 375
Malaperdas, George 243
Mamaloukaki, Christina 55
Manglara, Vasiliki 231
Mania, Katerina 55
Manoudakis, Hippocrates 188
Maravelakis, Emmanuel 55
Maria, Delazanou 266
Mavri, Mania 401
Mavroeidi, Katerina 401
Medici, Marco 321
Megalooikonomou, Pavlos-Stylianos 157
Melessanaki, Kristalia 104
Moraitis, Konstantinos 171
Moretti, Karolina 171
Moropoulou, Antonia 308, 335

N
Nitsiakos, Vasileios 222
Ntoulia, Persefoni 222

P
Panagiotidis, V. 125
Panagiotidis, V. V. 146
Panagiotidis, Vayia V. 137
Pange, Jenny 231
Pantazis, George 94
Papida, Sophia 104
Papoutsaki, A. 146
Parasyris, Antonios 298, 308
Patelou, Dafni 222
Paxakis, Nikos 308
Pentazou, Ioulia 188
Pentimalli Biscaretti di Ruffia, Anna Maria 213
Petrakis, Kostas 104
Petrakis, Stelios 298
Philokyprou, Maria 353
Polychronakis, Andreas 55
Pouli, Paraskevi 104
Proiou, Evangelia 401
Psalti, Athanasia 55

R
Rallis, Ioannis 364
Rempis, Nikolaos 298
Rodopoulou, Dora Chatzi 401

S
Sideri, Maria 401
Simou, Stavros 401
Sinachopoulos, Dimitris 243
Skamantzari, Margarita 171
Stamatopoulos, Michail I. 43
Stavridis, Stavros 401
Stefanou, Konstantinos 222
Stergios, Georgios 222

T
Thravalou, Stavroula 353
Tokmakidis, Panagiotis 3
Tsakoumaki, Marilena 55
Tsanaktsidou, Sofia D. 13
Turillazzi, Beatrice 321
Tzetzis, Dimitrios 3
Tzimtzimis, Emmanouil 3
Tzortzis, Ioannis N. 114, 364

V
Valianatou, Eleni 243
Vasileios, Pagounis 65
Vgena, Katerina 401
Vythoulka, Anastasia 308, 335

X
Xanthis, Agapitos 335
Xinogalos, Michael 55

Z
Zacharias, N. 125, 146
Zacharias, Nikolaos 137
Zafeiropoulos, Charalampos 114, 364

Printed in the United States
by Baker & Taylor Publisher Services